Life-Destroying

Diagrams

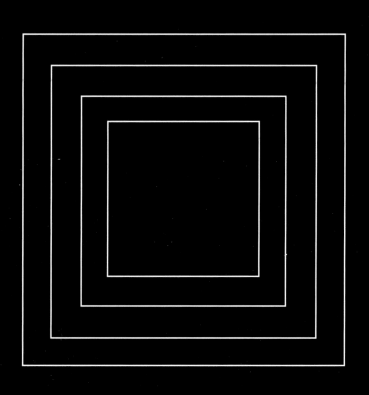

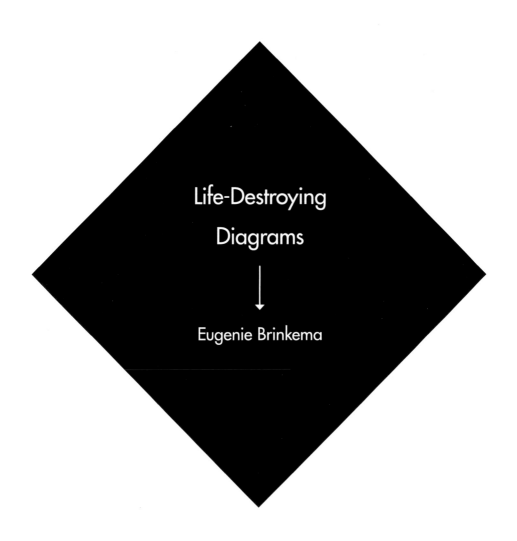

Life-Destroying

Diagrams

Eugenie Brinkema

DUKE UNIVERSITY PRESS ◆ DURHAM AND LONDON ◆ 2022

© 2022 DUKE UNIVERSITY PRESS
ALL RIGHTS RESERVED
PRINTED IN THE UNITED STATES OF AMERICA
ON ACID-FREE PAPER ∞
DESIGN BY AIMEE C. HARRISON AND
AMY RUTH BUCHANAN
PROJECT EDITOR: SUSAN ALBURY
TYPESET IN MINION PRO AND FUTURA STD
BY COPPERLINE BOOK SERVICES

LIBRARY OF CONGRESS CATALOGING-IN-PUBLICATION DATA
NAMES: BRINKEMA, EUGENIE, [DATE] AUTHOR.
TITLE: LIFE-DESTROYING DIAGRAMS / EUGENIE BRINKEMA.
DESCRIPTION: DURHAM: DUKE UNIVERSITY PRESS, 2022. | INCLUDES
BIBLIOGRAPHICAL REFERENCES AND INDEX.
IDENTIFIERS: LCCN 2021007173 (PRINT)
LCCN 2021007174 (EBOOK)
ISBN 9781478013433 (HARDCOVER)
ISBN 9781478014348 (PAPERBACK)
ISBN 9781478021650 (EBOOK)
SUBJECTS: LCSH: FORMALISM (LITERARY ANALYSIS) | CRITICAL THEORY.
| AESTHETICISM (LITERATURE) | HORROR IN LITERATURE. | BISAC:
PERFORMING ARTS / FILM / HISTORY & CRITICISM | PHILOSOPHY /
GENERAL CLASSIFICATION: LCC PN98. F6 B756 2021 (PRINT) |
LCC PN98. F6 (EBOOK) | DDC 809/.9164 — DC23
LC RECORD AVAILABLE AT HTTPS: //LCCN.LOC.GOV/2021007173
LC EBOOK RECORD AVAILABLE AT HTTPS: //LCCN.LOC.
GOV/2021007174

COVER ART: ADAPTATION OF STILL FROM *THE HUMAN
CENTIPEDE (FIRST SEQUENCE)* (TOM SIX, 2009).

DUKE UNIVERSITY PRESS GRATEFULLY ACKNOWLEDGES THE
LITERATURE SECTION OF THE MASSACHUSETTS INSTITUTE
OF TECHNOLOGY, WHICH PROVIDED FUNDS SUPPORTING
THE INCLUSION OF THE BOOK'S COLOR IMAGES.

TO EVAN ⟶

Contents

Illustrations

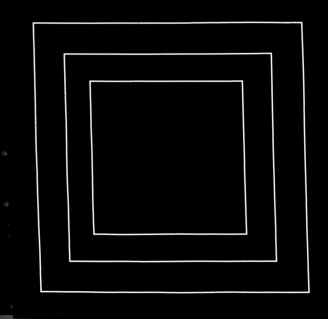

exordia

A white wall. Nothing distinct from the white wall.
(Enter All, centre centre.)

WITOLD GOMBROWICZ
The primary task of creative literature is to rejuvenate our problems.

GOTTFRIED WILHELM LEIBNIZ
(*Crossing left. Meeting him.*)
The best method is to make as many comparisons as one can.

ROLAND BARTHES
(*Crossing right. Meeting both.*)
The affectivity which is at the heart of all literature
includes only an absurdly restricted number of functions:
I desire, I suffer, I am angry, I contest, I love, I want to be loved,
I am afraid to die

(*All speakers now joining.*)
—out of this we must make an infinite literature.

LUDWIG WITTGENSTEIN
(*Aside.*) This book might well be equipped with diagrams.

A BURSTING VOICE (OFF).
EVERYTHING MATTERS.

A BURSTING VOICE (OFF).
ANYTHING MATTERS.

(Adopting various attitudes, Exeunt None.)

This book will argue the priority of the ~~political~~ formal interpretation of ~~literary~~ texts. It conceives of the ~~political~~ formal perspective not as some supplementary method, not as an optional auxiliary to other interpretive methods current today—the psychoanalytic or the myth-critical, the stylistic, the ethical, the structural [, the historicist, the new materialist, the affective]—but rather as the absolute ~~horizon~~ ground of all reading and all interpretation. This is evidently a much more extreme position than the modest claim, surely acceptable to everyone, that certain texts have ~~social and historical—sometimes even political~~ formal ~~resonance~~ aspects.

—Fredric Jameson, *The Political Unconscious,* adjustment

In his 1679 *Consilium de Encyclopaedia nova conscribenda methodo inventoria* (*Project of a New Encyclopedia to be written following the method of invention*)—an unpublished fragment, written in Latin, and only one of several plans for various (and variously structured) encyclopedias he developed—Gottfried Wilhelm Leibniz sets out to discover a work that would "comprise all the sciences that are based on reason alone or on reason and experience."[1] He presents the sciences to be considered in order:

1 — Grammar, "the art of understanding what the body of this Encyclopedia will convey to us" (in other words, an effort at a rational language);

2 — Logic, "the art of inferences, i.e., the art of judging that which is proposed";

3 — Mnemonic Art, "the art of retaining and recalling into memory what we have learned";

4 — Topics of "the art of discovery (*ars inveniendi*), i.e.[,] the art of leading our thoughts towards the elicitation of some unknown truth," which includes dialectics, rhetoric, invention, divination, cunning, algebra, &c.;

5 — *********;

6 — Logistics, "which treats of the whole and the part, of magnitude in general, as well as of ratios and proportions";

7 — Arithmetic, "magnitude by means of numbers";

8 — Geometry, "the science of place (*situs*) or figures";

9 — Mechanics, "the Science of Action and Passion," power, movement, statics, ballistics, &c.;

10 — Poeographia, "the Science of sensible (*sensibiles*) qualities";

11 — Homeographia, "the science of substances (*subjecti*) that are similar at least in appearance";

12 — Cosmography, "the science of the larger bodies of the world";

13 — Idographia, "the science of organic bodies, which are called species";

14 — Moral Science, "the science of the mind (*animus*) and its emotions (*motus*): knowing and directing them";

16 — Geopolitics, "which treats of the state of our Earth in relation to the human species. It comprises all History and civil Geography";

18 — Noncorporeal substances, "i.e.[,] of natural theology" (i.e., metaphysics).

His listing concludes, "This Encyclopedia should contain also a *Practical* part, dealing with the use of the sciences for happiness, that is, of how to act taking into account the fact that we are only human."[2]

Date: June 15, 1679
Edition: A VI 4 A 338–49; C 30–41

Science 15 is missing. Science 17 is missing. (One of them might have been Mathematical Geography; there are hints, traces in the drafts.)

Science 5 is the one that concerns us.

> 5 — Quinta est ars formularia quae agit de eodem et diverso, simili ac dissimili, id est de formis rerum, abstrahendo tamen animum a magnitudine, situ, actione. Huc pertinent formulae formularumque comparationes, et ex hac arte pendent multae regulae quas Algebristae et Geometrae in usum suum transtulerunt, tametsi eae non tantum circa magnitudines sed et circa alias considerationes locum habeant.

> The fifth is the *ars formularia*, which deals with the same and the different, the similar and the dissimilar, i.e.[, the art] of the forms of things, taking the mind away (*abstrahendo*) from magnitude, place (*situs*), and action. This art includes formulae as well as comparisons of formulae, and many rules that the algebraists and geometers have devised for their own use depend upon it, although these rules do not pertain to magnitude but to other factors.[3]

What precedes Leibniz's *ars formularia*—the discovery and comparison of the forms of things, the exploration of the same and the different—is the promiscuous category of the *ars inveniendi*, the art of deciphering, experimenting, interrogating, conjecturing, guessing, questioning, doubting in relation to unknown things. This is the technique of discovery that is the ground of the new encyclopedia itself, which folds to contain a thinking of this very practice. Techniques of wonderment thus give way to techniques of regarding same and different forms autonomous of their size, position, or action, which we might rephrase as follows: in order to pass from the most abstract rules (of language, of logic, of understanding) to the concrete study of place, action, and sensible qualities, two things are required—the speculative and the formal. These, for Leibniz, are the general powers that bridge theory and the world.

a work, then, not about form but of form

We need a thought which does not
fall apart in the face of horror.

— GEORGES BATAILLE, *The Accursed Share*

So if I draw a boundary line that is not
yet to say what I am drawing it for.

— LUDWIG WITTGENSTEIN, *Philosophical Investigations*

ONE

Horrēre

or

I am done with the neck.

In thrall to an etymology that details nervy vibrissae's standing on end—*a bristling, shaking, trembling; a shuddering; being roughed up, excited, stimulated by, moved by the terrible, the dreadful, from intense (& painful) feelings of fear, loathing, disgust, this icy unease, what chills all spines (a symptom; a sign), piercing and roiling shivers & unsteady movements (cf. the gestural recoil of abhorrence), a frisson, a thrill (some shock); even what sickens to tell* (horribile dictu: *opposite of miraculous, what wastes lovely wonder) or is revolting, or detestable, each nervous ascent of each rigid raised pilus, rippling skin and bloomy plain, pointing and stiffened and exhibiting, so then awful is soldered to body as what sudden strikes, rustles, waves (as in the sea), a fouled flesh now embossed with these displaced traces of all that undoing*—thinking has capitulated to this finely stippled field, purchased the ability to speak of Horror at the cost of keeping close to the sensitive receptions of the nape.

The Latin *horrēre*, hairs stood on end, itself from *ghers-* and the prickly, the spiky, what becomes stiff, sticks out, protrudes (as in the spines of plants, a leaf with coarse cilia)—such that *horridus,* from which arrives *horrid*, suggests the hispid and the hairy—this rude, unpolished line of fibers made erect, delicate but still too many of them, links *horror* even to the woollier, shaggier *hirsute*. Virgil writes of Cerberus in *Aeneid* VI, "Cui vates, horrēre videns iam colla colubris"—about the watchdog's several necks are glimpsed rising bristling snakes.[1] Try—you will fail—to make a verb of it. Horror is what is obtained or taken delivery of, experienced by or felt as and *done to*, a form of the *made* or what is intended, produced, or caused, not the performance of some doing. One may horrify solely as bequeathment: a giving of some quality in the act—but one does not, may not, horror as such. The *horrious* is what causes horror; the *horrible*, that capacity for dreadful realization indicated by the suffix class denoting possibility. Its shivering intensity may be paired with pity, with bitterness or unease, bonded to *le carnage* (for a Voltaire who repudiates both as faddish), figured as ataraxic in Edmund Burke's 1757 sublime (object of a "delightful horror, a sort of tranquility tinged with terror"), or its strangling aversion sewn to an unable-to-bear revulsion: when Mary Shelley's famous doctor glimpses his gray corpse-made creation, he gasps, "breathless horror and disgust filled my heart."[2]

> *(Augustine, in one of the most famous passages in* Confessions,
> *writes of the overwhelming moment when,*
> *for the first time,*
> *he knew God,*
> *"contremui amore et horrore."*
> —I trembled [violently shook] with love and horror.)*[3]

These terms for hideosity move between the literal and the figurative, such that the unshorn is also the rude, involuntary tremble, also a tone or mode of disquieting dread. (The Spanish *horripilante* and Italian *orripilante*, the literally hair-raising, are, evocatively, the grisly and creepy; the late eighteenth-century *Schauerroman*, a subset of the Gothic, is a shudder-novel.) Rough, coarse (as of cloth), and therefore ugly—the negative rotation of aesthetics, ill formed, what degrades the cultivation of form. And what a lack of clarity in form may compel: Brutus marvels to the ghost of Caesar, "Art thou any thing? / Art thou some God, some Angell, or some Devill, / That mak'st my blood cold, and my haire to stare?"[4] In *Dracula*, Stoker writes in Seward's diary of coming upon the terrible sight of Mina's blood exchange with the Count: "With his left hand he held both Mrs. Harker's hands, keeping them away with her arms at full tension; his right hand gripped her by *the back of the neck*, forcing her face down on his bosom. Her white nightdress was smeared with blood, and a thin stream trickled down the man's bare chest which was shown by his torn-open dress." The resulting horror, which is textually antecedent, performs a bodily reading of the scene—the affective turn circa 1897: "What I saw appalled me. I felt my hair rise like bristles on *the back of my neck*, and my heart seemed to stand still."[5] The reaction to the carnal tableau mimics the gesture that is its provocation—a transaction with substitutive body parts. Echoing the claret reciprocity between victim and bat, the novel turns on the figure of exchanged necks: At (the sight of) Mina's scruff, gripped (by aristocratic hand), Seward's (lived) column is convulsed (by raw affect). All neck, only necks, and neck a tender text that shows over and over the same familiar swell.

What is *horrent* or *horrendous* stirs and rouses the recipient not merely as raised flesh, but as though hackled with the projecting filaments of a beast (as in the stiffness prized for boar-*bristle* brushes, as in the uniform body and flagged end of boiled pig *bristle*). In his consideration of the muscularities of disturbance, Darwin treats the raising of these threads generously, at first focusing on the involuntary contractions of the *arrectores pili* on the capsules of separate hairs, now on end, as in the spines of the hedgehog. "Hardly any expressive movement is so general as the involuntary erection of the hairs, feathers and other dermal appendages," he writes in *The Expression of Emotions*. "These appendages are erected under the excitement of anger or terror; more especially when these emotions are combined."[6] When turning to the special case of humans, Darwin offers examples of the rough excitement seen in both rage and fear, mania and madness: "the bristling of the hair which is so common in the insane, is not always associated with terror. It is perhaps most frequently seen in chronic maniacs, who rave incoherently and have destructive impulses; but it is during their paroxysms of violence that the bristling is most observable." Strands function as an index of the mental state, visibly attesting to feverish disturbances of mind. If a lunatic is a lunatic all the way down, Darwin posits, it is "to the extremity of each particular hair."[7]

Entranced by this roughed-up, shuddering neck, critical work on horror and representation—whether in painting, literature, film, or other media; for necks extend, elongate: they *stretch*—has overwhelmingly, stubbornly, taken this etymological cartography as a nonnegotiable sign of the bad affect's essence, limit, purview, function, and conceit. Horror thus takes on the burden of all root-aesthetics dating back to Baumgarten's *aisthanomai*: I sense, I perceive, *I feel*. A disturbed viewer, reader, spectator is demanded by the force of the word's origin, this figuration that is seductively straightforward and simple—the positivism of goose bumps—while also poetic, evocative with all its rippled waves of flesh and nerve. There seems to be neither critical need nor desire to travel beyond the suggestion of a fundamental affective aim and purpose for the entire concept (or, perhaps it is in fact the case that horror fails even to be regarded as a *concept*, treated as nothing but an *affect*). Consider, for example, this proposition from James Twitchell's 1985 *Dreadful Pleasures: An Anatomy of Modern Horror*, an early and oft-cited study, and one that begins (and ends) with a horrēre tinged with necessity. Fixing on "the way nape hair stands on end," Twitchell argues that "the shiver we associate with horror is the result of the constriction of the skin that firms up the subcutaneous hair follicles and thus accounts for the rippling sensation, almost as if a tremor were fluttering down our back. From this comes the most appropriate trope for horror—creeping flesh or, more simply, the 'creeps.' [. . .] Medical science is now exploring the biochemical substance, corticotropin, that triggers this response by signaling the pituitary gland to produce hormones, but for our purposes just the hair on the neck will do."[8]

Theories of horror relying on this entrenched Latinate neck quickly become repetitive, rote, undifferentiated despite profound divergences in their theoretical approaches. Although in his influential analytic-cognitivist account *The Philosophy of Horror, or, Paradoxes of the Heart*, Noël Carroll expressly writes in opposition to the psychoanalytic hermeneutics on which Twitchell relies, he returns to sensation through the same spiny receptions of the back of the head. The affective priority Carroll attributes to his subject derives explicitly from an authority surrendered to source, even if bristling remains only a heuristic. "The word 'horror' derives from the Latin 'horrēre'—to stand on end (as hair standing on end) or to bristle—and the old French 'orror'—to bristle or to shudder," he writes. "And though it need not be the case that our hair must literally stand on end when we are art-horrified, it is important to stress that the original conception of the word connected it with an abnormal (from the subject's point of view) physiological state of felt agitation."[9] The sensorial claim furnishes a generic claim: "Novels are denominated horrific in respect of their intended capacity to raise a certain affect. [. . .] I shall presume that this is an emotional state, which emotion I call art-horror."[10] Carroll's recourse to provocation renders his cognitive-aesthetic philosophy of horror above all a philosophy of physiological feeling, one that does not require or grip a neck so much as stand on it.

Just as changes in theoretical allegiance do little to vary appeals to this etymological line, the decades-long evolution of horror studies has not diminished the priority of a bodily affect legible in flesh and follicle. A tidy finding of bearings folds this line of scholarship and makes it resemble itself in its citation of etymological authority.[11] Linda Williams quotes Twitchell extensively in "Film Bodies," her meditation on body genres (melodrama, horror, pornography) whose "success [. . .] seems a self-evident matter of measuring bodily response." "The aptly named Twitchell," she continues, "thus describes a kind of erection of the hair founded in the conflict between reactions of 'fight and flight'. While male victims in horror films may shudder and scream as well, it has long been a dictum of the genre that women make the best victims."[12] Although Williams's version of neck is now multiply surveilled on shuddering represented victims and bristling empirical spectators—and though that neck is particularized, given a relation to sexual difference—this model of a productive-receptive mimicry has not moved far from Tolstoy's late nineteenth-century definition of art as the means by which a creator "infects" spectators or auditors (admittedly, there, with the feeling during the act of creation; here, with the feeling represented within the creation), and the erection of strands on nape is still the fulcrum for affective criteria of generic "success." Williams's use of that word is telling; Carroll writes it often as well. So long as a definition of horror relies on dogma derived from neck, it will turn on the attainment of a specific, predictable outcome, which invariably returns to the demonstrated accomplishment of raised downy hairs. This is everywhere a language of purpose, a discourse of efficacy. Neck is a template predicated on the idealism of a positive aesthetic experience, realized with neither loss nor noise. Neck is a machine doing a good job. Neck names the well-behaving commodity.

Even Anna Powell's Deleuzian rejoinder to psychoanalytic horror criticism— with theoretical sympathies resolutely opposed to Twitchell, Carroll, and Williams—opens with a definition of her subject, "films designed to horrify by their depiction of violence and the supernatural," that turns on the by now familiar shivers—using language nearly identical to that of earlier critics. "The word horror," she writes, "is derived from the Latin *horrēre*, to bristle or shudder. Its historical usages incorporate sensory associations, such as 'roughness or nauseousness of taste such as to cause a shudder or thrill'; 'a painful emotion compounded of loathing and fear'; and 'the feeling excited by something shocking or frightful' which is 'revolting to sight, hearing, or contemplation'. These definitions emphasize the genre's affective potency, and intriguingly do not differentiate the impact of actual and fictional horror."[13] We might go on, assemble a vast archive of barely differentiated claims for horripilation, but the dissatisfaction is primed: *Is there only this one narrow neck in the all of critical history?*

Critical valuations have consequences. Twitchell puts it most nakedly. Following on his primary assertion from the neck—the insistence that "the experience of horror is first physiological, and only then maybe numinous," figuring horror as an immanent experience of the body and a body-addressing genre—he declares its upshot: "the instructions embedded in horror resist literary, especially formalist, interpretation."[14] If it is unsurprising that one result of neck essentialism has been a suspicion of, if not outright derision toward, critical approaches that are indifferent to the affected corpus, more troubling is that the privileging of neck has led to a contempt for all the marvelous detailed difficulties of formalist interpretation that engender theoretical reach and for which I advocated in *The Forms of the Affects*. To the point: there is a bartering of form for neck in this broad critical tendency, bristles purchased at a great cost. It is impossible to say which comes first: it is both the case that neck interiorizes a (sensitive, sensing) body to horror in order to impossibilize reading for form and that it interiorizes a resistance to reading for form in order to posit a (sensitive, sensing) body. Horrēre as an affective apodicticity, promising only to recover the isthmic and receptive, thereby forecloses modes of reading that would be generative and speculative.

Horrēre, more than any signifying monster, is the meta-trope unifying horror studies. There is an economy to the genealogical fix that horrēre locks in—but it is a restricted economy. If, within its own thinking, horrēre allows irruptions symptomatically (the return of the repressed, disturbing cultural leakages and excess), what it systematically refuses and suppresses is irruptive discontinuities in the neck-orientation of its name.

I take no interest in this neck, will derive no interest from it.

Although a constriction, although a slender structure, neck is also a strait. What connects (skull and shoulders; two bodies of water) is a channel, an outline of a fluid body, and channels above all beg to flow, to go otherwise.

Let us reread horrēre with care.

Suppose the problem was one of language all along. If etymological sedimentations beholden to the restrictions of a hairy, bristly map have engendered the critical obsession with a feeling, receiving, receptive body, might recovering a different tradition let us decisively move on from the neck?

Perhaps the trouble is with the Latin.

Our words are tired; they repeat, they are old. Words get worn. And so, then: Do we merely need some other ones?

The Greeks deployed an extensive vocabulary for the bad affective state we call fright, with tonalities varying according to stimuli, the sense of a justified or unjustified reaction, and valences related to experiences by individuals or groups. Within this substantial set, the most common words for fear were *deos*, *phobos*, and *ekplexis*, with nuanced resonances of, respectively, doubt, running, and shock.[15] *Deos*, from *du-, two, takes the sense of being unsure in the face of a double option or alternative (to be *in doubt* is to be *in two*): in *Iliad* 9.230–31, as everything hangs in the balance, Odysseus entreats Achilles, "We are afraid. It can go either way, whether we save or lose our well-benched ships"; in *Odyssey* 11.43, as Odysseus watches the shades drink blood he is seized with "chlôron deos," green fear, a favorite Homeric idiom sometimes rendered "pale fear" (think: blanching terror) and, classicists suggest, associated with the uncertainties endemic to the underworld or the supernatural.[16] (This terror inherent in doubled alternatives will be reimagined in twentieth-century structuralism as the hesitation between the uncanny and the marvelous—*An Event Occurs*: & was it a trick of the senses, an undermining of self and perception but against the field of a world preserved, knowable, firm *or* did this thing really happen as perceived correctly by the sure senses and now the world, before so stable and natural-seeming, is now changed, undermined, devastated? How to decide? *All is unsurety*—the duration of which Todorov will dub the Fantastic.)

Phobos takes the root "to run," but *phobeo* specifically means "I cause to run away," put to flight, that from which one moves violently apart, with an irrational and shivering, cold dimension; for example, Thucydides writes that "Night supervened, and the Macedonians and the mass of barbarians took sudden fright [*phobeisthai*], seized by that unaccountable panic to which large armies are liable."[17] The Greek grammarian Ammonius offered a treatment on the difference between deos, "a presentiment of evil [*kakou huponoia*]," and thus a project of mind, and the more corporeally bound phobos, "a sudden quivering [*parautika ptoesis*]"—and from phobos, of course, our modern sense of that thing from which one flees, the often idiosyncratic, often inexplicable, yet powerfully visceral cause of an outward display of great and panicked fear.[18] To be rough, to take an uneven surface (as on the sea), or to bristle (as in a mane), to ruffle, to shudder: the words that share the territory of horrēre are, first, the Greek *phrissô*, poetically as in *hote phrissousin arourai* (Menelaus's heart is stirred like the *bristling growing fields* of corn) in *Iliad* 23.599, and viscerally as in a chill, a shiver from great fear, as invoked by the chorus in Aeschylus's *Seven against Thebes* when they speak *pephrika tan ôlesioikon theon, ou theois homoian*, shuddering in dread at all this laying waste. (In his *Oedipus*, Seneca personifies horror as Phrike, *daimona* of fear, horror, terror, tremor, her name sharing the root *phrittō*, to shudder, to shiver.) Second is the rarer, often poetic or dramatic novelty *orrōdia*, affright, dread, terror, fear; *orrōdeō*, to be terrorized, to dread, to shrink from.[19]

—No, we have not moved so far from the telltale erectable hairs, from mistaking bristle for ontology.

New words, new new words: we were tired of the old ones,—but new words have not saved us here. The diachronic impulse to trace the transfer and crossings from Latin to Greek, to find our way to a neckless imagining, has returned the same shivering quake, merely adding the gesture of recoil: the spring or flinching that demands elasticity in the spine, muscularity in the back, what holds fast to body, strikes and rustles forcibly, disasters the stable ridge and waves the stem. Both Greek and Latin lines end in Goethe's *"Das Schaudern* ist der Menschheit bestes Theil," in which an overwhelming *sublime tremble*—smelt of fear, anxiety, anguish, awe—is the very finest experience of the human; and the critical track runs loyally straight on to now.[20] The history of the concept of horror is the very opposite of unfindable: it is, like its namesake, too much unconcealed, works on the surface of a skin. Neck persists; neck *insists*. It carries a lack of theoretical affect: assuredly displaces nothing, about which nothing is unknown. It is remarkably easy to remain with the body's narrow feeling field of muscle, chain, and nerve.

So much thinking is catastrophobic, sticking with violences to the neck because of anxiety about its overturning, frightened to bring its fecund disorders to a close. But necks veil a more disturbing violence; necks shield and delay confrontations with unsuspected modes of horror, ones linked to forces of order, systematicity, languages, schemes, shapes, and structures.

What is a philosopher?

— That is perhaps an anachronistic question. But I will give a modern response. In the past one might have said it is a man who stands in wonder; today I would say [. . .] it is someone who is afraid.

— Philosophers are numerous then, excepting Socrates and Alain—both famous for having been good combatants and having drunk hemlock without trembling [. . .]. But perhaps philosophical fear is of a more noble character.

— Not at all. Fear, whether it be cowardly or courageous, is intimate with what is frightening, and what is frightening is what makes us leave peace, freedom and friendship all at the same time. Through fright, therefore, we leave ourselves, and, thrown outside, we experience in the guise of the frightening what is entirely outside us and other than us: the outside itself.

— Then common fear would be philosophical fear insofar as it gives us a kind of relation with the unknown, thereby offering us a knowledge of what escapes knowledge. Fear: anguish. And we thus approach philosophies that themselves are not unknown. Yet there is in this experience a movement that collides as though head-on with philosophy. The fearful man, in the space of his fear, participates in and unites with what makes him afraid. He is not only fearful, he is fear—that is, the irruption of what arises and is disclosed in fear. [. . .]

— But is it thought that can be afraid? Are you not already using here a language that is symbolic, full of imagery or "literary"? It is the thinker who becomes frightened; he is frightened of what threatens his thought. And what does he fear, as a man of thought? Nothing other than fear.

— The philosopher, in this case, would be someone who is afraid of fear.

— Maurice Blanchot, *The Infinite Conversation*

Questions from the neck:

1) **What is frightening** (to me; to you; to group X; at historical period Y; across national differences Z)**?** Under the banner of which is discussed all monsters and monstrosity, cultural othering, allegorical anxiety, themes and tropes, epistemic uncertainties, ontological indeterminacies; all symptoms, sexual differences, bad families, doublings, abnormals; twists and pods and hybrids, the massified and excessive; a relentlessly replicating virus; all metaphors and fascinations; what is in between or violates categories (cf. abjection); when what was once imaginary appears in reality, the uncanny, the fantastic, the sublime, the dreadful or awe-induced terrible; true solitude or mobbish hordes, or the supernatural, or the natural, or what arrives from without or, then again, what is inborn or immanent (Mr. Edward Hyde; calls from inside the house; deposits in a skin, a stomach, a uterus, a brain); or all general hazy instability, modes of unmaking, societal transformation, antitheses of progress, underside of the Enlightenment, fallout of industrialization, Goya's "Sleep of Reason," the Nothing, pain, the pain of loved ones, dying, never dying, other people's panic, This Is the End (cf. There Will Never Be an End), self-folding fear itself, &c. (Relatedly: What does the frightening mean or express or symbolize in the context of a broader politics of representation; of what is it an allegory [of sexual/political/unconscious repression, with all the ideological implications related to normativity and naturalizing thereby articulated]? [The promiscuity of this question is legendary, as flexible as the signifier itself will allow in monstration, demonstration; it is extraordinarily generative, as evidenced by the influence of Robin Wood's famously open formula for horror—"normality is threatened by the Monster"—or as goes the claim in Jack Halberstam's *Skin Shows*: "Monsters are meaning machines. They can represent gender, race, nationality, class, and sexuality in one body."[21] Many of these claims are a glossed version of Althusser's notion of "expressive causality," which he attributes to {and vigorously critiques in} Hegel, in which narrative productions are the phenomenal expressions or reflections of cultural essences.][22] This praxis adjudicates inclusions [and traces exclusions], taxonomizing rules for membership, articulating expectations so tenacious that they are secured precisely through departures, self-conscious violations, and postmodern knowingness.) Inquiries into the ostensible timelessness of repeated, re-makeable, bad-time myths—appealing to Bettelheim, Freud, Jung, Jones, Campbell; or promising generous reach as in Wood's defi-

nition of the genre as "our collective nightmares"; or settling in vague bro-
mides such as Stephen Prince's claim that horror explores "fundamental questions about the nature of human existence"—are found alongside insistences
for the ineluctable specificity of a situated time or place or event (Auschwitz,
Hiroshima, Selma, Mỹ Lai; One World Trade Center; Chernobyl; or Juárez,
s-21, Abu Ghraib, and all the rest of all such things).[23] Here find emphasis on
the importance of the biological impropriety of scientifically uncountenanced
things (your large flies and mutants, half-wolves, and the undead) alongside
opposing claims that the monster, in fact, has died, has been replaced with
an ordinary sadist—as early as 1946, Kracauer wrote how "Nightmares are
seen in bright daylight, murderous traps are sprung just around the corner.
Everyday life itself breeds anguish and destruction"—or a violent normality in the guise of an awkward Norman Bates or an impassive killer named
Henry, himself to be replaced, still others propose, with the post-humanity of
the cyborg or a decentered technological gaze.[24] Much psychoanalytic work
is located herein, plus Marxist, cultural studies, feminist and queer, critical
race and postcolonial, most historicist, and national cinema contextual treatments; the broad nature of the investigation effortlessly places film, television,
and new media studies in dialogue with literary and visual studies. (Though
it comprises the largest group, by mass, of scholarly claims, all such writing
purports to grapple with and answer the same single question: What makes
the little hairs leap?)

2) **When, where, and how does this fright textually occur** (in film A,
with effect B, from aesthetic logic C, or across cycle D)? Here find the lists
of elements, the resemblances and consolidations of genre studies (ones that
emphasize narrative and trope in addition to those more concerned with
medium-specific *ciné-genre* characteristics), considerations of expressionism
against realism, lurid compared with avant-garde styles, spectacles and solicited astonishments; plus studies of the suspenseful dimension of offscreen
space or strategies of blocked vision (architectural occlusions, occasions for
partial or delayed glimpses), or, alternately, the wide-open expanse across
which every coming thing is visible but ineluctably unalterable; in addition:
elaborate treatments of shadows, staircases, fog, and I-cameras, of darkness,
violins, and syrup-blood, and attention to the explicit, graphic, gory; but also
mere suggestion, offscreen woundings only heard or Val Lewton-esque elegance, crafts of restraint. Here find aesthetic maps separating classic from
New, Hollywood from J-; here find auteurist signatures; here find histories of
technique that—justly—insist on the innovations of horror, whose lighting,

makeup, and effects trickled down to other modes of cinema. (Variant: How have these aesthetics of fright been produced, manipulated, transformed, branded, rebranded, and reinterpreted for global dissemination?) Add to this group the extensive catalogues, illustrated histories, fanzine portraits, and general fetishism of visual iconography, enthusiastic in place of critical, but parasitically related to scholarly work on horror. Although ample anthologized stills and beloved details are thereby produced from individual films, within the framework of this question the aesthetic is instrumentalized for the larger sake of a rippled nervous system—textual details are regarded for the sake of their effects, and aesthetic strategies are reduced to provocations that successfully produce the paramount frisson. All these (aesthetic, generic) *conventions* are thus taken as primarily affective (neck-oriented) *intentions*.

3) **How is the body** (this will be defined differently) **addressed, agitated, displaced, and moved in the instance of this fright?** Treated by phenomenological studies of horror, much cognitivist work, analyses of body genres (following Williams, that in which "audience sensation mimics what is seen on the screen," engendering an "over-involvement in sensation and emotion"), Deleuzian claims for the visceral agitations of the spectator, and more recent deployments of affect theory.[25] (This query may be posed very narrowly, as in Robert Spadoni's investigation of how spectators uncannily received early Hollywood monster movies by comparing "the first year of the classic horror cycle to a pattern of response that characterized general film reception during the immediately preceding sound transition years," or very broadly, as in Anna Powell's Deleuzian account of how the horror viewer "experiences corporeal responses as our senses stimulate the neural networks linked to organs like the heart (pace, pulse-rate), the genitals (warmth, tightness, moisture), and the lungs (depth and rapidity of breathing).")[26] While this question participates in long-standing discussions in aesthetics dating back to the eighteenth century about the specific sensations felt in the presence of representation containing certain qualities, also herein resides a good deal of work outside the humanities, including the measurement of physiological reactions, "self-reported arousal" metric compilations in neurobiology and social science, data about startle and scream (see Zuckerman's Sensation Seeking Scale), but also those who would ask, say, in the wake of a mass shooting, about mimicry and media effects, about the visceral pedagogy of violence, about being moved to move in the ways one saw on the screen (though it is never the investigator but always the faceless other who is vulnerably instructed by watching vile things). Finally, also here find, perverse ideological

bedfellow, predictive models by industry to anticipate audience appeal and arousal, to maximize the profitable elicitation of precisely such neck-borne responses.

4) **Why do spectators** (or specific group Q, e.g., adolescents, i.e. adolescent males [cf. not adolescent males]) **take pleasure in terror and fright?** (Variant 1: Why do spectators take pleasure in disgust or what repulses them?) (Variant 2: What is the [personal, social, historical, collective, national] purgative value of pleasing-unpleasing shock? [see: catharsis]) (Variant 3: Is this masochistic or sadistic? [3a, Or both, as in Philip Brophy's account of a gratification "based upon tension, fear, anxiety, sadism and masochism—a disposition that is overall both tasteless and morbid. The pleasure of the text is, in fact, getting the shit scared out of you—and loving it; an exchange mediated by adrenalin."])[27] (But still, despite all that, variant 4: Why would groups consistently represented as harmed—women, children, all queer identities— enjoy hours of sadistic-masochistic watching of designations of their destruction? [However, pause; suspend that question for variant 5: Not pleasure, but investment, as in Carol Clover's interest "in the male viewer's stake in horror spectatorship" {this turns on a theory of identification that will nullify variant 4; Clover dubs it "horror's system of sympathies"} {or, again, not pleasure, but compensatory thrilling-draining experience, as in Morris Dickstein's thesis that "Horror films are a safe, routinized way of playing with death (. . .) a way of neutralizing anxiety by putting an aesthetic bracket around it" (see, again: catharsis)}.])[28] (Variant 6: Is the fan's pleasure somehow otherwise [resistant, participatory, knowing {further var.: replace pleasure with connoisseurship; alt.: following Matt Hills in *The Pleasures of Horror*, regard that connoisseurship of subcultural capital as performative, which involves a methodological inversion, attending to the discursive texts of fans *in place* of reading horror texts}?]—[And furthermore: How has this changed in postmodernity? {Isabel Pinedo's urging} {alt.: How has this not changed at all in postmodernity?}])[29] Some psychoanalytic, most cognitivist, much feminist, most analytic philosophical, all fan studies, and almost all conservative deriding and general worries about the coarsening of culture are to be found herein (which itself replays the Plato-Aristotle dogfight about whether tragedy is corrupting or purgative, inciting or pedagogical).[30]

Perhaps the critic takes herself for a fan. Accordingly: **Question 3**, var., addendum: How is *my* body addressed, agitated, displaced, and moved in the instance of this fright, disgust, shock, &c.? **Question 4**, var., addendum: And why do *I* take pleasure, satisfaction, rueful glee, wild joy in this revulsion, fright, and thrill? For example, Powell: "I have chosen horror cinema because of my own engagement with it as fan and academic, and because I want to assert the genre's aesthetic complexity." Williams: "When my seven-year-old son and I go to the movies, we often select from among categories of films that promise to be sensational to give our bodies an actual physical jolt." Clover: "The initial dare took me into a territory I might not otherwise have explored, and against all odds I have ended up something of a fan. Like others before me, I discovered that there are in horror moments and works of great humor, formal brilliance, political intelligence, psychological depth, and above all a kind of kinky creativity."[31] One of the consequences of this tendency to phenomenologize the affective experience of horror and to make autobiographical (and confess to) its unpleasurable pleasures is a rabid evaluative drive—generic judgments of bad, better, and best in addition to omissions of texts solely because they are not to the critic's taste.[32] In a book whose subtitle promises a survey of modern and postmodern horror, Tony Magistrale apologizes for his (lack of) method: "I'm afraid there will be little here of interest to aficionados of zombies or the werewolf. [. . .] It is my belief that the zombie movie is better off dead. [. . .] For this writer, the cinematic world of the werewolf is similarly limited. [. . .] Precious few [. . .] films in this subgenre hold my interest for very long."[33]

Is it always the critic's own neck that must be saved in or by her writing? If so, it is at the cost of positing an ungeneralizable, untheorizable, and ultimately not all that compelling neck, which no one has ever derided better than the musicologist Eduard Hanslick in his critique of the "aesthetics of feeling": "We say nothing at all concerning the crucial aesthetic principle of music if we merely characterize music in general, according to its effect upon feeling, just as little, perhaps, as we would get to know the real nature of wine by getting drunk."[34]

(Who cares what you like? Who cares what you fear?)

Neck is a trap. Luring with promises of theoretical reach, it shows in the end only the faint traces of a small patch of stirred skin, and it offers nothing new in the way of thought about texts themselves. Neck is antithetical to speculation. Decide—as in *decaedere*, cut off, cleave—to be done with one's own dull column.

The final query, [Q4] Why would readers or spectators or viewers or users seek out occasions for unpleasurable feelings?, is fundamental to the broader aesthetics of the negative affects, ranging from Kant's prohibition on *Ekel* in *The Critique of Judgment* (1790)—for that which arouses loathing is an ugliness that "cannot be represented in a way adequate to nature without destroying all aesthetic satisfaction, hence beauty in art"—to Freud's rejoinder in *Das Unheimliche* (1919) that "As good as nothing is to be found upon this subject [the uncanny] in comprehensive treatises on aesthetics, which in general prefer to concern themselves with what is beautiful, attractive and sublime; that is, with feelings of a positive nature; and with the circumstances and the objects that call them forth, rather than with the opposite feelings of repulsion and distress."[35] In 1757, Hume posed the wonderment that has become a general model for this fourth question and its many variations: "It seems an unaccountable pleasure which the spectators of a well-written tragedy receive from sorrow, terror, anxiety, and other passions, that are in themselves disagreeable and uneasy. The more they are touched and affected, the more are they delighted with the spectacle."[36] That same year, Burke likewise derived from a theory of sympathy's substitutions that "It is by this principle chiefly that poetry, painting, and other affecting arts, transfuse their passions from one breast to another, and are often capable of grafting a delight on wretchedness, misery, and death itself. It is a common observation, that objects which in the reality would shock, are in tragical, and such like representations, the source of a very high species of pleasure."[37] (Burke and Hume share the language of "delight," a form of pleasure linked to the alluring, to charm; sublimity's awe is a pain that does not derange the body, that is not the force of violence itself, delightful horror above all a *delicate* horror.) More than two hundred years later, Hume's formulation still has currency: Twitchell follows the blueprint with his interest in "why we have been drawn to certain images in art and popular culture that we would find repellent in actuality," while Stephen King offers a worldly translation of this philosophical curiosity: "Why do people [. . .] *pay* to be horrified?"[38]

Carroll's version of Hume's tragic wonderment runs thusly in *The Philosophy of Horror*: "why would anyone *want* to be horrified, or even art-horrified?" This foundational question articulates the paradox of his book's title: "If horror necessarily has something repulsive about it, how can audiences be attracted to it?"[39] Why do all this to those poor necks? Although reviving the Humean aesthetic meta-concern, Carroll's preferred interlocutor is the lesser known 1773 meditation "On the Pleasure Derived from Objects of Terror" by the poet Anna Laetitia Aikin. For her, "well-wrought scenes of artificial terror" are not themselves pleasurable, but they engage "the pain of suspense, and the irresistible desire of satisfying curiosity," which "once raised, will account for our eagerness to go quite through an adventure, though we suffer actual pain during the whole course of it. We rather chuse [*sic*] to suffer the smart pang of a violent emotion than the uneasy craving of an unsatisfied desire." Aikin deploys the figure of fascination to extend the affective range of displeasures that can be made aesthetically endurable, from boredom to the extremest sympathetic suffering in cases of representational cruelties: "And it will not only force us through dullness, but through actual torture—through the relation of a Damien's execution, or an inquisitor's act of faith. When children, therefore, listen with pale and mute attention to the frightful stories of apparitions, we are not, perhaps, to imagine that they are in a state of enjoyment, any more than the poor bird which is dropping into the mouth of the rattlesnake—they are chained by the ears, and fascinated by curiosity."[40] (And, in a further rotation, Aikin the critic is also, in a manner, positively fascinated by these mixed captivations of fascination and curiosity—turning from aesthetic law to metaphor to put to *her* reader's imagination the death-bringing snares of the chaining by the ears of these pale, mute, hostaged children.) The poet concludes with a hierarchy of aesthetic evaluations, in which the highest promise of the gothic text, she submits, is the good feeling offered by "surprise from new and wonderful objects," such that, stimulating the imagination, "the pain of terror is lost in amazement. Hence, the more wild, fanciful, and extraordinary are the circumstances of a scene of horror, the more pleasure we receive from it."[41] Likewise, Carroll resolves his paradoxical presumptions in favor of a deeply pleasurable fascination and curiosity at precisely the category admixtures that constitute the provocative object of fear and loathing.[42]

Returning obsessively to the site of a phrasal trauma, the form of this last question cannot, it seems, be moved past, nor can thinkers shed the figure of the paradoxum: *that term for an absurd truth is the tic of a nervous criticism. Alex Neill responds to Carroll in an article entitled "On a Paradox of the Heart," while Berys Gaut quibbles with, and ultimately nullifies, the contradiction in "The Paradox of Horror"; years later, and considering both of those essays, Katerina Bantinaki pens "The Paradox of Horror: Fear as a Positive Emotion."[43] Offering a titular interrogatory that crystallizes the emotional puzzle, "Why Horror? The Peculiar Pleasures of a Popular Genre," Andrew Tudor turns his version of the query into a meta-inquiry—"precisely what we are asking is far from clear"—and then into endless iterations of the question, insisting it really should be "why do* these *people like* this *horror in* this *place at* this *particular time?"[44] Though a plea for proliferating distinctions, the fundamental tension of* [**Q4**]—What positive gain from negative *affects?—is only thereby scattered into a hall of mirrors, reflecting back an infinity of curiosities turning on the same self-negating oxymoronic terms: liking what is unlikeable, taking pleasure in displeasures borne out on neck.*

Dilemma: paradoxes tense a field; they yearn to be unknotted. And so, in place of an aporetic thinking with undecidability, this affective contradiction is constantly resolved. Each verdict forgets and forgoes the negativity in negative affects, supplants it with curiosity, fascination, palliative playing at anxiety, regressive wallowing in the culturally prohibited, gleeful temporary identification with othered sites, adolescent thrill-seeking, visceral temporal intensity, confirmation of fan identity, the delight of mixed sentiment, &c., all recuperating the abyssal negativity of unstable representations for something resembling a discourse of the diminution of pain or a neutralization of displeasure, a quiet reinstatement of pleasure—which is a judgment of value, a way of reviving a priority of the good, the establishment of noncontradiction at the cost of failing to read the negativity of negative affect as such. In other words, these resolutions deny the very object the theorist would contemplate in the first place.

These four questions that linger with the neck are often—indeed, usually—multiply present in critical work on horror and across diverse and otherwise irreconcilable camps: psychoanalytic, antipsychoanalytic, Marxist, feminist, cognitivist, analytical-philosophical, phenomenological, Deleuzian, &c. Within a span of a few sentences, Angela Ndalianis travels through the entire range of claims made possible by the set:

In New Horror Cinema, the label often given to this recent phase of the genre, the horror spectator enters a space that operates as a ritualistic violation of taboos and, in the process, fears and desires are unleashed that often threaten "normal" society and its onscreen ideologies [**Q1—What is frightening?**]: murder and displays of sadomasochistic violence, perverted sexual acts, incest and interbreeding, the return of the dead, cannibalism—these themes are at the core of New Horror [**Q2—When, where, and how does this fright textually occur?**]. Yet these themes rely heavily on the spectator's senses in order to achieve their full impact. New Horror, like all horror, relies on the sensorium, an integrated unit that combines cognition and the senses, the mind and the body [**Q3—How is the body addressed, agitated, displaced, and moved in the instance of this fright?**]. Horror media offers us a gamut of experiences—horror, laughter, fear, terror, the cerebral pleasures of intertextual play [**Q4—Why do spectators take plea-**

sure in terror and fright?]—and, depending on the sensory, emotional and intellectual encounters each example throws our way, we perceive, sense and interpret the fictional spaces of horror in diverse and distinctive ways.[45]

That the upshot of such an approach remains on the slender side of neck is made explicit in Ndalianis's subsequent declaration that "in conjunction with this cognitive and intellectual involvement is an insistent focus on the body on- and off-screen. Horror films, especially since the 1960s, have performed their textual journeys on the bodies of the characters that populate their fictional worlds. In turn, the bodily destruction depicted onscreen unrelentingly weaves its way offscreen and onto the body of the spectator."[46] The second shudder question, the one turning on the aesthetic, iconographic, or auteurist, is implicit across the above passage, as it appears in a chapter entitled "Horror Aesthetics and the Sensorium," which promises to examine "a key premise of horror: the tug of war that occurs between wanting to look and not wanting to look."[47] Ndalianis figures this tension in the history of the genre through the privileged figure of the extreme close-up of an eye. Attend, however, to what value is to be derived from such an attention to images on the screen: "as the zombie forces her eye closer and closer to the sharp splinter of wood [**Q2**], my perception responded physiologically to what I saw onscreen, triggered by the memory not of being attacked by a zombie, but of corresponding sensory and somatic responses [**Q3**]."[48]

Neck is what indentures form to feeling, placing [**Q2**] in the service of [**Q3**]. Neck aesthetics constitute that minimal attention to image, sound, duration, and structure sufficient to make a claim for the provocative impulse that stirs bodies. Form is thereby taken as means, put to work for affective claims: the text merely *in terrorem*.

It is not that critical language falters here or that the ineffable resists representation. Horror's risk is in its very etymological tidiness. Horrēre has rendered a reductive generic form marked at every turn by an ontological affectivity, whose essentialized joining to the moved corporeal scene has instrumentalized the aesthetic, blindly overvalued the spectatorial, colluded with the either cynical or fannish impulses of industry, exhausted the same theoretical models while entirely ignoring others, depleted the capacity to generate theoretical shock, and willfully ignored horror's capacity for a low formalism and the restricted forms, neutral forms, and speculations derived from reading for form that constitute an analytic (of finitude; of force; of ethics; of aporias of critique itself; &c.). This is why accounts of horror aesthetics have looked repeatedly at expressive lighting and suspenseful editing, but almost never at lines and shapes, constructed grids, formal games, rhythms unrelated to physiology, the nonhuman (without converting it to a provocation to a humanism of neck), eccentric typography, hypotactic structures, or the cold rigors of arbitrary restraint: for it is not immediately obvious how to make these things efficiently work for generic shudderclaims. Functionalizing the aesthetic, this theory can tell us nothing about the aesthetic, nor can it adequately grapple with formal elements that are indifferent to affect, opaque, neutral, blank, abstract. Thus, shadow will be overemphasized and number ignored; close-up of corpse valued at the expense of alphabet.

Paradoxically, well after *la mort de l'auteur*, a naive notion of intention is thereby brought back to the fold—for what is an affective tautology of horror other than an insistence on the centrality of intention-to-arouse-fright, not by a singular Romantic genius but by industry: the undead author as marketer, the text returned to a prestructuralist utopia of singular, successful, limited transmission of something shuddersome. Indeed, the entire impulse behind this critical tendency is a rabidly pre-poststructuralist fidelity to a model of nondifference between a word and a thing. Negativity is recuperated for a successfully expressed, successfully commodified affect-experience (criticism in collusion with a drive toward profit), and, paradoxically, the affectively disturbing is also thereby domesticated, contained and bounded by the idealisms of sensing and feeling that thrive at the site of the neck. Taken in this register, horror inverts Frege's definition of zero—what is not self-identical—and becomes that fullness which belongs to the concept *identical with itself*. Horror as the provocation of what horrifies. Horrēre has thereby constituted the finitude of the infinitely transformative task of *theoria*. In the midst of seemingly radical claims for the destabilizing, destructive, lustily entropic dimension of this mode of representation (all those dark themes! all those terrible tropes!), the body's fleshy connector functions as a way of keeping critical work on the side of essence, origin, totality, center, stability, integrity, unity, meaningfulness, put in the service of confirming noncontradiction and purity—all those anodyne ideals that will never fail to find their adherents.

If you wanted to write of difference. If you wanted to speak of change. If you chose to speak about the same but not presume it. If you wanted to think many, not one, or not even one but nothing, or what is becoming or unfurling or what isn't yet but might and how that might might take shape. If the body isn't enough, or if the body regarded differently might be enough but the body is not the neck and the neck is not enough. If you ache for other words. If you don't want to presume you already know. If you suspect that knowledge, in fact, is not the right term and suspect that knowledge might, in fact, be part of the problem if knowledge is presumed to afford the critic with something in advance. If you require surprise, to be surprised, to surprise. If you don't know beforehand what is missing or where things will go or how it will all end up and if that seems like the way to create something unforeseen even if it also does mean that no certain outcome would ever be guaranteed. If you wanted to think something new. If that feels risky. If you wanted to think something new and were willing to accept every risk.

CERVICAL FRACTURES

Neck is the supreme extratextual referent; it is what suspends, as in amber, infinite deferral, referral, difference, play—equilibrium of thought, neck is stasis. Necks are a single principle.

And so: What becomes possible if the theorist does away with the expressive-affective neck of horror, this flare so attractive for a mothy thought, this insinuating atlas that has so stubbornly gotten in the way?

Ossified concepts demand fracturing. And what, if not horror, teaches how nimbly bones can break.

—Neck thereby ruined, what now will prop us up?

The answer is a radical formalism, though it makes no promise to keep any skull or system afloat. For radical formalism—not a formalism in thrall to radical politics but radical as in *radix*, to return to the speculative *ground* or *roots* of what thinking can claim—involves reading without guarantee; its terms, affordances, and stakes cannot be declared and secured beforehand. It takes as its motto for theoretical ethos something like Heidegger's description of the primordial truth of existence: "The Situation cannot be calculated in advance or presented like something present-at-hand which is waiting for someone to grasp it."[49] An extraordinary vulnerability exists in this charge of being absolutely open to possible determinations. Reading without guarantee always risks defaulting on the contracts that purport to stabilize and restrain signification. Its promise, however, is enormous, allowing thought to proceed beyond the constraints of bad affect, to revitalize exhausted concepts, generating surprise in the unfolding act of reading itself—all that which is derived from its quality of being an uncertain investment, resisting economies that promise high returns and predictable yields.

One must begin with the priority of grid over neck, chart over feeling, design over affect, toroid over terror, drawn *graphikos* over the vividly graphic, arrangement (of textual form) over derangement (of represented corpus)—the totality of what can be neither paraphrased about a text nor instrumentalized for claims of intensity or experience. (Only pornography has been more durably regarded as exhausted by its affective provocations—and it, too, demands a resolutely formal reading. *Speculative pornography* is not an oxymoron.) I am not insisting that the transdisciplinary thinking of the most negative affect add to its tally a greater quantity of formal readings, nor that formalism is a *correction* or merely a new critical *emphasis*, but, rather, that rotations of the affective-expressive neck have operated at the explicit expense of speculative modes of thinking. The aim herein is a total effort to reapproach form as the root of all reading, and as what grounds theoretical work on every one of the figures—violence, cruelty, finitude, relation, ethics, care, and debt—that will carry across this book. What is revealed en route is a bond that sutures horror to philosophy as a site that (humiliatingly, problematically) also treats those figures themselves *as* problems of form. Perhaps at so late a moment it seems willfully odd to insist that, accordingly, this is not really a book about horror. But: this is not really a book about horror. It is a work that puts the extremest pressure on formalism's promise, reach, and aporetic limit at the site of extremities: of force, of construction, of thought. Horror will be the occasion where radical formalism is, as it were, *put to the test*, posing the question of the limits of formalism on its most difficult but urgent terrain—precisely where it might seem as though the raw materiality of destroyed bodies, of brutality and torture and the world's worst stuff demanded a renunciation of all abstractions and aestheticisms. That this is a book about form will not become visible—or, rather, the speculative stakes and risks of radical formalism will not become earned—until rather late in the text. Formalism reminds us that one must always begin thought from a particular concrete somewhere. Horror is one place to begin.

At stake in a radical formalism of horror is simultaneously a revision of our approach to the body, that body whose neck has so insistently been lodged at the center of critical concern. Insisting that a thinking of horror shed the neck and its affective teleology does not require renouncing the remainder of the body, only a wholesale shift in thought about what constitutes the body, what violence and force against the body are possible, and what bodies can formally do. Far from an idealism that would deny the materiality of the body, but equally divorced from an interest in the body as a discursive construction, horror regards the body as *nothing but formal material*, treating it as a compositional aspect that is navigated by, intersects with, interprets and is interpreted by, distorts and is distorted by, devastates and is devastated by, reconfigures and is reconfigured by, unfolding relations with countless other formal aspects that mutually and continuously interact, bearing out the potential for being otherwise. Bodies do not possess form, detaining it like a *thing*; rather, for horror the body is nothing but a trajective process of change that is formally navigable, which is to say givable and manipulable, and which does not disappear with an encounter with violence but in fact is positively enabled *by* it. This is not a matter of adding a formal consideration of the body as a supplement; it is to regard the body as a formal problem from the very beginning. It will, however, radically change the relation (strictly: the correspondence or connection) between the body and violence—one set of connective relations will be severed, while another will appear and be affirmed.

Quite late in *The Forms of the Affects*, I wondered, but left it alone: "Indeed, we might more broadly consider whether horror is the genre in which the body is formalized, given textual shape only to be subjected to the bare destruction of its form." We might indeed.

Consider Luca Guadagnino's 2018 reimagining of Dario Argento's *Suspiria*, which is orchestrated around the wild transformations, transfixions, and modifications of various female bodies, most spectacularly early in the film with the blackmagical joining of the bodies of dancers Susie and Olga (a corporeal sympathy), such that as Susie moves through space, dances, leaps, bends, and strains, Olga's body is forced to mimic the coordinates of the dance, will-less, volition-less, and art-less, which is to say dance reduced to its formal navigation of force on and through extremities, through limbs and joints and organs. The force of Susie's dancing forces Olga's body into new postures (plate 1). The dancing of one form, structured and purposive, is commuted to the dragging of another form, deprived of the freedom to choose aesthetic force, reduced to nothing but force qua force: Olga's form is dragged; that form is bent; its form is torn; this form's structural things (= bones) are made discontinuous (= broken; = fractured); the formal touching parts (= joints) are cleaved (= burst), their formal relation to container, to surface (= skin) made perpendicular (= pierced); one form (= unified) is made multiple, one form (= the upright, linear) is made different (= the spiraled, bent). Olga-as-form is neither deformed nor malformed: this She is taken for a This and the form of this This is re-formed. From the point of view of the feeling body—that is, neck—the scene is one of agonizing unending torture and the destruction of essential living quality. From the point of view of visible form, the same event is the construction of and generation of and attestation of new forms. *Torture* recalls its Latin roots from *torquere*—to twist, turn, wind, wring, distort—refusing to settle in itself the subject of what is twisted, turned, wound, wrung, distorted. *Suspiria* is not a horror film because of the presence of witches or any vague affective account of its effect on implied or empirical spectators; it is neither more nor less than a horror film because it attests to the state in which the deformation of the body from an anthropocentric perspective is formally generative of a new possibility for aesthetic construction, in other words, invents a new genre of dance from a compositional perspective. *Suspiria* demonstrates that the gestures of violence do not negate—violence is what positively ex-presses new choreographic potential precisely *because* horror regards the body purely formally.

Questions without necks:
    What does it mean to linger with the formal languages of any given text? This requires close reading, the digressions, deferrals, and inefficient detours of interminable interpretation. Texts are not to be reduced to the paraphrase of themes or itemization of tropes; broken is the empiricist circularity that confirms, in any given film, the set {horrific} determined in advance. This thought rebukes Twitchell's oft-invoked insistence that the affective-cognitive-physiological-sensorial priority of etymologically derived affect supplants the need to attend to the autonomous forms of texts and will work against what

Althusser dubbed in *Reading Capital* "the illusion of immediate reading," the myth of "an innocent reading."[50] To what use are put formal restraints (the compilation, the anthology, an abecedarium, but also the sequential, the enclosed, limited cartographies); and to what use are put forms such as the diagram, the ordinal; the cell or grid or table; graphs, maps, or sequences; formal rules; typography; the shapes of things; shapes themselves? Aesthetic, formal, structural dimensions are treated as indifferent to affective provocation; they bear out their own force. *Neutral horror* is no longer a zero-sum phrase. Jurisdictions of horror will now include being, relating, the relation of being and relating, and the relation of being and relating to form. Neck will come to seem less radical than grid, torture less brutal than diagram. More violence will be done in A, B, C than on flesh. What analytic (of finitude: as limit, of being, of thought) is thereby demonstrated, which is to say what analytic is put on formal display, or for which analytic is a purely formal display *necessary* for its demonstration? How does ontological finitude cut into and across aesthetic infinitude? What cold formalisms of philosophical thought on being and relationality are attested to in the formalisms of cinematic and literary objects? How to think the nothing, and for what reason? What is the feel of political terror and violence, not as a question of sensation but as a matter of rapidity, sensitivity, and mechanical action? How does an abecedarium, a list or a table, a chart or a grid, or a fascination with form itself bear out a specific kind of violence? And finally—with the aim of making as many comparisons as possible—what lines of thought are set loose by regarding horror as a deliverance *into* formality, not just for the aesthetic but for philosophy itself, that which intimately shares with horror the problem of how to think violence and ethics as nothing but problems of form?

a list, design, a table, a chart, a map, a grid, a database, a matrix, a line, a ray, an alphabet, order, a sequence, a diagram, number, system, set, a chain, an action, a rhythm, a color, a shape, a field, a spacing, duration, an increment, all thresholds, a pattern, extension, contraction, a toroid, a speed, a curve, a pressure, slowing, a field, a block, evasion, a figure, figures, and rubble and tread and sound or spool, silence, a word, light, lightlessness, repetition, a gap, a match, a difference, a givenness, a change, something, nothing, anything, but never a neck

First voice: How can theory reactivate an exhausted concept of horror?

Second voice: The problem is that the word already is *there* where this reactivation is called for.

First, again: Shall we merely say nothing, then?

How to think a horror that might be untranslatable, ambiguous and multiple, self-contradicting, self-annihilating—frustrating to the purview of genre in refusing a belonging, disturbance to the proper (horror that *does not want* the proper root that most intimately belongs to it: the height of *impropriety*)? Play as if to dishonor its name: forget *etymon*, true sense, from *etymos*, real, actual—give its form in active falsity, offer up only a lie. Exclude its familiar reified tones, and start over with the word, subject the concept to the urgent problem, the absurd difficulty, that is the promise of language itself, which is to say: confront it always again as though it had never been said first. Neologisms and hyphenations are not enough; contextual parentheses are not enough; elaborate and ever-finer taxonomic distinctions, the lexical equivalent of Freud's "narcissism of minor differences"—the careful midlevel ordering of horror versus terror against the sublime (different from wonder) and opposed to dread, related to loathing (var., contempt), not quite the grotesque, the uncanny, the fantastic, narrow monstrosity (contrast deformity [cf. freakery]) or the strange, or repugnance, anguish or the hateful, or , , , , , , , &c.—only defer down the long signifying chain another arrival at shuddering spine, disgusted gut, prickling skin—and these are all ways of still writing *Neck*.

If horror remains lodged to horrēre, the leech sucking off the host—though which is the fed-upon and which the segmented worm is an open question—then the critical risk is an etymology that seems to speak of plenitude, exhausting itself in its debts to what is prior; the word would be taken to exhaust the concept, in an exhaustion that converts a concept into a deixis for its affect, converting its affect into the commodity the object offers, and in doing so perversely works against Deleuze's insistence that concepts must above all be *generated*. Yet one is, as one is, stuck with exhausted terms, that liability for new thoughts. The question will always be how to retain the word without getting lodged in (trapped by) tautologies.

The crisis of horror, then, is that it requires horrēre be contradicted—say it for the new while denying that anything new might be said in its name; repeat, restate, reuse the very term under erasure.

On the other hand, of course, there can be no concept without a (provisional) word. We must retain it (—though not at any cost).

And so, the first task for thinking a nonaffective horror is to contemplate with rigor the form of a circle.

This is the fundamental problem of critical tradition, whether one of history, origin, development, or generic evolution: one cannot merely leap over the wasted heavy grounds of a concept to reinvigorate X without remaining stubbornly bound to them. We will not not write horror. As Derrida phrases this dilemma in *The Problem of Genesis in Husserl's Philosophy*, in his reading of the question of the origin of geometry, "The traditional sedimentations must be reduced in order for us to be able to return to the originary foundation; but at the same time it is because there is sedimentation and tradition that this return is possible."[51] If this methodological problem is a circle, the solution is also a formal figure, graphic and geometric. Husserl's proposed method in *Die Krisis der europäischen Wissenschaften* is that "we have no other choice than to proceed forward and backward in a zigzag pattern; the one must help the other in an interplay."[52] Husserl writes *Zickzack*—after all, what better to break into roundness than line? Disorderly, messy, a course of digressions and swerves, abrupt alternations between clarity and opacity, snaking oscillations between analysis and inclarities that block or frustrate, understandings that do not precede investigation—patterns that leave a record of dangerous, angular descents, of erring off course—all obliquity, a roughening up of graphic propriety. Unlike neck, that straightforward path on which one will never lose oneself, the energy of a zigzag is in its inefficiency as movement, recalling what Jean-Claude Lebensztejn beautifully dubbed "the extravagant patience" of Derrida's strategy of close, subtle, winding, indirect reading, reading that can surprise ("direct attention [. . .] through strangeness"), which generates new concepts in the act of reading as transverse travel. Detouring bends being themselves the point.[53]

A horror that does not stand on neck constitutes something unassimilable to genre's obsession with the genetic (origins) or the sorting tasks of *gendre*. Instead of taking horror from the point of view of neck's pleasures or unpleasures, this book turns to textual particulars, and in place of *genre*, it considers horror in relation to the *general*. Genre—whether conceived via the semantic or the syntactic—is miserly; the general is generous. In attending to the general, however, horror will come back around—and with great force—to violence and wreckage, to the inescapable limits of understanding, to the particular undoing of particular things and to the ruination of being. If there is anything interesting still to result from thinking with horror—if it is to be reactivated, reanimated—we cannot remain with the widespread assertoric bias of criticism, or what Andrew Tudor dubs "the empiricist dilemma" of genre, assembling an existing membership and then retroactively identifying shared characteristics in the group already assembled because it was determined to possess precisely those qualities in common in the first place. Genre ends up, as he neatly puts it, being what "we collectively believe it to be"—the archive held to be true solely as what already *is*, thus inherently on the side of the antispeculative.[54] For the rhythms of thought—at their best—disorganize their object of inquiry. The negative effort of critique is beset by the affirmative positing of new conceptual targets. The task, therefore, of unearthing the limitations of horror cannot remain with the project of unmasking what is already declared; it must also generate, through that interplay of what it is attempting to do violence to, a new form—that *something else something new* that is to be done.

And yet one cannot do away entirely with genre either. As Derrida frames this secondary dilemma in "The Law of Genre," "there is no genreless text; there is always a genre and genres, yet such participation never amounts to belonging."[55] The risk is in confusing the law of genre—a standard of unity, a test of distinctness, an establishment of limit—and the law of the law of genre, that while every genre contains a defining mark (by minimal definition), said mark is not itself within that genre. Any given work of horror is both classified and declassified by the problem of generic membership. Its impurity is a participation that is never a belonging. This is precisely what functions as an origin of interpretation, opening up fields of possibilities in relation to reading form. Consider the impasse of a purely generic reading of Drew Goddard and Joss Whedon's 2011 meta-horror extraordinaire *The Cabin in the Woods*, in which the film reflexively deploys stock generic conventions in its "upstairs" teenagers-in-eerie-location narrative, but requires that criticism relinquish precisely those aspects in order to grapple with the grid of possible database inclusions in the "downstairs" narrative conceit of panoptic controllers who manipulate the conditions of possibility "upstairs" (the meta-/hypertext grammatically and architecturally hypotactic). Rather than reflexively subverting conventions (the knowingness that so many critics have aligned with the quintessential postmodern horror sensibility), *Cabin in the Woods* effects platform leaps, spatialized and homologized in the glass grid of all possible monstrous narrative components that might have arrived in the textual universe "upstairs" but did not. If laws of genre explain the logic of inclusive membership, the law of the law of genre points to the failure to account for this grid from within any generic heuristic. *Neck can never account for database.*

One cannot entirely sever horror from genre, and yet a ready-made horror cannot think the *Zickzack* that is the methodological grapple required for undoing its name. The aim, then, is not to replace *horror* with merely another placeholder—one either indifferent to what has been said in its name or one that merely says the same name by way of a shift cipher. The charge is to notdefine, to suspend definition, to move in the space between and in the irresolvable blanknesses that beg to be filled in. Back to Husserl, Derrida neatly outlines the form of the dilemma: "If I empty geometry of its traditional, present, effective content, nothing will remain for me, or only a formal concept of geometry that will itself be constituted or derived. [. . .] Thus I will get to a description that will oscillate between an *a priori* formalism and an absolute empiricism."[56] This if-thus formulation is itself a conditional statement (if p is true, then q will result), performing the very dilemma thereby named: geometry can never be emptied such that truly nothing of it remains—for the very formalism of protasis and apodosis (of p and q) is foundational to pure geometry; writing cannot avoid the sedimentations of geometry to make a claim about geometry. (Geometry is a problem of genre as well. So many things are.)

Every reading method comes at a cost, and here our dilemma is a properly affective one, a matter related to love—it is, to the point, a problem of fidelity.

In *The Work of Mourning*, in his piece on (in the wake of) Barthes, Derrida posits an ethical dilemma for the friend who remains after the other dies. He casts this as "two infidelities"—"an impossible choice: on the one hand, not to say anything that comes back to oneself, to one's own voice, to remain silent [. . .] but this excess of fidelity would end up saying and exchanging nothing. It returns to death. [. . .] On the other hand, by avoiding all quotation, all identification, all rapprochement [. . .] one risks making him disappear again, as if one could add more death to death and thus indecently pluralize it." To recall through citation risks anesthetizing death's loss as pain, neutralizing friendship as love, and points only to the friend as dead; but to avoid quotation risks a re-disappearance, and so one must "do and not do both at once, with having to correct one infidelity by the other."[57] This accounting of the responsibilities of love in the midst of grief holds something of the fundamental difficulty of speculative thought derived from reading with form—itself a kind of amative project amid laborious troubles.

It's a fucking intolerable choice: On the one hand, if one remains bound to all that has been said in the name of horror (or anything that will be at stake in this book—finitude, violence, ethics, love, form itself), then critical work merely cites and reiterates the exhaustion of concepts; concepts and their specificity (all difference) disappear altogether and nothing new can be generated from their thinking. On the other hand, if one is indifferent to that density, one risks making the very subject disappear (killing it off, as it were, over and over again, at the origin). Even worse, of course, would be to be overwhelmed by the all-that-has-been-said and to thereby remain mute, repeating the dilemma of Cratylus of Athens: Aristotle's *Metaphysics* tells of a skepticism so extreme that he "finally did not think it right to say anything but only moved his finger."[58] So one must honor the impossible choice and *do and not do* both at once—correcting exhaustion and saturation (the *nothing-more-nothing-new-to-be-seen*; the *Has not everything been said on the subject of X?*; the *Doesn't death, or violence, or love, or _____ return us to meaningfulness as such?*) with bold indifference, with a callous refusal to remain faithful to accumulated saturations. The zigzag this book accordingly traces moves between a formalism of horror and a horror of formalism, a formalism of violence and a violence of formalism, a formalism of ethics and an ethics of formalism, and ultimately a formalism of love and a love of formalism, not allowing any single term to serve or stand on any other. Interest remains with the *Zickzack*: the disaffordance of critical possibilities, the disqualification of critical oppositions, lingering with the awkward, arduous, inefficient zigzag, holding fast only to the veering speculative potential of a great infidelity.

The words we know will be retained as worlds and as words; there will be no new words to save thought from the problems of sedimentation and exhaustion. But they will be retained as impossible and yet insistent; retained, but only unfaithfully. And then, as goes the essential promise of all close reading, the venture turns now to: let us see what happens.

We have heard that we do not know all it is that form can do.

What can form do in the face of horror?

It may be supposed that a little bit of formalism turns away from the material body subject to finitude, but radical formalism brutally, viciously, relentlessly, and movingly will bring thought back around to it. In time.

And in a manner we did not know was coming.

—Even when death as the possible impossibility of being is precisely what is seen to certainly be coming:

The mortals are the human beings. They are called mortals because they can die. To die means to be capable of death *as* death. Only man dies, and indeed continually, as long as he remains on earth, under the sky, before the divinities.

—MARTIN HEIDEGGER, "Building Dwelling Thinking"

Two things account for our conservatism: the strength of our original emotional reaction to death and the insufficiency of our scientific knowledge about it. Biology has not yet been able to decide whether death is the inevitable fate of every living being or whether it is only a regular but yet perhaps avoidable event in life. It is true that the statement "All men are mortal" is paraded in text-books of logic as an example of a general proposition; but no human being really grasps it, and our unconscious has as little use now as it ever had for the idea of its own mortality.

—SIGMUND FREUD, *Das Unheimliche*

"O cruel Death, give three things back,"
Sang a bone upon the shore;

—W. B. YEATS, "Three Things"

The list is the origin of culture. It's part of the history
of art and literature. What does culture want? To make
infinity comprehensible. It also wants to create order—
not always, but often. And how, as a human being, does
one face infinity? How does one attempt to grasp the incomprehensible? Through lists, through catalogs, through
collections in museums and through encyclopedias and
dictionaries.
[. . .]
At first, we think that a list is primitive and typical
of very early cultures, which had no exact concept of the
universe and were therefore limited to listing the characteristics they could name. But, in cultural history, the list has
prevailed over and over again. It is by no means merely an
expression of primitive cultures. A very clear image of the
universe existed in the Middle Ages, and there were lists.
A new worldview based on astronomy predominated in
the Renaissance and the Baroque era. And there were lists.
And the list is certainly prevalent in the postmodern age.
It has an irresistible magic.
[. . .]
We like lists because we don't want to die.

—UMBERTO ECO, Interview, *Der Spiegel*

We don't want to die.

Let's begin there.

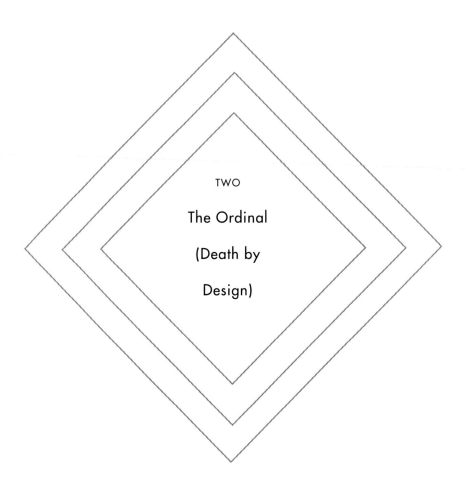

TWO

The Ordinal

(Death by

Design)

"I should have tried to find throughout nature the dividing line (*le point limite*), below which nothing exists. An example will show you what I mean. The newspapers the other day had an account of a workman who was electrocuted. He was handling some live wires carelessly; the voltage was not very high; but it seems his body was in a state of perspiration. His death is attributed to the layer of humidity which enabled the current to envelop his body. If his body had been drier, the accident wouldn't have taken place. But now let's imagine the perspiration added drop by drop. . . . One more drop—there you are!"

"I don't understand," said Olivier.

"Because my example is badly chosen. I always choose my examples badly. Here's another: Six ship-wrecked persons are picked up in a boat. They have been adrift for ten days in the storm. Three are dead; two are saved. The sixth is expiring. It was hoped he might be restored to life; but his organism had reached the extreme limit (*le point limite*)."

"Yes, I understand," said Olivier. "An hour sooner and he might have been saved."

"An hour! What are you saying? I am calculating the extremest point. (*Je suppute l'instant extrême.*) It is possible. It is still possible. . . . It is no longer possible! (*On peut encore. On ne peut plus!*) My mind walks along that narrow ridge. That dividing line between existence and non-existence is the one I keep trying to trace everywhere" (*Cette ligne de démarcation entre l'être et le non-être, je m'applique à la tracer partout*).[1]

Armand's focus in this passage from André Gide's 1925 *Les Faux-Monnayeurs* (*The Counterfeiters*), on the Drop, the Drop, the Still Possible, at the instant each transforms into the *One drop more*, the *It is no longer possible*, involves ordinal attention to forms of exactitude that catch up to being, the processual tipping point as predictable and certain as it is radical and absolute. This obsessive pursuit of *le point limite*, that line of demarcation between being and nonbeing, is given in the early modernist privileging of the figure of the precise instant. But the drive to know the extremest limit, beyond which there is nothing, is itself a feint, a kind of counterfeit. For one only ever knows from the point of view of being. That something might someday not be possible is the condition for the concept of the possible, but the no-longer-possible is not sensible or speakable except as the horizon that remains at a distance from the stable shore of what is. Even to declare *It is no longer possible* is to practice a syntactical fraudulence: such a declarative lingers with the grammar of being, the language that being boasts to imagine (read: cheat; read: invent) what it cannot, within itself, speak. The period that divides "On peut encore. On ne peut plus" likewise tenders a typographical deceit, simulating a punctuated space in which the irreversible passage of being to nonbeing could take place (as situated and actual, and no longer solely as horizon or extremest point). The same phrase might thus be said of the pause between being and nonbeing that Barthes declares of Gide's personality in a reading of his *journal intime*: it is that which "compromises itself."[2] The spacing on the page puts in order a false list, cunningly carrying through a sense of continuity that the extremest point can never make good on: by the time the list resumes with *On ne peut plus*, something will be grammatically compromised. We know, of course, of beings, that they do in fact die. *Not a one of us is wanting (for) death.* Yet this language of ridge, restriction, point—that "ligne de démarcation entre l'être et le non-être"—is geometrically and grammatically inadequate to the unfathomable, chasmic, and yet real divide figured in that one more drop of additive sweat that makes all the crucial difference.

This drama of the tiniest detail that is converted at the threshold of some disaster—thus producing the disaster at and in the moment of that conversion—is the fundamental logic of spectacle in the catalogue of demises that constitute the text of the *Final Destination* franchise, which contains five films (in addition to several comic books and novels) made between 2000 and 2011. There is something tautological and elegantly straightforward about the premise of the series: Death is the antagonistic force—the motivated cause of death itself. Each film begins with a character experiencing a causeless, contextless premonition of catastrophe in some restricted space marked by anticipated displacement (an about-to-depart airplane or ascending roller coaster) or blockage (a construction-congested bridge, a crowded car about to enter an unruly highway, spectator stands at a speedway), which leads to that protagonist and a select group of arbitrary others avoiding the portended death, which, as soon as they evade it, occurs *for others*. In time, however, despite this initial circumvention of a seeming inevitability, necessity is reasserted, and each surviving figure dies in turn, in some order related to the order in which they would have died had the foreseen catastrophe actually taken place, even if that order runs backward, as it does in *Final Destination 2*, reversal not a destruction of ordinality but only its inverted affirmation. Thus, the eschaton of each iteration of the franchise is the death of all the members of the opening premonition-evading set; that one nullified, a new set is posited and the sequence protocol begins once more in the next film. This ordinal insistence is what the films call "death's design," and the texts are peppered with didactic declarations of this logic via periodic appearances of a black-clad mortician intoning variations of the truism that one cannot evade or best the mortal state of being subject to a future, certain end. In the first film, he insists, "In death there are no accidents, no coincidences, no mishaps, and no escapes. By walking off the plane you cheated death. You have to figure out when it's coming back at you." The impossibility of defrauding or dodging a futurity marked by (one's) death is what brings about (everyone's) deaths. In the notation of universal quantifiers, each film tracks the difference between the existential quantifier $\exists$ and the universal quantifier $\forall$, or the movement from $\exists x$, *There exists at least one x not subject to the imposition of death's design* to $\forall x$, *All x's are subject to the imposition of death's design.*

Like *Les Faux-Monnayeurs, Final Destination* is grounded by the formal dilemma of how to handle a sequence that has something to do with death. With conjunction, continuity, order, and linkage (the excessive joiners and bonders, all ands and ors of polysyndeton, to carry the line or thread along—even if this overtly deceives), or with asyndetic difference, separation, breakage, rupture? Is death fundamentally limit, as in what ends by coming last, or does it offer a vitality of ordering, as, say, putting in place the temporality and sequence of an ongoing list? The five-film text endures at the fraught intersection of a stubbornly subjunctive tense confronting the facticity of a reasserted indicative: every listed death in sequence is simultaneously an irreal might-have/should-have *and* one that will and is.

This formula's rigor and purity; rejection of narrative suspense (substituting absolute certainty); privileging of obviousness over allusion; and replacement of stalker, psychopath, or assailant with the brute facticity of finitude have produced three modes of critical response, which represent a taxonomic shorthand for conventional treatments of horror. First, some scholars have aligned the franchise with postmodern horror's interpellation of a savvy player-spectator who is rewarded for their connoisseurship of the series (or, as the films are saturated with clues to be deciphered, a model of viewer-as-detective). Accordingly, like the *Scream* franchise, the films involve self-conscious nods to the history of horror, with a premise reminiscent of the 1983 low-budget film *Sole Survivor* and with characters named Alex Browning, Valerie Lewton, Billy Hitchcock, &c. Alternative endings in the DVD editions of the films contribute to this sense of a ludic franchise offering open-ended play. (In addition, typical of postmodernity's hybrid allusions, *Final Destination* seems to be at once modernist and ancient, high and low, taking as equivalent interlocutors 1950s horror gimmickry, Buñuel's *The Exterminating Angel*, and Bergman's *The Seventh Seal*; and while its obsession with waking visions and portents of death harkens back to a classical worldview—swapping the neck-breaking "hook-beaked eagle" of the *Odyssey* for ominous lightning, bodingly lyricized pop songs, and unsubtle reappearances of the number 180 (in reference to the flight number that is the disaster frame of the first film), plus its overt citation of Ecclesiastes 9:12 (the *nescit homo finem suum* bit)—the franchise is also structurally obsessed with what Barthes calls one of the fundamental "formal categories of modernity: that of the *sequence of phenomena*."[3] It tones every one of these registers at once.) A second set of critics has attended to the franchise's spectacular effects, particularly in the case of the stereoscopic language of the 3D sequels from 2009 and 2011.[4] This mass of arguments turns on the agitations, astonishments, and shuddering experiences endemic to spectatorial teleologies of horror: the horrological (mis)taken for an affectology.

Third, finally, the franchise has elicited accusations of being a cynical, reductive approach to genre. Reynold Humphries, relying on a political-psychoanalytic critique, condemns the films as "obscurantist nonsense whose only 'idea' is that death is an agency that has a 'plan' for each of us." He chides the franchise for its attempt "to deny death by foretelling the future," a denial that involves "a refusal to think in the present."[5] This approach illustrates a telling problem that a certain kind of critical tradition has in relation to *Final Destination*: the franchise is incompatible with any theory of horror that requires a monster or a concept of ideological repression or that regards horror as a machine for the generation of metaphors. *Final Destination* dispenses in toto with the master taxonomies by which horror is symbolically understood: no bad families or terrible places; no psychic, geographic, or domestic hauntings; and almost no interest in sexuality or sexual difference. In fact, overlooked in the critical rush to dub the films "teen exploitation" is precisely how much the franchise departs from the life- and self-practices of other horror subgenres ostensibly aimed at adolescents, in particular the indulgences in sex and drugs that signal impending punishment or that self-reflexively flaunt that convention. As soon as death's design is set in motion, these characters become stunningly sober: they are not trying to get laid or high, they are trying to evade trauma, catastrophe, and grave.

Violence reduces life to the bare building blocks of thought. One speaks as if learning a new language, those fragile reaching days when one only knows how to say *I am, I have, I want.*

Here, the characters' worlds are reduced even further to one repeated, tender plea: *not now, not yet, not now.*

If family and work are obstacles, it is not because they represent puritanical, bureaucratic, or oppressive disciplinary regimes, but because they are distractions from the urgent labor of staying alive by gleaning the signs that compose death's manifesting imminence. In place of the pursuit of pleasure, the *Final Destination* franchise is about anticipating, preventing, or at least delaying pain. (Which not a single being does. All these young adults, so recently *children*—every single one will expire.) As far as possible from ex-

ploitation, ironic camp, or ludic play, these films are constitutively bitter, an-
hedonic, paranoid, and sad.

Thus, although said to be ridiculous and gaudy, the *Final Destination* films
are *serious* in the sense that philosophy itself, according to Derrida, is "the at-
tentive anticipation of death, the care brought to bear upon dying, the meditation on the best way to receive, give, or give oneself death."[6] (—Or perhaps
it is our metaphysics that is nothing but campy doomsday schlock.)

Because death itself takes over the monster function, not only do these
films frustrate models of repression, they are instead very much about the
obvious, necessary, inevitably, and overtly foundational dimensions of death.
One of Humphries's chosen invectives, that the films are "inanities," is thus
apt in its literal sense of *inanis*, void (*inanitas*, emptiness, an empty space, also
uselessness), for hollowed out from a tautological horror formula in which
death is the guarantor of death are all models by which death is represented
by *something else* in the guise of a threatening cause. Once the *Final Destination* films do away with an entire rhetoric of monstrosity and metaphoricity
by privileging overt declarations of death's certainty, critical models incapable
of treating surface seriously come to their own impossible limit. For death is
less figure here than function. *Death is a structure, not a symbol.* And its function of being the possibility of finitude, of the possibility of ending, of being
the end toward which an ordered list is ordered, at which its end *will* end,
is *unthinkable*—it is critically unaccountable—apart from the specific overt
designs it takes. Which is to say: death in these films is not allegorical; it is,
above all, formal.

Among those scholars who do not dismiss the *Final Destination* conceit
outright, a common pejorative charge still circulates—that of the formulaic,
couched in modernism's valuation of innovation over iteration, building as
opposed to licensing.

(It is curious, this accusation against a text or a cluster of works for adhering to set forms. One might equally note that all franchise entries do the difficult work of articulating sameness. Carol White, in *Time and Death: Heidegger's Analysis of Finitude*, writes of her method, "I quote freely from the whole
chronological range of Heidegger's works since one of my basic premises [. . .]
is that he spent his life saying, to use his term, 'the Same.'"[7] Is it so obvious that
it is easy and uncomplicated for a film to say the same thing twice? Heidegger,
praising the same [*das Selbe*], contrasting it to what is merely equal or iden-

tical [*das Gleiche*], writes that sameness "is the belonging together of what differs, through a gathering by way of difference."[8] Far from the flattening work of the identical, the most formulaic franchise, in assembling as one precisely by way of what differs (minor details, the subtlest permutations), thinks sameness by way of confronting and thinking difference as such. So why deride in pop culture that which we revere in philosophy?)

When Kim Newman calls *Final Destination* a "proper franchise," it is to point to a presumed limitation in the films' material, the narrow, restricted, and overly exposed conceit of deaths-caused-by-Death.[9] If, however, one brackets the term's associations with a fast, cheap schematization of labor, a de-pejorativized notion of franchise going back to the Middle Ages ties *francus* to a special right or license that refers to a governable territory, to being at liberty or exempt from service, and also to uses of open and free language. The franchise is what is too blunt, too direct and declarative about its structure, marking with unburdened and liberal right the territory it delimits. So when *Final Destination* is charged with being a "proper franchise" to suggest something cynical, it is, to the letter, actually being accused of too little deceit, too much sincerity. And indeed, what is maximally formulaic in the *Final Destination* polytext—the most certain and exposed element of the five films—is the frank insistence that death comes last and ends something, that an order related to death figures it as (goes the titular notice) *final.*

Death is what is literally predictable :: what gives shape to the futurity of temporality as what has not yet happened :: to which being is slavishly bound :: and by which the figures in the films exist finitely in a structured time. In being what is possible and what is predictable—in other words, what gives textual shape to what has not yet happened—death, in its catastrophic ontological register, is not merely an a fortiori theoretical claim on the attentions of the films; rather, it is the formulaic *and* the formalist ground of this franchise. Death is what is above all seen to be certainly coming: *seen*, because it is given a visual correlate in signs; *to be certain*, because it is the tautological self-rule of the franchise; *to be coming*, for death is the correlate of the possibility in possibility, what has a noncontingent relation to the ordinal, takes a certain and fixed configuration, and is the ruled structure that governs the temporal progress of the text, orders what comes first, next, in sequence, and last.

This formulaic character of death—that it takes a nonarbitrary, certain configuration—is given visual presence in the franchise through death's bonding to specific figures: chart, schema, plan, list. That the films strictly adhere to—indeed, are entirely coextensive with (indeed, are accused of containing little more than)—these prescribed forms of sequence bringing about deaths suggests a metatext that is *presentational*, not *representational*. In its analytic of finitude—of beings who *are* insofar as they will at some point *not be*, this certainty a givenness and something that can be neither wished nor abstracted away—*Final Destination* deploys its structure as a cinematic thinking-through of the problem at the very heart of existential phenomenology, the death that, in Heidegger's formulation, is "that possibility which is one's ownmost, which is non-relational, and which is not to be outstripped [*unüberholbare*]."[10] In the Levinas-Heidegger dogfight—condensed in Levinas's complaint that "Heidegger deduces all thinkable signification from the attitude of man in regard to his own death"—*Final Destination* is formed around the confrontation between *one's own death* and *the death of the other*.[11] Formally foundational for the franchise is the question of whether death is a dissolution or an establishing of relations to others, for it is the death of the other that concerns the narrative progress of each film—until the precise instant that it is one's own final not-to-be-outstripped death that finally, definitively arrives.

If the privileged graphic mark in Gide is the line or ridge of demarcation, in the world of *Final Destination* everything turns on the form of the list. Death is inextricable from ordinal arrangement: the proper timing of death (deferred, delayed, premature, and yet unavoidable); the chain of particular deaths; evasive forms that upend taxonomic order (modes of substitution: saving someone's life; modes of creation: enabling new life that was not meant to be; modes of destruction: killing another in one's place). The films' obsessive attention to the arrangement of elements in relation to each other turns on the generalized figure of the *Then*, the indefinite but proximate position of what comes next. In lieu of the slasher mode's Final Girl, the *Final Destination* formula proposes only the *Next One*. To be next, to be accused of being next, to have mistaken whether one was in fact next—these *positions* are also *dispositions*: both placement in death's graphic, aesthetic, topological design *and* distributions of violence, anxiety, trauma, elation, relief, error, guilt, and so forth as each figure ultimately is disposed of.

(*Disponere*: to put in order, arrange, distribute. Each putting in place, each arranging in order, is here a dis-posing of some figure, such that ordering and ridding of noise or waste—by which the film means *beings*—become equivalent gestures.)

Because the structure of the films is governed by the proper order of deaths —an order that can be violated, superseded, tricked, undone, but that continually reasserts, even if only retroactively, its ordinality—*the franchise's fatalism is ontological, not tonal or generic.* Strictly, one's own (singular, future, certain, ineluctable) death is the absolute possibility of (one's) being, the inescapable condition that makes being in the first place possible: the no-longer-possible is internal to the possible. "Death is the possibility of the absolute impossibility of Dasein," goes one of Heidegger's best-known formulations for this interrelation in *Sein und Zeit*.[12] Death's possibility is already in the world of *Final Destination*—this possibility begins nowhere; it is merely a given condition from which the logic of the film advances. Critical positions that treat death expressively fail to articulate the most radical dimension of finitude: that it comes absolutely but not yet, that one exists finitely. Being, and not only franchise, is what is made according to a formula, whose course is predictable in the sense that its end (the possibility of its impossibility) is known in advance: for it is by its anticipated end that being is known and given at all. *Will die* cannot be modified by *probably*. The structure of finitude, because it is essentially and not contingently bonded to formal problems of design, is something that must be closely read for, and like the instant of finitude's arrival, it cannot be known in advance—*even as it is precisely what is seen to be certainly coming.* Otherwise, the critical act merely regards mutely each death that each time arrives. *Death's arrival is always chanced but never unexpected, not certain in any given instant but also never to be evaded altogether.*

Certain, but unexpected. But certain.

Far from having anything to do with supernatural horror, the *Final Destination* franchise is utterly immanent: it formalizes the violence of ontology itself.

Radical formalism—reading that proceeds autonomously from and independently of any account of some thing's history, context, function—is thus not a mode of prior theoretical determination, nor a method of reading among others that might be applied to *Final Destination*. Rather, radical formalism is a mode of reading derived *from* aesthetic objects, derived from thinking the intimate relation of death and violence and horror to questions of form. *If horror films formalize the violence of ontology and a violent ethics given structure through aesthetic elements, then* only *a radical formalism can account for how death functions in these texts.* The formal is what gives visible and temporal shape or configuration—molds, frames, sorts, and puts definiteness to figures, but also entails methods of procedure, the designed and composed—but also is what cannot be paraphrased about a text (the films' form: line, color, shape, texture, montage) and is the particular mode and appearance of structures therein (plan, design, list, schematic, diagram, map, chart, system), which both are and navigate, entrench and irritate, autonomous textual systems that both have form and birth new forms, not least of which is reading for form, which itself has form and births new forms.

Ahistorical abstractions *do things*. The formal forms.

That there is a more profound co-implication of violence, ontology, ethics, and aesthetics—that the relation of death to form demands an airing—with a larger co-implication of horror and philosophy as modes of speculative formal thinking, modes that extend to include all that appears to be nonhorror, including the realm of love itself—consider that project the horizon of this very book.

THE WAY DEATHS GO: POSSIBILITY :: IMPOSSIBILITY :: CERTAINTY

Whatever opinion we may be pleased to hold on the subject of death,
we may be sure that it is meaningless and valueless.
Death has not required us to keep a day free.
—Samuel Beckett, "Proust"

By dispensing with the question of whether death will arrive, *Final Destination* attunes itself to when, where, and above all how—the method, the means, the precise mechanical mode by which—death will finally and certainly take place in its dimension of being that which is possible.

This figure of possibility stains exegeses on the films, even when criticism does not quite realize it. As often happens, writing that derogates the text in question inadvertently deploys the most apt formulations for its analysis. For instance, "In terms of the serial killer or supernatural death film *Final Destination* is its *reductio ad absurdum par excellence*" goes an entry on the franchise in a survey of the horror genre.[13] As much as the films themselves, this claim is one worth closely reading. From the Greek *hê eis to adunaton apagôgê*, the Latin clause invoked here means "reduction to the impossible," or leading back to the absurd, a mode of argumentative proof that proceeds indirectly either by demonstrating that X must be true because not-X would be contradictory, false, anomalous, implausible, or impossible (its philosophical usage since Aristotle's *Prior Analytics*), or, in its ordinary-language usage, a form of rhetorical argument that attempts to refute a claim by carrying out its logic (X is false because it implies Y, which is ridiculous or impossible). (This mode of argument requires that the nature of contradiction or absurdity be agreed upon in advance: as goes Aristotle's summary, "Demonstration *per impossibile* differs from probative demonstration in that it posits what it wishes to refute by reduction to a statement admitted to be false.")[14] Some questions, then: If *Final Destination* is the reductio ad absurdum of "the serial killer or supernatural death film," precisely what argument or logical claim are those films purporting to make? What logic is being carried out therein to a point of impossibility? Or, what thesis proved by the demonstration that its rejection would be absurd and untenable? What conclusion (about death? about being? about horror?—it is unclear exactly what concept is advancing the proof) is thereby asking (and by and for whom?) to be accepted? (& Is it not interesting already to describe a horror franchise as advancing an argument? Is the franchise an extended thought experiment, a mode of logical reasoning, a speculative trial at something?)

Suppose that the argument of "the serial killer or supernatural death film" is a commonality to those two fairly distinct subgenres, perhaps some provisional hypothesis *p* that runs like this: Death is random but inevitable (it will arbitrarily but certainly come for you). Let us shorten that as *p* = "deaths will take place." To prove this, we will derive and assume the opposite: ~*p* is that "deaths will not take place." In the simplest terms, then, the franchise figured as argument runs: All will die. More generously: Each will die in time at a certain but unspecified time. (Or: Each will die prematurely in time at a certain but unspecified time, and if any does not die prematurely in time at that certain but unspecified time, another certain, premature, and unspecified time of death will, nevertheless, at some future, still unspecified, still certain time, certainly arrive.) From that preliminary assumption, we conclude that at a specific moment in time, death may or may not take place, but that during an infinite period of time, death will certainly in fact take place. But is that last statement contradictory, absurd, or impossible? Is it in fact not the essence of the noncontradictory and merely a restatement of the contingency of the manner and timing of death itself? (Any single death, after all, cannot both take and not take place at once—were that possible, Armand could not only trace but perch, linger for a long time even, on a very possible, very stable ridge of demarcation.) And does that not suggest that far from being a reduction to the absurd or impossible, the formulaic insistence of *Final Destination* succeeds in demonstrating the nonabsurdity, *the possibility* (which is to say that which may or may not take place in any given instant), of death?

The fairly glib critical evaluation should be taken seriously because the *Final Destination* films do present a form related to the possible, but one that is precisely the opposite of what the authors' formulation suggests: These films are structured by the *inverse* of a reduction to the impossible—and they are, in point of fact, impossible to reconcile to the *reductio*. They are entirely correlated to the mode of the possible. Until, that is, they are figured on the side of *It is no longer possible*, the possibility of the impossibility of being.

But even still, let us continue to regard the critics' words faithfully, even generously—Why not? For the reductio is a mode of argumentation that is also a style of reasoning, and in a lovely aesthetic addition to the term's appearance in logic, Adams Sherman Hill writes in his late nineteenth-century *Principles of Rhetoric* that "An argument which can be answered by *reductio ad absurdum* is said to prove too much,—that is, too much for its force as an argument; since, if the conclusion is true, a general proposition which lies behind it and includes it is also true. To show this general proposition in its absurdity is to overthrow the conclusion. The argument carries in itself the means of its own destruction."[15] Although the claim for a mode of reasoning related to the *impossibile* is inversely operative in *Final Destination*, the critical allegation picks up on the didactic dimension to the reductio, how it thrives amid the superficial, the polemical, the melodramatic, the overly and overtly artificial. And in this sense, the *Final Destination* films—with their maudlin memorial services, pop-psychological language of survivor's guilt, and histrionic grieving in the wake of the initial catastrophe; with their shamelessly presentational declarations of death's plan; with their figurations of menace in flashed lightning, affected underscores, hammy wind, and maximally visible, extremely close-up, slow and clear surface signs in the cause-and-effect sequences that lead to each death—have a tonal, if not logical, affinity with the reductio.

The *Final Destination* films, we might say, are constantly *proving too much*: there is a blatant obviousness in their visual language, a hyper-evidential demonstration of genre conventions, and also their glaringly, hortatively legible designs therein; —we might even say this is the ostentatious proving-too-much one sometimes glimpses in *counterfeit* objects, those that declaim too stubbornly their authenticity, thereby unconcealing their vulnerability. Instead of narratively privileging concealed, symptomatic, metaphorical, or displaced meaning, this franchise declares death's arrival and logic on the surface. (After all, the fulcrum between the first and second films is a female character named *Clear*—as in bright, loud, as in manifest, plain, evident, overt, behind which nothing hides; what is free from obscurity or ambiguity.) What appears stylistically as a proving-too-much is an aesthetic histrionics that is asymmetrical to the pressure required to advance the films' argument, a set of formal choices unnecessarily adequate to demonstrate the possible, in other words precisely the given, actual dimension of human mortality: what operates autonomously of analytics and would therefore seem to require very little (if any) demonstration or force for the persuasion of its claim, which will, with certainty, take place as a claim on being—whether logic supports its appearance or not.

In each iteration of the *Final Destination* franchise, the transitions of these modes of the possible to the no-longer-possible involve elaborately structured causal play with objects in the world that set off relations to other objects that in turn kill the various characters. The films' ethic of spectacle remains with Armand's desire to trace *le point limite*: *It is possible* (X dodges the seemingly agential flying knife), *It is still possible* (X nimbly jumps out of the way of the wildly falling statue), *It is no longer possible*—X stumbles into the road, elated to have conquered these ill-behaving objects, and is flattened by a bus. Although these death sequence set pieces are reminiscent of Bazin's account of Chaplin's improvisatory grapple with inanimate objects that refuse to be used in appropriate ways—horror here in sympathy with the comedic gag—they mostly resemble engineered contraptions to carry out a process whose telos happens to be a dead thing. When Wheeler Winston Dixon chides the franchise thusly, "modern American horror films are simply overblown killing machines. [. . .] [*Final Destination*] racks up one grisly death after another," he deploys an apposite figure for the way death takes place here—as though structured like an apparatus.[16]

This is not an underremarked analogy: a "Rube Goldberg–esque" epithet is uttered in almost every piece of writing that exists on the films.[17] Their death sequences share with Goldberg's mid-twentieth-century drawn inventions an overly complex system of indirect schematics that turns on a specific disjunction between the intricacy of some operation and the banality of its end (e.g., winning the battle for comfort in a cinema in the excellently named invention "Elbow Spikes to Keep Your Neighbors from Hogging the Armrest"), a delight in the unnecessarily complicated, in a purposeless asymmetry between effort of processual labor and requirements for achieving an end. Consider Goldberg's fourteen-point system, each part letter-labeled in a rigorous and precise notation, for his 1926 comic "Simple Way to Find Your Glasses":

FIGURE 2.1. Rube Goldberg, "Simple Way to Find Your Glasses," *Wilkes-Barre Times Leader*, January 27, 1926

As soon as you miss your glasses do a Charleston—string (A) causes ball (B) to hit dwarf (C) on head, squashing him so that button (D) flies off his coat and hits dinner bell (E)—oatmeal-spaniel (F) thinks dinner is ready and jumps forward, pulling string (G) and opening mouse-trap (H)—mouse (I) runs up mantelpiece to cheese (J) and nibbles at it—as cheese gets lighter, weight (K) falls on bulb (L) and blows auto horn (M), showing you exactly where glasses (N) are—when putting glasses down again, don't forget to set cheese and horn.

Goldberg's assemblages share with the *Final Destination* franchise an investment in the arrangement or disposition of elements already on the side of the aesthetic, aligned with the autonomous and purposeless since Kant—ornamentation in place of economy. While the process in its schematic rendering involves nothing but unnecessaries (in relation to what is oriented toward end)—for his drawn courses are nothing but digressions—the sequence that the schematic diagrams simultaneously formally restrict its ground and admit no unnecessaries (in its neat economy of letter-labeled process elements).

Goldberg's title does not lie. Although the later fourteenth-century sense of "simple" as modest or plain, lacking in complication, seems ironically invoked here, the Old French *simple* from the twelfth century and the Latin *simplus* were redolent of being straightforward, free from duplicity, and from there moved to valuative tones of being harmless and blameless, sweet if naïve, foolish even—and once again we are in the realm of the reductio: comic diagram and horror franchise are not duplicitous, they declare themselves to be without guile. Both texts are simple in that they are nothing but the order of operations that they present themselves to be. (And are they also thereby fundamentally *decent*?)

Goldberg's comics illustrate machines that carry out energy to some final end or destination through an avoidably complicated design. They are not locally arbitrary; precise sequence is paramount. The interactions, whether physical, chemical, or indirect, turn on the nature of chain reactions, which is to say that Goldberg's schematics are models of relations, the reciprocal and processual interplay of multiple, themselves unstable, things in the world. As are the spectacles of the post-premonition death scenes in *Final Destination*. The common aesthetic denominator between any sequence of Goldberg's inventions is a flattened and dehierarchized map of process outcomes: a first mover, a series of reactions, a penultimate and an ultimate step. The break between the final two elements in the previous list constitutes the provisional field for the line that Armand desires to trace, but the inventions, like the deaths in the films, figure that crossing as yet another schematic transition or relation more than a privileged shift of ontological orders. Armand's frustration at fingering the extremest point would thus be materially inscribed in the particular occasion of each death as much as in each diagram of each death. His failure to trace *le point limite* is given its abstract foreclosure in the hierarchized causal chain that is the precisely crafted sequence of events ending in yet another death in the films.

If the Rube Goldberg parallels align the deaths in *Final Destination* with the plastic absurdities enabled by animation—an aesthetic predicated on tensions between static images and the positing of sequential artificial movement— the death sequences are also reminiscent of the avant-garde objectal play in Peter Fischli and David Weiss's *Der Lauf der Dinge* (The Way Things Go [that title as apt for the horror franchise]). Their 1987 cinematic presentation of a one-hundred-foot-long constructed causal chain of interlocked actions turns on industrial materials including weighted tires, ladders, and soap drums, deploying fire and spilling water as chemical and physical triggers. (Attend to that tire; later in this book, it will animatedly return in the form of a moving toroid—though its reappearance, I warn you now, will mean *nothing*.) Despite appearing to feature a single complex, sequential chain reaction over the film's thirty minutes, the film contains dozens of nearly invisible *Rope*-like cuts. *Der Lauf der Dinge* presents a pure abstraction of the duration and force required for one thing to convert, through action on its thingness, to something else, the minimal force and essential waiting required to change something. As though a material, if anthrodecentric, revisiting of the famous opening line of Ovid's *Metamorphoses*—*In nova fert animus mutatas dicere formas*—what is put on display in the installation in the Swiss artists' film is purely the changing of material forms into new forms over the specific period of time (neither more nor less) required to carry that process out.

> *Processes are over when they are completed.*
> *Nothing runs out of time, it is merely that the running*
> *of a protocol exhausts its conditions.*
> *The destination is not final as fulfillment or culmination—*
> *every destination is final because it is last.*

An abstraction of a pure form of narrative in this constrained system world is thus rendered as: What will happen next; and what now? In Fabian Neuhaus's description of Fischli and Weiss's piece, "Similar to a chain reaction, a motion is unleashed that travels through a setting, constantly changing its form, shape and character."[18] If that displacement substitutes a body with changeable form for the classical development that would trace a narrative subject undergoing some modification, *Final Destination* films squarely place themselves on Fischli and Weiss's side, rendering each body in its particular sequence leading to its particular end as a brute thing that can be modified through minimal force into another thing: *It is / It is no longer.*

Interlocked physical affectivity requires both a highly vitalist worldview—things must be vibrant, stimulating, active, reactive, affecting, and affectable—and a closed system in which reactions in sequence can cause supplementary or branching reactions from an initial trigger—so long as no new influence exerts itself. In other words, the linearity and causality of the system that follows on the trigger, the initial release of stored potential energy, the succession and relation and connection to a collapse or explosion or spark or event, requires a maximal reduction of noise, a closure that prevents any external intrusion that might interrupt the linkages mutually affecting each other. The system must be reductive, restricted—must be limited—so that the concentrated showing of the pure transformation of isolated forms can take place.

In *Final Destination*'s formalism, the closure of system in which chain reactions can take place is also achieved through the manipulation and hyperbolic reduction of cinematic material. But in place of suturing cuts to counterfeit durational continuity, as in *Der Lauf der Dinge*, the horror franchise is a virtuosic study of the capacity of découpage to break apart unities and isolate

FIGURES 2.2 AND 2.3. *Der Lauf der Dinge* / *The Way Things Go*
(Peter Fischli and David Weiss, 1987)

details. The films' precise and restricted editing, which renders exquisitely composed partial and minor differences between images, does not suggest symbolic bonds between shots as in Soviet montage; rather, the strict sense of découpage as the dissecting analysis of a cut-up scene figures chemical, physical, causal, visceral, even haptic linkages between discrete objects in the diegesis. It is deployed less for expressive momentum than to eliminate the superfluous, to restrict through isolation specific elements that affect each other: it is therefore above all else a technique of formalizing objects, turning a polysemic visual field into a narrow, restricted set of cause-things that effect force on other things. Not an expressive linking, but a deconstructive severing—which, as technique, performs some task in a maximally indirect and unnecessarily complex way. For what is montage itself if not an écriture of indirection, purposeless and a formal absurdity, unnecessarily ornamenting, breaking apart, and visually complexifying what was originally in a simple spatiotemporal unity?

The first death after an evaded disaster in *Final Destination 3* places its restricted mise-en-scène in a tanning salon in which Ashley and Ashlyn, mildly differentiated, similarly buxom young women, put in motion, through a series of neutral gestures, a set of constraints that will ultimately lead to their conflagratory ends: Ashley places a cold drink on a table; Ashlyn turns up the heat a few degrees; forgotten music means a perusal of CDs on an unstable shelf that slightly dislodges its underlying support. A condition of possible future rescue is undone in the adjoining lobby when the salon owner steps outside and elects to use a tube of lotion to hold open an exterior door, the pressure against which oozes its contents out, preventing the stopping of the door that might return him to, at some future possible, not-yet-realized point, the interior of the space where the terrible things that have not yet taken place will, then, be in the process of taking place as the terrible things that will have, and by then already, irreversibly, taken place. These enfolded enclosures are sutured together through parallel editing between the closing bed lids and the slowly closing exterior door—each nude girl now folded in a bluely glowing bed; each bed in a room in a salon now locking out any potential interfering force. The machine of their death system, in other words, restricts the base for its operations and simultaneously excludes potential conditions that would interfere with its purity; this is a narrowing of constraints, a reductiveness to the bare, essential components that will set in motion the causal relations directly necessary to carry out the future mechanical process.

The girls are equivalent to Fischli and Weiss's tires.
These girls are things that can slide or fall or burn.

A small, seeping pool of melting condensation starts to puddle at the base of its origin in the slushy drink; its slow crawl into the clear contours of a flat, wide tear on a tabletop is cross-cut with the bronzing girls, all oblivious solipsistic pleasure from the sensual truncation of headphones and goggles. *Drop by drop . . . just one drop more—& there you are.*

All the while, the film cuts to its auguring, now deciphering, protagonist Wendy. In the methodology of the franchise, the first post-premonition death takes place in the midst of a for-now-living character's simultaneous realization of death's design, an understanding that will occur too late to forestall its inaugural membership. In this iteration, death's design takes the form of both an ordering of sequential occurrences in the reconstructed two-by-two seating arrangement on the derailing roller coaster the group initially escaped *and* the nature of that death in a sign system that turns on color and light, which Wendy reads into photographs taken on the night of the disaster, now blown up and studied for telling details à la Antonioni, London, circa 1966.

This scene's suspense is not epistemological—as what is being carried out is not in dispute—but durational, in the sense of deferral, postponement. Not uncertainty but delay—a temporal dimension formally manufactured through the analytic dissectability of space itself in montage. The *Final Destination* system asks its characters and spectators to *wait*, not doubt; to *wait*, not thrill; to *wait* as things go the way things go. Redefining subjects as temporal relations to themselves, this franchise regards beings as those-who-wait: selves who are nothing more than the capacity to *stand by*.

> First: It is not bodies but time that will be killed.
> Next: Recall that waiting means to stand guard, to guard with care,
> to observe with attention,
> to watch over—
> waiting is always a form of spectating,
> and spectatorship itself a kind of lying
> in wait
> (gait, lookout, sentry originally, though later an ambush or a trap),
> but waiting is always, in either case,
> endured.
> Finally: It is not always best to be done with waiting.

Upon reaching the ledge of the table, the water drips fast beads; they descend on the quickly successive pulse of the diegetic song "Love Rollercoaster," whose title and rehashed lyrical utterance refer to the carnival death scene from the beginning of the film. And it is a referral to the letter: there is no sly allusion here, only the transferring assignation of augury, a tracing or relating to first cause or source that was the original sense of the Latin *referre*— to carry back.

The disaster's unfolding, and simultaneous prolongation, is stitched together through a rigorous deconstruction of the image: a medium high-angle shot of the drink, a cut-in on the ironizing script on its side, through which runs a line of dripping water. When the droplets come into contact with the machine underneath the table, it sparks and steams—malfunctions in its prior obligations, but we might say it begins to function properly in the alternative death-telos for which it was (cinematically) designed. This is a conversion that turns, like the sweating, dripping cup, on the relation of elements of temperature. Temperature, of course, is in a nonarbitrary relation to death here: heat in the external natural world led to the acquisition of the iced drink; artificial cooling in the room led to the desire to increase the ambient temperature; and condensation formed as the interior drink took thermal energy out of the warmer air vapor in the room. These relations of discordance are set against the primary narrative mover for the entire death scene, which is the concentrated indulgence in artificial temperature through lamps that counterfeit exposure to daylight in the environmentally oxymoronic act of indoor suntanning.

The photograph that is revealed in retrospect to have formally anticipated these deaths is marked by another kind of solar forgery, which leaves its foreboding trace in a photograph of Ashley and Ashlyn from the night of the original accident (plate 2). The problem of light in night photography that ultimately augurs the salon fire is an aesthetic matter of the sensible characteristics of light that is also the absolute radiant scale measured in kelvins. The problem of *color temperature*—the manifest formal error of Wendy's too-red photographic image—is the sign of death's design that, in its cinematic form, will pivot on the problem of *thermodynamic temperature*, the conversion of ice to water to steam in the chain reactions that convert the thermodynamic system of the corpus from water and meat to melted fat and flame, as though each young body were the absolute black body object of Kelvin's scale, posited by the film and then heated to see what color changes would happen.

235, 240; the temperature readout internal to the beds incrementally leaps. *73, 74*: the room's thermostat climbs. At the crucial sunbed rise to *250*, the upper limit warned against in text next to its display, the victim-palettes start to glow and still and wilt. The parallel increases continue: *300. 78F*. At the latter reading of the ambient draft, the automatic air conditioning goes on, blowing a hard ray of pressure against the top of a coat rack, which falls (the scene's literal tipping point, its threshold of possibility) :: capsizing an artificial palm tree, which lands on the earlier loosened shelf, which weights itself on one of the pods and which, at Ashlyn's attempt to open the bed, slides to span the openings of the two glowing coffins, both locking against any timely departure, the dice of contingency thrown, the hand fixed, the processual sequence come to its realization, the final resting point of its possibility in the actuality of this—what has taken place as what was seen to have certainly been going to take place. This mode of death is at once literally an accident (what happens or descends upon you: *cadere*, fall) but is also not an accident (not nonessential or outside the course of nature: it is what occurrence will occur in the course of the nature of the interactions of the relations of heat, water, gravity, time). (No death of finite beings is ever really accidental, as in itself the whim of fortune or the nonessential quality of a thing.) Cutting from the glowing vermilion of the photographic warning, back in Wendy's house, to its displaced realization in the icy royal fluorescence of the salon—the chromatic shift mapping a temporal and evental one—the trapped girls' cheeks and chests palindromically respond by singeing to a burnished orange (plate 3). When the machine and they finally, screamingly, catch fire, returning the image of each to the bloodshot gold of fire's combustive flame, it fulfills a chromatic prophecy as much as an ontological one.

Death's design is signed in magnified, isolated details in the world of *Final Destination*. Its privileged framing of things at their tipping-point interactions with other objects hews to the aesthetics of the close-up as figured by Deleuze ("the close-up does *not* tear away its object from a set of which it would form part, [. . .] but on the contrary, *it abstracts it from all spatiotemporal co-ordinates . . .*").[19] The spatiotemporal abstractions of each cog of the death machine replicate on the level of aesthetics the violence of causal relations that effect each ontological disaster. In other words, the logic of editing here does not function as a representation of the disaster but levels with it as a presentational coequal: the series of broken-up, isolated images are constituted as causal units of the chain reaction that *is*, or, rather, will be (and will be legible only in retrospect *as*), the catastrophe.

System and finality are pretty much one and the same,
so much so that if the system is not finished, there is no system.
—Johannes Climacus, via Kierkegaard, *Concluding Unscientific Postscript*

The furthest reach—Armand's "l'instant extrême"—formally determines the methodic ordinality of "death's design" in each *Final Destination* film. Both the narrative procedural drive and the aesthetic priority given to découpage emphasize what occurs before, must arrive after, appears in turn as next, and comes last. Death puts in place a nonarbitrary order: that toward which the course of being is oriented. The endingness of things—as bodies, as elements in a design—is what is governed by the formalism of the list. For each sequence: Death is how the final thing happens. The franchise thereby offers a new media version of the old clock and sundial scratch: *vulnerant omnes, ultima necat*. It is always the last hour that kills.

The certain, nonoptional long-form sequence runs: premonition (of some catastrophe); evasion (of that precise catastrophe by some); actuality (of a slightly modified catastrophe for others); reassertion (of consequence: a few deaths, each the next death according to an undiscovered ordinality); realization of primary ordinality (on the level of design); run of sequence (whose ordinality is strictly followed); design sequence closure *or* aperture (depending on the installment, ranging from the temporary survival of two characters in the first film, deferring their deaths, which then take place, in the case of Alex, between the first and second film or, in the case of Clear, in the second film, to the radical closure of *Final Destination 5*, which is a prequel, joined to *Final Destination 1* in its final explosion, which is in fact the initial explosion from the first film, melding the entire franchise into a single, unified world—and thus introducing a further formal question: the relation of list to loop). Inverse of the fecundity of possibilities that governs any local detail in the spectacle of any single death, the possibility of being otherwise is excluded from the ordinal finality of death itself. Although a contingency that sets in motion causality governs the manner and editing of each death spectacle, the necessity of the methodology in which events come in order involves a logic of progression, a global following-through of sequence that mirrors the foundational following-through of sequentiality that is death's existential design, given in the most local form in the course of the tipping-point logic of each individual death. Microscopic, macroscopic, and conceptual levels are thus concerned with the particular order of listed things.

Inverse of living dead films, these are films of the finite alive—as though giving form to Nietzsche's thanatology in The Gay Science, *"Das Lebende ist nur eine Art des Toten"* (The living is merely a type of what is dead).[20]

This aphoristic claim is a map of taxonomic rank: life is a kind or species or genre of death, which is to say death, with its overall authority from which particularity and exception are derived, is not itself a genre but is, rather, aligned with the general. Beings exist finitely for this franchise: to be is to be provisional, oriented toward the future ineluctable horizon of one's own not-being.

Follow the Final Destination *films to their utmost reach, they formalize this proposal: Because any x ends absolutely, it takes shape at all.*

In the first film, gesturing at a contorted metal sculpture, the initial-death-surviving character Clear likens the aesthetic object to the premonition-bearing character Alex, saying it is "reluctant to take form," positing an epistemic and anthrodecentric lack in which the art thing does not yet know what it is. This declaration of a reluctance to take form is, however, a deceit, more counterfeit coinage. For of course the metal has taken form or it would not be perceptible as a particular shape, as the give of positive and negative space with a definite structure, in a bounded separation of material from external field. The sculpture cannot, in fact, help but take form—*form* is precisely how it is *given*. What the sculpture does, however, perhaps lack is a sense of the significance of that substantive form. Its opacity or abstract edge requires a reading—reluctance names only the hesitation of the will to grapple with form.

This reluctant wrestling with form—more so than even death—is the overt concern of each of the *Final Destination* films. (And note: Horror's unique capacity to speculate aesthetically on the concept of form will become more complex, more nuanced, and simultaneously more problematic by the time of its fullest consideration in the postscript to this book. It is worth observing, however, that the project of thinking form and death together has long been explored by theorists and artists: consider the architect George Nelson's *A Problem of Design: How to Kill People*, made for CBS's *Camera Three* program in 1960, a twenty-four-minute soliloquy in which Nelson carefully, with a flat, measured tone, details—squarely or subversively, depending on one's take—the aesthetic aspects and histories of the objects of violence-doing, from rocks and clubs to the atom bomb.) The franchise grapples with the twin dimensions of the concept that Raymond Williams identifies in *Keywords*: that the term "form" refers both to a (mere) visible, outward showing *and* to the essential specifying principle of some thing, spanning "the whole range from the external and superficial to the inherent and determining."[21] In grappling with a conception of form that is correlated to the inherent, determining, absolute facticity of finitude that is simultaneously given shape in manifest displays of self-showing signs that require ongoing, obsessive attention, the *Final Destination* films navigate the antinomy of form itself.

More precisely: the *Final Destination* films deploy a conception of death *in order* to navigate the antinomy of form.

In the first *Final Destination* film, Alex demonstrates this struggle in a reading of the seat chart of the Paris-bound airplane that is, at once, site of premonition, evasion, and arrived disaster. Death's design is the same design in each film: a list governing the relational position of those particular beings who will die in turn—it is always a sequential formalism. This design, however, is *signed* differently in each member of the franchise. Narrative progress is enabled by the possibility of temporalization (*this is how the next thing happens*—for a text, but also for the series, itself a sequence of installments), whereas each spectacle of death pauses the progression of list to focus on that which exists finitely as it confronts the arrival of its end (*this is how the last thing happens*—for [a] being). In place of the cardinal drive of much horror (an accumulated body count; piles of the dead or dying), this is an ordinal drive, one obsessed with the progression and succession of things, ranks, positions in sequence.

In addition to the master film-theoretical dualism of *narrative* (the melodrama of survivor's guilt) versus *spectacle* (the demises as attractions), *Final Destination* adds a third category of cinematic address: the *graphic*, the flat surface artifacts that express abstracted formalized information. In the first film, this takes the form of a seat chart of the aircraft that explodes after the death-evading characters were no longer on it as planned, a drawing that presents a spatial flattening of time, notating all possible deaths at once. Well into the film—after the burial and mourning of those who did not evade the conflagration and after the death of one of the premonition-affected survivors—Alex's attention is drawn to a television broadcast offering a new theory of the cause of the plane's explosion. The screened graphic zooms over an animated green background with small, white ordered rectangles, the field against which the seats of the cabin are superimposed, with pulled-out and line-connected orbs representing the grid of electrical connectors underneath the plane. The image switches to a close-up of a digital simulation of a spark, which sets off the catastrophic chain of events. This new graphic of the leak of combustible fluids simplifies the first, offering a reductive rendering of starred sequential bursts at each seat/punctum of ignition in electrical plottedness as the leak renders a trail from the initial spark through its course to the fuel pump and its final end in flame and disaster.

Final Destination cuts from this set of televisual graphics to a paused still of the second schematic image—the rendering of fuel path and final explosion—on a different screen. Over this screen's diagram, Alex places vellum, which preserves only the dark grid of the rows of seats. This layering of media constitutes another mode of formal variation and simplification: the muting of visual detail specific to the grid (i.e., specific to the level of the informational) enables an enhanced passage of light (a condition for an attestation of design), in which a new, different arrangement may take shape—or, rather, is no longer *reluctant* to take form. Over this thin paper, Alex copies out in marker the lines joining the components of the circuit at each point of the leak. (This is a tracing proper, recalling Gide's "cette ligne de démarcation entre l'être et le non-être, je m'applique à la tracer partout"; *tracer*: to draw, to plan, to map out). Alex then overlays this map of red vectors and starred explosions onto yet another table of seats, this one in black and white and containing the names of the seven characters who evaded disaster, each positioned at specific, spaced X'd-out boxes. The rectangles from the first seat chart are converted from empty plots in a grid to, when overlaid onto the critical one of the plane's electrical system, newly meaningful squares at which specific bodies in a past moment registered their presence. That is, the boxes move from being graphically equivalent abstract registers to being graphically nonequivalent. X marks each spot where the ineluctable specificity of a being once *was* at the point at which they *were* not yet not there, the diagram of the leak and subsequent explosion revealing a nonarbitrary order to the flat rendering.

The image is increasingly abstracted over the course of these proliferations of variations of the chart: in place of accumulated nuance, the final confrontation of an underscore image marked by no color, just the boxes and open fields of a white-space/black-line schematic of the plane's interior, and the second sheet, containing only the intersections and serrated bars of a red-lined course, suggests a dissection of totality. In extreme close-up, with his finger isolating each of these details in order, Alex points to each juncture on the last map, slowly navigating: "First was Tod, then was Terry. . . . They're

FIGURE 2.4. *Final Destination* (James Wong, 2000)

dying in the order they would have died. That's death's design." Hewing to the strict etymology of *order* as in position (Latin *ordo, orodos, ordin-*: row, series, line), as in those who live under a certain rule according to precise and methodical regulation, the relation of components is here assigned the quality of law—this fundamentalism of order given shape in the nonarbitrary presence of a drawn design. The grid as schematic presents all its elements at once, focusing visual attention at each turning point of the sequence: the inaugural spark, subsequent nodes of contact, and then the explosion, rendered through an upward, left-extending triangle—the blast figured as an intersection of lines, the violent energy of all those deaths converted to the formal energy of a diagonal shape.

The film thereby commits to a conceptual barter. It exchanges the scene of graphic violence (as in profane, obscene, gory) for violence as graphic (as in *graphikos*, writing, drawing). While the spectacles of any given death will commit to the former, the spectacle of the designs death has on the characters will be rendered entirely by the latter. Each extreme close-up of every isolated detail that Alex provides temporalizes these plots in relation: just as the montage of each death sequence breaks the arrival of violence into details, rendering the spatial temporal, the articulation of death's design temporalizes as ordinal the simultaneously present visual elements of the flat schematic. The deixis of Alex's finger flattens into a single image the declarative—Look; Here—at each point in time, while the editing that stitches together those isolated details is coextensive with the temporalizing of the list in sequence, thus realizing formally the multiple dimension of the notion of the *next*—the closest or nearest (a spatial proximity) and also what is nigh (a temporal proximity).

What comes in order—arrives first, comes next, and must by definition come last—for being that ends is not a neutral design question in relation to the broad designation of the horror film. In Alex's isolation of the labeled components of the final chart, the character Tod, T-O-D, has already died and died first, so what marks the origin of the list of deaths is the German signifier for death itself. First membership is coextensive with the intention to end of the entire self-folding list. This franchise thereby formalizes a problem analogical to Heidegger's absolute distinction between the two types of ending: "properly dying" (*Tod*—death—or *eigentlich sterben*, "actually dying," which is the dying proper to *Dasein*, uniquely what a human can do) and, on the other hand, "perishing" (*verenden*, stoppage, or "the ending of anything that is alive," as in *perire*, to leave, disappear, as in transpire, to go beyond a limit).[22] Because Dasein names not an event (what ends life), but the possibility of "no-longer-being-able-to-be-there," the disappearing of a form is in stark contrast to the endings experienced by human figures in these films (the ending proper to dying that is not like the endings of other things).[23] Death as temporal finitude (that being exists finitely) gives form to a radical horizon, the future possibility of Dasein's impossibility—such that "Dasein always already exists in just such a manner that its 'not-yet' belongs to it."[24] The infinitude of lists—that they promise the possible avoidance of end with not-yet-final accumulations of the "next"—is set alongside the most fundamental limit of human finitude, to which the film calculatingly commits on the level of the structure of chart. Alex's elongated, exhaustive, exhausting exegesis of this seating arrangement gives due patience to the unfolding by which one notates the aporetic structure of a death that assembles an orientation toward a future nullity. His close reading does not merely focus ever more refined attention on the details of this particular design; it performs the durational labor required for any close reading of any formal details of any particular design.

Read yet more into this schematic of the electrical system on the airplane. Read too much into it, toward the horizon of its extremest point. Any schematic diagram is a drawing showing the components or parts—and their interconnections, relations, and mutual implications—of some device, machine, circuit, flow, or process, enabling assembly, disassembly, repair, modification, reconstruction, &c. The conventional airplane cabin seat chart, with its grid of letters and rows to show the general arrangement of every seating position, here extricates singularity from the general to show the relations in space of only seven passengers. It is reconstructed to display the arrangement of particular bodies at a particular moment in time in their sheer, contingent impossibility, for those figures are precisely those who did not intersect with those electrical junctures during the leak and explosion. Alex's chart is thus a purely speculative diagram of where they *might* have been seated during the conflagration that precisely did not take place in the manner of this graphic attestation because they were *not* there when it did take place. The image displays an entirely virtual occurrence: what was possible and yet transformed possibility. But it also gives form to Heidegger's tonality of being toward death as properly an *"anticipation of this possibility"*—the diagram of the *closest possible* brush with death for those X's, what lodges them in the *formal* path of the explosion in a schematic of an event that it is only possible to give in the realm of design.[25] As though proceeding visually from the negative law of finitude, the diegetic images bear out this impasse: *"The closest closeness which one may have in Being towards death as a possibility, is as far as possible from anything actual."* "Death as possibility," writes Heidegger, "gives Dasein nothing to be 'actualized', nothing which Dasein, as actual, could itself *be*. It is the possibility of the impossibility [*die Möglichkeit der Unmöglichkeit*] of every way of comporting oneself towards anything, of every way of existing."[26] The schematic that Alex assembles is a temporal double: a description of what has passed (the explosion as fully realized) and what will pass (the order of deaths, what precisely did not take place such that it will, as though it had taken place, take place as the possibility of future not-yet-realized but realizable time). It also puts (drawn) line to "the absolute impossibility," the nothing-that-might-be-actualized of the schematic by which the seven figures are simultaneously in the disaster *and* not in the disaster, die then *and* will not yet have died.

This sequence of images moves between Christopher Alexander's typology of diagrams in *Notes on the Synthesis of Form*: what summarizes the pattern and exhibits the characteristics of the scene of the disaster (what he dubs a "form diagram"; his examples include a watercolor perspective of a racing car) and, simultaneously, in its addition of vectors, articulates the functional properties of the sequence that is the disaster. In being a "notation for the problem, rather than for the form," Alexander calls this second type "a requirement diagram," a purest example of which is a mathematical equation. The form diagram Alex composes presents the spatial coordinates for the articulation of the requirement diagram that will give ordinality to death's design. But Alexander is clear that if one seeks to translate "requirements into form," the two must be interrelated: "A requirement diagram becomes useful only if it contains physical implications, that is, if it has the elements of a form diagram in it. A form diagram becomes useful only if its functional consequences are foreseeable, that is, if it has the elements of a requirement diagram in it."[27] The implication of this interplay is that in inventing modes of design to show order, the form diagram must articulate futurity (its consequences become foreseeable) and the requirement diagram of the progress of the explosion and consequent fixing of death's design must retain the physical composition of the seat chart. Faithful to Bachelard's insistence that "tout ordre est un temps," there is no disarticulation of the chart from the temporal logic it puts in play.[28] Performing the most useful diagram according to the visual theorist, the articulation of space in the *Final Destination* seat chart corresponds entirely to an articulation of sequence, as though death's design were a resolution of the conflict between the two modes of presenting information and the sequence that produced the form of the design were a logical ordered outcome of a process of schematic translation.

Final Destination thereby gleefully inverts the prescription in Edward Tufte's *The Visual Display of Quantitative Information*: "What is to be sought in designs for the display of information is the clear portrayal of complexity."[29] For all that the franchise's narrative conceit is overtly and clearly declared, articulating death's design involves the complexification of clarity in the infinitely subtle, difficult, and layered orchestrations of design itself. In redrawing the cabin seating chart as it is reduced to the accident *that did not take place that way*, Alex-as-designer undoes any idealism of the chart as a mode of information that eases speed of understanding. The proliferating screens, surfaces, and media, in addition to the editing in close-up of each point of the explosion, offer only the complex portrayal of clarity. Alex's drawn schematic on vellum in collusion with cinematic form makes the chart *difficult* to read again, even as what the chart designates is the simplest fact of human finitude.

Horror—and this is a general law whose generality and particularity will deepen over the course of this book—does not perform negating, destructive work so much as it does its violence through the generative, positive fecundities of languages, laws, schemes, structures, constructions, orders, designs. Brutalizing is not an escape from form, but a wild flight into form.

Closely—painstakingly (what is *effort*, what is *exertion*)—reading for form decelerates understanding (and delays any final accounting), reinvests the simplicity of the obvious and self-evident with a complexity of unstable, shifting, and swelling signs. The significance of the raw data in Alex's schematic (*raw* retaining its flesh-sewn sense) is reclaimed through those multiple, layered, isolated, formalized, abstracted visual forms. This *final chart*, which is both last in the sequence of progressively pared-down images and a chart of the finality that awaits these seven beings as their determined futurity, melds the event that took place and the hypothetical event that did not take place but might have. This last image is adestined—out of historical time; entirely relegated to an aesthetic time—accordingly, it is also the sole site at which those who died and those who survived are present in the same (representational) plane at the instant of the catastrophe.

The dead and the living have nothing more *in common*.

Design—and nothing else—creates this impossible juncture at which the dead and living converge.

This graphic of the as-death-*would*-have-happened schematic gives form to a purely speculative conceit that does not admit the devastation of withness that is the world interceded with death. Drawing puts in place a counterfeit still-having-something-in-commonness between those who died in the explosion and those who survived the explosion but will not survive their own future deaths. This collapse of the registers of the virtual and actual makes this image idealized but also impossible—the chart attests to what structurally cannot take place, analogue to Armand's imaginary ridge. Alex's diagram is thus not merely one representational object contained within another (the film text): the diagram of the seat chart is a spatial schematic of the temporal progress of the film *Final Destination*. It registers a singular sequential disaster given cartographic form as a unity, which the cinematic text then takes apart into distinct segments. Death is both a limit—what comes last, what offers boundary to the plotted progress of each film—and, simultaneously, on the level of design, not an end but a way for the text *to be*, the very mode of its continual taking shape: the horizon of possibility against which the vitality of textual form—narrative structure, montage, temporal progress, the telling detail, meaningful signs, chromatic variation, drawn schematics—will take place at all.

This process involves a brutal, vicious exchange, however. For the map that can be read for its revelation of death's design involves expunging the visual field of those beings who in fact died in the actual, as taken-place, airplane explosion. In retaining solely those names of the seven survivors in relation to the virtual explosion that they uniquely did not experience, all the other names of all the other bodies represented graphically by all those empty, unnamed squares—now suggesting so many other rectangles: coffins, burial plots, checklists of the names in a disaster, allotments of entry in the largest list: that of the total of all dead—have to be erased. The names of the dead therefore are equivalent to all the other details that have to be excised in order to make the graphically reductive legible. Dead others—dead *friends*—are figured as textual clutter, as so much visual noise. This formal logic is also an ethical and political claim, and suggests a radically antimemorial, antimelancholic quality to design. The vitality of schematic interrelation itself sides with the register of beings that still exist. The diagram commits entirely to the *It is still possible . . . .* Alex's creative act of redrawing, in setting in place the ordinal purified of what disturbs sequence, remains squarely on the side of vitality, what expunges the dead for it is too interested in the living. In time, however, as each entry on this specific diagram also comes to die, it becomes clear that graphic vitality is not one's ownmost state—for each survivor, in turn, when they are *next* and when that next has arrived as the *now*, is expunged from this diagram of the remaining, as they have failed to remain. Ongoingness is not possessed by beings; rather, what goes on is a quality belonging entirely to the flexible, reconfigurable, mutable schematic itself.

The dead are graphic waste, an obstacle to clarity in the artifact—not just in this diagram, nor only in the conceit of the franchise, which is invested in the dead solely as formal elements to be eliminated as quickly as possible so that the attentions of the film can be redirected into the spectacular stillthere-for-now of the contingently remaining. For any regime of horror more generally, the dead are static, interference—they interrupt matters and contaminate texts, even as they may also be the condition of possibility for a text to take shape at all. The becoming-dead are as erased from each *Final Destination* film as they are from Alex's diagram, figured in their collective disappearance as irritations to graphic form.

It is thus neither the dead (as trace, as disappeared, as vulnerable alterity) nor the living (as vital pulsation) in which horror is invested: it is the living as they approach their certain death, it is that being exists finitely. What flatland design renews is that constant reconfiguration of the field against which this possibility of being's impossibility is measured, and by which it cannot be erased. Such an erasure would constitute a possible transference of death, an ontological impossibility equally for the philosopher and for horror. Although intimations of swapped membership on the list offer one mode of narrative organization and suspense—and although the second and fifth installments of the franchise suggest that new life or taken life can remove a figure from the list as such—in the end, the films brutally, without exception, conform to Heidegger's insistence that "by its very essence, death is in every case mine, insofar as it 'is' at all."[30] Even if membership is replaceable in the local logic of any given ordering, one's own death and necessary inscription on the list is marked by irreplaceability. While one can die for another as a sacrifice or displacement, Heidegger writes, "*No one can take the Other's dying away from him.* [*Keiner kann dem Anderen sein Sterben abnehmen.*] Of course someone can 'go to his death for another'. But that always means to sacrifice [*opfern*] oneself for the Other 'in some definite affair'. Such 'dying for' can never signify that the Other has thus had his death taken away in even the slightest degree. Dying is something that every Dasein itself must take upon itself at the time."[31] In Derrida's formulation: "I will never deliver the other from his death [. . .]. Death's dative (dying *for* the other, giving one's life *to* the other) does not signify a substitution (*for* is not *pro* in the sense of 'in place of the other'). If something radically impossible is to be conceived of—and everything derives its sense from this impossibility—it is indeed dying *for the other* in the sense of dying *in the place* of the other. I can give the other everything except immortality, except this *dying for her*."[32]

This impossibility of bartering death ruins every grand fantasy of evading the my-own-property-ness of death: deepest friendship; parental love; soldatesque loyalty; heroic sacrifice;—all those *far, far better things that I do, than I have ever done*. Done, always, for nothing.

The double logic of false sacrifice—that I cannot take the other's death away from them, nor can they die in my place as replacement—is staged repeatedly in the *Final Destination* franchise, as though it is a traumatic hitch that the films cannot move past. One character will interpret relevant signs related to another just in time, avert the disaster, grab the friend, throw his or her body out of the way, all to the sweet scored music of triumph, and yet every single time—soon after or much later, either between two of the films or right at the limit of a given film, often behind a cut to black—eventually, each one's own death is reasserted as necessary and absolute, unavoidably what will at some point arrive, not for the other (though also, always, eventually for the other) but for the self. This failure to forestall the spectacular demises attests to the nonsubstitutability of death as a problem of understanding. As Werner Hamacher summarizes the relation, "it is always dying, and by dying in this way it is infinitely finite. [. . .] [I]t is the infinite finitude of understanding. It still—and precisely here—understands itself in its Being toward death and *is* thus itself essentially the understanding of the absolutely incomprehensible."[33] The horror film relocates this "infinite finitude of understanding" to a relation between being and form. If being is "always dying" and thus is "infinitely finite," form is always giving birth to new forms even as it definitively takes shape. It is because design is reconfigurable as an infinite aesthetic that no X can take the (graphic) place of another. For any attempts to substitute for a schematic position will merely modify the form. The films attest to this not-to-be-outstripped quality of being finite through the infinitude of the modulation of design. One will always find that one's place in death's design is able to be notated; the possibility belonging to list (a purely formal possibility) ensures that. For *Final Destination*, ontological finitude is the plenipotentiary of aesthetic infinitude.

Inverting the possibility of an impossibility, which aligns with ontology, the realm of design is thus best given in this formulation: *the impossibility of a possibility.*

DASEIN VERSUS DESIGN, AND THE WORK OF READING

The *Final Destination* films present, on the one hand, spectacular deaths involving precise sequences of mutually affecting reactive events; on the other, they stage dilemmas of reading practices aimed at unfolding the logic of design determining those sequences. The franchise spends as much time on interpretation as on extermination. In the third film, when the hermeneutically burdened Wendy analyzes the enormous stack of photographs from the night of the amusement park disaster for the sign of death method that each image purportedly reveals, her readings move between those specific images and the deaths in the real as they come to take place—these deaths are also texts, which function as relays, compelling returns to and rereadings of the photographs, themselves compelling, in turn, returns to and rereadings of the real deaths-as-texts. This process resembles Barthes's account of the relation of the photograph and its caption: each is a distinct and separate space; they are "contiguous but not 'homogenized.'" Barthes continues of these cooperative registers: "It is only when the study of each structure has been exhausted that it will be possible to understand the manner in which they complement one another."[34] Whether it is the case that the photographs function as captions to the deaths, or whether it is the deaths that caption the photographs, is an unstable question—*both*. The ever-dwindling set of survivors in each of the films engages in repeated scenes of close reading, but even as these not-yet-dead speculate, misdirect, overreach, and, ultimately, understand the formal relay completely, it is always too late to modify or withdraw the outcome of their interpretation. The reading of any given set of signs risks falsely suggesting an exhaustion of reading, which is—*each time the characters attempt to thwart that design of death*—an anxiety about the perils of shutting analysis down prematurely. To prevent death—to stay on the side of life—is to prolong and dilate the limitless possibilities of close reading. Death's design—being given in the world, but its realization for each figure unsaid prior to the act of reading—requires an attunement of ongoing, not-to-be-outstripped interpretation.

Imperative of these films: Infinite exegesis! Do not cease to interpret!

The method of analysis advanced here, then, is not just one that requires perceiving and interpreting the signs of death's design, but an avowedly hysterical relation to reading that is determinedly suspicious of the meaningfulness of the world, and in particular of sites legible for a relation to design: all those photographs, charts, schematics, maps, lapses, tells, numbers, colors, shapes, &c. Living is translated into a hermeneutic fever. The films are thus methodologically pedagogical—they demonstrate an urgent formalism in which the reader must make as many comparisons as possible (—and, like any good theorist, the readers must also read their own readings lest their interpretations risk being taken as neutral, self-evident, what lacks form, a fatal error in a world in which nothing lacks form at all). Like Armand's obsessive drive to trace the precise instant at which the possible is no longer possible, the project of close analysis comes to preoccupy these texts entirely. While the formal language of editing in the presentation of the way being's possibility becomes impossible is reductive—with its spatiotemporal cutting and isolation of details—and is essentializing—as what remains is causally non-arbitrary for the process to be carried out—this restrictive formalism has its narrative realization in the hermeneutics of suspicion that converts to radical paranoia on the part of the characters. Editing's unavoidable visual emphasis on the every thing that is relevant is given its parallel in an allegorical orgy in which every

FIGURE 2.5. *Final Destination 2* (David R. Ellis, 2003)

thing is also interpretable and consequential. Put another way: There are no untelling details in this textual universe, only not-yet-adequate close readings.

The characters thus subscribe to an epistemology of exposure, a faith in the effective power of the demystification of signs that Eve Sedgwick aligns with the hermeneutics of suspicion in her famous essay "Paranoid Reading and Reparative Reading, Or, You're So Paranoid, You Probably Think This Essay Is about You." Ricoeur is the invisible interlocutor of *Final Destination* in his description of "the invention of an art of *interpreting*," in which "to seek meaning is no longer to spell out the consciousness of meaning, but to *decipher its expressions*."[35] These adolescent descendants of the Nietzschean, Freudian, Marxist tradition stake their lives on an infinite skepticism of surface. The asserted, didactic conceit of the films—that death will reassert necessity against contingent avoidance—makes the consciousness of meaning in the signs interpreted by the characters already available to them. What the young adults of the franchise then grapple with deciphering are precisely the shifting expressions by which that assertion of overt design takes place. As though inverting step by step, piece by sequential piece, Beckett's famous declaration, "There is nothing to express, nothing with which to express, nothing from which to express, no power to express, no desire to express, together with the obligation to express," *Final Destination* might be rewritten as the cinematic insistence: There is everything to express, every artifactual thing with which to express, everything from which to express, all power to express, every desire to express, *together with the reluctance and abrogation and ultimately futility of reading expression itself.*[36]

Opposite of a skeptical text, which asserts nothing can be known (or the hesitations and epistemic fragilities of the Fantastic), *Final Destination* turns on a passion of belief in the exposure made possible by interpretation. The films' paranoid charge places a naïve faith in unconcealment—rendering the supposedly exploitative, cynical, formulaic fare rather earnest in the belief that the act of deciphering signs will elude that which they signify, that making relations visible as such is an effective (transformative) mode of critique. One is always reading for the other (to warn the friend); one is always reading for the self (to attempt to forestall one's own not-to-be-outstripped death). In both cases, close reading is a specific mode of care born out of and derived from a confrontation with ontological horror. Violence compels a slow, deep attention to the details of design—what cannot be paraphrased or summarized, but must instead be read—and a formal disposition is not an evasion of the world's worlding, but the basal requirement for persisting in the world a slight bit longer.

Final Destination thereby wades into one of the most contentious debates in twenty-first-century humanities—polemics for surface reading in various post-hermeneutical turns—and advances this counterclaim: Close reading is not a retreat from the world, but one's only hope for remaining *with* it. Violence is not the limit of a reading for form, but what accelerates its burning necessity.[37]

It is fitting that this confidence in the efficacy of paranoid reading is the province of the surviving protagonists, for as Sedgwick argues, "paranoia is characterized by placing [. . .] an extraordinary stress on the efficacy of knowledge per se—knowledge in the form of exposure"; she continues that perhaps this is why "paranoid knowing is so inescapably narrative," and indeed the logic of paranoia—its insistence on meaningfulness, its epistemology of recovery—is the conceit of the formulaic narrative of each of the films.[38] The paranoiac imperative of *Final Destination* is faulty and yet necessary reasoning; it follows the formulation given by a critic writing on Schreber: "Paranoia [was] distinguished from other forms of madness in that its reasoning was, if *disordered*, not *without order*."[39] Above all, as Sedgwick figures it, "paranoia requires that bad news be always already known"; it is marked by an aversion to surprise, or, as D. A. Miller has it, surprise "is precisely what the paranoid seeks to eliminate, but it is also what [. . .] he survives by reading as a frightening incentive: he can never be paranoid enough."[40] Accordingly, one of the structural signatures of each film in the franchise is an epilogue in which a few characters imagine they have evaded death, have read the signs to safety; release their paranoia, which is to say *they have ceased to interpret*; and as a result find themselves—& too late & unmodifiably & certainly (& unusually cruelly)—in the midst of a suddenly legible arrival of their own about-to-arrive end. The films often conclude on this realization, cutting to black over the actual arrival of death, which is to say: the catastrophe given visual precedence in the closing moments is not the brutal transition to nonbeing, but the realization of the error of a premature abandonment of interpretation. The surviving characters' looks of horror—edited as shared glances of belated understanding—do not take as their objects pain or gore so much as the knowledge that they were not paranoid enough, but might have been, and now the surprise was able to take place. The fatal error each time is to have thought one was done with reading.

Although the films offer a sincerity of faith in the act of interpretation—interpretation as what is endlessly possible parallels death as what is ontologically possible—and although death finishes its local designed list because some last members ceased interpreting prematurely, they simultaneously present interpretation as fundamentally *inadequate* to alter the nature of being. Each *Final Destination* film brutally critiques, on the level of articulated spectacles, the naïveté of the paranoid interpretive stance that it simultaneously avows on the level of narrative. Ontology, *in collusion with editing*, reasserts the failure of ascribing radical transformativity to reading. Thus, while this is a franchise obsessed with epistemology, it is at once both epistemophiliac and epistemophobic. Instead of presenting the undeniable lure and risk of reading too much (a *vanitas* of paranoia that marks many texts of suspicion), the franchise presents the absolute necessity *and* radical insufficiency of reading into the signs of the world-as-text. The hermeneutic act is—quite literally—a matter of life and death, but it is always co-opted, in the end, by the latter.

In the enclosure of *Final Destination*: one must read, one has to closely read to survive (for a spell), and yet reading changes absolutely nothing at all about the structure of finitude. Reading for the form of death's design is the most important occupation of any actant—to the point that its duration structures all narrative unfolding—and yet it fails to forestall the nothing that is nonbeing. For each recovery of the visibility of death's design—permitting a deferral, permutation, or disordering of death's design—merely leads to a reconfiguration, a different ordering of that design; it is what cannot be blotted out but only manifests a (as) difference. Changing design does not negate design, it merely affirms the becoming of new design. And new design is not the endingness of design but the possibility of the not yet *more to be* of form.

From the viewpoint of narrative, everything turns on what would have hypothetically happened *had* the set of characters remained on the plane, on the bridge, on the roller coaster on which they did not remain, and yet in the end they might as well have stayed. But from the viewpoint of the unfoldments of design, *nothing* would have been possible (visually, formally, in terms of découpage) had they not initially escaped. Their bodies *had* to fail to be subject to violence so that the initial form of the film might be given; simultaneously, what is formed as the substance of the franchise is their future, sequential elimination from the world. These beings, then, are not subjects so much as graphic components in the reductive schematic of each film. Death in *Final Destination* is not without cause, ground, or a determinate reason to be; death is the very opposite of the incomprehensible whylessness of the abyss or horrifying without-ground (the Kierkegaardian *Afgrund*, an inscrutable void that is more than emptiness). Death, rather, is the means by which the determinations of an unfolding form take shape and can take shape again, by which a proliferating set of spectacular possibilities is unleashed over time.

Death is the aesthetic force of possibility in horror.

This is the totality of what is meant by the franchise's obsession with the concept of "death's design." The very concept of *design* bridges the relationship between the abstract purpose, plan, or function behind some gesture, action, or object *and* the representational conception or model that gives visual shape to that purpose, plan, or function in advance of its material realization. "Death's design" is simultaneously the manner of being marked *for* death, as in the Latin *designare*, to mark out, choose, appoint ("death's design" as *intention*; as in: Death has *designs on you*), in addition to suggesting death's (own) design, its presenced mode in some distinct arrangement, signified in specific representational instances (even the way the horror franchise itself is designed *for*, as in, in the service of, death).

Death *designates*—we are, in being, designed for death; and Death is *designated* in form.

Unlike possibilities that can present themselves as questions in classical Kantian fashion (for example, the general posing of "What can I know?"), being *designed for death* means the impossibility of asking: How do I know whether to die at all? (We never need ask this.) The unquestionability of this query arises out of the concrete nature of what is given: that existence *is* oriented toward its own nullity. Thus, the exceptions to death's design—its possible permutation, reordering, upsetting—are less narrative elements than formal ones that delay or accelerate arrival, upset composition, and ultimately permute *design* (as in intention and purpose), but which, in turn, open up new, previously unthought avenues for *design* (as in arrangement and order). There is no mode of possibility in *Final Destination* for disordering the intentional-functional dimension of design without putting in play a different aesthetic design; that latter mode of design is marked by infinitude. For in this franchise about what is fundamentally terminable and terminated, what is interminable is design as such.

The structuring opposition of this franchise is not normalcy versus the monster, as in Robin Wood's famous formula for horror, but *Dasein* versus *design*.

And the infinite referral, deferral, and play of unobliterable *design*? Over time, it triumphs, in the end, in time, over being, every time.

What is given, then, in the *Final Destination* form is not just a model of a finitely existing being whose own future certain death is not to be outstripped. The films, we might say, move a step further than Heidegger: for more fundamentally given in relation to this death is the givenness of a formal disposition to infinite becoming. Formal generation, more than one's own death, is what is not to be outstripped. The aesthetic structures and haunts existence as much as does finitude. Horror revises existential philosophy's insistence that being's most fundamental *responsibility* is conferred by death, insisting on—by which I mean giving form to—the manner in which a fundamental *aesthetic responsibility* is conferred by being-toward-death. Set against modes of dissection is the fundamental adequacy of design: design is what reasserts itself, reconfigures itself each time against the concreteness and surety of the finitude of beings. Death is not the outstanding or future event that ends human life; rather, finitude constitutes the ongoing horizon of being as its not-yet. It is always oriented toward the future: "As such, death is something *distinctively* impending," writes Heidegger.[41] Thus, of being we can say that it is infinitely finite, that it is nothing but the anticipation of the possibility of its own impossibility. The anticipation of death opens up the possibility of the possible as such by disclosing that so long as being still is, *at least* one more possibility remains for existence (to not be); that *at least one more* (an ethic shared by list) reveals the measurelessness of possibility. "In the anticipation of this possibility it becomes 'greater and greater,'" Heidegger writes; "that is to say, the possibility reveals itself to be such that it knows no measure at all, no more or less, but signifies the possibility of the measureless impossibility of existence."[42] In the anticipation of the realization of death's design that becomes greater and greater, we might also say that each *Final Destination* film approaches asymptotically the reductio, the ostentatious proving too much, the obviousness of the tautological formalism of the logic whereby death is the cause of death.

But while Dasein is marked by the infinitely finite and the infinite finitude of understanding, what opposes this is what is *finitely infinite*: what takes specific, particular, restricted form against the infinite, limitless possibility of variation, variability, recombination, and a not-to-be-outstripped ongoingness. For while Dasein *is* (exists) finitely, design *is* infinitely. The material body ends while the immaterial abstraction of death's design is what by its essence goes on, continues, reconfigures itself across each text and disperses across the franchise, and *cannot be destroyed*. It is the infinitude of design against which the finitude of being is measured, contrasted, and limited in its possibility. Being, in being handed over to design, is formally given in these films as what above all *ends*. Each closing cut to black hews to Heidegger's notion that in ending "there is essentially no representation." Like being, which exists finitely toward death, the films are governed in their formal unfolding by the horizon of a not-yet-arrived ending, which itself truncates representation, but toward which unfolds the possibility of all representation.

For Heidegger, Death names not an event but the specific possibility "of no-longer being-able-to-be-there." Design, likewise, does not name a fixed formal event, but rather the possibility, plan, protocol, or yet-to-be-formalized nature of some future making or taking shape. *Design names the possibil-*

ity of the being-able-to-be-there of form itself. For Heidegger, the possibility of the impossibility of being shapes, alters, clouds, and stains every other possibility available and open to the subject; and *Final Destination* literalizes and radicalizes this approach to finitude—refusing for its franchise or its characters to act as though death were contingent, optional, occasional (Heidegger calls this delusion being distracted by the everyday diversions of life, but consider how much horror—and thought; and living—diverts in precisely this way). The critical complaint about the shameless, obvious, tautological machine of *Final Destination* is coextensive with its single-minded drive to refuse this diversion. The films do the same thing with the realm of the aesthetic: design is not taken as a contingent, optional dimension of possibility, but the impossibility of a possibility, the rapturously open, never outstripped, infinitely becoming otherwise, never-taking-*final*-form that belongs to—that *is*—the formal.

Far from the "ontological imperialism" that Levinas accuses Heidegger (and philosophy back to the Greeks) of advancing, in *Final Destination*'s showdown between aesthetics and ontology there is an *aesthetic imperialism*, a philosophy of formal power. One must closely read form, has to hysterically interpret, must read as a matter of (local) survival, *and yet* reading does not change the fact of certain future death,—*though still yet* what one reads, design itself, formal reconfigurability in the mode of design, is what persists as the field against which every one will perish. Locally, the ontological reasserts itself over the aesthetic (despite reading, each still dies in time), but globally, the aesthetic reasserts itself over the ontological (design's *infinitude* is secured precisely because of *being's* finitude). At one point in the first film, a not-yet-dead protagonist—all any of these beings are— declares in a moment of deluded triumph that if he sees death's design, he can intervene; that if he intervenes, "I change the design." But this local truth only counterfeits the consequence that death's design will be anticipated infinitely. A *changed* design—the logic by which the five films are structured, what they demonstrate as their complex schematic—is just the difference proper *to* design. Destroying design (upending the order, intervening in order to put in place another schema) is not equivalent to destroying a body: Design does not perish in its alteration. Although the devastations of being impossibilize being, the devastation of form positively forms other forms. Inverting Heidegger's ordinal priority of finitude over infinitude—in which *Unendlichkeit* is the Un-endlichkeit, posterior to finitude and derived from it—*Final Destination* posits a priority of infinitude in the plenitude of design itself, the fullness of permutation, modification, and variation set against being's finitude. The formal is figured as the field against which that which does not go on does not go on.

Dasein is what can be destroyed absolutely—that for which its impossibility is possible—and what exists, what *is*, because a projection of its destruction is possible, because its future not-being is certain. *Design* is what can never be destroyed because its devastation is constitutively subsumed into its renewal, what *becomes* precisely because it can always become something otherwise. Far from any model of horror as the negative affect bound up with anxiety at the loss of being, or on the side of spectatorial shock at the graphic, spectacular demises (assimilable to the claim that death has designs on being)—horror is in collusion with the possibility of the interminable recombination of form itself, the infinite potential of design to endure—to *be* not yet final. The finite infinitude of the aesthetic is what assures, and what secures, this most terrible thought: that horror is not on the side of the It-is-no-longer-possible. Horror resides in the It-will-always-be-possible. Design figures the infinitude against which loss (and what is losable) is formalized. In the *Final Destination* franchise's relay between aesthetics and ontology, the violence of ontology is the lifeblood and motor of the aesthetic, what postpones its formal system ever being finished, what in fact makes impossible the possibility of its end.

Death's infinite design ensures that the next death is always to come.

FIGURE I.1.1. Hans Holbein the Younger, Letter A from *Todesalphabet, The Alphabet of Death* (1524). Woodcut, 2.4 × 2.4 cm. Block cut by Hans Lützelburger. Drawing by Heinrich Loedel after Hans Holbein (1856), 8 × 23 cm. Source: Bridgeman Images.

FIGURE I.1.2. Vítězslav Nezval, Letter A from *Abeceda* [*Alphabet*]. Typographic design by Karel Teige. Prague: Otto, 1926. © Karel Teige—the heirs c/o DILIA.

FIGURE I.1.3. *A* (Jan Lenica, 1965)

Abecedarium

To let it be understood that there was no question here of a love story [. . .], to discourage the temptation of meaning, it was necessary to choose an absolutely insignificant order. Hence we have subjugated the series of figures (inevitable as any series is, since the book is by its status obliged to progress) to a pair of arbitrary factors: that of nomination and that of the alphabet. Each of these arbitrary factors is nonetheless tempered: one by semantic necessity [. . .], the other by the age-old convention which decides the order of our alphabet. Hence we have avoided the wiles of pure chance, which might indeed have produced logical sequences; for we must not, one mathematician tells us, "underestimate the power of chance to engender monsters."

—ROLAND BARTHES, *A Lover's Discourse*

There is no monster or there is a monster but the monster is the grammar of a form.

What the film demonstrates, above all, after all, before all, *for* all—what the film is *for* is the alphabet itself. It is an experiment in the constraint of the abstraction of alphabetic ordering, constraint being an essential condition of any formalism whatsoever. And so what, other than a resolutely formalist reading, could ever make sense of all this?

The 2012 horror anthology film *The ABCs of Death* consists of a set of twenty-six shorts, each four to five minutes long, each made by a different director hailing from one of a dozen countries, each of whom was given total freedom in fulfilling the mandate of the project.[1] Every director was assigned a letter and given the task of choosing a single word beginning with that letter and staging a variety of what the title indicates: a story regarding at least one death, the conceit of which arrives in spelled-out blocks at the end of each segment—for example, "D Is for Dogfight"—the letter and title recasting the prior scene to, at times, redundantly name the obvious conceit ("M Is for Miscarriage"), at times declare a theme (as in the araneological "E Is for Exterminate"), at other times offer a specific designation of the death-achieving weapon ("H Is for Hydro-Electric Diffusion"), while, at other times, deploying letter to retroactively ironize the preceding tale, as in the first segment, which begins at the beginning, with the most insinuating letter, or, as Derrida puts it, "the first one, if we are to believe the alphabet and most of the speculations that have concerned themselves with it."[2]

From the red glossy flat of a meal tray, a camera zooms out to reveal a man quietly residing in bed, all the accoutrements of illness and debility cluttering his room. A woman bursts in and, nervous, hesitant at first, begins to brutalize him with a knife; the encounter is messy, awkward, drawn out, uneven in its rhythmic punctuations, and at the piercing of his jugular, the burbling of his trachea, the frenzied violence stills and wilts—only to resume in a swell as she recommences, throwing boiling water on his face and striking his body repeatedly with a heavy pan, whose violence as hard rhythmic strikes is supplanted with sounds from outside the room and home: sirens, crashes, screeching. A negation, a repudiation, breaks the silence: "It wasn't supposed to be like this," the woman confesses, and not without some tenderness. "I've been poisoning you since last year. You were supposed to die in a few months, slowly, like up to now. Nobody would realize it was me. Everything would have worked out. It would have been over with." His reply, his sole offering in the film—exhausting the language of a certain Jobian logic of suffering—is a whispered, "Why?" Crawling into bed, leaning against his shoulder, she replies, "Because I've been listening to the news all morning and I've run out of time." Apologizing, she continues, "I'm sorry, it was going to be better. But we didn't have time." The image pulls out from the couple, each of whom is dying and will die in their own unique way—though in her case the spectator is still seconds away from knowing that—and returns to red in the fabric of a curtain separating this space from the increasing cacophony in the streets. The segment concludes with its recontextualizing title: "A Is for Apocalypse."

The four-minute short turns on a series of juxtaposed alternatives: man versus woman; husband versus wife; private murder versus public cataclysm; secular versus cosmic rampages; the one versus the many; the lone versus the All, which of course will ultimately include, as the All to be undone in the apocalypse, the wife whose death is also named by the titular letter's appended word. The variety of death on the level of letter, naming apocalypse and not torture or poisoning or burning or stabbing, subsumes the intimate into the universal. The film thus weighs two forms of *particular* violence (poisoning against piercing and scalding) given as two regimes of rhythm (slow prolongation against rapid irruptions), while ultimately neutralizing both in favor of a meta-opposition between two broader *general* regimes of violence: any individual instance of any individual death against the total endingness of life and ultimate finality of earthly time of *Apokalypsis*.

Apocalypse means unveiling, uncovering, revelation, and what "A Is for Apocalypse" exposes is the conceit of the anthology film that it inaugurates; it lays bare the work's large-scale alphabetic structure, which will subsequently be iterated twenty-five more times. Radical endingness is the beginning, and in the beginning is the disclosure of a form. In disclosing this form, the film also constitutes an apology—the woman's reflexive, "I'm sorry, it was going to be better. But we didn't have time," a statement that bonds aesthetic judgment to aesthetic rule: posing the question of the evaluation of the film as a whole as indistinguishable from the limitations that will constrain each of the twenty-six letter segments. Two requirements equally apply here: in addition to alphabetic sequencing, the compiled shorts are required to account for an ending of life. There is no thinking the latter without accounting for the former. The film is not about the concept of death, let alone the percept of death (let alone the affect of death)—death is neither idea nor thing nor sensation. Rather, the work anthologizes, properly speaking—gathers and collects, as of an extraction from a flower (*anthos*)—forms of death as uniquely *giveable* in and through the schema of the abecedarium. The A-part declaration, *It was going to be better / But we didn't have time*, is thus a true apology in the sense of a justification, an *apologeisthai* spoken in defense of the text to an assembly of people, a reasoned reply to possible accusations of a formal error or misdeed on the level of the truncated, restricted structure of the works to come. There is no announcement or unconcealing of form that is not a defense of form in advance, framing the question of a study of varieties of death as indissociable from the nonvaried ordering of alphabetic structure and the simultaneous pressure of a strict durational limit. One might accordingly regard the alphabetically ordered compilation horror film—that it is a nonexhaustive catalogue, a mode of accumulated listing in which ordinal structure is derived from letters—as neither more nor less an advocate for (read: an *apologia* for) the generative value of a strict formalism as an Oulipo experiment such as Georges Perec's 1969 *La Disparition*, the lipogrammatic novel that avoids the letter *e* save for its insistent, repeated appearance in the author's name.

Abecedaria have a few essential formal components. Above all, they comprise a listing of the graphemes of some alphabet (here, the twenty-six letters of the Latin alphabet) *in order*. As Brian Rotman writes:

> [T]he logic of the alphabet is deeply and inescapably serial. Its laws are those of sequence, succession, concatenation, juxtaposition, and ordering along a one-dimensional line: from the original fixing of the letters in the abecedarium, to sequences of them to form words, sequences of words through linear syntax to form sentences, successions of sentences to form texts, and so on. Alphabetic ordering enables, among other things, dictionaries, thesauruses, indexes, Dewey classification of books, the whole apparatus of bibliographical scholarship, encyclopedias, and concordances, not to mention nonsense verse, crossword puzzles, secret codes, and Borges's dizzying fiction of an infinite self-cataloguing library.[3]

In addition, an abecedarium may include obsolete, unvoiced, or conjoined letters. Although frequently deployed by poets and visual artists, abecedaria have a rich history as a pedagogical tool primarily aimed at children's literacy and upbringing, especially for the teaching of prayers. One of the most famous of these is the seventeenth-century *New England Primer* and its numerous variations, including the *Bay State Primer*—which begins "In Adam's Fall / we sinned all; Thy life to mend / This Book attend," and which was cinematically redeployed for that classic of structuralist film, Hollis Frampton's 1970 *Zorns Lemma*.[4] The use of the alphabet for didacticism was enough of a seventeenth- and eighteenth-century commonplace that by 1899, Hilaire

Belloc penned *A Moral Alphabet* ridiculing the sanctimonious certitudes of Victorian abecedaries (e.g., "C stands for Cobra; [. . .] Moral: This creature, though disgusting and appalling / Conveys no kind of Moral worth recalling").[5] Polemicists and satirists (in particular, satirists satirizing polemicists, whose affective rage is so often twinned with moralizing) have long exploited abecedaria; Bertrand Russell's ironical *The Good Citizen's Alphabet* (1953) delightfully begins with "ASININE—What *you* think." Whereas at other times they comprise sincere, democratizing efforts at pedagogy, as in Leo Stein's *The A-B-C of Aesthetics* (1927) or Ezra Pound's *ABC of Reading* (1934).

The abecedarium as a poetic form typically deploys alphabetic order at the beginning of successive lines or stanzas or sections, as in this economical run:

ABC

ROBERT PINSKY

Any body can die, evidently. Few
Go happily, irradiating joy,

Knowledge, love. Many
Need oblivion, painkillers,
Quickest respite.

Sweet time unafflicted,
Various world:
X=your zenith.

Far older examples exist, the most famous being the Hebrew letters that structure Psalm 119, Chaucer's fourteenth-century A. B. C. *(La Priere de Nostre Dame)*, and Edward Lear's nineteenth-century *Alphabet Poem* and *Nonsense Alphabet*. Walter Abish's experimental *Alphabetical Africa* (1974) follows a rather severe abecedarial guide for each chapter, constraining words in the first to those beginning with A, those in the second to those beginning only with A or B, those in the third beginning only with A, B, or C, and so on, each chapter accumulating subsequent letters until the twenty-sixth explodes with the possibilities of the words of a full alphabet, only to remove, in the second half of the novel, letters in a reverse order, all Z words disappearing in chapter twenty-seven, then all words beginning with Y, &c. Nor is twenty-first-century poetry a stranger to the abecedarium's ludic potential, as in Jack Collom and Lyn Hejinian's "The Abecedarian's Dream" from their collaboratively composed *Situations, Sings* (2007). In Louis Lüthi's 2018 metafiction *A Die with Twenty-Six Faces*, the narrator L. introduces a collection—we might say an *anthology*—of alphabet books, "books with letters for titles," such as Perec's *W, or the Memory of Childhood*, Louis Zukofsky's *"A"*, John Berger's *G.*, Robert Calasso's *K.*, Pynchon's *V.*, &c. In L.'s collection, only *L* is missing; however, Lüthi's book itself bears a large *L* on its cover, so it is not, in fact, missing after all but itself comprises yet another alphabet book.

The abecedarial form also begs to have its array of letters bonded to other restrictions and constraints, as in the use of number in the Danish poet Inger Christensen's 1981 *alphabet*, which lets succession simultaneously become densification—compounding formal restraints by way of accounting for a crystalline givenness of the concrete details of the world:

1

apricot trees exist, apricot trees exist

2

bracken exists; and blackberries, blackberries;
bromine exists; and hydrogen, hydrogen

3

cicadas exist; chicory, chromium,
citrus trees; cicadas exist;
cicadas, cedars, cypresses, the cerebellum

[...][6]

Christensen's alphabet is an incomplete one, fitting for the impropriety of its concurrent use of number. The poem's fourteen sections comprise A through N, each section beginning with the successive letter. But within each letter-named section, words accumulate according to the Fibonacci sequence—albeit a flexible Fibonacci sequence, which, one might well argue, means that it is precisely *not* built on the Fibonacci sequence but on its shadow or perhaps its skeleton, an edged spectral almost-Fibonacci. Instead, that is, of the rapid growth of 0, 1, 1, 2, 3, 5, 8, 13, 21, 34, 55, 89, 144, 233, 377, 610, &c., Christensen ignores the first two entries (0, 1), beginning with 1, then 2, then 3, then 5, each number applying not to the atomic problem of word but of line—one line for A, two lines for B, three lines for C, and suggesting ordinality only to upend it and reassert a different logic of sequence at five lines for D and eight lines for E, thirteen for F, and rapidly reaching the listing monumental-ity of 233, 377, &c., losing control of line and its precise register of exponential growth because of the additional formal (material) restriction of the size of the printed page.

The abecedarial form is also predictable catnip to artists: think of Erté's alphabet paintings, the forty-year series begun in 1927 in which the shapes of letters are made through various intertwined female figures, some of whose silhouettes and bony structures loan line to letter while others submerge or embed the corporeal form within a field of color and movement that gives rise to letter. The year before Erté began his project saw the construction of one of the great works of Czech modernism, *Abeceda*, a collaboration be-tween the dancer Milča Mayerová and constructivist Karel Teige: Mayerová choreographed the (twenty-five letter, Q-omitting) alphabet while Teige set typographic form to her postures in a ballet photomontage. Where Erté's re-fined, sinuous forms are redolent of the language of Art Nouveau, Mayerová's wrist- and ankle-bent postures confront, push on, and puncture Teige's stark and dynamic arrangements, staging nothing so much as the fecundity of ex-pressive variations of angle. (One lure of any alphabet—to take the body's plasticity for an infinitely generative letterform. This endlessly seductive proj-ect also animates the 2018 *Physical Poetry Alphabet* by Douglas and Françoise Kirkland, whose staging of contortionist Erika Lemay is set against lush colors and a nearly rococo mise-en-scène, performing the interplay of stark graphic restriction against the virtuosic reconfigurability of the human form.) Or con-sider Jasper Johns's 1969 *Alphabet*, a set of twenty-six letters superimposed in order, whose arrangement devastates the clarity of letter, unconcealing in its place formal problems of a different sort of abstraction related to line, to negative and positive space, to gutters and margins of the image, to questions of proportion and the relation of roundness to edge. Or spend a hypnotic quarter of an hour with the magnified oily whorls of a fingertip as it languidly erases each member of a glass-wetted alphabet in Ann Hamilton's 1994 *abc* only to, through the reversible ontology of video, appear to rewrite it letter by letter. Or regard the six minutes of Martha Rosler's 1975 *Semiotics of the Kitchen*, in which the alphabetically listed clutters of a kitchen (e.g., chopper, eggbeater, hamburger press, spoon) and their slow stilted gestural demonstra-tions become a violent accumulation and pressurized video performance of barely suppressed feminist rage.

Death often runs through abecedarial texts, especially pedagogical ones—not least because it functions as an idealized punishment for the consequences of failing to heed moral and theological provisions. But in its particular navigation of mortality, *The ABCs of Death* shares closest kinship with Hans Holbein the Younger's 1524 *Das Todesalphabet* (Alphabet of Death), in which the etched letters are contained within a square depicting the power of death over subjects of all classes (and with no narrative interaction between the subjects and letters, just a purely formal relation of intersecting lines), or, jumping ahead four centuries, with Edward Gorey's *The Gashlycrumb Tinies* from 1963, which accumulates the untimely demises of children, one letter at a time. The letter in those dactylic couplets, however, designates the proper name of the dead, not the method of departure (for example: "M is for Maud who was swept out to sea / N is for Neville who died of ennui").[7] If the Renaissance reminder of *vanitas* is a declaration of the equality of subjects in the face of mortality—one that privileges death's reach above all else—Gorey aestheticizes and inverts this claim, offering deaths in order to advance the reach of the formality of the alphabet itself, such that the flat accumulated listing of curious demises, each declarative resoundingly avoiding explanation or justification beyond the final causal dimension of what *deaths them*, suggests that cause itself is reducible to the necessity of alphabetic progression. Put another way, in Gorey, listed deaths minister to the aesthetics of the abecedarium itself: each named child dies in order in order to deliver the correct alphabetic sequence.[8]

The letters in *The ABCs of Death* do not offer proper names, nor, indeed, are they functionally symmetrical or predictable: despite the ostensive clarifying function of each letter, there is no consistency in how any letter relates to the minutes that precede its naming. "G Is for Gravity" declares the literal, neutral cause of death in a piece with a first-person point of view that documents little more than the hands, placing bricks in a bag, paddling into water, of a body that will tip itself into a suicide. But what to make of "J Is for Jidai-geki," which names a class of Japanese period dramas, one subset of which is the swordfight, warrior, or samurai film? What bonds letter to text in *this* case are the metatextual conventions that govern the representation of violence: neither a diegetic weapon nor a narrative context, but a subgeneric cause of death that points to the larger formal causation of death that is the alphabetic structure of the entire anthology film set of which this film is a single member. Nor is temporality consistently alluded to: the title "M Is for Miscarriage" appears as a redundant declaration of a death that has already taken place, as the restricted event of the film involves a woman running through a house to find a plunger to dispose of matter stopping up a toilet (rendering a brutal elegance to Ti West's respect for the conceit of the anthology—a little piece of film about a little piece of dead tissue). Other letters function to declare not a death already taken place but one that is filmed in its commission. Still, yet others name a tone or mood that asymptotically approaches death without ever intersecting or interacting with it proper: "C Is for Cycle" titles the stylistic logic of a looping Doppelgänger story, while "S Is for Speed" retroactively highlights that short film's accelerated style—provocatively making something of an argument that aesthetic style itself constitutes the manner and mode and agent of death. Some of the shorts begin in medias res and are fashioned as though they are a segment excised from a larger, coherent work; others follow a self-contained narrative line that ends at death. As a result, what these shorts share in common is precisely their asymmetrical nonrelation. Thus, as often happens with horror, it is the critical complaint that isolates the formalism at play: if a commonly cited failing of the anthology film is its "unevenness," that is precisely what the textual units have in common, what one must take most seriously. For what the short varying films share is the quality of being *uneven*: unequal, unlike, irregular, *different*, while simultaneously appearing in an order that is regular, predictable, certain, and irreducibly iterable in its sequence, sequentially definitive until it comes to an equally definitive end.

One effect of this asymmetry is the consequence Foucault locates in his well-known reading of Borges's certain Chinese encyclopedia at the beginning of *The Order of Things*:

Precisely because it puts them into categories of their own, the Chinese encyclopedia localizes their powers of contagion; it distinguishes carefully between the very real animals [. . .] and those that reside solely in the realm of imagination. [. . .] The quality of monstrosity here does not affect any real body, nor does it produce modifications of any kind in the bestiary of the imagination; it does not lurk in the depths of any strange power. It would not even be present at all in this classification had it not insinuated itself into the empty space, the interstitial blanks *separating* all these entities from one another. It is not the "fabulous" animals that are impossible, since they are designated as such, but the narrowness of the distance separating them from (and juxtaposing them to) the stray dogs, or the animals that from a long way off look like flies. What transgresses the boundaries of all imagination, of all possible thought, is simply that alphabetical series (a, b, c, d) which links each of those categories to all the others.[9]

Wonderment, that is, or what is "impossible to think" as Foucault words it, is not the curious ontology of, say, the Nazi stripper fox of "H Is for Hydro-Electric Diffusion," but the "narrowness of the distance" separating *H* from *I*, which is to say, what separates Nazi stripper foxes from "I Is for Ingrown" and its entirely possible, not statistically unlikely image of a woman being murdered by a man, a mode of death so common that the term *femicide* was coined to name it. What disturbs thought is precisely "that alphabetical series" which sets those two modes of death in their two worlds, one alternate and one ours, and those two sets of terms, anthropomorphic animals and the ordinary cruelties of gender-based violence, alongside each other at the remove of the distance of two letters that come in sequence. Thus, as Foucault continues: "The mere act of enumeration that heaps them all together has a power of enchantment all its own" as "proof of the possibility of juxtaposition."[10]

Theory is so often the doublet of art. This is an enchantment that comes at a cost. It is fitting that Foucault's reaction to Borges is the very same affective adulteration solicited by the horror anthology—laughter and horror; delight and queasiness; enchantment and discomfort. The philosopher writes, "Ce texte de Borges m'a fait rire longtemps, non sans un malaise certain et difficile à vaincre" (This text of Borges made me laugh for a long time, though not without a certain discomfort [uneasiness, queasiness, sickness] that I found difficult to overcome [defeat, beat, conquer, shake off, override]).[11] The stubborn trace of bad affect is due to Borges's text's arousal of a "suspicion that there is a worse kind of disorder than that of the *incongruous*, the linking together of things that are inappropriate; I mean the disorder in which fragments of a large number of possible orders glitter separately in the dimension, without law or geometry."[12] Monstrosity thus is redirected from the encyclopedia's impossible beings to a "monstrous quality that runs through Borges's enumeration."[13] That brutal, possible deaths of miscarriage, of suicide, of spider bites, are set against fantastic and impossible ones functions as positive proof of the possibility of the anthology, the collection, the catalogue as such, demonstrating the enchantments of enumeration and classification themselves—in other words, proof of formal fecundity in a listing of ontological finitude. (One might repeat the final lesson of the previous chapter: death's infinite *design* triumphs in time, every time, over the finite being of *Dasein*.)

In the midst of the uneven, the asymmetrical, the inconsistent, oddly joined and imperfectly structured, the ground zero of the cinematic compendium is the twin requirements of its order and structure: the titular bonding of alphabet to death. Death is not an ontological certainty so much as a formal certainty. It is also, therefore, what seems to promise *meaning* in the midst of the structural play with order. This involves what Barthes calls the fundamental "temptation of the alphabet": "to adopt the succession of letters in order to link fragments," to valorize "an unmotivated order (an order outside of any imitation), which is not arbitrary (since everyone knows it, recognizes it, and agrees on it)."[14] The large-scale form of the abecedarium would thus seem to promise the euphoria Barthes describes as "no more anguish of 'schema,' no more rhetoric of 'development,' no more twisted logic, no more dissertations! an idea per fragment, a fragment per idea, and as for the succession of these atoms, nothing but the age-old and irrational order of the French letters (which are themselves meaningless objects—deprived of meaning)"—a pure site to play out the meaning or meaningless of order itself, a testing ground for the fecundity of the arbitrary.[15]

> *Inverse of the temptation of the alphabet to adopt succession thus to link (some) fragments = the temptation to sabotage the alphabet, to wreck succession thus to fragment (all) linkages.*

When the Dutch design collective Experimental Jetset partnered with the sub-underground musician Ian Svenonius to form the installation *Alphabet Reform Committee*—which ran in late 2018 at the Volksbühne Pavilion in Berlin— its ostensible purpose was to explore "the notion of the city as a platform for language," a project in sympathy with abecedarial experiments like *Zorns Lemma* and Lynne Sachs' *Abecedarium: NYC*. Their project, however, had one crucial difference: instead of celebrating the typographic fecundities of urban spaces, *Alphabet Reform Committee* took aim at the hegemony of sequentialism that is the formal logic of the alphabet itself. It advanced, that is, one of the other fundamental temptations of the alphabet: to destroy it absolutely. In the installation space, voices intone impossible suggestions: ranging from "B should go where the T used to be" to "I like S at the beginning of the alphabet." What becomes clear is that alphabetic *reform* is always a gesture at *de-forming the formalism* of the alphabet: no reform without razing, ravaging, wrecking. And why this urge to reform, which is to say destroy, the alphabet? It is the correlate of its overwhelming terrorizing, territorializing insistence: fitting that Jan Lenica's 1965 animation *A* turns on a typographically turgid letter haunting a man in his apartment, blocking his passage, bouncing indolently, refusing to be chiseled or willed away, smashing and stomping and piercing—the tip of the (any) A a sharp and potent weapon—and kicking and obliterating the fellow, until finally he will cease to be molested by the abu-sive A, will calm and relax for the briefest of moments, only to back into, and slowly turn toward, a newly appearing, newly menacing B. The realization of this appearance of new, next letter is a pure register of horror.

Alphabet is a cruelty: we have known this since at least 1927 when Mr. Ramsay in Virginia Woolf's *To the Lighthouse* imagines thought like the al-phabet, "ranged in twenty-six letters all in order," but he, despite "running over those letters one by one, firmly and accurately," stops on the letter Q, is unable to move past Q, unable to fathom what comes next, gets stuck (trapped, stranded, deserted) in its callously linear progress:

> He reached Q. Very few people in the whole of England ever reach Q. [...] But after Q? What comes next? After Q there are a number of letters the last of which is scarcely visible to mortal eyes, but glimmers red in the dis-tance. Z is only reached once by one man in a generation. Still, if he could reach R it would be something. Here at least was Q. He dug his heels in at Q. Q he was sure of. Q he could demonstrate. If Q then is Q—R— [...] A shutter, like the leathern eyelid of a lizard, flickered over the intensity of his gaze and obscured the letter R. In that flash of darkness he heard people saying—he was a failure—that R was beyond him. He would never reach R. On to R, once more. R——[16]

In *The ABCs of Death*, that this testing ground of alphabetic order and its brutal progressive sequential insistence happens against the overdetermined site of repeated deaths would seem to beg Barthes's related warning: "This or-der [...] can be mischievous: it sometimes produces effects of meaning; and if these effects are not desired, the alphabet must be broken up to the advantage of a superior rule: that of the breach (heterology): to keep a meaning from 'taking.'"[17] If the promise of alphabetic order is that it "banishes every origin," its twin risk is that "perhaps in places, certain fragments seem to follow one another by some affinity; but the important thing is that these little networks not be connected, that they not slide into a single enormous network which would be the structure of the book, its meaning."[18] *The ABCs of Death* hews to this resistance to allowing any single unified meaning of death to take: it avoids demonstrating any overriding theme (again: its formalism is what pos-itively produces an affirmative, generative unevenness). The potential of each letter (any letter) is its infinite associations against the specificity of any given arbitrary assignment as word. This is the tension we see at once with the let-ter *A*, which appears, more than the other letters, to govern—indeed, loans as *alpha* its very name to the alphabet, and seems in its reflexive reference to brevity and insufficiency to render a formal judgment on the compilation as a whole. The *A* segment, that is, insinuates a figuration of meaning—the ambiguity of whether it offers an origin, whether it is a fragment sliding into and forming a network of larger, connected meanings. This short demands that we grapple with the question: Is it significant that the figure of the apocalypse, its radical eschatology—its complete ending, devastation of all beginnings—should inaugurate the film's alphabetic progression, come first in letter as what, quite literally, need be the disaster that comes last? This question is set against the arbitrary constraint that the first letter must come first, an ordinal priority that is indifferent to the ending-dimension of the named concept represented therein, co-opting this film instead for the gesture of opening and beginning that is by rights the province of (any) A. Both sites of possible meaning are thus undone: *A* as the privileged letter of initiation, and Apocalypse as the privileged sign of termination; *both* are co-opted instead neither for A nor for Apocalypse but for position in the anthology merely as that letter which precedes B and is itself preceded by nothing. (Keep and hold fast to this *A* and *B* for the duration of this book; they will eventually return, albeit with an important third term added—will painfully, inescapably reappear, but now crawling low on suture-stitched knees, as only *a*, *b*, *c*.)

In Erté's composed graphic alphabet (this is Barthes again), "the letter becomes primordial (ordinarily it is a capital); given in its *princeps* state, it reinforces its essence *as letter*: here it is pure letter, sheltered from any temptation which would link it to and dissolve it into the word (i.e., into a contingent meaning)."[19] In our cinematic abecedarium, the site of repetition—the flat equivalence of the appearance of the blocks declaring "Letter Is for Word"—is likewise pure letter, the letter-as-isolated-figure the sole site on which the meta-film could be constructed as having any coherence. Like Deleuze's account in *The Logic of Sensation* of the figural as what deforms the figurative (his privileged violence of sensation against the violence of representation), the illustration of death in each film's narration (a figurative account) is deformed by, disfigured by, the isolation of each letter as alphabetic figure. The alphabet is thus formally prior to the assembled films; the figural, prior to the figurative. Each story (or figuration) of death is primarily a story of disfigurement; the letter thus functions dialectically to figure via the alphabet as what has been unfigured or disfigured on the level of the short's narrative. It would misunderstand the form of the film to read only these words into which these letters contingently dissolve, just as it would misunderstand the relation of this film to death to co-opt its abecedarium entirely to the accumulation of a sequence of letters. The question is how to hold to the solitary letter entry and the specificity of finitude without privileging either; this is the precarity of the meaningfulness of death and the seeming nonmeaningful (anti-meaningful; mere) formalism of alphabetic ordering.

The alphabet thus functions in this film as a *primer* in both senses of the word: as grammatically instructional—as in a book of prayers or a schoolbook, or more broadly as an introductory work on a topic—but also as preparatory in relation to a certain finitude that is figured iteratively through the alphabet. If the abecedarium evokes the idea of the first (hour, stage, service, part) of something, it simultaneously evokes other senses of *primer*: as in to cover with a first coat in preparation for more material (that undercoating what ensures a stronger future adhesion of subsequent layers, what loans durability to the bond). This layered system is given in a formula, and that is the title format for each of the twenty-six segments: Letter Is *for* Letter-beginning Word (as in "A Is for Apocalypse"). *For* takes a double sense here: *for* as both designation and representation, but also *for* as in offering or gift, suggesting that the alphabet itself bequeaths the certainty of death that it each time, differently, and yet predictably, names, *preparing for adhesion to future material*.

Death, however, is and is not the alphabet's to give.

This problem of the "for" is the same one that Heidegger and Derrida make a problem for the thinking of dying for the other, which in the preceding chapter took the form of the impossibility of evading "death's design"—that *for* the grammatical complication that is an ontological impossibility, as when Heidegger insists, "By its very essence, death is in every case mine, insofar as it 'is' at all," and as Derrida makes clear: "Death's dative (dying *for* the other, giving one's life *to* the other) does not signify a substitution (*for* is not *pro* in the sense of 'in place of the other')."[20] The bequeathment of the *for* in the title to each of the twenty-six short films is likewise a designation of an indirect relation, what letter loans to word—and not unlike the ontological dilemma that no one can die *for* the other, no offering of the abstraction of the letter for the particularity of the word and the specific death it names signifies a substitution of the letter for the meaningfulness of that word, nor does it obliterate the infinite other possible words to which that letter might have loaned its abstraction and its position, in the place of the death contingently but concretely named and narrated. The letter each time offers its designation to the word, but it does not give it away; it both bequeaths the certainty of the death named by the given word and retains its position as pure ordinal entry (that which, formally, it *cannot* give away).

What the abecedarium in this film is a primer for, then, is each time what comes in order—what arrives first, comes next, and must by definition come last, being *what* ends, the ending proper to dying that is not like the ending of other things, including lists, including alphabets. This problem of order and preparation is not a neutral one in relation to the specific abecedarium of this film: death of course is that which one is always in a manner preparing for (what one *is* beforehand) and what one cannot prepare for, yet what will certainly arrive as prepared for by being and without any overt preparation required. We are, in being, *primed* for death, what we do not in fact—the sole thing in fact—we do not require a *primer* to learn.

A different alphabet, although the point is: it is always the same alphabet.
A different end, although the point is: it is always the same end.

A man is sick.
He is suffering.
This man is dying.

Starting in 1988, Deleuze agreed to sit for a series of interviews with Claire Parnet filmed by Pierre-André Boutang, with two stipulations: the resulting film would not be broadcast until after his death, and it would be structured a certain way according to a restriction, a device, one that he declares has arrived from the outside, having come to him as a decision with whose rule he will abide but which he did not make. The footage begins with Deleuze speaking, addressing Parnet: "Tu as choisi un abécédaire. Tu m'as prévenu des thèmes et là je sais pas exactement les questions, si bien que moi j'ai pu réfléchir un peu aux thèmes. Répondre à une question sans avoir un peu réfléchi c'est pour moi quelque chose d'inconcevable." (You chose an alphabet [for the form of the film]. You warned me of certain themes (though I do not exactly know the questions), so I was able to think a bit beforehand about those themes. Answering a question without having thought about it a little is inconceivable to me.)

Death runs through *L'abécédaire de Gilles Deleuze* in numerous ways: in explicit conversation (during a discussion of territorialization, Deleuze speaks of an animal seeking a territory of death) and through the grain of Deleuze's body—the jagged rasp of his cough, his exhaustion set against the vitality and grace of his speech. But above all, the abecedarial form—with its spontaneous speech and alphabetically ordered themes—is framed in relation (defended: once more we are lingering with apologia) as a structural conceit enabled, even uniquely afforded, by death. Safeguarded in advance from the spontaneity of the form and his likely cursory answers, Deleuze is calmed by a condition of the game: "Il y a une clause qui me sauve: cela ne sera utilisé, si c'est utilisable, qu'après ma mort" (There is a clause that saves me: it will only be used, if it is usable, after my death). Thus, in this project of speaking while alive solely for a projection that will appear only after his death, Deleuze describes himself as already become-archive: "Je me sens déjà réduit à l'état de pure archive de Pierre-André Boutang, de feuille de papier et ça me remonte beaucoup, ça me console beaucoup [. . .]. Je parle d'après ma mort. On sait bien qu'un pur esprit [. . .] n'est pas quelqu'un qui donne des réponses très profondes ni très intelligentes, c'est un peu sommaire." (I already feel reduced to the state of a pure archive of Pierre-André Boutang, a paper sheet, and it calms and consoles me a lot. [. . .] I speak from my death [after my death]. We know well that a pure spirit is not someone who gives very profound, very intelligent answers, just a little summary [digest, sketch, perfunctory remark].)

And so it begins—*A is for Animal*, and with the figure of the bestiary in Deleuze's writings they are off.

Here, Deleuze is speaking *avant sa mort* with a certain liberty promised by declaring it a speaking *d'après ma mort*, declaring himself what has become-archive in this testament *for* death, bequeathed as an archivable gift on the condition *of* death. This is Deleuze constituting his own memorial in advance, and constituting it as the ineluctability of alphabetic structure, what is contained between "A *comme* Animal" to *Boire*, Culture, Desire, *Enfance*, Fidelity, Gauche, onward to Joy, eventually Resistance, ending at "Z *comme* Zigzag."

(First resistance to abecedarial completion: Upon arriving at W, Deleuze insists there is nothing to say, *nothing* contained within W, while Parnet persists, asking about Wittgenstein, asking about Wittgenstein *as word*. From this nothing-to-say Deleuze repudiates an overwhelmingly destructive and regressive tendency in contemporary philosophy ["ils cassent tout"—they break everything]. This is what the pure spirit of letter enables and brings forth: to start with the nothing-to-say and to end with the vigilance of philosophical thought itself.)

(Second resistance to abecedarial completion: While the exhaustion of alphabetic order in the abecedarium is the structure of its formal constraint, it is the rare abecedarium that does not take liberties—such liberties, of course, being the negative possibility afforded by the positivity of any constraint. As the alphabet comes near the close of its series, Parnet will declare X unknown, and Y unspeakable ["*indicible*"—unutterable; ineffable], arriving rapidly to Zed, to the end, to the final term, and with it, the unknown and ineffable condition of the future broadcast of the footage as it is still in the act of being filmed: the unknown and unspeakable, unutterable and ineffable, occasion and moment of Deleuze's future death in which this speech, as it is still in the act of being uttered, will become known because now, which is to say *then*, it will constitute a speaking *après sa mort*. When Parnet comes to *Z*, the final letter, Deleuze says "Just in time!" No word after. —Only all these words after.)

In speaking philosophically in relation to death—death being what gives form to the philosophical thought therein—this alphabetic primer is a primer *to the letter*: a practicing of death (a speaking after death) while still alive. The hours of footage are neither a representation nor a documentation of Deleuze as philosopher, but rather constitute a textual practice that figures an essential *act* of philosophy. The film is not figurative (of the philosopher; of a narrative of a philosophical life, let alone death), but rather is figural of philosophy as practice, in the sense that Socrates insists in the *Phaedo*: "A man who has really devoted his life to philosophy should be cheerful in the face of death [. . .]. [T]hose who really apply themselves in the right way to philosophy are directly and of their own accord preparing themselves for dying and death"; this argument is derived from the separation of unaided intellect from contaminations of the body, and the claim that that state is a living that is "as close as possible to death," such that "true philosophers make dying their profession."[21] *L'abécédaire de Gilles Deleuze* is thus an exercise in philosophical discipline, monstrating a concern for the dying of the self, textually unfolding in its sequentially ordered fragments of thought that the "aim of those who practice philosophy in the proper manner is to practice for dying and death."[22]

The film itself is a *melete thanatou*.

And this practice for dying and for death explicitly hinges on the structure of the abecedarium. Deleuze insists at one point that there will be no unpublished work upon his death, that he has no "reserve knowledge." The alphabet is likewise without reserve; it runs its course, has nothing remaindered as a set, to the point that alphabetic beginning and ending define totality: from A to Z promises exhaustion, no other letters, nothing else remaining. In these interviews, Deleuze is preparing for what will be shown after death in a certain, nonarbitrary order of being and nonbeing.

Except, one thing more.

In 1994, Deleuze contravenes the rules of the game. Negating the comfort offered by his opening remarks—what comes textually *prior* to A, what *primes* A to take place in the first place—that he is comforted knowing he is speaking from *after* his death, pure spirit the alibi for the unscripted partiality and spontaneity and sketchlike aspects of his thoughts—Deleuze agreed to a broadcast of *L'Abécédaire* on European television before its proper time. That is to say, before he is after his death. His explanation is that because his health, his body, had so worsened, "C'est comme si j'étais déjà parti" (It's as if I were already gone).[23]

And indeed, Deleuze died by suicide in late 1995 while the interviews were still being broadcast.

Analogue, Malone Dies:
The feet are clear already, of the great cunt of existence. Favourable presentation I trust. My head will be the last to die.[24]

Analogue, Dante and the Lobster:
Well, thought Belacqua, it's a quick death, God help us all. It is not.[25]

What solicits attention here is a formal homology.

Deleuze's poignant phrasing puts together a general condition and the most particular if also impossible utterance, what can be spoken only by contravening itself: "C'est comme si" and "j'étais déjà parti." It is *as if* or *as though* the case that *I were already gone* (*already dead*), a statement made possible by the latter remaining *as if* or *as though* and not *in itself*. But it also constitutes another bond of death to alphabetic ordering, for the structure of *L'Abécédaire* also repeatedly deploys *comme* in naming its commitment to abecedarial form, as in "*A comme Animal*," in which *comme* names likeness (the as-in), names the exemplary premised on so-as-ness. *As in* is not quite the same as *as if*—the first names a relation whereby some latter Y is a particular (specific, given, but nonexclusive) example of a general case of the (infinite) former X, whereas the second names a form of likeness and resemblance, a comparison not of the particular and general but of two particular states, one of which may not be true but is *possible*. Abecedarial form gives rise to the infinite possibilities for completion in the concrete decision of any *A comme* [   ], while what makes Deleuze's *as if*, *as though* unlike any others is precisely the finitude that marks the final clause as what the sentence must suspend (what cannot yet have taken place) but what, with certainty, will, at some future point, definitively take place. What will not remain impossible. What, in sequentiality, will reassert itself as definitive and inescapable, even if it has yet to arrive at the moment that its possibility (and likeness) is uttered. Abecedarial form is thus violated in order to be reasserted. Instead of speaking *après* his death, Deleuze speaks before it, while speaking, simultaneously, *after* it: as in *chasing* it, in pursuit of it, in imitation of it, intending to overtake it. He speaks further than his death by speaking before it speaking after it.

Deleuze's rescinding of the sole requirement that the film be shown posthumously turns on that *comme*, the same *as* of each letter's title, the same grammatical gesture of comparison or likeness, *as if, as though, as in*, in other words, the impossible bequeathment that we also see with "for" in *The ABCs of Death*—what the abstraction of [Letter] loans to the contingent [Word] it names, but imperfectly, and without completeness. To remain on the side of speaking the "*as if* I were already dead" is to loan likeness, but without taking away the absolute specificity of the future position from which one definitively will not and *cannot* speak those words. It loans its similarity and sets in place a juxtaposition only to retain a radical difference in terms. It reserves the irreplaceable dimension that belongs equally to the sequence of members in any alphabetic set and the order of being one that will die.

These two abecedaria—*The ABCs of Death* and *L'abécédaire de Gilles Deleuze*—are not analytics of finitude, they are enunciations of it; they offer not an interpretation of death, but an attestation of its unbreakable relation to sequence, to order, certain and predictable, iterable and yet utterly each time unique, systematic yet variable, being what, each time, ends—precisely as its form guaranteed, from the very beginning, it would.

INTERLUDE II

Rhythm & Feel

At the climax of Montaigne's 1580 essay *"De la cruauté"* (On Cruelty)—the moment at which he arrives at the central provocation, that "even in the case of Justice itself, anything beyond the straightforward death-penalty seems pure cruelty"—after his provision of a mimetic ethics in the "Nothing tempts my tears but tears," but before the surprising essayistic swerve from the tortures of the dying to his concluding plea for a general duty toward animals, the philosopher tells this vivid story:

> A few days ago a soldier in prison noticed from the tower in which he was held that a crowd was gathering in the square and that the carpenters were at work constructing something; he concluded that this was for him; he determined to kill himself, but found nothing which could help him to do so save a rusty old cart-nail which Fortune offered to him. He first of all gave himself two big jabs about the throat, but finding that this was not effective he soon afterwards gave himself a third one in his stomach, leaving the nail protruding. The first of his gaolers to come in found him in this state, still alive but lying on the ground weakened by the blows. So as not to waste time before he swooned away, they hastened to pronounce

sentence on him. When he had heard it and learned that he was to be decapitated, he seemed to take new heart; he accepted the wine which he had
previously refused and thanked his judges for the unhoped for mildness of
their sentence, saying that he had made up his mind to appeal personally
to death because he had feared a death more cruel and intolerable, having
formed the opinion that the preparations which he had seen being made
in that square meant that they wanted to torture him with some horrifying
torment. This change in the way he was to die seemed to him like a deliverance from death.[1]

This parable dramatizes the violent fecundities of imagination: the hypothetical tortures of an elaborate execution are taken to be so horrific that the
prisoner would rather deploy a rusty nail to throat and belly to avoid it, thus
auto-realizing something of the dreaded slow and tortuous wounding, ending in gratitude for the promise of a milder, quicker beheading from without.
But it is simultaneously a story about—and its textual unfolding is governed
by—matters of precise timing, and orders of coming first, coming next, coming last. The formal category of the sequence governs every event described:
the crowd assembling; the material erection of the scaffold; the series of two
wounds to the throat; the subsequent finding that after that, one persists in
remaining alive; then (consequence and subsequence) afterward a third to the
belly; the reading of the sentence; only then the acceptance of wine; &c. "Et,
voyant qu'il n'en avoit peu esbranler sa vie, s'en donna un autre tantost après
dans le ventre" (And, seeing that he had not yet shaken his life, he quickly
gave himself another in the belly) crystallizes the passage's formal ordering:
having not *yet* shaken off life, there is the giving of oneself *another* wound at
some point soon *afterward*. The relation of the body to its imminent destruction involves—it is unthinkable here outside of—a precise arrangement of
events: ones scheduled, deferred, then quickened and readied. Forced dying
happens, above all, in time. And the specific tonality of that time involves the
interplay of the slowness of bleeding out (that "yet" in "yet alive") followed by
the urgency and haste in the rapid reading of the actual sentence. If the parable is about degrees of latency in relation to abstract timing—the improper
dying of the body *too soon* (before the execution takes place) and the quick
reading of the institutionalized sentence before it is *too late*, plus an oversen-
sitivity to the hypothetical *slow* time of the dying the prisoner imagines and
the future *quick* time of the certain beheading that takes place beyond the
edges of the narrative itself, in other words *after* it—it also poses the broader

question of the relation of violence to what delays and what accelerates, to the entire formal category of rhythm, to questions of pacing, tempo, beat, rate.

Violence thus becomes unthinkable outside of what Barthes dubs *bathmology*, what he calls in *Roland Barthes par Roland Barthes* "a new science: that of the degrees of language."[2] Writing of the sequence of the effects of champagne in his preface to Brillat-Savarin's *The Physiology of Taste*, he likewise insists on "one of Modernity's most important formal categories: the gradation of phenomena" and again calls it a "bathmology," "the field of discourses in so far as degrees come into play."[3]

Bathmos: a step in a staircase; a step or a degree, a threshold or interval; a rank or grade or standing. From the same root as *bathos*, a level of dignity, from depth and fullness, but also as in the sudden (we remain with questions of pacing) shift from the lofty to the commonplace, as in Alexander Pope's invented, Longinus-satirizing rhetorical figure of bathos in his 1727 "Peri Bathous, Or the Art of Sinking in Poetry"—a failed, ridiculous attempt at sublimity. And there is certainly something of the bathetic in the nonsublime anti-grandeur of the prisoner's near-death—not the grand tragic project of a *passage à l'acte* suicide nor a whispering dignified expiration, but the unintentionally anticlimactic absurdity of piecemeal harms to a self who will die soon thereafter anyway. Not pathos, but a cringe-inducing awkwardness. The sheer embarrassment of having read the scenario so wrong, having been that earnest, that panicked, so *serious*. Derisive glances shared by the jailers. Everyone all a bit mortified at how the thing had to go down.

> *Bathesthesia is also a term for a body's sensitivity*
> *(to stimuli: pain, pressure, vibration, movement)*
> *in relation to deep structures in the body.*

In his essay "Image et violence" Jean-Luc Nancy sidesteps the question of "images of violence"—ones that are "indecent, shocking, necessary, heart-rending"—for the more provocative question of the violence of images, an assaultive intensity irreducible to its legibility in relation to what he dubs in "The Forgetting of Philosophy" the realm of meaning: "the element in which there can be significations, interpretations, representation."[4] In doing so, he offers a general definition of violence as "the application of a force that remains foreign to the dynamic or energetic system into which it intervenes."[5] Violence "denatures, wrecks, and massacres that which it assaults," exhausting itself in a "pure, dense, stupid, impenetrable intensity."[6] The generality of this structure—that of a force external to a system in which it intervenes—enables a proper promiscuity of violence. A system might be a leg, a liver, a nation, one lidded jar, everything gravitationally bound, a landscape, a chromatic palette, the food supply, a line of inquiry, our neck-punctured prisoner, philosophy itself, any one of which *as system* might experience a *systemic* force that intervenes and denatures it.

My arm—the application of a force—a cracking sound; the line of the ulna, radius, or humerus presently running otherwise: my arm, now wrecked in its angular qualities of extensive armness, my arm denatured. Or, a field of monochrome (a swath of red, of blue, of black)—the application of a force (say, sudden new light), which intervenes into that chromatic system and wrecks, massacres the chromatic constancy in every direction, forces the intrusion of a visible difference, &c. This is violence too.

And so, although this is not where he takes his thinking, one can glimpse in Nancy's definition the potential for a pure formalism of violence—one that is irreducibly linked to a capacity for a generality of violence to be thought speculatively, which is to say as a theoretical possibility of form itself, and not as a demonstration of given instances. Violence, instead of naming either concrete cases or intensity quaquaqua, thus correlates to the plastic ground of form, its essential capacity to reform, deform, and take shape otherwise as reformative and deformative possibilities internal to its giving of system in the first place. (And if there is a correction, then, to make to Nancy, it is on the terrain of the term *foreign*—"the application of a force that remains foreign to the dynamic or energetic system into which it intervenes"—for what a proper formalism of violence reveals is that dynamic and energetic systems gives rise to their own forces, ones that precisely do not remain foreign to systems but, in their capacity for disturbance, give rise to system in the first place. What is *outside, out there, at the farthest reach*, that is, will always turn out to have been *inside*, in the interior of the interior. That does not make violence any less violent.)

In regarding the relation of forces to system we require a vocabulary to account for that formal sensitivity to formal stimuli, to variations in pressure, to the applications of forces into the dynamic/energetic systems in which they intervene, one that speaks directly to the brute responsiveness of formal gestures to formal gestures, and one that returns us to that primary question of the relation of violence to the aesthetic category of rhythm, to a sensitivity to changes in pressure that delay or accelerate the reactivity of the components of a system. We require, in other words, a thinking of *feel*, not in the sense of *feeling* as it is routed back through the Old English *felan* (to grasp), accumulating with it various empiricisms and the priority of sense experience that regards feeling only ever as a matter of touching and (thus) perceiving.[7] Rather, the feel of violence requires an accounting in the sense in which an object is said to have a certain *feel*: a question of the tautness or the slackness of mechanisms, by way of accounting for sequence, rhythm, pacing, and the diagrammatic arrangements of elements that are how a formalism of violence in horror goes. (*Feeling* without *Bodies That Feel*: yet another way of writing *not neck*. We are never not writing *not neck*.) The matter of touch at the heart of feeling is thus not excised but perverted, turned away from the body and toward material: touch as in the feel of an instrument, the *touch* or *feel* that a mechanical apparatus bears out in its formal arrangement, as in the mode of the responsiveness of keys to touch, as in the soft or slow or hard or fast action of a particular piano: a slow or loose action feels mushy, floppy, slack to the touch, compared with the brittle, crisp, and sharp feel of a particularly sensitive instrument in which response is governed by rapidity. A tight feel can become overly tight, resulting in a stiff, awkward feel: imagine stuck, rusted keys, keys that cannot breathe.

The feel of an instrument relies on the interplay of the total relationship between its mechanical components: well-lubricated pivots and joiners and springs, with a level of tension to counterbalance the weight of other components, an action tight enough to produce smooth movements in the playing of the instrument yet not so tight that it results in brittle or constricting movements, or, even worse, a tightness that overly resists the force applied to the mechanical elements. (Getting the latter wrong is not just a problem of tone—it is also how instruments break, how they can be *ruined*.) A low action in a guitar might render a vague fuzziness or buzzing; in a horn, it might produce a dampened sound or slightly depressed pitch—which, of course, might be desirable at times. Some performers are willing to take the risk, or loss, for the sake of tradeoffs in possibilities in technique. Glenn Gould, prizing a particular feel, had all of his pianos dissected and reassembled with a famously fast action, making their keys incredibly sensitive to touch, offering no resistance, mutating the piano into something more like a harpsichord. Another way of phrasing this is that on the level of the speed of the material, Gould's adjusted action produced a differential between the key pushed and the string struck that was as minimal as possible. *Feel* names relative responsiveness to stimuli, the amount of physical effort necessary to make an instrument do what it is designed to do, the requirements of velocity and pressure that bring about effects. It is thus a general name for a system's sensitivity to variations in pressure. Rereading violence through the question of feel, rendering it a matter of acute or dull textual sensitivities to stimulation, generates the ground for a thinking of the carnage of horror as irreducibly linked to formal questions of tempo.

FROM HIS MOTHER'S WOMB / UNTIMELY RIPP'D

À l'intérieur (Bustillo and Maury, 2007), given in English as Inside (with resonances of Inland, Inward, Internal, Domestic, Within), opens with a muffled voice speaking, "My child, my baby, finally inside me," matched to the image of the interior of a pregnant body (a uter-optic shot aligned with the perspective of a womb-cam), at which point amniotic calm and float suddenly gives way to a violent crashing jerk. The fetus, in the middle of the frame in a middle distance, is, in this instant, spatially reoriented, its form made to consume the totality of the foreground as it is thrown toward the camera, brutally smashing against the fourth wall, here rendered border of the body and also limit of the visible. The catastrophe arrives, as they do, without warning; it alters the tonality and pacing of the fetal figure, from the languid, light, loose movement of floating to that sharp, heavy jerk from the blow of the accident. At the culminating impact of violence the screen is entirely obliterated with the forced-forward flesh, its tones of yellow and red the exhaustion of the screen, the encounter of force with fetus a shattering of the integrity of the frame (amniotic, chromatic, cinematic). Violence moves the distribution of elements in the womb, redescribing foreground/middle ground relations, radically shifting temporal rhythms and spatial openness or restriction. The force of the impact destroys, above all, the slack of the drowsy heavy floating movement—makes that cadence out of place in the space in which that cadence had been entirely, previously, at home.

The film then cuts to the sound of heavy rain and reorients the image outside of the body to reveal a car accident, expressionist steam and fire, a dead father, a bloodied but still living mother, Sarah, and a featureless second car. The syrupy blood dripping from faces matches the pouring torrents of rain, the totality of the image orchestrated around the elasticity of varying viscous ropes. Four months later, on Christmas Eve, a grieving Sarah prepares alone for her delivery the next morning. (And one among many perversions of the film is that a trial of labor will, in fact, take place, though it will involve labors of desperation in place of dilation, and although delivery will arrive, it will be an involuntary and untimely birth, the womb ripped open by an inducting and external force.) Locked and alone in her Parisian house, Sarah refuses to answer the door to a woman shrouded in black, referred to solely as La Femme, but who menacingly calls Sarah by name, and who knows of her husband's death. The police visit, assure Sarah that nothing is awry, promise to check in later, and leave. They are brusque because they have a competing claim to their attention: the film takes place against the distant backdrop of riots at the outskirts of the city (evoking the late autumn violence in Clichy-sous-Bois in 2005), in televised glimpses of cars burning and a reference to Sarah's photojournalistic work which, were she not *inside* tonight, would have her *out there* documenting the disorder taking place. When Sarah goes to bed, the woman appears in the home, awakens Sarah by plunging scissors into her navel, at which point Sarah flees to her fluorescently bright bathroom and locks herself in. Various helpers arrive but, in spectacular and quick fashion, each is dispensed with, and in the end, in the midst of an elaborate confrontation between the two women, La Femme reveals that she was the other driver in the initial car accident and miscarried as a result of the trauma of the collision. In the midst of this revelation, in one of several surrealistic turns in the film, one of the police officers presumed dead seems to reanimate; he confuses Sarah with the attacker, and La Femme switches from predator to incidental savior, killing the officer and protecting Sarah (if only for the sake of protecting the unborn child within), and likewise exchanges role of assailant for midwife, bringing forth the child through a savage, forced cesarean delivery. The final shot pans over a dead Sarah on the stairs in a house drenched with blood while La Femme cradles the infant in the dark, on a rocking chair, to its shrill mewling cries. *Now her child, her baby, finally outside her.*

On the surface, *À l'intérieur* seems so undeniably vicious, even by comparison with the canon of extremities in contemporary horror—in its initial brutal fetal slam; in flooding the late pregnant body with terror; in making the already grieving suffer—demonstrating what Montaigne refers to as the essential form of cruelty: "to invent unusual tortures and new forms of murder, not from hatred or for gain but for the one sole purpose of enjoying the pleasant spectacle of the pitiful gestures and twitchings of a man [*sic*] dying in agony, while hearing his [*sic*] screams and groans."[8] He writes how "the poets particularly emphasize the descriptions of such horrors as something deeper than death," condemning the doing of violence for the sake of spectacle—which is, on one level, entirely what this film *is*.[9] On the other hand, narratively, with its exchange of one lost fetus for a regained one, the film involves the most purposeful, explanatory (and classical) defense of violence—a horror logic model of proportionate punishment and retributive justice. There is, in other words, an uneasy juxtaposition of the extraordinary cruelty of the spectacular scenario set against a rigorous and systematic narrative explanation for its origin—a tension between a wild formlessness of violence, one that devastates boundaries of bodily integrity and literally turns one body inside out, and, simultaneously, a violence that is not purely destructive but respects and enacts the exchange of like for like, and which founds a natal-maternal union previously rent asunder, re-forming a semblance of the dyad with which the film began, albeit at a delay. La Femme's violence is barbarous but its proper aim is telic, concerned in its formal articulation not with the rhythms of retaliation so much as with those of redistribution.

Set aside any shuddering bad-affective feelings associated with the horror genre—those neck logics of narrative affects (grief, anxiety, rage, motherlove) and spectatorial ones (disgust, horror, perverse glee, whatever)—and instead grapple with the feel of horror and the sensitivity with which this film formally reacts to stimuli. Consider, first of all, À l'intérieur's temporal structure. Its eighty minutes break down thusly: a five-minute prologue that establishes the violent conceit (the crossing and exchange of blows that is the car accident) and then three twenty-five minute segments.

1. The first part follows Sarah on the night before birth—her final doctor's appointment, refusals of company, fantasies of her dead husband, the preliminary (shunned) arrival of La Femme—through the departure of the first three police officers, who have assured her that the house is empty and secure. This segment concludes with Sarah retiring to bed.

2. The second part begins with a ruptured awakening as scissors are plunged into her abundant stomach. This period of time contains a series of rapid turnovers in violence-eliminating salvation and violence-enabling destruction: Sarah's boss arrives, her mother arrives, more police arrive and are killed, one after another after another in this frenetic middle segment.

3. The final third of the film begins as the last police officer enters the house, after every other enterer is dead—but this time he arrives with a narrative, rhythmic, and racial difference. A young Arab teenager named Abdel has been picked up by the police during the riots; despite his maintained innocence, the officers take pleasure in promising how, as soon as they have checked in on Sarah, they will book him at the ur-

ban stationhouse. When the last officer has no choice but to go into Sarah's home, he handcuffs Abdel and ties him to the officer's body with a long leash—"like a dog," notes the prisoner (like a less mucoid *funiculus umbilicalis*, notes the critic).[10] This segment follows the final (failed) attempted rescue, the untimely ripping and excision of the fetus, and the death of Sarah.

The film thus takes its model for narrative development from the formal prescriptions of Aristotelian *Poetics*, but alongside an unavoidable association of the *omne trium perfectum* with other trimestral forms in play in the film. That gestational morphology suggests: a prologue that functions as the narrative conception of the evental structure; then three segments or trimesters, each with a different tonality, feel, significance, and sensitivity; culminating in a birth, albeit one that obliterates the maternal body, that leaves the child in the arms of a mother who did not previously house it.

The feel of each of the three main sections—in the sense of their mechanical, formal sensitivities—is remarkably different, most notably in the exceedingly fast action and nimble feel of the middle section in which figure after figure enters Sarah's home and is rapidly dispensed with. The second segment is extraordinary for the formal efficiency of its depletion of elements. Redescribing each new arriving body as a systemic intrusion, the rhythmic design of this section is orchestrated around the diminishment of the forceful impact of those additions to the film's textual system. Each supplement is matched with a furiously quick response of abatement, the only waste the residue of each rapid balancing in ever more red streaking walls and floors and faces. This film has a cast of only fourteen: two medical professionals who appear only in the first few minutes, a dead husband, the two central women, Sarah's mother and boss, six police officers, and Abdel. The middle section of the film kills off half of the cast—Sarah's mother, boss, and the officers—and the deaths occur with the most nimble, quick action possible, most spectacularly in the case of Sarah's mother, who, from first arrival in the frame to falling out of the frame in her death, is present on screen for a mere sixty seconds. She arrives to check on her daughter, demands of La Femme a sharp "Qui êtes-vous?" and rushes upstairs to Sarah, locked in her bathroom in terror, simultaneously safe and yet imprisoned in the violent fluorescent brightness of that small, cold room.

Radical formalism's refusal to treat the feel of violence in horror within the episteme of somatic, visceral, affective, embodied strong sensations is not without its precedents in the history of aesthetic thinking. Consider, for example, the Greek concept of *ekplexis*—shock, astonishment, excitement, figured as an intense emotional reaction linked to a frenzied textual surprise. In *Poetics*, in his discussion of the emotions that may be aroused by either the tragic spectacle itself or, in the hands of the more skilled poet, by "*the very structure* and incidents of the play," such that "even without seeing the things take place, he who simply hears the account of them shall be filled with horror and pity at the incidents," Aristotle offers a taxonomy of horrible, pitiable incidents (done, or not done; known or unknowingly).[11] Among enemies or those indifferent to each other, wrongdoing does not move us to pity; where there is love, however—and his privileged case is within the family—wrongs may be quite terrible indeed. Here, Aristotle adds the dimension of understanding that is key for the emotional tenor of the work: "The deed of horror may be done by the doer knowingly and consciously, as in the old poets, and in Medea's murder of her children in Euripides. Or he may do it, but in ignorance of the relationship, and discover that afterwards, as does the Oedipus in Sophocles. [. . .] A third possibility is for one meditating some deadly injury to another, in ignorance of his relationship, to make the discovery in time to draw back."[12] If the injury is done in ignorance and understood only afterward (anagnorisis: the critical discovery), here the experience for hero and audience is of an astounding, shocking, thrilling recognition: Aristotle gives this emotional effect that assails out of nowhere but also is sequential, comes in order in time, blazing in to change everything forever, as *ekplektikon*.

And so, when our panicked, hysterical Sarah, having been pursued mazily by the demonic figure in black to land, finally, in the blinding white of her upstairs bathroom, is, it seems, about, possibly, to be rescued from the derangements of La Femme, to be saved—for her mother has arrived, has accused the intruder, and now has charged upstairs, is on the cusp of quelling the viciousness, cauterizing the pregnant body's open, pouring wounds—her *mother* is there—she is here, to be, once more, as all mothers at least one time are, on the side of life, her mother, who immediately senses the danger and rushes upstairs to *ma fille*, her trapped and slowed daughter, her daughter, who, in her blind terror, frantic and worn down from the sheer skinweight hours of that (still early) night, at her mother's arrival at the heavy door, Sarah, bloodied mouth and chest, wild orby eyes, and the marshaled insane courage of the traumatized, hears that a body is on the other side of the bathroom wall, gasps a single breath, throws open the door and stabs right through the neck of the figure at the threshold, but it is mother, her mother, it is her mother and not the murderer at all, and she sees this, she knows this absolutely instantly yet already too late, early enough for her mother to register surprise, to touch the arc of red, to look at her daughter, uncomprehending, to stagger backward, to feel the throaty jets, to turn away, to fall out of the frame, time for Sarah to understand, to see what has happened while it is still in the process of happening, to crouch to her knees, to cry *maman*, to plead, to refuse, to wail out that disbelief—and yet to know certainly that this has taken place and all that has yet to take place will because her mother—*Maman! Maman!*—will no longer be a possible future arrival, but had indeed arrived, to care, to restore, and was instead faced with violent metal from a soft familiar source, and this look, this downturned fall, Sarah's cry, *maman*, the elongated final syllable of a child's shrieking howl, as daughter slides to the floor, curves into her spine under the grounding weight of all gravities, knowing truly and certainly and nakedly what has transpired, every moan-awed No that understands an irreversibility, and if begun by someone else still this death of *her* mother was at *her* hands—this is anagnorisis, what Aristotle promises as ekplektikon. Violence was not averted in time. The pathetic knowledge came in the doing, which is to say: too late to be undone.

The feel of this second section of *À l'intérieur* is given in the rapidity with which its form responds to intrusions of force—whether that force is chromatic and illuminative (the first part's swampy yellow darkness, the bleakness of the night giving way to a staccato puncturing of that fog in the green-white fluorescence of the bathroom); the frenetic editing, including the nimble and hyper shot/reverse shot grammar of alternation that is how the mother's death comes about—the breakneck back and forth and back and forth that within seconds results in the laying waste: of mother, of hope; or the intrusion of force that is a new body (each body itself above all a formal element, which is to say an element to which form reacts to the intrusion with a sensitive response). The feel here is fevered, frantic, nervous, unstable, and Sarah's mother's death is inextricable from the overly keen responsiveness of the grammar of montage. Violence is thus not what is experienced as too fast (as in psychoanalytic theories of trauma) but is given as the aesthetic quality of too-fastness, overreactivity as such. Every action is hypersensitive, running out of control, and indeed, the pathos of the rapidity is that structure whereby realization arrives only at the instant that that turnover is understood to have been too rapid. The system was too sensitive to the intrusion of force. And thus Sarah, like Montaigne's jumpy prisoner taking nail to throat and belly, acts too early, miscalculates and misreads the situation such that events happen before their proper time, and therefore happen wrongly in a time in which the realization (understanding) of violence is simultaneously a realization (enactment) of deadly injury to another in ignorance, unable to make that discovery in time to draw back and strike a different note altogether. As in Montaigne's allegory, our prisoner carries out a mistaken and infinitely worse sentence.

One of the measures of instrumental "fast action" is the briskness with which one can reattack a specific key, the nimbleness of retraction so that a key is ready to be struck again—a measure of the rapidity with which repetition can take place. The middle-term killings in *À l'intérieur* involving fast formal action exchange every iteration of interior/exterior positions (each additive entry that must be eliminated) with the maximal efficiency in turnover, albeit at the cost that this feel involves the aims of violence going astray. This rapid conversion in agential position each time a body is nimbly, promptly done away with enables, with the most minimal possible lag, the possibility for a repetition of the scenario, a recurrence of the same exchange with yet another arrival of a possible savior and yet another elimination of that figure from without as it enters the inside. At the moment of this structure's inversion—in which the interior moves into the exterior (the forced cesarean delivery)—film form is likewise efficient and quick and light: although one might expect a work of extreme horror to linger over the details of the surgery that culminates in Sarah's death, it instead absorbs that event easily, exchanging the spatial position of the fetus with alacrity, so that the next next thing can occur. The feel of violence, as a measurement of form's vulnerability to perturbation and the temporal latency required or not required to account for that perturbation, instructs us in this general rule: moments of passage, which are the overt sites of representational violence in the film, are also where the text is most quick, rapid, light, and lively in processing and absorbing these (crises) in exchange.

In the third and final segment of the film, however, form radically changes once more, and its feel becomes dull, sluggish, heavy, and slow. Formal intrusion and difference become stuck, mechanisms have difficulty turning over in response to the forces that impinge on them. This change in feel occurs in relation to the case of the only death shown in this section, that of the chained Arab teenager Abdel. (Sarah also expires in this part, but her death occurs offscreen; after the scissors to the abdomen, the incision to the uterus, the removal of the baby, Sarah is reduced to the volume and redness of her blood, her fading sob of "maman, maman." A later image confirms the complete destruction of Sarah's form on the stairs, her offscreen death symmetrically mirroring the never-represented death of La Femme's child in the opening crash.) Abdel, who comes not only from the outside but from the outside of the outside, arrested and imported from the Parisian *banlieues*, dies in a slow, self-conscious duration amid a strangeness of light and awkward elaboration of gesture, in which the feel of horror changes to a muddy, nontransformative mush, in which form struggles to strike again, in which a force external to its systemic constraints does not merely denature the film's formal system but grinds it to a near standstill.

In a near-black image punctured by an agitated oval of piercing brightness —a furiously waved-around flashlight, its beam a derangement of illumination amid the pitch of the room—the officer to which Abdel is bound promises to unleash him if they can only find more light. Within and set against that chromatic deprivation, there are clear sounds of a gunshot, Abdel's screams that La Femme is still in the house, and his frantic efforts to recover the keys off the now-corpse of his chained partner. In close-up, dizzyingly underlit from the flashlight's loose, unstable aim, the image cuts to Abdel's point of view, showing scissors slowly reaching up into a blank dark space; then his face in profile, reacting with terror; then the scissors raised again in overlapping editing and an elongation of duration, his face shaking before the definitive plunge; then the slow sinking of the scissors into meat; then a several-seconds-long shot of the scissors glinting in the partial light; then his head from behind, staging the scissor's material intersection with his scalp; then his hand almost imperceptibly slowly raising, shaking, touching the metal handles, the pour of blood, his eyes open still, his hands twitching toward La Femme and only then, finally, his body's heavy, definitive fall to the earth.

Abdel's dying takes an awkward, drawn-out two-and-a-half minutes to fully transpire, and the editing presents the meeting of scissors and scalp in a careful and studied articulation of perspectives—from the front, side, back and overhead. The languid, nontransformative formality of Abdel's death suggests that unlike those overly fast figurations of the inside and outside exchanging with ease in the middle section, his relation to interiority and exteriority is not like that of all the others previously expunged from the film. The modulating feel of the different sections unavoidably suggests something of the form of the contraction: an alternation of extreme hardness (of the abdomen) and tension (of the uterus) with their respective softening and relaxing; just as periodic, wavelike constriction and tightening moving into repeated deflation and stretching is how the work of labor occurs, the laboring of film form likewise maps out a precise modulation of pressures in order to progress the work forward. Until the point at which it gets stuck—and the film's visual and rhythmic language begins to work against narrative progress, slowing to systematically study light and gestures, losing its lively step, clinging to the image, fastened and weighted down.

From the feel of violence as a principle of rhythmic sensitivity to formal stimuli, we thus derive a *formal exception* for the figure of Abdel.

To return to Nancy's definition of violence as "the application of a force that remains foreign to the dynamic or energetic system into which it intervenes," a formalism of violence requires an attention to the responsivity and sensitivity of any system to its denaturing, its relationship to rapid or languid transformation in response to any application of force.[13] The denaturing of a system (of duration, of lighting, of montage) at Abdel's death suggests that something has become blocked on this occasion—a textual dystocia. It is the case that we cannot understand *À l'intérieur* if we cannot answer this question: Why is Abdel the site of slow and mushy, thick, dull form, where the film cannot nimbly strike so that it can with minimal latency strike again? Why is it at the death of this minor character that the film's rhythmic qualities grind to a halt, that form gets choked and does not turn over efficiently? Put another way: *Why is Abdel the cinematic analogue of stuck instrumental keys?*

TOPOLOGIES AND MISREADINGS

If we take Abdel *as* the awkwardness of his death, it is instructive to note how he is awkward in a more fundamental, spatial way, as the importation of the banlieues. A banlieue is a city's "outskirts," from *ban* (to command but also to forbid, to proclaim but also to outlaw) and *leuca*, a league of distance or extent of territory. In other words, it is the measure of distance in which juridical action may still by right take place (the farthest reach that permits the police to arrest Abdel). Étienne Balibar gives it a formal designation as "a frontier, a border-area and a frontline"—and like the Derridean parergon, this setting, in its banishment, simultaneously functions as a center that grounds the interior of the city.[14] Abdel is not a figure of relief entering the inside from the outside to help (like Sarah's mother, her boss, the police), nor is he equivalent to the figure of predation entering the inside from the outside to wound-cum-reckon (like La Femme). Rather, he is a figure from the outside of the outside (the Parisian banlieue) who is brought into the inside of the inside by force. As Balibar describes the inhabitants of the banlieues, they "can be characterized neither as absolutely outside nor as really within the social system, but only in the paradoxical terms of an *internal exclusion*."[15] *À l'intérieur* is explicit in its preoccupation with this figure of an internal exclusion and its relationship to the maternal object(s) at its center: the literal fortress walls and symbolic designations of the Parisian enclosure have historically been dubbed *l'enceinte parisienne*, thus suggesting that any thinking of Sarah's body is unavoidably linked to a thinking of the national body. But Abdel is less a metaphor for the banlieues than the rhythmic register of the feel of *unwilling intrusion*. This is not a sensed feeling (of marginalized subjects, of life under structural violence) but the feel of violence, how its formal attestation goes. Abdel's structural counterpart is thus the *unwilling extrusion* of the fetus in the violent cesarean delivery. The impropriety of this spatial position is what manifests as the formal stuckness in which his presence renders transformation resistant, in which it becomes difficult, nearly impossible, for form to turn over rapidly, for its arrangement to become otherwise.

Upon being dragged inside the house, tied to the officer on a leash, Abdel sees the corpses plural and screams "Get me out of this terrible place!," an indictment of will-less enclosure that one might link to the ontological condition, what it is to be thrown, without cause or decision, into the sheer facticity of where one finds oneself. His continual calls to "Let me out" match La Femme's repeated insistence—the simultaneous drive of violence and redistribution—to "Let me in!" The film thus turns on an imperative whose logic moves both ways: the demand to cut something out or the demand to be cut out of something.

This is the general form of a cesarean imperative. The term *Caesarean* has competing linguistic origins; a discredited one claims it for the method by which Julius Caesar was delivered, whereas another tradition derives it from a Roman legal code that stated that, in the event a mother dies before giving birth, the fetus must be cut out of its mother's womb, with evocations of the Latin *caedere* (to cut), also the root for scissors, which are the instrument of violence and opening and mother-obliterating delivery in the film. The film's cesarean drive involves a series of encroachments, sectionings, partitionings, the continual opening up to different arrangements through new intruders into interior spaces: the ur-intrusion of vehicular force against body; the intrusion of La Femme into the home; the opening of the front door by figure after figure, each opening promising assistance and each opening thus generating a rapid response of elimination in order to maintain violence's formal equilibrium; the breaching of Sarah's body in auto-affective surgery she per-

forms on her own trachea (bandaging the hole with duct tape); the unautho-
rized cesarean section on the stairs, &c. When Abdel screams "Let me out!,"
he seems to be an exteriorized figure of the fetus, one who, unlike the infant
(who is *in-fans*, without speech), can voice this demand. And indeed, there
is a curious intimacy in La Femme's murder of him—its choreography also
suggests a kind of care, even the upturned point of view of the fetus that will
later be cut out of Sarah's body. On the other hand, Abdel, required to follow
the officer's body through space, is a form of slowed and difficult movement;
his struggle to navigate this space while tied to another makes him also function as another pregnant figure in this film in which pregnancy is, above all,
a temporal slowing of actability, a decreased rate of movement, a restriction
in alacrity in fleeing. Abdel also dies with his eyes open, in an image that will
be repeated in the final shot of Sarah's corpse. He is neither an allegory for the
fetus (despite the structural parallels) nor a proxy for the pregnant (despite
the kinetic parallels), but rather figures their intersection, which is to say that
he unconceals a general structure of bound but severable relations. Abdel is
neither a character nor a metaphor, nor is horror here concerned with his
sensuous feelings nor spectators' feelings about him; rather, he is a vulnerable
relation of spatial proximities that brings the film to a rhythmic crisis in its articulation of mechanistic possibilities. Abdel is a specific assemblage of formal
qualities. And in Abdel's death, bound but severable relationality extends beyond the body to the issue of political interpretation itself, which is to say that
the grounds of critique are derived *from* the formalism at the heart of horror's
navigation of the worst hemic violence.

In Arabic, *Abdel* means servant [of]. (Its etymological root *'abd* can also
mean slave, albeit with resonances of "the worshipper." His theophoric name
thus bonds him to God as tightly as the boy is earthly bound to the law by a
leash.) What does this emblem of the neglected Parisian banlieue serve, as a
figure? It is because of the draw of the police to the site where violence is always taken as possible (out there amid the *black-beur* youth) that they fail to
see the actual violence taking place in the interior of the interior. Not unlike
Montaigne's prisoner's misreading of the particular form of violence that is
yet to come, Abdel thus serves as a bad interpretation of the map of where violence resides. His structural position as the unwilling intruder demonstrates
a misreading of space by the law. The film ends, with great difficulty, by cutting out and eliminating this (mis)reading of the banlieues for the sake of re-
establishing the final shot, the representationally overdetermined image of a
singular mother cradling child. (It does not take an extraordinary leap to see

in this image the privileged emblem of nationalism, Mother France nursing Romulus and Remus to nurture and thus sustain the nation figured as an imaginary unity, a fantasy that rests on constant formal logics of violence as excision without end.)

À l'intérieur thereby proposes two competing spatial frameworks marked by different relations to sensitivity: the cesarean imperative to cut things out and partition, mark distinctions, let one in, let one out (which does great violence in its drive to violate borders in order to establish them); and a second model with a softer action, where, in fact, mechanisms are adhesive, instruments get stuck, and systems do not move forward without noise and loss and difficulty, without injury. Both are linked to violence, but the differing tonalities of each mode of action suggest that though the cesarean cut is fast and quick, nimble and responsive, it is too quick, arrives in untimely anticipation that gets the sentence wrong, whereas the site of mushy action abandons the possibility of striking a new key in time. What remains inefficient and fastened to the present is this site at which an exterior attached by force to the interior is forced into that interior from which it is simultaneously cast out. The film cannot sever itself from Abdel (his presence sticks to the film, slows it down, dulls its action), and yet it eliminates him. His death is certain, but the film will grind to a halt in order for this excision to take place. Two objects are, then, tied by cords and bound by severable relations, each designating a competing formal system: if the fetus is pure reaction (what records the effects of violence) and is ultimately birthed live, its bond severed and left behind, Abdel is pure absorption, where representation cannot get going to something new, quickly, nimbly. The film's rhythmic form thereby submits interiority—what is inside, inward, within—to a violent critique, putting under duress the presumption of a great difference between the interior and the exterior. In an inversion of Foucault's famous description in Madness and Civilization of the madman sent to sea "put in the interior of the exterior," experiencing a banished enclosure within the outside, Abdel instead experiences a banished exclusion within the interior.[16] He dies, remaining unwillingly tethered there. Abdel formally attests to the rhythmic difficulties of transforming the relations that comprise the diagram of living in common that is (as diagram) what violence targets for disruption, dispersion, wrecking, rearrangement.

This is an aesthetic version of the conclusion the philosopher Byung-Chul Han arrives at in Topologie der Gewalt (Topology of Violence), that precisely because "violence occurs not only at the interpersonal level," it is imperative "to *formalize* it into a negative tension between the interior and exterior, in order to be able to register and describe this macro-physical form of violence, which cannot be constrained to the conflict-filled intermediary space between the self and the other. At that point the violence can be described as an event that prevails but cannot be internalized."[17] Han's reading of violence as rift, rupture, corruption, &c. makes clear that any philosophy of violence must be neither interpretation nor symbology, but, as goes his title, *topology*. The question of exclusion at the heart of any thinking of the political thus turns less on feelings of exclusion (or any conventional affectivity of political life invoking shame, resentment, rage, fury, hate, fear, horror, terror) than on the feel of politics as a question of the capacity or resistance to (rapidly, nimbly, languidly, not at all) strike—ever—a new note.

À l'intérieur constitutes an aesthetic thinking of the relations between forms of continuity and cessation, addition and annihilation, supplement and depletion, and the exchange of rapidity with a dull languidity. It is a presentation of the sensitivities and speeds of violence: its arrival too soon, too late, too quickly, too slowly. Like Montaigne's story of the prisoner, what is most terrible in *À l'intérieur* is a misinterpretation so reactive that it cannot fail to create the worst of all possible results, whether it acts before its time or whether it slows to a crawl. The political is thus rendered the slow action of conversion to what has not yet come to be, constitutively out of sync—cruelly, brutally so—in its responsiveness to unexpected stimuli. A formalism of horror unconceals the total structure in which the force of violence will always react too soon and thus misread with consequence, and yet also be stuck in place. The feel of violence is precisely the impersonal play of the arrangement of these inextricable elements that precariously live among each other: Paris, the Arab, the chain, the law.

Lapsus

It means a fall. These things that drop from heights, these descents of degrees and sinking downfalls, gravity's cruel reductions, they land on earth, on dirt and soil, in loam. Every corpse a lapse. Also a temporal question (a passage of some period of time; a flight of time; time out of joint; elapsing, expired time; or missing time, if time can go missing); also one of potency (the forfeiture of legal right; what slumps or goes to ruin); also a slight error or minor failure, if time or power can be said to err or fail, even slightly. Any decline into disuse. The *Historical Thesaurus of the Oxford English Dictionary* offers more than thirty major routes to the word through thesaurus classes, including:

the world > the earth > water > flow or flowing >
flow [verb (intransitive)] > slowly or gently ▶ lapse (1832)

the world > time > spending time > spend time
[verb (intransitive)] > waste time ▶ lapse (1667)

the world > matter > condition of matter > bad condition
of matter > deteriorate in condition [verb (intransitive)] >
be dilapidated or ruined > fall into ruins ▶ lapse (1620)[1]

There are competing topologies: the continuity of the Latin *lapsare*, to misplace a steady footing, the slipping or gliding, the stumbling that keeps feet in contact with ground in the process of failing in precise placement, an ongoingness of an extended passage of losing—gliding sometimes sweet, gentle even—and simultaneous suggestion of the rupture of a termination, a void, an interval or aperture, a break, a breach, a gap, an irremediable mistake—lapses in judgment potentially fatal—a slip of the tongue, the memory, a pen; that soaring "Karma Police" repetition—"for a minute there / I lost myself"—and a weakness, a moral slip with the consequence of the absolute (cf. the history of people's—usually women's—unique ruination by hard swerves away from rectitude). What points to the presence of the lacuna or gap or absent thing itself, or to the surround that offers continuity and ongoingness—relation—in the midst of some excision or momentary blunder; what therefore poses the minimal presence of some form of difference in the ongoingness and continuity of some system, including, let it be said, the positive force of the systems that ground theory. In "My Chances / *Mes chances*," Derrida writes, "A lapsus is revealing in the sense that it gives another truth its chance."[2] If we introduce a ruination or break in the continuous history of thought about horror, what possible something else, what precise *another*, appears there where negative sensation's bristling hairs have been continuously and durably lodged?

Sometimes, what becomes visible in a lapse is what was there all along, the most familiar of all perceptible things. Revealed is a simple closed form, even the most basic geometric shape.

Came a time when things of the belly and the underbelly no longer provoked laughter, blushes, or disgust.

Nutrition, elimination, and fecundation became pure (as in themselves they are). There were no more shadows in the picture of human acts; no more secrets known to all and hidden by each.

Death lost all its imaginary power, and was clearly seen as a condition of life. It now was understood that life changes its tenants as a man changes his shirt. It was also understood that these changes of its individual possessors are as essential to life as are changes of the drafts of air he breathes to the living man, and changes of the molecules of water are to an advancing wave.

Man became as pure as an angel or animal; for "impurity" is simply a *mixture of the two*. Tired of being neither angel nor beast, he decided to be sometimes one, sometimes the other; now "body" and now "spirit."

Shame, anxiety, and gloom, fear and hope and love were banished by the Great Change. Poetry died out; algebra and sensations were the only fashionable pursuits.

Thus ended the strange affective world of man; the world of emotional upheavals, passions, perturbations, spurious values. The realm of the nervous system was split in two, the "soul" vanished into thin air; and thought was no longer harassed by parasites and harmonics of a visceral origin. Permanent functions were no longer thrown out of gear by events or ideas. "Things" were forbidden to have more meaning than they have existence, and more effects than they have meaning.

— PAUL VALÉRY, "Thoughts in the Rough"

And things, what is the correct attitude to adopt towards things? And, to begin with, are they necessary? What a question. But I have few illusions, things are to be expected. The best is not to decide anything, in this connexion, in advance. If a thing turns up, for some reason or another, take it into consideration. Where there are people, it is said, there are things. Does this mean that when you admit the former you must also admit the latter? Time will tell. The thing to avoid, I don't know why, is the spirit of the system. People with things, people without things, things without people, what does it matter, I flatter myself it will not take me long to scatter them, whenever I choose, to the winds. I don't see how. The best would be not to begin. But I have to begin. That is to say I have to go on.

— SAMUEL BECKETT, *The Unnamable*

FIGURE I.3.1. *Rubber* (Quentin Dupieux, 2010)

INTERLUDE III

Objects, Relations, Shape

> The fundamental obstacle for the abacists was, of course, the
> peculiar use of the zero sign by the algorists; a sign which af-
> fected values of numerals wherever it occurred but had no value
> itself, and which appeared as a number in calculations though
> it answered to no positive or real quantity.
>
> —BRIAN ROTMAN, *Signifying Nothing*

Borges opens his 1962 essay "The Fearful Sphere of Pascal" with a hedged proposition: "It may be that universal history is the history of a handful of metaphors," subsequently turning to the figure of the *sphere*, eternal, without end, complete and radically uniform, praised by Xenophanes as the figure of theological perfection, and offered in Plato's *Timaeus* as a model for closed utopia itself, what disseminates a constancy of force in every direction, what leaves—and, indeed, requires an abstention from—remnant, excess, departure, and the intervention of external modification. By the end of Borges's genealogy of this figure, however, in the wake of what he calls "the dispirited century" of the 1600s, in which "the absolute space which had inspired the hexameters of Lucretius [. . .] became a labyrinth and an abyss," a figure like

Pascal will dub the sublime silent universe a *"fearful* sphere"—thus requiring a rewriting of his opening supposition: "It may be that universal history is the history of the different intonations given a handful of metaphors."[1]

Now substitute for perfect/terrible sphere a related another of the handful —that of the circle—and one sees the same shifting relations of intonations: exulted extension to abyssal aperture. What is infinitely full and complete, infinitely devoid and lacking—either totality (completion, union, continuity, as in Hegel's famous declaration in *Philosophy of Right* that philosophy "forms a circle," becoming a self-enclosure, but also recurrence, as in Nietzsche's dubbing of Zarathustra an "advocate of the circle") *or*, on the other hand, emptiness (lack, a hole, subtracted and fundamentally a frame around what, in failing to accountably be there, gives shape to what is, necessarily contains the possibility of a being-there in the not-there at its center).[2] Either semiotic caging of *something* or generalized figure for *nothing*, what is given in antinomic intonations, some fearful/some great (circle's *perfection* also *vicious*), the entire set derived from the central dilemma of being a sign that can be taken to signify nothing, posing the fundamental question of whether nothingness is ontological. The circle is a problem for thought—it cannot be done away with.

Quentin Dupieux's 2010 Calvino-esque, Greek chorus-containing, genre-deconstructing film *Rubber* follows an abandoned tire that rises from the dirt of a dump (rubbish as both nonsense and waste) and begins to roam on what the diegetic spectating chorus takes to be a psychokinetic murder spree. Dupieux, better known as electronica artist Mr. Oizo and for his work with the puppet Flat Eric, mostly eschewed CGI, working with puppets and remote controls to figure this staging of a tire crossing the open space of the California desert, crushing bugs and trash before beginning a series of encounters that explode objects within spaced proximity to the tire: a bottle, a rabbit, a man, many bodies. Following an anthrodecentric model, the tire is an ambulatory thing encountering other things; if a pure form of the force of violence, it simultaneously recasts violence as the interaction between things in space, not a wrecking imposition on some external or privileged system. A tire merely inflicts itself formally on its environment: its outer perimeter is marked by grooves, the treads that compress weight into the ground, perturbing earth. And, of course, to *rub* is to scratch, scrub, a gesture of erasure; from an earlier sense of an obstacle, hindrance, impediment, what is rough, uneven. The tire, in this sense, transforms—it deflects objects and bodies off course.

On the one hand, the tire is exceptionally noisy: not *le grain de la voix* but *le grain du pneu*, a sonority governed by hapticity, a cacophony derived from exploring the variable pressures of rustle, grit, sand, gravel, or the irregular treble shrill of a glass bottle rotation under the pressure of rubber's tentative forward roll, or the rustling vibrating swell of squeak and electric static in each instant of cathartic explosion. But if one logic of sonority privileges the tire, competing sonic fields—a background insect buzzing; the muted sepulchral tones of the bleak desert air—suggest multiple parallel soundtracks, all rather indifferent to the presence of the tire. On the other hand, because this tire does not speak, we might also say that its noisiness divulges *nothing*. What divulges everything, makes sense of this nothing and turns it into a something, is the diegetic chorus, whose polyphony ascribes affect, motivation, and agency to the tire, reading its proximity to a showering naked woman as desire; articulating rage in the wake of an exploded body; condemning and enjoying its spectacular proximity to (which it reads as: a causing of) violence; and converting its mechanical vibrations and twitches into signs of psychokinesis, the technique of animation at a distance that does away with the requirement of physical interaction for physical modification. The chorus is what gives the tire a gender (He), taking seriously what will only be declared in the final credits, where the tire is billed as Robert, a name that, if pronounced in French (*Robert*), confuses nomination of a being with the nomination of material (*rubber*), performing the homonymic slippage from object to subject that the chorus is in the film in order to constantly risk.

In the midst of these encounters, a conceptual problem of critical language presents itself: to declare that the tire *makes* things explode—let alone to declare this film a narrative of a killing spree—is to figure each encounter of spatial proximity a scene of material causality, to figure spacing of tire and future exploded object as a scene of destruction. But the tire is a destroying machine only from two points of view that are not obviously authorized: the point of view that inserts causality into the proximity of the tire and the body-made-corpse, and a decidedly human point of view. Indeed, although *Rubber* is an index of recurrent sequences that follow the general form of encounter and explosion, it can be declared an *escalation* of target from bottle to rabbit to man solely from the imposed anthropocentric perspective of the binocular-spectating chorus. From the perspective of spectacle and object, the tire is not a destruction machine but a creation machine: making new forms out of dehierarchized bodies, beheaded forms, blood splatter aesthetic forms, creating (which is to say unconcealing) the potential of a human body's material

FIGURE I.3.2. *Rubber* (Quentin Dupieux, 2010)

as its form is reconfigured in what is solely a murder from the point of view of the human.

The critical question is whether the second half of the film disqualifies this latter position.

For the chorus is poisoned halfway through the film by a bureaucrat whose job is to get rid of the spectators so that the investigation into the increasing body count can end. One refuses to take the bait, and his insistence, "I want my show"—a self-interested observer bearing out a pure drive of spectacle in place of the descriptive and reflective functions of the choral stasimon—compels the meta-fictional narrative to continue, which it does until he approaches too close to the tire, object of his fascination. Despite his insistence, "I'm not a character; I'm just watching," his head too is devastated. The tire, seemingly reanimated in a tricycle, rolls down the desert stretch, accumulating a massified set of tires, until they arrive, finally, at the base of the Hollywood sign.

If the first half of the film offers the thing of the tire as a surface that confronts an *I* and stands in opposition to it, the ending in the wake of the poisoning and murder of the chorus and the lone holdout spectator suggests a persistence to the thing beyond its constitution as an object. So *Rubber* seems to signal an abandonment of a certain right of philosophical jurisdiction over objects, appears to manifest a space in which humans are not posited as sovereign but are figured among disparate entities, which here would include, at minimum, tire, dirt, blood, car, water, desert, all those things that equally exist in the assemblage of the film. Precisely because of its investment in an empty form, the film navigates concerns central to diverse and seemingly incompatible projects, ranging from Kafka's modernist wonderment in "The Cares of a Family Man" at the Odradek creature, "a flat star-shaped spool for thread" that is "not only a spool, for a small wooden crossbar sticks out of the middle of the star, and another small rod is joined to that at a right angle"—and the anxiogenic conclusion, "Can he possibly die?"—to a post-human inquiry into speculative aesthetics and thing theory's "secret lives of things" or "metaphysics of things."[3] In fact, *Rubber* appears to be a preeminent example of what we might dub *object-oriented horror*, vested in object agency and what Ian Bogost calls the "self-expression of objects," and couching its interest in moving beyond the human by staging the explicit disposal of the chorus in anticipation of a hypermaterialist confrontation with violence, endorsing a different model that "requires us to admit that [objects] do not exist just for us."[4]

Rubber thus stages an encounter between two competing questions. The first, derived from object-oriented concerns, runs something like, "What is it like to be a killer tire?"—in which materiality, rubber, withdraws from perceiving judging audience that only has impressions to make *about* its allure, readings to propose *about* its qualities, an account that remains firmly indebted to the narratively inscribed and inscribing metaphoricity of objects. The second interrogatory framework squarely centers on the anthrocentric point of view and is exemplified by the formal tagline for the film, which addresses some *us*, asking, "Are you tired of the expected?" This query figures *the* tire as *to* tire, as what is tiring, wearying; evoking textual exhaustion, generic tedium, promising stylistic reinvigoration for both diegetic and nondiegetic audience.

But to this confrontation of incompatible questions, for all that the film seems to hew to something like Graham Harman's insistence that "a real object [. . .] is first produced from the outside through causal interactions," the film is also explicit that these interactions take the form of a spectacular violence.[5] Or, rather, to read the film as staging violences—as opposed to just any set of causal interactions—requires the point of view of the chorus. In their poisoning, the ground of a critique of violence is thereby provided in order to be done away with, abandoned coextensively with a posited acriticality toward violence itself: the tire just *goes on* in the wake of evaluation and judgment. *Rubber* thereby wades into one of the more tense contemporary theoretical debates about objects, entities, relations, and realisms: the standoff between relational ontology and object-oriented ontology. Whereas the former emphasizes mutual relation over substance or essence—displaying a marked tendency toward regarding mutual affectivity and intermingled intimacies in a Romantic, idealist manner—the latter strenuously objects to the former, finding an emphasis on relation to constitute violence against the uniqueness of particular objects, demanding a nonrelational ontology in which no object is ever fully reduced to its relations. Taking sides on the matter, *Rubber's* accumulating corpses suggest that relational ontologies are violence incarnate. Thus, in place of flat ontology's celebration of expanded modes of "living with"—as in Eileen Joy's insistence that "turning one's attention to animals, objects, post/humanism and so on is precisely about thickening our capacity to imagine more capacious forms of 'living with'; it is precisely about developing more radical forms of welcoming and generosity to others, who include humans as well as trees, rocks, dogs, cornfields, ant colonies, PVC pipes, and sewer drains [. . .] [becoming critically] interested in what I would even call the 'tender' attention to and care of things, human and inhuman"[6]—in Dupieux's world those amplified relations among fields of things end only in an accelerating body count. *Rubber* literalizes, even gleefully affirms, the effects of force by actants—the tire is, above all, effectual, attesting to its potentiality as object on objects to format them otherwise: to bring out that the decapitated corpse is a different thing than the head-bearing body. The film proposes that violence is not absorbed and brought to a close by sensitivity to the mutual relations of objects, but rather is spectacularly *increased*.

So, when the collective voicing judgment of the ethical comes to not be there, what happens to violence in this account? Is a critique thereby also abandoned? (Are we left with only blank stares at the relations of things, at which there is no more it is possible to say?) Is the film merely an anti-art valuation of nullity, an attempt to uninflect or disinflect the provocations for violence, stripped of its allegorical lures, here rendered pure repetition of effect with no discernible cause—one that recalls Robert Smithson's claim that minimalist artists engaging nullification "re-created Malevich's 'non-objective world,' where there are no more 'likenesses of reality, no idealistic images, nothing but a desert'"?[7]

The uncertainty of both interpretations
allows one to assume with justice that neither
is accurate, especially as neither of them
provides an intelligent meaning of the word.
—Franz Kafka, "The Cares of a Family Man"

The thing is: the tire is not only a *He* (as insists the chorus), but nor is it only an object—it is not only *Robert* and not only *Rubber*. It is also a torus.

This homological problem bonds agent of violence with consequent: the philosophical notation that marks the in-betweenness of the corpse, what Blanchot dubs its strangeness, that it is "neither the same as the one who was alive, nor another, nor another thing," a double quality that relates to both the aesthetic problem of resemblance and the self-deconstructing concept of Nothingness.[8] The tire is neither the same as the claim for the anthropomorphically invested Robert, nor is it the same as a speculatively invested Rubber, *nor is it entirely another thing.*

For what is *there* in the film is above all a shape—a distinct figure in a particular givenness. Specifically, the pneumatic tire has a toroidal shape—a surface of revolution involved in revolving a circle around an axis—whose visual form is given multiple variations across the film. Because a torus is the product of two circles, when even slightly canted and seen from the side, the harmony of the form is flattened, creating a variety of nested ovals, distentions and anamorphic curves, and these ovals, of course, also are what are known as ellipses, the purest definition of which is a geometrical curved figure with one diameter longer than the other, though regard these ellipses mathematically *and* as the "and so forth" of aposiopesis, what indicates an unfinished dimension falling short, usually in language, but here an eccentricity oriented in relation to the ideal form given in the topology of the tire, which is to say the form necessary for thinking Borges's handful of metaphors in the first place, for the handful is not curious about minor deviations but about shape and structure in themselves, the lure of this framed absent center to be taken for a positive figure for nothing. And this film always was to involve the problem of the specificity of distinct forms: Dupieux's initial script was called *Day of the Cubes*, but an antipathy for CGI led to the tire, one figured as preferable to the cube because "the tire is empty, it's kind of silly, and there's nothing in it."[9]

On the problem of the specificity of distinct forms

It is not only the torus in *Rubber* that demands a radically formalist reckoning in order to come to terms with horror, violence, bodies, objects, &c. How else other than through an exhaustive reading of form could one account for Richard McGuire's 2003 short *Micro Loup* (Micro-wolf), whose whimsical animated violence comprises a virtuosic play with point of view, completely abstracted and designed vertically, in which everything of the world is seen from above looking straight down, rendering a minimalism in the image that is also a maximalism of diagrammatic form, requiring that the spectator imaginatively fill in missing details, but also giving a wealth of visual information in the interaction of positions and spacings between agent of violence and its recipients, whereby beings are thin white loops (continuing our homonymic word play, which bonds *Robert* to *Rubber* and *loup* to *loop*) and disappearance of being is given as the sudden disappearance of circle, precisely because of the formal manipulation of scale, such that criticism could not possibly account for this abstraction of the disappearance of being without attending to *shape* as a vital form in its own right? And how else other than through an exhaustive reading of form could one analyze Junji Ito's horror manga series *Uzumaki* (The Spiral) or its 2000 cinematic version by Higuchinsky in which a city is beset by—cursed by; contaminated by; infected by; consumed by; driven mad by; completely wrecked by—*spirals*? How else other than through an exhaustive reading of form could one dissect the architectural violences of space and wall, of room and (as) trap, of deliriously numerous outer and inner shells, mapped also by formalisms of varying colors, of Vincenzo Natali's 1997 *Cube*? How else other than through an exhaustive reading of form could one reckon with the interrogatory typography of James Whale's 1931 *Frankenstein*, in which the opening credits list The Monster as "*?*"—thus demanding a reading of the alternatives (blanks, pseudonyms, asterisks or carets, ellipses, an obelisk, why not an interrobang, or empty space-enclosing brackets, the graphic aggression of a full-width solidus, or perhaps one lovely ornamental hedera)—any one of which *might*, as typographical mark, have appeared in its stead, as opposed to the eroteme that is there, sign of wondering epistemology, positive attestation of some concealment, presence of missing information, thus rendering name of extra-cinematic star akin to a form of *data*, but also suggesting the glyph's use in other modes including algebraic chess notation in which a *?* indicates a bad move, an error, a mistake—not unlike the bad move, error, mistake of birth that our creature comprises in the Gothic game about to unfold—but also crises of philosophy, as in Heidegger's diagram in the second logic course in which futural *Dasein* is cast back on itself, two vectors, one moving forward, one retreating, with a large *?* at their rightmost approach to each other, of which he writes that the interrogation mark signifies the inscrutable "horizon that remains open," itself posing a further reading of the role of the interrogatory mark in so much of Heidegger's work (*Was ist . . . ? Was heißt Denken? What is Philosophy? How is it with the nothing?* &c.), not to mention the broader role of dwelling in skepticism and the interrogatory ethos condensed in aporia smudging his philosophy writ large?[10]

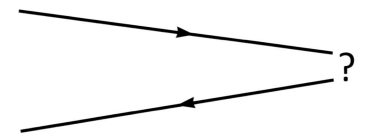

FIGURE I.3.3. Interrogatory mark, based on a figure from Heidegger, *The Metaphysical Foundations of Logic* (section 266)

And for that matter, how else other than through an exhaustive reading of form could we account for the grotesque shapes and descriptively impossible color—and the form of analogy that is thus required of color, complicating color's aesthetic philosophical history as mere charm that itself is *opposed to form*—of Lovecraft's 1927 "The Colour Out of Space" (or the strange light fields and expressionist gray studies of its cinematic reimagining in Huan Vu's 2010 *Die Farbe* or the psyche-delic purple-pink histrionics of Richard Stanley's 2020 version)? This question itself is an open form; infinite variations: How else other than through an exhaustive reading of form could we consider the negative space and wide-angle reach that is the condition for both violence and the predations of cinematic movement in David Robert Mitchell's *It Follows* (2014)? How else other than through an exhaustive reading of form could we account for the aesthetic quality and potent quantity of sunkenness that marks the broadest possible regime of racialized violence in Jordan Peele's *Get Out* (2017)? &c.

This question is asked seriously:
How else? What do you propose?

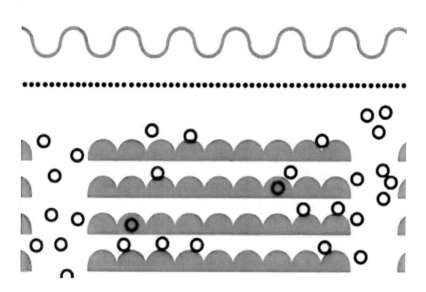

FIGURES I.3.4–I.3.6. *Micro Loup* (Richard McGuire, 2003)

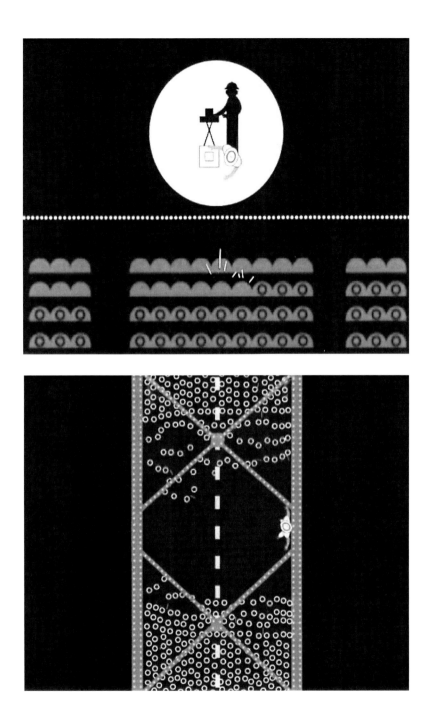

The figure of negation is given independent repeated permutations in *Rubber*—the chorus' intonation that the spectacle is "lacking in purpose," the final diegetic spectator's complaint of an "inadequate ending," and, most importantly, the avowal in a reflexive pronouncement at the beginning of the film that the entire work is an homage to the idea of "no reason," which it declares to be the essential element of style. The topology of the tire thus accumulates inflected figures for absence (of meaning, reason, provocation, cause), each one generating ever more somethings in all these metaphors for nothing. They come to comprise the duration of the film, accumulate alongside the rings that roll across the frame. This is the same paradoxical structure by which a discourse is said to be "full of gaps and full of lights, filled with absences and overnourishing signs" that Barthes writes of in *Writing Degree Zero*.[11] The critical generation of this structure results from a confusion between nullity, the quality and thing itself of nothingness, and what we might dub *nullitology*, the very full, very nonvoided consideration, description, and study of the nothing, the science of nonbeing, nonentity, empty space, absence, limit, vacuum, the uncreated, prior, and void—of which one can say so very much.

Horror is thus held by Blanchot's problem of the writer's double bind (we might say vicious circle) that "he is not free to be alone without expressing the fact that he is alone," in which *the text is not free to express nothing without expressing the fact that it is expressing nothing*.[12]

The tire is a visible hole; it is thus *in the way*, with resonances with Carl Andre's 1968 definition: "a thing is a hole in a thing it is not."[13] It is a boring (the making of a hole) that within this negative gesture challenges its claims to being boring (tedious). By virtue of being something *for* form—in the most fundamental way, what is there, a form that imposes itself on form, is animated, is proximate, spaces things in the frame—it cannot only be, which is to say give the measure only of, *nothing* as such. But nor can we make the tire *something* without in essence keeping the chorus alive, without writing over their poisoning, their elimination, their silence. The circle is not an object so much as a kind of longing for an object; it is the shape that gives shape to abstraction. Despite all the noisy observations in the film, there is nothing more to be said about a circle: a circle is its external form, it shows all that it is possible to nominate about it, exhausts its discourse, is without reserve.

Rubber is a meta-formal thinking of two competing theories of affect: *the chorus versus the torus*. The chorus designates affect as a matter of feeling (rage, desire), requiring the tire be taken as a He, ascribing cause and motive, converting the form of the tire to a sign for a question of positive meaning that enables a figuring of violence as destructive and ethically negative. The torus, by contrast, for which the tire is impersonal form, shape, texture, its tread a pure inscriptive force, is oriented toward a violence that is to be regarded as a deliberate change in forms, which is to say an initiative that is ethically neutral, and (because) it is above all aesthetically generative.

Film language itself bears out this encounter and difference—which is to say, it is cinematic form that regards and explores this formal problem of the circle. Three different large-scale visual regimes operate on the level of framing and editing: one that recalls the resolutely anthropomorphic basis of film grammar (for example, in match cuts and shot/reverse shot patterns emplacing tire in the historical role of subject of the diegesis interacting with the separate objects of the world); another formal system that emphasizes the tire as object encountering other objects, focusing through close-ups and extreme close-ups on the textures of mutually affecting materials, rubber, and sand; and a third regime that shows the toroid, always from the side, in a planimetric expanse against world rendered background, flattening the image, lining up the two circles of the torus such that they offer the perfection of a single graphic circle, rendering tire neither Robert nor rubber but shape, and establishing a rigid geometry to the tableau. In other words, these three visual regimes of cinematic form themselves navigate the tire *as though* it were Robert, rubber, and a toroid, teasing out the tire from an anthropomorphic, nonanthropomorphic, and formalist perspective, demonstrating above all the fecundities of cinematic form itself to comprise a critical stance on its central visual figure.

FIGURE I.3.7. *Rubber* (Quentin Dupieux, 2010)

The first half of the film constitutes a finding of the nothing as an observed animated thing; the second half leaves it behind. But it cannot be left behind completely if one wants to be able to say something about a violence with an orientation toward the human as unlike any other regime of force. This poses a problem: How can horror deal with (the) nothing without merely negating something? One must negate while preserving, abandon what is also left in place. For what is to be abandoned cannot be abandoned completely. Instead, *Rubber* puts under duress the supposition that violence requires the language of something or nothing precisely by formalizing how horror might hollow itself without merely negating, to instead arrive at a place—slow, quiet, dull, spaced—where the horror film has nothing to express, a state derived *from* the formal generality and abstraction of the circle, and not from giving its metaphor yet another inflection. Any promise of an affective affordance of horror is thus recast as a disaffordance of a critical valuation cast as a critical perspective. It is not the case that horror is the site of an affective engagement with the ethical problem of violence; rather, horror is the name for a neutralization of any substantial claim that an affective ethics might express. *Horror is the name for the state in which the ethical has nothing to express about violence.*

Žižek, in his thought experiment "*The Birds* Without Birds," imagines the way in which a different version of Hitchcock's natural horror film might have been punctuated with the occasional appearance of birds as symbols of the repressed family drama. By contrast, for Hitchcock, the birds are not symbols: "They play a direct part in the story as something inexplicable, as something outside the rational chain of events."[14] Their presence comes to obliterate the significance of the domestic drama, which becomes mere pretext; the birds "block, mask, by their massive presence, the film's 'signification,' their function being to make us *forget*, during their vertiginous and dazzling attacks, with what, in the end, we are dealing."[15] Žižek's thought experiment is supremely productive because it fails in relation to *Rubber*. The film without the tire would be nearly unchanged: one could imagine the same reflexive chorus watching for something to happen, seeing (and griping about seeing) only nothing—just as they do in the film; one could imagine the same periodic corpse-making, the same police investigation. But with one central problem: the absent cause would bend the film to the language of suspense. With nothing in the frame to indicate how it was that bodies were being decimated, choral and spectatorial curiosity would turn on the desired revelation of the positive reason for the narrative unfolding. What the presence of the tire in the scene does, then, is not symbolize or allegorize anything in the pretextual narrative, but nor does it function like a bird, making spectators forget the pretextual narrative; instead, the tire makes it impossible to forget the vacuity of the pretextual narrative, makes it impossible to dissimulate that something is happening in this film.

To read *Rubber* as expressive of a prior and external stance on ethics, one must lose the circle, an impossibility from the position of taking form seriously, but to fail to lose the circle is to be unable to move past the something or nothing which remains coextensively beholden to the circle. Critique must make itself free of the sedimentations of the circle, though this loss is not an abandonment in the sense of an absolute leaving behind; one must repeatedly encounter the circle—to put it in its place. Heidegger offers this formulation for what comes in the wake of discovering Nietzsche's thinking: "Only when we have succeeded in finding it may we try to lose again what that thinking has thought. And this, to lose, is harder than to find; because 'to lose' in such a case does not just mean to drop something, leave it behind, abandon it [*es hinter sich lassen und preisgeben*]. 'To lose' here means to make ourselves truly free of that which Nietzsche's thinking has thought [. . .] and so leave it at the place where it by its nature belongs."[16] The matter is: How to put the nothing where it belongs? A reading encounter that requires one find and lose, preserve and abandon, demands remaining between the divergent possibilities of settling the relation between reason and no reason, neither remaining faithful to the nothing or something nor imagining one might abandon that language altogether, leave it behind or cut it loose from its moorings *in* and moorings *for* philosophical thought. The tire, rather, as oriented toward the ideality of the circle is at once not without nothing (complete in itself), nor nothing (empty)—but above all, in this remaining-between it is *almost nothing*.

The almost nothing: not a center, not an object nor a force; it is a spacing, a shape and a proximity, what the film continually (infinitely; what goes on and on) attempts to erase either through irony or choral anthropomorphism (though it cannot quite), but nor is it indifferent to violence. It signals the almost impossible relation of something to violence, leaves behind the barest trace of an encounter: tread to earth, what wears down, the rubber that makes the minimal form of contact to ground—and, while it is not something, nor does it figure or explain or posit the nothing, nor does it leave behind completely those dimensions of the circle. It formalizes them, but in the most bare, spare way possible.

The *almost nothing* is the minimal dimension of the formal that gives the measure of something. Heidegger, in "What Is Metaphysics?" famously wrote "das Nichts nichtet," *the nothing nothings*, a negation of negation that will function as the target of Rudolf Carnap's vitriolic 1931 critique of continental syntax as what deploys language to form nonsense (he dubs it *rubbish philosophy*). Minimally at stake in the phrase "the nothing nothings" is that the nothing does not annihilate—it brings Dasein before beings in Heidegger's formulation: this negated negation shows that beings *are*. Reimagine this as: *the formal forms*; this possibility of representation distinguishes shape to abstraction, gives the minimal measure of form, but *for no reason*. This formal forming is not a static or singular giving of shape, not a simple coming to shape, but the restlessness of the movement of formation itself, what ceaselessly gives shape to abstraction and equally ceaselessly undoes itself. It is only its formal process. And the ongoingness of reading with form—always without guarantee—is likewise restless; it rolls on.

A formalist reading of the toroid reveals that *Rubber* arrives at the point at which it has nothing to express, but nor is it without ground: that ground is not causal but morphic, that the circle is there. Violence is thus not catastrophic, but it is catamorphic: a generalization of the folds of changing forms. For *Nothing is without form*. And the only way to arrive at an abandonment that takes leave of what would be lost in its place is through a paradox: it is through obsessively reading the forms of and in the film, taking seriously and giving priority to the circles, ovals, ellipses, splatters, holes, and textures, that the film comes to positively attest to this *almost nothing* to express. *Rubber* relinquishes, which is to say abandons, transfers the rights to what can say something about violence, yields violence to the almost nothing-to-express, not unlike the great philosophical conversion bequeathed to posterity from modernism, whereby the expressionless or inexpressive is neither obscurity, passivity, nor deficiency, but is the positive and obligatory condition for aesthetic production. The abandonment of the something-to-express does not exclude a critique of violence but rather spaces it like the aesthetic topologies given in the film, exposes the impossibility of expressing any relation adequate to bridge that space. Derrida, among others, reminds us that to abandon can also constitute a giving (*abandonner* contains within it *donner*). As Blanchot words it in *The Unavowable Community*, "The gift or the abandonment is such that, ultimately, there is nothing to give or to give up."[17] At the limit of horror, the voided possibility of declaring violence in the absenting of the human point of view does not retreat from critique but points to the impossibility of any final, closed critical stance.

In order to grapple with violence, the torus must be thought before the tire. But it must be thought before the tire infinitely—a formal affect never arrives at the expressive affect for which it would serve as the instrument of textual demonstration, as disposable means to a critical affordance. A circle cannot be paraphrased, but nor is it a thing. Its flat formalism demands an abandonment of the expectation that *either* the sentience of the thing *or* the choral perspective on the thing would be adequate for an account of force. In attesting solely to the almost nothing, *Rubber* forms a spaced possibility that topologizes the positive limit of the ethical. The formal affectivity of horror is the terrain on which a critique of violence is precisely good for nothing.

> *Is an ethical critique of violence necessary?*
> *— What a question.*

You shouldn't be here.

This should have gone differently.

We do not rush toward death, we flee the catastrophe of birth, survivors struggling to forget it. Fear of death is merely the projection into the future of a fear which dates back to our first moment of life.

We are reluctant, of course, to treat birth as a scourge: has it not been inculcated as the sovereign good—have we not been told that the worst came at the end, not at the outset of our lives? Yet evil, the real evil, is behind, not ahead of us. What escaped Jesus did not escape Buddha: "If three things did not exist in the world, O disciples, the Perfect One would not appear in the world . . . ." And ahead of old age and death he places the fact of birth, source of every infirmity, every disaster.

— E. M. CIORAN, *The Trouble with Being Born*

i. A film asks this seriously,
asks this *sincerely*:
How hard is it to kill nine-year-olds?

THREE

Grid, Table,

Failure, Line

There are only affects, ancients, and bureaucrats, except that there are forms.

By this I mean that Joss Whedon and Drew Goddard's *The Cabin in the Woods* (2011) is nothing else but the interplay of the affective universe of suffering (horror, terror, fear, shock, dismay, a beat resignation) alongside the mythological substrate of giant ancient gods, ritual sacrifice, evocations of "Ph'nglui mglw'nafh Cthulhu R'lyeh wgah'nagl fhtagn," and the metaphysics of evil alongside the surveillance, global positioning, informatics, technical glitches, protocol guidelines, office banalities, and distributed operations of corporative logic. Pain; Prehistory; System. The resolute verticality of the structure, by which the tortured youths in the upmost level are manipulated by the impersonal machinery below them, themselves answering to the sub-

subterranean collective demands of the gods, can be shorthanded as: there is a downstairs to the downstairs. There is a below to what is below. Architectures of declension—caverns, basements, graves, deep waters, descending elevators. (A cinematic universe not of line, but of ray: a part of a line running endpoint to infinity, but only in one direction.) There is no upstairs to the upstairs, no site of transcendence; the cabin-level world reveals no stars. There are only affects, ancients, and bureaucrats all the way down.

Except that there are forms.[ii]

Forms function not as exceptions but as objections to the divisions on which the cinematic universe is constructed. Form neither names nor mediates the differences between upstairs and downstairs, or downstairs and even further downstairs, or late capitalist bureaucracy and ancient mythology, nor does it set in relation affect and system. Form does not passively suffer its appearance, nor is it servant to a metaphoricity of each level. Rather, form intervenes in affect; it intervenes in the ancient; it intervenes in bureaucracy; it puts in place a problem that does not disappear with the total disappearance of being in the eschatology that is the end of the film. Grid, table, database, pool, matrix, array, hexagon, cell, frame, extension, corner, line, part of line . . . *Accept that there are forms.*

THE BUREAUCRAT'S UNCONCEIVED CHILD

This is what we must make sense of: What if violence is very, very difficult to do? What if horror is nearly impossible to bring about? How can that be? — Violence seems so overwhelmingly likely, flesh so self-evidently soft (so raw-meaty, so fleshy). Agatha Christie taught us that *Murder Is Easy*; *Snuff*, that life is cheap; Mouffe, Derrida, Weil, Arendt, Benjamin, Schmitt, Freud, Nietzsche, Hobbes, each offers a form of constitutive archeviolence, an irreducibility of violence that governs every possibility of relation, a foundational risk of violence, sometimes prepolitical, sometimes linked to necessity, sometimes

ii. This formulation is an homage to Badiou's writing in *Logics of Worlds: Being and Event II*, that "*There are only bodies and languages, except that there are truths*," which itself is an homage to Mallarmé's *Coup de dés*, and the "*nothing has taken place but the place, except, on high, perhaps, a Constellation.*" The philosopher will lose the poet's *on high* and the *perhaps*. The formalist will retain these as lost while adding a new little bit more in the end.

bound to phenomenality itself.[iii] Primary or secondary, divine or mythic or symbolic, state or intimate, structural or unforeseeable, what violence never seems to be is fragile, occasional, deficient, vulnerable to failure, ever at risk of being *inadequately violent*. And yet, what if? But then why would we be so afraid all the time? (And yet; what if?) —All of history seems to contradict even the notion of this thought.[iv]

Two discourses of violence are presented simultaneously in *Cabin in the Woods*, each marked as a form of *possibility*. It is possible for violence to take place. It is also possible for violence to insufficiently take place, for violence to not be violent enough when measured against a prior external standard that objectifies violence: for insufficient pain to be brought; for nonviolence to trouble or disturb violence; for violence to not arrive in the precise order, manner, or intensity desired. For there to have been zero fatalities (for some event to thus have been a total wash). Not a horror (generic, political) espousing the vulnerability and disposability of bodies, but the vulnerability of violence itself to deficiency (material criteria), meagerness (economic criteria), imperfection (aesthetic criteria). Insufficient violence is marked within the bureaucratic level and logic as *failure*, attested to from the earliest minutes of the film by Lin, a member of the chemistry sector who declares with great concern that Stockholm has "gone south"—leaving in play only Japan and the United States, as each of the other possible national rituals has failed to produce the requisite violent sacrifice of the young that will appease the demands of giant, evil, ancient gods.[1]

These alternative global scenarios are visible on multiple diegetic screens in the extensive surveillant operation center that measures, monitors, and intervenes in the cabin-level narrative. After the adolescent protagonists select a young girl's diary—within the constrained options of the artifactual, metonymic objects in the cabin's basement—and read the Latin therein that summons the Buckners—the "zombified pain-worshipping backwoods idiots" with "a hundred-percent clearance rate"—the bureaucrats Hadley and Sitterson turn to their control room's bank of screens, each of which displays a different global location playing out its particular scenario of violence: Berlin, scene of a raging fire; Kyoto, with an *onryō* floating in the middle of a

---

iii. cf. Heraclitus's Fragment 53, "War is the father of all and king of all"; Ice Cube, "Seems like I'm viewin' a body every other month"; God's burning anger, seeking to destroy, to negate absolutely, in the dialogues with Moses in *Exodus* 32; &c.

iv. And yet. What if?

FIGURE 3.1. *The Cabin in the Woods* (Drew Goddard, 2011)

classroom as petrified schoolgirls flee to the margins and bolted doors of the enclosure; Rangoon, showing something like a military encampment. Later, after the failure in Japan, where evil has been defeated and the ghost Kiko's spirit resettled, the film cuts to one of the embedded screens surrounded by a black border, making the nested diegetic image coextensive with the outer screen, thus collapsing the generality of *Cabin in the Woods* with the particularity of each alternative site, flipping channels between the newly (catastrophically) pacified scene in Kyoto and then: Stockholm, where a helicopter flies over a ruined snowy landscape; Buenos Aires, showing a dead and defeated Godzilla; and Madrid, with a burning castle on a mountainside. Each site, captioned by geographic name in the lower middle of the frame, is written over in the center of the image with a repeating, flashing, red typographical marker: FAIL.

Failure, from the Old French *falir*, both to be lacking and to not succeed, to err or make a mistake, and to come to an end, from the Latin *fallire* and *fallere*, to trip, cheat, elude, be defective, moves between a relation to an outcome and a relation to temporality. A disappointment of expectation or purpose, intention or protocol, failure also marks a cessation of function (to run out, to come to an end, to cease being or to become exhausted). In each global horror scenario in *Cabin in the Woods*, violence stumbles, horror disappoints, a violence that would be *sufficiently violent* eludes the event as its protocol runs through, and its violence was lacking, was inadequate and insufficient, was not equal to demand—and now time has run out and now time has come to an end. Each national operation thus ends in failure in the sense of both imperfection and cessation. This failure is irrecoverable, irreversible, nonnegotiable, total. Force was averted, its vitality drained away, which is to say that a horror that would be enough to appease a greater horror has not succeeded in taking place, and in this failure to be All, a violence that is not-All has been shown to be *possible*. Sidestepping the essentialist questions (what is horror? what is violence?) and simultaneously sidestepping more modest and situational questions (where is horror? where is violence?), the bureaucratic logic instead attests to an outcome with only two possibilities: wholly successful or absolutely not. The horror scenarios that have failed to take place sufficiently or completely—without residue, partiality, noise, or supplement; which have missed their mark—ultimately leave only the scenario playing out in the United States, which will also ultimately fail to manifest the requisite horror that is the entirety of what is required for radical failure (total human endingness) to fail to take place.

Even the most predictably successful violent scenario—the Zombie Redneck Torture Family, chosen every year by maintenance and shared with Ronald the Intern, the scenario that literally *maintains* and *interns*, preserves the horror formula for the market—will be a formula that is not formulaic enough *this time* (and catastrophe requires only one time) to enact the correct procedure by which sacrifice and substitutionary atonement is successful and violence is All—which is to say, *it is therefore shown to not, in fact, be formulaic* (its set form is shown to be unsettleable). The scenario induces unspeakable pain and suffering in *particular* instances as it runs through its ritual form in this *particular* case, in this *particular* film, and yet it is shown to be insufficient as a general protocol. And yet, precisely because there is a violence that falls short, that is not-All, a violence that *is* All, which will achieve its force with maximal sufficiency, will, in the future, at the edge of the film, take place—with vitality, with triumph, with nothing lacking—in the final, successful arrival of the unappeased wrath of the ancient gods,[v] which is

---

v. Ancient godly rising purely a consequence of failed protocols, and thus neither for the sake of experiment (epistemic drive) nor from "aesthetic interest alone […] with the world for a canvas," as in Dr. Baines's proposal in James Blish's 1968 *Black Easter* to "let all the major demons out of Hell for one night, turn them loose in the world with no orders and no restrictions."

marked at the edge of the film (beyond it) as the possibility that the film gives rise to (though this possibility is not contained within representation itself), devastating the totality of human life, rendering possible the failure (the end, in time, at the proper and expected time, with success of intention and outcome) of All human being—that which will lose vitality, die away, which will now and forever be marked as a planetary historical failure.

While the cellular unit of each individual instance of the failure of violence to be All is the nation, the cellular unit of the total instance that is *not* a failure of violence—the positive attestation of a violence that *is* All—will be the Anthropocene itself.

This violence that is All will never be marked as an instance of failure—no typographical FAIL is to be superimposed over the United States' scenario—because this failure will function as the limit of appeasement (a failure to stave off its arrival), and therefore the total set of what will thereby arrive as a violence that is All includes as things to be destroyed: the cabin, the corporation, the labs, the red phone, the red system purge button, any remaining bureaucrats, the surveillant technology, the bank of screens, the machinery that renders the typographic superimposition, the pixels that display the word as red; and with the annihilation of all those who live in language and the assemblage of words adjacent to red, also slated for eradication is all, every, each human notion of redness in itself.[vi]

Violence will not fail to arrive this last time, will not become extinct and die out, run short: what will become extinct, die out, run short, will be human life itself, failing because dying, failing as disappointed, what is let down, expiring, Being redefined as that which will perish, that which is no longer to be produced. The *All*, the universal in logic, is the realm of general prop-

---

vi. —So your blush your rose your crimson and sunset ruby oxblood scarlet, *rood* and *blozend* and *read*, *rouge* and *vermiel*, *ahmar* and *aka* and *rot* and *kokkino*; the site-specific rustiness of *falu*, *rosso* and its long bond to *giallo*; cinnabar and its seductive toxicity, medieval roasted minium; all riding hoods and furious eyes and precious holy wounds; the luscious ugly beauty of ruined strawberries, and the scent and the memory of the scent and the love of the memory of the scent of cumin and smoked paprika and a slight vinegar burn in the oily glisten of the crushed *guindillas* of *mojo rojo*; Macbeth's terror of a green converted in "the multitudinous seas incarnadine"; Plath's execrated tulips; Anne Carson translating Sappho, "As a sweet apple turns red on a high branch, / high on the highest branch and the applepickers forgot— / well, no they didn't forget— were not able to reach / . . . ."*

* *All that which is at stake in cutting a long story short.*

ositions. If, on the one hand, the violence that is All is brought about by the failure of a sufficient violence to be All in the local and particular contexts of each regional scenario, the ending of the film asks us to regard the generality of the universal in conflict with the particularity of the individual, and to try to imagine a horror that would be universal,[vii] which cannot, however, be represented within the particularity of the scenario as it is still unfolding in real time. A violence that is All, that arrives because some violence was not-All, will not fail to render humanity a failure that is All, that will come to an absolute (total, irreversible, cinematic) end. However, *Cabin in the Woods* offers this structure up via an ethical reorientation, one that proffers disappointment at particular failures of violence and an ironic celebration of its alternative, an exuberance of the universal fleeing the restrictions of the particular in the final arrival of a theological violence that does not fail to be All.

There are two critical ways of regarding the not-All: The first is as lack, deficiency, disappointment (against an originary All that would be knowable, full, sufficient), in which case the not-All would mark a departure from perfection, a diminishment of a prior, given, stable plenitude. The other way of regarding the not-All (the mode that gives rise to Lacan's identification of the term with the *extra* pleasures of feminine jouissance) is that unlike the All, governed by limit, border, and finitude, the not-All has no limit, is not constrained by the essential restrictions of being All, and thereby calls into play possibilities for experimentation, for new relations, for as-yet-unthought newnesses. It, and not totality, promises the boundless, limitless apeiron. The not-All, evading the totalizing logics of the All, leaves open room for excess, noise, residue, disturbance to completion, which is to say: for something unexpected to happen. And indeed it does: on the level of form, the film's unfolding colludes with each national site of horror being not-All against the not-yet-arrived horizon of a violence that would be All. It is precisely the lack of totalization that marks the possibility of the ongoingness of the world and the cinematic inscription that is *Cabin in the Woods* in the context of an only speculative violence that endows it with finitude,

vii. A project of universalization shown to be a feint, given (literal) body *as impossible* in the very particular appearance with which the film ends: the not at all universal anthropomorphic gigantism of a single hand plunging up through the hypotactic world levels with its discernibly national, even New England regional, evocations of a Lovecraftian metaphysics, the hieratic scale of this hand resituating a priority of the human form over the monstrous mutations presented previously.

that borders and shapes and limits its representational and temporal attestation. The violence that is not-All gives rise to the resistant system, the final system purge that spectacularly unfolds the unforeseen possibilities of a catalogue of nightmarish monstrous alternatives. But if there is a conservative aesthetic impulse here, it is that the finitude of a violence that is All will constrain and produce a restriction of the play of possibility in its definitive arrival as a violence that does violence to failed violences, arriving successfully and bringing about an adequate (which is to say: effective) endingness to the ongoingness of the film.

Cabin in the Woods thereby admits the existence of All, Some, or None, but it does not regard them equally. *None* will die (zero fatalities; a total wash—the Japanese scenario); *Some* will die (the American scenario); *All* will die (the endingness of all human life, which is marked as suspended just past the horizon of cinematic representation). Those terms, however, reside in a hierarchy, because the All will include those members of the set None and any remainders belonging to the set Some. Thus no negative term exists for the All—neither Some nor None stand as a rejoinder to completeness. The All is not not; it takes no logic of negation; it works by subsumption. There will be only the unary: all One, no Two. This All names endingness without exception: permadeath of the human experiment. What solely retains a bond to the infinite play of the not-All, the contingent, unstable, fragile possibilities of what is not restricted by finitude, what admits the multiple (is not the One) will therefore arrive within a system that is neutral to violence. The not-All will thus be redirected from the failures of violence to be All into the ongoingness, possibility, play, multiplicity, &c. of form; (—but we are not quite there yet).

Failure, a project of disappointment, a misadventure of expectation, a nonperformance, rendering of something wanting, is also, as a general mode of unsuccessfulness, a kind of *miscarriage* (as goes one definition of *fail* in Samuel Johnson's *Dictionary of the English Language*)—what won't work, doesn't work, what might not work. *Cabin in the Woods*, in fact, opens with a presentation of two contexts for failure—the failure of violence to happen with adequacy or sufficiency, extensively enough, its wreckage in the right order or completely (Stockholm: gone south)—and the possibility of the failure of something else altogether. In the opening lines of the film, in medias res, to the bureaucrat Hadley's complaint, "It's hormonal. I mean, I don't usually fall back on, you know, 'it's women's issues,'" his colleague Sitterson asks, "But childproofed how? Gates and stuff?" Hadley's response, "Dude, she did the drawers! We don't even know if this whole fertility thing[viii] is gonna work and she's screwed in these little jobbies where you can't even open the drawers." To Sitterson's resigned, "I guess sooner or later," Hadley insists, "Yeah, well a lot later. She did the upper cabinets. Kid'll be thirty before he can reach them. Assuming, you know, we have a kid." From hedging, he consigns himself to negative fortune, insisting, "It's a jinx. It guarantees that we won't get pregnant."[2] *Cabin in the Woods* arrives amid these two instances of failure—put another way, failure is primary, there is no cinematic world prior to this assertion of the possibility of multiple modes of deficiency: the failure of something to happen satisfactorily (the failure of horror's wrecking work being sufficiently *All*), and the failure of something to happen (the child may not be conceived: an event may not take place *at all*). Failure names an economy of excluded fractionality. One cannot be *a little bit* pregnant; one cannot appease ancient gods *partially*. Failure to be All is failure full stop.[ix]

viii. Does it require pointing out that what a fertility treatment is is a manipulation of hormone levels, not unlike the bureaucrats' manipulation of the teenagers' hormones via pheromones? The film is rather transparent on this parallelism, that the world level of the bureaucrats is equally one of surveillance (the Director, of the control center, via the interpellation of the room's red phone), also one of inadvisably ignoring warnings (Mordecai's prophetic warnings to Hadley and Sitterson that Marty the Fool might derail the ritual, which, in the end, he does), also one of choices and of transgression. All this is to say: the All includes the impersonal bureaucracy that monitors and manipulates from below—of course it does: this allnesseverything being the very thing that *All* names. Hadley and Sitterson are not exempt from the world they simultaneously manipulate; downstairs is contained within the system set of which it is a part, and it will thus also be extravagantly destroyed when the violence that is All finally appears.

ix. First complication: from an aphoristic point of view, one cannot be a little bit pregnant, fine. From an epistemic point of view, one can be entirely uncertain whether one is a little bit pregnant, and from the point of view of mensuration one can, in fact, be a little bit pregnant: *and there it is, a positive test, but the numbers aren't looking good and it's probably just a chemical pregnancy—or it* was, *before the bleeding I mean; I guess I know now that that's what it* was, *though I didn't know it at the time and maybe I wish I guess I wish I wish that I didn't know now.*

> [Language lesson: While it might seem as though the present perfect tense is the one in which one *has been* a little bit pregnant, the present perfect tense ought to be used to refer to actions that began in the past and are still in progress. It is therefore preferable to write "was" or "were" to refer to something done in the past that now, and forever, no longer applies, e.g., *I was a little bit pregnant*, and not, *I have been a little bit pregnant*.]

Or, *How long had it been since the heartbeat was missing, and when was the last beat and the beat before the last beat?*, or, *What is it called (What am I? [*always the question*])* *when only the sperm has been implanted or when the embryos have just been transferred* *and now it is all about the levels and test after test and when precisely does it feel sure* *enough to say Yes, —to believe, to be willing to hope, to imagine that more might come* *next?* What the bureaucrat's wife—unseen, unnamed, elsewhere, yet there in the cinematic world—is doing is *waiting***, waiting to see if the referenced fertility treatments have worked, or whether—and who knows how long she has waited, how many times they have tried, whether this is the first, still-optimistic go of a committed long haul or the final last achingly yearning but by now a nakedly pessimistic gasp—

and bitterly weeping,   *goddamnit*
I just can't do it
     (do it again

—they have failed.*

    * And if they are still trying because the previous time, of however many goes, didn't work, did some acquaintance then, smug with unctuous sympathy, say, *Don't* *worry wife, you can always try one more time. It isn't* the end of the world+ *you* *know, you can always try again.*

       + That insistence, always cruel, sometimes, as here, is also not true.^

          ^ (You're wrong, you think; Fuck you, you think; I can't, you think; It must, you think; bargains, you think, and *Please*, you think, and whys, you plead, and Broken, you think; Damaged, you think; Defective, you think; other things, you think, only this, you think; Wasted time, you think; every regret, you think; His fault, you think; Thinking not the point, you think; Thinking not the point entirely the problem, you think.)

    ** *Waiting* seems to be the lot of certain women in *Cabin in the Woods*—as with Anna Patience Buckner, whose very name connotes a submission to the slow prolongations of time, whose failed willingness to endure her name, whose keen drive to announce the end of waiting ("I have found it. In the oldest books: the way of saving our family") brings about the catastrophes that *await* the teenagers, and whose diary entry is about *awaiting* the restoration and the great pain, &c. Waiting for the embryo that has been implanted to take—embodying that total but fragile state of expectation, of uncertainty in which the possible child may have been conceived but not being sure yet, not having ascertained whether a treatment, a protocol or experiment will work or will fail, whether it will have worked or will have failed—the bureaucrat's unconceived child notates a case in which one is also *not sure* what is being killed at the end of the world: nothing, or the very beginning of a little something.

Here are some things that she will never know:

the sour back-of-ear smell
the deadweight rump-raised sleep posture
a sudden intake of air, inversion of a scream, at some surprising trivial
    thing giving undiluted joy
new fearlessness at having now only one single fear
the milkgrease sweaty hairline smell

There are others.
There will not be any others.

In Japan, the failure of the horror ritual—the failure of violence to be sufficiently violent—is shown to result from a process of redistribution. Two-thirds
of the way through *Cabin in the Woods*, in the midst of Dana stabbing, and then
fleeing from, the brutal zombie family, the film cuts abruptly from the pitch of
the cabin-level nighttime to a stark white screen and the shrieks of the *onryō*
amid the schoolgirls, singing as they hold hands and form a circle around the
quivering, pacified specter. "The evil is defeated," pronounces the other site's
heroine in the film's other film. "Now Kiko's spirit will live in the happy frog."

This faint, light-disturbing *yūrei* is a dead child: still wearing a white burial
kimono, her youthful face tortured by the unrest of the bloodless, she is converted from a haunting menace to a peaceful enshrinement. She receives, in
other words, in this other film, in this other national cinema, in this other
scenario of terror, a proper placement through funerary, mournful rites and
rituals, given a lodging in the afterlife through being encircled by the children
and their singing of "Donguri korokoro," a song about a rolling acorn and a
loach who play together until the acorn is homesick, finally redirecting the
spirit into the frog at the line, "Bocchan issho ni asobimashō"—"Young one,
let's play together!" The invitation to communal life, embodied in the circular community of gripped hands, is an ethical enactment of being-with, and
it ultimately defeats evil—which is to say that it renders the Japanese horror
scenario a failure from the point of view of the sacrifice protocol. Unlike the
betting pool of the bureaucrats—a game of collectivity in which each member
is in competition against each other—the circle formed by the schoolchildren
involves playing together, inviting the tortured ghost into the fold and thereby
transforming an antagonistic spirit into the generality of cooperative spirit. In
so doing, the positive commitments of a relational ethics and the redistribution of care produce a failure of violence to be All. Friendship thereby names
a residual *insufficiency* of violence. Following on the critical tradition that regards the not-All as that which is not restricted by the finitude of the All, the
Japanese scenario's relation to a violence that is not-All opens up a creative
line of flight into other genres altogether. Like the conversion of malevolent
to peaceful spirit, horror is converted into a story about political possibility
(collectivity, cooperation, transformation, ongoingness, a relation of the human to the animal); destruction and vengeance are replaced with magical
thinking, which becomes the grounds for channeling (territorializing) a new
social organization, with an attendant conversion of forms (the centrifugal
dispersion of shrieking bodies versus the centripetal holding of hands in a
ring); and terror and panic are affectively converted into love and celebration.

To Sitterson's furious question, "How hard is it to kill nine-year-olds?" the answer is: it is at least somewhat hard. (It is not not hard.)

The bureaucrat's child may or may not have been conceived (it is only ever possible), but it is never to have been born. The violence that is absolute, certain, and definitive is the eschatological horror that annihilates every human life on the planet, including the bureaucrat's possible child and his wife who yearns to conceive that child—and carry and trial in labor and safeguard for, and love and teach and laugh clean care sick for, pick up [   ] put down [   ] and feed hand right to left to mouth and clean hand left to right to mouth pick up [   ] put down [   ] and loud and less again again—and all the children who are, and all the conceived and unconceived children whose conditions of possibility, generation, and regeneration are thereby extinguished. Also to be killed are these nine-year-old schoolgirls who survived the tortured spirit but will survive neither the day nor the end of the world, who will die at the hands of ancient gods despite having appeased the horror that they directly faced. They did not, in the end, avoid violence, their redistribution of horror but some rearranged deck chairs amid a catastrophe newly arranged by their scenario's failure, which is to say, by that very rearrangement—joyful triumph now exposed as delusion.

The structural analogue to the systemic fact that in *Cabin in the Woods* there is a downstairs to the downstairs is that *there can be a failure of a failure*. The temporal analogue to the fact that there is a downstairs to the downstairs and that there can be a failure of a failure is that *there is a younger to the youths*. Marty and Dana, as much as they are punished for being young, so tells the Director of the logic of the violent ritual sacrifice, also punish the younger to the younger (the children; the unconceived child). *There is no possibility of any one evading violence that is All as it definitively arrives, nor is there a possibility of evading a doing of violence to someone else in the passivity whereby a violence that is All is allowed to arrive.*

Cabin in the Woods thus offers one way of thinking planetary disaster and total extinction, given in this maxim: It may be very difficult to kill some nine-year-olds; it is rather easy to annihilate everyone.

Easy, because it is, all told, inactivity that brings about the violence that is All—Dana's failure to shoot Marty to complete the ritual, her refusal of a decision, her apology for a weak attempt, her insistence that "I probably wouldn't have," his unwillingness to offer himself in sacrificial exchange for the ongoingness of humanity. Dana and Marty do not teleologically suspend the ethical for a greater leap of faith in the possibility of ongoingness; the youths merely slump against a wall and *wait* for the endingness of the human experiment, letting the last horror ritual fail, thus allowing the great violence that would be All to successfully take place. Marty and Dana are neither evil nor treacherous, but they are resigned. Able to act with minimal agency to prevent the arrival of a violence that is All, they weakly refuse. Not-doing is the great determinant of catastrophe. But why? Friendship, of course. Who kills their friends?

But if one mode of friendship is opposed to violence, friendship itself does not take a stable predictive relation in *Cabin in the Woods*. It is, after all, the offering of an invitation to play together—the promise of a new and communal form of amity—that ensures the failure of the Japanese ritual and creates the condition of possibility for a future bringing-about of a violence that is All. Friendship in this case does not resist violence but enables and produces it. Likewise, Marty and Dana's ethics of friendship, her refusal to kill him and render a requisite order of deaths that would stave off the failure of an otherwise successful American ritual, induces the violence that is All, fails the ritual but succeeds in bringing about the endingness of being (for all humankind, all history, all futurity). The encircling by the schoolchildren recalls a complaint Marty voices about the system of the social: that far from crumbling, it is consolidating, fortifying, enclosing; it is *binding*. Cooperative schoolchildren, like bureaucrats, are on the side of the continuity of existence: they, as much as the quasi-governmental agency manipulating the components of Foucauldian biopower, aim at the ongoingness of life (not for All, but at least for Some). It is the Virgin and the Fool, Dana and Marty, who remain on the side of anti-preservation, anti-violence-that-would-not-be-All. Marty's critique of the social, that it has not produced sufficiently rapid—adequately devastating—upheaval, is in full support of the violence that is All in the context of a scenario in which he simultaneously imagines that violence as his antagonist. Marty refuses to die in order for Dana *or for any one else* to go on.[x]

x. Not for his friends elsewhere, or for the schoolchildren, or for any other children, or for his parents (who he worries will think he is a burnout when they see the surveillance footage that, of course, they will not and never see for they are included in the total set of those who will die—whom he will *let* die), or for untold strangers. Nor for the sake of ideals or abstractions: recall that the first images of the cabin-level world are Dana's dormitory room littered with her drawings on the wall, her sketchbook charcoals of the professor with whom she is in love; —so Art, Love, Family, none function

Relational ethics thus functions as no guarantee of nonviolence.

All this is to say: in this film's schema, one cannot *generalize* friendship's relation to violence. And as a result, one cannot generalize an ethics: an ethics of friendship bonded to nonviolence is a possibility (which retains its promise of new relations and the generation of differences, alternative arrangements), and an ethics of friendship bonded to violence is a possibility (what will arrive, as necessity, concretely, in the here and now of the final eschatology, the event that will definitively end a *generality* of all human life because of one *particular* friendship). The ethical as such thus comes to name contingency and not necessity—particularity, and not what is in the realm of the universal.

Horror more broadly attests to a vision of politics that is really an inconsistency-tolerant ethics. It follows out its consequences strictly, seriously, and above all *to the end.*

---

as metanarratives of being, in the end, something to live for. The most potentially seductive lure is epistemophilia—Dana and Marty's final stated curiosity* about yearning to have been able to see the "giant evil gods"—and yet that impossibility also voids any commitment to any other reception or production of knowledge that might rescind the passive commitment to the imminent endingness of everything.

* The film's greatest feint is the impossible witnessing of the instant of one's own death: Dana's "I wish I could have seen them" (the enormous malevolent beings), and Marty's reply, "I know." It is the case that the film itself will see past the obliteration of these speakers, will take a metaphysical position above the cabin (related feint: camera purports to occupy the structural position of missing stars), being there to see the plunging of the monstrous hands projectively grasping toward the final obliteration of representation of all that *is*, which includes the field of the spectatorial zone, prior to the radical cut to black, thereby realizing Dana and Marty's wish for the sake of a future *someone else*, illustrating the deceit by which a final term hypothetically remains behind the annihilation of All in order to bear witness to it. This is reminiscent of the double structure in Blanchot's lines at the strange lightness of an evaded execution in *L'instant de ma mort*: "I imagine that this unanalyzable feeling changed what there remained for him of existence. As if the death outside of him could only henceforth collide with the death in him. 'I am alive. No, you are dead.'" To remain to see the endingness of All is to be dead yet to be still alive, to be alive to see how very dead one is at that very instant. This is what the concluding shot assures in a false flattering of ongoingness. And yet the film does not reveal the in-itself violence that is All, but rather, by positively testifying to its showing, the film unconceals precisely the perpetual *abeyance* of a violence that would be All. Thus does a representational violence that is All never arrive except as deceit, cheat, counterfeit, inadequacy—except as yet another (here, cinematic) failure.

Cabin in the Woods documents a logic whereby, for the explicit sake of the friend, one will not sacrifice oneself for the friend. A violence that is All, that includes within its All the agonizing death of the friend, as well as the deaths of all possible friends, is defended precisely for the sake of the category of the friend. Neither Merman nor Angry Molesting Tree nor Dismemberment Goblins nor {   } . . . *friendship* is the ur-horror in this catalogue of multiple possible horrors. Friendship is the nightmare for ethics. Not in Kierkegaard's sense that in the suspension of the ethical the individual asserts herself "over against the universal," acting as "the particular" (as in Abraham's acting in the "form" of sin) and making the self the exception to the universal; rather, the friend functions as a failure of a general ethics, without the positive gesture of acting as the particular.[3] In *Cabin in the Woods*, friendship neutralizes a certain stance, it voids the universal without positing a particular. It does not show anything *in common* among types of friendships (what it means to evade the universal: what applies to everyone and applies every time), and in that way, friendship comes to name something unrepeatable, paraconsistent, purely contingent, and without any generation of a concept. The ultimate philosophical consequence of horror is thus an attestation and formalization of a state in which an ethics of nonviolence would be something wholly accidental.

In the final confrontation between the Director and the two remaining protagonists, well after the deaths of their other friends, right after the deaths of the bureaucrats, the Director explains what is at stake: "The other rituals have all failed. The sun is coming up in eight minutes; if you live to see it, the world will end." To Marty's retort, "Maybe that's the way it should be. If you've got to kill all my friends to survive, maybe it's time for a change," the Director replies, "We're not talking about change. We're talking about the agonizing death of every human soul on the planet. Including you. You can die with them. Or you can die for them." (Marty: "Gosh, they're both so enticing.") In this exchange, the Director is both right and wrong: right, this end is not a change in the sense of turn-taking within a logic of the Same or a substitution of like, as in any barter or exchange, but wrong, this change *is* a change in the sense of undergoing a formal alteration, making something other than what it was. The agonizing death of every human soul on the planet is not change in the sense of a progression of liberal politics, but it is change in the sense of the difference of a difference. Thus, for all that *Cabin in the Woods* can be regarded as both member and critic of postmodern horror for its reflexivity and depth of allusions—suggesting comparisons to the *Scream* franchise; *John Dies at the End*; *Tucker & Dale vs. Evil*; the meta-horror of *The Final Girls* or *Behind the Mask: The Rise of Leslie Vernon*; the abstraction of *It Follows*; and literary works like Thomas Olde Heuvelt's novel *Hex*, in which surveillance networks confront ancient mythos—in many ways the film is less invested in the constraints of genre than in problems of the general as the question of contemporary politics and ethics (general failure, general violence, general change, a general ethics, general annihilation, &c.).[4] This is particularly visible in the last judgment pronounced by a wounded Dana, slumped next to Marty, the Director now dead, the world now conscripted to endingness from the failure of a sufficient violence that ensures the arrival of the violence that will be All. Her general verdict: "Humanity. It's time to give someone else a chance."[xi] In this final conversation, Dana and Marty end up ventriloquizing a version of the late-twentieth-century doctrine of accelerationism: that the world would be better off being forced to a rapid combustion of its worst tendencies. As Steven Shaviro words it, "Accelerationism is best defined—in political, aesthetic, and philosophical terms—as the argument that the only way out is the way through. [. . .] The hope is that, by exacerbating our current conditions of existence, we will finally be able to make them explode, and thereby move beyond them."[5]

The film's protagonists declare allegiance, however, to a very particular strand of the concept. The term initially came from Roger Zelazny's 1967 novel, *Lord of Light*, in which a group of revolutionaries called the Accelerationists seek to take society "to a higher level" through rapidly transforming social relationships to technology, with an explicitly political aim: "There would no longer be any gods, only men." In the novel, accelerationism is described as "a simple doctrine of sharing" and "an act of charity" that "would be directed to the end of raising their condition of existence to a higher level,

---

xi. Dana, however, is absolutely wrong in her interpretation of the scenario at hand: it is not time to give someone else a chance. The endingness of all human life is not *time* (not contained within time—it signals the anarchival and the end of historical time), not for some *one*, not a horizon that admits *someone else*, and not *chance*. Her declaration feigns a futural possibility foreclosed by the horror that will be All, for Marty and Dana's passivity is not vested in producing a new world: destruction is guaranteed, not contingent; All, not partial with the possibility of excess or residue; not about the unthought or surprise or the new. Rather, there is no political or aesthetic plan for what might come beyond or after the violence that is All.

akin to that which we ourselves occupy."[6] This utopian impulse toward transformation and elevation is retained in some contemporary forms of critical thought, including this final tenet, for example, of *#Accelerate: Manifesto for an Accelerationist Politics*:

> 24. The future needs to be constructed. It has been demolished by neoliberal capitalism and reduced to a cut-price promise of greater inequality, conflict, and chaos. This collapse in the idea of the future is symptomatic of the regressive historical status of our age, rather than, as cynics across the political spectrum would have us believe, a sign of sceptical maturity. What accelerationism pushes towards is a future that is more modern—an alternative modernity that neoliberalism is inherently unable to generate. The future must be cracked open once again, unfastening our horizons towards the universal possibilities of the Outside.[7]

This version of sharing and unfastening recalls the Japanese schoolchildren's drive toward a different arrangement of the social in their redistribution of spirit and promise to play together—a reconstruction of the future, a making-new of what is to come. Marty and Dana's advocacy of accelerationist logics, however, hews far more to the nihilistic version found in works like Benjamin Noys's *Persistence of the Negative* and *Malign Velocities*. There is no sense of the better world to come in Dana and Marty's passivity that allows all human life to be violently ended, and they loan sympathy instead to something like philosopher Nick Land's account of the "thermospasmic shock wave" as "undilute chaos," such that "disorder must increase, that regional increases in negentropy still imply an aggregate increase in entropy." Land's vision, a mash-up of death-drive theories and nihilism via Bataille, culminates in a model whereby "any process of organization is necessarily aberrational within the general economy, a mere complexity or detour in the inexorable death-flow, a current in the informational motor, energy cascading downstream, dissipation."[8] Or, as Marty rants earlier in the film: Society is "filling in the cracks with concrete. Everything's filed or recorded or blogged. Chips in our kids' heads so they won't get lost. Society needs to crumble. We're all just too chickenshit to let it."

By affiliating with this particular strand of accelerationism, Dana and Marty are also part of (the end of) the project Badiou identifies with the twentieth century writ large—what he dubs the *passion du réel*, the passion for the real, "the idea that things had to take place, here and now, that they had to *come about*, to *realize* themselves [. . .]. For instance, the notion of the appearing of a new humanity, or that of a total revolutionary overthrow of existing societies, or the creation of a new world."⁹ This drive involves an unfolding series of purifications: "In order to arrive at the real, to produce it, a method was needed to eliminate the old world, to eliminate all the habits and things of old. In my view, a large part of the violence of the century, the extreme political cruelty that dominated its first sixty years or so, was rooted in the conviction that ultimately no price is too high for an absolute beginning."¹⁰ Badiou links this passion for the real to a "will to formalization," a drive to attain a "radical simplification that would allow one to extract the kernel of the opposition between the new and the old in its purest form."¹¹ When Badiou argues that one consequence of this formalization is a devastation of the local (local difference, local differentiation) under the total weight of the global, he seems to perfectly describe the mode by which the specific *mise-en-abîme* representational economies of particular national film traditions—Europe, Latin America, Japan—each fail (contain horror; that is, are not sufficiently violent) in relation to the broader arrival of a pretention toward universalism via the American genre scenario. If, however, the brutal simplifications of politics, homologized for Badiou in the stark simplifications and extreme formalizations of avant-garde practices of the previous century, are given shape here—in that the film's ending gives body, as it were, to "the conviction that ultimately no price is too high for an absolute beginning," that the agonizing death of every human on the planet is not too high a price to pay for an absolute beginning of a difference—it is the postmodern horror touch that deprives this conviction of conviction, that renders it a *passivity* as opposed to a political *project*. That the "absolute beginning of history" would involve resigning oneself to the resurgence of ancient, formerly omnipotent, gods—that is, of the absolute nonbeginning of history but rather its vengeful return—suggests that a twenty-first-century rereading of the twentieth century ends less in a will to formalization than with a will-less *whatever*. A radical simplification of the "give someone else a chance" that is capable of the same extreme cruelty and indifference to the cost of eliminating the whole of the present, now old, now former world. No bang, few whimpers. A little stoned, a shrug.

Except that there are forms.

INFINITE POSSIBLE CONTINGENCIES (EXTENSION)

A human is that being which prefers to represent itself within finitude, whose sign is death, rather than knowing itself to be entirely traversed and encircled by the omnipresence of infinity.
—Alain Badiou, *Being and Event*

Topology is not "designed to guide us" in structure. It is this structure.
—Jacques Lacan, "Second Turn: The Discourse of the Analyst and Interpretation"

Horror is not only about violence, and violence isn't only about violence. Both are also about the processes of the formalization of abstractions.

Every architectural-structural-textual level of *Cabin in the Woods* gives aesthetic body to a schematic or arrangement proper to it: the hexagonal network grid of the cabin level; the three-dimensional matrix grid of glass cubes in the architecture directly below that level; the written table organizing the betting pool of potential options for the American scenario's agent of violence in the control room; and the subterranean gods' appeasement or disappointment bonded to intaglio and hollow lines of stone-sculpted relief filled in, partially and ultimately inadequately, with the sacrifices' blood, its incisions forced with the course of a viscous pigment, thus converting a form of sculpture to something more evocative of printmaking. Although the vertical hypotactic levels of enunciation in *Cabin in the Woods* have been read as a formalization of the metatextual (the puppeteers, bureaucrats, and Director taken to reflexively stand in for the machinery of cinematic production and the marketplace of horror film as formulaic commodity), the film is far more akin to a *textualization of the meta-formal.* Above all else, the film is about the properties of varying formal systems. These forms are not metaphors—for society, or information, or power, biopower, the necropolitical, &c.—; they are the structures themselves.[12] There are forms.

1. THE GRID (GPS & THE BEE AS GEOMETER)

The grid arrives in *Cabin in the Woods* as both metaphor and visual material; as figure and as graphic; as anxiogenic, abstracted symbol of a totalizing disciplinary/surveillant regime and as an illuminated network of intersecting lines. Its double invocation takes different spatial topologies: *that which one seeks to get off of* (a cartographic model in which evasion, which is to say *grid failure*, is possible), and *that which one cannot avoid encountering as force* (an affecting-affected form of sufficiency, which does not admit failure or exception or off-ness). In the language of the logic of violence, the former is a grid that retains the possibility of being not-All; the latter is a grid that is marked by being All.

The first grid is invoked early in the film. Only minutes after the introduction of the upper textual cabin-level narrative, as the college students begin their generically familiar departure of suburban and familiar setting for the (unknown, rural, differently classed, &c.) escape, Jules announces a cartographic failure: "I hope this is the right road. It doesn't even show up on the GPS. It is unworthy of global positioning." To this worry, Marty insists on the positive value of software breakdown: "That's the whole point," he rants. "Get off the grid, right? No cell phone reception; no traffic cameras; go someplace for one goddamn weekend where they can't globally position my ass." This first grid is lodged within epistemologies of geolocation and technologies of identification, connected to matters of precision and adequacy, but also of failure: of which it is possible for error or nonperformance to render one *off* the grid. The second grid is an illuminated material network, a hexagonal electrical grid that Curt forcefully encounters during the climax of the cabin-level narrative when trying (and failing) to escape the predations of violence by leaping an abyssal canyon on a motorcycle, and which is foreshadowed earlier in the film by a soaring bird's staticky confrontation with its voltaic network of lines.

These two grids do not name the same object, episteme, or form. The grid Marty invokes, which he celebrates getting and being *off of*, is inextricably linked to techniques of mapping and the long history of navigation. But the world of the protagonists in *Cabin in the Woods* involves a distinctly modern mode of positioning; as Marty notes, there are no stars in the blackest sky above them, which is to say that missing are the astronomical markers that guided the ancient exploration of territory,[xii] particularly maritime ex-

---

xii. Before they are those to be tortured, to be killed, to be ritually sacrificed, in taking to the road for the sake of displacement from suburban campus to rural cabin, the college ploration, now lacking the determinations that might orient one in and at and in relation to the underfoot earth. The instruments in play are thus not fifteenth- and sixteenth-century astral observations and measurements, nor seventeenth- and eighteenth-century charts and maps and clocks, nor nineteenth- and early twentieth-century radiogoniometry and positioning via transmission signals, but the late twentieth- and early twenty-first-century regime of GPS, a Global Navigation Satellite System reliant on US military satellites made available for commercial use and enabled by and integrated with the disseminated receivers endemic to an era of mobile privatization. Ineluctably bound to the language of recovery and failure, and the possibility of getting lost (the problem, historically mortal, of lostness for which such positioning was a designed solution), global positioning traffics in information, data that can be converted to applications: determinations of velocity or localization, with attendant conversions to forms of monitoring, tracking,

---

students initially are evaders of geographical limit. In that sense, though not quite navigators, they are akin to explorers, and their transgression is initially that of cartographic boundary. Because the structure of the film is the departure from a starting place and the attempt to return to it (announced in the lyrics of OK Go's "White Knuckles," which plays at the first rupture between textual levels: "You'll never get that taste, out of your mouth / You'll never get the paw prints, out of the hen house now / And you can't go back, same way you came / Round all the pieces up, but they just don't fit the same"), the film's long line is an iteration of the ancient narrative form of a *nostos*,* albeit here a failed** one.

 * The history of navigation is more broadly the history of the affects of *nostos*—terror or rage at a lack of orientation, deep grief at the possibility of a failure to return+ home. *Nostos*, whose frequent bond to *algos*, *algia*, pain, elides the multiplicity of affective attachments—ranging from longing to disgust, doubt to heroic certainty—was always already an aesthetically mediated question of the felt practices of navigation: as Anna Bonifazi puts it, "In Homer, *nostos* means first and foremost 'return home from Troy by sea.' It refers both to the return itself as experienced by the Achaean heroes and to the poetic telling of that experience."

  + This return, however, being conceptualized differently in ancient and modern regimes of longing; James Phillips neatly summarizes the opposing forms as, "Odysseus longs for home; Proust is in search of lost time."^

   ^ And of course, one could also argue that in reasserting monstrosity in the form of giant, evil, ancient gods, the horror film qua generic template is here nostalgic for a lost affectivity bound up with sensible and monstrative forms prior to the reflexive ironizing of the postmodern era, a textual longing for lost, now drowned, modes of horror representation.

 ** —because they die, a common, though not exclusive, reason for such failures—

surveilling, finding, refinding, failing to lose. In the cabin-level world of the film, optical measurement systems are thus explicitly negated in favor of algorithmic systems: a replacement of drawn angle with code.

The complex global positioning system under which the protagonists operate evokes omnipresent regimes of tracking and surveillance (under the guise of navigational guidance and ideologies of service and security), but it simultaneously contains within itself numerous modes and varieties of deficiency. Failure is not of the order of the One (possible or not; *a* failure, *the failure*) but is multiple:

inaccuracies
gaps in coverage
unanticipated unavailability
lowered power
inadequate receivers
a lack of reliability
difficulties with density
margins of error (a twelve-foot radius; a three-foot radius)
the possibility of missing signals
glitches
frauds and spoofs
jamming
cyberattacks
timing flaws and desynchronized time stamps
search domains confronted with their limit
intervals and diversions
variations in satellite geometry
possibilities of atmospheric interference
design change or error
signal blockages
mislabeling
missing addresses
delay effects
multipath errors from local obstructions
systems that can multiply fail
systems with limited fault tolerance
systems that can multiply fail amid systems with limited fault tolerance
crashes

The promise of exhaustive mapping is given form[xiii] against the necessary inclusion of the minimal miscalculation that inserts a limit in the ideology of the total. It is only because one can fall off of it that the positive assertion of the grid Marty jubilantly celebrates is possible.[xiv] Accordingly, this grid is central to the regime that contains the "electrical glitch," the power reroute from "upstairs" that signals Marty's evasion of the Buckner family's torture (or, rather, evasion of their violence being All)[xv] and his ruining of the bureaucratic plan for a successful sacrifice—his manipulation of the electrical network that (initially) prevents the cave being blown in and (initially) subverts (opens up, enables, maps a successful route for) possibilities of escape for the remaining survivors. The vulnerability of this grid is precisely what renders the failure of the American scenario, heralding both the imminent system purge's cacophony of extraordinary horrors and the violence that is All that ends everything whatsoever.

It is fitting that this electrical glitch, a failure of infrastructure and network that fails to blow the tunnel and collapse the cave at the crucial moment of potential escape, occurs amid the scale and scope of the mountain range, road, and abyss, sites that intervene between the world from which the youths have departed and the rural setting from which they will, to a one, not return. The natural grandeur of this particular locale, though seemingly an eighteenth-century figure of classical Kantian sublimity—reason intimately interacting with sensation, with the concept's attendant notions of vastness,

---

xiii. The Latin *forma*, for all that it meant figure, shape, appearance, plan, also, at one point, very long ago, referred to a surveyor's map.

xiv. This promise is always an inadequacy as a positive internal requirement, for a true adequacy of map would cease to function as representation—as glimpsed in Borges's thought experiment in "On Exactitude in Science" (itself a reimagining of Lewis Carroll's "Sylvie and Bruno Concluded"), in which cartographic art was eventually able to create a "Map of the Empire whose size was that of the Empire, which coincided point for point with it."

xv. A violence to the formulaic certainty of their generic form, a devastation of their "one-hundred-percent clearance rate"—which is to say: an insertion of the statistical noise dubbed a margin of error,* the smallest allowed amount of miscalculation of that percentage.

* Although an allowable miscalculation, margin of error, of course, is routinely responsible for the catastrophic consequences of the accident, the crash, the explosion, the wreck, &c.+

+ In the previous sentence, what precisely does *allowable* mean?

boundlessness, and power—is, via the electrical malfunction, transformed into the twenty-first-century notion of "the technological sublime," a contradictory structure in which, as David Nye frames it, the observer interprets "a sudden expansion of perceptual experience as the corollary to an expansion of human power and yet simultaneously evokes the sense of individual insignificance and powerlessness."[13] The glitch reorients the film from natural sublimity to the digital sublime via the affective operation of technological failure.[xvi] As Eugénie Shinkle writes on the question of material breakdown in gaming: the technological sublime is explicitly marked by "a collapse of con-

xvi. It is worth recalling the crucial role of failure already operative in Kant's theory of the sublime in *Kritik der Urteilskraft*. Briefly, we know that Kant distinguishes between two kinds of sublimity that overwhelm disinterestedness, are "absolutely great" (*schlechthin groß*), and are beyond all comparison (Kant writes "absolute, non comparative magnum"): mathematical and dynamical. In the former, sublimity is linked to the problem of comprehending vastness and magnitude (snow-gray, periphery-exceeding "shapeless mountain masses towering above one another in wild disorder with their pyramids of ice"); in the latter, it is a question of force, potency, power, dominance [*Gewalt*], as in "volcanoes with their all-destroying violence," or a "boundless ocean set into a rage." In either case, the imagination, in attempting to apprehend the object of such power or scale, *fails*: "This idea of the supersensible [. . .] is awakened in us by means of an object the aesthetic judging of which stretches imagination to its limit, whether that of enlargement (mathematically) or of its power over the mind (dynamically)." Reason's drive for imagination to represent the object absolutely (as a whole impression, as an absolute magnitude, as a totality of power) is frustrated, and the object is therefore contrapurposive for the imagination. This failure, however, constitutes a negative exhibition and makes the sublime (newly; subjectively) purposive: it is thus "a pleasure to find every standard of sensibility inadequate for the ideas of the understanding." Hence the negative affective pleasure of the sublime: displeasure at imagination's failure is tinged with pleasure that imagination is inadequate to reason, exposing a greater freedom (above, transcending, beyond [mere] sensibility; above, transcending, beyond [mere] nature). The negative pleasure of the sublime rests on this failure; the affect "pleases immediately through its resistance to the interest of the senses." The sublime involves a "feeling of the deprivation of the freedom of the imagination by itself, insofar as it is purposively determined in accordance with a law other than that of empirical use." A failure of imagination to be All, we might say in the vocabulary of violence's possibilities, involves the expansion of itself, inducing an affect that is All: "Imagination, although it certainly finds nothing beyond the sensible to which it can attach itself, nevertheless* feels itself to be unbounded precisely because of this elimination of the limits of sensibility." Failure exposes, and is required for, this generation of the beyond.

* Are we too shy to say what is nakedly happening here, what this "nevertheless" really means? Reason is humiliating imagination—and a taken-aback imagination finds that it likes it. Gets a taste for it. It will, in fact, come to *crave* it.

trol and meaning, and it is felt when gameplay is brought to an abrupt halt by the *failure* of interface. Failure events in videogames can take the form of minor hardware malfunctions like bugs, glitches, slow running, poorly designed artificial intelligences (AIs), and so on." More catastrophic failures, "such as crashes, random memory corruption and irrecoverable hardware failure [. . .] have more serious consequences for the subject."[14] In the case of the latter sort of failure event, she writes, "the unimaginably large, extroverted, operative sublime—which many videogames attempt to simulate visually—is replaced by an unimaginably complex 'introverted' sublime, which is incapable of presentation to the senses."[15] Failures of interface rupture perceptual experience to such a degree, Shinkle argues, that the result is a subject who is "disabled and dispersed—no longer part of the gameworld." What appears in this encounter is "not a meaningful game form and extension of reason, but an inexpressive intelligence, a pure, depersonalized power, a technological other."[16] In the encounter with this inhuman other, the sublime experience "is emptied of the transcendence that the term originally comprised."[17]

There is, however, in *Cabin in the Woods*, that second grid. This other grid neither admits nor requires exception; it functions negatively in relation to the possibility of failure. There is no getting off of this grid: it is only ever (and only ever again, and only over and over) encountered as the sufficiency of its form, because the irreducible givenness of this grid rests on the adequacy of line. This grid will not, cannot, fail to be All. There is an unfreedom to this grid. In formalizing its own presence, it is something akin to Levinas's *il y a* (the "there is")—an impersonal, anonymous, unavoidable, resolutely insistent form. While Marty celebrates the prospect of getting off of the grid, for Curt it is just the case that *There is a grid.*

Comprising a mere fifteen seconds of screen duration, the sequence in which Curt encounters grid (so amenable to a reading in relation to genre convention—here, a mock-heroic action-adventure climax) begins with a reduction of the film's visual material to the difference between a field of darkness and a single point of light. When Curt revs the engine of his motorcycle, as he turns it to face the canyon, the camera's frontal position, aligned with the abyss he purports to leap, displays the round unity of a single blinding headlight against a detail-obliterated background. Light will pose the primary question of the emptiness or fullness of this space, the thingness of the negative, a matter that will be hystericized within diegetic seconds by Curt's subsequent crashing encounter with an electrical grid, at which Holden frantically sputters: "He hit something. There's nothing." The question of whether there is *nothing or something* will be a question that light uniquely unconceals: diagramming, giving form to, the lines of a grid that reiterate that paradox, illumination bearing out the violence of the broader structure in which the teenagers in the upper level find themselves. There *is* nothing. And yet Curt hits something. He brutally, body-destroyingly encounters a formal arrangement, which is not a thing—which *is* nothing—and yet which enacts total force on him at discrete moments of a junctured, mutually affecting encounter. He hits something, yet there's nothing. He dies because he hit something. There is nothing.

At the moment of the initial leap, the motorcycle is shown in perspective, its right to left movement emphasizing the horizontality of the mythology of escape (and of progress: toward the law, hope, rescue, return, home, &c.), the screen a homogeneous field of darkness, the soundtrack saccharine, soaring. Then, the suddenness of the life-ruining encounter of bike and grid. It is given in a sonic and luminous violence: a loud static crackle that obliterates musical line; a brutal visual collision that devastates kinetic line. At the impact, horizontality and its varied ideologies are replaced with a resolute verticality, a partially illuminated electrical grid shown in an oblique, canted perpendicular and extending beyond the borders of the cinematic frame. The grid is not illuminated as a single or homogenous form, but as a dynamic and internally divisible series of lines of electric flow: where Curt directly contacts it, the full expanse of lines blazes and scatters light, sparking ferociously across the frame. The negative space of the potential for crossing—the openness of the abyss, previously signaling the possibility for new forms of movement—is thereby filled with the positive aesthetic force of electrical discharge, whose bright spitglints overtake that empty space. Amid this first contact, there are extensive blank patches, the lines only shadowly visible, and discrete threads of electrical activity running a jagged and sharp up-and-down graph of varied amplitudes and uneven distributions across the compositional field.

The film cuts to Dana screaming and then cuts back to the grid from her perspective, a newly frontal view that transforms the grating into a recognizably ordered and organized pattern, illuminated in patches of adjacent hexagons in the local area of Curt's repeated impact as he falls farther into the abyss of the canyon. That frontal view is made oblique once more through a series of shots from Dana and Holden's elevated vantage point as the grid is reencountered again and again in smaller, because more distant, patches until the grid lines return to pure attestations of the presence of light: small pulsations receding into the space, not of an expansive mountain road but of

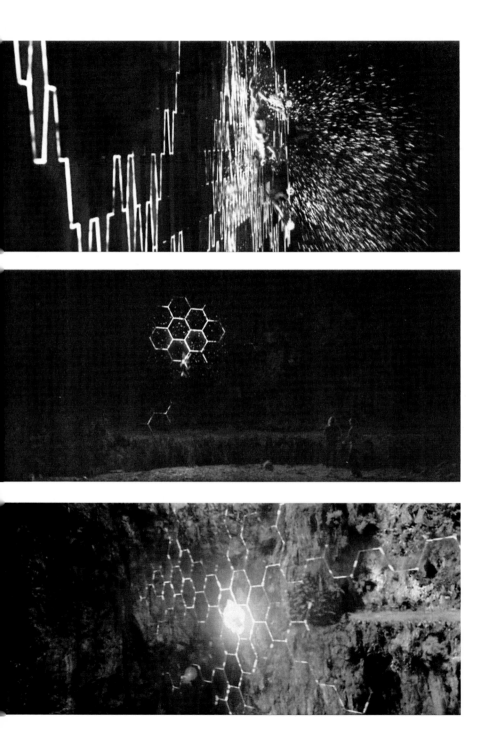

FIGURES 3.2–3.4. *The Cabin in the Woods* (Drew Goddard, 2011)

a deep mountain maw. The sole uncanted grid—what offers the most non-oblique image of its repeating hexagonal form—appears only once in a single frontal point of view, the vantage at the instant of Dana's shrieking "No!" The formal purity of the grid is thus aligned with a negative horror at its positive realization.

Earlier, when the soaring bird encounters it as fore-announcement, the grid is shown also canted from the side, but with an approach from the left, continuing the film's interest in an extensive visualization of this grid as a form that is involved in demarcations of space, with which things interact with force, and yet which *is not itself a thing*.

Bird is neither sign nor symbol; it is nothing but the occasion to display the lines of the grid (in that precise sense then, of course, it is—or rather it thereby becomes—something, the something of *something is happening*).

And what does that bird hit? It hits something. There's nothing.[xvii]

> *This bird is not a pigeon. But a pigeon is also a bird.*
> *Much later, well after we have left horror behind,*
> *only, perhaps, to rediscover something of it in the midst*
> *of a thinking of love —*
> *although what else motivates Curt to take this leap other than tenderness*
> *for the friends he yearns to save from future harm —*
> *these two avian figures materializing in light*
> *may,*
> *as it were,*
> *come to resonate with each other.*

Curt's death sequence de-abstracts the grid's sense of a distributed network of satellites and information data applications and spatial protocols for transmission, identification, specification, positioning, and targeting by putting materiality and light back into the grid. With this gesture of re-electrification, the hexagonal forms also thereby enable a writing of *line* back into grid, recalling the *Oxford English Dictionary*'s definition of "an arrangement of parallel bars with openings between them; a grating."[18] This sense of grid is inextricably bound to the formal quality of crossed bars: the syntax of an infrastructural framework; the designed grids (and gridlock) of urban planning; what

xvii. (Except that there are forms.)

distributes and controls[xviii] a flow of something in its quality of being "a net-work of lines, esp. two series of regularly spaced lines crossing one another at right angles; *spec.* one provided on a map as a means of specifying the location of places and objects."[19] The encountered grid therefore leaps back to the origins of the word as a shortened form of *gridiron* and *griddle*, utensils for cooking and broiling, and also medieval instruments of torture by fire.

Force is not allegorized in the hexagonal electrical grid; it is *geometrized.* And this question of the form of force paradoxically makes Curt's encounter with grid a properly affective one, not for any sense of an emotive property (of hope, courage, horror), but rather, as a case of *affectus* to the letter: the scene stages the mutual intensities and interacting forces of some A and some B.[xix]

xviii. Which is one reason why Bernhard Siegert declares of the grid that it is a cultural technique unique to modernity,* capable of "turning humans into retrievable objects." He continues: "The ontological effect of the grid is that modern concept of place and being-in-one's-place [. . .]. In other words, it presupposes the ability to write absence, that is, to deal equally efficiently with both occupied and empty spaces. This concept of place is thus inextricably tied to the notion of order."

  * If not modernity writ large, there is critical agreement on the grid's relation to at least modernism. As in Le Corbusier's polemic for rigid symmetrical grids and intersecting lines in the foreword to his 1924 *Urbanisme* (*The City of To-morrow and Its Planning*): "Modern art and thought—after a century of analysis—are now seeking beyond+ what is merely accidental; geometry leads them to mathematical forms, a more and more generalized attitude." Here, grid is inextricably linked to transparency, reason, rationality, rationalization, industrial efficiency, scientific management, &c.

    + Le Corbusier's polemic is reminiscent of Dana and Marty's final drive to nihilate and start over—their deluded deixis to the "someone else" imagined to have a chance—as in the architect's insistence, "WE MUST BUILD ON A CLEAR SITE.^ The city of today is dying because it is not constructed geometrically. To build on a clear site is to replace the 'accidental' layout of the ground, the only one that exists today, by the formal layout."

      ^ That the grid is continually linked to clearing fields, to *newness*, is reiterated in Rosalind Krauss's famous essay on the subject and its relation to modern art: "By 'discovering' the grid, cubism, de Stijl, Mondrian, Malevich … land in a place that was out of reach of everything that had gone before. Which is to say, they landed in the present and everything else was declared to be past."

xix. In the terminology Grégoire Chamayou offers in an exquisitely long footnote in *Théorie du drone*, Curt and the grid do not *co-exist* so much as they are *co-present* in a field of reciprocal if not symmetrical effects on each other. Co-existence, for Chamayou,

This hexagonal grid has two[xx] salient formal qualities: First, it is a grid repeat pattern, which is to say that it extends without visible border in four directions (up and down, left and right) beyond the edges of the cinematic frame. Second, its hexagonal cell texture is seamless, lacking gaps[xxi] or negative space

merely requires that two terms exist at the same time. "Co-presence," however, "assumes more than that, namely the possibility for one term to affect the other or to be affected by it (a relation of causality). In other words, co-presence is defined by an instantaneous but not necessarily actualized possibility of a real relationship. Yet another way of putting this is to say that co-presence is defined by the accessibility of one term to the other. To be co-present they must be within reach of each other." This, from a book about the question of the drone and the explicit forms of violence enabled by a co-presence that is nevertheless not symmetrical; for Chamayou, therefore, the concept is always a question of force and *range*. Which is to say, it is an explicitly formal question of areas of variation between limits on some given scale: Curt and the grid are *in range* of each other. What it means for there to be a grid that one will not fail to locate oneself *on*—that one cannot fall off of—is that *there is at least one grid* whose range is infinite. Co-presence* does not require reciprocal awareness; it merely requires sharing in common an extent of territory.

> * Chamayou: "The prey and its predator lurking in the shadows are co-present even if the former is not yet aware of this (or even if the prey cannot yet see the predator). For there to be co-presence, all that is necessary is that one of the terms involved should be included in at least one field in range of the other. There are paradoxical forms of unilateral co-presence in which entity A can act upon or be affected by entity B, while entity B is not in a reciprocal position. Here, the prefix 'co-' indicates no reciprocity in the relationship but simply a common inclusion."+

>> + Other in-common inclusions in *Cabin in the Woods* include the multiple textual worlds and levels (cabin level affected by and affecting bureaucratic level and sub-subterranean level; sub-subterranean ancient theological level affected by and affecting bureaucratic level and cabin level). Each level is not reciprocally or symmetrical visible to every other, but each term is *within range* of the others. Also co-present to each other are the various fields of forms of violences, and although the climax's glass matrix suggests a co-existence of discrete monstrous alternatives, the system purge is what makes them into a network of co-present atrocities, able to nonreciprocally and asymmetrically affect each other. They may have occupied adjacent cells in the glass matrix, but proximity is not the sole factor; it is the system purge that puts them *within range* of each other.

xx. There are many more than that.

xxi. One compelling formal aspect of the grid—any grid—is its reductive, radical simplification, its effort to constrain, and to not merely reallocate but redescribe the complexity of some system. The grid's stark indifference to complexity, its simplicity both of line and angle but also of conceit (as opposed to network, as opposed to system, both of which can accommodate, even court, complexity), involves a paring down to barest internal to the grid, given in the form of hexagonal tessellation: a regular tiling (meaning edge to edge by congruent polygons) in which three hexagons meet at each vertex.

There are thus two modes by which the image of this grid lacks interruption: the grid extends to infinity in every direction; and hexagonal tiling itself is a maximally optimal, seamless mode of tessellation.[20] In metric geometry, as we have known since the sixth century, only three polygons can tile a plane: squares, (equilateral) triangles, and (regular) hexagons. Let me put this another way. Close your eyes. Cram your darkness full with as many circles as possible. Now do the worst imaginable violence to these vulnerable shapes. Stretch, bend, push, bludgeon, assault, and terrorize their edges to maximally fit in more, to shove and cram and squeeze them on your mind's screen. Leave no dark gap unfilled; permit not even the tiniest sliver of space. These shapes of yours will have distorted under all that pressure, but symmetrically so. And hexagonal tiling will name the result: the densest way to arrange circles in two dimensions. This seamlessness gives rise to the idealism of the form, one linked to questions of sufficiency, saturation, density, and discourses of natural efficiency (visible, as the form is, in bees' honeycomb,[xxii] snowflakes, bubbles, graphene, crystals, &c.). From these associations arose a long-standing metaphysical and theological interest in hexagonal tiling in contemplations of perfection, harmony, and teleology.

Every—any—grid pattern lacks a center. (Krauss: "The absolute stasis of the grid, its lack of hierarchy, of center, of inflection, emphasizes not only its anti-referential character, but—more importantly—its hostility to narrative.")[21] This cinematic hexagonal grid extends outward from the local junctural point of contact with Curt, but any other site of force would have likewise radiated and made visible the repeating pattern and infinite extension of the grid. Nonhierarchical, boundless, the grid's pattern is one of extending distribution and total saturation. The abyss is in this way double and self-contradicting: at once empty (full of nothing, negative space, a bottomless ex-

---

graphic elements. The hexagonal grid is the minimally present form whose extension induces a maximal (optimal) sufficiency and density of tessellated space.

xxii. In "The Honeycomb Conjecture," the paper giving a general proof of the proposal that "any partition of the plane into regions of equal area has perimeter at least that of the regular hexagonal honeycomb tiling," Thomas C. Hales goes so far as to write, "In part because of the isoperimetric property of the honeycomb, there is a vast literature throughout the centuries mentioning the bee as a geometer."

pansive pit; the *Afgrund*, without ground, void) and entirely full (completely saturated by the form of the grid); it is the empty set, empty, which is to say *nothing*, what is open to nothing and exposes and frames it, and yet it is also still a set, also, that is to say, *something*.

As a form, hexagonal tessellation is one of general optimality and economy. One of the curious foundations for the honeycomb conjecture in its invocation in biology is that its starting place involves a presumption of scarcity,[xxiii] an anxiogenic relation to issues of quantity: it rests on the assumption that, as the philosopher of mathematics Mark Colyvan words it, "bees have a limited supply of wax and need to conserve it while maximising honey storage space." In other words, "hives built under such constraints *must* have a hexagonal structure."[22] But what constraint induces the hexagonal structure of the grid that Curt encounters? It is a constraint of system, not sugar. What is in limited supply is not storage for honey but the stowage of the image. The restrictive system is the boundedness of framing, the parameters of screen, a limitation to the visual extension of space, which comes to a finite end in the material ground of the mediated image. Put another way: what constrains is cinematic form itself. The solution for which is also formal. Because the grid is a schema of maximal density, the full saturation of its formal properties and capacities is not only enabled by the finitude of screen but required by it. The regular hexagon—marked by the highest degree of symmetry, in both equilateral and equiangular directions—does not represent but unconceals optimal saturation, with neither noise nor error, and with no lack or vulnerability, no possibility of failure. Because the hexagonal repeat pattern is a problem of intensity and density given via the problem of measurement, it names the general abstraction of any model of maximal extension. *It does not geometrically, which is to say graphically, which is to say formally, admit a possibility of getting off or evading the seamless extension of this grid.* This negation is the positive condition for the grid within the constraints of cinematic form.

Cabin in the Woods makes a geometric-aesthetic study of the arrangement of the grid; its formalism is, properly, an investigation, an exploration of

---

xxiii. Darwin describes the structure thusly in *The Origin of Species*, in a passage lavishly praising the hive-bee: "The motive power of the process of natural selection having been economy of wax; that individual swarm which wasted least honey in the secretion of wax, having succeeded best, and having transmitted by inheritance its newly acquired economical instinct to new swarms, which in their turn will have had the best chance of succeeding in the struggle for existence."

the properties of these arranged lines—of which the frontal view is only one among the infinite potential perspectives that framing might have, and yet did not—but yet might have—provided. Obliquity does not evade the totalization of grid—that the infinite extension of line is coextensive with a violence that will not fail to be All—but it does introduce a possible second-order transposition: it submits the possibility that other forms will be co-present *with* this form, that those forms will mutually affect each other, setting loose speculative possibilities belonging to neither realm alone. Which is to say that it is not the case that discrete forms are lodged in *Cabin in the Woods* (ready in wait like so many underbed threats) so much as the film itself is a tessellation of dispersed, yet interacting, complex, and mutually affecting and mutually interpreting forms, which themselves generate and give rise to further ones. This horror film in its own large-scale formal structure is itself a network, a number of systems themselves connected in a grid topology in which individual aspects of the large-scale form are connected via others in multiple and distributed dimensions.

The film's formalism is a hyperformalism. These forms reciprocally interact, rendering multiple, unstable, unpredictable, in-flux new forms. Accordingly, the text itself is a model of the absolute necessity of a radical formalism. In its staging of forms interpreting and engaging with other forms to generate unforeseen possibilities, it gives rise to a nonanthropomorphic, antihumanist model in which forms and structures speculatively grapple with other logics, including those of violence and endingness—and do all this solely in and via the realm of the aesthetic. All the theoretical terms in play—possibility, not-All, being All, finitude, infinitude, indifference, impersonality, offness, failure, selection (the someone else, the another, to be given a chance; the *You shouldn't be here*; the *This should have gone differently*)—every one of which is essential for any thinking of ethics and violence in *Cabin in the Woods*, and all of which are equally essential for any thinking of the versions of critique (accelerationist, antifutural) with which the film sympathizes—require nothing other than lingering with and extravagantly reading the geometries and forms and structures that themselves theorize, encounter, and give rise to these very terms. The seriousness of every speculative claim about these stakes will derive *from* a resolutely formalist approach—not despite it.

Cabin in the Woods is thus not to be read from the point of view of an applied, secondary formalism that engenders speculative thought about an ethics of violence, force, destruction. Rather, the film *is* a formalism that engenders speculative thought about a violence that *it itself* regards wholly formally.

The seamlessness of the hexagonal repeat pattern, such that there are no gaps in coverage, no margin for error, no offness—it *does something*; there *is* nothing—itself is the radical formalism of optimal violence, one that is indifferent to the representational world, glimpsed only in moments of co-presence and mutual affection. This second grid is what invites the comparison of the divergent senses of the word: as what stands for force, power, discipline, surveillance, extensive bureaucratic manipulation, and what takes material-graphic shape as a network of lines and the properties of a form under varying conditions and constraints. Getting off of the first grid is a matter of subject positioning as a question of technological inscription and its possible successful evasion; but hitting the grid is a question of displacement to other parts of a formal field with no possibility for evasion. Marty's avowed triumph is exposed as only ever an illusion: grid as line emphasizes the *thereisness* and the coercions of the grid.

However, there is no "the" grid.

Rather, it is more apt to say that cinematic language takes the optimality of the isoperimetric honeycomb form and actively subverts it, deploying the cinematic potential of framing to feign a honeycomb that would in fact take unequal lengths and cede its relation to total saturation—torquing the grid in order to morph its regular form into something mutable, unpredictable, visually dynamic—only to brutally reassert the idealism of the form in the single frontal point of view that reiterates the optimal tessellation of the grid. If the rigidity of grid remains on the side of violence—that system is inclusive—the dynamism of the grid is purely located in the realm by which cinematic form visually, extensibly, geometrically negotiates the form of the grid. That its lines extend beyond the edges of the cinematic image suggests that the former is not completely contained within the latter but extends beyond the margins of the work.

What puts pressure on grid, what attempts to imagine it as not-All, is thus a secondary navigation: cinematic form, whose framing and reframing and canted and oblique lines and angles induce a speculation of the possible not-Allness of the grid. Cinematic language is thus not in collusion with the totalization of grid form; rather, it deploys framing to continually reapproach its offlessness. The Allness of the grid, its infinite extension, its diagrammatic obliteration of offness, is the givenness of a violence that is unavoidable, that unimpeachably reasserts itself, that is assertive. There is no—and there never will be any—*off the grid*: or, rather, what is off the grid is yet another grid:[xxiv] an

xxiv. If the grid of cinematic form is one[xx] of the grids off the grid—such that there is no *off the grid*—there are two main others: the betting table*** and the matrix**** of glass cubes from which alternative selections for the agent of scenario's violence might have been selected. Horror arrives in a world already interceded by form, what gives rise to the condition of possibility for violence to at least potentially be All, even if any given selection fails to be All. The (grid, table***, matrix****, bank of cells) is not a metaphor* that would function as a fixed symbol for "culture industry" or "horror film"; rather, these forms are the manipulation of flexibility and infinitude that formalizes the radical impersonality of different, other, potential selections.**

> * Nothing is underneath or behind the grid, it does not loan or transfer its sense to anything else[+]; the grid is only its formal extension and optimal saturation. This is the law of insisting that the grid not be taken as metaphor. Grid taken as metaphor is the grid mistaken for *monster*: as demonstrating, displaying, warning, showing a figurative sign of an elsewhere, prior, external X (power, the scope of disciplinary society, &c.). Rather, the grid is monstration without a referring system of signs: it does not demonstrate or show something else, it is the (infra)structure that it is. The film thus follows the course of modern psychoanalysis, attesting to a replacement of mythology with topology: like Lacan's Möbius strip, Klein bottle, cross-cap, or Borromean knots, structure is neither illustration nor metaphor nor convenient heuristic, example, or pedagogical tool: structure does neither more nor less than manifest the structure that the structure is.

> > [+] The Greek *metapherein*, to transfer, carry over; to change or alter; from *meta*, over, across; from *pherein*, to carry or produce or convey.[^]

> > > [^] also, "to bear children" (cf. *matrix*, der. from *mater****)

> ** Take, as just one example of that formalization, the table***: what is nothing else but its capacity to add, grow, subtract, exchange, and the linkages and relations between possibilities that it puts into play. The table is different from metaphor* because its flat, dehierarchized form does not transfer meaning to other sites, but attests to the indifferent selection between an array of possible cells, as one is as present as equally as another. It holds in place the refusal to subordinate one sense to another by the form's blank, flat, dehierarchized insistence on any cell's possibility of being selected. The table, put another way, is *metaphor rewritten from the standpoint of geometry*—metaphor without the modification of meaning: a *transfer* of diagrammatic position, a *change* or *alteration* in coordinates that is, however, neutral to any conversion of sense.

> *** What is a table, generally? And what is a table, precisely, here, in which it names

orthogonal extensive one that forecloses the routes of egress or evasion that the former holds out as lure. The grid is exposed as a strident flatness: nothing under or behind, just extension of line and pattern. Violence ultimately, unavoidably, definitively arrives. And yet, in the midst of this, the possibility of a not-

the whiteboard written up to track the parimutuel betting of the bureaucrats and chemists and maintenance workers and interns in the downstairs level? And how is any table, or this particular table, like or unlike a matrix****, a database, a grid? For one, *table* is the oldest of the words, the twelfth-century slab or board or plate (as in *tabula*: plank; writing table; but also list, picture, panel). From the tablet of stone, what bears inscription (as in laws; commandments—those of Solon, those of Moses), by the fourteenth century it will mean "arrangement of numbers or other figures on a tabular surface for convenience" and by the fifteenth, well, a great deal more,+ and with convenience duly set aside. The table shares with the matrix**** the formal property of the display of data from a data set into cells++ that are organized in rows and columns that are flexible and not predetermined.

FIGURE 3.5. *The Cabin in the Woods* (Drew Goddard, 2011)

The whiteboard table of betting options is a coordination of two sets of variables: the choice selection of monstrosity linked to objects available as possible sources of horror in the cabin basement (Dismemberment Goblins, The Scarecrow Folk, The Bride, &c.), and in a corresponding, chromatically variable register, wagering on that contingent selection by a department or designation of a collective (Data Archives, Zoology, Engineering, &c.). Some selections are not claimed; others are claimed twice,+++ a growth in collective membership that proportionally minimizes the value of such a selection. This table is resonant with its usage in computing, per the *Oxford English Dictionary*: "A collection of data organized in a notional set of rows and columns; *spec.* one stored in memory in the form of a series of records each of which has a unique key stored with it," each unique key here being a different selection of possible sources of horror from the larger data set of all

All neutral to violence but that can at least speculate a future beyond or *oblique* to violence is given in the cinematic formal navigation of grid form. And yet, even so, however, cinematic form is also, of course, constrained by its own debt to finitude: the ineluctable assertiveness of line at the border of the image.

---

possible agents of violence (which is to say: anything that could properly be called an *agent* at all). The whiteboard table notates the possible betting options for the contingent selection of the means by which these particular adolescents will particularly die in this particular scenario (which retains its unexceptional status at this point, despite the fact that it will be exceptional, above all, for failing to be All, for therefore being the last and final—the last and final being what is not like anything else precisely for its foreclosure of another selection or a different choice or someone else's possible turn at a contingent particularity).

+ *table*, fifteenth century, "a systematic arrangement of numbers, words, symbols, etc., in a definite and compact form so as to show clearly some set of facts or relations; esp. an arrangement in rows and columns, typically occupying a single page or sheet. Formerly occasionally: an orderly^ arrangement^^ of particulars,^^^ a list; a list of rivals or competitors showing their positions relative to one another, arranged in descending order of ranking; a league table"; "details in a concise form; a synopsis, a conspectus"; a sketch,^^^^ a plan, a model.

^ Then again, tables being what are so often *turned*.

^^ Tables being what are regularly *set*.‡

‡ Then again then again, tables being what are so often turned.

^^^ Table: the conjunction of image and law. If a statement of particulars, is there such a thing at all as a table in general?***

^^^^ *Tabula*: a board or plank, a writing table, a picture, one painted panel; that small flat slab just *waiting*, waiting like a waiting woman waits: waiting for writing, or for writing that might come again after the writing marks that did come were expunged. *Rasa*, fem. past participle of *radere*, to scrape away, erase. Proto-Indo-European roots meaning to scrape or scratch also mean to gnaw, to eat away, to abrade, corrode, *destroy*.

++ a small room in a monastery, a small monastery, a small room; a store room, a hut, a unit of a prison or asylum, a compartment, a grave; an excavated cavity, a chamber in a building, "typically intended for or inhabited by a single person": hence a form of isolation, restriction, separation, individuation, a form of not-togetherness, not-with, not-among, not-many^; what results from dividing a surface by linear partitions, cutting it up, breaking it down; and all those small rooms in a monastery, small monasteries, small rooms, from *cella*, from *celare*, to hide, conceal, via the *kel-* tree of terms for cover, conceal, save from exposure, shield from big and public spaces, share this root, also, as well, with *shame*. (The latter also is, or at least can be, a way of dividing a larger structure.)

This sequence of the encounter of body and grid is thus not a narrative climax in which escape is thwarted and hope devastated for a subject so much as it is a *formal climax* in which cinematic form—and nothing else—interprets the form of the grid, which is given as a series of formal attestations. The vi-

---

^ In relation to the whiteboard table, the bureaucrats have formed a betting *pool*: what puts resources into common stock, what is shared in common‡ and combined for common benefit. The money collated forms a collective stake, and in the particular case of the particular selection from the particular choice made by the particular protagonists in this particular scenario, the dividends must be shared, split further, put in common even after the winner has undone the being-in-common of the pool with its redistribution of the common benefit to the new benefit of only a few.

‡ What is shared most in common in *Cabin in the Woods*, what puts in common the All of humanity, is the endingness of humanity: the purest form of being-with at the instant of the annihilation of (all) being, and thus of withness too.

+++ This table induces overt disagreements about what it means to be chosen once versus to be chosen twice. At the reading of the Latin^ from Patience Buckner's diary and the corresponding selection of the Zombie Redneck Torture Family, won and thus split by maintenance and Ronald the Intern, Sitterson points to the winning tabular cell, this finger functioning as an index to the interpretability of table and thus game; he later extends both hands in deictic^^ function to distinguish, to a voiced objection, the categorical distinction^^^ of Zombies from the Zombie Redneck Torture Family, insisting they are not the same (in other words, that a choosing of one is not a choosing of two).

^ Via this Latin book, *Cabin in the Woods* can be regarded as a showdown between the *grimoire* and the *grammaire*: between an account of violence as ineluctably, necessarily bonded to ancient ritual and its invocation through the bad book of magic spells (what the reading of the Latin performs as source of horror; what is recognizable, which is to say grounds for laughter, in Marty's protestation, "I'm drawing a line‡ in the fucking sand here. Do not read the Latin!") versus a grammar of horror, a general study of the morphological properties and rules by which (any) ordering of horror is possible, of which the grimoire is merely the contingent one in this particular scenario—such that any other would have functioned *syntactically* as equivalent.

‡ Marty here is voicing the essential logic of the cinematic◊: the film, *formally*, being nothing but the multiple drawing of various modes of lines.

◊ And not for the first time. Though Dana's reading of the diary calls up the particular violence of the Buckners, which will ultimately fail as local scenario to be All, it is the case that the film honors the law

olence of violence is speculatively available solely at the site at which *form is reading form*. But there is an additional movement, and thus it would be more appropriate to write that the film is (cinematically) formalizing a (cinematic) formalizing of (grid) form. It is *formalizing formalizing form*. This reflexive

---

of violence whereby the victims choose how they die by way of the object in the cabin basement with which they most robustly interact. For Marty, the figure who ultimately decides how he (and Dana, and all who are) will die, touches the object that is ultimately successful in bringing about the violence that is All: he unspools a roll of celluloid. And it is ultimately the film itself that will kill off human life in its need for a violence that is sufficiently All that its representational on-goingness can finally end.

^^ *Deixis*, to the letter, a drawing attention to something by means of point-ing (a reference by way of gesture by way of body, specifically by way of extending digit) is one of a network of interests in the film in the question of the hand, including the fingertip delicacy of rolling a joint, the caressing of hands against the pelt of an open-mawed stuffed wolf, hands whaling on glass in furious rage: and it is, of course, the touching—the picking up and turning, the holding, flipping, playing, sorting, stretching, unspooling of the objects in the basement that determines the arbitrary selection of the nonarbitrary manner of future death. The hand is more abstractly but no less powerfully invoked at the Director's explanation of the ritual's reliance on ancient archetypes of the Whore, the Athlete, the Scholar, the Fool, the Virgin. To Dana's rejoinder that she is not in possession of the requisite vir-ginity, the Director replies, "We work with what we have"; there is, in other words, an exploitation of what is available, a naming of the essentially im-provisatory form of *bricolage*,‡ the using of materials *found at hand*.‡‡ This artisanal inheritance of media and materials useful for being proximate, for being ready to use, for serendipitously appearing for use, also, of course, is reminiscent of the *mise-en-abîme* ontologies, intertextual references, found footage splicing (on the bank of screens of other national scenarios) and slurry of signs‡‡‡ that is *Cabin in the Woods*, not inventing concepts ab ovo, but using the generic, textual tools of those who have come before, which carry with them traces of their past cinematic appearances and which pro-duce the disarranged, even chaotic and cluttered effect of the film as a prox-imity of different periods and styles (Lovecraftian mythology set alongside contemporary surveillance technologies, &c.‡‡‡‡).

‡ Lévi-Strauss, *The Savage Mind*: "In its old sense the verb 'bricoler' applied to ball games and billiards, to hunting, shooting and riding. It was however always used with reference to some extraneous movement: a ball rebounding, a dog straying or a horse swerving from its direct

multi-meta-formalism bears out the obligatoriness of the grid—the brutal and radical impersonality of its thereisness, its assertion, extension, and inescapability—while simultaneously speculating through the canting of line, and in a mode that is itself indifferent to violence, about the possibility, just the mur-

---

course to avoid an obstacle. And in our own time the 'bricoleur' is still someone who works with his hands and uses devious means compared to those of a craftsman."

‡‡ Lévi-Strauss, continued. Of the *bricoleur*, "His universe of instruments is closed◊ and the rules of his game are always to make do with 'whatever is at hand,' that is to say with a set of tools and materials which is always finite and is also heterogeneous because what it contains bears no relation to the current project, or indeed to any particular project, but is the contingent result of all the occasions there have been to renew or enrich the stock or to maintain it with the remains of previous constructions or destruction."

◊ a universe, we might say, without stars

‡‡‡ Lévi-Strauss, continued: "Both the scientist and 'bricoleur' might therefore be said to be constantly on the look out for 'messages.' Those which the 'bricoleur' collects are, however, ones which have to some extent been transmitted in advance."◊

◊ Derrida, "Structure, Sign, and Play in the Discourse of the Human Sciences": "If one calls bricolage the necessity of borrowing one's concepts from the text of a heritage which is more or less coherent or ruined, it must be said that every discourse is *bricoleur*."

‡‡‡‡ cf. Evocations of the *Twilight Zone*'s "Five Characters in Search of an Exit."◊ Enclosed in that cylinder: "Clown, hobo, ballet dancer, bagpiper, and an army major—a collection of question marks. Five improbable entities stuck together into a pit of darkness. No logic, no reason, no explanation; just a prolonged nightmare in which fear, loneliness, and the unexplainable walk hand in hand through the shadows. In a moment, we'll start collecting clues as to the whys, the whats, and the wheres. We will not end the nightmare, we'll only explain it—because this is the Twilight Zone."

◊ cf. Pirandello's *Six Characters in Search of an Author*.§

§ cf. Baudelaire, Poe, Baudelaire's translations of Poe (i.e., modernism<)

< cf. German aesthetic theory's influence on modernism>

> cf. &c.

^^^ Nothing but a manic proliferation of multiple distinctions: that is what the film multiply is :: Japan versus the United States; failure versus success;

muring possibility, of a different configuration, which itself will remain uncertain and yet will have been momentarily conceivable, which is to say imaginable, which is to say visible, as what something yet nothing, thinnest lines of light, from a certain angle, and except for the briefest of moments, has revealed.

---

upstairs versus downstairs; ancient versus modern; enough versus not enough; first as opposed to last; grid but not table; the virgin or the whore; being from a nightmare and being that which nightmares are from; &c. Truman, the new security guard who arrives for this particular scenario's run, whose appearance allows occasions for pedagogy and explanation (of the ritual; of the betting pool), declares that he has been "prepped" for what will occur during the ritual, to which Hadley responds, "Did they tell you that being prepped is not the same thing as being prepared?" *Prepped*, as in trained, practiced, made ready for, versus *prepared*, brought into a condition for some future action, inclined or disposed beforehand; the one more a matter of habitus, the other a state of mental readiness; the one a preliminary to a trial, the other an able adaptation to precisely what one was not given to be expected as a preliminary to that very same trial.‡

‡ *Use the distinction in a sentence*: one can be *prepped* for violence (as trained in response, as likelihood for which one is ready); one is never *prepared* for violence (as its wrecking work works by failing to arrive as the future action one expects).

**** A matrix is the specific type of structured grid that stores or displays data.+ The dimensional structured format that displays the raw data of horror's agency—the "not something from a nightmare," but the "something nightmares are from"—is the downstairs-level bank of glass cubes that extends in all directions, each cube/cell containing an individual figure for violence, materializing the abstraction of selection, the another, another chance, contingency, the indifference of the selection of violence (violence *formally* unapproachable without the concept of *selection*) against the nonneutral difference of a scenario (any scenario) that succeeds and the particular one that catastrophically fails. (Unlike the table's column-row logic of expansion constrained by the finitude of the edges of the whiteboard, this extension exceeds the boundaries of cinematic frame, suggesting the ongoingness of list, which is to say: infinitude.) This glass cube matrix is in motion, endlessly unfolding new forms of adjacency: the cells slide, push, recede, project, they reorder themselves—hyper and frenzied, they are *energized*, rushing toward and away from the spectator, up and down and left and right. Less Sol LeWitt *Color Grids, Using Straight, Not-Straight, and Broken Lines in All Vertical & Horizontal Combinations*, more Aleksandr Rodchenko *Hanging Spatial Construction*; less Carl Andre, more Sarah Morris. That violence is particular and discrete, each agent isolated in a cell, is clear from the mode of egress: the "access drop"++ in which any one of these cells—or, ultimately, many of them at once—are moved either to the upstairs of the downstairs (the cabin-level world) or to the center of the downstairs (the control-level world). Marty and Dana themselves are trapped in a cube, shown to also be a selection, an option, an alternative for the origin of violence—and, indeed, they are the ones who, if they fail to be All in the ritual sacrifice logic of local appeasement violence, do successfully bring about the violence that is All through that very failure, demonstrating once more that there is no outside to the grid,[xxiv] which here is the same thing as declaring that there is no possible position that is located beyond the extensive structure of violence.

FIGURE 3.6. *The Cabin in the Woods* (Drew Goddard, 2011)

+ For this reason, among others, the term *matrix* is often used synonymously[^] with *table*.***

[^] While a matrix, which structures data by storing and displaying it, can have horizontal rows and vertical columns exactly like a table, it can also, by being a broader term for the storing and display of data, take and store and display said data in a range of forms.[‡]

‡ Accordingly, matrices are generally considered far more flexible[◊] than tables[◊◊]; the latter conventionally has a set number of those horizontal rows and vertical columns, whereas a matrix may vary in size dynamically, even name a table with multiple columns within a single row, to which new rows and new columns may infinitely—which is to say not destroying form, difference (variation, alteration, newness) being what *enables form* and what *form enables*—be added.

◊ Uterus, womb, origin, in the fourteenth century, from the Latin *matrix*, pregnant animal, or put another way: from *mater*, mother.[§]

"Place or medium where something is developed," "supporting or enclosing structure," and only centuries later, an "array§§ of possible combinations of truth-values."

§ A film about a mother who will no matter what not be a mother despite wanting, we are told, very badly to become, to be a mother, adjacent to a formal matrix that cannot help but be a matrix: source of some form being originated and produced; the other, not and never.

§§ "What is found at the historical beginning of things is not the inviolable identity of their origin; it is the dissension of other things. It is disparity." (Foucault, "Nietzsche, Genealogy, History")

◊◊ As a verb, *to* table, also, of course, is to postpone consideration of a matter or a resolution, to shelve§ what had just moments before been *on* the table, to entomb in a drawer, for the sake of another urgency, and also to do so indefinitely.

§ *Table*: what is submitted in the same gesture by which it is put aside.

++ This language of *access* a further bond of matrix to database,^ which is likewise a structured set of data, with the added sense, however, of what is accessed or manipulated by means of software. Databases are systems; they above all have to be *managed*.

^ Itself from the twelfth-century *base*, "a notional structure or entity conceived of as underlying‡ some system of activity or operations; the resources on which something draws or depends for its operation."

‡ What lies *under* the system of activity that is the film's resolutely vertical structure, what builds upward from the manipulative bureaucrats to the sacrificed youths, is, of course, the lowest reach of malevolent ancients, whose formal register of satisfaction or its un- is the wall-carved figures of the archetypes of sacrifice—the Whore, the Athlete, the Scholar, the Fool, the Virgin—whose indented outlines◊ do or do not fill with sufficient blood-as-pigment.

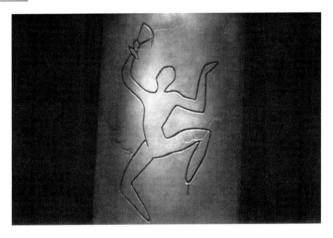

FIGURE 3.7. *The Cabin in the Woods* (Drew Goddard, 2011), detail.

◊ The carvings, formally minimalist, maximally restrictive (literal enclosures for some quantity of something that flows), minimally ornamental yet maximally differentiated, resemble the aesthetic technique of intaglio.§

§ Intaglio, more precisely, names a range of techniques, including etching and drypoint, but their common denominator is that an image is engraved< or incised<< into a hard surface and the sunken register, for example in printmaking, holds the ink. This image type is the opposite of sunken relief—the sculptural technique that removes the background (e.g., of wood or stone), lowering the field against which the sculptured material appears to be raised, and which required and was bonded to the vicissitudes of sunlight, exploiting strong light to reveal hard-edged outlines and shifting shadow formations. By contrast, in this subterranean world, a world without sun, these spare depressions take on no depth: they cast no shadows (cf. the aboveground being a world without stars). Not the elevations of relief (*relevo*: to raise), these thin trails thus constitute yet another of the film's sunken forms, a minimal descent or declension from plane, here of material, homology to staircase, elevator, subordinated narrative levels, temporal pastness, &c. The intagliated hollows of these faceless outlines, eyeless and blank, instead are filled with a coursing forking blood—or they are not, as in the case of a violence that fails because it is not-All, in which blood is redescribed as insufficient pigment, inadequacy in relation to depth and reach of pigment, the violence that is not-All a catastrophe of border and hollow and line. What is chiseled into stone each time are continuous contours defining the basic shape of a human body but with stylized variations in pose and gesture: each figure is erect but in a contorted posture: a leg raised in leaping merriment; a head downbowed in modesty. There is an exhaustion of line within the constraint of a local system (which is to say line rejoins with itself, is not a broken or segmented line: one that might, in material terms, spill or leak its stuff). A graphic generality exists in the carvings: figures that play with the form of the human but are resolutely working through a process of abstraction, reducing the complexity of the anthropomorphic to the simplest possible morphic forms. These outlines sit alongside equally simplified tropic forms, for each continuous line of each carving makes a diagram of the body's formal bond to objects (to fabric, to dress, to spear, to book and pen), thus showing the human form as *in* culture, as *in* history, as *in* the world—as static and drawn (i.e., as dead), but as writing, fighting, seducing, refusing (i.e., as alive). Figures, but figures who do things. Who do specific things. And do not do others. And who soon do nothing else. Human life in its vital and interactive and relational liveliness is transposed, that is, to nothing but line, line made hollow tube, hollowness made nothing but map for the trajectory of any dark fluid. Line not merely the medium of drawing, not extension or Euclid's "breadthless depth"; here line is converted into channel edging the promise of the open: that in which something courses, runs, goes. In which something circulates or goes in a new, different direction, which is to say: goes somewhere where it is currently not.

< from *grave*, v., to dig, to scratch, to scrape; n., an excavation in earth; both from *gravis*, what is heavy, loaded, burdensome, teeming, distended>

> lit. and fig.: pregnant

<< *incisus*, to cut into, as in stone or marble, or as in skin, as in surgery; what may, therefore, at some future point, far off or perhaps sooner than expected, require a few carefully placed stitches>

> a prick, a puncture, a stab; sudden local pain; but also contortions of laughter; a single motion in sewing; or the movement of a needle through the edges of a wound—

Two Violences

↓

Not genre, never again genre—but perhaps (possibly) the general.

A general distinction: there is a violence of *consumption*; there is a violence of *digestion*.

The violence of consumption takes in, absorbs, exhausts; it devastates some resource. This is the violence of burning and dissipation, draining and squandering, to bleed or milk or just suck dry; from the Latin *consumptio* and *consumere*, "to use up, eat, waste."

You consume me really means *You waste me*.

Eating, the preeminent activity of the ruining work of consumption: ingestion, intake, uptake, the deglutition of liquid and imbibing; respiratory labor and depletions' expenditures; and of course the devouring maw, the insatiable hunger of the lip-licking consumer, falls to this logic as well. What we are talking about when we talk about violence is usually this violence, and its broader notions of possession and destruction—a greedy gulping incorporation, a complete eradication, a wolfing *down*, a cramming *in*, a finishing *off*—all rely on embodied oral violence, and the sense that ingested food is the preeminent assimilable, expendable object, for its metaphorical capital. Or consider Fassbinder's *Angst essen Seele auf.* Is there any doubt that one is speaking of total extinction here? *Essen*—so transparent, so powerful a word, its meaning survives the broken grammatical distortion of *Fear Eat Soul Up*.

The violence of digestion is of an altogether different order. Digestion— from *digerere*, "to separate, divide, arrange"—suggests the activity of breaking down through mechanical or enzymatic action into substances for use, a conversion that promotes better assimilation through fragmentation; a taking apart into constituent elements in place of a using up, and often a release of new energies, as in the metabolic breakdown that occurs during catabolism—we might say: not annihilating, but creating. The privileged form of this decomposing violence is the assimilation of food in the bowels—assimilation as *function*, a conversion, a softening or dissolving, an arrangement that involves a rearrangement, a mode of analysis, even the elegant labors of codification that are the complex alimentary system.

In short: Ingurgitation obliterates its objects, while peptic action systematizes its objects. Consumptive aesthetics: what deploys form to *devastate* its objects (which may include bodies, which themselves are also forms). Digestive aesthetics: what deploys form to *arrange* its objects (which may include bodies, which themselves are also forms). Pain, domination, depredation, ruination, brutalization, obliteration, negation, the destructuring that Heidegger means by *Abbau*—a total dismantling of the layers of some system—on the one hand; and, on the other, procedurals, schematization, testing and sorting, positioning, ranking, measuring, classifying, grouping, filing, distributing, organizing; the writing of assembly languages, index notations, all array logics; the force of putting into place the formal extent of structures.

A. A violent order is a disorder; and

B. A great disorder is an order. These

Two things are one. (Pages of illustrations.)

—WALLACE STEVENS, "Connoisseur of Chaos"

how it was I quote before Pim with Pim after Pim how it is
three parts I say it as I hear it

— SAMUEL BECKETT, *How It Is*

The identification of the same in the "I" is not produced as
a monotonous tautology: I am I. The originality of identification, irreducible to the A is A formalism, would thus
escape attention.

— EMMANUEL LEVINAS, *Totality and Infinity*

And I only am, I can only be, I *must* only be starting from
this strange, dislocated bearing of the infinitely other in me.
I must carry the other, and carry *you*, the other must carry
me [. . .], even there where the world is no longer between
us or beneath our feet, no longer ensuring mediation or
reinforcing a foundation for us. I am alone with the other,
alone to him and for him, only for you, that is, yours: without world. I am left with the immediacy of the abyss that
engages me on behalf of the other wherever the "I must" —
"I must carry you" — forever prevails over the "I am."

— JACQUES DERRIDA, *Rams*

It was a humorously perilous business for both of us. For, before we proceed further, it must be said that the monkey-rope was fast at both ends; fast to Queequeg's broad canvas belt, and fast to my narrow leather one. So that for better or for worse, we two, for the time, were wedded; and should poor Queequeg sink to rise no more, then both usage and honor demanded, that instead of cutting the cord, it should drag me down in his wake. So, then, an elongated Siamese ligature united us. Queequeg was my own inseparable twin brother; nor could I any way get rid of the dangerous liabilities which the hempen bond entailed.

So strongly and metaphysically did I conceive of my situation then, that while earnestly watching his motions, I seemed distinctly to perceive that my own individuality was now merged in a joint stock company of two; that my free will had received a mortal wound; and that another's mistake or misfortune might plunge innocent me into unmerited disaster and death. Therefore, I saw that here was a sort of interregnum in Providence; for its even-handed equity never could have sanctioned so gross an injustice. And yet still further pondering—while I jerked him now and then from between the whale and ship, which would threaten to jam him—still further pondering, I say, I saw that this situation of mine was the precise situation of every mortal that breathes; only, in most cases, he, one way or other, has this Siamese connexion with a plurality of other mortals. If your banker breaks, you snap; if your apothecary by mistake sends you poison in your pills, you die. True, you may say that, by exceeding caution, you may possibly escape these and the multitudinous other evil chances of life. But handle Queequeg's monkey-rope heedfully as I would, sometimes he jerked it so, that I came very near sliding overboard. Nor could I possibly forget that, do what I would, I only had the management of one end of it.

—HERMAN MELVILLE, *Moby-Dick*

Ivan Ilyich asked Gerasim to sit down and hold his feet and he had a talk with him. And it was strange, but it seemed to him that he felt better while Gerasim was holding his feet.

—LEO TOLSTOY, "The Death of Ivan Ilyich"

The mute conversation which, holding the hand of "another who dies," "I" keep up with him, I don't keep up simply to help him die, but to share the solitude of the event which seems to be the possibility that is most his own and his un-shareable possession in that it dispossesses him radically.

—MAURICE BLANCHOT, *The Unavowable Community*

Death is the death of other people.

—EMMANUEL LEVINAS, "The Other in Proust"

thus our life in common we begin it

—SAMUEL BECKETT, *How It Is*

Monday

Me.

Tuesday

Me.

Wednesday

Me.

Thursday

Me.

— the famous opening of the first volume of
WITOLD GOMBROWICZ's *Diary*

:

And so:

Being or relating, that is the whole question.

—MICHEL SERRES, *Le Parasite*

I is I.
A is A.
B is B.
A, B, C.

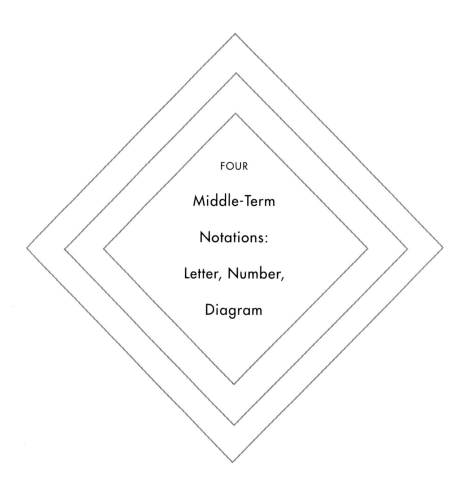

FOUR

Middle-Term

Notations:

Letter, Number,

Diagram

The *fistula in ano*, an infected tunnel that connects the anal canal and a secondary opening in the skin, that external perianal opening which may be visible, and which usually results from anorectal pustules that produce the hollow damp antrum, the cavity that will have to be evaluated for depth and extent of the tract, and from which built-up debris renders (as in hot oil, tried from the fat; as in presenting for inspection or consideration; as in payment due, as though a tribute) a foul-smelling drainage and thin yellow exudate, a bloody brown percolation from the blocked septic glands, a forced draining in another organ that may allow feces to pass to the skin, & note it can be chronic, and of course, once ruptured, what is suppurating results also in swelling and chills and great pain ("a nice little abscess will form, with an idea inside, point of departure for a general infection," promises Beckett in *The Unnamable*), usually requires, as abscesses generally do, some form of surgery. And when the fourteenth-century English surgeon John of Arderne details his technique for treating anal fistulae in his definitive treatise on the subject—his *Practica* the first medieval surgical manuscript to be accompanied by copious illustrations of operations in hundreds of colorful marginalia, at the limit of linguistic description, carefully coordinated with the text but aiming to move from the word to show the fistulous holes, the curing needle going into the tender mouth of the "depe wonde," or, in the most spectacular example, one that replaces procedure with affect, the pain of the *iliaca passio* in a twisted spiral, depicting not the guts but the observer's speculation of their agony—he writes, as a preliminary to the image, each time carefully writes, the Latin phrase for *as is here shown*.[1]

Sicut hic depingitur:

I. (DETAIL)

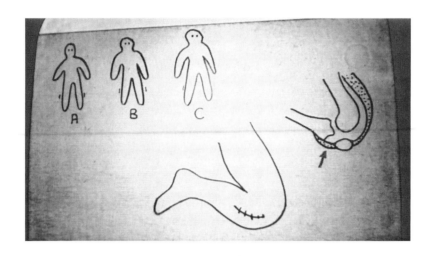

II.

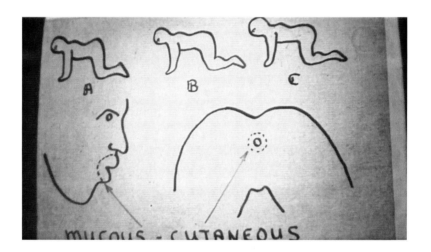

III.

IV.

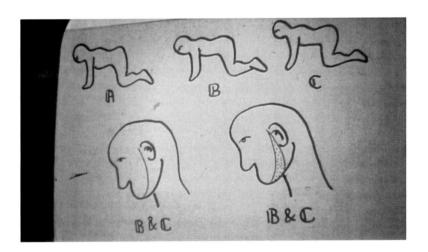

V.

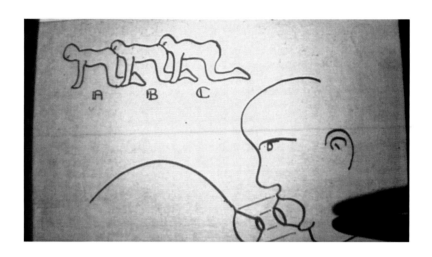

VI.

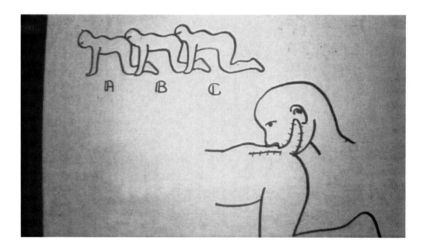

VII.

The conceit of Tom Six's *The Human Centipede (First Sequence)* (2009) is simple enough to describe, and surely that simplicity accounts for some of the extreme reactions generated by the film and its sequels, *The Human Centipede II (Full Sequence)* (2011) and *The Human Centipede III (Final Sequence)* (2015). A German doctor named Joseph Heiter, an expert in the act of separating conjoined twins, has become obsessed with creation in place of destruction. Having previously sewn together what he calls "mein lieber Dreihund," but having lost the three-dog creature to death, he acquires new bodies, two American girls and a Japanese man, to fashion a human centipede through the methodology that rendered the franchise infamous: a surgical procedure that joins multiple bodies into a single alimentary canal—anus to mouth, anus to mouth—in order to make possible the unwilling progression of, as Heiter pronounces: "A Siamese triplet connected via the gastric system. Ingestion by A, passing through B, to the excretion of C."

There is little more to *The Human Centipede* than this technique of brutal sequencing—the text is consumed with the thing that the title names. But the film is invested less in the historicity of the made or its becoming than in the investigation of the *Dingheit* of the thing. Thus, the actual surgery (and its pretext for spectacular specular gore) is largely elided, eager as the film is to indulge a fascination with how the novel composite figure will move, act, eat, shit—which is to say how the abstractions of parts A, B, and C will relate to the constructed whole.[2] This having been accomplished, the film ends perfunctorily. A too-quick resolution brings two police officers into the house only to be killed by Heiter at the same instant they kill him, right before which figure A slits his throat as an act of rebellion and right after which figure C, rigid hand entwined with the friend whose spine is her horizon, dies from an infected wound, the flankflesh already gunmetal gray. And so, the film ends on the weeping and hysterical middle-term figure, Lindsay—or, rather, B—alive, attached to death from the front and to death behind, and in a house with no more living figures, either those who would torture, those who might save, or those desperate others who suffer with her.[3]

This being alive while being riveted to the dead is a fate inextricably bound up with the cultural imaginary of the conjoined body, most famously in the case of Chang and Eng Bunker, the nineteenth-century brothers who were the source of the term *Siamese twins* after their exhibition on a global curiosity tour. One morning in 1874, when they were in their early sixties, Chang suffered a stroke and expired in his sleep, and Eng woke to find his dead brother attached to him; he himself died a few—

*how long that long and lonely how lonely that lonely how long how
lonely how quiet that long so lonely and quiet and long that lonely
alone now lonely so quiet alone*

*how quiet alone how heavy that quiet how many that many and
long how long alone how lonely that quiet, how long long quiet
how long how heavy how heavy that quiet, how long how long
how many how long how heavy how long long heavy how many so
heavy how many now quiet and lonely and quiet that lonely that
quiet alone and heavy and long*

*now long now lonely now heavy now many how lonely long quiet
how heavy that many so heavy not long long knowing long dying
alone now one and lonely and dying alone so many not long not
many no many*

—hours later.

(1) The twins shared a liver.

(2) Their autopsy was publically disseminated as entertainment. As an ordinary nineteenth-century spectacle.

(3) For decades scholars repeated the lie that Eng died of fear from the fright of being tethered to his mortified kin, living still while attached to his own decomposing flesh.

(1) That particular night the brothers slept on the ground floor.

(2) This was because of Chang's paralysis from a stroke four years prior.

(3) The paralysis made climbing and descending steps difficult. Or impossible. It does not really matter which.

(1) If we are to understand this death through simple arithmetic, as 2 − 1, the fifteenth-century *Crafte of Nombrynge*, one of the first algorisms to appear in England and itself a translation and interpretation of the thirteenth-century *Canto de Algorismo* of Alexander de Villa Dei, will be

helpful in this regard: "As for the first thou must know that subtraction is the withdrawing of one number from another."[4]

(2) This is a form of subtraction in the sense that Aristotle writes *aphairesis*: a taking away by way of removal. Such a subtraction, for the philosopher, also names a kind of abstraction. In *Metaphysics*, for example, he writes of arriving at a concept of matter by "taking away" that of form; in *De Anima*, one can arrive at knowledge by "taking away" aspects or qualities of the sensible.[5] This mode of negation does not mean that something does not remain. The Latin *abstrahere*, root of abstraction, means to drag away or detach, from *ab-*, off, and *trahere*: to draw, to pull, to drag—as along the ground. Subtraction, from the Latin *subtrahere*, to take away or draw off, from *sub-*, under, and again from *trahere*: once more to draw, to pull, to drag—as along the ground.

To *abstract* and to *subtract* thus notate only the topological difference in being dragged off or in being dragged under.

(3) To take away is not always the worst thing. There is also to leave in place.

A TO B TO C

Invested as it is in the facticity of its titular term, *The Human Centipede* displays the form of the human centipede twice: once in a presentation of method projected for a diegetic audience of the three gurney-bound victims— these images are drawn, surgery not the only manual operation in the film (*serurgerie* from *kheirourgos*: what work is done by hand)—and then again in an illuminated representation of the golden realized (fleshed-out) creation, knees gauze-wrapped and stained red, stitches the material joiners of lips to anal verge. The first presentation of centipedal form occurs twenty-eight minutes in; the second, forty-eight minutes in, at almost the precise halfway point of the film (as though it centered its structure [of course, *iff* the second, light-soaked sight of the thing in itself is indeed the {affective, generic} ground of the work {—more on that claim, infra}]).

Violence in the act of creation turns, in *The Human Centipede*, on the mechanics of a digestion engineered to mimic the mechanics of ordinary digestion, despite its extension over three bodies made one. Feeding figure A, Heiter shouts as incitement, "Feed her!" in reference to the inevitable exchange of intake for a waste that will become gavage for figure B that will in turn pass once more to waste as intake for figure C, who will finally, in the alimentary logic of the construction, excrete the waste of the waste of others who have been bonded to the self. Digestive form is thus put to the service of violence, not through its perversion but through a strict fidelity to the material law of its course. Unlike certain horror films, which commit to the inversions of vomit, making the mouth the anus within digestive schematics (*The Fly, The Exorcist, Audition, City of the Living Dead, Bad Taste*, &c.), *The Human Centipede* retains, indeed requires, the correct arrangement of esophageal length and pacing, order and function. And this precise plan of digestion is precisely demonstrated. If there is a monster here, it is neither the made thing nor its mad creator, but *monstrare* to the letter: a showing, a teaching, a putting on display. The invisibility of digestive processes is given visible form through a presentation of images before these processes are embodied in illuminated flesh. Thus, for all that popular and scholarly reactions to the film's conceit have emphasized an immediacy of negative affect (whether shock, horror, disgust, contempt, revulsion), because the film's violences are routed through specific representational schemas, lest we fall prey to what Althusser dubbed in *Reading Capital* "the illusion of immediate reading," these schemas must closely, slowly, carefully—that is: *with painstaking care*—be dissected.[6]

In the first scene of showing, having relocated himself and his victims from the glass-paned modernism of aboveground house to the enclosed fluorescence of basement laboratory, Heiter puts on a stark white lab coat and walks to a podium, faces his audience of three, and, in a simple but representationally resonant gesture, turns on a light—(with all the metaphysical associations unavoidably bound to light, light, the poet reminds us, "the visible reminder of Invisible Light").[7] The word *heiter*, in addition to suggesting the affectively light (cheerful, amusing, merry, lighthearted), also suggests bright or clear (nuanced like *klar*). *Heiter* is a word that can refer equally to atmospheric and to affective conditions—an entire metaphysics of mood that cuts between the state of the world and the state of a mind. If Heiter is, in fact, too heiter—too serene, too genial, too fair and mild in affective disposition while conducting the activities of his horrible research—he is also throughout the film associated with what is *heiter*: what is bright, what is clear and *lucid*, analytically, epistemically, and literally.

There are eight slides in all, moving from the abstraction of three notated figures A, B, and C into their joining A to B and B to C, working through an isolation of the conditions of mechanical possibility for the composite form:

the ruination of knee extension that brings the figures low, the cutting of the mouths of B and C, the grafting to the anuses of A and B. ₁The first image Heiter places on his *en abîme* projector contains only three blank shapes, the outlines apart, distinct, individuated in space but devoid of quality, unmarked in relation to sexual difference, and utterly decontextualized save for their reduction to the minimal contour required for an anthropomorphic sketch of an upright form. Generic, bare, spare—embodiment converted to an operation of line—the figures are particularized solely by the notation assigned to each: A B C. This sequential ordering of the figures—A to B to C—is nonoptional, not only because the figure displays a structured sequence with first, middle, and last terms, but because the script's directionality conforms to the readerly, a primer for a kind of literacy of the compositional arrangement. Were the centipede to be flipped, turned around such that its diagrammatic presentation were to read C to B to A, its ordering would retain a spatial relativity of first, middle, and last terms and a claim for transitivity, albeit a finite one. But with alphabetic order preserved, C is not an end, nor a term gesturing at the cyclical, but merely the next term in a minimally defined but extensible sequence. All that is required for this sequence is a third term, an order neither of the one (the all-alone) nor of any dia-logics of the two. (Later in the film, the *One, Two* will suggest a different arrangement altogether, one bonded to failed collective organization and situational transformation.) Three or ten or twelve (as in *The Human Centipede II*) or the titular etymological trace of the hundred (*centum*) or five hundred (as in the final part of the trilogy) or five hundred thousand (—it does not matter): what *three* points to in this ordering is the multiplicity, the bare opening to the *et alia*, the *and the rest* (i.e., *all the possible others*).

These figures are not only generalized as any A, B, or C, they are not even cleaved from Heiter until he names himself as other: the projector initially throws the three figures onto a hybrid screen, the outline of A cast onto the white of the doctor's lab coat. Only at the break of individuation at the declaration "I'm Dr. Joseph Heiter" does his face stand aside from the three shapes. (His body functions as screen in the eighth image of conjunction as well, articulating, blocking, and grounding the final stage of the operation at once.) Heiter's opening pronouncement over this image, "Good news: Your tissues match," is the brute declaration, without history, blank and without provocation (assertive in the strictest sense) that the conjunctive operation is *possible*.[8] The possibility of joining is thus articulated over the self-evidence of the human form as presence. Put another way, violence is possible because of this minimal condition that beings *are*—the constraint on freedom is declared as an event that requires solely what the visual logic avows: that the human *is*.

The Human Centipede turns on a technique—and it is not a technique of construction or a technique of power so much as a technique of representation. The film presents a delineated figure, marked out by lines, written by hand, attesting to the structure of something unified and self-enclosed, of the joining of A to B to C. Elemental human form is bonded to an elemental notation for conjunction in a precisely ordered sequence. The film, in other words, displays a diagram, which means that it turns on a mode that has essential formal characteristics. Diagrams are reductive, usually drawn images, with limited colors and limited elements and with an internal reduction of each of those elements; this visual reduction produces a marked openness in the image, typically a field of white space with black marks. They are governed by a unity of image, with parts often "correlated by means of a geometric notation system," as is the case here.[9] The designation of the components, even once joined, thus giving form to the joinedness of what is joined, is key. In creating a taxonomy of visual representations in his 1967 *Semiology of Graphics*, Jacques Bertin distinguishes a diagram from a network from a map from a symbol with the crucial provision that a diagram establishes divisions of one component and another; the diagram explicitly turns on the separation of parts and is always, in some way, about the elemental.[10] The diagram's externally imposed formalism and reduction, furthermore, are in the service of describing some action or process through constrained components; they represent, as the *Oxford English Dictionary* has it, "the course or results of any action or process, or the variations that characterize it."[11] In *Discipline and Punish*, describing the Panopticon and its polyvalent applications, Foucault dubs the form of the diagram "a functioning, abstracted from any obstacle, resistance or friction."[12] Not an archive or repository, the diagram is a cartography of an ideal.[13]

(1) In *The Manhattan Transcripts*, Bernard Tschumi's notations of events of death, set alongside each other are theoretical drawings, works in progress, transcripts of the interrelation of objects, movements, and events juxtaposing photographs, schemas, collages, axonometric projections, all in order that these "plans, sections, and diagrams outline spaces and indicate the movements of the different protagonists" in varying events of violence.

(2) For example, MT3 "The Tower" depicts a fall from a Manhattan tower block, and the "drastic alteration of perceptions caused by the fall is used to explore various spatial transformations and their typological distortions." The preface for MT3 outlines the narrative of a horrific event of great melodrama, or a melodramatic event of great horror, set next to a photograph of an imposing building—"The Fall . . . First it was just a battered child, then a row of cells, then a whole tower. The wave of movement spread, selective and sudden, threatening to engulf the whole city in a wave of chaos and horror, unless . . . . But what could she do . . . now that the elevator ride had turned into a chilling contest with violent death?"[14]

(3) Tschumi dubs *The Manhattan Transcripts* a book not *about* architecture but *of* architecture.

(1) In MT3, Tschumi's schematic displays a tower, a street, connecting rooms in relation to the fall as nothing but vertiginous modifications to diagrammatic positionings of line.

(2) This is the case in the event of *any* fall.

(3) Once more, we are speaking on the order of the general.

  IIHeiter's second slide retains the three outlined figures of A B C in a minor form—one cannot declare them to be in the background, for the image is nonperspectival; rather, they hover, bordering the metonymic violence of the excerpted impersonal knee, stitched crudely in an exterior hatch, a red arrow pointing to an isolated detail of the ligamentum patellae that will be severed first. Heiter's pronouncement that "knee extension is no longer possible" brings the figures in the subsequent slides on all fours, the deixis denoting the modifications of the form of the figures presented in order to be destroyed (this is identical to: presented in order to be modified). IIIIn the third transparency, local demarcations are made based on positionality in the sequence: from B and C, the teeth will be pulled from the upper and lower jaws. The lips from B and C and the anuses of A and B are to be cut to the measure of the dotted circles "along the border between skin and mucosa." The dotted lines that indicate cutting move from the descriptive to the creative, more akin to a blueprint or surgical map that does not trace a prior action but plots one that has yet to occur. ₁ᵥIn the fourth transparency, the grafts are prepared, lifted from the underlying tissue.

This fourth slide, the sole image that does not contain the three lettered forms, is an abstracted, maximally impersonal illustration of joining. The image of linking is lifted from the linked things that even so fragilely might serve as its representational or surgical ground; grafting, figured as flesh extending from shape, is thus written in line (*dia* + *graphein*) as pure operational potential, exposing the general form of the body as open to a capacity for *being joined*.

ᵥThe fifth sheet shows the three figures in profile—all the while retaining their lettered designation, all the while down on their nerve-exposed, oozing knees—as local suturing is articulated: the red line of the graft between B and C slices the outline of the mouthless head from chin to cheekbone. ᵥᵢThe graft having been shown, the images follow suit: in the sixth transparency, the three profiled forms share as a singular line the rump border/face border, each track of spine leading into the gentle swell of the head that follows. ᵥᵢᵢThe seventh page offers the cross section of the redundant flesh, showing the pedicle grafts of skin from anus to mouth, exhibiting how the nose of one will rest lightly on the coccyx of the neighbor. ᵥᵢᵢᵢAt the last piece of cellulose, the titular figure assembled, its letter designations stubbornly adhering, Heiter stands as ground of the image for which he is responsible as he pronounces this thing: "a Siamese triplet connected via the gastric system."

VIII.

When Barthes reads the plates of Diderot's *Encyclopedia*, he poses the question: "Consider the astonishing image of man reduced to his network of veins; here anatomical boldness unites with the great poetic and philosophic interrogation: *What is it?* What name to give it? How give a name? A thousand names rise up, dislodging each other: a tree, a bear, a monster, a hair shirt, a fabric, everything which overflows the human silhouette, distends it, draws it towards regions remote from itself, makes it overstep the divisions of Nature."[15] And as though honoring Barthes's wonderment, Heiter will likewise conclude this "astonishing image" of his own, of man reduced to conjoined alimentary length, with an answer to that "poetic and philosophic interrogation." He ends his presentation by giving it a name, declaring the answer ontologically—"A human centipede. First sequence." Flesh is reduced to knee, chin, mouth, tooth, anus, skin, hole, line—all parts elements in a precisely notated sequence. In the final diagram of centipedal form, a red tunnel of exteriority shows the logic of passage, this chromatic shift marking the telos of the black-and-white diagrams: what goes into A will pass through B to its resting place in C, as though figuring major, middle, and minor terms in a coprophagic syllogism.

> *What is it?*
> —*Being is letter.*
> (Everything follows from this.)

(1) In Heiter's diagrams, flesh is reduced to line in a demonstration of an analogy common in the eighteenth century—as in Diderot's "*Fibra enim physiologo id est, quod linea geometrae*" (The fiber is to physiology what the line is to mathematics [geometry]).[16]

(2) Diderot takes the general form of this affinity from Albrecht von Haller's *Primae lineae physiologiae* (First Lines of Physiology), wherein the physiologist—amid polemics for adding to the study of anatomy the role of movement and the development of concepts of irritability, sensibility, elasticity, and nervous power—likens fiber to line in geometry in particular, not mathematics in general. Of mathematics-aesthetics, geometry-aesthetics, mathematics-physiology, geometry-physiology analogies there are many in the history of the thinking of both line and flesh.

(3) Diderot's celebration of line—and its spontaneity, its formal joy—engenders his famous aesthetic valuation of the sketch. (This is a Diderot who will be very familiar to readers of Barthes, who himself had great affection for writerly and graphic sketches.) "Sketches frequently have a fire that the finished paintings lack; they are the moment of the artist's zeal, his pure verve, undiluted by any carefully considered preparation, they are the painter's soul freely transferred to canvas," Diderot promises.[17] The sketch's reliance on line renders an unfinished but infinitely more vitalized image than the completed picture. Other lines with which Diderot was fascinated included musical strings, which, like the graphic line, attest to the fiber's vitality, both fiber and string subject to vibration and capable of transmitting those vibrations.[18] In a Diderot who sounds like Deleuze (due to the overt Spinozism in both), a fiber is "soft, elastic and pultaceous, long without being wide, or wide without being extended"—its heterogeneity resists total dissolution, its system best described as "the gluten or fluid element of the fiber, [which] contains water, sea salt, air and oil in combination; together they form a whole that is neither water, earth, nor oil, or anything that dissolved in analysis." In other words, fiber is an assemblage—and its decomposition releases, frees up and disperses, "intensities."[19]

(1) In a memorable comparison, in *Elements* XVII Diderot views the fiber "as an animal, a worm":

> The animal is composed of such beings and nourishes them. This is the principle of the whole machine.
>
> Its growth is but the growth of a worm. (*Sa formation n'est que la formation d'un ver.*)
>
> If you want to witness the similarity between the muscle fiber and the worm, pull on it, and you shall notice how it squirms, coils up, and slithers.[20]

(2) Shall we sit with tiny unpleasant figures for a moment and set in proximity this A and some B in the form of a rule: What the *ver* is to Diderot, the *mouche* is to Barthes. (For an example of the latter: "A fly bothers me, I kill it: you kill what bothers you. If I had not killed the fly, it would have been *out of pure liberalism*: I am liberal in order not to be a killer" in the *J'aime, je n'aime pas* listing of *Roland Barthes by Roland Barthes*; sign of

disordered movement in thought, in 1975 Barthes wrote that "we read a text (of pleasure) the way a fly buzzes around a room: with sudden, deceptively decisive turns, fervent and futile"; of the lover's discourse in 1977, it is "no more than a dust of figures stirring according to an unpredictable order, like a fly buzzing in a room."[21]) Perhaps all French philosophical thought shares singular figures, this fly that Barthes does or does not kill, the very same fly "dragging himself along, stupefied, sunning himself and rubbing his antennae one against the other" that Roquentin does "the favor of squashing" (to the Autodidact's horror) in Sartre's *Nausea*.[22] And is this then the friction between the existentialist and Barthes: the one does the fly the favor of killing it, the other lets him live, but only to appear liberal—the fly that lives and the fly that dies the singular difference with which everything about some philosopher might be said?

One possible C: Bataille was likewise obsessed with flies; they are distractingly visible across his writings, as though his pages were the lower frames of fifteenth- and sixteenth-century trompe l'œil paintings.

(3) All these worms and flies bedding down in the words of philosophy, landing, unpredictably but without fail, as on a pool of expelled sourest fluids.

A Further Aside on the Topology of Different Types of Lines

Undulation is likewise the formal cornerstone of William Hogarth's eighteenth-century aesthetic theory in *The Analysis of Beauty*, an elaborate polemic on behalf of a particular kind of serpentine line, the S-curve, a boundary that draws the eye through the greatest possible movement of varied forms. Hogarth's aim is to consider objects "merely as shells composed of lines"; accordingly, his principle of the beautiful stems from an experiment on the body of a thing:

> let every object under our consideration, be imagined to have its inward contents scoop'd out so nicely, as to have nothing of it left but a thin shell, exactly corresponding both in its inner and outer surface, to the shape of the object itself: and let us likewise suppose this thin shell to be made up of very fine threads, closely connected together, and equally perceptible, whether the eye is supposed to observe them from without, or within; and we shall find the ideas of the two surfaces of this shell will naturally coincide. The very word, shell, makes us seem to see both surfaces alike.[23]

Hogarth's aesthetic philosophy thereby originates in an act of disemboweling—gutting the substance of a cavity, ravaging and decimating, exenterating and extracting and clearing out the total mass of its creamy, gloppy inside stuff. To open it up, as if for novel passage. Hogarth's assurance of a scooping out "so nicely," so neat and with precision and rigor, is a form of cleaning, purgation, even potentially of care, but it also, unavoidably, despite that great politeness, suggests a necessary measure of relentless excavatory violence.

From this gutting of every object follows a newly precise taxonomy and valuation of those newly abstracted and extracted lines. Hogarth lists them in order—first, those objects composed entirely of straight lines (the cube); distinguished second from those objects composed of circular lines and straight lines ("the capitals of columns"); as opposed to those third that include the addition of waving lines consisting of contrasting curves in one plane ("as in flowers, and other forms of the ornamental kind"); finally, and most crucially, the fourth possibility, "those composed of all the former together with the serpentine line," a line marked by waving, winding, twisting, as in "the human form."[24] The last two are the "line of beauty" and the "line of grace," respectively, for waving and serpentine lines are those most varied in form, and thus, according to Hogarth's theory, in which well-ordered composition is the manipulation of variety, they are the most beautiful. A straight line, impoverished by a capacity merely to "vary only in length," is bested by the serpentine line, which by its "waving and winding at the same time different ways, leads the eye in a pleasing manner along the continuity of its variety."[25] This perceptual density is a frustration to representation: "all its variety cannot be express'd on paper by one continued line, without the assistance of the imagination, or the help of a figure [. . . .] [T]he precise serpentine line, or *line of grace*, is represented by a fine wire, properly twisted round the elegant and varied figure of a cone."[26] The abstraction of this quality of this final kind of line—the aesthetic dimension of curving-quality, the aesthetic dimension of undulation-quality—is not given shape by Heiter's diagram, but itself is what gives shape to the diagram of conjoined centipedal form, which is to say the diagram of a line of the edges of bodies joined *as drawn line—as nothing but the shape of their shell*—and not bodies as filled bowls or substance. The diagram thus effects the formalization of the aesthetic theorist's formalism; it is what puts on display the abstracted linear *qualities* of a certain type of quality of line. If this smacks of an essentialism and an idealism, those qualities likewise belong to the order of the diagram.

Heiter's centipede, I wrote above, is displayed twice over, once diagrammatically and notationally—in line and letter—and once in depth, flesh, skin, as a field of full and rounded light. The presentation of the centipede is thus, superficially, given a metaphysical metanarrative: planned and consummated; speculated and lived; letter and flesh; system and functioning; static line and heaving movement; what written, what reality; inked line against feculent taste; text, thing; form for form's sake, the real matter.

(1) Gustatory version of this tension, following Barthes: "when written, shit has no odor."

(2) He writes this, notably, in relation to the impossibilia defended in Sade in which possibility solely remains discursive, negative to reality. Indeed, the libertine speaks in *Juliette* of works recovered from Herculaneum: "In all these paintings one remarks a wealth of postures and attitudes which almost defy natural possibilities, and which testify either to great muscular suppleness in the inhabitants of those countries, or a great disorder of the imagination."[27]

(3) Likewise here.

The visual alternative to the diagram, which displays the thing in itself as promised by the drawn procedure, illuminates and exposes the long line that traces the elegant sloping of conjoined flesh, each hand gently resting on each adjacent thigh (plate 4). The fleshy image of accomplished centipede restages and recasts the compositional elements of the transparency presentation: the white of screen and lab coat is exchanged for the white of fabric and gauze; the cold blue light of the projector thrown to the incredibly warm light of the revelation. The fulfilled creation faces to the right, is akin to the reverse of the final slide (the meaty body now, quite literally, the opacity of that transparency)— no longer notated according to the order of alphabetic inscription, for these bodies have lost their written letters. The arrangement of limbs in strict parallel, the undulating line thereby formed, the rolling golden light: the image is compositionally classical—oh let it be said: it is *beautiful*.

(Though on the technical-philosophical question of beauty, Hogarth's privileged line is ambivalently promised here: on the one hand, the serpentine vitality of the human form is assuredly enhanced by the joinedness of multiple human forms, what extends and vitalizes—on the order of line—the possibility for variation: the swell of a single knee to a lone hip less aesthetically compelling than the rising roll *from knee to hip to waist to shoulder and down to neck and up to rump and down to ribs and up to sternum then down to arse and up once more toward head.* On the other hand, the body is what disturbs the ideality of that line as pure line by threatening everywhere to give Hogarth's shell and surface guts, stuff, all that inward content that was to have been scoop'd out so nicely—that is, a contamination of line by all that is not line.)

This presentation of the embodied centipede occurs amid a compounding of meta-representational figures, the scene of revelation saturated with aesthetic densities: a painting of symmetrical conjoined bodies on the wall, its upright central mass forming an axis perpendicular to the sprawling horizontal tripartite creation; a series of receding spaces in the back of the tableau, blocks of layered windows, grids of glass providing depth. Heiter, in general, is associated with an ever-expanding series of mediating figures: the film opens with him studying a photograph; he deploys the light-lens-mirror structure of the projector and transparencies; his house features numerous large-scale photographs and paintings of surgeries or conjoined twins; and, in this crucial scene in which the figure of the title is presented to the film's audience, Heiter holds up to the terrible thing he has cruelly created a flashing camera and then an ornate round mirror. This mirror is shown from the side, from the matte back, as it reveals each newly joined, newly destroyed but also newly created face to itself, displaying what Foucault will call in his exegesis on the mirror in *Las Meninas* "that enchantment of the double," what restores the visibility of what had remained invisible.

Representationally, a mirror is a confrontation. When Heiter forces it on his victims, the glass gives back what has been taken away: the ability to see the self one at a time; it reflects a redoubling of the direct face of terror, made inaccessible through the logic of the new machine. This image, crucially, includes the reverse side of representation: spectators are shown primarily what Foucault dubs the "lustreless back" of the mirror.[28] The film is thus in sympathy with the mode by which seventeenth-century Dutch art, which made an essential study of the mirror, deployed it: for allegorical doubling or reflexive self-consideration, what might introduce the presence of the painter in order to stress the fictional dimension of the scene, or, if canted, might reflect a figure whose back is to the viewer in order to offer more information or show something otherwise invisible in the outer frame. (The film even seems to deploy mirror in collusion with camera in the manner of a collector's *Wunderkammer*, with its reflective glass set between drawers so that a treasured object might be viewed from every angle at once.)[29] The tableau frames the made thing, stages the centipede in the context of this representational depth (of space, of meaning): it displays violence as fully realized (as full and fulfilled), and it displays the centipede as a fundamentally aesthetic object.

This revelatory moment, this golden light and these limbs in graceful sequence, the blood and knees, the several anuses and pulled teeth, *this thisness* is what the diagram called into being. The fundamental critical question, then, is whether this image is here in order to show the insufficiency of the earlier diagram, to suggest its lack or privation. Does the fleshy monstrosity supersede its stark outlined plan? Was the diagram for the sake of this image, a means or mere tool to bring it about—as in the understanding of diagram as preliminary sketch, as quickly inked possibility, what is not yet realized as opposed to some actual project? In conventional generic topologies of horror, it seems self-evident that violence is on the side of the made thing—its blood, festering wounds, oral-anal intimacy, the revealed construct where what passes is not a red line marking gastric progress but the stinking juices of that anti-willed process itself. At best, diagrammatic labor would be subsumed by the motif of the torturer's presentation of his tools as a prolegomenon to suffering, as a sign of the pain that itself will destroy signification.

But now consider: Is it conceivable that it is *this* image—despite its representational complexity, depth, and referentiality, its rigorous composition, aesthetic pleasures, and affective solicitations—that is not enough, that lacks some abstract power that belongs to the diagram alone?

For the diagram diagrams. And what the diagram of *The Human Centipede* diagrams is an inalterable enchainment in a specific sequence. The diagram formalizes the fact of being riveted, stitched and sewn, to an inescapable order related to one's own finitude bonded to others who precede and come after the self. The film's account of enchainment rests on the purest relations articulated by Heiter's diagram: bound up with first, last, middle terms and involving a not-to-be-outstripped givenness of one's place in that sequence. The entirety of the question of violence in *The Human Centipede* turns on the violence of an unmodifiable position, a rivetedness to a certain notation: the formality of a written inscription that is violent in excess of any order stained with blood, vomit, pus, piss, shit, agony, weeping, terror. The diagram is what poses the formality of the problem of escape from the sequence that it *is*.

(1) The diagram's notation of a joining of A to B to C is so insistent that it governs the relation of the components of the franchise itself, which is structured as a metatext consisting of three segments: *The Human Centipede (First Sequence)*, *The Human Centipede II (Full Sequence)*, and *The Human Centipede III (Final Sequence)*. The films overlap from A to B and from B to C, the last minute of the first film opening the second; the ending of the second opening the third. But as a result, the suturing of these three works is an example of poor surgical technique, for closure is said to be "well approximated" when the edges of a wound fit together without undue tension and with minimal skin overlap—what is known as "stepping," when mismatched heights produce an asymmetrical result, unsightly, thick scarring, and any number of poor results. (In cases where a wound has irregular edges, it can therefore be helpful to trim the skin before placing the sutures; in cases where the surrounding skin is not viable, a delay in closure may be advisable, lest one fasten, with all that time, with all that labor, only for the site to develop a new infection, for it to fail to survive.)

(2) The crucial image of figure B is the hinge between the components that, in sequence, compose the first two parts of the large-scale text. The premise of the 2011 sequel is a meta-cinematic one in which Tom Six's actual first film is a diegetic object that has become the obsession of a vile, mute, developmentally stunted man named Martin. The film opens with the last few minutes of *The Human Centipede* filling the screen, only to zoom out at the credits to reveal that it is being played on a video monitor—in the great aesthetic deception, the window thus becomes a frame, and the films form a sequence, with the scene of B alone at the end, sewn to death, functioning as their graft. Martin, the ultimate fanboy, attempts to exceed his cinematic model by creating a twelve-person centipede, but in one of the darkly comic dimensions of the film, because he is not a surgeon like Heiter—whose conceit is required for the verisimilitude of the seriously taken surgery of the first film—Martin's initial efforts at grafting kill his first victims, as one might expect, and once down to ten, stymied by the reality of anatomy, he ineffectually staples and tapes them together. In the sequel's climax, representation is inverted, as one of the actresses from the first film (C, now playing herself) comes to audition for a "Quentin Tarantino film"; mistaking Martin for her driver, she ends up as the head of the sequence this time,

not its culmination, though were the *en abîme* centipede to meet its fictional avatar from the first film in a transontological realm, she would literally function as its hinge, having been the last term and now constituting the first.

The climax of the sequel involves Martin's attempt to digestively prove the functioning ontology of the constructed centipede: if the expanded alimentary system works, he has made the diagram into a thing, fulfilled the plan that it names. Feeding the first figure, nothing happens, so he injects each term in the sequence with a laxative that eventually leads to a hyperecstatic bursting of excrement from the final member but also in between the sutures of the creature. This explosive, graphic instant, however, is a decoy for what truly takes diarrheal form in the film. Literally, from the Greek *diarrhoia*, a *flowing through* (the German *Durchfall* is literally a falling through), this mode of intensity—a fluidity, a groaning out of the body—is not, in the sequel, a foul substance that is shown in the image; rather, what flows through the film is the diagram itself.

For the key feature of the first film to which the second returns with obsessive attention is the diagrammatic notation, and not just in explicit visual citations as when Martin resketches Heiter's images as he prepares to make the twelve-person centipede. Rather, one of the most remarkable formal details of the sequel is that it is shot entirely in black and white, with one exception: at that climax, the ontological laxative test, the film departs from its formal system—at the instant of the explosive diarrhea, a sudden shock of warm brown fills the frame. In *The Human Centipede (First Sequence)*, the aesthetic exception to the black line/white wall system of Heiter's diagrams was the tube of red mapping the course of digestive progression through the expanded alimentary canal. The singular chromatic instant in both films is thus aligned with digestion's passage (the equation would read something like color = movement, or color functions as deixis: pointing to the progress of movement). *The Human Centipede II*, then, with its antichromatic rigor and metatextual replication of the logic of the original slides, does not take apart, digest, deconstruct, or process the diagrams of the first film—it, in a manner, with its black-white-chromatic-exception world, is coextensive with the visual logic of those diagrams. It *reiterates* the diagram. It is equivalent to yet another slide presenting the form of the diagram's reductive, insistent notation.

FIGURE 4.9. *The Human Centipede II (Full Sequence)* (Tom Six, 2011)

(3) The third film likewise begins with uneven wound edges, here effecting a metatextual leap in which the first and second films in the franchise are commodified media objects (their DVD cases are bandied about). Like the opening of *The Human Centipede II*, the final installment begins with the last minutes of the previous film, the frame comprised entirely of the pile of suffering joined bodies with which the second film ends, moving out to the credits, then pulling out from those credits and leaving behind that film's black-and-white logic to shift to color stock and prison warden Bill Boss watching (and loathing) the second film. He opens the shades in his office, and to his accountant Dwight's question, "What do you think?" Boss replies, "Jesus Christ, I fucking told you these movies were shit. Literally. They stink." Although the ontology of this world is one in which the two previous films by Tom Six exist as objects, there are bleeds between levels: Boss is played by Dieter Laser, Heiter in the first film; Dwight is played by Laurence Harvey, who is Martin Lomax, the asthmatic protagonist of the second film.

The Human Centipede III (Final Sequence) is consumed with Dwight's project of persuading the warden that making a human centipede would be an economical answer to the overcrowded and underfunded carceral system and a more effective deterrent to crime. Accordingly, one of the innovations of this final film is that there must be a technical provision made for inmates' future release from prison, and thus a way around the permanency of centipedal conjoining. A solution is devised. Instead of cutting the knee ligaments, they will induce temporary paralysis. Leather straps instead of sutures provide the requisite oral-anal joining; these leave only a slight scar upon release. For the prisoners sentenced to life and those on death row, however, Boss devises a new morphological variation. The final form of the final film is not a centipede at all but what Boss dubs a human caterpillar: bodies sewn anus to mouth in a connected gastric system, but arms and legs cut off, preventing movement and any possible resistance. The limbless joined structure of the human caterpillar instructs in a crucial lesson that theology, philosophy, and horror equally teach: that one can always be degraded further, that becoming-lower—*as a formal quality*—is always on the order of the possible.

One might describe each of the three films in relation to one privileged mode of rhetorical address: in the first film, the diagram of the human centipede is invoked as a tool for pedagogy (instruction to the future victims; the abstract presentation of methodology); in the second, it functions in relation to dramatic imitation (the strict repetition via tracing of an action, part of the broader realm of mimesis); and in the third, the centipede is presented as idea, and a particularly utopian one at that, rendering the dominant mode that of persuasion (and the diagram as example and as exemplary). Dwight insists that with inmates sewn anus to mouth there will be no more prison fights or assaults on guards, and fences will no longer be required (a fantasy of a self-sustaining punitive system). As part of this persuasion, he invites the real director, Tom Six, playing himself, to the prison to talk about the "medically accurate" aspect of the centipede methodology from his two films. When the discussion turns to the question of surgical possibility, Six produces the diagrams from the first film in a dossier containing an "operation report and the drawings," ostensibly produced by a doctor in Amsterdam. (Later, Six remains in the prison, eager to see the surgery in the flesh, as opposed to in latex special effects—aghast, the director is unable to watch the results.)

The diagrams, pedagogical in the first film; mimetic source material in the second; become by the third film evidential, and evidence, in particular, of a question of technical possibility/feasibility and political efficacy/desirability. The drawn images exist already in the first film, presented in real time; in the second, they are traced and copied, repeated and remediated; in the third, they are linked to a prior report, brought to bear as an entry in an archive. The diagram thus traces broad differences in a series of regimes: the *Pedagogical, Mimetic, Evidential*; or *Presence, Remediation, History*. Furthermore, what the centipede itself is also varies across the three films. In the first, it is a form of research, a form of experiment; in the second, the human centipede is a provocation to art through homage and citation; in the third, the centipede is invoked as a punishment, as revenge and deterrent, as economical and strategic answer to a problem. In other words, the franchise progresses from a form of knowledge to an aesthetic practice to a technique of power and discipline. The form's abstraction thus enables a ranging over *Epistemology, Aesthetics, Politics*. What concerns us in every one of these sequences is the middle term. For from the point of view of the logic of the diagram, the structure of the three films suggests that it is Aesthetics that joins together the realms of Knowledge and Power.

And yet, the subtitular particularity of each entry in the franchise is given more than a number locating it in its metatextual sequence—each is also nominated by a qualifier: *First Sequence, Full Sequence, Final Sequence*. It is immediately apparent that those terms do not refer to the same categories of identification: while *The Human Centipede (1, 2, 3)* names the countable positionality of ordinal listing, the individual cinematic entries are signed under the regime of a sequence abstracted from number.

Again, what concerns us, *and always now*, must be the middle term.

For the middle part of the sequence exceeds its ordinal designation. In place of *first, second, last; first, middle, final; first, subsequent, conclusive*; &c.—any of which might have sufficed to mark difference and progression—instead we have *First, Full*, and *Final*. Contained within the extremes of origin (First: the Adamic; the inaugural) and end (Final: telos; the eschatological) is a claim for the fullness of the form. *Full Sequence* does not suggest finitude, but a plenitude of membership, an exhaustion and completeness and repletion in the middle position of this (or any) sequence. This *Full Sequence* is the film in which the human centipede is not invoked for the sake of epistemological gain or political utility, but for the sake of *aesthetic seriousness*. It is thus the middle term of the Aesthetic—middle and thus unavoidably bound to while also surpassing, also surviving past, Epistemology and Politics—that contains the fullness of the logic of sequentiality itself. (And of course this second film is also the great formalist exception among the three films, committed as it is to a maximally restricted aesthetic language of black and white and a virtuosic sonic catalogue of grain and grunt in place of word.) Above all, *Full* leaps from the linear language of enumeration, length, or position to speak to matters of *volume* and completeness, suggesting "containing or holding as much or as many as possible; having within its limits all it will hold; having no space empty; filled to capacity," while also evoking the utter satiation that eating and drinking provide. Fullness is what is "complete, perfect; entire, whole; thoroughgoing"; a realm of ideality marked also by denoting the entirety of some system.[30]

It is the middle term where the general fullness of an implication is borne out.

| IS |

Man approaches man. He is stitched of responsibilities.
Through them, he lacerates essence.
—Emmanuel Levinas, *Humanism of the Other*

In his early essay *De L'évasion*, from 1935, Emmanuel Levinas insists that "The need for escape—whether filled with chimerical hopes or not, no matter!—leads us into the heart of philosophy. It allows us to renew the ancient problem of being qua being."[31] Levinas is clear, though, that the sense in which he takes *l'évasion* (escape; fleeing; avoidance; flight) is neither an ordinary-language, nor poetic, nor conventional philosophical sense. Beginning with a negative definition of his key term, Levinas rejects any understanding of escape as an evasion of brute or low reality; a true understanding of escape regards it neither as the rejection of social convention or physical laws into the marvelous, nor as a Romantic escape of the material of the body or the spirit's servitude to bare need. These motifs are merely translations of "the horror of a certain *definition* of our being but not that of being as such." They concern themselves with "going somewhere" as destination, futurity, elsewhereness, and thus fail to speak at all to a more radical form of escape.[32]

—Regardless of the scatology and carnage, the juniper-green rot at the edges of the mouth: most horror is a kind humanism. It retains a horizon of possible escape from the violence therein depicted (even if, as often is the case, that horizon remains suspended outside the borders of the text— belonging to it only as the excised). It is nearly always the case that the possibility of nonviolence remains unscathed, indeed, gives pathos to the presence of violence itself. The horror that remains with what Levinas derides as the naïve view of escape emphasizes minor departures: what frees the self from the force of other beings, what cleaves the self from the aggressions of the not-I. So very many things can be a refuge (the Real; Law; Revenge; History; Allegory; Death [the privileged evasive destination for horror: how quickly it loses interest in the dead, renewing it solely in the case of a secondary refuge out of death into un-deadening]—each an escape to *somewhere else*, each a fantasy of the transcendence of violence). In this view, the suffering desire for an escape from violence is given renewable hope through its link to possibilities of antiviolence, nonviolence, or an end to violence. Violence as such thereby need not ever truly be considered.

By contrast, *The Human Centipede* is not about escape *to* somewhere in this minor sense, but about a different concept of escape altogether: the brutal aspiration only to *get out* (Levinas writes *sortir*). Not to elude or flee the house, the doctor, the foulness, the terror—not to do something else or something new; true getting out is "assimilable neither to renovation nor to creation"— but to evade the structure one oneself is. Not transcendence, but what Levinas dubs *excendence*.[33] Violence does not produce a need to go or be or dwell somewhere (else), but rather the extremest existential suffering to not be (what) one *is*.

When Levinas considers an invitation to escape that might actually take the measure of being, this figure turns on the possibility of a break with the self. In the crystallizing line of the essay, "Escape is the need to get out of oneself, that is, *to break that most radical and unalterably binding of chains, the fact that the I [moi] is oneself [soi-même]*."[34] This need to escape is not a result of privation (it is not because I cannot live many lives, nor because it is impossible to say what I mean, nor is it the finitude through which my temporality is given); rather, "In escape the I flees itself, not in opposition to the infinity of what it is not or of what it will not become, but rather due to the very fact that it is."[35] The very identity of being thereby "reveals its nature as enchainment." The brutal existence of the I is what is at stake in this radical form of evasion.

In theorizing this notion, Levinas turns to a contemplation of affects—suffering and malaise, anxiety and nausea, and, in a final rotation, the figure of shame. Shame's intensity is the mark of our "inability not to identify" with the being of I. The affect is thereby severed from its bond to the moral or deviations from the normative to instead name the confrontation with the need to get out of oneself, and the concomitant realization that this desire is unfulfillable. It is therefore the affective mode formally bonded to the *impossibility* of a true mode of escape: "the fact of being riveted to oneself."[36] In positing his definition of shame as being annexed to oneself, Levinas turns to the cinema, citing the case of Charlie Chaplin's Tramp figure in *City Lights*, in the scene in which he accidentally swallows a penny whistle whose telltale sound announces (discloses) him each time he hiccups. The whistle "works like a recording device, which betrays the discrete manifestations of a presence that Charlie's legendary tramp costume barely dissimulates."[37] The tramp cannot hide from others, but more importantly he cannot hide from himself or escape the fact of his breathing, hiccupping, bodily existence—which is to say, each continuing effort to persist in a living body announces the inescapable facticity of the present material that he *is*.

Levinas's figuring of shame as a structural condition with a correlate in the structure of being speculatively suggests formal correlates in other spheres, including aesthetic ones. When the philosopher writes, "It is therefore our intimacy, that is, our presence to ourselves, that is shameful. [. . .] What shame discovers is the being who uncovers himself," the diagram of the centipede shows a sympathetic nakedness, unconceals the bare logic of sequencing in the joining of A to B to C.[38] The weight of being—that one is stuck with oneself, that one *is* in a particular impersonal sequence—is what is exposed in crudely drawn line. The impotence of A, B, and C is not in relation to failed transformation or weakened commitments of community; it is the "powerlessness to take leave of that presence," the exposure of the unmodifiable form of being.

That the suffering of the need to escape expresses "the presence of our being and not its deficiency" results in a wholesale revision of the relation of need to lack.[39] Shame is dehisced from figures of limitation (weakness, vulnerability) but rather resides in the plenitude of one's presence to oneself. This rivetedness of I to self also positively induces an inescapable enchainment to a responsibility: "Shame is founded upon the solidarity of our being, which obliges us to claim responsibility for ourselves."[40] There is, therefore, for Levinas, an abundance to being: the inability to break with the self is not privation, but is the fullness of a "condemnation to be oneself," such that "there is in need something other than a lack."[41] Accordingly, in the most extraordinary figure in the essay, the philosopher calmly notes that suffering does not necessarily expose being as finite: "One heartrending need is the despair over a death that does not come."[42]

B

In routing its violence through the representational mode of the diagram, *The Human Centipede* gives form to the desire to escape and the structural inability to escape in the more radical sense by which Levinas theorizes it: the brutality of being's inescapable rivetedness to itself.[43] The film reveals the extremest formality of the violence of this suffering. Violence is not in the sewing and stitching of the thing; violence is in the nonmodifiable givenness of diagrammatic attestation—the *notational* impossibility of any true getting out.

The diagram diagrams.

Its form does not admit exception. Abstracted from all obstacles, its reductive, radical formalism is an idealism and a plenitude. The sequential arrangement that the film's diagram displays is an assemblage that does not admit difference, modification, or undoing; the value of the abstraction of Heiter's diagram is that it presents the formality of a model of bondedness in a three-part structure that is stronger than the threads of surgical sutures. Any violence against middle-term Lindsay may compel a (minor) desire to transcend the brutality (to live to tomorrow, go back to school, bear children someday); *but there is no extra-diagrammatic possibility for B admissible within the assertions of this particular sequential form.* To escape the diagrammatic inevitability named by the structural position of B can be articulated solely as the unfulfillable need *for B not to be B.* The violence of the diagram is beyond any violence of force, disgust, torture, surgery—those are the violences of light, of depth and perspective. Notation contains a horror utterly other than that of representation.

For a body's vitalism might strain against the corpus to which it is joined. This is precisely where blood leaks into the stained wound-cloths of the realized golden-light image of the embodied centipede—a red not of idealized passage, but of the *failure* of that perfection in the fragile joining of material forms, a red that signals a fleshly joining that might become unjoined—that was made and therefore retains its bond to what might be unmade or made otherwise. Indeed, among the most striking visual elements of the revelation of the material centipede is the carefully composed graphic match between the black tattoo marking the lead's skin and its repeated shape in the stain of blood at the gauze on the knees, calling attention to the artificiality of that blood, marking it as, above all else, a compositional element that points to the contingent constructedness of this centipede. This same red blood stains the film's narrativization of the illusion of the minor form of escape that Levinas derides. Stabbing Heiter, biting him, rendering him unconscious, A orchestrates a plan for evasion as generic adventure: "We have to get out of here," he cries in Japanese, addressing a plural first-person in a language that only he can comprehend. He holds up his right hand and says to the American girls *ichi* (one), holds up his left hand, says *ni* (two). Ichi. Ni. The three-made-one awkwardly coordinate their knees and hands on the measure of the simple pattern, which signifies not in itself but in relation to the alternating meaningfulness of the body's bifurcation. At a curved staircase the collective pauses. Then: ichi, ni. The alternation slows, the bodies strain to coordinate their collaborative gestures over the duration of the climbing; the sutures pull, the white gauze stains, and Heiter awakens. The attempt at escape comes to nothing. The *One, Two* of cooperative action only reddens and rends the struggling creature; the stairs, scene of their attempted transformation within the givenness of their formed structure, drip with gluey black blood. The *One, Two* attempts to transcend structure: make it work, as in profit from it; accept its properties of joinedness and *nevertheless, despite violence, which is to say within violence, without evading violence,* strive toward futurity. The attempt at ongoingness involves the feint of becoming a new actor, one predicated on the transformative potential of community. The attempt to climb out of the basement is a literal attempt to climb out of (*trans-scandere*) the violence of the structure. But the *One, Two* fails. It does not transform the sequence, nor does it transcend the brutality of ordering. The film displays the uselessness of action, the nothing-more-to-be-done that is inscribed in advance as the cruel unmodifiability of the diagram.

The diagram is not posited in relation to an exteriority, freedom, history: instead, the film's grounding attestation is that *the diagram is all there is*. This is why attempts to co-opt the diagram for historical allegory are so problematic, *pace* the mass of criticism on the first film that attributes to it symbols ranging from the opposing alliances of the Second World War to the production and consumption dynamics of global late capitalism. These approaches lend *The Human Centipede* a horizon that denies the necessity of the diagrammatic arrangement, return to it a possible discursive *escape* from the brutal attestation that the film exhausts: A to B to C. That is all. One can speak ceaselessly of the allegorical resonance, the promise of an intelligibility to the diagram (and its denial), a field of realizations that makes another figure appear in the stead of the diagram. Content with conceiving the diagram in relation to an infinite number of outsides, such a move cannot broach the question of the diagram as such, for its formalism leaves no space for the positing of variation, and the condition of possibility for its inscription is the inadmissibility of variation.

A diagram is its form. Nothing before, nothing after, nothing outside: it is solely its arrangement of elements. It does not refer, allude, resist, suggest; does not free or seek or condemn or mean; does not name, produce, consume; should not be put to work (critically; for any outside). The brutality and self-sufficiency of centipedal form—the joinedness of A to B to C—is given as the self-assertion of the diagram, that which admits no exception to the form that it is. A, B, and C are subject to violence not as constraints on their freedom or from a force external to and against their beings, but as the positive constraint of the givenness of a specific and particular arrangement. But the diagram does not bequeath this as property, nor does it represent it a posteriori: the diagrammatic possibility of sequencing A to B to C is given solely as the necessary notation of alphabetic order. The diagram is the nonspontaneity of a claim that posits itself as an existential fact: diagrammatic form de-monstrates what it *is*. Every diagram does not admit variation without invalidation; its form cannot be modified without it becoming a different form, which is to say: another diagram altogether. This particular diagram of enchainment thus cannot be interrupted, transcended, or evaded—it is the privileged *eidos* of ineluctability: nonremittable, inalterable. Its violence is its formal irrevocability. This formalism thus enables the presencing of a structure that is not generic, but which is general. And thus, to the extent that violence here is in the enchainment to an inescapable position in a notated sequence, the diagram is coextensive with the wrecking work of violence itself.

For Josef Heiter is not Josef Mengele. Contrary to a naïve allegorism, which remains only with the cuts, the stitching, the plaything skin—eye color experiments; twins selected and measured and injected—he is no angel of death. Nor, however, is Heiter Heidegger, despite seeming to function as the mouthpiece for ontologism. Heiter is *heiter*, merely the whiteness of light; he is that brightness through which the diagrammatical is illumined, given to presence, made visible. He is the necessity of violence, its clarity, its genial, diagrammatic, unmodifiable self-evidence. (Adorno, on Kafka: "It is not the horrible which shocks, but its self-evidence.")[44]

A horror that formalizes the violence of ontology and the violence of enchainment not only gives rise to formalisms; in a further rotation, a horror that formalizes violence is itself solely accountable via radical formalism. (We have seen this before in this book: in charts, tables, grids, an abecedarium, a toroid, in rhythm and design and shape and line—the totality of the wrecking work of violence that will not be speculatively thought *despite* a formalist reading, but solely *from* it.) Enchainment is not a theme; the centipedal form, despite its cultural cachet, is not an allegory machine. To reduce the diagram to a theme is to utterly miss its relation to violence, to treat it as something that the text itself can *get out of or evade.* The joined A to B to C cannot both be the diagram it is and admit an interpretive space in which B escapes the notational logic by which it follows A and precedes C in a sequence that runs: A then B then C. To allegorize the diagram is to fail to hold the film responsible for what it directly presents, to fail to see what is given in order to be seen.

One consequence of the formal strategy that makes the diagram coextensive with the violent project of the film is that *The Human Centipede* does not exaggerate how relation works: rather, it displays what is in sequence about beings. This failure to fall to exaggeration is another case of the film's stark simplicity, its reductive formalism of which the diagram is the privileged textual mode. For, as in the formulation given by Alexander Düttmann, "Every justified exaggeration is no longer an exaggeration. Once justified, exaggeration is either an external device or a necessary limitation of thought. In both cases, it ceases to be an exaggeration *constitutive* of thought and its claim to truth; indeed it ceases to be an *exaggeration* that could be regarded as constitutive of thought and its claim to truth."[45] *The Human Centipede* makes the seemingly exaggerated qualities of conjoining a necessary, nonexaggerating dimension of finite being—the inscription of alphabetic order not only justifies but domesticates this structure; thus does the diagram display the inevasible correlation of bodies to each other in sequence by displaying it as the absolute condition for form to take shape at all. The film is not an exaggeration of being's enchained relation to the other, but nor is it a representation of relation, which would require a position of exteriority from which this structure would be thinkable without being subject to it—would, in other words, require the reverse side of a mirror. *The Human Centipede*, rather, is more akin to an aesthetic attestation of a formalization of the ethical, an attestation that ultimately addresses philosophy itself.

A creeping, pressing (as in acute and urgent; as in forcing and straining) violence stirs within Levinas's philosophical account of being consigned to being. In ethics as first philosophy, one is riveted, not only to being, but to an unremittable obligation one did not and will not elect to accept. The weight of being, what Levinas dubs the "condemnation to be oneself," is also "seen in the dialectical impossibility of conceiving the beginning of being—that is, of grasping the moment where being takes up this weight—and of being nevertheless driven back to the problem of one's origin."[46] The weight of being is not merely the inability to break with the self; it is also the infinite responsibility to which being is committed. *The Human Centipede* attests to the most fundamental tension in Levinas's account of rivetedness—tension not as in contradiction, but as in its most vulnerable stress point. For this ineluctable inescapability is intrinsically bound up with what Levinas calls "guiltless responsibility," a certain obligation that our unremittable presence commands in the ethics of alterity for which his work is best known: that our presence arrives in a world in which incomprehensible others precede us commits us to a responsibility that is absolute, but also to an indebtedness that we can never completely fulfill—the dissymmetry of *I* and *other* exposes my finitude as *respondent* to the infinite demands the other makes on me. Being as being-for-the-other is both ethic and condemnation; it is a demand *I* can neither avoid nor flee, nor ever fully meet.[47]

Perhaps the great project of philosophy is to find the violence in philosophy itself. (For his part, for example, Levinas will call Kierkegaard's notion of noncontinuity—the *dépassant* or passing-beyond of the leap—the surging ground for "Kierkegaardian violence.")[48] And likewise, we see this creeping figuration of violence in the shift from early to late Levinas in his figuration of the other. The early work, culminating in *Totality and Infinity* (1969), turns on the generous language of welcoming the other or being open to the alterity of the other. But the latent hostilities grounding the notion of infinite responsibility derived from the plenitude of being start to seep out, to leak between the sutures of ego to *autrui*—and by the time of *Otherwise Than Being* (1974), Levinas declares that responsibility as a being-for-the-other arrives at the point of being more akin to the ensnarement of a prisoner. The other who *concerns me*, with whom I must *be concerned*, is also the other about whom I will ultimately *be very concerned*. Whereas in *Totality and Infinity*, "the subject is a host," by *Otherwise Than Being*, "the subject is a hostage"—one who comes second, who only ever issues an "après vous, monsieur."[49] *Après, always après; —and what is B except what is après A, and what is C except what is after B, and so on, and so on . . .*

Thus, "in responsibility for another," Levinas instructs, "subjectivity is only this unlimited passivity of an accusative which does not issue out of a declension it would have undergone starting with the nominative."[50] This radical passivity is reducible "to the passivity of a self only as a persecution, but a persecution turns into an expiation. [. . .] The self of this passivity [. . .] is a hostage."[51] (Derrida's "A Word of Welcome" in *Adieu to Emmanuel Levinas* is a long unfurling of this "host as hostage" relation, and the intimate kinship—etymological; structural—of host and hostage as a broader theory of substitution in Levinas.) Being "held by the other" pulls then on a triple sense: at once, rivetedness and enchainedness (being stuck to, held by the other as debt); but also, being held by the other as fascination (the other entrances, even blinds one); and also, finally, being *held up* by the other—being detained; being not only captivated but also being captive. This responsibility for the other also, for Levinas, "provokes this responsibility against my will, that is, by substituting me for the other as a hostage. All my inwardness is invested in the form of a despite-me, for-another."[52] These responsibilities did not arise from decision or free consideration (they did not wait for the commitment to be made): again, in *Otherwise Than Being*, Levinas reiterates that "responsibility for the Other is not an accident that happens to a subject, but precedes essence in it, has not awaited freedom [. . .]. I have not done anything and I have always been under accusation—persecuted. [. . .] The word *I* means *here I am*, answering for everything and for everyone."[53] Beings *are*; they are thrown back on themselves: "This means concretely: accused of what the others do or suffer, or responsible for what they do or suffer."[54] The analogue for this structure in the logic of Heiter's presentation is his brute, declarative assertion, "Your tissues match." This is not a rhetoric of rivetedness but the correlate of its unbearable certainty: the intolerable rivetedness to the self as tissue (as code, as information, as material by which sequential joining can be correlated precisely because it *is*). Alphabetic order also does not await decision or risk deserting itself; its ordered necessity is the opposite of contingency, it is neither reasoned nor decided nor decidable.

Horror is the formal realization—the idealization, diagrammatization, and presentation—of this total structure. The cold logic of the diagram by which B follows A but precedes C deploys formality *for* enchainment. The final reckoning that leaves only figure B alive in the house displays, on the one hand, the sheer presence of being, its living continuation, its inescapable facticity and persistent vitality that is sutured to dead others. The diagram both declares without debate and yet is indifferent to the fact that this body is present, that it is there. On the other hand, however, this is a self who persists not as the one alone, but *in sequence*, enchained and riveted not only to her own presence but also to figures A and C: in other words, this is an impossible-to-flee self who persists as the B term in a diagrammatic relation by which an A necessarily comes before and a C necessarily comes after. One is heteronomously obliged to the other, after the other, before the other, responsible for the other, and this precedes any autonomy. Beings are given in the world only as and in a state in which the other precedes the I, never to be either A (the phantasmatic first) or C (the phantasmatic last). *B is anteceded: this is the opening of the ethical.* To be the middle term in the sequence—so let us be clear that *to be* is to be this middle term—is to be sutured to the inescapability of our own presence unavoidably bound up with the certain witnessing of other terms who suffer and who die and for whom we *are* wholly responsible.

(1) Hegel famously wrote in the *Logic*: "Everything rational is a syllogism."[55]

(2) He also insisted that the middle term in the syllogism, the *medius terminus*, was the most important feature of its form, what unites two others in its schema—the thesis, antithesis, synthesis; the universal, particular, and individual. Thus the syllogistic relation is "the *unity* of the extremes, the *middle term* which unites them, and the *ground* which supports them."[56] This middle term is neither grammar's joiners nor to be thought as a purely mediating function, for it itself is the result of prior mediations and thus retains a bond to both the concrete and the abstract. (From the viewpoint of syllogism, a judgment is "not a connection drawn through the *mere copula* or the empty 'is' but one drawn rather through a determinate middle which is replete with content.")[57]

Syllogistic form is a form and therefore can be found in many surprising places; for example, in his *Philosophy of Nature*, Hegel writes that "the chemical process is therefore a syllogism; and not merely the beginning of the process but its entire course is syllogistic. For the process requires three terms, namely, two self-subsistent extremes, and one middle term in which their determinatenesses come into contact and they are differentiated."[58] He further writes, "Since the real difference belongs to the extremes, this middle term is only the abstract neutrality, the real possibility of those extremes; it is, as it were, the theoretical element of the concrete existence of chemical objects, of their process and its result. In the material world water fulfills the function of this medium."

One example of a famous triad in Hegel's dialectics is Being (thesis)–Nothing (antithesis)–Becoming (synthesis).

(3) The first three definitions of *middle* in the *Oxford English Dictionary* are "a. Designating that member of a group or series, or that part of a whole, so situated as to have the same number of members or parts on each side of it: said with reference to position in space, time, order of succession or enumeration, or the like. Sometimes modifying a plural noun," and "c. Of a point, line, area, or volume [. . .] : equidistant from the ends or boundaries of a thing; situated at the centre, central."[59]

The middle definition is "b. Designating the second in age of three siblings." Unremarked is the positional term for the remaining one of two dead siblings. Or the remaining one of many dead friends. Or the remaining one of three dead strangers.

(4) Across Hegel's philosophy, one can find triadic structures that contain four terms and others that contain only two.[60] What, precisely, is thus meant by *triadic*? What does it *guarantee*?

Before he makes the centipede, Heiter promises figure B (at that point, Lindsay) that her suffering will be the worst in the middle-term position, as retribution for her earlier attempted escape. And indeed her suffering is the worst, for she must ingest the shit of figure A but, simultaneously, through the sheer labors of her gut system, it is she who is positioned to do violence to figure C, to the other, enchained to *her*, who comes after her. Figure B can neither escape the fact of having a body that persists but nor can she escape the way in which that self is sutured to finite others. She is in the singular position of unavoidably being done violence to, and unavoidably doing violence to others. And yet, despite the fact that A (apologizing, all the while) does his necessary violence (i.e., ultimately has to defecate), Heiter notes during an exam that B is constipated; he prescribes a laxative that he never gets around to administering. We might rephrase this as: *Something gets stuck at the level of being*. There is a blockage in this position. B's violence against the other remains suspended, unrealized yet infinitely possible: the fact that the fact of her being imposes on the other, indebts her to the other, takes the place of another, is purely notated on the level of a supposition of her being: not due to any realized violence her body actually does. In other words, B's imposition on C is a pure correlate of being B—her always *possible* violence against the other exists solely on the diagrammatic level. What the diagram displays is the logic of notation by which Lindsay cannot be turned into B and yet fail to be in the sequence that gives formal urgency and seriousness to the totality of the ethical. This is why the diagram is not the mere privileged representational form of Heiter's violence: the diagram, in giving the relation of components to each other, in positing the sequential dimension of sequence—what could not be outstripped from sequence without destroying sequentiality—is coextensive with the very violence of the ethical.

(1) Although modernist masterpiece and postmodern excretory horror text might seem unjoinable, any B can follow any A through the formalism of sequence. Beckett's 1964 *How It Is* (*Comment c'est* [1961]) is a diagram of precisely this question of brutal corporeal enchainment: "What we were then each for himself and for the other."[61] What the horror film fastens through sutures and alimentary conjunction, the novel phrases as a "slight overlapping" of flesh: "Pim and me part two and Bom and me part four what that will be / to say after that that we knew each other personally even then / glued together like a single body in the dark the mud / motionless but for one right arm."[62]

It is the shared general insistence on joining that concerns us here:

for as we have seen part two how it was with Pim the coming into contact of mouth and ear leads to a slight overlapping of flesh in the region of the shoulders

and that linked thus bodily together each one of us is at the same time Bom and Pim tormentor and tormented pedant and dunce wooer and wooed speechless and reafflicted with speech in the dark the mud nothing to emend there

there he is then again last figures the inevitable number 777777 at the instant when he buries the opener in the arse of number 777778 and is rewarded by a feeble cry cut short as we have seen by the thump on skull who on being stimulated at the same instant and in

the same way by number 777776 makes his own private moan which
same fate

something wrong there[63]

In fact, the concept of the diagram is not infrequently invoked in accounting for Beckett's formalism in this complex, metatextual, self-
interrupting work of unpunctuated paragraphs. (It is not infrequently
invoked in exegeses on Beckett in general; one only has to linger a bit
with his plays in particular to note the constant appearance of diagrams,
as in the geometrical figures that bookend the 1981 television play *Quad*,
the schematic of pacing and direction of steps that open the 1976 play
Footfalls, or the diagrammed angles of perception and perceivedness in
his 1969 script to *Film*.) Leo Bersani and Ulysse Dutoit explicitly use
the term in *Arts of Impoverishment* in their reading of origin and com-
mencement (as evoked by the French title), writing that *Comment c'est*
"diagrams a type of being (the being that is human) structured as the
unending repetition of its own origination. As if the deepest structure of
being could never be anything but that: the beginning again of its own
beginning."[64]

(2) There are a thousand points of possible connection between *How It Is*
and *The Human Centipede*, but beginning requires only one: the two
works share a common and uncommonly intense interest in the aesthetic and metaphysical figure of *crawling*—a term that conjoins posture
and rhythm, the agonizingly slow dragging of oneself along the ground,
as in a dying limb-cracked dog, as in the movement of the most base-
born insect, as in the vital practice of the worm—and also as in the tentative uneven explorations of the child, what tests (and risks) the total
newness of its (the) whole world. Crawling presumes lowering: what it
means to dwell on the ground, to be ontologically reduced, which is to
say diagrammatically reoriented toward the material humiliation that is
a downing to dirt, earth, mud; to slither, to slither awkwardly—"when
we crawl in an amble right leg right arm push pull flat on face."[65] *Circa
1200*, creulen: *to slowly draw the body across the ground, to drag oneself,
to claw*. The clawing crawling of attached bodies exaggerates clawing
crawling's sluggishness. Of the rhythm of such conjoined movement,
Beckett writes, "our slowness the slowness of our procession from left

to right in the dark the mud." Posture and rhythm here are secondary to the constitution of the diagram that gives rise to the syntax of difficulty that determines both aesthetic characteristics. *How It Is* and *The Human Centipede* share a drive toward a language of infinitely greater abstraction coextensive with a thinking of unavoidable violence in the structure of being-with.

But what *The Human Centipede* relegates to letter by way of a reductive formalism of a diagram of being's enchainment, *How It Is* treats via a reductive formalism of being's coordinates (left right; north south), via vertices, lengths, and angles, and via number—which is to say: what *The Human Centipede* relegates to a system of writing (drawing; alphabet), *How It Is* treats via mathematics. And so, in the opening lines of part 2 of Beckett's novel, after the dismissal of "no more figures" and its supplanting with "yes vague impressions of length length of space length of time vague impressions of brevity between the two," something of a conclusion is drawn: "no more reckoning save possibly algebraical."[66]

Accordingly, Andrew Gibson's description of Beckett's work as "much closer to mathematics than it is to most literature. Like mathematics, it is characterized by its powerful will to abstraction; its radical withdrawal from a world of which it none the less retains a residual trace; its frequent concern with extraordinary paradoxes and what seem to be irreducible problems and impossibilities; and its formalization of material that is threatened with drastic inconsistency."[67] This double will— toward abstraction and formalization—is set against an equally powerful ironization of mathematical formalisms and an attention to the "limits of formal mathematical systems," such that "mathematics is no more adequate than language to a complete description of the self and world."[68]

(3) What letter formalizes in *The Human Centipede* and what number formalizes in *How It Is* is an abstraction of the condition of being a (any) middle term in the minimal form of a sequence, which is to say the cruel logic of joinedness by which one is simultaneously always torturer and tortured. As Bersani and Dutoit describe the structure, "In this perfectly organised world, at every moment, everyone—whatever the number may be—is either enjoying a victim or suffering at the hands of a tormentor, or he is either crawling toward his victim or confident that a tormentor is on his way."[69] In part 3 of Beckett's novel, this formal depiction—which is to say, a depiction that is unnamable, ungiveable

except through a formalism—notates a series of sequences taken from an infinite set, infinitely extensible, but in the work of literature only contingently given: 814326, 814327, 814328. Crucially, Beckett begins with the middle term and works outward from there, positing the arbitrary origin of 814327, which gives rise as logical consequence to an antecedent term and a subsequent one, each one giving rise in turn, and again as logical consequence, to a further antecedent term and a further subsequent one:

> number 814327 may speak misnomer the tormentors being mute as we have seen part two may speak of number 814326 to number 814328 who may speak of him to number 814329 who may speak of him to number 814330 and so on to number 814345 who in this way may know number 814326 by repute [. . .]
> rumour transmissible ad infinitum in either direction
> from left to right through the confidences of the tormentor to his victim who repeats them to his
> from right to left through the confidences of the victim to his tormentor who repeats them to his[70]

Just as Heiter's B will *necessarily* ingest the shit of A and *necessarily* be poised to do violence to C—this necessity the unstrippable givenness of the form of the alphabetically notated and diagrammed sequence—one is simultaneously victim and tormentor by the logic of ordinal listing: any middle term in any minimal sequence being what is extensibly bonded to a something before, a someone after. One *is* in *The Human Centipede* and *How It Is* only ever in a world interceded with alterity, an alterity that does not guarantee the (or any) good but does nevertheless stand as the ground of a formalization of an ethics. There are differences between the texts, of course. (Everything is a particularity, especially within a thinking of the general.) Beckett's formalism of number suggests simultaneously more infinity and more arbitrariness—via the ongoingness of number, via number's listing that starts in the middle—while the film's notation of A, B, C suggests the contours of a closed system, albeit with substitutable parts: there has already been another A before the first film's A; there will be future As in the metatextual leaps as well; and there will be hundreds of middle terms, there could be thousands; there are millions. B is nothing if not an infinitely re-occupiable impersonal position.

A and C are the playthings of theology. For ontology, ethics, and aesthetics, it is no concern but B all the way down.

THE HUMILIATION OF METAPHYSICS

Contra Eugene Thacker and his *Horror of Philosophy* trilogy, what philosophy should ultimately recognize of itself in horror is not a question of tropes of the unknowable or representations of the unthinkable, but rather an unbreakable debt to formalisms. In particular, an unbreakable debt to formalisms by way of thinking B. Horror shares with philosophy, with mathematics, with Beckett, a drive for ever more abstraction; the writer was the supreme chronicler of the tensions inherent in this pursuit—always struggling "to maintain a faith in the power of abstraction in a world apparently surrendered to the logic of embodiment," which resonates loudly with horror's stubborn etymological, historical, and critical bond to sedimentations of the concept of an embodied negative affect.[71] In horror, the drive toward an infinitization of formalization means that violence (the next death in death's design; the infinite re-formation of the body in the generativity of torture; the suspension and voiding of critical positions) is *always* formally possible—always possible precisely because it is formal.[72] All the same, in this drive toward abstraction, horror is not an allegorization of philosophy. It is precisely the opposite: horror is the uneffacing of philosophical metaphoricity, a formalization that is a lowering, an abasement, a humbling boot to the face: it demeans and degrades philosophy by showing it *to be nothing but a formalism*.[73]

Horror humiliates metaphysics: brings it down to the rotted ground (lit. *humilis*, lowly, from *humus*, earth). As though a lost girl with kneecaps broken, horror drives all lofty light low, down from rectitude to make it crawl sad-bellied and aching in moist sad muck. Neither expressing philosophy (to thematize it) nor materializing it (as science fiction literalizes Romanticism: the twin scenes of, I saw you and my head exploded), horror uneffaces the pretty abstractions of philosophical claim.[74] *The autrui are unknowable?* Perhaps they will speak different languages, Japanese, English, all the while muffled by a tongue's permanent pressure against the open sphincter of the other. *You will regard the other die?* Here then is the very being you must watch tremble, give in, expire. *You are the tormentor of the other?* This One had a mother. To her this unknowable other was tiny socks, was nipple bites and belly kicks, malformed drawings and stones shoved in pockets. *You are responsible for the other?* Very well, you will be the hostage of the other until the day you yourself die. There is vomit and pus and *hurt*, there is boundless violence in this insistence of unremitting debt. —Quite right, and you shall eat the shit of the other, taste his sickness; you are saddled to this heavy life and shall remain sewn to the other even after their death, will feel the pulsation of the body softening into rot, will smell their body oldening and old and dying and dead and after. This body will stink. It will always stink.

Horror mortifies the philosophy described by Derrida as consisting of its metaphors, in which the first meaning and first displacement are effaced and forgotten: but in rubbing and wearing its metaphors away, uneffacing not to restore or illuminate, there is only a lowering with neither recourse nor alibi.[75] Thus horror works over philosophical metaphor in the strictest sense, drags it along the ground (draws it away: recall the labors of *trahere*), wears raw philosophy's inherited abstractions. Uneffacing, which is to say forming anew, supplementing in place of removing, unobliterating by creating, positing, forming, writing instead of rubbing, *making* in place of destroying the bondedness of enchainment and intertwinement, horror humiliates as creative praxis. Thinking, we know, is condemned to representation, and philosophy, we might say, is condemned to notation. Horror generatively humiliates philosophy by reminding it of its own bondedness to the diagram, to abstraction, to notations and formalizations, to speculative gestures such as Levinas's critique of sameness in *Totality and Infinity*, which turns on the formalism "A is A."[76] It is no coincidence that Richard Rorty's constant charge against Levinas is that his ethics amounts to nothing but an empty formalism.[77] (Or that Hegel used the same phrase in *Philosophy of Right* in critiquing Kant's categorical imperative.)[78]

Horror: what puts metaphysics in the mud, and thereby gives it its certainties—"the mud the dark I recapitulate the sack the tins the mud the dark the silence the solitude nothing else for the moment."[79]

Levinas's philosophy indebts being completely, but it does not commit being to the good because it severs itself from decision or acceptance of infinite debt: enchainment is impersonal, irrevocable, diagrammatic. It is this reminder of an unremittable enchainment to formalism that above all humiliates metaphysics; what first philosophy is is a dragging to the ground that which supports all secondary decision and thought. This is a ground that is taken literally by *How It Is* and *The Human Centipede*: a formalization of being that is lowered to the brutal thereisness of scum, muck, sludge, mire. This is a humiliation, but it puts process and movement to that lowering, to *humilis*: horror does not merely humiliate metaphysics once, it makes it crawl long in that mud, exposes the vital straining of abasement, that one is not left unmolested, corpsestill in prostration, but rather renders a mortification that is *ongoing*, by which I mean: in *being*, one must *go on*. But only lowly, only on ground, infinitely on belly, in the dark, in this mud,

> —one's entire world reduced
> to the earth's sad
> and dirty
> oils.

And if this writing has posited its own minimal form of a sequence as *Film–Philosophy–Literature*, or perhaps *Image–Philosophy–Word*, it remains the case that the middle term has it the worst, what will always both do violence to and be done violence to by A and C, by its previous and subsequent terms, slightly overlapping, sutured into one system, inelegant surgery at that, these terms that are unavoidably bound to each other, tormenting and tormented *by* each other. Ad infinitum.

The Human Centipede plays out the structure of enchainment in the cruel formality of relation; the dimension of being unmodifiably already in sequence is what the diagram displays, and what cannot be otherwise in the reductive shape that it gives. Horror (what is said to bristle the hairs, what is said to wreck through fear and disgust) is not there, in this film, in images of the dying, the suffering, the excreting; it is in a black line on a white plane revealed via a slide through which light passes. What the film ultimately cannot digest—indeed, the very essence of what is indigestible for thought itself—is the dimension that the diagram gives as its form: a simple ordering of elements that goes *A to B to C*. This attestation through the reductive formalism of the diagram is not graspable by a criticism that presumes it knows the object it seeks to capture (for symptomatic, historical, or generic analytical purposes), or that has decided in advance that the conceit of any film is but a paraphrasable theme and that the critical task is reduced to articulating how that theme has guaranteed connections to predetermined affects or strong sensations. Drag horror past the imperialism of bad affect. If thinking regards *The Human Centipede* and remains on the side of felt shock at the illuminated relation of mouth to anus, or with scatology as allegory or provocation, it has in fact *avoided* a confrontation with horror altogether. Violence is instead in the joining of abstract irrevocability in notation, in drawn line and letter. For what a formalist reading of *The Human Centipede* uniquely reveals is that this is not a text about contingency (being in the wrong place at the wrong time) but one of givenness and necessity, the necessity of the structure of being (that being is always in the right [the only] place at all time—*stuck*, that is, with being itself); that violence is not given over in the opened explicit graphic body, but in the reductive formalism of a spare graphic diagram; and that horror is not offering a model of violence as a force external to a system that wrecks it, but one that is constitutive *of* systems and structures in which one is given and to which one is inescapably riveted.

Except, one thing else.

Although *The Human Centipede* is clear on its central ethical stance—horror as first philosophy—making this attestation of the bondedness of being at the level of form and with no ground but form, it also, however, as a morphology of the diagram, introduces at least one further term: an unexpected opening up to violence that, in other contexts, we might call the problem of *care*.

During an escape in which she alone had progressed toward a chance at freedom, Lindsay decides to return for Jenny, risking everything to drag her unconscious friend out of Heiter's house. Lindsay's action, the cause of her later placement in the position of figure B, occurs in the wake of the presentation of the surgical slides, and the attempted rescue displays a contingent form of the necessary sequentiality of their diagram. In other words, it sets the abstraction of an unmodifiable responsibility for the other against an affirmative election to be responsible for the other. While diagrammatic form reveals the former, cinematic form uniquely notates the latter.

The sequence begins inside Heiter's house as the camera shows Lindsay and Jenny from the front, the one friend grasping the other under each arm and straining to pull her out of the tall rectangle made by a broken floor-to-ceiling window, whose verticality and narrow aspect ratio is cruelly set against the robust horizontality and heaviness of the two figures dragging along, dragged along, wet low ground. Lindsay and Jenny are dressed identically in blue patient gowns in preparation for the surgery that will in fact, but has not yet, but will, take place.

(1) Many types of lifts, carries, and drags are taxonomized in manuals for emergency responders.

(2) For example, there is the one-person arm carry; the fireman's carry; the pack-strap carry; the tied-hands crawl; the two-person seat carry; the human crutch. Some manuals break these down further into one-person and two-person rescue techniques, further distinguishing those extrication techniques requiring a team of rescuers, and also distinguishing urgent from nonurgent moves. Dragging methods include the emergency clothes drag; the blanket drag; the arm drag; and the arm-to-arm drag. If the first of the previous list is used, and if the patient's clothing has buttons, one must ensure that the top two are undone in order to prevent a violent and counterproductive choking in the midst of a saving.

Lindsay dragging Jenny is a perfect demonstration of the arm-to-arm drag, in which the extractor places her arms under the patient's shoulders and through their armpits and, while grasping their arms, drags the patient backward. Arm-to-arm dragging is classified as a one-rescuer technique.

(3) *Advanced Emergency Care and Transportation of the Sick and Injured* sternly advises: "You should use one-rescuer techniques to move a patient only if a potentially life-threatening danger exists and you are alone."[80]

> *Of course, even in cases where a one-rescuer technique is performed, the very presence of the someone who is to be moved means that one is never precisely entirely alone.*

Once Lindsay and Jenny are outside the house, the camera flips its axial position and will henceforth only either stand behind Lindsay or show the bodies from the side. Humiliating itself—which is to say, resting on the ground—the camera's vantage behind Lindsay and Jenny reveals a strangely moving composite form, but one that figurally resembles something close to the singly human: Lindsay's straining legs are visible, Jenny's arms are outstretched limply and awkwardly, but the (other) legs that are dragged and the (other) arms that are gripping are blocked by the position of the camera, and therefore the retreating grunting figure retains the illusion of a self-contained subject moving toward a chimerical escape.

The film, however, then cuts to a different vantage point, and in this reframing from the side the moving figure now is (re)revealed as containing too many extensions for one trunk, a point of view that makes clear the burden of multiple limbs in an arrangement where one body is set behind the other, bearing its full weight. This juxtaposition is a demonstration of a claim about joining: if the first image promises the fantasy of a being all alone who might evade joining, the second brutally recalls the awkward and stilted, inelegant, arduous lived labors of joining. But the figure itself does not change—the framing does. In other words, it is the mutable perspectives of cinematic van-

FIGURES 4.10–4.11. *The Human Centipede (First Sequence)* (Tom Six, 2009)

tage *and nothing else* that attest to the already inscribed presurgical dimension of Jenny and Lindsay's conjoined being. Film form here is thus equivalent as thought to Levinas's claim that ethics is first philosophy and does not wait for decision: for cinematic framing and the relation of these two images reiterate that what appears from one angle to constitute an election to return for the other, to drag something separate along with the self, is—from another angle—merely the heaviness of being in which the other was already a limb-part part of the self.

When Adriana Cavarero, in her philosophical critique of rectitude—a "postural geometry of ethics" that philosophy has presupposed at the cost of other models—describes the implications of the Levinasian rupture, she writes that "emphasizing vulnerability is not a matter of correcting individualistic ontology by inserting the category of relation into it. It is rather to think relation itself as originary and constitutive, as an essential dimension of the human." In its most radical version, "which liquidates any residue of individualistic ontology, the relational model does not in fact allow for any symmetry at all, but only for a continuous interweaving of multiple and singular dependence. At its most extreme, it is exemplified by scenarios in which the protagonists are altogether unbalanced." This last word insinuates itself. Relationality, Cavarero writes, means "our being creatures who are materially vulnerable and, often in greatly *unbalanced* circumstances, consigned to one another."[81] Mother to the child. Friend to the friend. Stranger to the other. Everyone to anyone. Horror, once again humiliating metaphysics by uneffacing its metaphors, here literally unbalances its awkwardly moving bodies, refusing symmetry or grace for those creatures by deploying cinematic form to show, then hide, then reveal once more the total absence of reciprocity in their conjoined and burdened interwoven being, limping and shuffling together along.

The worst violences, attested at the abstracted sequential level of diagrammatic enchainment, perversely formalized (perverse because literal, taking place on the back of letters), and available to thought solely via the grand humiliation of philosophy, are what the logic of an ethics of relation exposes one to. But visual form adds to this law one further rotation: Friendship is what *cinematically* discovers and reencounters Lindsay in the centipedal form abstracted by the diagram. Lindsay is the hostage of Jenny—the vulnerable other who may be the beloved friend is still just so much dead weight. Yet one must drag it along. And one will drag it along. Care, that is to say, makes one inherently *many-footed*. What marks the particularity of an ethics of friendship is that one accepts with a measure of tenderness this structure that did not wait for decision or commitment or the assumption of responsibilities: one issues a Yes to the condition of being to which one *is* conscripted. Lindsay refuses the possibility of an escape that was not to be in order to remain in the position in which she already was. *She gives up something that she did not have to a cumbersome someone who did not want or ask for it.* Film form's own diagrammatic arrangement of sequence thereby unconceals that one type of vulnerability to violence is coextensive with the very debts of a chosen devotion.

Horror, in that sense, is just another name for how love goes.

Sicut hic depingitur.

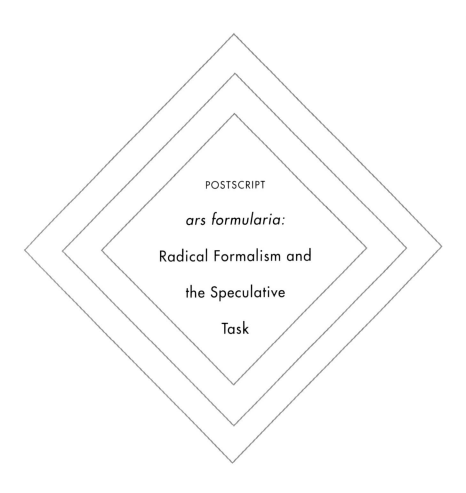

POSTSCRIPT

ars formularia:

Radical Formalism and

the Speculative

Task

Hatreds of formalism are all alike. Accused of abandoning the world, its misfortunes, its tumults and things, one is asked to accede to Fredric Jameson's call for a "literary or cultural criticism which seeks to avoid imprisonment in the windless closure of the formalisms"; Yves Bonnefoy's midcentury condemnation of formalist poetic practices in *L'improbable*, "La vraie malédiction en ce monde est d'y être réduit au jeu" (The true curse in this world is to be reduced to playing games); or, earlier, and with a leap outside the humanities, the intuitionist Ludwig Bieberbach's 1919 polemics against modern styles of mathematical thinking, "The tendency towards formalism must not cause us to forget the flesh and blood over the logical skeleton."[1] Alone at night, in a soft pause before sleep, on some level you agree.

Or, you don't.

What, precisely, are we talking about when we talk about formalism? One may speak of formalists (who may or may not embrace the term), the formalistic (nearly always a pejorative epithet), Russian formalism (not to be collapsed with Czech structuralism, which developed from a different line of philosophical thinking, namely, the abstract formalism of Johann Friedrich Herbart, which became dominant at Prague University), new formalism (not to be confused with—because in part it rejects, though it is also in dialogue with aspects of—New Criticism), New Formalism (not to be confused with new formalism, this refers to the late twentieth-century poetic movement that promoted a return to metrical verse [q.v., the unapologetically feminist formalism of Marilyn Hacker]), evaluative formalism (e.g., Aristotle's *Poetics*, setting out calculated rules and rigid codifications for aesthetic objects; Kant will reject this model for its confusion of judgments of taste with judgments of logic), restricted formalism (restrictiveness and a representationalist conservatism being what Kant's aesthetic doctrine in turn is often accused of, to the point that Robert Kaufman grounds the literary-critical phenomenon he dubs "Everybody hates Kant" in a critique of what is taken as "bourgeois formalism"), philosophical formalism (late Lacan, some Badiou), mathematical formalism (e.g., game formalism; cf. Frege's scorching critique of term formalism), neo-formalism (the cognitivist and constructivist-adjacent movement in film studies associated with David Bordwell and Kristin Thompson's use of formal devices as orienting cues for spectators), moderate formalism (defended by philosopher Nick Zangwill), or extreme formalism (like that of theorists such as Clive Bell and Roger Fry, or the musicologist Eduard Hanslick, but also artists such as Malevich or Pollock, some but not all expressionists, the 1920s Polish formists, &c.).[2]

Proliferating further variations: in "What is New Formalism?," her summation of the previous decade's return to aesthetics in literary theory, Marjorie Levinson writes of a "practical division between (a) those who want to restore to today's reductive reinscription of historical reading its original focus on form [. . .] and (b) those who campaign to bring back a sharp demarcation between history and art, discourse and literature, with form ([. . .] disinterested, autotelic, playful, pleasurable, consensus-generating, and therefore both individually liberating and conducive to affective social cohesion) the prerogative of art. In short, we have a new formalism that makes a continuum with new historicism and a backlash new formalism."[3] Dubbing the former "activist formalism" (Susan Wolfson's term) and the latter "normative formalism," Levinson posits that the former regards a study of form as essential to the critical moves of materialist and historicist readings—compare that with what Tom Eyers via Paul de Man calls a "speculative formalism" in which the impasses of literary, specifically poetic, form constitute a philosophically serious engagement with history and the political—whereas the latter, norm-setting formalism, regards form as the ground of the aesthetic, thus also bonding it to the generality of the accusation against formalists that their interest is always ultimately in "art for art's sake."[4] (So once more, we have rearrived at the question of that claim of some abandonment of the world.)

There is a formalism that means not-historicist, though Barthes famously insisted in *Mythologies*, "I shall say that a little formalism turns one away from history, but that a lot brings one back to it."[5] There is a formalism that means not-materialism, but de Man concludes that in Kant's third *Critique*, "[It] is this entirely a-referential, a-phenomenal, a-pathetic formalism that will win out in the battle among affects and find access to the moral world of practical reason, practical law, and rational politics. [. . .] The radical formalism that animates aesthetic judgment in the dynamics of the sublime is what is called materialism."[6] For every formalism that is an ecstatic reverie (with overlaps with various Romantic sentimentalisms; with other overlaps with a range of aestheticisms)—think Oscar Wilde's "mere colour, unspoiled by meaning"— is a formalism devoted to completely dissevering sentimentality and analysis (W. K. Wimsatt and Monroe Beardsley's affective fallacy; Viktor Shklovsky's "By its very essence, art is without emotion").[7] Complicating things, there is a profound interest in social and cultural forms and formations and the form of events in thinkers of the political from Adorno to Althusser to Jameson, an investment that manifests in the midst of profound and diverse antipathies toward aesthetic formalisms and formalists.[8] (And what to do with this: long before the contemporary showdown between historicism and deconstruction, the Marxist philosopher Lukács wrote his early work *Die Seele und die Formen*, translated into English as *Soul and Form*, though losing in the process the titular plural that governs his exploration of numerous invented and reinvented forms, which are always particular—including literary ones such as the essay, the lyric poem, tragedy, but also the form of the Platonist, the form of Kierkegaard's *Lebensphilosophie*, the form of longing, and also that of love, &c.—and which both emerge *from* and encode the expressions *of* life.)[9] Some have written *formalism* and actually meant *structuralism*—though Barthes insisted that "one cannot speak about structures in terms of forms, and vice versa."[10] (Lévi-Strauss opens his well-known essay on Propp with a similar if less forceful separation: "Structuralism exists as an independent doctrine which, indeed, owes a great deal to formalism but differs from formalism in the attitude it has adopted toward the concrete."[11] [Then again, in 1975 Michael Kirby called his new formalist theater "the Structuralist Workshop."]) Sometimes, one will say (or accuse) *formalism*, but really mean *modernism*; Clement Greenberg wrote of *formalism* in order to praise *abstract expressionism*. In her 2015 book *Forms: Whole, Rhythm, Hierarchy, Network*, Caroline Levine extends her notion of a "strategic formalism" to specify her focus on "all shapes and configurations, all ordering principles, all patterns of repetition and difference"; as a result, when she writes of form as a question of arrangements and organizations, she unquestionably is denoting something more akin to forms, and in writing forms she is clear that she is writing politics ("It is the work of form to make order. And this means that forms are the stuff of politics")—and thus, by *formalist* she really means something much narrower: progressive activist.[12]

Certain dialects of thinkers pronounce the formalist the one most concerned with *genre* or *style* or *technique* or *language*. Others, the one who attends to *pattern* or *fugue* or *sonnet*. The sixteenth-century music theorist Gioseffo Zarlino insisted on the absolute purity of the *numero sonoro*, or *sounding number*. Le Corbusier liked to announce his focus on *invariants*.[13]

To some critics, formalism, while purporting to name a neutral method, invisibly advances a valuation of certain types of avant-garde work while diminishing explicitly politicized movements. So proceeds one critique: "Insofar as modernism is a modern formalism, it is by definition opposed to the possibility of a political avant-garde, which is necessarily concerned with meanings. Eisenstein is considered by formalist critics only in terms of formal innovation," his theoretical work "selectively reduced" to issues of montage and composition.[14] Formalism can thus refer to an exceptional range of stances, methods, techniques, valuations, and critical and speculative trajectories: it can suggest an interest in a medium specificity such as *literaturnost*, the critical target of the Russian formalists (the literariness or literaturity of literature), or following Jean Epstein the *photogénie* of cinema; or, instead of honoring and expressing material (or substance, content, subject, matter), it can consume or destroy or erase it, as in Schiller's "only through form can we expect true aesthetic freedom. This is the real artistic secret of the master, *that he eradicates the material through form*" (dass er den Stoff durch die Form vertilgt); it can suggest a method of reading (one among many or a singular one); it can suggest an interpretive stance or strategy or positively

organize a movement of aesthetic practice; it can refer to the aim of a simplification of structure (as in the irreducible thirty-one functions comprising
Proppian morphology; or the formal categories that shift from the sixteenth
to the seventeenth century—linear/painterly; planar/recessional; tectonic/
atectonic; multiplicity/unity; absolute/relative clarity—posited in the art historian Heinrich Wölfflin's 1915 *Kunstgeschichtliche Grundbegriffe*), or it can be
defended as what resists historicists' simplification of structure by infinitizing
interpretation, recalling Derrida's strategy of subtle, winding, indirect reading, inducing not generalities of social context but particularities of individual
texts; and by formalism one as often suggests a self-reflexive formalism that
examines the nature of form itself (poetic, sculptural, diagrammatic), including the forms of thinking that animate, for example, views on the foundations
of critique, including the very and varied forms (Malabou: *plasticity*; Laruelle:
decision) of philosophical speculation.[15]

Or—Busy motor of rejection, epithet grounding negative polemics, form
is, at heart, what disciplines (literary and cultural studies, art criticism, post-
poststructuralist film theory) are ever trying to move away from, move beyond, move *past*. One speaks of *formalism* because it is so very complicated
to speak of what one inherits; in targeting formalism, one has in mind *before*,
one groans *not that old song again*.

Often, it is merely the thing one wants to ditch.

Making matters even more difficult, few interpretive methods in the study
of representation display an utter indifference to some aspect of a work's composition, form, aesthetics, or structure, so what does it really mean to insist
on the critical priority of reading for form? It does not, on the face of it, involve a retreat from other theoretical, political, or ethical commitments. As
Ellen Rooney words it, all that is required for taking form seriously is "refusing to reduce reading entirely to the elucidation, essentially the paraphrase of
themes."[16] Drawing on Cleanth Brooks's famous "heresy of paraphrase" in his
1947 *The Well Wrought Urn*, this insistence—that a poem is not an attempt to
represent the world or its purported exterior, hard, really realness, neither a
collection of themes nor a container of ready-made symbols nor an analogue
to content, reducible to its "subject matter"—requires merely that one ground
interpretation in the description and analysis of structure. Brooks qualifies
and complicates that claim, however, writing:

> Though it is in terms of structure that we must describe poetry, the term
> "structure" is certainly not altogether satisfactory as a term. One means

by it something far more internal than the metrical pattern, say, or than the sequence of images. The structure meant is certainly not "form" in the conventional sense in which we think of form as a kind of envelope which "contains" the "content." [. . .] The nature of the material sets the problem to be solved, and the solution is the ordering of the material. [. . .] [T]he paraphrase is not the real core of meaning which constitutes the essence of the poem. For the imagery and the rhythm are not merely the instruments by which this fancied core-of-meaning-which-can-be-expressed-in-a-paraphrase is directly rendered.[17]

Most definitions of formalism begin with this suspicion of paraphrase, this investment in the *what is* of aesthetic material; take, for example, Robert Lehman's "approach to art objects—literature, film, painting, and so on—grounded in an attention to these objects' spatiotemporal qualities, their *phenomenal* qualities, which might allow for the transmission of a content or a meaning but that are not themselves *intrinsically* meaningful. As a critical practice, then, formalism would prescribe consideration of meter, line, composition, rhythm, movement, shape: all those characteristics that are supposed to make an art object what it is."[18]

Whether, in fact, formalism is a method, a theory, a mode of reading, *the* mode of close reading, a technique or strategy, or a type of critical disposition is perhaps the most contentious question in twentieth- and twenty-first-century debates about aesthetics. To now further bedevil matters, what we are talking about when we talk about *form* is infinitely more complex than in the case of various formalisms (—and I will not even attempt here to grapple with *format* or *formalization*, let alone, God help us, *platform* and various platformalisms). That is because the term *form* is always multiple and contradictory, starting with the problem that the unary Latin *forma* replaced both Greek terms *morphē* and *eidos*, which poses the fundamental dilemma of form as double: that it refers both to a minor showing; mere appearance; a visible, outward shape (cast in wood or stone) or display (as of religiosity) or attention to superficial *rather than* substantial qualities (resonances with the formula and the formulaic), *and* points simultaneously to the specifying principle of some thing, an inward kind or essential type. For Aristotle in the *Metaphysics*, form names "whatever we ought to call the shape present in the sensible thing," rejecting the Platonic conception of an immaterial, insensible, immutable Form available solely to mind.[19] (At stake, in part, is the question of whether there can be forms of negations.) One might, however, reject the neatness of such a binary—the Platonic versus the Aristotelian; the eidos of abstract idea versus the morphē of visible shape—and pluralize form further. The philosopher and historian of art Wladyslaw Tatarkiewicz, for example, in "Form: History of One Term and Five Concepts," proceeds from the contrary, positing that "the many opposites of form (content, matter, element, subject matter, and others) reveal its numerous meanings."[20] These include (1) the abstraction of the "disposition, arrangement, or order of parts, which will be called form A" (its opposites include "elements, components or parts which form A unites or welds into a whole"); (2) what is concretely "directly given to the senses" (its opposite is content); (3) the "boundary or contour of an object" (its "opposite and correlate is matter or substance"); (4) the "conceptual essence of an object" (the Aristotelian *entelechy*), whose opposite is the "accidental features of objects"; and (5) the Kantian notion of "a contribution of the mind to the perceived object" (its opposite and correlate "consists in what is not produced and introduced by the mind but is given to it from without through experience")— these latter two pose the difference between substantial and a priori form. (The first three ideas, Tatarkiewicz writes, "are the creation of aesthetics itself," whereas the "remaining two concepts of form arose within general philosophy and then passed into aesthetics.")[21]

Because "form" is a passive description of outward appearance while simultaneously a determining active principle; because it can refer to an immaterial idea or a sensible shape; because it may mean the formation or arrangement of something in and of itself or, by contrast, the formation or arrangement as determined in opposition to ideological or historical development; and because of the minor distinctions of its varied usage in aesthetics and in metaphysical philosophy, Raymond Williams phrases its essential tension thusly in *Keywords:* "It is clear that in these extreme senses form spanned the whole range from the external and superficial to the inherent and determining."[22] What is literally pro forma is done for the sake of form (all formalisms thus proformalisms) but always in the sense of being done merely for the sake of form (and not, presumably, for something—pick your particular topology—deeper, higher, beyonder, *morer*).[23] In even stronger formulations, Angela Leighton contends that "while most abstract nouns lend themselves to philosophical whittling, to definitions which reduce their sense for clarity and use, form makes mischief and keeps its signification moveable," and Peter Osborne regards formalism as the "enduring *problem*" raised by the relationship of French Theory to art criticism and practice in late modernity.[24] Any reading for form is made possible by the tensions generated by the aporias of the concept of form, which, themselves, as readings that have and grapple with form, give rise to new iterations of those very tensions. Thus, in contending with a conception of form that is correlated to the inherent, determining absolute that is simultaneously given shape in manifest external displays, the sensible quality of form that requires close, detailed, obsessive attention and ongoing reading, formal readings are always also meta-formalisms, navigations of the antinomies of form itself.

How could we ever read the sedimentations of the concept of form without availing ourselves of a concept of form?

In setting out my defense of "radical formalism" in *The Forms of the Affects*, on the one hand I had in mind foundational assertions like the severing of aesthetics from subject in Maurice Denis's famous 1890 symbolist manifesto, "Définition du néo-traditionnisme": "It is well to remember that a picture—before being a battle horse, a nude woman, or some anecdote—is essentially a plane surface covered with colors assembled in a certain order."[25] Insisting that close reading attend to line, light, color, texture, space, scale, duration, montage, mise-en-scène, and that only such a close reading for form would reveal the possibilities of the affective turn, I turned to the question of form's relationship to theory:

> Given that Bordwell explicitly positions neo-formalism against what he terms "Grand Theory," my approach to affect recovers and reintroduces the insights and problematics of continental theory in dialogue with form instead of necessarily opposed to it. Not neo-formalism but *radical formalism*. This I mean quite literally: heeding its own etymological *radix*, radical formalism returns to roots, presses on what is essential, foundational, and necessary in formalism itself. A radical formalism in film and media studies would take the measure of theory for form *and* take the measure of form for affectivity; this vital formalism, in the sense of what is both affective and urgent, returns to the roots of formalist analysis, and extends their reach.[26]

My interest then and now is not in a radical formalism that would instrumentalize readings of form for the sake of (in thrall to) the projects of radical politics (as in Craig Dworkin's *Reading the Illegible*, in which the formal experimentation of unreadable avant-garde texts reveals a "politics of the poem"), nor in the formalism that Laura U. Marks deploys to argue for a radical materialism—"the irreducible materiality of electronic media is that mutable particle, the electron."[27] Rather, a *radical* that dredges *radix* returns to the speculative ground of what formal thinking can claim and situates reading for form as the rootedness of theoretical claims themselves—what produces the stakes of the moves of speculation, what should be *prior* in the sense of both ordinality and priority. At stake in radical formalism is how to move past thinking *about* form to the question of thinking *from* form. Many formalists merely think about form and do so in the service of a sense of form's strategic utility to make other claims—(they also thereby risk performing the supremely antiformalist gesture of thematizing form). Levine's interest in *Forms*, for example, in how "attending to the affordances of form opens up a generalizable understanding of political power," urging literary critics to "*export* those practices, to take traditional skills to new objects—the social structures and institutions that are among the most crucial sites of political efficacy"—is an investment in reading forms insofar as they can be instrumentalized for the sake of something else, converted into confirming the logic of the political or social, which retroactively gets established as prior to and external to the formal; thus forms never themselves pose the question of the political, of efficacy, of site, of export, of practice, &c.[28] Into avowals of the various "affordances of form," shared by a broad cohort of new and activist formalists, the speculative potential of radical formalism inserts negation.

Knotted roots open up the question of the *disaffordances* of formalism, its capacity to trouble, disrupt, even void grounds of meaning, to render readings that are bad investments, interpretive stances that do not return thinking to substantives, but open up a thinking of nonunderstanding, finitude, limit, passage, the not-something, arrival at the nothing, abeyance, inaudibility, without obliterating those scenes by recalling them to languages of presence, humanism, idealism, plenitude, utility, economy, value, &c. Radical formalism is strictly *indifferent* (impartial: no more inclined to one than to another) to affordances *tout court*; it is not demonstrative, it is prospective. Although affordance and disaffordance formalisms share a discomfort with historicisms, Levine's interest in a "formalist cultural studies" that would take "the very heterogeneity at the heart of form's conceptual history" and distill it into five functions (for her, all forms contain, differ, overlap, travel, or operate politically) everywhere risks a model of textual recovery—finding form, finding formal affordances (*finding* being implicit in one of her founding claims, that "forms are everywhere structuring and patterning experience"). Projects of finding and recovery, however, operate at the expense of the ongoing generation of new and unforeseen lines of thought.[29] The point of radical formalism is not merely to displace contextualist readings, but to activate and launch the speculative potential of texts, one only available through readings that proceed without guarantee. Which is the heart of what reading form entails. One does not know in advance what is as yet undiscovered. Reading cannot secure a gain on its investment through promises of prior and external affordances precisely because aesthetic objects do not immediately render the world. Form, by another name, is the measure—and force—of their difference. Thus all affordance formalisms write around the great potential of reading for form, which is precisely that it neutralizes and suspends and disimplicates critical oppositions, inserts irresponsible difficulties, unsteadies, unseats, works over yes and even wrecks.

Reading for form is a proceeding. But without guarantee. But a proceeding.

THE VIOLENCE OF A (CERTAIN) FASCINATION WITH FORM
(And what thereby introduces a potentially fatal late-stage complication, requiring a reimagining of formalism as *process*)

Is formalism without risk?
Would it be worth anything without some risk?
> General form: Is anything worth something without some risk?

We might redescribe this risk through some listed worries: Is the formalist the one who is a bit too fascinated with form? Are topologies of violence, philosophies of finitude, and films of horror fastened to their own fascination with monstrations of cruelty and death-bringing things? And which is worse: a fascination with extreme violence or an extreme fascination with form? From what do we ask theory to shield its eyes: fascinating aestheticized if revolting spectacles or the repellent exhibition of a fascination with *something that is nothing but* an aesthetic attestation?

Versions of these questions date at least as far back as the founding texts of metaphysics. Consider the story of Leontius in Plato's *Republic* who, "on his way up from the Piraeus under the outer side of the northern wall, becoming aware of dead bodies that lay at the place of public execution at the same time felt a desire to see them and a repugnance and aversion, and that for a time he resisted and veiled his head, but overpowered in despite of all by his desire, with wide staring eyes he rushed up to the corpses and cried,

There, ye wretches, take your fill of the fine spectacle!"[30] The Greek for the spectacle is *kalon*, fine or beautiful, admirable or noble, a judgment of a worthiness of being-attended-to that is simultaneously reproached in a form of self-disgust, an ironic juxtaposition of the language of the ideals of beauty and the appetitive lure toward what is ugly, base, at once debased and debasing. But is censure directed here at the affective attraction that draws attention counterposed against a revulsion that compels retreat, or is it directed at the aesthetic attraction that draws attention toward fineness or beauty? The word *kalon* names both moral and aesthetic goodness, and it thus unseats a certainty about which is the riskier form of fascination: that with what is morally degraded or that with what is aesthetically elevated.

Despite a modern sense of the captivations of fascination and its discursive associations with sublimity, awe, wonder, attraction, desire, &c., fascination was long bonded to forms of extraordinary violence, in particular in its ancient relation to wounding, transfixion, the exercise and direct action of maleficence, the denaturing work of force—a bond both etymological (*fascinare*: to bewitch, enchant, with evocations of witchcraft) and mythological-critical, as in Sibylle Baumbach's summation of the privileged trope of fascination, the petrifying gaze of Medusa, as "a double image of fascination and counter-fascination: she also resembles an unspeakable event, functioning as both a symbol of and a talisman against trauma in a myth that deals with physical and visual assault."[31] In this way, the vicissitudes of the concept of fascination are not so unlike the transformations of the word *passion*, which moved in just a few centuries from the early medieval sufferings of Christ on the cross to a seventeenth-century absorption into the episteme of the sentiments—what Diderot dubbed "penchants, inclinations, desires and aversions carried to a certain degree of intensity"—rendering "passion" akin to enthusiasm, strong liking, even figuring it as the lusty core of erotic love.[32] (Fascination, paradoxically, despite its etymological, intellectual-historical, and mythological debt to transfixion and stasis, what stuns and stills, has always thereby been able to be put to work for the busiest mobilities of philosophical labor: the frenetic machine of sublation, what defends against the losses and risks of the negative as such.)

In the long history of the relation between aesthetic and ethical philosophy, violence is the constant companion of fascination, but unsettled is the matter of which is the greater risk, a fascination with aestheticized violence or a violent fascination with aesthetics. Inserting a rotation and infidelity at the heart of their intimate relation, the general problem of horror names the aesthetic mode that formalizes what it is for fascination not to mitigate violence or make violence tolerable, even pleasurable, but to *constitute* a mode of violence. Horror attests to the violence *of* fascination, or, rather, of a specific type of fascination, a fascination with visible form, and a fascination that is itself a mode of violence that disturbs and deeply troubles the very formalism for which this book is advocating. In formalizing a mode of violence that involves a fascination with form, horror thereby becomes a privileged site for a testing of formalism's own aporias, ultimately bearing out something of a law for an ethics of formalism—what amounts to a formalism that refuses to linger with visible forms, continually relocating itself with what undoes visible form, but formally so. Radical formalism reveals that horror constitutes an ultraformalism that puts on display form's own (terribly) risky and unavoidable bond to violence, requiring not that one renounce reading for form but, in fact, mazily pursue it to its furthest possible, unforeseen, interminable reach.

Pascal Laugier's 2008 film *Martyrs*, sometimes assimilated to the regime of "New Extremism" or nominated as "torture porn" (itself a designation and denigration of what ostensibly ought to constitute an object of spectatorial or critical fascination), constitutes a fertile field for thinking the way in which horror speculatively grapples with the violent nature of a certain logic of fascination, not least because from the viewpoint of the agential cause of violence in the film's narrative, it is nothing but the alibi of a fascination with form all the way down.

 Martyrs takes a strict AB structure, with a hypotactic relation between the two halves, and with such a violent cleaving at film's midpoint that many viewers are ferociously disoriented. It opens in medias res with a young girl, Lucie, running toward the camera in a frantic state of corporeal disrepair and abuse, the cause for her hysteria unfolding through psychoanalytic and anthropological discourse over the first half of the film, a narrative of unimaginable torture experienced as a child. The mute, traumatized creature, now safely in an orphanage, is befriended by a girl named Anna, who becomes her protector. Without warning, and still in the first part of the film, the text leaps ahead fifteen years to a previously unseen family, dwelling for five long, contextless minutes of screen duration on the banality of their morning rituals and unremarkable domestic conversation. At the doorbell, a grown Lucie stands in the frame. She murders the two adults and two children in an explicit, protracted, nearly wordless sequence. When Anna shows up to care for her friend, she and the spectator are left in doubt as to whether Lucie invented a bond between her childhood abuse and this anonymous family, and the film's near lack of dialogue, overt refusal to confirm causality, and Lucie's hallucinations and eventual suicide frustrate epistemic closure, framing the narrative as either a revenge tragedy that has concluded too quickly, or an ironic if vicious melodrama about the potentially asymmetrical and unpredictable reactions to violence by those who suffer extreme trauma.

The second half begins when Anna, cleaning up the various corpses and blood splatters in the home, at the exact midpoint of the film, opens the doors to a wooden hutch and, upon finding a staircase down into the basement, proceeds to descend into the cavelike walls. This B-part, which begins as causelessly and wordlessly as did the opening, ultimately validates Lucie's account of events, confirms that the murdered parents did have a direct hand in her abuse as a child. Simultaneously, the B-section dispenses entirely with the narrative of the first part of the film as a subject of concern or attention. The second half of the film, in other words, withdraws any and all cathectic spectatorial investments in the story of Lucie, which are as unceremoniously buried as are Lucie and the family's corpses, thrown into a ditch by a group of bureaucrats after Anna's descent into the basement. The mass grave does not just include the cast of the first half of the film, save for Anna—it also functions as a brutal dismissal of the epistemic, ethical, and formal conceits of the first half. Part A has been endured solely to be rendered irrelevant; it solicited an aesthetic interest in order to announce through a *volta* that the text itself no longer retains any interest (meaning: no longer finds value) in its own preliminary structure.

The underground, which is to say, second part of the film, while producing epistemic closure as to what happened years ago with Lucie, introduces a new rhetorical mode governed by epistemic abundance. If the first half is marked by extreme doubt, the second opens with excessive confirmation, overtly presenting what is now happening (with what motivation, cause, reasoning) and what is going to happen (with what process, methodology, consequence). A woman known only as Mademoiselle explains to Anna that she is in charge of a sect obsessed with the literal question of metaphysics, the *ta meta ta phusika*—What is beyond, which is to say, after, the *physics*: What is beyond the world of being? After decrying how easy it is to create a victim (she intones the protocol: "You lock someone in a dark room. They begin to suffer. You feed that suffering methodically, systematically, and coldly. And make it last."), Mademoiselle praises the counter-case of the martyr: "Martyrs are exceptional people. They survive pain, they survive total deprivation. They bear

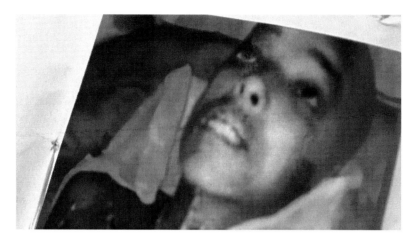

FIGURE 5.1. *Martyrs* (Pascal Laugier, 2008)

all the sins of the earth. They give themselves up, they transcend themselves. [. . .] They are transfigured."

Martyrs demonstrates at least three modes of a fascination that is coupled with violence: first, and most plainly, the narrative superstructure that retroactively sutures together the two cleaved halves of the film, the cult's fascination with the martyr as a rare, exceptional case of perseverance through suffering, a remaining alive while glimpsing death, a fascination with the knowledge to which the ecstatic martyr uniquely has access and which the cult seeks to gain (a Gnostic fascination); second, the cult's and the film's shared visual fascination with the image of the martyr in their experience of this liminal state, given in the magnified photographs of tortured martyrs on the wall and in Mademoiselle's photographic archive of transformed, transfigured faces presented in one arrested tableau after another through a haptic, pretechnological montage as she turns pages in a perverse album.[33] The figure that condenses Gnostic and visual fascination is the last stage of martyr production: the suspension and flaying of Anna's body, an act that recalls that a lineage dating back to Francis Bacon bonds scientific experiment and the discovery of knowledge to the language of torture, as in his advocacy of putting nature "on the rack," forcing it to reveal its inmost secrets.[34] Third, finally and simultaneously, when *Martyrs* is taken as a preeminent example of "new extremity" or "torture porn," it is taxonomized in accordance with a presumed commercial investment in a positive fascination with a viewer's own capacity to endure intense negative affective experiences via an aesthetic that privileges the opened body and unflinching images of fluids, viscera, all manner of abject stuff and matter, with minimal metanarrative diversions or alibis. *Martyrs*, in this sense, is taken to enact an extratextual fascination with a spectator's capacity to endure an encounter with a narrative and visual demonstration of the metaphysics of endurance.

The film thereby attempts the same project as the sect—to formalize the conditions for the possibility of fascination with a visible appearance, with the possibility of a successful demonstration of a limit, a project to which spectators and adherents are bound as their (sole) drive. The film *is* the sect's obsessive efforts to martyr Anna, dispensing with extraneous projects and ending at the task's culmination. Not unlike Blanchot's reading of the *Odyssey*, in which the entire text is organized around Ulysses's meeting with—and fascination with and survival despite—the Sirens, *Martyrs* is organized around a single event: the martyring-but-not-yet-extinguishing of Anna. Blanchot's formula for the means by which a fascinating encounter is converted into the communication of fascination begins with the general formulation that "something has happened, something which someone has experienced who tells about it afterwards, in the same way that Ulysses needed to experience the event and survive it to become Homer, who told about it."[35] The narrative of fascination with an "exceptional event," however, is also a transformation of that endurance: "If we regard the tale as the true telling of an exceptional event which has taken place and which someone is trying to report, then we have not even come close to sensing the true nature of the tale. The tale is not the narration of an event, but that event itself, the approach to that event, the place where the event is made to happen."[36] *Martyrs* is likewise the aesthetic place where the event of fascination with a body enduring the limits of the extremest cruelty is *made to happen*, not narrated about or reported on but the event itself of encountering, studying, attending to, being fascinated by the visible form of that limit state of transcendence. The text is *nothing but* that event, occurring solely to the extent that Anna persists in enduring it, the sect *nothing but* the effort to make that unbearable event of survival (despite what is taking place) bearably take place, being above all that duration of the toleration of the intolerable in time. For Blanchot, it is the fascination with the violence of the encounter and survival of the Sirens that is the necessary precondition for the telling of the encounter as event. In *Martyrs*, commuting speaking to a visual register, the final title card traces the etymology of *martyr* back through *marturos* to the French *témoin*, meaning *witness*—leaving resolutely open and undetermined with whose witnessing the film is most fascinated. Whether the tortured (body; subject) or the spectatorial (body; subject) is the ultimate martyr of the work is the central question that the film invites.

It is not the right question to ask, however, because it operates at the expense of a different interrogation altogether. Or, put another way, one should not take the film's posing of this question at face value or in good faith. It is not the inquiry that actually permits a confrontation with how violence works here. For these accounts of fascination in relation to *Martyrs* share one problematic presumption: that fascination functions as a positive analogue of attention, curiosity, the drive to look offsetting an affective negativity opposed and exterior to it. These approaches are marred by their fundamental inability to speak to the aesthetic language of the second half of the film without converting it into a mere instrument of visual displeasure or an index of intensity for a spectator fascinated by their own capacity for enduring that displeasure. Unable to read the way in which the torture sequences of the second half are formalized in *Martyrs*, torture would thus critically be taken as the positive object of fascination, its violence thereby erased by its conversion into any other fine spectacle. Instead, one must linger with a more discomforting thinking of fascination that suggests that the only way to account for force in *Martyrs* is to read the film as part of a philosophical lineage that posits a fascination with form as *itself* constituting a mode of extremest violence.

This reversal is at the heart of Derrida's "La forme et la façon," his preface to Alain David's 2001 *Racisme et antisémitisme*. There, Derrida views David as suggesting that the "originary crime" of racism and anti-Semitism is "privileging form and cultivating formal limits," that the violence of racism is given directly in an investment in a limitation by form, that the motor of the negation-work of catastrophic violence is an obsession with a purity of form that posits within its own thinking a threatening contamination of that purity. Derrida writes that the violence of such evil pivots on "rien d'autre que la *forme* elle-même, la fascination pour la forme, c'est-à-dire pour la *visibilité* d'un certain contour organique ou organisateur, un *eidos*, si l'on veut, et donc une idéalisation, un *idéalisme* même en tant qu'il institue la philosophie même, la philosophie ou la métaphysique en tant que telle" (nothing other than *form* itself, the fascination for form, that is for the *visibility* of a certain organic or organizing contour, an *eidos*, if you will, and thus an idealization, an *idealism* itself insofar as it institutes philosophy itself, philosophy or metaphysics as such).[37] Note how the promiscuous *même* runs through Derrida's accusation against *la fascination pour la forme—même*, as in *very, even, the same, itself,* a self-folding, self-referring accusation of a kinship, an even-the-very-sameness-as-itself of a fascination with form that belongs equally to violence and to philosophical thinking.

Unlike (and in some tension with) other of Derrida's treatments of racism—for example, his reading of apartheid in "Le Dernier Mot du racisme," the piece in which he pronounces "there's no racism without a language," such that it "is not that acts of racial violence are only words but rather that they have to have a word"—here the violence of racism and anti-Semitism is fastened to a fascination with a *visible* form.[38] If the linguistic violence of racism in the earlier piece "institutes, declares, writes, inscribes, prescribes," and is a "system of marks," what "outlines space in order to assign forced residence or to close off borders," by the time of "La forme et la façon," it is visible form (*la forme*: shape, appearance) that marks distinctions and boundaries, that inscribes and outlines space.[39] The subtitle for Derrida's preface indeed vows "(plus jamais: envers et contre tout, ne plus jamais penser ça 'pour la forme')"—(never again: against all odds, do not ever think of something as being just "for form's sake"). What is never to be done again is to act "pour la forme," what is done only superficially or perfunctorily or rhetorically (—or what is to happen never again is the insistence that something done is *merely* for form's sake, only just a formality, or the standardized, empty politeness of what is *pro forma*). The problem here is that of qualification: mere, only, just. The danger of being *pro* forma, however, is also the risk inherent in all formalisms. The more resolute the formalism, the more this risk of a violent fascination with form, an acceptance of its perversion, an accedence to its idealisms.

Acknowledging that it is a surprise that "une chose aussi abstraite, la *forme,* la *limitation,* la *limitation par la forme*" (such an abstract thing, form, limitations, the limitation by form) is to be regarded as so horrific, as what "déforme la forme, à savoir le monstrueux" (deforms form, namely the monstrous), Derrida continues to wonder, "Comment le désir de la forme et de la limitation formelle peut-il produire du tératologique?" (How can the desire for form and for formal limitation produce the teratological?) Although vicissitudes of form may produce monstrous anomalies, the monstrosity of form as such is bound to its givenness, the desire for a radical limitation by form.[40] Racism and anti-Semitism are thus but an iteration of the idealism of philosophy's fascination with the question of essence, the foundational "What is it?" of the study of being in Western metaphysics. Philosophy, misrecognizing its own debt to the notion of the "objectivity of form," is unable to see how its own passion for a purity and generalizability of formal delimitation colludes with the monstrosities of the worst violence.

This risk is derived from a broader problem that, Derrida argues, inheres in the entire philosophical history of thought of form, a diagnosis one can find in his earliest works on Husserl. In the sweeping synthesis that is the first pages of "Form and Meaning," he pronounces that Greek terms for form, whether *eidos* or *morphē*, constitutively "refer to fundamental concepts of metaphysics."[41] Therefore, "As soon as we utilize the concept of form—even if to criticize *an other* concept of form—we inevitably have recourse to the self-evidence of a kernel of meaning. And the medium of this self-evidence can be nothing other than the language of metaphysics. [. . .] The system of oppositions in which something like form, the formality of form, can be thought, is a finite system."[42] The consequence of form's quality of being identified with the metaphysical canon of appearance, sense, presence—"only a form is *self-evident*, only a form has or is an *essence*, only a form *presents itself* as such"—is that any thought imagining itself free of the sedimentations of metaphysics is, in writing of form, nothing but its loyal hostage.[43] Whether Platonic or Aristotelian does not matter: "All the concepts by means of which *eidos* or *morphē* have been translated or determined refer to the theme of *presence in general*. Form is presence itself. Formality is whatever aspect of the thing in general presents itself, lets itself be seen, gives itself to thought. That metaphysical thought—and consequently phenomenology—is a thought of Being as form, that in metaphysics thought thinks itself as a thought of form, and of the formality of form, is nothing but what is necessary."[44] Though I am eliding nuances in Derrida's thinking—and revisions and complications that intercede between this earliest work, from 1967, and the preface written decades later for David's book—it is the through-line by which form is "what is presented, visible, and conceivable" that makes possible, indeed makes necessary, makes *inevitable*, the later account of a collusion between a metaphysical account of form and a logic of racism and anti-Semitism that is fascinated with evident form. David's book, as Derrida ultimately frames it, thus comes to constitute a critique of form as such, putting "form on trial"—and in turn, by way of resistance, David's counterproposal is a new phenomenology that would be based around the limitless and a responsibility to an affirmation of what is unlimited (with strong resonances of the ethical thinking of Levinas, to whom David was close in work and in life), to interrupt form and exceed a formalism of limits aligned with visibility and the gaze.

However, however,—despite and enacting every danger he has described, Derrida's preface is *nothing but* a thinking of, a being-in-the-service-of a thinking of, a being what is *for*—as in toward, as in thinking before, in the face of, in the presence of, for the sake of, an advocacy of—this very problem of the question of form (for philosophy, all philosophizing being pro forma). Thus, in his own writing, Derrida will promise an erasure and effacement of the labor and discourse of the metaphysical philosophy that he simultaneously writes and is bound to (is *fastened* to)—"J'ai déjà commis les deux péchés (philosophiques! si la philosophie peut pécher!), les deux délits incriminés par Alain David. Ce serait d'ailleurs une seule et même faute: délimiter en *donnant forme* ou en *croyant voir* une *forme.*" (I have already committed the two sins (philosophical ones, if philosophy can sin!), the two offenses incriminated by Alain David. It would be one and the same fault: to demarcate by *giving form* or in *believing to see* a *form.*)[45]

Form endures; it prevails; it persists, insists, carries on.

If for David and Derrida the violence of metaphysics is indistinguishable from its overt fascination with visible form, Jean-Luc Nancy pushes this logic even further, suggesting that particularly excessive violence involves a fascination with a specific form, writing in "Image et violence" that violence is not only monstrous but monstrative: violence is what "exposes itself as figure without figure."[46] All violence thus makes an image of itself, imposing and enacting a specifically visual fascination with a specific aesthetic possibility. As Nancy writes, "Cruelty takes its name from bloodshed (*cruor*, as distinct from *sanguis*, the blood that circulates in the body). He who is cruel and violent wants to see blood spilt. [. . .] He who is cruel wants to appropriate death: not by gazing into the emptiness of the depths, but, on the contrary, by filling his eyes with red (by 'seeing red') and with the clots in which life suffers and dies."[47] Cruelty is a fascination with "a little puddle of matter," precisely what representation seeks to stand in place of and supplant.[48] If for Derrida the violence of philosophy shares the violence of racism's fascination with form, for Nancy, representation stands as the violence of cruelty's fascination with rendering a specific form (that "seeing red" which metonymizes an encounter with a form that can stand in for the real of matter).

The reason, then, that the thinker of horror must move away from the claim that *Martyrs* is about or performs a fascination with violence to consider the more radical thesis that the film performs the violence of a fascination with form is that the second half of the film is nothing but a forty-minute

FIGURE 5.2. *Martyrs* (Pascal Laugier, 2008)

study of purely formal propositions—the pulsations of forced feeding and its call-and-response retching; the rhythm of frantic, frenzied straining against metal chains that bind, and the texture, sound, and movement of those chains, their glinting light tones, the astringent sounds of their tight rings; the backlit limb-stretched heaviness and shapes and folds of motor restriction; the glottal choking panic of the pale, mute girl, Anna's hysteria taking form in the texture of stridorous breaths. Having erased and withdrawn the narrative of the first half, having declaimed an exhaustion of the conceit of the second half, there is nothing textually left to do but distend Anna as a form until a sufficient transformation occurs. This rendering of a martyr does not involve the torture (which is to say: the twisting and torment) of a body so much as the distortions of pressure, tension, duration, rhythm, chromatic intensity, and the modulations of light in which the body is posited as nothing but the varying results of a series of formal constraints and navigations: torture and destruction and flailing and skinning nothing but time- and light- and chromatic-modulating processes.

While the sect is narratively fascinated with the singular, particular limit case of the martyr's strange ontology, transfixed into a privileged instant in the photographic stills in the basement archive—fascinated, that is, with martyrdom as *end* (as *peras*: the limit or boundary of being at the reach of possible still-being-alive-in-death)—the textual object *Martyrs* is durationally fascinated with unfolding forms of violation, with martyrdom as *means*. The two fascinations are both fascinations with form but they do not line up: one is fascinated with the form of the martyr, the other is fascinated with the distensions to aesthetic form that martyring effects. A robust theory of form is therefore required to account for the multiple ways in which a fascination with form as a type of violence manifests here. For a fascination with form is not quite like fascination with any other thing. Not unlike fascination's etymological vicissitudes, in which it names both the most unpleasurable and death-bringing captivations and positive attraction and epistemic-affective conscription, the complexity of the very concept of form, such that it is a passive description of outward appearance while simultaneously a determining and shaping active principle, registers a fascination that is unstable, potentially double, refusing to disclose what precise register of appearance or essence, shape or structure, surface or depth, it addresses.

The film's fascination with processes of manipulating aesthetic form (and not violence as *topos*) moves through a study of the lines of force of the chains, the rhythms of struggle and passivity, the negative space of the darkness, each of which extracts formal qualities of rhythm, space, color, angle, line, to arrive at the final step of the transformation and extraction protocol: Anna's suspension in a large metal wheel and the peeling of all the skin of her body save for her face. Like the ur-account of flaying in *Metamorphoses*, the death of Marsyas in which Ovid writes, "He screams; the skin is flayed off all his form, and he is but one wound," the target of fascination, what is unable to resist violence, is also that Anna "*nisi vulnus erat*" (that she is now "nothing but a wound"—nothing *except* one continuous raw wound).[49] We already know from Nancy that the blood that spurts will be *cruor* (*cruor undique manat*), a showing of the blood that spills redness as quality—and with no covering of skin, as with Marsyas, *salientia viscera possis et perlucentes numerare in pectore fibras*: one is able to count the throbbing entrails, and the naked nerves appear, are made transparent. They come *to light*.

The violence of a fascination with form is not a case of force levied against a subject; rather, this event marked by a lack of resistance to harm is addressed to the visible form of the body, what torture distorts—in other words continually makes otherwise, against itself. The body becomes the site of the violent transformation of a limitation, transfixion, and modification by a series of formal constraints. The body is not made monstrous by transformation: the body is what is given *as* its infinite capacity for a teratoformalism—its monstrosity is identical to its infinite formal reconfigurability.

Eisenstein, writing of a wholly different textual body—the animations of Walt Disney, which he treats as pure meditations on the "mutability, fluidity, unexpectedness of form"—gives to "the rejection of the constraint of form, fixed once and for all, freedom from ossification, an ability to take on any form dynamically" the name "plasmaticity."[50] This infinite capacity for the variability of form—which he also links to natural variation, in particular in fire's flames—is linked to particularity and contingency amid the total field of what something might have been and might become: "A being, which is represented in a drawing, a being of a given form, a being that has achieved a particular appearance, behaves itself like primordial protoplasm, not yet having a stable form, but capable of taking on any and all forms of animal life on the ladder of evolution."[51] He opposes the inexhaustible transformational movements of plasmaticity, to both take and abandon any form, to the mere figurability of a static identity that he calls plastic. If infinite potential, plasmaticity also names the capacity for a process of becoming different that is indifferent to origin and is not a one-time departure or break from a prior form. It names not the distortion of a given form, but the particular contingent formal givenness—which starts anywhere, merely from any single place—of a particular variation set against the general potential for any other formal variation against which every form and every distortion of form is *possible*.

(Immediately after describing formal variability as plasmaticity, Eisenstein writes, "Why is watching this so fascinating?"[52]

—Once more, we cannot shed this word, this stubborn term signaling a cruel captivation.)

The destructive formalisms of Futurism, modernism, and their legacies are well known—in polemics for tipping, exploding, breaking, burning as the ground for aesthetic generation. But a crucial distinction is found in a correction offered by the Swiss artist Roman Signer, whose aesthetic philosophy celebrates force and whose work focuses on material, physical, or chemical transformations (chairs thrown through windows; catapults; shotguns; crashes and explosions): "Die Sprengung schliesst von ihrer Natur her die schnelle Veränderung ein: Eine Form geht in eine andere über. Das muss nicht immer die Zerstörung sein. Die Sprengung hat viele Möglichkeiten und Ausprägungen, die noch überhaupt nicht ausgeschöpft sind." (The explosion inherently involves a rapid change: one form becoming another. It does not always have to be destruction [ruination; devastation]. The explosion contains many possibilities and aspects that have not yet been exhausted [that have yet to be explored].)[53] Signer accounts for explosion as a question of exploring rhythm (specifically the rapidity with which properties can change), which is to say that explosion as the dynamism of form is analyzable solely in terms of the failure of formal properties to (yet; ever) be exhausted. From this point of view, not only is there no destructive aspect (literally un-building: *de-/struere*), but indeed *there is no possible destruction*: only an infinite and inexhaustible restructuring of infinite and inexhaustible formal properties. This is what (all) it means for something to happen.

But if *Martyrs* is sympathetic to this view, it also poses a further, finer articulation of the relation between the generative and speculative work of destruction's restructuring, engaging its exploration of the limitlessness of formal variation as it is set against the finitude of the terminable human body. This yoking is closer to the project governing Sade's *120 Days of Sodom*, in which the textual effort to exhaustively catalogue violence (a gesture at finitude marked by magnitude) exists alongside a formalism of infinite permutation and permutability; that is, the finitude of the body is confronted with and beset by the limitless aesthetic possibilities for new violences. The libertine desire for infinite torture (and thus a desire that would be unextinguishable) forcefully encounters—and again and again, this *again* constituting the duration and logic of listing that governs the maximalist work—the infuriating vulnerability of the human form, which is a frustration precisely because it has (it *is*) the necessity of extinguishability, which will mark the end of every torture, will comprise the necessity of the failure of every effort at some point in a prolongation of torture. The brutal formalisms of torture—while it is still possible—thus turn on rotating diagrammatic positions (interior/exterior, A/B, male/female, back/back), as in, "97. A sodomist: rips the intestines from a young boy and a young girl, puts the boy's into the girl, inserts the girl's into the boy's body, stitches up the incisions, ties them back to back to a pillar which supports them both, and he watches them perish."[54] It is fitting that the work's Addenda, the notes on the draft that appear after the fourth part and the Supplementary Tortures, ends with a turn to enumeration. Sade concludes the whole project by writing, "Upon one page in your notebook of characters draw the plan of the chateau, room by room, and in the blank space next to this page, itemize all the things done in each room."[55] This auto-directed demand is an attempt to formalize that primary tension: the infinitude of listing set against the finitude of duration (those 120 days); the infinitude of desire set against the finitude of bodily extinguishability; the infinite imaginative possibilities of new tortures set against the material finitude of the literary object itself, which itself has borders, which begins, which ends, which itself took thirty-seven days to pen.

Recall the *ars formularia* from Leibniz's *Consilium de Encyclopaedia nova conscribenda methodo inventoria*, the craft and technique, art and science, with which this book began and the *ars* under which its thinking has taken place. This discovery and comparison of form independent from and irrespective of considerations of size, position, place, activity, or action is, as a study of the same and the different, what Herbert Breger dubs "the foundation of a theory of qualities" in Leibniz's philosophy.[56] The comparison of form is a finding of difference, which is nothing other than a change in form itself, and thus the discoveries and comparisons of form are always also discoveries and comparisons of forms changed and changing into other forms (again, resonances with Ovid's *In nova fert animus mutatas dicere formas corpora*).[57] Indeed, Breger views the totality of Leibniz's *ars formularia* as the study of transformations writ large—broader than the local transformations of algebra or of geometry or of topology, but rather the study of the possibility of changes in form qua form. He elaborates:

> To recognize the existence of a transformation means to see similarities and connections between specific problems and objects from a higher level of abstraction. On the higher level of abstraction, a formal theory of transformations can then be erected; one can then talk, for example, of symmetries in the sense of group theory, of Euclidean transformations in geometry or of permutations in combinatorics. [. . .] It is the aspect of transformations that causes Leibniz to subordinate algebra as the science of magnitude to combinatorics as the science of forms and similarities. Leibniz occasionally speaks of an "ars formularia" as well, which is concerned with the same and the different, with the similar and the dissimilar, thus with the forms of things, independent of size, position and action. With the help of this *ars formularia*, Leibniz obviously intends to try to develop a method and theory of transformations and their applicability. The

similarity of geometric positions and geometric figures, important for the analysis situs, is for Leibniz a special case of regarding forms or qualities in metaphysics.[58]

The insistence that a serious study of form is necessarily a serious study of transformation extends from Leibniz through present theories of plasticity, notably in Catherine Malabou's work, which revisits and rereads philosophy (i.e., metaphysics) as itself constituting a rethinking of form as conversion: "From Hegel to Heidegger and then from Heidegger to Derrida, a grand formal adventure unfolded, a revisiting of form that now prohibits us from confusing form purely and simply with presence, for form has secretly transformed itself. Today form reveals its true colors: form is plastic."[59] To study shape is to study changing shape, to regard form is to regard form's dislocation; or, in Malabou's words, "it is the question of *the differentiated structure of all form* and hence the *formal or figural unity of all difference and articulation*."[60]

It is because it could be otherwise that form is at all.

(And if this sounds like a story about fragility,
about what can and most likely will break, what will break over and over again,
and if it thereby, and improbably in the midst of all this
violence and wreckage,
recalls something of love and of lovers,
—hold tight to that sense, endure that impression of their intimacy.)

The question is not what this study of changing formal properties represents (behind or underneath it, as it were) but what it poses in itself.

In the middle of a reading of Pasolini in *Cinema 2*, amid a description of *Salò* as constituting one of several "geometrical demonstrations in action [. . .] [in which] unbearable corporeal figures are strictly subordinated to the progress of a demonstration"—and while describing Pasolini's technique of substituting "formal linkages of thought for sensory-motor [. . .] or figurative linkages," achieving a "truly mathematical rigour"—Deleuze turns to the question of a light that does not reveal what is concealed in objects but that enables one to see an object's opacities.[61] He quotes the critic Serge Daney on scenographic flatness: "The question [. . .] is no longer: what is there to see behind? But rather: can I hold my gaze on what I am seeing anyway?"[62] Deleuze continues, "What I am seeing anyway is the formula of the unendurable. It ex-

FIGURE 5.3. *Martyrs* (Pascal Laugier, 2008)

presses a new relation between thought and seeing [. . .] which constantly sets
the thought outside itself."[63] And so: *Can I hold my gaze on what I am seeing
anyway?* If this is one of several possible questions for the sect, for the spectator, for the philosopher, it is a nonoptional question for the formalist, the one
whose reading tarries with precisely the what-I-am-seeing-anyway, the target
of a study of form itself. What I am seeing anyway—this is a methodological
matter that is also an ethical matter. Can I commit to hold my gaze on that?
(And could I linger, will I hold and wait and witness, and especially, when and
as what I am seeing anyway is undergoing transformation, is slipping away
just as—*as*—it comes?)

    Martyrs' presencing of the limit state of a torture that twists, turns, and
distorts form involves a slow zoom into the flayed face of Anna-cum-martyr.
Juxtaposed against Anna's stasis and transfixion, the camera's relentless pro-
jective movement beyond the borders of the body, beyond the limitation of
line into a pure field of color, beyond the image to a blinding field of white
light, exposes the materiality of the cinema and the condition of possibility
for appearance as such. Film form here is fascinated—that is, transfixed and

FIGURE 5.4. *The Passion of Joan of Arc* (Carl Theodor Dreyer, 1928)

wounded—by an encounter with pure abstraction, arriving at the blankness of a screen waiting to be given form by inscriptive representation at a time that remains in the future, speculative and inaccessible. At this crucial moment, *Martyrs* is also citing one of the more famous instants of martyring in the history of film, Dreyer's 1928 *The Passion of Joan of Arc*, which itself poses the question of fascination's bond to violence, affect, and formal restriction. Deleuze calls *The Passion of Joan of Arc* "the affective film *par excellence*" for setting in place a double relation: the first is the narrative state of things, the all of the what-is-happening that he dubs "the trial," and the realm of emotions as properties, such as the "anger *of* the bishop and the martyrdom *of* Joan," &c.[64] This first relation establishes a difference between the historical and the emotional, but it still links emotion to individual subjects. The second relation, however—what Deleuze dubs the genius of the film for constructing "the difference between the trial and the Passion, which are nevertheless inseparable"—is the more essential project: "To extract the Passion from the trial, to extract from the event this inexhaustible and brilliant part which goes beyond its own actualisation, 'the completion which is never com-

FIGURE 5.5. *Martyrs* (Pascal Laugier, 2008)

pleted,'" what is beyond its local causes and in excess of individual historical subjects.[65] Faciality is no longer the privileged site for a legibility of emotion but the setting for a distension of film form that extracts passion as a desubjectified affective potential in its awkward angles, distorted framing, and broken up mise-en-scène. "The affect is like the expressed of the state of things," Deleuze concludes, "but this expressed does not refer to the state of things, it only refers to the faces which express it and, coming together or separating, give it its proper moving context."[66] This pure form of affective intensity—a swill of anger, martyrdom, rage, suffering, &c.—is ineluctably bound to form. No longer narratives about emotions or emotions as properties of characters, aesthetic language bears out the pure intensity of passion itself.

This encounter with nothing but form, this attestation of how the shown shows itself, how illumination is illuminated, and what holds together the cinematic image, is not parasitic on the violence of torture that has denatured Anna: rather, *Martyrs* unfolds *in order* that Anna be converted into yet another formal element available for being given otherwise. The martyring is not an act of negation or destruction: rather, the deformation of the body is a pure experiment in variation, that is, the formation of new forms. It is not, as Tim Palmer has it, that new extremisms and horrors are a *cinéma du corps* that can only regard *Martyrs'* "sadistic torture chambers" as "an on-screen interrogation of physicality in brutally intimate terms."[67] Such an approach remains fastened to a critical fascination with a visible form called the body. Rather, these extremisms are nothing but cinemas of form; or, if cinemas of the body, they are nothing but cinemas of the body as the body is rendered nothing but a question of form. The interest of horror—as in its investment, what it profits from—is not in fascination with a fixed, visible object, but fascination as the action of changing forms into new forms. And the violence of a fascination with form is this: to the extent the text commits to a fascination with formal possibility, it nullifies any textual place that would nominate torture's violence as being on the side of negation or erasure or ruination. Torture, from the point of view of form, is inherently generative.

From the beginning, this book has not been interested in, has not derived interest from, genre—but it is deeply interested in the general. And so here we approach a general definition of horror: *Horror is a formal act of decision.* Not as in a gesture of resolution but *decision* as in its decisiveness: its particularity that is not something else. Horror is the formal act of decision to regard the body as a form subject to formal constraints, restraints, possibilities, and re- and de-formations and re- and de-formative possibilities.

Horror is the attestation of any general state
in which torture is ethically neutral
but aesthetically affirmative.

To refuse to regard the body as a form (in other words, to retain torture for a humanist critique of violence) is to linger solely with the first half of *Martyrs*, to put torture to work for what Nancy dubs in "The Forgetting of Philosophy" the realm of meaning: "the element in which there can be significations, interpretations, representation."[68] In that case, the human body would retain the sedimentations of the human subject, the torture would remain an ethical abomination (such readings *of* violence constituting laments *for* violence). But this requires that we shield our eyes and *do not look* upon the second half of the film. To look, however, to encounter the aesthetic attestations of the second part of *Martyrs*, is to encounter the body stripped of meaning, speculatively put on display as formally navigable, which is to say as indestructible because its form can always be made otherwise. Horror is not the affective-aesthetic mode that puts on display violence done to bodies. Horror is the affective-aesthetic mode in which violence can *never* be done to the body because the body is made a form, violence to which produces a new form; the body is posited as that to which infinite variations in its formal constitution are possible.

Levinas anticipates something of this structure when he writes in "*Il y a*" that "Horror is nowise an anxiety about death," but rather, that it is the *There-is* "which returns in the heart of every negation," such that "the impossibility of death, the universality of existence even in its annihilation" is true horror. He continues: "To kill, like to die, is to seek an escape from being, to go where freedom and negation operate. Horror is the event of being which returns in the heart of this negation, as though nothing had happened."[69] For Levinas, it is the *il y a*, the anonymity, impersonality, and irremissibility of being that causes recoil, and a homological move has been visible across this book: for *Final Destination*, it is that death's design ensures that the next death is always to come; for *Rubber*, that the toroid goes on; for *Cabin in the Woods*, that there is no off the grid, for off the grid is merely another grid; for *The Human Centipede*, that one *is* in being the diagrammatic figure of B and that a reductive formalism of alphabetic order names the graphic obligatoriness of that position, and so on. And so on.

Horror has never been about finitude in isolation, but about processes of infinitization set against and ineluctably crossing, being crossed by, interacting with multiple forms of finitude (mortality, materiality, framing, exhaustion). Horror; torture; reading; fascination—each names the realm of apeiron, the unlimited and limitless, while each is, simultaneously, within its own thinking, bound to the violence of the boundary, the limit, the edge, the end.

Infinitude and finitude constitute a homotopy: the two mutually and continuously deforming one another.

What form speculatively launches is never, therefore, *nothing* and *something*, but always only *something* and *something else*.

The reversal that regards violence against the body as infinitely impossible precisely because formal variation is infinitely possible comes, of course, however, at an extraordinary critical cost. There can be no inherited critique of violence within a speculative grappling with horror because horror imagines violence only ever as monstrative, as the condition of possibility for generating the aesthetic. This is coextensive *with* its formal language, which is to say that the motor of possibility for its textual continuance is the infinite destructibility of the human imagined as the infinite variability of its form. The conventional reading of *Martyrs* as demonstrating a fascination with violence never need think horror as such because horror is continually converted into the anti-horrifying, entirely genial, and positive lessons of liberal critique. However, to take a fascination with form seriously as a form of violence requires that the theorist herself defend this with her own speculative fascination with closely—even obsessively, always with an unhealthy fixation—reading the details of textual form. This is the extremest violence: the transfixion of criticism by the very logic of force one would purport to think, now no longer from the safe distance of the outside, but squarely in the absorptive maw of the structure of fascination itself.

Reading is an act of decision as well.

Formalism is not a question of what one reads (for); it is a question of how one reads. Radical formalism is aimed not at the results of reading—for political affordance; for a prior understanding of the value of critique; or worse yet for the sake of a prior understanding of the fixed, specific political affordances critique ought to return and make good on. Radical formalism is aimed, at once ambitiously and modestly, at revitalizing the form of reading itself: it is *method*, a pursuit, a proceeding—it is merely a way of going. Instead of deriving (borrowing, leeching) the value of reading from existing and prior valuations, it grounds itself in the ineluctable specificity of the textual object with which it thinks and by which it is thought in turn. Radical formalism is, once more, an act of decision, which at root is a term best thought as a formal problem, the *de-/caedere* that is a cutting in two, which is to say a division that is a multiplication of an aspect of something's form. Radical formalism is not in any way a new *way* of thinking—for a thinking of form, per Derrida's warning and nervous recapitulation, is as old as our thinking of thinking is in the West—but it is absolutely and always a *new* way of thinking, for the most robust attention to form is precisely to attend to what is unprecedented: unprecedented by anything, that is, except the concrete particularity of the textual object itself, whose form is irreducibly contingent. Because a theoretical practice that proceeds by way of grappling with form guarantees nothing, because its fascinations are shared with modes of violence, closely reading for form is an act of decision that cannot, however, be obviously claimed for antiviolence. The potentially fatal complication would be if closely reading for form were an act of decision that committed one to forms of speculative violence.

Therefore, the unavoidable question for the formalist is not unlike the question that the metaphysical philosopher puts to himself: *How and when and where and with what inevitability have I potentially erred here?* —How, thusly, then, to proceed?

If formalisms (as aesthetic or interpretive strategy) share an isomorphic structure with violence in a fascination with visible form, what antidote or reinvention of formalism sidesteps this unwanted intimacy? One answer is to fight tooth and nail, skin and all viscera, against the conversion of form to the intelligible, and to refuse to allow form to remain defined in Mademoiselle's or the sect's (or the film's, and plenty of weak formalists') partial sense of a visible static shape or appearance: refuse, that is, transfixion's fixations, and put back into formalism its motor, its movement, its process, its circulation. Let it stir; let it churn; let it go; —risk some loss (of control, interest, profit, payoff).

One must transform formalism itself. To transform formalism is itself a process and promise of form, its mutability, its intimate bond to the *ars inveniendi*. This requires relinquishing the association of formalism with the recovery of (static, knowable, fixed, given) *forms* and instead demanding that formalism name an unsatisfied, relentless, interminable grappling with the antinomies of form, including form changing, which is to say being marked by the difference that gives form in the first place (that it *is* precisely because it could always be otherwise), and includes the navigations and processes by which form gives form to form—visual form giving a nonidealist form to the obliquities of a toroid, cinematic form interpreting the form of a canted grid, literary form working over the form of enumeration, &c. —failing to produce readings that pay out dividends (call them ethical metanarratives; historical analogues; political critique; whatever). The theorist must instead retain reading as *process*, the dynamic business of interpretation, itself infinitely mutable, with what in form remains speculative and as-yet unthought, naming the antidote to a violence that would take the form of a fascination with a concrete appearance. In the language of wonder that continually edges fascination, critical praxis must never convert fascination with form as the drive of the unfolding of thought to a fascination with forms as limited, bounded, precedented, given—including the very ones with which *Martyrs* seduces: that

Anna and Lucie are female; that they are both non-White; that the film moves through nothing but institutions, ones theological, psychiatric, familial, &c. One must, that is, not locate forms or find forms or recover and derive affordances from forms, but rather, one must always read *with* form, *without* guarantee.

The task is to take absolutely seriously the film's final cruelty from Mademoiselle as a charge for thought. It takes a double form. After she alone has received Anna's ecstatic whisper, Mademoiselle insists, "It admitted of no interpretation." Of her sect's access to whatever it is that admits of no interpretation, she cruelly declares "Doutez," proceeding to commit suicide and steal away the revelation with her forever.

Doutez: although the English translation of the film's dialogue gives it an epistemological register, subtitling it as "Keep doubting," the verb *douter* names a broader register of temporal waverings: to hesitate, procrastinate, linger, defer, put off, delay.

A formalism of the Doutez names a truly radical formalism, letting form function as the infinite deferred ongoingness of uncertain speculative claims; —what names a demand for the processual work of reading; what refuses to let fascination resolve into the mere recovery of prior forms, retaining what admits of nothing but an unceasing questioning, in perpetual parenthetical worries about errors of thought that must nonetheless impose themselves; what remains bound to, lingers with, the vital energies of deriving no interest or profit from reading and yet continuing to tarry with reading nonetheless.

> I will try
> to fasten into order enlarging grasps of disorder, widening
> scope, but enjoying the freedom that
> Scope eludes my grasp, that there is no finality of vision,
> that I have perceived nothing completely,
> that tomorrow a new walk is a new walk.
> —A. R. Ammons, "Corsons Inlet"

Where there is the great restlessness of doubt, there is the infinite general potential for particular surprises, which are possible only in the hesitating detours of unfolding thought that vacillate and waver. If there is a fascination at the heart of a radical formalism that would enable speculative thought—and resist Derrida's and Nancy's warnings of a formalism perfectly amenable to co-optation by violence, cruelty, fascism, racism, &c.—it is nothing but the risk of allowing the theorist's fascination with form to never arrive at a final, decisive interpretation, nor to imagine that any aspect of form does not require further reading, including the form of a (any; *this*) reading. The antidote to what admits of *no interpretation* is what admits of *nothing but interpretation* all the way down. An ongoing risk of a fascination with form that wields itself as a form of violence is risky because ongoing, ongoing because risky. Neither God nor grammar promises the conjunction that would keep aesthetics and brutality sufficiently dissevered. And yet, there is no other way true thinking can go if it is not merely to shield its eyes from the start.

Hatreds of formalism are all alike.

Every love of form will have to love in its own way.

PLATE 1. *Suspiria* (Luca Guadagnino, 2018)

PLATE 2. *Final Destination 3* (James Wong, 2006)

PLATE 3. *Final Destination 3* (James Wong, 2006)

PLATE 4. *The Human Centipede (First Sequence)* (Tom Six, 2009)

PLATES 5–8.
Amour Fou (Jessica
Hausner, 2014)

PLATE 9. *Stranger by the Lake / L'inconnu du lac* (Alain Guiraudie, 2013)

PLATE 10. *Stranger by the Lake / L'inconnu du lac* (Alain Guiraudie, 2013)

PLATE 11. Jean-Baptiste-Camille Corot, *Souvenir of the Environs of Lake Nemi* (1865). Oil on canvas, 98.4 × 134.3 cm. Bequest of Florence S. McCormick. Source: Art Institute of Chicago.

PLATE 12. *Blue Is the Warmest Color / La Vie d'Adèle—Chapitres 1 & 2* (Abdellatif Kechiche, 2013)

PLATE 13. Egon Schiele, *Zwei Mädchen, in verschränkter Stellung liegend / Two Girls, Lying in an Entwined Position* (1915). Gouache and pencil on paper, 32.8 × 49.7 cm. Graphische Sammlung Albertina, Vienna, Austria. Photo: Bridgeman Images.

PLATE 14. *Blue Is the Warmest Color / La Vie d'Adèle—Chapitres 1 & 2*
(Abdellatif Kechiche, 2013)

PLATE 15. Egon Schiele, *Zwei Freundinnen / Two Friends* (1912). Gouache and pencil on paper, 44.4 × 30.2 cm. Private collection. Photo: Bridgeman Images.

PLATE 16. *Blue Is the Warmest Color* / *La Vie d'Adèle—Chapitres 1 & 2* (Abdellatif Kechiche, 2013)

PLATE 17. *Blue Is the Warmest Color* / *La Vie d'Adèle—Chapitres 1 & 2* (Abdellatif Kechiche, 2013)

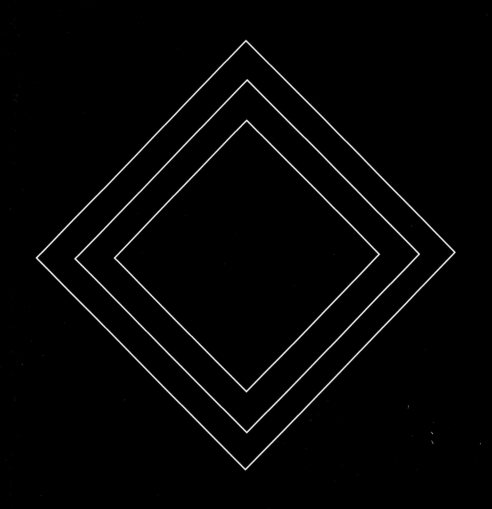

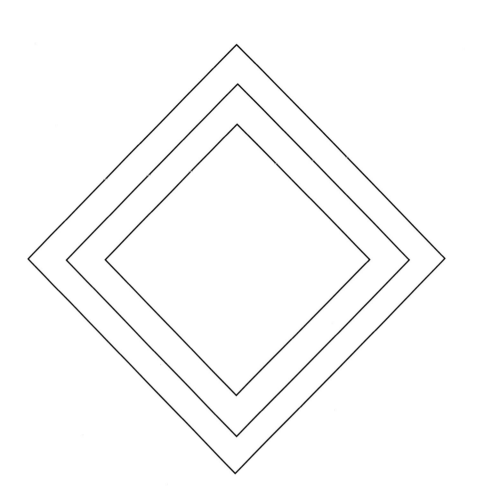

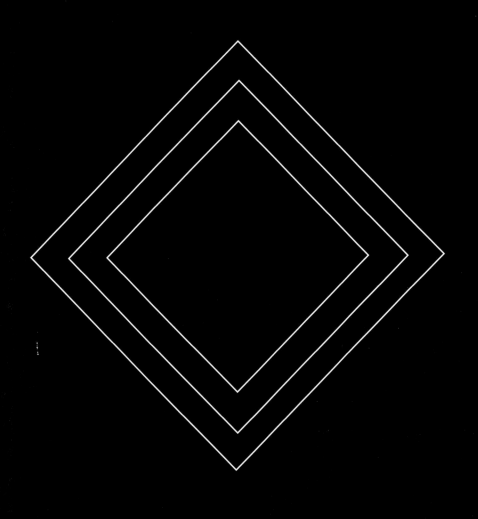

All the new thinking is about loss.

In this it resembles all the old thinking.

—ROBERT HASS, "Meditation at Lagunitas"

LOVE AND
MEASUREMENT

Michel Serres's *Rome: The First Book of Foundations.* Writing of a series of relations—of plague to war, hosts to guests, friends to enemies—the philosopher advances this rule:

> God is not the inverse, it is not the opposite of the wolf. The opposite of the wolf is an opposite wolf. They have the same wet muzzle; they wag the same tail; they show the same fangs. The opposite of evil is an opposite evil; the opposite of violence and murderous cruelty is a symmetrical and twin horror. [. . .] Love is not the inverse, the opposite of hatred.[1]

His elaboration of this formal law specifies that because love is of every value, being what does not specify, exclude, limit, or determine, love's "omnitude of values" includes hatred. (Serres: "'I love you' doesn't specify place; 'I love you' doesn't exclude anything, lets everything in, is ignorant of status, determination"; he further describes love's "bouquet of omnitude" — hold fast to those swollen bunches of flowers.) This refusal to exclude is also its great exposedness: love risks knowledge of what threatens it from within. What is most proper to love — peculiar to it, what individuates or differentiates it as distinct (distinct concept; distinct affect) — is the impropriety of what would devastate it. Hatred's operation, by contrast, brings the multiplicity of valuation down to some unary position: "Hating is folding every position over a single one; hating ravages the possible; hating is determining, negatively defining a single element in the inclusive possible of love. Hatred is at the heart of knowledge, which always begins with double negations."[2] Because hating assigns place and site, it is coextensive with forms of knowing, but hatred by this definition is also powerfully reminiscent of the order-making work of the static model of form on which the previous chapter warningly ended. And thus, Serres concludes the striking passage by offering this general definition: "Hatred is not merely antithesis; it is already the thesis. Love is the geometral of places and sites."[3]

This formulation serves as ichnography for what follows: a plan, the blueprint.

Vitruvius, in his *Ten Books on Architecture*, describes the aspect of design that is ichnography thusly: "the representation on a plane of the ground-plan of the work, drawn by rule and compasses."[4]

THE GEOMETRAL

Jessica Hausner's 2014 *Amour Fou* can be well misapproached in the following way, by beginning with the stage of the historical film. Set in 1811, *Amour Fou* formally, deliberately, and at a studied distance focuses on the professional melancholic Heinrich von Kleist, only a few years after the publication of his *Die Marquise von O . . .*, well in the grips of *Lebensmüde*, sallow and nervously postured, his thumbs perennially tucking into the bellies of his hands, and on Henriette Vogel, a passive, pallid, flower-arranging, Lieder-performing wife and mother who declares herself mildly intrigued by that novel's study of a woman whose passion for her idealized lover is not obliterated entirely by his violence against her (impregnation during unconsciousness; the chivalric rape; what takes place behind the infamous dash that Dorrit Cohn dubbed "the most pregnant graphic sign in German literature").[5] Kleist spends most of the film trying to persuade his cousin Marie to commit suicide with him as a gesture of her undying love ("Would you care to die with me? You'd make me very happy," he requests) — to which she does not react with revulsion or horror but with irritation at the repetition of the pleadings and with frowns of distaste at the impropriety of the appeals, in particular once she is engaged to another man. In the midst of her ongoing rejections, Kleist reluctantly targets Henriette as a woman who might "understand his suffering" and desire to become immortal as one, advising her, "You seem to be an outsider just like me. You are also lonely. Bereft of friends. And nothing really matters to you. You love nothing, and nobody loves you." Despite her protestations that she loves her child and her child loves her, that she loves her husband and her husband loves her, Henriette's body appears to be taken with Kleist's suggestion, and in the wake of a vague, newly emergent illness misdiagnosed by doctors as a tumor that is swiftly killing her, she reconsiders Kleist's request and the stiff figures politely agree to die together.

Various aborted attempts and repeated rescheduling—the double suicide above all a logistical nightmare—are intercut with Kleist's periodic disappearances to attempt (yet again) to persuade an increasingly put-off Marie, still the true target of his *Liebestod* fantasy. But as the fateful event approaches, a suggestion that Henriette's ailment might in fact be more neurotic than necrotic complicates her protestations of a desire to find eternal engulfment with the restive Romantic writer. Possessing new knowledge from her husband that she perhaps will not have to die so soon after all, that cure might reside in a trip to Paris to see a doctor of the spirit, to his insistence that marital loyalty is firm and that he will spare no effort in keeping her well, Henriette tells Heinrich that there is a possibility of ongoing life. The two nevertheless take their trip to the countryside, the one that was initially intended for the planned climactic event. Her illegible face and the film's antipsychological predilection for tableaux of mannered posture and gesture opacifies any sense of internal deliberation or hesitation or decision one way or the other. Remaining with the well-misapproached attitude, there are occasional subtly coded suggestions of Henriette's changed mind, including an aborted effort to apologize to a Heinrich who speaks over her and declares with new determination, "I'm sorry I ever doubted you," and an image of Henriette, half-shadowed in golden light, unable to sleep the night before the life-ending event. The following morning they wordlessly, awkwardly crunch over icy winter branch and bramble, Henriette's pale yellow dress at vivid odds with the bluish gray cast of the setting. Within the frame, the two bodies are composed with a rigorously maintained distance between their progressing forms save for one moment in which Henriette trips, forcing a sudden spatial contraction, and Heinrich touches her, undoing the plotted reach between them more than establishing a newly amative one. This procession takes seventy seconds of screen duration, continuous save for one cut following the diagrammatic disruption of their momentarily touching forms.

But abruptly there is a noticeable and jarring jump, one that is discordant both in scale and kinetically, setting in place a set of multiple differences. The framing changes radically: in place of long shots of figures framed against a wild landscape, the new image is a medium shot of Henriette, her face turned away from the camera; whereas in the previous shot the figures move away from the camera, in the second, Henriette is completely still;

from a focus on two figures, the image attends to only one; from a mobile mark of chromatic offness, the yellow coat now takes up the middle fifth of the frame, dividing the static image in two; &c. The cut and these differences point to the fact that something in the formal system of the film and of the two parties' relation has changed, but the cut also covers over an unknown period of time prior to the arrival of this particular moment, which is to say it keeps something of the appearance of the critical moment in reserve, fails to make it known or knowable. From the image of the back of Henriette's head, she slowly turns toward the camera, a visible smile playing on her face (an answer to a question, or demand, or presence offscreen, or any number of possible provocations, every one of which would have happened behind the cut, as it were). As Henriette silently stares at the camera her smile fades, her eyes cast down, and behind her she and the spectator hear, but ultimately only the spectator sees, Heinrich approaching directly behind her, pulling out his gun. She begins to say, "Heinrich, what I wanted to say . . ." and turns to face him. Another cut, to Heinrich pointing the gun directly at the camera; he fires, and we hear Henriette fall dead offscreen.

It takes Kleist multiple tries to effect his own suicide, the successful one never shown on screen (the film's interest remaining with the fumblings themselves) — each technological failure inserting an ever wider gap of distance between the two deaths, each subsequent effort inserting an ineptitude and inefficacy of action into the schema of an idealized simultaneity of perishing. Duration thus appears precisely where instantaneity is demanded by the idealism of the form of the event. Failing to replicate Tristan and Isolde's "without parting / dearly alone, / ever at one, / in unbounded space, / most blessed of dreams!" — the famous frenzied erasures, displacements, and chiastic, diagrammatic exchanges of Wagner's second act:

TRISTAN

You Tristan,
I Isolde,
no more Tristan!

ISOLDE

You Isolde,
I Tristan,
no more Isolde!

No names,
no parting;
newly perceived,
newly kindled;
ever, unendingly,
one consciousness;
supreme joy of love
glowing in our breast![6]

—*Amour Fou* is entirely a staging of varying forms of parting, separate consciousnesses, distinct names, and the banality if not bathos of death, one the survivors will misread as testifying to a secret affair despite the fact that Henriette and Kleist are not stirred lovers, never share a kiss, rigorously and impersonally (and rigorously impersonally) maintain the very distance the erotic suicide pact attempts to eternally, formally, efface. They are never *Both* but always one and the other, each one each one and each one never the other, never more never the other than in the separate each alone absolutely distinctly isolated moments of each individual death.

The film's deaths-producing ending puts in place at least two possible misreadings—one internal to the film, the other external—though Serres has instructed us in this crucial point: *the opposite of a misreading is merely an opposite misreading*. The first misreading is made by Henriette's husband who—at the autopsy's revelation that neither cancer nor tumor was residing in his wife's body—concludes of the double suicide, "It was out of love after all," presuming Henriette's consent and positing some *Liebe* to retroactively affirm (and to posit the genre of) a Liebestod. The opposite of this misreading is an opposite misreading, which insists, by contrast, on a resolute lack of consent and a replacement of love with violation: this is the critical effort to describe the film as a feminist parable of a woman's growing "self-consciousness." As a critic in *Sight and Sound* extends this line of thought: "The only way this woman of burgeoning strength, courage and freedom could ever have gone along with one man's pathetic wish for her to kill herself was, in the end, to be shot in the back without her consent."[7] (This claim extrapolates a great deal—psychology, will, judgment—while also resting on a crucial descriptive error: Henriette turns; she is precisely *not* shot in the back.) Both Vogel and critic fixate on the alternative posed by the possibility or impossibility of dying together as an act of love—

either the fulfillment or decimation of the values of Romanticism; either an oblique sincerity (for diegetic figures who do not witness the event) or a mean and critical irony (for a spectator who does). If the abandoned husband ventriloquizes an affirmation of de Rougemont's famous thesis that the history of the Western lyric aligns love with passion and that "passion means suffering, something undergone," such that "death is revealed as having been the real end, what passion has yearned after from the beginning," the critic converts auto-destruction to assassination and thereby invents two murders: Henriette's by Heinrich, and that by which Henriette's death stands as feminist allegory, as in Lacan's famous dictum in his *Discours de Rome* that "the symbol first manifests itself as the killing of the thing [*le meurtre de la chose*]."[8]

Perhaps we should be wary of so readily killing the thing.

The common question that both misreadings arrive at is whether *Amour Fou* restages *Die Marquise von O . . .*: Is this the case of a mutually consented suicide or a suicide-murder (seduction converted to rape; love-death converted to assault)? Any attempt to answer, however, requires what the endingness of Henriette's death forecloses—which is to say: it fills in the rest of her sentence that is suspended, constitutively half-finished, ontologically partial, and thus eternally incomplete.

There is, however, a completely different way of approaching *Amour Fou*. This second approach is structured around the generality of the question of whether this—or, really, *a*—distinction can be made. It does not matter which distinction, and it includes the distinction that that first account of the film demands: the gap between the opposing readings of the deaths. But it just as well might concern the distinction between

sane love and mad love;
dying together and dying alone;
joining and parting;
a free death and an unwilled one.

Or it might ask about the distinction between restricted and unrestricted economies—for Jean-Luc Nancy, for example, the "common suicide" of lovers, "an old myth and an old desire that abolishes limit and touch at the same time," attempts to establish an operative community, one that strives toward an immanence that assimilates the other, obliterating the alterity that is the ground of the inoperative community.[9] Or a distinction might oppose letters and oral agreements;

neurotic as opposed to corporeal ailments;

proper requests and rude ones;

Kleist and Goethe;

Henriette and her daughter Pauline;

angels and devils;

singers and listeners;

Rivette's *L'Amour Fou* and Hausner's;

Rohmer's Kleist and Hausner's;

planes and diagonals;

those who are subject to taxation and those who are not;

Prussia contra Britain contra France . . . .

Or whatever.

The broad question of whether distinctions can be made hinges on how one grapples with a figure that might seem as far as possible from suicide and love: specifically, the problem of a patterned wallpaper. Much—everything, to be precise—will depend on how one regards, reads, and accounts for it. There is no privileged shot in *Amour Fou*, but there is a privileged general arrangement—a broad horizontal field of wall in which anthropomorphic and objectal figures are staged centre centre in a flat frontal tableau. Within this schema, the film is structured by obsessive returns to the pasted-up decorative reach of a specific wall covering in the drawing room of the Vogel's well-appointed house, its pattern sometimes profoundly blurred, sometimes acutely sharp, always extending to the edges of the screen, interceded and interfered with, masked or exposed by the light that marks the progress of the day, the light that shades or illuminates, blocks or reveals, distributes light and dark, and effects visual noise in the mutual interference of detail, line, and color: the pattern's distinctness muddied in the dim illumination of an evening salon; visible solely in thin and shadowed vertical columns alternating with the blackest shadow in a late-night hypnosis session; crisp and painfully clear in the light of a morning spent writing a letter; &c. Light distributes this wallpaper, arranges its form: light extends its pattern omnidirectionally but always within simultaneous formal restrictions of band and border, depth and shallow.

The film impossibilizes a relation of indifference to this wallpaper: more than a decorative signature, the autonomy of its visual interest requires a reckoning. The wallpaper matters precisely because it poses—within itself—the question of whether it will be read scenographically or geometrically. The alternative is the one launched with the help of Serres: that between a love that is geometral and a hatred that is a something else. That something else, what wrecks the geometral and is given as the scenographic, involves an assignation specifying a fixed (critical, historical, aesthetic) position. Broadly, the terms *geometric* and *scenographic* deal with problems of setting, place, and spaces given or crafted, but their difference poses a tension between *angles* and *affect*. *Geometric*, from *geometria*, points to the measurement of earth or land (the -*metry* element functioning as in *metron*, *metros*, and *meter*). By contrast, the term *scenographic* derives from Aristotle's aside in *Poetics* that Sophocles added to the tragic form *scenery*, or *skenographia*. *Skene*, "tent" or "stage," initially implied a fundamentally temporary structure, and the word came quickly to specify drawing in perspective or the art of staging objects or theatrical scenes in perspective.[10] *Scenographic* thus refers not to measurement but to the arrangement and formation of an impermanent decorative space for imagined, represented places, a constructed architecture for the presentation of artifice. And from those associations, by the twentieth century the term referred to the totality of built elements that establish an atmosphere for a theatrical presentation. Scenography harnesses a placed space for expressive, communicative ends, while geometry turns on what the space and its relations are before, outside of, and indifferent to all that.

Serres takes the term *geometral* from Leibniz, a figure who has haunted these pages from the very beginning. In *Le Système de Leibniz et ses modèles mathématiques*, Serres rereads Leibniz's corpus as scenographic variations on the same conceptual ichnography, following on one of the central insights he takes from Leibniz: that "scenography represents objects in perspective, and ichnography is the elevation, that is to say, the horizontal plane or geometral."[11] (Leibniz will translate/elevate this distinction to an extraordinary visual law, elaborating on the question of spectatorial placement in one of his many letters to the theologian Bartholomew Des Bosses: "The difference between the appearance of a body for us and for God is the difference between scenography and ichnography"—which is to say, a singular, fixed particular human perspective against the infinite, plural, multiple, different points of view attributed to an omniscient, omnidirectional capacity.)[12] By *geometral*, then, Serres is invoking the nonfixity of positions or assignation, but also all possible appearances of marks—what is many-valued, infinitely-valued, substitutable, a description of virtual relations, the ground plan that summarizes and contains within itself a multiplicity of scenographies. As he words it in *Genesis*, "Once more, what is the ichnography? It is the ensemble of possible profiles, the sum of horizons. Ichnography is what is possible, or knowable, or producible, it is the phenomenological well-spring, the pit. It is the complete chain of metamorphoses of the sea god Proteus, it is Proteus himself. It is thus inaccessible. We are tied down to a spot, our limitation, our definition is our point of view, we are chained to scenographies."[13] Louis Marin, recalling that the term's etymology derives from the Greek *ichnos*, "print," writes of ichnography, "The outline on the ground at the surface level is nothing but the trace that would be left by the building if it were to be destroyed by time, by the violence of meteors or men." Thus, "the design, the preliminary drawing of the construction project, is *its* ruin."[14] Ichnography thus names a giving of form that contains every undoing of form: what is there as what is already ravaged.

The bond between the geometral and ichnographic is as follows: the former's formal restriction and *inflexibility* is precisely the origin of and capacity for its extraordinary permutation and compositional *possibility*. If the scenographic reminder is that the theatrical stage is an artificial yet affective space, the geometral insistence is that that space is an irreducibly and infinitely *logical* one, denoting the capacity of space to be described in relation to abstract dimensions of composition, as a diagrammatic field of shapes, lines, points, figures, corners, the parallel or perpendicular, the tangential, skewed edges — Euclidean geometry above all being a lexicon of form: the angular, the circular, the rectilinear, and their composites.[15] To read wallpaper in terms of line, form, rhythm, or proportion is precisely to refuse to describe it either symbolically or allegorically or from the point of view of atmosphere, mood, affect — all that is bound up with the scenographic construction of an artificial space for particular expressive ends. To read the wallpaper from the scenographic point of view is to emphasize the degree to which its visual presence as ornamentation renders any scene a domestic tableau, a claim that bonds *Amour Fou* to problems of artifice and history and posits a series of expressive connections derived from (and thus served by) aesthetic form. A radical formalism of wallpaper, by contrast, advances the geometral of place — one that approaches a proper thinking of love as the omnidirectional itself, disaffording a claim for the meaningfulness of love as borne out in its disclosure — one that would either attest to it as presence (Vogel's misreading) or attest to it as violent negation (the critical misreading). Rather, the geometral emerges in forms that neutralize meaningfulness, disqualifying the critical disagreement over the film's ending and instead giving priority to the problem of wallpaper as a matter of infinite potential. Prioritizing the geometral over the scenographic, angle over affect, grid over scene, the ichnographic over the theatrical, does not enable a thinking of love's *expression* through the diagram or grid or increment, or through omnidirectional extension, each of which would thereby be instrumentalized for its utility in demonstrating a *concept* of love — rather, love has to be thought via angle, grid, ichnography, as the sole manner of sidestepping the double risk embedded in either adjudication of the position of love in the ending of Hausner's film: sentimentalism, in accepting the positivity of love's idealism, or ironic cynicism, in discounting it. Either requires the assignation of a specificity to love, one that the geometral keeps perpetually open — unassigned and unassignable. A geometral treatment of wallpaper lends a formal thinking of love that preserves the secret of the film's ending as inaccessible by refusing to specify a critical place for the distinction between love and violation: in containing every multiplicity of scenographies, the ending attests to *both*, to *all*.

Barthes, in his Preface to *Critical Essays*, refutes the common understanding of the task of art as that which must "express the inexpressible"; to the contrary, "the whole task of art is to *unexpress the expressible*."[16]

The wallpaper in the Vogels' drawing room consists of a repeating pattern: small black flowers with slightly unevenly sized petals oriented in slightly different rotations are separated from each other by a network of vertical hourglass-like undulations. The technical term in pattern theory is *ogee*, a figure based on the S-curve, with both concave and convex contours, and whose aesthetic mark is one of radical limitation: its repeating curved grid minimizes choice for unit placement of the central motif. Ogee patterns are uniform networks, and because of their tight restriction of motif placement, the dark weight of these flowers comprises strong diagonal lines that, with the vertical curves, create the pronounced visual noise of multiple directions of energy at once. As instructed in *Principles of Pattern Design*: "The graceful ogee is derived from the lozenge or diamond [. . .]. By superimposing a properly adjusted network of such wave lines on a lozenge diaper, the ogee network emerges. Ogees may be vertical, like glass Christmas ornaments, or horizontal, like stretched fishnet. The object is to make the shapes fit the contours of the neighboring ones without leaving awkward slivers of space between. The sine curve is another, mathematical means of arriving at the ogee network."[17]

The scenographic approach to wallpaper also turns on a grid of relations, this time, however, to the expressive meaningfulness of flowers autonomous of the ogee pattern's lines, asking instead: Is there a relation between these decorative flowers and the lush real ones Henriette is constantly arranging in vases that half obscure her from the camera; or a relation

> between these and the finite flowers she speaks of under hypnosis ("I'm afraid. It's the flowers. They frighten me. [. . .] I can't bear to see their sweet beauty. It reminds me of the fact that they will fade");
>
> or with the trampled "sweetest violet" in Mozart's setting of Goethe's text "Das Veilchen" performed in a salon at the beginning of the film;
>
> or ———?

And are the flowers there to be read as signs of the feminine, or to convey an affective charge related to the claustrophobia of the domestic *huis clos*; are they there to be thought as property of the film's mise-en-scène, meaning substance, but also imprisonment related to modes of oppression — "I am my husband's property, and I should never dare to demand freedom" declares Henriette during a conversation among the men of the film about the new tax that "everyone now must pay," taxation being a form of bearing burden? Does the film's visual language bear the burden of these many dark flowers — is it *taxed* (as in harassed; as in fatigued) by them?

And so on goes the network of expressive associations.

This scenographic drive is the approach taken in the culminating moments of an otherwise resolutely formalist reading of *Amour Fou* in Sue Thornham's *Spaces of Women's Cinema*. Finding a kindred spirit with the feminist films of Chantal Akerman, Thornham describes *Amour Fou*'s movement as "contained and repetitive, and its framing distanced, formal, geometric," with framings that "echo Vermeer's domestic interiors, with their doorways opening onto tableaux of domestic life, their draped curtains that half obscure our view, their geometric floor tiles which lead us into an inside room but only as far as the facing wall, and their figures centrally placed but often with their backs to us, refusing the intimacy that the painting's domesticity seems to invite."[18] Attending to the compositional arrangement of bodies during the first of three diegetic recitals, she writes, "In the space between the two groups a dog poses with a solemnity equal to that of the two groups, and behind it in the diamond-patterned wallpaper we see the suggestion of a concealed door."[19] Evoking David Bordwell's concept of the planimetric shot, in which the camera is perpendicular to a flat rear surface, with its "sense of stiff ceremony" and "static, geometrical frame," Thornham attends to Henriette's dialectical movements that alternate between "tightly choreographed lines" and near-static postures of domestic duty: letter writing, flower arranging, in a mise-en-scène that does not regard exterior landscape as a release from structure but as yet another structured enclosure.[20] Despite the care and insight of this close reading, Thornham retreats from the problem of form, taking pains to afford enclosure the status of a symbol, converting the geometric reach of border and extension into a conception of unfreedom. "Two symbols in particular define this enclosed world," she posits: the wallpaper and the film's flowers. Linking *Amour Fou* to Charlotte Perkins Gilman's "The Yellow Wallpaper," Thornham continues, "Though not quite yellow, and far more geometric than the 'uncertain . . . flamboyant' pattern described in Gilman's story, here is a version of her imprisoning wallpaper. Its pattern and muted colours are echoed in the domestic clothing of both Henriette and Pauline, so that they seem to fade into its walls as it entraps them there."[21] In becoming symbol, the formal quality of wallpaper is relegated to the realm of scenography, standing as expressive *of* something else, constrained to the service of the symbolism of stultifying bourgeois norms (of family, domesticity, gender, love, duty, &c.).

Reading's decisiveness: if, by contrast, the flowers in the wallpaper are to be regarded and read as that which is *there* as their repeated graphic extension in every direction at once, the reductive consequence of the specificity of this organization of visual elements is that the wallpaper does not mean at all, but unconceals in its form the workings of the omnidirectional. Like the logic of the rhizome—beginningless, endless, foundationless, coming and going, always in the middle, and above all *conjunctive*, as in the famous "and . . . and . . . and . . ." that Deleuze and Guattari formulate in *Mille Plateaux*—from the standpoint of the geometral, a scenographic assignation of a fixed and certain place to love, what involves limitation, exclusion, and the determination of site, becomes useless, absurd, but above all impossible.[22] For in limiting, excluding, and determining site, thought has already missed love, has already specified it within the knowledge regime of hatred.

The essential problem with the scenographic approach is that it treats wallpaper *as* the idealism of its pattern—pattern as presence, pattern as locatable attestation, pattern as ornament, ornament as confinement, confine- ment as unfreedom, form as content. But the formal rhythms of the wallpa- per do not exist in the abstract, dehisced from the simultaneous navigation of pattern by cinematic form, whose intercession of angle, manipulation of light and scale, and deployment of deep and shallow focus put into the re- peated extending pattern the quality of infinite possible *difference* against which the sameness of extending pattern is distinguished. As Henri Focil- lon states of the simple form of an ornament in his classic 1934 *La Vie des formes*:

> Not only does it exist in and of itself, but it also shapes its own environment— to which it imparts a form. If we will follow the metamorphoses of this form, if we will study not merely its axes and its armature, but everything else that it may include within its own particular framework, we will then see before us an entire universe that is partitioned off into an infinite variety of blocks of space. The background will sometimes remain gen- erously visible, and the ornament will be disposed in straight rows or in quincunxes; sometimes, however, the ornament will multiply to prolixity and wholly devour the background against which it is placed.[23]

There is no *the* wallpaper. Put another way, wallpaper is neither being nor set value: it is multiple formal dimensions; not fixed, it moves and picks up speed, it goes in an infinite *and . . . and . . . and . . .* as a question of which direction to extend. *All of them; every possible and all at once.*

In a scene early in the film, in which Henriette and her daughter face opposite each other at a large round table, Pauline at smileless work on a puzzle, Henriette penning a letter to Heinrich, at least four visual regimes of wallpaper are in play: (1) as Henriette takes paper and ink from a cabinet, the background, in sharp focus, presents two walls meeting at a white verti- cal joiner of molding, the ogee pattern extending outward from the middle of the image simultaneously toward the left and right of the screen (plate 5); (2) as Henriette moves across the room to sit at the table and prepare for writing, the structure behind her, now a flat expanse deprived of the an- gles of the two walls meeting, is rendered entirely out of focus, the shallow emphasis and bright light that brings Henriette into visual relief destroying every aspect of pattern (what is no longer visible includes repetition; the decorative; the detail; omnidirectional extension; and the design itself—a form marked by regularity of mark is now a form marked by a constancy of blurred marklessness) (plate 6); (3) when the image cuts across the axis of action to Pauline, the wallpaper is violently brought into its most acute, sharp relief in a riot of uniform pattern (plate 7); and (4) upon the return to Henriette, parts of the back wall now in focus play against the light tones that make that background only partially visible, in an extension of sunlight toward the right side of the screen and patches of pattern-obliterating darkness on the left (plate 8). The measure of difference is thus multiply given in the changing relations of pull and proximity, sharpness, framing, scale, and light. Echoing in its own voice one of the crucial lessons demonstrated in chapter 3 by *Cabin in the Woods*, in its cinematic formal navigation of the form of the grid—that that film is a tessellation of dispersed yet interacting, complex and mutually affecting and mutually interpreting forms, which themselves generate and give rise to further forms, such that the film's formalism is a hyperformalism in which form is reading form, (cinematically) formalizing a (cinematic) formalizing of (grid) form, and thus *formalizing formalizing form*—*Amour Fou* involves a cinematic formalism of manipulated light, scale, depth of field, and framing, all of which read the formalism of an ogee pattern as it is formalized in a decorative object. If depth of field, framing, and light cinematographically induce regimes of difference, on the level of montage the scene evokes that of similitude with variation, for the editing structure (Henriette's frontality toward the camera, bearing a smile that fades, cutting to a previously unseen arrival) anticipates the form of the final encounter of Henriette and Heinrich that results in her death with, however, this difference: in place of the lover's approach by which he is invisibly behind, toward whom Henriette turns on a horizontal axis, the bleak relation here is that of the daughter visibly opposite, she who turns down, vertically away from Henriette.

Because the geometral is omnivalence, for Serres the compass is the supreme geometral form: it *is* the very potential to point in every direction. What the geometral approach to wallpaper claims—and this is the entirety of what it can claim; this exhausts its grounds for claim—is that there is no determining element that assigns a fixed place or site (and thus no science or philosophy of wallpaper possible). "Love is the geometral of places and sites" proposes only extension in all directions without specifying any single determinate element or path. *Amour Fou* regarded geometrally disqualifies every attempt to specify the secret of its ending (which is coextensive with the secret of love—there where it unfathomably is or ultimately is possible, or there where it is not or ultimately cannot be); and it disqualifies it through the aesthetic obsession that multiply intercedes the film with variable, multiple differences.

　—What is the proper object of a thinking of love? Is it lovers or is it forms? Is it subjects or grids? A related question: What is the form of knowledge proper to a thinking of love? Science? Art? Philosophy? Is it only one? Nancy is emphatic in "L'amour en éclats" that philosophy is always *missing* love proper, translating it from affect to concept, speaking around it. Is affect the proper register, then, for a thinking of love? It is, after all, what is opposed to philosophy in the film: Marie, replying to Kleist's final request to demonstrate her devotion by dying with him, replies, "I've always enjoyed philosophizing with you, but now you're ruining my good mood." Philosophy ruins a good mood, but one might equally say that a good mood can ruin a philosophy. Mood seems to miss love as much as philosophy does—the problem being that both equally rely on specifying love *as* thesis or *as* antithesis, situating it in a fixed and certain conceptual place, in other words that which is proper to the realm of hatred instead.

　Derrida, taking up Novalis's well-known claim that "the authentic philosophical act is suicide" [*Selbsttötung*: the putting to death of oneself, the annihilation of self], maintains that "what remains to be thought *together* is the first kiss *and* suicide, the principle *and* the act of authentic philosophy, their youth *and* their discipline, the act *and* the action."[24] But *Amour Fou* has the advantage (for philosophy, if philosophy can be said to accept advantage) of containing neither a first kiss nor making visible an uncomplicated suicide: neither an act nor an action, neither inauguration nor fulfillment, but their absolute suspension, frustration, extension: their orientation as only ever possible, as contained as value within the geometral that is the containment of all possible values. The secret of the film is that it contains no secret, or, rather, no fixed place for the secret, no specifying of the secret—it is unspecified in every possible direction. For those who would put it to work to think consent, (un)freedom, the political, or the meaningfulness of love or death, its impropriety is that it is indifferent to how Henriette would have ended that sentence; it is *neutral* that the autopsy reveals that she was not dying after all. It is not surprising that Kleist is one of the privileged figures in *Mille Plateaux* for what Deleuze and Guattari figure in his writing as "a violence of affects that causes an extreme confusion of feelings" for its manipulation of "catatonic freezes and extreme velocities, fainting spells and shooting arrows."[25] This, however, is where Hausner's formalism is more radical than that of French philosophy: Deleuze and Guattari describe the risk of lines of flight, the danger of their *"turning to destruction"* or the *"passion of abolition"* — warning that Kleist's flight turns *"into a line of death"* — and *Amour Fou* will not worry this, pure and simple.[26] This flight will not disturb its form but names what gives lines and extensions, directions and rhythms *to* its form.

Any reading that would fixate on consent as the opposite of unfreedom misses the more radical stance that the opposite of consent is an opposite consent. The opposite of love is neither violence nor hatred, neither cruelty nor indifference, neither force nor violation. *Amour Fou* invites the geometral thinking of love without falling to hatred's knowledge of fixed places — this is what lets the film retain the secret of love as the property of form itself bonded to its ineluctable *impersonality*. It is not a singular love that individuates some *I* (that is one's most private, most individual and distinct property), nor is love shared as a mutual or public common property (contra Bataille and Nancy, it does not form community). It does not *do* the totality of tasks to which thought has set to love and which love contains. *Fou*, after all, for all that it means crazy, mad, wild, stray, lost, ecstatic, drunk, insane, passionate (as in Breton's namesake text, as in Rivette's namesake film — each of which positions *amour fou* as the madness of freedom itself), also can qualify an apparatus or object whose movement is out of control, unconstrained, wild, *une voiture folle*, for example. All *amour* thus is amour fou, not for its passion or madness but for its uncontrollable, undisciplined mobilities out of order, what does not work properly in balance or function. Improper love is what is ill-adapted to securing what is one's own: geometral because it is abstract potential without recourse to the specification of place, name, substance, faculty, property; neither owned nor given away, neither freedom nor violence, what is unassigned and extensive, secret and yet unavoidably there. *There* alongside its every possible negation.

Love always discharges blanks.

That does not mean that it does no damage.

The secret of love is neither kept to oneself nor shared between several — the secret is that the opposite of love is an opposite love, already contained within its bouquet of values — it extends in every direction at once, even toward the indecency of violation, even toward the realm of what would certainly wreck it from within.

Love's omnitude of values contains already, then, both of these questions:
Why shouldn't love end in violence? (— *Amour Fou*)
Why shouldn't violence end in love? (— *L'inconnu du lac*)

◼ ◼ ◼ ◼ ◼

Different interlocutors, different lovers, different settings, a similar landscape, a kinship of restrictions, the same love, though it is never the same love, beginning with the same disagreement, those very same two words.

◼ ◼ ◼ ◼ ◼

LENGTH; OR, LOVE.....????.......!!!!!!!!!!

As for the Silurus, a cut-throat hee is wheresoever hee goeth, a great devourer, and maketh foule worke: for no living creatures come amisse unto him, he setteth upon all indifferently.
—PLINY THE ELDER, *Historie of the World (Historia naturalis)*

Toward the beginning of a conversation in *Cinema Scope* between the Portuguese filmmaker João Pedro Rodrigues and Alain Guiraudie, director of the 2013 *L'inconnu du lac* (*Stranger by the Lake*), speaking of the rigid, reductive formality of Guiraudie's film—which takes place over ten days in a radically confined setting within a rigorously plotted order of shots of the limited register and reach of a parking lot, a lake, its shore (itself invisibly partitioned into zones for cruising and for amity), an adjacent forest for watching or for fucking—whose boundaries collectively function as the restricted ground in which desire and murder play out, a space that is a frame, which is to say both rigid structure and circulation of evidence related to a crime—Rodrigues says of the work, "It's very *geometrical*." Guiraudie apparently agrees, only to metanoiacally recall or convert this pronouncement. "Yes," the director replies, "very *'scenographic'* I'd say."[27]

Those two designations, we already know, are starkly incommensurable. Lit. negation of *mensurabilis*: they have no common measure. Reading continues to take place at the site of that nothing-in-common.

L'inconnu du lac focuses on two sets of three figures, distributed by anthropomorphic type. The first begins and ends with the romantic, idealist Franck; his older, achingly desired love object, Michel; and his corpulent, observant friend, Henri, who will ultimately give himself over to Michel's violence as a sacrificial warning to Franck. The narrative turns on Franck's immediate and intense craving for Michel, which does not wane when, on the second day of the ten, he covertly watches Michel and his current lover in the titular lake and sees in a spare and dark long shot the disappearance of the second body under the line of the water and the slow reemergence of only Michel to the shore. The subsequent days follow Franck's erotic investment in Michel as it arcs through curiosity, amplification, love, tacking toward ambivalence, fear, and a soft loathing, all while a police inspector makes inquiries to the previously closed community of semianonymous cruisers, their count now down by one. By the end of the film, Michel has murdered both the inspector and Henri, and the light closes on Michel entreating out in the dark for a frightened but still present Franck to return to him — he who never to the end gave up entirely on his desire, never gave Michel over to the police. The film ends with a symmetrical exchange of calls without response: the exhaustion of this first cry of names and Michel's departure from the enclosed stage and then the final minutes of day and film, which present in near darkness an ambivalent Franck who wanders the pitch of the woods alone, finally whispering, trying, then baying Michel's name once, then again, again, and again. Franck cries out for the one he wants, which is to say the one he wants *nonetheless*. (All true wanting takes this form.) These men constitute the central narrative triangle — one that stages opposing models of eros: *amor*, a destructive, dissymmetrical passion turning on the grammatical opposition between the lover and the beloved, set against the mutuality of *philia*, the reciprocal goodwill among friends — which is to say structures that play out Platonic versus Aristotelian conceptions of the most ethical form of love.

Alongside this first triad, and composing a symmetrical if markedly different form of relations, there are three nonhuman figures: a corpse, a place, and a fish. More precisely, give this as a corpse, a place, and a measurement. This tripartite structure is not a triangle of desire, as in the amato-graphic narrative, but a setting in place of relations of comparative *quantity*. This is most visible in the film's account of the coming to be of the corpse, the disappearance of Michel's lover's body, which is structurally isomorphic to the famous formulation given by Aristophanes in *Symposium*: love as the yearning to be grafted together from Zeus-made halves, the fusing of an originary being split asunder, which is numerically offered as "being two you shall become one" (*hen ek duoin*, "one out of two"). The formula for murder is merely that two figures in the lake become one — that a pair of inky marks in a field of blue are supplanted with a single dark stain at its center — through loss in place of love's joining complementarity.

The second inhuman term in this set is a figure of place: the closed land-scape against which the ten days are structured. Invoked in nearly the same way in every piece of criticism on the film, landscape is taken as its spatial limitation and restriction, or the unity of the setting, and as its pronounced aesthetic qualities, shaded by differing quantities of light. This is the sense in which the film is read in *CineAction*: "While the space is confined, it is a natural setting and the film is attuned to its visual beauty, the sun, the water, the beach, the trees, and the sky. [. . .] The space becomes tactile and pro-duces a sensuality that is conducive to the men's nakedness and the sexual desire that motivates their presence on the beach."[28] In the wake of the cen-tral, which is to say inaugural, which is to say unexpected, act of violence (whose force *is* this contingency) — the vision of the subtractive form that has taken place in the lake — Franck, hidden, watches Michel depart for the eve-ning over a pronounced duration (eighty seconds from the two-into-one in the lake until Michel steps onshore and then two and a half further minutes for him to finally, languidly, leave the beach for the parking lot). When Mi-chel finally departs, the film cuts to a series of studies of the sky, composi-tions of clouds tinged with fading light, given as forms of shape, line, nega-tive space, color, and colorlessness (plates 9 and 10).

Although the violence of the coming to be of the corpse is given in the purity of the down-by-one formula, landscape here risks being taken as the environmental caption upon which the meaning of that formula is grounded. Light in particular solicits this approach, both for its Romantic associations with sublimity and contemplation and for its relation to the prospect of muta-bility. The art historian Charles Harrison's reading of Jean-Baptiste-Camille Corot's *Souvenir of the Environs of Lake Nemi* (1865) is instructive in this re-gard: Harrison describes the interplay of "the dramatic evening light, timed, it seems, after the sun has dropped below the horizon but before it has sunk too far for its glow still to tinge the undersides of the clouds," in reference to "the faunlike male bather in the right foreground, braced for the sudden movement in which he will pull himself out of the water" (plate 11).[29] Corot's tableau establishes, as Harrison puts it, a relation between "a moment of anticipation conceived in paradigmatically visual terms—the moment of impending loss of light—and a moment of anticipation of sudden physical movement."[30] In Guiraudie's film, the about-to-be-lostness of the nearly gone light in the landscape is set against the about-to-move unfixity of Franck from his voyeur's hiding place, where he has seen absolutely one event too many. The stillness and duration of the murder tableau and the pause invested in the length of light remaining to the crucial second day of ten are each broken with the resumption of movement, narrative, the what-next-now-what wake of wanting the one who has done such violence. The framing of light in the primitive landscape set of sky and Earth, in other words, transports the film from the vision of horror to living in and with its aftermath. Illuminated landscape, taken this way, is the medium of the resumption of new possibilities for action or decision. As the specificity of Corot's tableau fixes around those imminent changes, each on the cusp of arrival, each suspended as the available *souvenir* of the painting's title, Harrison's reading of these suspensions in relation to an "engaged spectator's own muscular anticipation" and sympathetic response turns these relations into means to bring about a physiological, sympathetic, and above all sensorial end, and puts the restricted landscape to use as the scenographic, as an arrangement of elements to call forth to the imagination of the viewer powerful effects. *Souvenir*, from *subvenire*, "to come to mind." In this critical tradition, landscape's aesthetic features are fundamentally scenographic, the scenographic is atmospheric, and the atmospheric is above all affective: it moves the mind, engages imagination.

We have moved no further, then, than that initial disagreement over a word.

Landscape as scenographic stage that expresses meaning is invoked in nearly all of the criticism in French and English about *L'inconnu du lac*. In *La Vie des idées*, Fabien Gris writes of the film that "c'est sur la scène à ciel ouvert de ce théâtre très codifié—l'unité de lieu y est rigoureusement maintenue" (it is on the open-air stage of this highly codified theater that the unity of place is strictly maintained).[31] The affective scenery is the privileged sense by which the director describes landscape's bondedness to desire: as figuring the conjunction of place, space, and queer relationality. Showcasing his debt to the Romantic tradition of atmospherically grounded sensorial reception, Guiraudie explains: "I wanted to return to a single space—to a scenography, a dramaturgy, a geography that would be extremely simple and immediately legible. I wanted to be able to appropriate a place, be *present* in it, take possession of it and populate it with characters I could manipulate freely. All of this to go back to the question of desire."[32] This, then, is the restricted sense in which the restricted setting of the landscape of shore and forest has been read: that the location is photogenic, that it is the scene of and for eros, the setting inextricable from the modulations of affective triangulation that structure the narrative. This treatment of landscape regards the space, the light, and the lake as above all an affective map for plotting sentiments of arousal, terror, disgust, and anxiety.[33] When criticism focuses on the text as "a drama of love and death set at a rural cruising spot," emphasizing the enclosure, isolation, and restriction of the space in which eros and violence circulate, or casts the film as one in which Guiraudie "entrusts his visuals—landscape, the actors' gestures, their naked or half-dressed bodies—with the communicative work that spoken language performs, sometimes to excess, in his earlier films," then landscape is taken as equivalent to the scenographic, and the scenographic is taken as the ground for an analytic.[34]

The geometric, by contrast, as what is concerned with plan and section, with properties of figure, what notates an omnitude of values and contains a multiplicity of scenographies, attests to a brutal, uncompromising measurability of the world. This movement from analytic to geometric is the progression from anything else whatsoever to a radical formalism. In *L'inconnu du lac*, the contacted workings of violence and erotics are placed into this rigorously plotted, scrupulously formed scene around a lake not in the attestations and choreography of an impersonal intimacy, or what Leo Bersani calls the "sexual sociability" of cruising; not in the unsimulated cum shots whose glistening texture is both studied and staged through the filtered chiaroscuro of sunlight; not in any post-AIDS allegories of risked (and arousing) peril through connectedness with anonymities; and not in the montage of the mediated and embodied exchanges of glances through which desire, suspicion, evaluation, and love circulate. Rather, in the master opposition that we cannot shake, Rodrigues was right and Guiraudie wrong about his own film, for something simultaneously horrific *and* on the order of love enters *L'inconnu du lac* through an impersonal form of measurement. Landscape gives the measure of violence — not as setting's expressive geography, but as geometry.

This returns us to the third term in the second set of inhuman relations: there is the corpse, the illuminated place, and now to that fish. Geometry is brought into *L'inconnu du lac* through a brief exchange that takes place four minutes into the work. Franck and Henri, previously unknown to each other, establish the ground for their philia through a conversation about the lake from which Franck has just emerged, one that turns on the reported, disputed presence in the lake of a *silure*. To the affective question condensed — Henri's opening query, "Doesn't the silurus scare you?" — a series of conversational negotiations ensues about the unseen fish: *Dix mètres? Cinq?* Henri insists to Franck's skepticism that a silurus four meters long has definitely, assuredly, been seen, and so a five-meter one is surely possible: after all, "de quatre à cinq mètres, c'est pas loin." This silure, when mentioned at all in the critical mass, has been codified as a figure of anxiety, or as an allegorical monstrosity that lurks in the lake, a condensed symbol of risk associated with that space, from the most literal reading that dubs the reference to the ten-meter-long fish "une tension dramatique" to claims for it as the linchpin that appropriates the film to the language of thriller or horror, as much for its entwining of sex and death as for its setting of violence in the idyllic but secluded place-that-is-nowhere.[35] As goes one account of the closed community of cruisers, "Like the silurus, perhaps they've just been lucky until now, evading death by not being in the same place at the same time. But death has come [. . .], and like all good horror films, it comes out of the lake."[36] In this move, *silure* is taken for thing. And perhaps this is found to be persuasive. The silurus, after all, is not a neutral or arbitrary choice here: in the *Ninth Book of the History of Nature*, Pliny, speaking of the silurus in the section "Of the Names and Natures of many Fishes," dubs our voracious figure "a great Robber" who "devoureth every Animal; often dragging under the Water the Horses as they swim."[37] (A note to Pliny from the 1848 Wernerian Club edition cites the delightful proverb "Every fish preys on some other one, but the Silurus on all.")[38] The French word *inconnu*, which can refer equally to a person who is unknown or to the unknown in general, is also, in an obscure usage from the nineteenth century and earlier, the word that names a shee-fish, in other words, the wels or European catfish, or the *Silurus glanis*. So, titular permutations in French themselves suggest a collapse of the stranger by, from, near, or of the lake (the one I cruise, observe, evaluate, am evaluated by, fuck, ignore, kill); an unknownness from, of, or comprising the lake (as such); and also, finally, the indeterminate figure said to reside in the depths of the lake. If criticism wants to make the claim that the silure is one of many monstrous figures in, of, and from the lake—that it puts a thematics of monstrosity and death into the water, anticipating Michel's violence and the corpse that will be produced therein—there appears to be evidence for that.

Except for one thing. There is no more *the* silure in *L'inconnu du lac* than there is *the* wallpaper in *Amour Fou*. That figure functions only in the allegorical or affective sense if criticism, in essence, fleshes the fish out for the film, resolving the very question of its qualities and existence that is put under duress in Franck and Henri's conversation. For what the silurus is to the text is not body (wet, monstrous, voracious) so much as a problem of measurement. What the silurus *is* is a disagreement over ten meters versus five meters versus four meters. The ontology of the silurus is an uncertain claim of measurement; in this way, it is literally a variable, a symbol for an as yet unknown number. Its ontology is nonstabilized, it is only the more or less. In being the different-but-not-by-muchness of *quatre* versus *cinq mètres*, the silurus is the not-so-very-far distance made in the comparison of quantity. What, other than a strict formalism, could ever make sense of *this* silurus?

Unlike other types of mathematics, geometry does not turn on abstract quantities—it is profoundly antialgebraic because it does not involve comparisons in relation to abstractions. Instead, geometry is about comparing measured things. Nothing is permitted in a geometric proof except that which is measured by comparison to something already measured; geometry exists in reference to the prior, to comparisons of the existing. Guiraudie's film offers an algebra in its fundamentally numerical formula for death, which involves the same terms that are in play in the formulas it offers for different modes of love—

the $2 - 1 = 1 + 0$ (murder);
the $1 + 1 = [1,1] + x$ (desire);
the $2 \pm 1 = 2$ (Henri/philia);
the $\frac{1}{2} + \frac{1}{2} = 1$ (Aristophanic love)

. . .

. . .

. . .

. . .

. . .

The geometric, however, undoes metaphoricity, erases the parenthetical translations of those algebraic forms, and designates a relation to the lake that is radically indifferent to two bodies versus one body emerging from the water to instead turn on three posited line segments and the matter of whether they are congruent. The geometric points to the act itself—and nothing else—of comparing lengths. Likewise, Franck's insistence about the silurus, "I would have seen it by now," and Henri's rejoinder, "You've never been in the same place at the same time," redescribe the overdetermined contingency (of love or violence, it matters little) entirely as a matter of localization and the relative position of figures. The origin of Franck and Henri's relation of nonerotic amity arrives through a geometric insistence, one whose conceptions are formal and diagrammatic, not allegorical.

A geometric approach inverts the critical grammar of lake. Instead of marshaling an entire cartography of meaning that turns on prepositions—Henri's insistence that he likes sitting by the water or the various tonalities of "l'inconnu *du* lac" (of, from, in, by), all those notations that show spatial, temporal, and logical relations—and instead of figuring the unknown as a thing in this prepositional relation to the scenographic lake, the geometric puts in play the unknown of what the lake is in its critical regard. The lake, like Franck's final calling out of Michel's name, is ahermeneutic. The film thus stages the formality of death by way of a lacuna in its presencing of the unknown(ness) of the lake as an expressive sign. (That missing portion of a manuscript, that resolute blank—*lacūna*: a hole, a pit? It is derived from *lacus*: hollow, opening, but also basin, also pond, also reservoir, cistern, bin, lake.) The film encounters the unknown, establishes a relation with it through a separation—spacing an interval between geometry and scenography, between measurable and affective landscapes, between love and violence, eros and thanatos, desire and revulsion, shore's security from lakeish peril, and placing varying distances between them, making insufficient any claim for their capacity to attest to a definitive expressive conclusion, including the definitive expression of ambiguity.

The film thus does *not* not-mean. It abrogates the capacity of violence or desire, or death or love, to stand *for* meaning, to afford critical readings purchase. It is not enough to say that some film frustrates meaning or evacuates metanarratives or ambiguates allegory—the frustration of meaning still derives from the sphere of meaning, the nonmeaning internal to meaning, the silence that gives shape to voicing. The more urgent question is how to stage the unknown without recalling it to the known, how to attest to the ahermeneutic dimension of the final call of Michel's name—in other words, what cannot be reduced to either the claim that desire can outrun fear or its negation, but that which nihilates the very ground for making that evaluation. The lake is an interval but not between two concrete registers of space or the location of a look and its scanned object; rather, the lake is the interval between the idea of landscape in its scenographic register and the formality of landscape as a series of measurable distances that indicate no privileged single vantage on or by which to read them.

The geometric thus produces an impersonal relation within thought, establishes an impasse within accounts of the relation of horror conceived as broadly as possible to love conceived as broadly as possible. In place of queer theory's fixation on the impersonal relations of sex that govern the circulation of desire, glance, gaze, and cruising, this impersonality is lodged at the center of interpretation itself. Debates about designating nomenclatures of membership (Is the film Hitchcockian? a thriller? queer horror? It must be named—) miss the generic forest for the trees: what is horrific here is not a positive nomination but the opacity of violence and love. The silure is not the monster from the lake: the silure names the monstrousness of an impasse of reading form as affording an expressed meaning. In turn, the film's aesthetic language poses the dilemma of whether the scene is equivalent to the film's relation to desire: that is, whether constructed space is *there* to represent something about the capacity of erotic passion to not only survive but even sustain the revelation of the lover as bringer of death. Is light there to disquiet or to lure? Is the topography of the landscape descriptive? Are the zones arrangements that turn into allusions? A geometric approach, however, does not regard violence as a matter of force between agents, not a failure or aporia of the ethical, nor love as its antidote, nor desire (or community, homosociality, dialogue, sacrifice) as affirmative forms of relationality. Rather, a formal reading merely tarries with the positive force of irrelationality, the *energeia* of a nonaffective, nonsignifying, and impersonal geometry.

Brutal measurability permits the question of love to remain unknown yet nevertheless establish axiomatic and describable relations compatible with a radical indifference to what is being measured or described. While the scenographic (and all its attendant concepts: affect, atmosphere, allegory) figures what is composed and structured to be seen and felt, the geometric evacuates the "what is seen and felt"—it is the generative making unknown of all of those dimensions. Love thereby remains *l'inconnu*. The film's spacing, its measured distance from the interpretability of the relation or relative positions of desire and love to brutality and violence, emplaces affective extremes in the uncompromising figure of measurability without meaning.

◪ ◪ ◪ ◪ ◪

Amour Fou: *Parting without ever having joined.*
L'inconnu du lac: *Joining and then not parting (for now).*
——————: *Joining, then parting, and never to rejoin.*

◪ ◪ ◪ ◪ ◪

NEGATIVE SPACE (ON NO LONGER BEING LOVED)

1 *Tu ne m'aimes plus?*
   Non. Mais j'ai une infinie tendresse pour toi.[39]
   Probably it was nothing all that loving, not much, and nothing now is missing. You are everywhere but the center but it is too late, or never again, and it is too late, too late, it is too late this time, it is late it is hard all has waned it is over, and in the end you were not enough.
   To no more be the thing that is wanted: a levigation of heart. *Infinite tenderness* can mean affection without end or what is raw without balm. If the latter case, one is stained forever: invisibly inked a hematoma's purple & black &

2 *Blau*, cont. (Goethe)[40]
   "779. This colour has a peculiar and almost indescribable effect on the eye. As a hue it is powerful, but it is on the negative side, and in its highest purity is, as it were, a stimulating negation [ein reizendes Nichts]. Its appearance, then, is a kind of contradiction between *excitement and repose.*"

(Reiz und Ruhe: *stimulus, attraction,* but also *lure,* also *charm as of a woman, what luster is alive* & *peace, quiet, rest, repose,* but also *quiescent, inactive,* also *neutral,* also *dormancy as of inoperative love, deactivated,* in other words *broken* and *faulty, what is dull and/or* [but mostly &] *what is dead*)

"780. As the upper sky and distant mountains appear blue, so a blue surface seems to *retire* from us."

(zurückweichen: *to back away, to pull away, to fall back, to give way,* but also *to shy away* [*shame away* and *shrink,* so close to *wither*], the more violent *to flinch,* the fear-linked *to blench,* and *to recede, retreat, weaken, withdraw—*)

"781. But as we readily follow an agreeable object that flies from us, so we love to contemplate blue, not because it advances to us, but because it draws us after it."

(And in so wandering off, in being what departs, blue is no longer the lure but the recoiling that distances *as its lure*; we haul after withdrawal, not withdrawing thing, dragged after and not yet closer, perpetual retreat, all leaving and still not close. Every time Zeno's Achilles, each time the pathetic weepy runner.)

3 Everything henceforth will be a question of negative space.

4 It takes place in between its two titles: Abdellatif Kechiche's *Blue Is the Warmest Color / La Vie d'Adèle—Chapitres 1 & 2* (2013) has been characterized if not caricatured as a love story, a first love story, a coming-out story, a best lay of your life—& *it will never be that good again*—or a feminist/resolutely antifeminist/queer/redemptively heteronormative/male gaze-displaying/female desire-demonstrating work so often that it bears pausing and pointing out the very obvious, very simple fact that the film is, at heart, in truth about depletion—about the retreat of a world-positing-world-destroying love, what bruising toll is taken by a draining away of affect, by love's bleed, passion's absenting and its vicious whimpered end.

The work attests to the form of no longer being loved.

(4a)   In the logic of the chromatic febricity of the English title, the film is structured by a cooling.

(4a, alt.) Or, so go the chapters of the French: a succession of plenitude and lack, partible divisions that cancel each other out; one gains freedom at the other's direct loss: zero-sum.

(4a, alt.) Or, in the language of Goethe, the text itself is a stimulating negation.

(4b)   What we are speaking of is not purely a negation but a negation that forms a positive difference, posing: What is the affective specificity of the losing of a directed affect? What is the specific tonality of this no-longer? It has nothing in common with the bittersweet feeling of no longer loving. To no longer be loved is not like to no longer love nor like to no longer be disgusted, to no longer grieve, no longer hold in contempt, to have unmoored hot shame or no longer inspire a recrudescent fear; nor is it a static anhedonia, nor or or—No; it is merely the changing pressure of a unified system: the intensification into a new state at a structure's one-sided waning of affect.

 One is, strictly speaking, dislocated from the form of love: a joining of mutually affecting forces.

(4c)   Stendhal describes how "to love is to enjoy seeing, touching, and sensing with all the senses, as closely as possible, a lovable object which loves in return."[41] One wonders then: What is the temporal order of undoing love at the breaking of that *which*? A love no longer returning forms a spacing: devastates the as *closely as possible*, interpolates an interval.

(4d)   Suppose you are loved. What happens next is either: nothing at all or you are no longer loved. For as long as you are loved, nothing new is happening and no event is next until something else intercedes. Love is surprise, the encounter is what by definition was what was not seen to be coming—but nothing is surprising in love itself until the sudden instant that love on someone's part is no longer.

(4d, cont.) Jean-Luc Nancy: "It is possible that one day I will no longer love you, and this possibility cannot be taken away from love—it belongs to it. It is against this possibility, but also *with* it, that the promise is made."[42]

But I am speaking of this not as possibility but as necessity: when what belongs to love as its no-longer limit has arrived, absolutely and decisively.

5   In the rush to adjudicate *Blue/Adèle* in relation to stale motifs of identity politics, generic debates about pornography, trite arguments over the verisimilitude of sexual practices—and in thrall to readings that coopt every text for a flattening and naïve demonstrationism of prior, stable, fixed categories of cultural knowledge—Kechiche's film has been treated to paraphrase and evaluation not only divested from a consideration of form but resolutely indifferent to the specific insights that radical formalism might generate in relation to affective intensities. As a result, affectivity has been taken for a positive nomination instead of a structuring repudiation (love, in place of its withdrawal); aesthetic elections have been (mis)taken for themes (extreme close-ups as exhibiting the meaning of intimacy); form has been instrumentalized for a simplistic model of spectatorial reception (extreme close-ups as productive generators of intimacy); and largely unremarked is the rigorous composition of the text on the level of light, color, line, figure, ground, and the mode by which the internal divisions of the film are governed by a series of dialogues with intertextual figures.[43]

Those include—& this list is far from exhaustive—Marivaux's eighteenth-century *La Vie de Marianne, ou Les Aventures de Madame la Comtesse de ****; Jean Anouilh's twentieth-century *Antigone*, and more precisely Antigone's refusal ("c'est le jour où elle dit non, et c'est le jour où elle va mourir" [The day she says no is the day she will die] offers a teacher as the essential form of tragedy); Sartre's *Les Mains sales* and "L'existentialisme est un humanisme"; Francis Ponge's surrealist poetry of things, *Le parti pris des choses*; HK's Leftist protest anthem, "On lâche rien"; Pabst's *Pandora's Box*; the films of Kubrick (—the great painterly colorist of the cinema); Julie Maroh's title-loaning source-text graphic novel, which further suggests one might consult the history of color temperature in eighteenth-century Aesthetics or, why not, the relation of warmth and coolness to animation more broadly, dating at least as far back as the Middle Ages; Gaspar Noé's *Enter the Void* and its siblings' pact of storgic love to never ever, ever *ever* leave each other; the Klimt-versus-Schiele debate; *Beaux Arts* magazine; the Western discourse of Artists and their Muses; Neoclassical sculpture; Courbet's *L'Origine du monde*; Picasso (—of the famed Blue Period); sentimental literature and its polyphonic tears of love; the Ugly as excluded from the Fine Arts; the children's book *Le Loup est revenu!*; the nursery rhyme "Lundi tout gris"; Alain Bosquet's poem "La Trompe de l'éléphant" (*Pas besoin*)—and *we have only lingered with the first two chapters.*

(5a) The literary intertexts constitute structuring breaks at regular intervals, passages read aloud functioning as epigraphical cleaves in the rigorously partitioned cinematic work. This is a quick sketch (—we really ought to diagram it): the first half of the three-hour film is governed by three large sections, each of which is inaugurated by a recitation in Adèle's high school classroom (with a visual logic of figures isolated from a blue ground; more on that infra):

(i) *Marivaux*—and a discussion of glance, encounter, love, and regret, then a scene of eating, the appearance of a boy, first exchanging glances with Emma in the street (i.e., being taken off guard by a shock of blue), uninspired sex with the boy, their break up, a protest march; &c.

(ii) *Anouilh*—and a discussion of refusal, tragedy, childhood, death, then a kiss at school, encountering Emma at a bar at night (introducing a second free-floating haunt of blue), schoolyard cruelty, sketching and sweetness in the park; &c.

(iii) *Ponge*—and the question of the natural, perversion, inevitable vice, then a museum, eating in the park, the rigorously composed ecstasies of Adèle and Emma's first fuck (forming a first internal symmetry with the first segment, repetition with a series of differences: spontaneity supplanting the rote, girl supplanting boy, lust supplanting convention [and also a series of formal differences: the light is otherwise, the angles are new]), another protest, this time for gay pride (forming a second internal symmetry with the first segment), dinner with each set of parents, a birthday party, more sex (whose duration, intensity, and fleshy explicitness is required: one has to know what precisely our heroine will be losing, will have lost).

At one hundred minutes in, a hard cut signals a temporal leap by the loss of blue—Emma's hair is suddenly an ashy blond—and the first three acts are over.

The second chapter, as it were, is also structured by epigraphic readings of three texts aloud, this time in inversions in which Adèle is now the teacher, no longer the student (forming another set of symmetries with the first half), exchanging schoolyards and patterning itself after the first chapter in order to rotate or negate key elements—for example, Adèle no longer eats her father's pasta, she makes the pasta to serve to Emma's friends; the aesthetic objects on display no longer appear in the museum but are Emma's works, in the home; and, crucially, rutting is what does not happen as it did as Emma's cool spurning of Adèle's attempts at seduction supplant the unbounded yesses of the first half. (Sex: what never happens again quite as it did.) The second chapter symmetrically moves outward, quoting and citing the constituent elements of the first chapter in order to effect this one-to-one negation, moving back toward the opening of the film: Adèle fucks a man, then she is alone again, undone as she was at the start.

There is no love; there is love; there is not-love.

Everything is given form in order to come apart.

& so on.

(5b) And, of course, other logics and structures—other diagrams— might be drawn: consider the temporal relations between the ferocious intensity of the first time the two women's naked bodies slam into each other (seven minutes), the ferocious intensity of the fight that cleaves the two (seven minutes), and the brutal declaration at a dark café toward the end of the film that the one still loves while the other does not (fourteen minutes from encounter to end as though summing the total affective quantities of the first and second seven-minute sequences). Aristophanes's numerical metaphysics of love again insinuates itself, the *hen ek duoin* a machine to proliferate formulas, but now:

No longer sharing love in common, $1 + 1 - 1 = \{\varnothing\}$
One's world reduced to null set in the *Tu ne m'aimes plus?*
    — You don't love me anymore?
        At the confirmation of the withdrawal — *Non* — one
        now *has* precisely nothing.

(5c) All this and we have not yet begun to treat blue. When Emma's
      new lover says to a supplanted Adèle at the final gallery show
      that the former lover is "still here" and points to a sketch of Adèle
      on the gallery wall — a drawn nude stained with blue splatter — it
      begs the question: What does it mean to be there as figure in
      line; or, its variation: what does it mean to be present as a shock
      of color, the form of the very first encounter with Emma, the
      smoky blue of her hair not signing meaning but constituting in its
      sudden appearance the essential dimension of the contingency
      of love? The film is saturated with blues — soaked with them, and
      too many: Kleinian, navy, cyans, near-blacks, violet grays, and
      white-tinged pales; it is paired with, alongside or cut through,
      blue's color-wheel negations of golds and burnished yellows; it
      appears as a rupture of the new, sudden in the frame, or it rises
      or retreats, attaches to fabrics or takes on the status of a Figure
      or bleeds beyond the screen as extensive infinitizing ground.
          Or it does a thousand other things (undiscovered; all waiting
      without guarantee: most apparent to the eye as presence,
      color still always requires a reading).

(5d) In Maroh's graphic novel that loans its English title to the film — a
      very different text, not just medially but in sentimental arrange-
      ment, one that turns affectively on mourning and melodramas
      of love realized too late — blue is a sign of transition between
      the present and past, between inner and outer textual frames.
      Color breaks up space, inaugurates a temporal break in worlds.
      (Color: a pure form of visible difference.)

(5c, cont.) *The film nullifies any neutrality toward blue.* It risks being
      overtaken by a color (i.e., risks being overwhelmed by a formal
      detail).

(5e)   The opening shot: a dusky blue mailbox in the middle ground, blue signing the crystallization of passage, site of what is sent out, what is received, where things and messages fundamentally cross. Adèle walks toward the camera, away from its rectangular structure, that form not stained by a supplementary charm of blue (*pace* Kant) but *given* form by the limited extension of blueness.

(5f)   The final shot: the vibrant flare of Adèle's sapphire dress in agonized departure—from Emma and her new lover—walks that dress and its hourglass of blue down a street, bearing its saturation as movement that departs, that withdraws as she walks away from the camera, unable to move quickly enough to leave blue behind.

(5c, cont.) How does a reading of blue as compositional element relate to affective appearance and waning, to temporalities of suddenness and elongated duration, to scales of magnification and intimacies of proximity and details in miniature or estrangement and spacing? Blue does formal work. Blue also does affective work—perhaps; it might; why not—but one cannot know what that is in advance, so closely, slowly, consider again: What unremittable work does blue do here?

(5f, cont.) One can retreat from blue in many ways:
        —"A nude woman, ugly, spread out on opaque blue grass under some palm trees." (Louis Vauxcelles, *Gil Blas*, 1907, on Matisse's *Nu bleu, Souvenir de Biskra*)
        —"If I met such a woman in the street, I should run away in terror. Above all I do not create a woman, I make a picture." (Matisse)[44]

(5g)   How else might one read for formal affectivity? These bodies proximate and they space: this is what all the fucking is about. It is ineluctably graphic—not explicit or obscene but as in *drawn*, as in given in schema and line. Any reading of the extended (in duration) and extensive (in space) stagings of Adèle and Emma's bodies entwined must not speak in indifference to and ignorance of the specific forms they take—careful not to write over the limbs and tongues and curves and planes as compositionally complex; a radical insistence to consider skin as color and light, fingers and calves as angles and border. Above all, thinking must remain wary of a generic topology that evaluates the tiresome field of the sexually arousing (whereby one generic test succeeds) or the aesthetically arousing (whereby its generic test fails). For in this film it is impossible to get around: Sex is not a thing, but nor is it a relation. Sex is a form of composition, a way bodies take up and use space, a question of ornament, line, color, scale, figure, ground, balance, emphasis, texture, material, rhythm, expansion, cry, weight, collapse. The two women suck and stir and writhe and grasp—and thereby create and unconceal different geometric shapes, new rhythms, distended lines, &c. To write about love and sex *without* recourse to attentively reading form is to designate no critical claim, precisely because love and sex are designated *in* form. And so: Where is the image heavy and light, balanced or unbalanced? How are the figures locked within rigid hierarchical grids: vertical then horizontal ones? How does the schema of the interlocking bodies relate to fore-, middle-, and background, and where do they concentrate lines, blending distinct figures into a composite or fluid one? And how are these figures *given* in relation to the bare stage of horizontal blocks of white and blue, devoid of ornament, flattened and flattening? Two people are fucking—but that does not mean we are done with reading.

To the contrary: Sex is a meeting ground of forms, of which bodies are but by no means are the only ones.

Two bodies' intimacy, after all, is the compositional dimension by which, for a brief and fragile and sometimes extraordinary time, they share one interior line.

(5h) N.B. in a spare, flat tableau the erring single foot, what extends its awkwardness to the left at an angled remove in the cinematic (plate 12) and painterly (plate 13) frame precisely to loan weight and density to the entangled mass block from which its vector flees.

(5i)   Corpus can be color. Each time Adèle and Emma's bodies cross, the paired tones of blue and gold are thrown to the margins of the image as though a condensation and ninety-degree rotation of Schiele's two 1912 friends, their figures unfixed in space, all axis and crossing, difference given in *gouache* (that opaque material also, of course, known as bodycolor).

(5i, alt.) Bodies are fundamentally shapes. Each time Adèle and Emma's bodies right-angle form (plate 14), the paired blue-gold coronas mirror-reflect and reorder the vertical hierarchy of Schiele's amative ovals (plate 15).

(5i, cont.) Unpack this carefully composed cinematic tableau, with its uneven distribution of blanknesses: whitewall background fields interrupted by the dark excision of a rectangle; the artifice of candles (inadequate to the light cast on the two figures in the space: they precisely do not lend to the bodies the seductions of glow, the mysteries of shadow); the open window gesturing at a beyond to the flat representational space; the glint of blue just beyond its reach; the timelessness and abstraction of the setting; the white drapery of classical sculpture (cf. curtains cloaking nudes) thrown to the bed rendered horizontal platform; &c.

6 All this is not (yet) a reading. It is only a first chapter or two, and part of a longer story. It remains only the insistence that any critical claim to make about *Blue/Adèle* would do well to linger with the complex details of the epigraphic structure, the forms of symmetry and dissymmetry between the parts of the film — to give formal body to its series of repetitions and their differences. To ask: How does the text establish an opposition between feeling and understanding (look, perhaps, to the Bosquet); between sculpture and drawn sketch; between the Ugly and the Beautiful? How is the affective singularity of no longer being loved a formal problem, and how does reading for form illuminate the dimensions of this loss? No reading could take the measure of all of these questions, but a robust account must read for some of these aspects of what the text is beyond summations or paraphrase.

Blue/Adèle is a particularly urgent ground for resisting the false notion of form at first sight, turning as it does on intensities of sentiment, intensities of color, each apparently manifest as presence, their conjunction a fundamental test of the problem of the relation of form to affect at its most acute stage: when it is disappearing, when it is nearly not there at all. In considering the agon and agony of no longer being loved, reading must take the measure of blue, of line, of space, shape, texture, brilliance, duration, gesture. Otherwise one risks never being taken by surprise by the particularity of this film, this text precisely about the world-positing-world-destroying disorientation of being taken surprise by love.

Otherwise: what it is to no longer be loved will never rise to the level of a specificity.

—And just ask around: everything painful is a specificity.

7 "One loses control of reading; that is its infinite promise."[45]

8 "*La Vie de Marianne* is not so much a novel about the body as a novel about the effects of the body on those who are confronted with it. The color of Marianne's eyes is of no import to the internal coherence of the novel, but the effects they have on others is of fundamental import to the narrative. The various responses to Marianne's appearance provide the framework for the narrative, ranging from lust (M. de Climal) to infatuation (Valville) to sympathy (Mme. de Miran), and it is therefore these responses Marivaux emphasizes."[46]

—But what happens when the effect on the body of those confronted is to retreat from effect, to declare that, faced with these specific eyes and tears and lips and skin: *you are the thing that no longer affects me?* Then there is no more in you to still prompt love. You become that which calls forth no response.

9 In organizing itself around the dimension of affective separation—the distancing and no-longerness of love, inseparably in a relation to the positive element that is withdrawn, such that they, as it were, mutually sketch each other—*Blue/Adèle* is obsessed with figure/ground relations, put into the film in an aesthetic shorthand: a fifty-second scene in which Emma and a doctoral student of art history and philosophy establish a set of oppositions in a disagreement about Egon Schiele and Gustav Klimt, the former aligned with a regime of unlikely positions, the body as gesture, what is twisted, obscure, dark, morbid, as

opposed to the decorative, florid, and ornamental. This is a well-worn opposition (the familiarity is the point: it constitutes a signature of obviousness), one that opposes formally ordered, meticulous, patterned surfaces and brilliant palettes to brutal, awkward, figural distortions, what is indecorous instead of decorative, strangely angled instead of geometrically patterned, what is defiant to norms of beauty, even ugly. Another way of naming the opposition between Klimt and Schiele is between formalism (cold, all surface, all geometry) and affective intensity (what distends figure, what gestures wrack and wreck the body). (As just one example of that shorthand: "A metamorphosis was thus completed: by substituting emotional affect for decorative effect in the interplay of color and form, Schiele had unmasked the sensual, sinister world that had always been buried beneath Klimt's seductive surfaces.")[47] This is yet another version of the claim for an antonymic relation of the decorative against the expressive, line against emotive power of line, affect as what rescues an aloof, detached formalism, &c. In this tradition, any affect is always (taken to be) the warmest color.

(9a) The aesthetic microallegory crystallized in the worn Schiele/Klimt opposition is thus a metacommentary on the very way in which one might read the affect of love and its loss in relation to form in the film. Consider, then, how it hinges on the word *florid*, what Klimt is accused of; Schiele, opposed to.

Florid is a fighting word: what is excessively beautiful, what is gilded, overwrought, too decorated, excessively ornate, & is also what feels too much—a florid sensibility, what is fervid—& is also reddish, ruddy, rosy: in other words, too *red*; all that is not blue. What *flourishes* (*floridus: in bloom*, in other words: alive, living) is opposed to morbidity (what withers, is diseased, is dead)—so of a petal, a body, a sentiment.

10 As *Blue/Adèle* turns on an affective withdrawal, negative space becomes the privileged compositional site for the affirmative staging of retreat, nowhere more strikingly than in the crystallization of a unique configuration of love: the kiss.

FIGURES 6.1.–6.3. *Blue Is the Warmest Color* / *La Vie d'Adèle—Chapitres 1 & 2* (Abdellatif Kechiche, 2013)

In lieu of a negative space that surrounds and demarcates a joined form, here the composition involves the establishment of an illuminated space between the lovers' faces that is posited, withheld, constructed, then demolished in pulsations on the rhythmic capitulations of the lips. Compared with the lovers' final encounter (not last, for there will be others, but the encounter marked by its avowal of a finality of love), in which the black imposition between Adèle and Emma *as figures* cleaves their relation both to each other and to ground, where darkness gives the sharpest possible line of separation, the chromatic oppositional logic of the kiss demonstrates the give of illumination, of lightness as a form of *conjunction*. Light is not constant here, however; the pulsing of the sun flare establishes a relation between line and what overtakes line. This image poses the question of how to posit a withdrawal as process—not an arbitrary consideration in a study of no longer being loved. Light is what cleaves but thereby activates negative space; kiss is what unifies but thereby works over edge. The distinctness of each singular face is obliterated not by a shared interior line, as in Schiele's pairings of friends and lovers, but by an overwhelming luminosity. The sun flare attests to the intrusion of negative space as force; it erases the boundary between the figures and simultaneously erases the hard line of demarcation between figures and ground. So the showing of illumination in the kiss effects a double obliteration: a devastation of any shared line of the two forms and an obliteration of the distinction of figures from ground.

The spacing that is the measure of love—an intimate crossing that can always withdraw again—is *there*, affirmed in form, as a spacing offered in order to be ravaged. (This is what, above all, one gives in love: the condition of possibility for a laying waste.) The negative space posited then erased gives shape to what is unrendered: it establishes the distance crossed in love, demonstrates the dissolubility of structure itself. Light animates withdrawal as the positive intensity of *what is most vibrant in its retreat*. (Once again, recalling the formulation given by Goethe: this is the realm of a stimulating negation. *Ein reizendes Nichts*: a most lovely nothingness.)

(10a) cf. the sun flare that surrounds Adèle alone, two and a half
hours into the film, after the end of love, as she floats in a field of
blue (plate 16). Here, light's glister spoils the neat cleaving of fig-

ure from ground as a matter of outlined form, a matter of the one all alone, and not of the two.

(10a, cont.) Color is thereby commuted from potentiality in the world (what is encountered as the new) to the givenness of compositional ground for what remains, for what has no choice but to go on as things now are.

(10b) Put another way: The chromatic development of the film traces an excentricity of blue as it becomes a concentricity of blue. What moves toward Adèle (crossing the street; erupting behind her in the bar; the appearance of color as shock: of the new, of vitality, of passion) is carried away *by* her, borne on her person in the final shot of her blue dress withdrawing, retreating, spacing, putting in place a visual distance from the camera (plate 17). What Adèle encounters as difference (all that is Emma's body) she withdraws on her person. (What it means to no longer be loved: it does not mean there is not love; it means that there is no *withness* to love.) The discordant encounter with blue, with all its possibilities and futurities — excentrically dispersive — is commuted to the containment of a blue deprived of that possibility as a new necessity, the staining residue of what had once surprised. Blue that drew one into the world now draws itself inward, retreats, condenses. These are the contrary movements of blue, the differing geometries at stake in a blue that is thrown to the margins of composition — from which the body is excerpted — and a blue concentrically composed and put under pressure.

(10c) One way to describe what no longer being loved does: it rearranges light.

11 The text is unfinished. Which text? Marivaux's for one; its eleven sections

◨ ◨ ◨ ◨ ◨

love or formalism or
love and formalism or
a love of formalism or
a formalism of love

◨ ◨ ◨ ◨ ◨

SIMILITUDE

> omne animal diligit simile sibi
> —Ecclesiasticus 13:19

The film is zoned, it is generalized, it traffics in nominal categories. Awash in rules, punishments, distinctions, lessons, it also contains several panto-mimes: as in dumb, mute performance; as in the art of conveying emotion through gesture; as in *pantomimus*, dancer; as in *mimos*, imitator. It takes equal interest, then, in the law, in gesture, and in the gestures (inaugural, impersonal, symbolic, violent) proper to the law.

Yorgos Lanthimos's *The Lobster* (2015) constructs as its central situation a dystopian disciplinary society in which the Law of the City is that Single people (whether through inertia, divorce, death, or any of the other many ways one may fail to be part of a Couple — [Is it not the easiest thing in the world for others not to be in love with us? Is that not the lesson of everything read up to now?]) be transferred to a Hotel where they must find an amative Match within Forty-five Days. It is forbidden to be One alone. The Hotel has many Rules: no bisexuality, no half-size shoes, no masturbation. (If this latter prohibition is violated, a Hand will be burned in a Toaster.) Each morning, the Singles dine Alone among the incomplete patrons, each facing the empty expanse of two-top Tables; one of their Arms is bound behind their Backs to show the logistical difficulty of life not-as-Two. A Single who forms a Match based on dishonesty is Punished by being turned into The Animal No One Wants to Be. If the Singles fail to make a Match, they will be sent to the Transformation Room to be turned into the Animal of their Choosing and released into the Woods wherein the faction of Loners — who have been hunted by the Singles for Points in the form of an Extension of that forty-five day Deadline — engage their Resistance labor against the Two, in turn setting in place an equally disciplinary counter-society governed by unyielding valuation of the One, in which to Kiss, to Fuck, to Couple, to Dance-while-touching, to Love are strictly forbidden at the cost of corporal brutality. The Punishment for Flirting is The Red Kiss, in which each Loner's Lips are slashed with a razor and they are forced to kiss; there is also The Red Intercourse. Each Loner must dig their own Grave.[48]

At the film's start, David, short-sighted, just left by his wife, arrives at the Hotel with a dog — his brother, who had stayed at the Hotel previously (but did not successfully mate) — and meets the other Singles. One man has a lisp; one girl gets nosebleeds. One Single is a painfully solicitous woman doling out cookies and offers of sexual favors; another is heartless. Limping Man tells the story of his morphogenesis, a trait obliquely bequeathed to him by his mother's failure to Match:

> My mother was left on her own when my father fell in love with a woman who was better at math than she was. She had a postgraduate degree I think, whereas my mother was only a graduate. I was nineteen at the time. My mother entered the hotel, but didn't make it and was turned into a wolf. I really missed her. I found out she had been moved to a zoo. I often went there to see her. I'd give her raw meat. I knew that wolves liked

raw meat, but I couldn't figure out which of the wolves was my mother so I used to give a little bit to each of them. One day I decided to enter the enclosure. I really missed her and I wanted a hug. I climbed the fence and jumped in. All the wolves charged at once and attacked me; all but two who stood motionless. My guess is that one of those two must have been my mother. The zoo guards got to me quite quickly and took me to the hospital. Thankfully I didn't lose my leg. I just have this limp, which is also my defining characteristic. My wife died six days ago. She was very beautiful and I loved her very much. She had a limp too.

David eventually flees the Hotel and joins the Loners, falling in love with a woman who, just like him, is nearsighted. Only in the City—where the Loners periodically play-act their participation in Couples to escape surveillant Policing for Singles, demanding proof in the form of a produced Marriage Certificate—are David and the Short-Sighted Woman free: imitating the rituals of partnership, they are able to indulge the truth of their passion, the entrapping structure of the cruel law enabling new intimacies and enhanced sentiment, performing a general version of the psychoanalytic lesson that desire proceeds from the risk of censure. The Leader of the Loners, upon realizing that David and the Woman have formed a Match, has the woman blinded, and the film concludes with the two of them escaping the Forest for the City, ending with the now sightless woman waiting at a table in a restaurant while the still-sighted David, in the bathroom, does or does not blind himself with a knife in order to reconcile himself to be like once more the woman he loves.

The entire film is a meditation on this *like* as the basis for a formal thinking of love.

Of Lanthimos's cinematic formalism one might say a great deal: about his studies of claustral spaces (as in his other films, situations take shape within hermetic, restricted environments); of the characters' highly restricted and codified bodily gestures (as choreographed codes replace unsayable speech, in particular of love in the context of its prohibition); of the interplay of the beautiful and vicious (as natural light and exquisitely slowed motion in chase scenes in which Singles hunt, tranquilize, and brutalize Loners convert violence's edges into arcs of the balletic); of the discordant possibilities of soundtrack (as in the film's use of voiceover by the Short-Sighted Woman long before her character appears or as in the histrionic, hyperexpressive, and overwrought canon of Beethoven, Shostakovich, Schnittke, and Strauss in discordance with the spareness of the mise-en-scène); &c. And yet, the text's compositional richness exists in a constant assemblage with the figure of love that veins *The Lobster*: the arbitrariness of love, the demands of love, the fragility of love, the compulsion to love, the question of the possibility (or impossibility) of love. The film's aesthetic language does not demonstrate a concept (let alone a percept or affect) of love so much as the film's theory of love is itself ineluctably *formal*, and the film's rigorous attention to forms of matching is in the service of an abstraction of the amative, a theory of love sustained by a tension between similitude and difference, and one that is profoundly at odds with privileged philosophical dogmas of eros, including the hegemonic figuration of Aristophanes's *hen ek duoin* that has supplied us so far with so many formulas turning on questions of addition, completion, and a world describable in relation to ones and twos. That Lanthimos's cinematic formalism is set alongside a formalism of love, however, does not place the former in the service of a demonstration of a prior conception of the latter: rather, the latter radically revises the very question of how the former is read. Thus, it is not the case that *The Lobster* is *about* love—one ought not (as in a review in *Film Comment*) speak absurdly of "David's turbulent inner life"—but rather, the film is a thinking of love through the impersonality and exteriority of form itself.[49] A radical formalism of matching radically redistributes love according to inhuman terms of correspondence and similitude, beset by force that takes the form of unlikeness. Fidelity is not interpersonal nor the analogue of affection: rather, the film's concept of the fidelity of love is derived *from*, and is solely legible *as*, a constancy of form under threat from variability.

No longer "Love is not love / Which alters when it alteration finds, / Or bends with the remover to remove." Rather, in *The Lobster*, love is solely love which alters when it alteration finds. And nor will it have to hunt down this alteration like stumbling prey; alteration will not fail to light upon love.

(—And perhaps nothing less, in fact, should ever really move us.)

In the scenario constructed by *The Lobster*, every Single at the Hotel has a defining characteristic, and character names are given as Limping Man, Lisping Man, Nosebleed Woman, and so on. Although some criticism has largely identified these as essential vulnerabilities or sharable wounds (tritely pop-psychologizing), a defining characteristic can also be beautiful golden hair or an affection for butter cookies. Formed Couples include the Hotel Manager and her Partner, who, we are told, both have nice voices;

there is a Couple who both love to ski. A Couple who both studied social sciences. Singles are encouraged to match on the basis of these defining characteristics—in both their human and, if they fail, future animal forms. (As his choice of a lobster, David would have a second chance at love, the Hotel Manager advises, but only with a like form: "A wolf and a penguin could never live together. That would be absurd.") The valuation of sameness as the ground of assortative love is so strong that a subplot involves Limping Man, whose time is running out, and whose closest match is a woman with a sprained ankle—an insufficient ground for lifelong homogamy—self-inflicting epistaxis by brutalizing his face against nearby objects, smashing his bones into the edge of a pool or a table, and not once but as a regular and ostensibly permanent part of his life's roster, in order to fraudulently partner with Nosebleed Woman.

In place of a formula for eros as completion of deficiency, reforming an originary unity, and also in place of eros as bound to alterity (in which love of the other is what fails to sacrifice or obliterate the absolute otherness of the other—as in Levinas's account of femininity as what appears "not merely as a quality different from all others, but as the very quality of difference"), *The Lobster*'s general amative form is radically exteriorized in the matchable characteristics (vulnerabilities, deficiencies, porosities, capacities) of the partners in body or practice (nosebleeds, limps, nice voices, and short-sightedness as properties of anatomy structurally equivalent to hobbies and academic studies as the practices of subjects).[50] This love does not demand identicality; it accepts chirality—it solicits likeness. The film's world thus seems to pull from an ancient account of similitude as the ground of love, as in Aristotle's highest form of friendship in the *Nicomachean Ethics* as that which is based in two people of similar virtues and characters. Aristotle, in fact, shares with the Law of the City a sense of the fragility of this structure whereby the friend or lover must not only have but must *maintain* certain qualities, asking in book IX "whether friendships should or should not be broken off when the other party does not remain the same"?[51] He continues, "if one accepts another man as good, and he turns out badly and is seen to do so, must one still love him? Surely it is impossible, since not everything can be loved, but only what is good. What is evil neither can nor should be loved; for it is not one's duty to be a lover of evil, nor to become like what is bad; and we have said that like is dear to like."[52] (Complications and nuances are admitted by the philosopher and refused by the City, however: Aristotle also writes that if a good man has only become a little bit bad, the true friend is bound to morally redeem and make him virtuous once more—dissimilitude an occasion for a restoration of similitude as the ground of partnership as opposed to what ensures its immediate nullification.)

Whereas Aristotle's model of likeness emphasizes a similitude of virtues, however, Lanthimos appears to draw more closely from a related, but crucially varied, account of love: Thomas Aquinas's notion of *unio amoris* (love as union) in which the lover is taken as "another self" in a union of affection based on "formal sameness" (two are one). Compellingly insisting on an intimate bond between affectivity and form, for Aquinas, the lover's unity is an affective structure based on this formal matching—similitude (*similitudo*) is itself a cause of love.[53] Making clear that likeness is always a matter of similitude *in* formal qualities— and not, say, lodging with another in empathy or sympathy; or willing the good for another as though they were the self—Aquinas turns to a privileged, if also problematic, figure of quality, that of color: "For the fact that two people are alike in having some form means that they are, in a sense, one in that form: thus two men are at one in their membership of the species 'humanity,' and two white men at one in their possessing the form 'whiteness.' The result is that the affections of the one are bent upon the other as being one with himself, and he wishes well to the other as to himself."[54] Permuting Aristotle's account of the love of friendship as "one soul in two bodies," hewing closer to Aquinas's valuation of a likeness of formal qualities, Lanthimos rearranges this as One characteristic in Two bodies—from soul to limp, from soul to lisp, the film demonstrates an apparently identical philosophical valuation of similitude, one merely thrown to gait and misarticulation.

The Lobster, in seeming to display allegiance to this model of love as predicated on likeness, however, also simultaneously appears to model an account of *antilove* associated with the valuation of characteristics. This turns on the tension between *qualitas*, the attributes or properties of the beloved, and their existence as a haecceity, as the particular and irreducible *this* that they are. Notice, for example, how anathema the form of love in *The Lobster* is to the Barthesian account in the *Tel* (or "Thus") entry in *A Lover's Discourse*, which begins under the header, "Endlessly required to define the loved object, and suffering from the uncertainties of this definition, the amorous subject dreams of a knowledge which would let him take the other *as he is*, thus and no other, exonerated from any adjective."[55] The stubborn alterity of the one I love derives from that "thus," what separates the lover from the beloved as other (other body, other being). This is the fundamental difficulty of love—the distance between *I* and *You*. Cixous names this in her *Book of Promethea* as: "Never am I you. That is what is astonishing. [. . .] That is what is too much for my love. I like your soul right down to the bone, I know the taste of every inch of your nerves, but you I do not know you I do not know."[56]

The dilemma Barthes names is a very ancient one in the philosophy of love: if I love a spun-out list of attributes (your honesty, flint-colored eyes, or deft lover's fingers; your blue hair, gorgeous cock, or melancholic disposition; or your enthusiasm for radical politics; or your affection for the poetry of John Berryman . . .), then, as Barthes says, "I might well, someday, replace [the beloved]"— for qualities, nameable, generalizable, nonessential (on the order of what Aristotle dubbed *kata symbebekos*, what is incidental, accidental to the substance of something and belonging to it only as property) are by definition interchangeable. Others, surely, also are wild about *The Dream Songs*. Manic Panic's Atomic Turquoise comes in a jar. But what cannot be substituted is the unique situatedness of the beloved, and so Barthes writes, "I accede, fitfully, to a language without adjectives. I love the other, not according to his (accountable) qualities, but according to his existence; by a movement one might well call mystical, I love, not what he is, but *that he is*."[57] If Barthesian love is a love wholly without adjectives, in which "the whole love cannot be inventoried without being diminished," the amative according to *The Lobster* appears to be nothing other than a proliferation of adjectives, each person only the precise catalogue of their defining characteristics. The film thus seems to hold simultaneously to a model of love based on similitude while defining similitude from the antilove stance of possessing similar qualities.

But in fact Lanthimos nullifies *both* the derided and privileged forms of love that Barthes offers. There is no I-love-*that* you are, but nor is there precisely an I-love-*what* you are, for love, instead, is lodged in the matching of qualities themselves and not in any attestations of the lover. (Once more we arrive at this question: What other than a radical formalism could make sense of a thinking of love as a formal structure—the matching of qualities themselves?) Consider the *I-love-you*. This spoken promise of love is displaced in *The Lobster* onto the matching gestures of the body, the invented language David and his short-sighted lover adopt in order to communicate among the Loners: "We developed a code," the Woman intones in voiceover, "so that we can communicate with each other even in front of the others without them knowing what we are saying. When we turn our heads to the left it means 'I love you more than anything in the world' and when we turn our heads to the right it means 'watch out, we're in danger.' We had to be very careful in the beginning not to mix up 'I love you more than anything in the world' with 'watch out, we're in danger.'" This gestural system is an arbitrary collection of signs that acquire meaning from their differential, oppositive relation—like structuralist trees or psychoanalytic bathroom doors. In place of the I-love-you as the general performative promise that grounds love, there is only the turn to one side, the partaking of the directional difference of purely contingent, relative spatial orientation: left contra right.

Love in *The Lobster* is not interpersonal but nor is it solipsistic: it is an arbitrary but absolute fidelity to an arbitrary similitude given through arbitrary but absolute fidelity to an arbitrary signifying system.

But because love is lodged in the form of matching itself, similitude is constantly beset by the threat of dissimilitude: what may slightly permute and thereby destroy matching absolutely. A double violence is thus possible in this world: a Single can fail to find or make a Match (thus ending in the violence of *trans*formation, a process whereby negative force against a human form positively generates a new animal form) and others can unmatch you, condemning you to this structure; or, having successfully and happily Matched, matching—as in *gamakon*: fitting well together—can itself be unmade through changes (willed or unwilled) to characteristics. Matching can be made *not* to fit things together well; newly discordant qualities can render the membership of a set ill-fitting. What decimates similitude? This is what is called *difference*. The film neutralizes judgments of violence except in relation to a single criterion: to what degree force has inserted difference into a structure. Matching is beset by a difference that is prior to it and that threatens it from every side: the Deleuze of *Difference and Repetition* would warn the Singles, "Repetition can always be 'represented' as extreme resemblance or perfect equivalence, but the fact that one can pass by degrees from one thing to another does not prevent their being different in kind."[58] When David, feeling the pressure of deadline, mimes cruelty to pair up with the Heartless Woman, when she tests this by killing his brother, and his response of a slightly cracking voice reveals the truth of a stirring grief—and it is thus *her* betrayal *by him* that the scene documents, he whose similitude was deceptive—the act of torturing the dog is no more or less violent than when the Loners break into the Hotel and at gunpoint demand that the Hotel Manager's Partner quantify his love on a scale of fifteen (he gives it as a fourteen, that distance of one comprising the infidelity) and answer which of the two would be willing to live without the other. At his affirmation that he alone—which is to say *differently*—could live without his wife and his willingness to execute her, the fact that the gun is ultimately revealed to shoot only blanks, is apposite: for the devastation has already taken place, a difference has been introduced, and no worse violation is possible. (Again: Love always discharges blanks, and this does not mean that there is no damage.) Violence in *The Lobster* is solely directed at the likeness of matching. The blanks literalize equally the empty content of a force whose violence is that of transformation and a love whose guarantor is a formal similitude that can be shattered.

The blinding of the Short-Sighted Woman by the Leader of the Loners, then, should not be read as a force against the body's nerves and organs. The blinding is neither more nor less than the insertion of difference into the likeness of two entities who share short-sightedness in common. From the point of view of the film's formalism of love, the blinding by force is absolutely *equivalent* to a hypothetical case in which the Leader had the woman's sight perfectly but unwillingly *corrected*.

This is the risk of such a thinking of love: Infinite violence against matching is possible because infinite variability is in fact what possibility *is*, and indeed is what *is* prior to sameness.

Thus, the final scene of the film—in which David is poised in the restaurant bathroom with a knife, tip just to the eyeball, caught in the flinching suspension, the duration of decision—as the Short-Sighted Woman waits back at the table, waits for the decision to be made—is not an image of violence about to take place, but a response to a violence that has definitively taken place with the intrusion of dissimilitude between him and his match. Self-blinding here would in fact be a mode of antiviolence, would bring similitude back into consonance. *The Lobster* thus does not end with epistemic confusion—this is the fundamental misreading of the film, when critical reaction turns to the *Will he or Won't he?* permanent wonderment of the screen that goes sharply black—the Can-David-go-through-with-it? the What-are-we-willing-to-do-for-love? question. For either answer is wholly inadequate to a serious thinking of love by imagining a (any) final or singular gesture of devotion. Rather, the film ends within the suspension of a fidelity to similitude that is only required, as fidelity, in the midst of the intrusion of difference. This is not an epistemic confusion; it is an aporetic structure. It is only in the face of the difference that threatens similitude that one can act *for*, which is to say on behalf of, matching. Nothing other than this impossible case in which David both has and has not blinded himself deserves to be called love, and what love requires is not fidelity to a partner (not that humanism in collusion with the law) but fidelity to the unavoidable intrusion of difference, what gives form to matching by constantly besetting it with possible modifiability. The geometral approach to love contains both scenographic possibilities, but also *every other possible one*.

Love is neither thing nor mystical: it is process. Agonizing process.

The Lobster comes to a textual limit over the image of the Short-Sighted Woman waiting for David because the question of love is always to what degree the other will remain faithful to the infinite becoming that love requires. Nothing David is undergoing with knife and mucosa is as excruciating as the duration of waiting for that knowledge — for blindness will not and cannot represent a telos of a love that cannot potentially be threatened again with variation. No final accounting can be provided — no final reading produced; no ultimate guarantees offered; no fixed and certain outcomes; no ground to be located in bloodied eyes, promises, utterances, nor any encoded gestures that might invent new languages for love. For difference that besets similitude is not negative, external, exterior, or a posteriori — it cannot be outrun, it cannot be outstripped from the very form of matching itself. What is internal to matching is infinite potential unmatching. There can be no sameness unscathed by the difference that forms as otherwise that which forms at all.

And this insistence is where *The Lobster* offers a serious provocation to philosophical theories of the amative by demanding that philosophy account for the formalisms on which its thinking is dependent.[59] For while much has been thought about the formalism of love, in other words a formalism proper to love — indeed, that is what philosophies of love offer — very little has been said about love as fidelity to a general logic of form, a love at once impersonal, inhuman, processual, and affirmative not despite but because of the destructive-generative force internal to it — in other words, a love proper *to* formalism. For the constantly-beset-by-difference that is the model of violence against matching (which is to say against love) is another way of naming the positive force of formal experimentation: the ongoing affirmation of characteristics that *are, can, will* always become otherwise and that proceed without guarantee.

Philosophical formalisms of love conventionally turn on the *One* (union, completion, the wholeness of the *hen ek duoin*, fulfillment, communion, fusion, transcendence, a withdrawal from the world) or the *Two* (difference, dislocation, differentiation, alterity, or Badiou's theorization in his 2009 *Éloge de l'amour* of love as an evental project involving a quest for truth in the construction of "a world from a decentred point of view other than that of my mere impulse to survive or re-affirm my own identity" — in numerical terms, a stance that involves a life made "no longer from the perspective of One but from the perspective of Two," a construction of "the world on the basis of difference").[60] But whereas Aristophanic love involves prior and future union out of present division, and Badiou's love involves prior and future diversity out of present univocality, Lanthimos denies to the present lived moment an experience *either* of One or of Two. Love, instead, is the minimal movement that makes the one and the two — union and dispersion; similitude and the minimal difference required for there to be dissimilitude — different. Love is the experiment that not only makes a test of the infinite possibilities of qualities moving into different qualities, but is faithful to it even in the face of its patent, idiotic absurdity. Love is neither a state of restitution nor an experience, nor is it, as Badiou has it, a construction of a truth. Love is neither state nor experience nor construction because love is the likeness, the ideally matched mate, of the work of form. And here we would do well to return and newly consider Lanthimos's compositional investment in studies of slow motion, the aesthetics of natural light, languid or manic gestures, his time-out-of-joint voice-overs, his use of symmetry, discordant music, studies of hands, restricted settings, language games, &c. — for if formalism is at heart a presencing of the contingency of characteristics, and if love is not a timeless ontology of unified substance but the process of coming into a matching given form by what will ravage (which is to say deform and unform) it, then it is not the case that aesthetic formalism exposes something essential about Lanthimos's philosophy of love, but that the film's philosophy of love attests to an understanding of the labor, the violence, the risk, and indeed the passions of a fidelity to every possible different detail of each studied and actual aesthetic composition. The difference of unmatching is positive without being unifying: it is the affirmative condition of formal ongoingness, formal experimentation, the aesthetic and fundamentally impersonal project of exposing singularities — what is because it could have been absolutely anything else. Violence is reimagined as not negation — what besets and destroys similitude — but as the affirmative condition for recoupling from perpetual uncoupling. Love is thus the correlate of decisive contingency, and it bears within itself the imperative to remain with what is thereby exposed.

Love is what instructs in the closest thing to a general ethics of formalism: Because anything matters, everything matters. Because everything matters, absolutely anything matters.

Love requires more than what is possible because what it requires has not yet been asked of it (—this is its infinite form). It is not arrival or substance but the not-to-be-outstripped difficulty of the impasse of forms of matching, constantly beset on all sides neither by law nor by apathy, neither by betrayal nor by scarcity, but by the internal possibility of difference that will require matching anew, again, always again, and always again, and so on, so onward. There is nothing more to love—or to aesthetic decision, or to reading with form without guarantee—than fidelity to the most fragile thing imaginable: a configuration of the particular way something is as it could have been and will be and is already becoming otherwise.

Till death do us part.

■ ■ ■ ■ ■

They walk, the lovers of Beckett's *Enough*. Steps are, above all, counted: "At an average speed of roughly three miles per day and night. We took flight in arithmetic. What mental calculations bent double hand in hand! Whole ternary numbers we raised in this way to the third power sometimes in downpours of rain."

Base three numbering: three digits, all nonnegative, and now to love's familiar One and Two is added a Zero.

A portion of a lifetime is spent this way. "We did not keep tally of the days. If I arrive at ten years it is thanks to our pedometer. Total milage divided by average daily milage. So many days. Divide."

Our story was always going to end this way.

"No more rain. No more mounds. Nothing but the two of us dragging through the flowers. Enough my old breasts feel his old hand."[61]

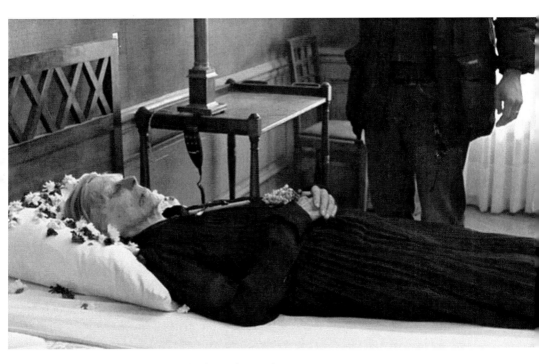

FIGURE 6.4. *Amour* (Michael Haneke, 2012)

We might one final time say: The dead and the living have nothing more *in common*.

"Je n'étais pas *comme* elle, puisque je ne suis pas mort avec (en même temps qu') elle," goes Barthes's *Mourning Diary* entry of May 1, 1979.[62] The one is not *like* the other, for a true similitude would require that A die *with* (at the very same time as) B — but to know, to write the death of the other entails always the slightest delay, an incremental degree of difference that ends withness absolutely but in turn engenders witnessing: the Derridean ethic of friendship, itself indebted to Blanchot, that one of the two in an intimate relation will see the other die, thus wait, thus keep, thus mourn, thus take a relation to the *thus*, in other words what follows, to be what comes after, what persists as the second term in a fundamental relation of sequence.[63] That nothing *more* in common is what the living hold in common, the community of vitality given minimal integrity by its shared commitment not to property or substance but to the possibility of an infinitesimally greater (undisclosed) quantity of time. A relation to the form of the more: what is disallowed for the dead for whom all is over, from whom any quantity of not-yet-arrived futurity is estranged — for whom nothing more *is* or will ever *be*.

Although they hold nothing more in common, it may be that the dead nevertheless present to the living an ethical pedagogy, instructing in the "strength in unchangeableness" in their dimension of being truly faithful, absolutely constant. This is Kierkegaard's insistence in the penultimate section of his 1847 *Kjerlighedens Gjerninger* (Works of Love), written as discourses and published under his own name (displaying, however, both maieutic and stylistic features of the pseudonymous works).[64] The philosopher describes a certain "occasion for making a test of what love essentially is [. . .]. In truth, if you really want to make sure about love in yourself or in another person, then note how he relates himself to one who is dead."[65] "Den Kjerlighedens Gjerning at erindre en Afdød" (The Work of Love in Remembering One Dead) turns on the specific ontology of the deceased: a slack departed figure who "is nothing actual," who "is *nobody*" and is "not an actual object"; the dead one is an "*Ikkeværende*," a nonbeing.[66] Instead, the deceased "is only the occasion [*Anledning*: chance, event, occasion, cause] which continually reveals what resides in the one living who relates himself to him."[67] Love in remembering one dead — and the unremittable duty of memorializing, given in his admonition "weep softly, but grieve long"—is pronounced by Kierkegaard to be the most free and most unselfish love. That duty is absolute but indeterminate: "How long cannot be decided in advance, because no one remembering can with certainty know how long he shall be separated from the dead."[68] For Kierkegaard, who rejects an idealist tradition in which love is inclusive, anti-discordance, what seeks union, annuls separation, and dissolves particularity (all true love a communion, all eros a monism)—as in Hegel's law that "genuine love excludes all oppositions"—love requires and derives from difference, dissimilitude, disunion, the nothing-more-in-common of the living and dead positing the condition of possibility for the work of love itself.[69]

The dead unconceal and lure a supreme form of ethical love due to their negative structural relation to demand. Like almost every philosopher or theologian who has contemplated the amative, Kierkegaard confronts the dilemma that a love commanded or demanded, unfree love, coercive love, habitual or recalled or reciprocated or beneficial love, love from law or love for gain, does not appear to be true love at all. For this reason, self-love that takes itself as its object and a lusty desire that takes lack as its object equally risk appropriating, incorporating, sublating, and thereby using, accruing value from that which would be whispered *beloved*. In "L'amour en éclats" (translated as "Shattered Love," though the French better captures the sense of exploding, dazzling, splintering fragments of glass and also brilliance, splendor—and ultimately, though I digress, it is not time yet, but there will come that point at which we will not want to sidestep the role of light in love. Lumen insinuates itself . . .), Nancy invokes this exclusion when he writes that "an entire analytics [. . .] of the amorous operation as calculation, investment, completion, retribution, and the like" is absolutely foreign to love.[70] It is not merely that profitable love abrogates any claim as love; rather, any structure that would even admit the possibility of an amative yield compromises entirely love's ethical-affective promise. The dead, however, are all silence and stilled. For Kierkegaard, they are that which can make no repayment (the lover's love is a matter of total indifference to the dead; love cannot transform or modify ontology); the dead do not call themselves to the living's memory (commanding neither force nor seduction, their recollection is neither posed nor imposable); and they can do nothing coercive to demand or extract remembrance—(unlike the wet soft child, the dead do not cry: the baying infant's wailing reminder an affective and memorial constraint on even the most purportedly unattached parent). The dead do not and will not

love the living in turn: "It is so hopeless; it is such a thankless job," Kierkegaard writes, "such a disheartening occupation to remember one who is
dead! For one who is dead does not grow and thrive toward the future as
does the child: one who is dead merely crumbles away more and more into
certain ruin. One who is dead does not give joy to the rememberer as the
child gives joy to its mother, does not give him joy as the child her joy when
to her question about whom he loves most he answers, 'Mother'; one who is
dead loves no one most, for he seems to love no one at all."[71]

The melancholy of deceased silence is set against an asymmetrical vitality to the pulsating recollection of the now-absent presence, now no longer, now moldering and rotting—"He remains quiet this way down there in
the grave while the longing after him grows, so dejecting that there is no
change conceivable except the change of dissolution, more and more!"[72]
This dead one is the most abjectly helpless, the most vulnerable, for their
remembrance is constantly beset by the new impressions of what comes after their being and the crumbling integrity of recollection, which they cannot bolster. "The loving memory," Kierkegaard warns, "has to protect its
freedom in remembering against that which would compel it to forget,"
which is nothing other than the ineluctable ongoingness of time. What Kierkegaard plots sequentially Barthes will thicken: "What separates me from
maman (from the mourning that was my identification with her) is the density (enlarging, gradually accumulating) [*c'est l'épaisseur (grandissante, pro-
gressivement accumulée)*] of the time when, since her death, I have been
able to live without her, inhabit the apartment, work, go out, etc."[73] Inverting the form of Freudian melancholia—in which its pathological version
of mourning work fails to withdraw its sticky cathexis from the departed—
Kierkegaard and Barthes share the worry that the truly horrifying scenario is
not that one remains forever bound in the stasis of a transformationless grief,
but that it will be in fact far too easy to move on, almost inevitable that one
will *not* remain in melancholia's pleasurably suffocating amber.

On the one hand, love is a private self-folding remembrance, the most
intimate test in the relation to the one who is dead. On the other hand, love
is conscience, writes Kierkegaard—"and thus is not a matter of impulse and
inclination or a matter of feeling or a matter of intellectual calculation."[74]
Neither sentiment nor passion, neither suffering nor a private, particular endurance, this heart is pure, sincere, and bound—it is a matter of universal
duty, abstract and general. In either case, love is distanced from—wholly
and essentially indifferent to—affect, intensity, movement, and vitality. For

Hegel—against whom Kierkegaard writes here—there can be no love without vital force: "True union, or love proper, exists only between living beings who are alike in power and thus in one another's eyes living beings from every point of view; in no respect is either dead for the other."[75] From love's exchange between living beings, Hegel moves outward to define love itself as a "sensing of something living"; the begetting of love in the "living child, a seed of immortality"; and the lover's dyad as a new form of vital body: "Each separate lover is one organ in a living whole."[76] By contrast, for Kierkegaard, the most profound form of love mortifies an organ in that living whole, sets in gangrene to putrefy amid the live body: love as poor circulation, a strangulated hernia, embolic clots, gnawing sores, and checked nutrition, or the carious tooth dissolving, what irritates or stills vital fluids, or the dead tissue not yet sloughed off, like scale or shell, the core of a boil or thin sheets of skin. Love is hereby recast as each lover distinguished—separated, made to no longer *be* in common—by the one that is a necrotic organ in a whole slowly rotting, devoured from within by an unfurling, unremitting difference.

Because Kierkegaard's model of love is one of uncompromising rigor: free, faithful, true, and above all disinterested—all inwardness, self-denying, abstract and general—a critic like Adorno will dub the love toward one dead as comprising "the best and worst of [Kierkegaard's] philosophy."[77] Adorno's profound dislike for Kierkegaard's doctrine will, predictably enough, be that its unyielding abstractness ignores social relations, but there is something more—a critical stance that is almost an aesthetic emetic, writing with a distaste bordering on disgust for this work of love, a horror at the philosophical demand that (as Adorno puts it) "love behave towards all men *as if* they were dead."[78] Kierkegaard's absolute insistence on indifference at the center of the structure of the affectively intense state of the amative seems to especially unnerve Adorno. Inverting the promissory recovery of mourning by which the lost or absent object is regarded *as though* it were still present, in this work the positive living presence of the beloved is provisionally and analogically regarded—by the very act of love—as if it were the very same as what is not. Violence takes the form of a homology, force lodged in similitude itself: in being loved, one is made *like* one who is not. One's own inmost still-living being is thereby rendered fictive, as though being itself were conditional.

We know well in the wake of Heidegger how grammar aporetically stutters here: In this regard, there *is* no *being* loved.

Adorno casts the inwardness and disinterestedness of this model of love as a violence that drains moral estimation—"the rigorousness of the love advocated by Kierkegaard partially devaluates the beloved person"—and turns into a negative ethics: "The overstraining of the transcendence of love threatens, at any given moment, to become transformed into the darkest hatred of man."[79] The unyielding abstraction of this model, Adorno finally insists, is bound to the existent, fails to grapple with the relations required for an adequate critique of the social (loving the neighbor, in this model, "can neither help him nor interfere with a setting of the world which makes such help impossible"), while itself merely offers what he calls "a reified and fetish love."[80] He therefore dubs the love toward one dead the best and worst aspect of Kierkegaardianism precisely insofar as he sees performed in *Works of Love* a symptomatic diagnosis of the social logic by which the only possible love *would* be love for the dead neighbor because the neighbor has decayed in modernity. There are strong echoes of the Kantian good in the existential philosopher's thinking. When Adorno paraliptically makes one of his key points by denying it, writing that "it is unnecessary to point out how close this love comes to callousness," one hears echoes of Nietzsche's "good old Kant: the categorical imperative smells of cruelty," from *Genealogy of Morals*.[81] This lexicon of a cold, cruel, callous abstraction marked by its equal obliquity to affective passion and intimate or social relationality—what reaches its apogee in the nonreciprocity of the love of those who have passed away—what names the speculative proposition of a generality of love that would behave toward all *as if* they were already dead—is the radical formalism of Kierkegaardian love.

In the midst of this accounting, Kierkegaard makes a curious aside about the dwelling space of the dead, and in doing so he formulates a poetic map for his philosophical amble. (By poetic read Romantic, echoes of Thomas Gray's "Elegy Written in a Country Churchyard"—philosophy and poetics equally photophilic.) "Go out," Kierkegaard instructs, "when the morning sun peeps in among the gravestones with shifting lights and shadows, when the beauty and friendliness of the woods and the different forms of life and the twittering of the birds almost let you forget that you are among the dead." The thought experiment continues, shifting from dappled vital matter to a temporal leap:

> Then it will seem as if you had entered into a foreign land which has remained unacquainted with the confusion and fragmentation of life, into

the world of childhood, consisting only of small families. Out here, in fact, there is an attainment of what in life is vainly sought: equal distribution. Every family has a little piece of ground for itself, all about the same size. The view is about the same for all of them; the sun shines equally over all over them; no building rises so high that it takes away the sun's rays or the refreshing rain or the fresh air of the wind or the music of birdsong from a neighbor or the one across the way. No, here there is equal distribution. In life it sometimes happens that a family which has lived in luxury and prosperity must cut back, but in death all of them have had to cut back. There can be a slight difference — perhaps a foot in the size of the plot, or one family may have a tree, which other inhabitants do not have on their plots. Why do you suppose this difference exists? It is a profound jest to remind you by means of its littleness how great the difference was. How loving death is! For in this inspiring joke it is precisely death's love which with the help of this little difference reminds one of the great difference. Death does not say, "There is no difference at all"; it says, "There you can see what the difference was: half a foot."[82]

Despite the initial insistence on parity in the distribution of ordinary sublimity, a little variation insinuates itself. *Half a foot?* There you can see what difference is.

What is to be done with the curious oscillation between forms of similitude and difference in this accounting of Kierkegaard's formalism of indifferent love? The entire "Work of Love in Remembering One Dead," in fact, pivots on claims for a collapsing equality and dispersion: at once, Kierkegaard will write that in death, one has "power over the diversities" of life, emphasizing that the dead "are of one mould, this kinship of death"; at the same time, a positive smallest difference continually irritates this claim for unmarked oneness.[83] Going out to the dead, one glimpses not only the extremest abstraction of Kierkegaardian love but also a strained coexistence of unity and wholeness with modes of barely perceptible variation and a stubborn multiplicity. Let us consider with seriousness this little great difference marked out in measurement as a matter that governs the relation of love to death, death to life, and is unconcealed through and as the manifestations of plotted minor spacing.

For this general structure insinuates itself across Kierkegaard's thinking of finitude. "At a Graveside," the third of the *Discourses on Imagined Occasions* and a text that is an inverse companion to "The Work of Love in Remembering One Dead" (while the latter is about the ongoingness of remembrance, the former posits the radical decisiveness of death's ending), repeats the paradoxical logic of simultaneous unity and partibility, similitude and difference. There, Kierkegaard writes that unlike life, which cannot resist time's progress, death "has this power; it does not dabble with the decision as if there were still a little left over; it does not chase after the decision as the living person does — it carries it out in earnest. When death comes, the word is: Up to here, not one step further; then it is concluded, not a letter is added; the meaning is at an end and not one more sound is to be heard — all is over."[84] Death's decision, its absolute stillness and radical finitude, is cast in relation to its *refusal* of the one-step-further: even the most minute "as if there were still a little left over" is given solely to life. Death is the death of mutability as a formal possibility: that is the generality of its decisiveness.

And yet, all the same, when one goes out to the dead there *is* some minimal structure of plotted variation — that jesting "half a foot." We have, therefore, opposing topologies, a tense and antinomic structure: the all-is-not-yet-over is internal to death's decisiveness, it *is* what ends; finitude takes its form from this foreclosure of one-more-sound, the letter-added, the one-step-further. But if thinking wanders past that, death's love reminds one of the persistence of the littlest possible difference, externalized in the most trivial, minor plotted variable alteration in zoned space.

Go out to the dead and there, in the midst of the law of the *All is over!*, regard the barest form of the increment.

a love of formalism

Doors stop and separate. The Door breaks space in two, splits it,
prevents osmosis, imposes a partition.
—GEORGES PEREC, *Species of Spaces and Other Pieces*

Michael Haneke's *Amour* (2012) opens with an opening — from the pitch of a saturated black screen, symmetrical large doors explode inward. The rupture is violent, intrusive, and brutal, and simultaneously an aesthetically oxygenating aperture in that this initial breach is what lets light in and inaugurates representation. Reflexively recalling the wreckage of barrier between stage and audience that is a flung-open proscenium curtain, in the instant of the breaking that posits the threshold to the apartment, that of the elderly couple Georges and Anne, the spectator is revealed to already be within this space. Rushing forward are figures of law and care, a firefighter who announces his presence under the sign of the grammatical problem of being: *C'est les pompiers . . . est quelqu'un?* This wonderment of whether anyone is at home will circulate aporetically throughout the film — in a nightmare, Georges will stand in the same threshold of the door, peering outward, posing to the damp horrorspace of the corridor, "Il y a quelqu'un?" at which point a sudden-appearing hand over his struggling mouth anticipates the pillow he will later press over Anne's face. In both cases, it is an ontologically and grammatically impossible question: there *is* no one there, the language of being what cannot be said when what resides *is* no object, no thing, the nothing of nonbeing, equally the corpse and what is-not in the dream.

The firefighters move through the dim natural light of the bourgeois apartment, unsealing enclosures, to encounter, in a room with an already-open window, that secondary architectural framing of light and, laid out on the bed, a dead body set in gray and rest. At the encounter with the entombed body at its core, the spectator is retroactively placed as belonging to a form: residing in the interior of the minimal definition of a grave, lodged where a dead body has been housed, space not excavated out of earth but a cairn assembled out of room and door and bed and tape. *No need to go out to the dead — for you are already there.* Despite lacking the undertaker's tools of caps, glues, wires, and sutures, the features of the face of this corpse have been set: mouth closed, lids shut, body dressed, flowers strewn — though none of this process has or indeed will be shown. Time is chromatic and olfactory: the instant of death is distant enough that the body stinks, but not so long that the corollas are no longer yellow and purple and white; the body has decayed but the flowers have not, and the film begins in the space of that difference, the precise gap in the asymmetrical, incremental changing of the quality of flesh and petal.

Amour composes itself around making a space for this death that appears at the beginning of the film, in which the prologue confirms the incontrovertible certainty that is how finitude works: by being what ends, decisively — the "All is over!" of "At a Graveside." At one point, while the central activity of the living is their interminable dying, Georges and Anne's adult daughter, Eva, asks her father about her mother, "What will happen now?" His answer, "What happens now is what's happened until now. It will go steadily downhill for a while and then it'll be over." But while Georges gives linearity to the narrative of decline and telos to death's break, this being-over-with is how the film begins: so what will happen is subsumed by what has already happened: what has happened and what will happen have both happened: the decisiveness of death's end has already occurred. The film in its temporal structure thus constitutes an act of remembering one dead, and it does so under the sign of love.

The once-more intrudes—*Amour* opens with three prologues: the opening into light, space, home, death; then, precisely three minutes at a piano recital given by one of Anne's former students, which constitutes the sole segment of the film shot outside the couple's Parisian apartment and which reflexively stages a diegetic audience staring back at Haneke's viewers; and third, the arrival home after the concert, introduced in medias res as Georges says to Anne, "They used a screwdriver," commenting on an attempted break-in, the visible signs of which mark their front door. In this final arrival, once more the spectator is already within the dark space of the apartment, as though the more professional burglar, residing uninvited and in wait. If the film thereby poses an ethical question as a topological concern—the question of from where violence will arrive: as an intrusion from the outside or from already within the home—it settles the matter early on when Anne has a stroke, and the film follows Georges's patient, tender, erotic, exhaustive, exhausted, brutal tending to her increasingly alinguistic, decomposed state—the two-hour film an unflinching unfolding of these declensions, with an emphasis in long takes on the raw physicality of Georges's care for Anne—what critics praise or why the film is declared unwatchable (one dubs it "deliberately tortuous").[85] This agonizing exposure of the labor of care and the systematic humiliation of the body's endurance of endtime is linked to a series of substitutions: Anne's instructions for moving her paralyzed body exchange the vocabulary of care for the lover's pedagogy in pleasure; marital dining together is supplanted with feeding the other, at times prying open the lips by force; —until, flatly but decisively, and with no final declarations of affection, Georges spontaneously suffocates Anne, at which point the film turns to a triad of epilogues, symmetrically answering the form of the opening: a pigeon appears in the apartment; Georges imagines a re-enlivened Anne and follows her out of the home; and, in the final moments, Eva enters the now empty rooms with parted doors, walks through the space of the home, crossing its stage, and sits down by herself, alone amidst the limpid light.

Like its prologues and epilogues, *Amour* appears to constitute a triple accounting: in its construction of the home becoming tomb, it is a thanatography, a writing of Anne's death; it is also, simultaneously, as an account of Georges's relation to one dying and to one dead an amatography, a story of love; and, finally, it is a rigorous mapping of the restricted interior of the apartment, this enclosure of rooms that remains at the end of the film when neither Georges nor Anne do. The film thus constructs two primary configurations: some relation of love to death, and a formal articulation of space. The critical task is not to synthesize or hierarchize these dimensions, but to force them to an encounter: What is this text doing by putting on display careful dimensions of increment and threshold in its construction of space while simultaneously moving toward an extraordinary act of violence in the context of the erotics and exhaustions of care for the other? As with the tension in Kierkegaard between the All-is-over and the little great difference, there is a fundamental disproportion between the precise formal measure of space and the affective extremity of the film's title and subject, the finitude of house set against the radical limitlessness ascribed to love, care, grace, which is one reason why many critics have written — in error, by the way — that *Amour* constitutes a departure from Haneke's violent earlier work and have absorbed the film into discourses of sentimentality and humanism, the thawing of his earlier *"emotionale Vergletscherung"* (emotional glaciation) films. Any thinking of *Amour* will turn on whether space is taken to serve meaning as its ground, space having *interest* in meaning, that which love or death can profit from, what makes some understanding of love or death communicable. For representation in the closed system of the film is inaugurated through a failure to avoid a confrontation with the sight of the dead. In this way, *Amour* functions as a palliative for Benjamin's famous concern in "Der Erzähler" (The Storyteller) that the innovations of nineteenth-century bourgeois society — the social lineage to which Georges and Anne squarely belong — have pushed dying and the dead "further and further out of the perceptual world of the living. There used to be no house, hardly a room, in which someone had not once died. [. . .] Today people live in rooms that have never been touched by death, dry dwellers of eternity, and when their end approaches they are stowed away in sanatoria or hospitals by their heirs."[86] Inverting Benjamin's aesthetic law, in which "death is the sanction of everything that the storyteller can tell. He has borrowed his authority from death," figuring what might possibly constitute the communicability of meaning as such, Haneke refuses all that death loans. For Haneke builds a cinematic room to house death and dying as a luminous problematic that situates non-meaningfulness in the instability of the home's formal relations.

Grappling with the configuration of love and death does not seem to require that the critic take seriously forms of space.[87] The ethico-amative question is the obsession of criticism, always framed as whether Georges's suffocation of Anne is the culmination of a logic of love (the extremest fulfillment of amour: where love fully *is*) or its radical absence (the extremest limit of amour: where love *is not* or is surpassed). As just two examples of readings that fall to this opposing logic: Garrett Stewart defends the first position, dubbing the suffocation "the final act of love, the *geste d'amour* [. . .] fulfilling the tacit promise to end [Anne's] suffering," while Roy Grundmann locates in the film a violence intrinsic to love, submitting that "compassion," even in "romantic love, is never completely altruistic [. . .] [but] emerges [. . .] as selfishness incarnate."[88] The former risks sentimentality; the latter courts cynicism. My argument, however, is that the double alternative of the film's ethical crisis is unthinkable except by taking seriously the seemingly unrelated and nonethical dimension of spatial incrementality as it constructs a series of figures of Threshold. To give this claim in a stronger formulation: The critical antinomy that asks whether *Amour* demonstrates that the act of violence is the fulfillment of love or its voiding poses the wrong question altogether—absolutely false because it is the question that must come second in a list in which something unnamed by that alternative comes first. For prior to the suffocation (thus, to be clear: prior to the ethical and the grounds for its adjudication) is incrementality as such—and only from a formal grappling with incremental difference can one arrive at a thinking of how the film itself constitutes a work of love in the face of death. Not only does such an approach not evade the question of whether injurious force is love's totality or limit—radical formalism, given due seriousness, disimplicates the stance that criticism must indeed choose one of these interpretations.

For *Amour* is not at heart a film about a marriage, nor about a family; neither is it primarily about inwardness or care, nor about suffering or grief, nor hope, nor the affective realm at all. For all that its reception, scholarly and popular, has turned on diegetic and spectatorial anguish at watching Anne slowly and knowingly and miserably expire—for all the carefully composed close-ups of spittle and the thin lips, the shame of assistance in undressing after inadvertent urination—for all the discomforting duration of the count of ten, eleven, then twelve, thirteen, to fourteen, fifteen, of the pale loose-skinned leg lifted in stiff and pointless exercise—for all its resemblance to the contract of conventional love in partnership: what an unveiled yearning to grow old with the other looks like; what awaits those for whom only in death will they be parted—for all that the film begins with the nonneutral image of the dead human body—indeed, for all that the film signs itself under the saturated name for the paragon of passion, promising a Platonism of Love in itself as such—for all this, *Amour*, in its arrangement of elements, is concerned with none of these nor with the elementary of an appropriating meaningfulness that they invoke or attempt to force. Haneke's film is neither about love's fulfillment in violence nor love's supersession in violence. *Amour*, rather, is a film about forms of comparison.

as many comparisons as possible

Return to the half-a-foot; it can go by many names. Next call it sixteen seconds.

The space of Georges and Anne's apartment—its severely limited setting the most striking aesthetic aspect of the film—is constructed through a precise language of incremental steps across its interior. Haneke's anti-psychological formalism, his commitment to structure over character, his scrupulous—sometimes even taken to be callous—investment in line, light, and duration, here take shape in the precise plotting of the distance between the apartment's rooms, in particular its kitchen and bedroom. The temporal and spatial enclosure of the entire film within the walls of the couple's apartment (save for those three minutes in the prologue) has been treated in most of the critical work on *Amour* as allegorical, that is, as scenographic: the limited cinematic setting taken either as an analogue of marriage's inmost register of sensual care or to figure the familiar as potentially imprisoning, sign of love's claustrophobia, its cut-offness from the world. In this approach, the dark, cluttered, if lovingly curated mise-en-scène serves as a material allegory for the couple's intimacy, turning on their shared constructed life, staging their witnessing of each other's histories in this minimalist chamber play; the haute-Parisian hallmarks—the landscape paintings; classical music LPs, CDs, and scores; beautifully bound books; elegant furniture; and Haneke's pronouncement that the layout was modeled on his parents' apartment in Vienna—are taken to function as a broader bond to the director's decades-long critique of the emotional glaciation of a certain type of bourgeois subject. This approach to space in *Amour*, for all that the Adorno critical of Kierkegaard would be pleased, is profoundly restricted in the speculative claims it can make about the film. Not only does it figure the apartment purely as a layout minable for its relation to figuration, narrative, allegory, recovering love and death for meaning, it also focuses on the interior substance of the bounded space as representation: what a marital bedroom signifies, the humiliating hermeneutics of abjections in the bathroom, the symbolism of the rooms' suffocating enclosures. This critical stance converts time to space in privileging enclosure over duration; converts space to spaces, prioritizing symbolic densities of rooms over diagrammatic possibilities of layout; and converts spaces to metaphors for social relations — in the process becoming multiply incapable of speaking to form, in other words what cannot be reduced to a paraphrased narrative of space and what abstracts spacing from particularities of meaning. And without being able to address the film's figuring of incrementality, there can be no accounting for the irreducibility of either violence or love here.[89]

Nine minutes into *Amour*, sitting at the kitchen table eating breakfast, speaking in the slack soft intimacy that is the easeful routine of lovers of decades, at an indeterminable point something will retroactively be revealed to have changed: Anne's still comportment that seemed like listening is converted into a little great difference when Georges's questions to her — "What's going on? What's wrong?" — receive no response. He rises and turns on water in the sink to dab onto his wife's neck; he leaves the kitchen, and the camera patiently, gently remains with him as he walks across the apartment's large foyer to the couple's bedroom, a distance that takes sixteen seconds lintel to lintel by the measure of the aged, bent body. In the bedroom, he hears the water go off, sign at a distance that Anne has resumed her presence to the world; he returns, the identical journey indelibly charged with the world-upending difference of the sound of water on, sound of water off, again taking sixteen seconds. This passage from the two far reaches of the bounded setting covers over the breaking of the stroke, and over the course of the film it clinically articulates the logic of time and space that, incrementally crossed, points to the difference in events that take place over it.

The rabid incrementalism of Haneke's film constructs an interior governed by a larger question of the measure of difference and its positive relation to space. Although its most concrete form is the extended duration, always shot continuously, of this crossing of the distance from kitchen to bedroom, the crystallizing labor of increment is the construction of a series of thresholds at the margins of the apartment—a large window; the front door of the inaugural breach—each a bare framed rupture between *out there* and *in here*. The cinematic navigation of the interior diagrams the formal conditions of possibility for this space; prior to the grounds for any ethical critique are these thresholds sealed tight and brutally opened, the incremental transgressability of little great differences between one register and another.

That register of the one-step-more extends from space to include being. After the first stroke, Georges comes home to find Anne having failed at attempting suicide: her body lies slumped on the floor under a large open window toward which progress was frustrated by the impaired sensation in half her body. She reproaches him for his incrementally earlier than expected arrival, and declares twice, to his horror: "Je ne veux plus"; I don't want any *more*—it is the a-bit-moreness, the minimal ongoingness of an increasingly intolerable life that she deems unbearable. Death's decision will abolish any *plus*, any more of life, and yet death's arrival requires what the paralyzed body cannot accomplish: the just-a-bit-more toward the window that at some incremental tipping point of weight would have led to the decisive.

> Anne is not a character so much as the figure who potentializes
> decremental change until All-is-over.
> Anne is a form. She is there *to die;*
> she is there as a perpetual process of declension.

The Threshold in its most general, abstract sense is the point at which an incremental difference creates a change of state; it constitutes the most minor possibility of difference, indifferent and belonging to neither of two registers that it puts in an unbreakable relation. Threshold does not belong to the realm of beings or things, nor is it derived from or secondary to identity; it is the rift, a spacing between realms; Threshold is difference. As in Heidegger's reading in "Die Sprache" of "Ein Winterabend" by Georg Trakl, which emphasizes the third stanza, and in particular the second line, the only one in the past tense, prior to the world of light and thing—"Wanderer silently steps within; / Pain has turned the threshold to stone. / There lie, in limpid brightness shown, / Upon the table bread and wine"—pain is not an internal sensation. "We should not represent pain anthropologically as feeling [*Empfindung*] that makes us feel afflicted [*wehleidig*]. We should not think of the intimacy [of pain] psychologically as the sort in which sentimentality makes a nest for itself," writes a Heidegger who might as well be Haneke. Rather, from his reading of Trakl, Heidegger figures pain as what "tears asunder; it separates, yet so that at the same time it draws everything to itself [. . .]. Pain joins the rift of the difference. Pain is the difference."[90] Pain is thus given as the structure of the sustenance of Threshold, what rends, what divides realms and constitutes a relation of spacing, the no-more-in-common: of two objects, two scenes, two registers, two domains, two beings, two forms. Threshold, *Schwelle* in Heidegger, is the place of stepping "from one realm over into another"—a ridge or barrier or edge that figures the instability of the liminal. Like *Amour*, Trakl's poem opens by positing a basal difference between outside and inside, taking as its inaugural aesthetic concern the manner in which the threshold is "the root standing to uphold the entire door. It supports the middle where both the outside and inside interpenetrate each other. The threshold is the in-between."[91] It *bears* what is in between—supports, as in weight; endures, as in suffers. If the dead one in Kierkegaard is the occasion that reveals love to the living in its most absolute form, the difference between outside and inside is the occasion for a thinking of spacing in the most abstract, general manner. What gives the measure of that difference between inside and outside in the burst by which *Amour* opens is the light that gushes with unseeming vitality across, unconcealing, this first rend.

The extremest and most abstract form of Threshold is thus lodged in the light that sets in play a difference at the apartment's door, what materially opens and becomes the ground of a promise of love. After the first stroke, Anne, having returned home, insists that Georges vow never to take her back to the hospital. She repeats this formulation even as he fails to answer, her insistence reposing this demand as a pure extraction to which no spoken response would be adequate or adequately secure. Phrased another way: the promise does not arrive but approaches incrementally an affirmation of its reception. The work of love thereby takes an avowedly spatial register, and marital debt shifts from the bonding performative of "I do" for the witnessing of the other's life to the "I promise" not to ever again force the crossing of the threshold of the apartment. Later, after Anne's second stroke—an hour into the film, from one shot to the next a temporal leap bears out a violent rupture in her capacities of language—Eva and her estranged husband visit her parents, and, in an argument about whether to put Anne in a nursing home, Georges frustratedly exclaims that he will not do so, that he promised he would not. This exchange between father and daughter, critically overlooked and dismissible as the narrative ground of a domestic melodrama, is, in fact, a map of the essential formal concerns of the film. For in this scene, Georges offers two comparisons: to Eva's proposal that her mother be sent to a hospital, Georges refuses, saying that she would only be sent to a *maison de retraite médicalisée*, a nursing home, saying of such places, "Ce qu'on fait dans ces maisons, [on] peut très bien faire ici"—*what they do there, we can do here.* He then offers this rejoinder to his increasingly upset, protesting daughter: *I presume you understand that I love your mother as much as you do* ("J'aime ta mère autant que toi").

A comparison of resemblance without identity is predicated on there being a minimal form of specific difference between the terms. *Amour* turns on a *There* against *Here* and a *My Love* against *Your Love.* The gap between *ces maisons* and *ici* is the rift that establishes the renewed amative promise, linked to the specificity of remaining in (this) place, to refuse to be taken past the threshold of the *maison* (as in one's home) into the *maison de retraite*, which is to say a promise to remain etymologically with the Latin root of *mansionem*, home, as opposed to *maneo* (where one resides but does not intimately dwell)—at the cost, however, of securing an uncertain but definite future time at which the home will be commuted to a grave. The minor but decisive difference between the *maison* and the *maison de retraite* is the threshold of the apartment, what sustains the adverbs' separation and is thus syntactically equivalent to the comma separating "what they do there, [break, *koptein*'s cut] we can do here."

While *There* and *Here* are the difference on which the promise is demanded and what is sustained by the aperture to the apartment, the other comparison, "I love your mother as much as you do" (*J'aime ta mère autant que toi*), points to an entirely different Threshold. For a work titled *Amour*, there is a notable absence in the film—what Barthes figures in *A Lover's Discourse* as what takes no meaning, has "no usages," is "without nuance," and is fundamentally "extra-lexicographical"—the holophrastic *I-love-you*.[92] For Nancy, even more than for Barthes, there is no love without this promise: "love's name," he writes, "is not 'love,' which would be a substance or a faculty, but it is this sentence, the 'I love you.'"[93] This promise, so crucial, also however secures nothing and is always in vain: these blank words bring nothing about, name no thing, and deploy language in a manner that cannot be authenticated. Nancy gives this formulation as "the words of love, as is well known, sparsely, miserably repeat their one declaration, which is always the same, always already suspected of lacking love because it declares it."[94] Love is not merely an abstract designation; its spoken promise is always an empty designation, a something that is not given (given as *not* there) in its offering. (One sees this best and most cruelly in another of Haneke's films: in *71 Fragments of a Chronology of Chance* [1994], a husband mutters "I love you" to his wife; she reacts with shock and resentment, presumes he must want something; he is humiliated and the exchange triggers violence—he slaps her.) But in *Amour*, I-love-you as an offering between Georges and Anne is nowhere. In its place—supplanting it, usurping it—is the promise not to take Anne back over the threshold of the home. This is the promise that cuts across love, what secures nothing but lets its law appear, here a law of space that rejects the sublation of *Here* to convert it into an *ici* that would now be *There*. When Anne finally does leave the apartment, the promise of love contravened, it is either not shown (the offscreen removal of corpse) or visible only as an ontological deceit (in the realm of fantasy in which imaginary figures of Anne and Georges take leave of the home and film in the second epilogue). Love's explicit declaration is given—and givable—only in the formula of the second comparison, the one not of space but of amative quantity: the *J'aime ta mère autant que toi*.

That "autant que" not only points to the radical dissymmetry in these two forms of love—the child's for the mother, the lover's for the beloved; the one who appears and leaves, the one who remains and cares; the one without debt, the other bound to home and to promise. The "as much as" is also predicated, as a linguistic and logical claim, on a measurability of each love, a task that belongs to the realm of not-love. In *Phaedrus*, when Socrates offers the discourse of Stesichorus, refuting the claim that the lover is mad and favor should be granted to the nonlover as sound of mind, he says "the affection of the non-lover, alloyed with mortal prudence and bestowing a small measure of worldly goods, will beget in the beloved soul the narrowness which the common folk praise as virtue."[95] The nonlover's miserly thrift is given as *oikonomousa*: management, ordering, a regulating, a parsing out. Anne Carson's summation in *Eros the Bittersweet* returns to the question of profit and interest: "It is a deadly stinginess by which the nonlover eludes desire. He measures his emotions out like a miser counting gold."[96] To functionalize love and subsume it to economy is not to unlove, which belongs to eros: love can always end, of course; more precise to say that love *is*, if it can be said to be, precisely *because* it can end. Rather, to subsume love to economy—to love to a degree, to love by allotment, to love in proportion or to offer (or take) but a share, to love any extent (or volume, or reach, stock or store), to budget one's love, to accommodate it to regimes of expenditure, revenue, return — is to *not love*. Although a quantitative increment moves the body across the space of the film (and economically: literally the *nomos*, rule or law or custom of the *oikos*, at once the family, their property, and their house), the change from not-dead to dead or not-love to love is not incremental or hierarchical (one is not more dead than another) but absolute, decisive, a break. There is death — what is its decisiveness — and everything incrementally up to the point that *All is Over!* is a form of difference. This is the radical self-negation of claiming, "I love a little," "I love in part," "I love as much."

This density of love, its resistance to comparisons of quantity that it simultaneously invites, is internal to philosophy's grapple with the amative. Nancy's "L'amour en éclats" opens with an elegant summation of how "the nature of love is shown to be double and contradictory, even though it also contains the infinite resolution of its own contradiction." Because love absorbs all these terms — "the access and the end, the incomplete being and the completed being, the self and the beyond of the self, the one and the other, the identical and the different" — love is the "contradiction of contradiction and noncontradiction."[97] Now add to Nancy's accounting, following Kierkegaard, the absolutely decisive and the little difference. For any incrementality puts unbearable pressure on the love of completion and fulfillment, the love organized as what maintains even in its surpassing. To say "some quantity of love" is to subordinate love to the calculated gain of an investment, to partibility, portioning, dissection, interest. To declare that there is some extent of love, a measure of love in A as in B, is to offer measured love (always as an internal limitation: *mesurer*, to curb, to moderate). And to offer measured love is to offer no love at all. In this view, love's bliss does not need to be cloistered from its opposite, neither from hatred nor cruelty nor violence; — Love needs to be protected from the increment.

And yet, in *Amour* the comparison of quantity is nevertheless made. One cannot unmake the *autant que toi* — this is the ethical charge of close reading: one has to grapple, with seriousness, with what is. In offering the relation of "as much as," I-loving and you-loving situates Georges and his daughter; the very existence of the comparison arranges them in a structure. It emplaces them: as Barthes has it, "The person with whom I can [. . .] talk about the loved being is the person who loves that being as much as I do, the way I do: my symmetric partner, my rival, my competitor (rivalry is a question of place)."[98] If the two types of place bound up with There and Here are the radically different *maisons* sustained by the threshold of the apartment, the loving in *my place* loving in *your place* points to the absolute difference of two beings: that Georges's body is not the same place as Eva's. The threshold that separates them is not that of *une maison de retraite* but the threshold of action: the *j'aime ta mère autant que toi* is broken apart by the act of force against Anne. What disproves the posited similitude of as-much-as is an event of violence. Georges's bringing about of Anne's death is the threshold and finitude of the "as much as"—what determines fully that these two terms do not love the same. The suffocation is what rends loving in Georges's place from loving in the daughter's place; it is the syntactical cleaving in this claimed comparison. Thus, smothering of the beloved, door frame, comma—they formally function the same. Because violence is what does violence to the formal claim of a comparison of quantity, what effects the most evanescent incremental difference in love and devastates the ground of the as-much-as, *violence* secures the incomparability of love: it structurally forecloses the measuring dimension of not-love. *Amour*, once more, is neither a story of love nor of death, not the private account of a marriage nor a diagnosis of the bourgeoisie; it is a film about forms of comparison, and these are the elemental terms at stake: things that can be compared incrementally and that are sustained by Thresholds, and registers that cannot be compared for which the violence of an act is the difference and which in so constituting negate (all) possible grounds of comparability.

"I love your mother as much as you do" is fundamentally a geometric claim: a comparison without recourse to known quantity—but it is an ephemeral geometry. The formulation compares two immeasurables, two potentially infinite, indescribable loves. To compare unique loves is to bring them into a unity that desecrates the uniqueness of each. Amative calculi offered on the level of language thus falsify the representation of love's difference. *This is not only a formal problem but the very problem of form*: what, in being modified, becomes decisively otherwise—what must be irretrievably losable in order to be at all. Redistributing love according to the inhuman terms of similitude and variation; quantity and the incomparable; Thresholds set in light, marking inside from outside; a violence structurally equivalent to a punctuation mark; a difference between a There and some Here, *Amour* regards love through the abstract, general, impersonal, and indifferent lens of the variability of form itself. Love is neither feeling nor remembrance; it is infinite difference. The speculative gesture of this reading is that there is a homological structure to formalism and love. *Amour* does not display a love of formalism in order to demonstrate or put on display a prior and external formalism of love (incremental logic is not there to serve a Kierkegaardian theme), but, rather, there is a love proper to a thinking of form that derives from its inmost logic — abstract, general, impersonal, indifferent, callous, even cruel.

such a love that would be proper to form

Return to material, to wood and to beam. If the light-giving, light-given threshold to Georges and Anne's apartment puts in relation the intimate but chasmic rift between *There* and *Here*, there is an aperture that figures the in-between in a slightly different way: the central window in the apartment's vestibule, which constitutes (vertically) and casts (diagonally, onto the floor) a narrow field of brightness. Through this aspect ratio a pigeon enters and is shooed away by Georges, and after that the film moves rapidly toward its unbearable crisis: forced water, Anne's refusal to drink, Georges's hard slap; final stories; the suffocation; Georges sealing their bedroom; and then, a pigeon appears again, not through the window but inside already, walking on the apartment floor. Like the spectator, it is realized and given as already within the space. Georges hears its beating, approaches it, closes the window; he stalks it, eventually covers it in a blanket, cradles it; we never learn its egress or fate — it remains within the apartment, like Anne-corpse, Georges-image, and spectator. Writing a letter to an unknown addressee (and using the *tu* form), Georges's script offers, "You won't believe this. A pigeon got into the apartment." So the great critical error, of course, would be to take this pigeon as a symbol. For the pigeon is not merely a lure for symbolism — it is the lure for a particular symbolism: the pigeon, which linguistically derives from the word for dove (the Old French *pigeon*, *pijon*, means "young dove," and in many languages, pigeon is not distinguished at all from dove; morphologically, they are the same), sacrificial bird, figure of escape or messaging, figure of love in the Song of Songs, that is also, as in Judah's anguish in Ezekiel, sign of mourning — (one will "moan like doves" in grief). The pigeon is there to pose the question of the meaning of feeling or its meaninglessness. It demands a reckoning, poses the difference (which is to say invites the comparison) between that which represents and that which merely is (in light). Haneke, though often and willfully an unreliable reader of his own work, has an excellent response to this, insisting in an interview, "I don't know what the pigeon means. All that I know for certain [. . .] is that the pigeon appears."[99] Indeed it does: from somewhere, from *there*, this thing that was not previously *here*, *appears* and is shown in and through light.

The epilogical pigeon functions as a final Threshold—Final because it is Next after the decisiveness of Anne's *All is over!* The pigeon is a pure event of continuance, a something that happens to mark the minimal ongoingness of the world in the face of the death of Anne. The threshold between what you can and cannot, will and will never relate to the other whom you love, now dead, is impossible to figure and yet absolutely and radically real. Nothing approaches the truth of the real more closely than this dissimilitude: next to the drained eye of one recently deceased, one who is still living sees *more*. It is there even if it is also completely uncertain. The pigeon as such is indifferent, but its pulsing vitality as presence attests to the minimal difference between life in which Anne's death has yet to arrive and the world in which her death has in fact taken place: it constitutes the smallest, most trivial gradient of the new, and therefore the pigeon is not an anagogic symbol, but this bird is an event. Of one of Georges's stories of his childhood, Anne says, you never told me that before; and now this pigeon will be the first of these other stories of the infinite set: the always-one-more-story that one will at some point be unable to tell to the beloved who is dead. The pigeon is the jest that reminds "by means of its littleness" how great the difference is: its entrance unconceals the rupture of the world in which Anne existed as alive and this one, the threshold that marks as otherwise the world intercalated with death. These worlds invite comparison, but they are not *as much as* each other by the measure of a profound and simultaneously absurd, arbitrary, fluttering increment.

Amour does not symbolize something meaningful about love; indeed, it deploys its indifferent, rigorous aesthetic language as a positive force that negates all grounds for symbolizing *anything* meaningful about love. Crucially, the film is not titled *l'amour* (love as an in-itself), nor *son amour*, his love, nor *mon amour*, object I love. Instead, the title places the film under the sign of sentiment without definite article. This articlelessness simultaneously elevates and diminishes (incrementally shifts) any accounting of love linked to essence: elevates it through its association with the poetic tradition, as in Verlaine's 1888 collection *Amour*, yet diminishes any claim toward nominating a positive substance. In fact, dropping the article suggests nothing so much as *amour*'s alphabetic inscription in a catalogue of affects, more akin to a dictionary or encyclopedic entry, an abstraction divorced from its lived form. It also thereby places *amour* in dialogue with the other articleless word that saturates the text: as the film moves inexorably toward Georges's act of violence, Anne begins a near constant wailing of "mal" from her bed. *Mal*: hurts, badly, wrong (also heartache, also pain), an adjective used with corporeal verbs of state. A nurse attempts to comfort Georges by insisting that Anne's cry is a reflex, that the dying "always say something"—that it could as well have been "maman, maman, maman." (Though, of course, it wasn't.)

Amour is not about anything at all. It is no more a showing of *le mal* (evil) than it is a study of *l'amour*. *Mal* is invited into the film not to mean nothing but not to mean, to function as the linguistic form of death's quality of being contingent but decisive: that the dying "always say something" is the order of the decisive, and whether it is *amour* or *mal*—or *maman* or anything else—is the brutal indifference of contingency. In place of meaning, *Amour* displays the revealed world of light and thing as an attestation that love *is* not in any *here*—as either its fulfillment or as its failure. Thinking love outside of placement—arriving solely as passage—Nancy writes, "love is the impossible, and it does not arrive, or arrives only at the limit, while crossing."[100] It is its coming-and-going. And Nancy will call that which love unveils: finitude, simultaneously a radical incomprehensibility and a limit internal to its form. "Love does not transfigure finitude, and it does not carry out its transubstantiation in infinity," Nancy insists, "Love cuts across finitude, always from the other to the other, which never returns to the same."[101] Love, like existential being, *is* what is oriented toward its own nullity.

Love is not only the site of a decisive failure or refusal of meaning or narrative, the totality of what is put to *mend* rifts and differences in meaning; beyond that, love is what devastates figuration as such. The aesthetic question, then, will always be how to render love without representing it, how to think a critique of love without substantializing what elides difference. As Nancy phrases it, love is "always present and never recognized in anything that we name 'love.'"[102] *Amour* names love—the articleless title announces itself as just such a naming—but its formal language fails to offer itself as a presentation of a positive substance that would falsely claim to be adequate to love. The film does not settle the little great differences of its various rends: it incrementally approaches Threshold, indifferent to whether that threshold is a wooden partition or a bit more of life; formal incrementalism merely commits to the in-between that refuses to lodge its meaning in physical, metaphorical, or critical places. Love is maintained in difference, and love maintains difference: Love is the threshold between the presence and absence of love itself. Thus a radical formalism concerned with the disposition of comparisons, of incremental differences—one that demands a reading prior to the terrain of marriage, death, violence, the ethical—is not only *a* mode of getting at love here, but the sole manner in which love's abstraction is not converted into one or the other side of the threshold it does not just name but itself sustains.

We have already seen how the metaphysics of love, the philosophical formalism of love, has been durably cast as numerical since the account Aristophanes gives in *Symposium* that the longing for wholeness involves the *hen ek duoin*, the one-out-of-two, and running right up through Badiou's insistence in *Éloge de l'amour* that love is a construction of a truth that involves seeing "the world from the point of view of *two* rather than *one.*"[103] It is finally time to move past these prejudicial ones and twos, for love is less numerical than properly *mathematical:* love as an abstract notation resembles algebraic procedure, inviting the comparison of the presence or absence of something lacking ontological ground and commitment, designating above all the undefined.

Nothing is easier to assign to meaning than love.

Amour does not make a test of love so much as Love—in the abstract mode by which it is given here: articleless, contextless, general—is the supreme occasion for a testing of the thinking of form. Like Nancy's accounting of love as "double and contradictory, even though it also contains the infinite resolution of its own contradiction," such that it figures the "contradiction of contradiction and noncontradiction," the radical dilemma of form (the dilemma at its root) is irresolvably double and contradictory—that it names both an immaterial idea and a sensible shape. The heterogeneity at the heart of the concept of form thus gives the measure of the essence of the contradictory. Love, in posing the contradiction of contradiction and noncontradiction, takes the form of the structure of form itself: what is neither inside nor outside, neither essence nor appearance, but what gives shape to the impasses thereby posed. A formal thinking isomorphic to love renders a kind of love made not in the twining of bodies but in the act itself of reading for form.

Amour's spare, brutal, even callous incrementality constitutes a profound reduction of elements, a decremental approach toward the minimal definition of a serious form of love. *Amour* does not read love or mean love—the film is not *about* love; nor does it affectively report or communicate it. (This is always a question of exhaustion. As Nancy reminds us, "has not everything been said on the subject of love?")[104] Haneke's film, instead, and with all the counterpressure of what resists exhaustion, vitalizes the thinking of the amative by taking the *measure* of love. What a formalism of increment and threshold bound up with modes of comparison and difference allows is a lingering with the speculative. Falling neither to a love that would be infinite, universal, and eternal, dissolving temporality and risking a flattened sentimentality, nor rendering solely the individual singularity of a particular love, *Amour* offers a speculative relation to love without taking shelter in the concrete register of an expressed meaning that could only repeat that exhausted everything that has already been said on the subject. Taking the measure of love in lieu of assigning it to meaning allows its indifferent, general, decisive abstraction, sidestepping all speaking about love, always false because it names it, inadequately faithful to what in love *is* speculative.

But at last, consider then: Do you think it so easy to fail to fall to meaning? Do you think it so simple to not speak about?

Go out to the dead, consider carefully those features of the corpse, gentle, still, pale, small, and set—now regard how Anne frenziedly struggles in the suffocation, how the pathetic meat of the body fights in saddest spasms the not-one-step-further when it overtly arrives. For a love that gives the critical purchase *nothing* in return (no profitable allegory, no ethical evaluation, neither social relations nor their improvement, no interest at all to be derived from reading—now rendered unsure and unwise investment), can you linger with the half a foot, the sixteen seconds, the There and the Here, the as-much-as, plotted spacing, the dissimilitude of more, dimensions of apertures, the bird that appears, omnidirectional extension, four versus five, patterns and grids, diagrams and design, commas, cuts, alphabet and shape, difference and sequence and color and space, pace and interval, rhythms, repetitions, tables, list, line, letter, and only the light if from all this is derived nothing, absolutely and decisively.

—Reader, could you still engage this callous form as *work*?

□ □ □ □ □

FIGURE 6.5. *Amour* (Michael Haneke, 2012)

Acknowledgments

For a long time I wanted to write something called "The Erotics of the Colleague." Not that one wanted or went to bed with those contingently housed in the same university department—though, of course, some do—nor to invoke those midcentury campus novels where sherry at faculty parties instigates often disastrous concupiscence, but rather in the straightforward sense that I am fundamentally moved by the nature of the association with the colleague, and that, in wanting to explain and acknowledge what a true colleague can be, I find myself unable to distance this figure from the language of the erotic in a Barthesian sense: as what undoes or suspends or troubles a unary sense of ourselves, where blurred is the seam between intellectual passions that belong to us privately, as if a secret property, and an expanded sense of what we might, given the right occasion, find ourselves caring about from the outside. Collegiality strikes me as a variation of the fundamental erotic situation: that slurry of pleasures, anonymities, responsibilities, intimacies—all that is at stake in hosting others, in being hosted by another. A profound collegial relation might result from a thousand brief encounters or one heady, absorbing weekend. And part of what makes a good colleague undoubtedly overlaps with what makes a good lover: enthusiasm, willingness, a mix of boisterous self-regard and pronounced selflessness. Lovers and colleagues make themselves *available*: they put themselves at others' disposal.

Perhaps this ought to have come first: What, after all, is a colleague? An associate or partner, one who shares an office, vocation, practice, labor, or common purpose, from *com*, with, together, from *leg-* (as in *legare*, to bind or tie; to entrust, to send as an envoy or delegate, as in *legate*, that deputy who represents the province), all this from a root for *to collect or gather*. Strictly speaking, colleagues are united, joined in alliance, leagued. A colleague, etymologically, is one who has been chosen *at the same time as another*, but as our world is no longer one of conscripted deputies to the pope, let us rephrase this as: the colleague is one who has chosen, and what a colleague has chosen is to work with another, to convene with another. It is that *with* that concerns us. For it is the *with*, the *together*, that renders collegiality a lived practice of sympathy: only in place of a feeling-with it is a thinking-with, an ongoing, deliberate, chosen act of collecting together, gathering together, conspiring to be together, for the sake of thinking with the other, at the same time as the other.

Colligāre, to entangle.

A kind of diagrammatic exchange is thus possible between certain kinds of colleagues: *having time in short supply, I nevertheless created the time to think as if I were you, in your place, to try to think your thinking with you, as you would ideally have thought it, and this is what I think you meant to say, even if I myself would never have said it, and am only saying it now as if I were you with your interests and for your sake.* True colleagues keep time with the rhythms of others' obsessions; they hold fast to questions that originate from other people's curiosities and not from indulgences of the self. To find oneself lingering in the company of an idea that in no way concerns you but to concern yourself nonetheless: this is to have a colleague.

In its ideal form, as in many ideal forms, *to have* and *to be* constitute the very same thing.

A deep amity, a small and quiet ethics, an act of a singular kind of care. Also, a form of affection, sometimes devotion; also, a form of recognition, sometimes the deepest understanding.

Consider: Julia Kristeva, writing to Barthes in 1977, "It's been more than ten years (already!) that I've been reading you, and finally always this way, at each departure, and afterward—a gift of happiness in lightning flashes."

When I write, then, that Brian Price is one of my closest colleagues and one of my dearest people, it might be an error to regard the latter as the more intimate public admittance. After all, this is the collegial side: for the fourteen years in which I have presented my—usually new, raw and unfinished—scholarly work in front of him, I have, every single time, kept the hard copies of the paper on which I scrawled his questions, provocations, recommendations, doubts. These treasured scraps, ripped napkins and the backs of conference programs, remain in my company until the final work is done and the question, provocation, recommendation, doubt—even (or especially) if not followed to the letter—has at least been taken seriously.

Colleagues can bestow generosities that are wholly unknown in other relationships.

So when I confess, for example, that I am always slightly on the lookout for articles and phrases and texts that might be of interest to Abe Geil or Marah

Gubar, and they to me, or that without quite realizing it I am dispositionally attuned to keep close to mind what Tim Dean, Meghan Sutherland, and Kyle Stevens are working on, and they to me, it feels utterly redundant to name them also as cherished friends. What quantity of care or trust isn't already in play when we have spent *years* talking and reading, thinking together with each other's work?

Some of those listed below began our acquaintance as my students; some, as my teachers; some belong to bodies I've never crossed paths with in person. (A few, as sometimes happens, their names I do not know.) Some I have written to, and they to me, for well over a decade, while my association with others is mere months long, but this is my collegial world at the moment of this writing, and if I remain lucky it will be outdated and incomplete at every future time of its reading.

If lists seduce with the promise of infinitude, that openness is itself an object of my deep and renewed gratitude. Thank you to all.

Abe Geil

Adam Lowenstein

Akira Lippit

Amy Villarejo

Andries Hiskes

Anna Backman Rogers

Anonymous 1, running up after a talk to ardently recommend *Micro Loup*

Anonymous 2, who shyly, rightly, right on the cusp of taking leave, urged a return to Hogarth

Anonymous 3, that raucous dinner, entirely spent on *The Manhattan Transcripts*

Arthur Bahr

Ben Dalton

Bernd Herzogenrath

Brian Price

Bruno Perreau

Caetlin Benson-Allott

Carol Dougherty

Caroline Jones

Caroline Levine

Catherine Bernard

Catherine Clark

Catherine Wheatley

Daniel Morgan

David Rodowick

Devon Ress

Diana Henderson

Donna Kornhaber

Elena Gorfinkel

Elisabeth Bronfen

Ellen Rooney

Emily Pollock

Emily Watlington

Erika Balsom

Ernst van Alphen

Esther Peeren

Gabriele Rippl

Hanjo Berressem

James Buzard

James Cahill

Jason Middleton
Jay Scheib
Jeff Scheible
Jenny Chamarette
Joaquin Terrones
Joel Burges
Johannes Voelz
John David Rhodes
John Paul Ricco
Julius Greve
Karen Redrobe
Karl Schoonover
Kate Rennebohm
Kieran Setiya
Kristel Smentek
Kyle Stevens
Laura Finch
Laura Frahm
Lee Edelman
Libby Saxton
Lilia Kilburn
Lisa Coulthard
Lisa Dwan
Lucy Bolton
Lynne Joyrich
Maggie Hennefeld
Marah Gubar
Marisa Fryer
Martine Beugnet
Mary Fuller
Maryn Wilkinson
Meghan Sutherland

Mieke Bal
Mikko Tuhkanen
Nadine Boljkovac
Nico Baumbach
Nikolaj Lübecker
Noel Jackson
Patricia Pisters
Pooja Rangan
Rey Chow
Rosalind Galt
Ruth Perry
Ryan Pierson
Sandy Alexandre
Sarah Cooper
Sarah Dillon
Sarah Keller
Sarah Osment
Scott Durham
Scott Kryzch
Scott Richmond
Seb Franklin
Shankar Raman
Stephanie Frampton
Stephen Tapscott
Steven Shaviro
Tanya Horeck
Tim Dean
Tina Kendall
Tom Eyers
Tomáš Jirsa
Veronica Fitzpatrick
Wyn Kelley

In addition to my colleagues of a decade in the MIT Literature Section, who indulge my enthusiasms even if they do not want to hear too much about the lowest of my texts, I am grateful to our section's staff: Alicia Mackin, Daria Johnson, Jessica TranVo, Emmie Hicks, Belinda Yung, and Laura Ryan each have made my working life possible and better in a thousand ways, and I am deeply appreciative.

I owe an especial acknowledgement to the variable annual cohorts at the World Picture Conference, where so much of this work was presented in its earliest instantiation, in addition to audiences at numerous universities, whose generosity of thoughtfulness and skepticism in equal measure made their mark over the years I worked on this book. In 2018 and 2019, I had the extraordinary luxury of finishing the manuscript among some of my favorite colleagues in my singularly favorite city—Abe Geil and Patricia Pisters generously hosted me as a visiting scholar in Media Studies at the Universiteit van Amsterdam. They, along with Mieke Bal, Ernst van Alphen, Maryn Wilkinson, and Esther Peeren—ably at the helm of the Amsterdam School for Cultural Analysis—fostered an environment uniquely both convivial and intellectually exciting.

Two anonymous reviewers for Duke University Press offered a mix of line-by-line care and broad-picture perspective on this maximalist project, for which I am deeply grateful. I hope that both reviewers recognize in my remarks above that having benefited from such readings is precisely why collegiality strikes me as a deep form of unrepayable debt.

Books are made possible by a particularly intense if short-lived professional world. It is such a pleasure to publish with Duke, and I have been the fortunate recipient of the editorial labors and talents of Sandra Korn, Susan Albury, Aimee C. Harrison, and Amy Ruth Buchanan. Christine Riggio and Andrea Klingler were of enormous assistance with the art program and copyediting, respectively. Courtney Berger remains the editor of my dreams. She lived this project in countless exchanges and conversations for the full seven years that it took to materialize, and her great support for it in substance and style has been profoundly meaningful to me, never wavering even during the years-long, ultimately abandoned, slightly eccentric plan for it to be bound *tête-bêche*. Her advocacy and enthusiasm have buttressed my work, and she, too, is a dear colleague.

Writing takes *time*; it takes time while other things in life require tending, and this need be remembered. I am lucky to have had wonderful childcare provided by Sarah Carr, the teachers at Curious Kids kinderopvang in Amsterdam, and the Waldorf School of Lexington, Massachusetts.

My parents, John and Leonie Brinkema, continue to amaze me with their profound kindness, indefatigable curiosity, and vocational passion. I learn as much from them now as I ever did, and it is one of the greatest joys of my life that we have all aged into choosing each other over and over again as best friends as adults.

You gave me Barthes's unpublished correspondence and inscribed it, "Well, *I* think this is romantic."

Well, hell. I have never understood the notion of a love so overwhelming that the two sit in a thick, inexpressible silence—you know what I mean: the two-lovers-on-a-park-bench bit from *Einstein on the Beach*. There has never been love with me without talking with me, without last night's conversation picked up midthought upon waking, or nine hours in a car with the same poised album waiting to be played once there's a lull but there's never a lull, or the rushed fragments of a story, a child in each arm, ten minutes to say one simple thing, at the end of long days, but somehow it gets said, or *what are you working on?*—always *what are you working on, what now, what did you write today?* The world is threadbare when you're gone; quiet, still, and dull. Simply put, you are the good thing that happens.

For over twenty years, Evan Johnson has been the one I want to tell and from whom I simply have to hear.

Nothing goes without saying, so say it: My happiest fact is that we share a life. You have given me time to write as a share of your stock of time, at cost to your work; I know this, I see it. Your reading is the one I wait on and yours are the only edits I can receive with absolute openness; even when I don't, I always suspect I ought to take them all. A check on my excesses, an enticement to others, filtered through your illegible ink-scrawled comments, my work finally becomes what I wanted it to be.

With a hard crystal certainty, I am aware that in writing and in person, I am not for everyone. It has always been more than enough that in both I am for you.

Confidential to Sebastian and Beatrix:
This is what I also did
when you were very small.

Notes

EXORDIA

1. Witold Gombrowicz, *A Kind of Testament*, ed. Dominique de Roux, trans. Alastair Hamilton, intro. Maurice Nadeau (Champaign, IL: Dalkey Archive Press, 2007), 87. Leibniz, "Methode de la certitude et l'art d'inventer": "la meilleure Methode qu'il y a c'est d'y faire le plus de comparaisons qu'on peut, et des indices les plus exacts, les plus particularisés, et les plus diversifiés qu'il est possible" (the best method is to make as many comparisons as possible, and the most accurate, the most particular, and the most diverse indices possible). Here, and for Leibniz's proposal for a new encyclopedia, I have relied on the collection of Leibniz's essays found in Gottfried Wilhelm Leibniz, *The Art of Controversies*, trans. and ed. Marcelo Dascal (Dordrecht: Springer, 2008), A VI 4 961, A VI 4 338–49. Roland Barthes, Preface, *Critical Essays*, trans. Richard Howard (Evanston, IL: Northwestern University Press, 1972), xvi–xvii. Ludwig Wittgenstein, *Notebooks, 1914–1916*, 2nd ed., ed. G. H. von Wright and G. E. M. Anscombe, trans. G. E. M. Anscombe (Chicago: University of Chicago Press, 1961), 12e. Fredric Jameson, *The Political Unconscious* (Ithaca, NY: Cornell University Press, 1981), 17.

2. Leibniz, "Encyclopedia," in *The Art of Controversies*, 134–39.

3. Leibniz, "Encyclopedia," 136.

CHAPTER ONE. HORRĒRE OR

1. "Cerberus haec ingens latratu regna trifauci / personat, adverso recubans immanis in antro. / Cui vates, horrēre videns iam colla colubris, / melle soporatam et medicatis frugibus offam / obicit" (These realms huge Cerberus makes ring with his triple-throated baying, his monstrous bulk crouching in a cavern opposite. To him, seeing the snakes now bristling on his necks, the seer flung a morsel drowsy with honey and drugged meal). Virgil, *Eclogues. Georgics. Aeneid: Books 1–6*, trans. H. Rushton Fairclough, rev. G. P. Goold, Loeb Classical Library (Cambridge, MA: Harvard University Press, 1999), Book VI, lines 417–21, 561.

2. "Aujourd'hui tous nos mauvais versificateurs emploient le carnage et l'horreur à

la fin d'un vers." Voltaire, "Remarques sur Sertorius," in *Oeuvres completes de Voltaire*, vol. 9 (Paris: Librairie de Firmin Didot Frères, 1855), 609.

Edmund Burke, *A Philosophical Enquiry into the Origin of Our Ideas of the Sublime and Beautiful*, ed. T. O. McLoughlin and James T. Boulton, in *The Writings and Speeches of Edmund Burke, Volume 1: The Early Writings*, ed. Paul Langford (Oxford: Clarendon Press, 1997), 288. Burke's theory of "delightful horror" is a rejoinder to John Locke's reduction of all affects to degrees of either pleasure or pain, themselves mutually exclusive conditions and the one the negative of the other. Burke's account of the particular delight of a certain type of pain linked uniquely to aesthetic feeling proposes mixed sentiments that are processual in addition to composite and multiple: a cessation of pain produces a certain form of relieving pleasure that then returns to what Burke dubs "indifference," and a cessation of pleasure involves a certain form of unpleasure named as disappointment or grief. A pain that does too great a violence is merely terrible and holds no delight.

Mary Shelley, *Frankenstein: Or the Modern Prometheus* (1818). Oxford World's Classics. (Oxford: Oxford University Press, 2008), 39.

3. Augustine, *Confessions* VII.10.16. See the first volume of James J. O'Donnell, *Augustine: Confessions, Latin Text with English Commentary* (Oxford: Oxford University Press, 1992).

4. Shakespeare, *Julius Caesar*, act 4, scene 3, lines 278–81.

5. Bram Stoker, *Dracula* (Oxford: Oxford University Press, 2011), 262 (emphasis added).

6. Charles Darwin, *The Expression of Emotions in Man and Animals*, in *From So Simple a Beginning: The Four Great Books of Charles Darwin*, ed. Edward O. Wilson (New York: W. W. Norton, 2006), 1314.

7. Darwin, *Expression of Emotions*, 1435.

8. James B. Twitchell, *Dreadful Pleasures: An Anatomy of Modern Horror* (Oxford: Oxford University Press, 1988), 10.

9. Noël Carroll, *The Philosophy of Horror, or, Paradoxes of the Heart* (New York: Routledge, 1990), 24.

10. Carroll, *Philosophy of Horror*, 14–15.

11. Or something stronger than resemblance—overt critical recycling. Linda Badley, in a passage that explicitly cites Twitchell, repeats his etymological claim: "Horror is also the most physiological of genres—with the possible exception of pornography. [. . .] As pornography's purpose is to arouse desire and stimulate pleasure, horror's is to arouse and exorcise latent fear. [. . .] At its simplest, it delivers a frisson that originates as a somatic response. Horror comes from *horrēre*, which refers to the 'bristling of the hair on the nape of the neck' [. . .]. The phenomenon has been taken to its logical conclusion in images of the body that evoke the greatest possible physical response." Linda Badley, *Film, Horror, and the Body Fantastic* (Westport, CT: Greenwood Press, 1995), 11.

Likewise, Bruce Kawin intones in *Horror and the Horror Film*, "in Latin the verb *horrēre*—the source of 'horror'—means to tremble, shiver, shake or shudder, not necessarily because of disease, but in some cases because of fear; it also means to loathe and to dread as well as to bristle, to stand on end as hair does, and to be rough. The hair-raising shudder is part of the term. [. . .] There it is: rough, nauseating, dreadful, frightening, hair-raising, repulsive, unspeakable, nameless, loathsome—an odd foundation on which to build an art." Bruce Kawin, *Horror and the Horror Film* (London: Anthem Press, 2012), 4.

12. Linda Williams, "Film Bodies: Gender, Genre, and Excess," *Film Quarterly* 44, no. 4 (summer 1991): 5.

13. Anna Powell, *Deleuze and Horror Film* (Edinburgh: Edinburgh University Press, 2006), 8.

14. Twitchell, *Dreadful Pleasures*, 11, 17.

15. For an exhaustive catalogue and analysis of words related to fear and bravery in the Homeric epics, see Robert Zaborowski, *La crainte el le courage dans l'*Illiade *et l'*Odysée (Warsaw: Stakroos, 2002). See also Gregory Nagy, "The Subjectivity of Fear as Reflected in Ancient Greek Wording," *Dialogues* 5 (2010): 29–45; David Konstan, "Fear," chapter 6 in *The Emotions of the Ancient Greeks: Studies in Aristotle and Classical Literature* (Toronto: University of Toronto Press, 2006); and Part I, "Theoretical Views About Pity and Fear as Aesthetic Emotions," in Dana LaCourse Munteanu, *Tragic Pathos: Pity and Fear in Greek Philosophy and Tragedy* (Cambridge: Cambridge University Press, 2012).

16. John Miles Foley, "'Reading Homer' through Oral Traditions," in *Approaches to Homer's* Iliad *and* Odyssey, ed. Kostas Myrsiades (New York: Peter Lang, 2010), 29.

17. Thucydides, *The Peloponnesian War*, trans. Martin Hammond (Oxford: Oxford University Press, 2009), 250.

18. See Konstan, *Emotions of the Ancient Greeks*, 153–54, for a critique of Ammonius's distinction.

19. See H. G. Liddell and R. Scott, eds., *A Greek-English Lexicon, with a Revised Supplement*, 9th ed. (Oxford: Clarendon, 1996).

20. Goethe, *Faust II*, line 6272: Shuddering [the shudder; to shudder] is the best part of humankind. Constantine translates this as "Best faculty in man's the thrill of dread." Johann Wolfgang von Goethe, *Faust: Part 2*, trans. David Constantine (London: Penguin, 2009), 56.

Nietzsche will echo this in a fragment in the *Nachlass* from 1872–73: "Das Erschrecken ist der Menschheit bestest Theil" (Terror is the best part of humanity). The philosopher of laughter (and dance) was also very much a philosopher of the shudder. Friedrich Wilhelm Nietzsche, *Nietzsches Werke: Schriften und Entwürfe 1872 bis 1876* (Leipzig: Druck und Verlag von C. G. Naumann, 1896), 209.

21. Robin Wood, "The American Nightmare: Horror in the 70s," in *Hollywood from Vietnam to Reagan . . . and Beyond*, rev. ed. (New York: Columbia University Press, [1986] 2003), 71. Judith (Jack) Halberstam, *Skin Shows: Gothic Horror and the Technology of Monsters* (Durham, NC: Duke University Press, 1995), 21.

22. See Louis Althusser and Étienne Balibar, *Reading Capital* (New York: Verso, 2009).

23. Wood, "American Nightmare," 70. Stephen Prince, "Introduction: The Dark Genre and Its Paradoxes," in *The Horror Film*, ed. Stephen Prince (New Brunswick, NJ: Rutgers University Press, 2004), 2. On horror as historical allegory, see Adam Lowenstein, *Shocking Representation: Historical Trauma, National Cinema, and the Modern Horror Film* (New York: Columbia University Press, 2005), 1–16.

24. Siegfried Kracauer, "Hollywood's Terror Films: Do They Reflect an American State of Mind?" *New German Critique* 89 (spring–summer 2003): 105; originally published in *Commentary* 2 (1946): 132–36. "The monster, as we know it, died in 1963 when Hannah Arendt published her 'Report on the Banality of Evil' entitled *Eichmann in Jerusalem*" (Halberstam, *Skin Shows*, 161).

25. L. Williams, "Film Bodies," 4, 5. See, for example, claims such as, "My other anchoring point is the body, especially the moment of visceral contact between the viewer's and the character's, as foregrounded in examples of graphic Horror, mutilation or torture. This cinematic moment [. . .] is, for me, the epitome of the moment of affect: the point at which our bodies may be moved by those we see on the screen." Xavier Aldana Reyes, *Horror Film and Affect: Towards a Corporeal Model of Viewership* (New York: Routledge, 2016), 3.

26. Robert Spadoni, *Uncanny Bodies: The Coming of Sound Film and the Origins of the Horror Genre* (Berkeley: University of California Press, 2007), 2. Powell, *Deleuze and Horror Film*, 5.

27. Philip Brophy, "Horrality: The Textuality of Contemporary Horror Films," *Screen* 27, no. 1 (January–February 1986): 5.

28. Carol Clover, *Men, Women, and Chain Saws: Gender in the Modern Horror Film* (Princeton, NJ: Princeton University Press, 1992), 9. Morris Dickstein, "The Aesthetics of Fright," in *Planks of Reason: Essays on the Horror Film*, ed. Barry Keith Grant (Metuchen, NJ: Scarecrow Press: 1996), 69.

29. See Matt Hills, *The Pleasures of Horror* (London: Continuum, 2005), 73–90; and Isabel Cristina Pinedo, *Recreational Terror: Women and the Pleasures of Horror Film Viewing* (Albany: State University of New York Press, 1997), 12–14.

30. For example, in a *New York Times* article about the inaugural issue of the journal *Horror Studies*, the lede is deferred until a time-honored question is posed: "With gruesome television series about vampires, werewolves, serial killers and zombies earning huge ratings, and a new cinematic bloodbath opening seemingly every week, the cultural appetite for horror raises a curious question: why do so many of us enjoy being disgusted and terrified?" Jason Zinoman, "The Critique of Pure Horror," *New York Times*, July 16, 2011. A useful survey of approaches to the broader aesthetic paradox can be found in Aaron Smuts, "Art and Negative Affect," *Philosophy Compass* 4, no. 1 (2009): 39–55.

31. Powell, *Deleuze and Horror Film*, 8; Williams, "Film Bodies," 2; Clover, *Men, Women, and Chain Saws*, 20. That attention to the specific iconography on screen returns not only to the felt experience of the body, but to the felt experience of the critic's body, is a broader shortcoming in theories of affectivity that rely on a

phenomenological theory of embodiment, about which I have written elsewhere. See Brinkema, *Forms of the Affects*, 26–46.

Of the confessional tendency, most notably there is this: "I first started paying attention to horror movies when I was a teenager dating Karla Decker in the 1970s. Karla was a leggy cheerleader who was usually distant and physically unapproachable [. . .]. In the darkened theater of a gripping horror film, however, Karla became uncharacteristically animated: She required me [EB: !] to hold her clammy, manicured hand, put my arm around her trembling shoulders, and supply a brave chest to shield her exquisitely beautiful face from the terrifying action occurring on the screen in front of us." Indeed. Tony Magistrale, *Abject Terrors: Surveying the Modern and Postmodern Horror Film* (New York: Peter Lang, 2005), xvii.

32. As Stanley Solomon pronounced in 1976, "It seems to be incontrovertible that the horror genre in the American cinema has been primarily exploitative, artless, frequently without taste or restraint or sense, and generally unworthy of serious attention." Stanley Solomon, *Beyond Formula: American Film Genres* (New York: Harcourt Brace Jovanovich, 1976), 112.

33. Magistrale, *Abject Terrors*, xvii.

34. Eduard Hanslick, *On the Musically Beautiful: A Contribution towards the Revision of the Aesthetics of Music*, trans. Geoffrey Payzant (Indianapolis, IN: Hackett Publishing, 1986), 6.

35. Immanuel Kant, *Critique of the Power of Judgment*, 2nd ed., ed. Paul Guyer, trans. Paul Guyer and Eric Matthews (Cambridge: Cambridge University Press, 2000), 190. Sigmund Freud, "The 'Uncanny,'" in *Writings on Art and Literature*, ed. Werner Hamacher and David E. Wellbery, foreword by Neil Hertz (Stanford, CA: Stanford University Press, 1997), 194.

36. David Hume, "Of Tragedy," in *Eight Great Tragedies*, ed. Sylvan Barnet, Morton Berman, William Burto (New York: Meridian, 1996), 433. The 1757 essay was first published as the third dissertation in Hume's *Four Dissertations*, of which the fourth was his companion work on aesthetics, "Of the Standard of Taste."

37. Burke, *Philosophical Enquiry into the Origin of Our Ideas of the Sublime and Beautiful*, 221.

38. Twitchell, *Dreadful Pleasures*, 9; Stephen King, *Danse Macabre* (New York: Gallery Books, 1981), 28. The general form of this question is impossible to shed; one begins to paranoiacally glimpse it everywhere. Kristen Wright's recent version of the paradox wonders almost identically, "How can something that we desire suddenly become disgusting? And how can something that is monstrous elicit both of these opposing emotions?" Kristen Wright, *Disgust and Desire: The Paradox of the Monster* (Leiden: Brill Rodopi, 2018), vii.

39. Carroll, *Philosophy of Horror*, 158. This question is given multiple variations throughout his text: "Why are horror audiences attracted by what, typically (in everyday life), should (and would) repel them?" and "How can horror audiences find pleasure in what by nature is distressful and unpleasant?" Carroll, *Philosophy of Horror*, 159.

40. Aikin, "On the Pleasure Derived from Objects of Terror," in *Gothic Readings: The First Wave, 1764–1840*, ed. Rictor Norton (London: Leicester University Press, 2000), 282–83.

41. Aikin, "On the Pleasure Derived from Objects of Terror," 283.

42. Carroll's theory of art-horror requires a monster—it conceptually fails without it—precisely because that figure is the nonarbitrary site of revulsion and fear that simultaneously constitutes a riveting attraction and curiosity, enhanced and sustained through narrative structures related to disclosure. He thereby resolves his paradoxical presumptions in favor of a fascination at the very category admixtures that constitute the provocative object of fear and loathing. The very broad promise, then, of a philosophy of (all) art-horror is achieved at the expense of conceptual reach: the theory requires a scientifically uncountenanced monster (Carroll does not admit *Psycho* as a horror film) in a carefully structured narrative form (he does not admit non-narrative elements), in which emotions are the "rivet" bonding viewer to objects on screen, keeping them cognitively engaged in this process of satisfying curiosity. Those three reductions negatively supply the capacity to make a positive claim for the resolution of the aesthetic paradox.

Julian Hanich, in a rejoinder to Carroll's privileging of the cognitive over the sensory, remains also with the formula so durable since Hume, titling his 2012 book *Cinematic Emotion in Horror Films and Thrillers: The Aesthetic Paradox of Pleasurable Fear*. Hanich's phenomenology of horror attends to the lived experience of "the emotionalized body, the cinematic surroundings, the threatening film, the captivated co-viewers." Decrying the emphasis on representation and "interpretive methods" that have ignored the experiential dimension of fear, Hanich, like Twitchell, explicitly opposes his project to formal readings. "Focusing on experience implies that we stop treating films like de-contextualized 'texts,'" Hanich posits, "but take them as events that take place in special environments. We should refrain from looking at frightening films as autonomous aesthetic products, but situate the embodied viewer within the spatial and social surroundings of a specific site of exhibition." And to his word, if not his credit, Hanich does describe nuances of experience without considering texts as aesthetic objects. This is particularly apparent in his language of aim-achievement when he turns to alliterative phenomenologies of variations of fear ("frightening fascination," "startling scares," "apprehensive agitation"). In perceptual reference to matters of "increase of loudness" and "deliberate distraction," and "filmic strategies of suggested horror," the formal is subsumed into the felt, textual aesthetics rendered mere strategy, which is to say: a plan aiming at achieving *something else*. Hanich does away with catharsis theories, resolving his version of the paradox in favor of a pleasurable "subjective *intensity* including remarkable metamorphoses of the lived body and the foregrounding of time as well as valuable instances of *collectivity*" (emphasis in original). This model is not only invested in the bristle; it is one whose paradox-resolution is coextensive with (it happens, as it were, on the back of) an agitated neck: the rippling of erectable hairs is the source of the calming of paradoxical turmoil, a bodily tautology given meaning from functionalized aesthetic strategies.

Julian Hanich, *Cinematic Emotion in Horror Films and Thrillers: The Aesthetic Paradox of Pleasurable Fear* (New York: Routledge, 2010), 15, 16–17, 24.

43. Alex Neill, "On a Paradox of the Heart," *Philosophical Studies: An International Journal for Philosophy in the Analytic Tradition* 65, nos. 1/2 (1992): 53–65; Berys Gaut, "The Paradox of Horror," *British Journal of Aesthetics* 33, no. 4 (1993): 333–45; Katerina Bantinaki, "The Paradox of Horror: Fear as a Positive Emotion." *The Journal of Aesthetics and Art Criticism* 70, no. 4 (2012): 383–92.

44. Andrew Tudor, "Why Horror? The Peculiar Pleasures of a Popular Genre," *Cultural Studies* 11, no. 3 (1997): 461 (emphasis in original).

45. Angela Ndalianis, *The Horror Sensorium: Media and the Senses* (Jefferson, NC: McFarland, 2012), 16.

46. Ndalianis, *Horror Sensorium*, 17.

47. Ndalianis, *Horror Sensorium*, 32.

48. Ndalianis, *Horror Sensorium*, 34.

49. Martin Heidegger, *Being and Time*, trans. John Macquarrie and Edward Robinson (New York: HarperCollins, 1962), sect. 307, 355. All references to *Being and Time* cite the section and page number in the Macquarrie and Robinson translation.

50. Althusser, *Reading Capital*, 17.

51. Jacques Derrida, *The Problem of Genesis in Husserl's Philosophy*, trans. Marian Hobson (Chicago: University of Chicago Press, 2003), 164.

52. Edmund Husserl, *The Crisis of European Sciences and Transcendental Phenomenology*, trans. D. Carr (Evanston, IL: Northwestern University Press, 1970), 58.

53. Jean-Claude Lebensztejn and John Johnston, "Star," *October* 1 (spring 1976): 88.

54. Andrew Tudor, *Theories of Film* (New York: Viking, 1973), 138, 139.

55. Jacques Derrida, "The Law of Genre," *Critical Inquiry* 7, no. 1 (1980): 65.

56. Derrida, *Problem of Genesis in Husserl's Philosophy*, 166.

57. Jacques Derrida, "The Deaths of Roland Barthes," in *The Work of Mourning*, ed. Pascale-Anne Brault and Michael Naas (Chicago: University of Chicago Press, 2001), 45.

58. Aristotle, *Metaphysica* (Metaphysics), trans. W. D. Ross, in *The Basic Works of Aristotle*, ed. Richard McKeon (New York: Random House, 1941), 745–46.

CHAPTER TWO. THE ORDINAL (DEATH BY DESIGN)

1. André Gide, *The Counterfeiters*, trans. Dorothy Bussy (New York: Vintage Books, 1973), 287; translation slightly modified.

2. Roland Barthes, "On Gide and His Journal," in *A Barthes Reader*, ed. Susan Sontag (New York: Hill and Wang, 1982), 4.

3. Roland Barthes, "Reading Brillat-Savarin," in *The Rustle of Language*, trans. Richard Howard (Berkeley: University of California Press, 1986), 250.

4. The interested reader should see Caetlin Benson-Allott, "Old Tropes in New Dimensions: Stereoscopy and Franchise Spectatorship," in "Genealogical and Ar-

chaeological Approaches to 3-D," special double issue, *Film Criticism* 37/38, no. 3/1 (spring/fall 2013): 12–29.

5. Reynold Humphries, *The American Horror Film: An Introduction* (Edinburgh: Edinburgh University Press, 2002), 191.

6. Jacques Derrida, *The Gift of Death*, trans. David Wills (Chicago: University of Chicago Press, 1995), 12.

7. Carol J. White, *Time and Death: Heidegger's Analysis of Finitude*, ed. Mark Railowski (New York: Routledge, 2016), li.

8. Martin Heidegger, ". . . Poetically Man Dwells . . . ," in *Poetry, Language, Thought*, trans. Albert Hofstadter (New York: Harper and Row, 1971), 209–27, 216.

9. Kim Newman, *Nightmare Movies: Horror on Screen since the 1960s* (London: Bloomsbury, 2011), 394.

10. Martin Heidegger, *Being and Time*, trans. John Macquarrie and Edward Robinson (New York: HarperCollins, 1962), sect. 251, 294.

11. Emmanuel Levinas, "Ethics as First Philosophy," in *Is It Righteous to Be? Interviews with Emmanuel Levinas*, ed. Jill Robbins (Stanford, CA: Stanford University Press, 2001), 126.

12. Heidegger, *Being and Time*, sect. 250, 294.

13. The entry continues: "No psychological traumas turning a child into a psychopath, no witchcraft, no vengeful spirits. In the high-concept world of *Final Destination* the cause of death is Death, and not even a scythe-wielding skeletal figure, just Death itself." Colin Odell and Michelle Le Blanc, *Horror Films* (Harpenden, UK: Oldcastle Books, 2007).

14. Aristotle, *Prior Analytics*, in *The Complete Works of Aristotle*, vol. 1, revised Oxford translation, ed. Jonathan Barnes (Princeton, NJ: Princeton University Press, 1984), sect. 14, 100.

15. Adams Sherman Hill, *The Principles of Rhetoric* (New York: Harper and Row, 1895), 330.

16. Wheeler Winston Dixon, *A History of Horror* (New Brunswick, NJ: Rutgers University Press, 2010), 201.

17. See, for example, Kevin J. Wetmore, *Post-9/11 Horror in American Cinema* (London: Continuum, 2012), 93: "Death then uses Rube Goldberg devices to bring about horrible painful death to those marked to die"; and Stephen King, "What's Scary: A Forenote to the 2010 Edition," in *Danse Macabre* (New York: Gallery Books, 1981), xxviii: "*Final Destination*: I love all these movies, with their elaborate Rube Goldberg setups—it's like watching R-Rated splatter versions of those old Road Runner cartoons—but only the first is genuinely scary, with its grim insistence that you can't beat the Reaper; when your time is up, it's up."

18. Fabian Neuhaus, "urbanMachine," in *Studies in Temporal Urbanism: The UrbanTick Experiment*, ed. Fabian Neuhaus (London: Springer, 2011), 19.

19. Gilles Deleuze, *Cinema 1: The Movement-Image*, trans. Hugh Tomlinson and Barbara Habberjam (Minneapolis: University of Minnesota Press, 1986), 95–96 (emphasis in original).

20. Friedrich Nietzsche, *The Gay Science*, trans. Walter Kaufmann (New York: Vintage Books, 1974), 168.

21. Raymond Williams, "Formalist," in *Keywords* (Oxford: Oxford University Press, 2015), 94.

22. Heidegger, *Being and Time*, sect. 240, 284.

23. Heidegger, *Being and Time*, sect. 250, 294.

24. Heidegger, *Being and Time*, sect. 243, 287.

25. Heidegger, *Being and Time*, sect. 262, 306 (emphasis in original).

26. Heidegger, *Being and Time*, sect. 262, 306–7 (emphasis in original).

27. Christopher Alexander, *Notes on the Synthesis of Form* (Cambridge, MA: Harvard University Press, 1964), 87.

28. "Or le temps est un ordre et n'est rien autre chose. Et *tout ordre est un temps*. L'ordre des ambivalences dans l'instant est donc un temps." Gaston Bachelard, *L'intuition de l'instant* (Paris: Le Livre de Poche, 1992), 105.

29. Edward Tufte, *The Visual Display of Quantitative Information* (Cheshire, CT: Graphics Press, 2001), 191.

30. Heidegger, *Being and Time*, sect. 240, 284.

31. Heidegger, *Being and Time*, sect. 240, 284 (emphasis in original). (This formulation is the target of Levinas's objection, calling out Heidegger's privileging of "his own death" above all.)

Dennis Keenan words this irreplaceability as a question of property: "The death that cannot be taken away (*abnehmen*) must be taken upon oneself (*auf sich nehmen*). I must appropriate death, I must assume this possibility of impossibility, if I am to have access to what is irreplaceably mine." Dennis King Keenan, *The Question of Sacrifice* (Bloomington: Indiana University Press, 2005), 140.

32. Derrida, *Gift of Death*, 43 (emphasis in original). To follow this logic, responsibility is what "relates me to what no one else can do in my place. [. . .] [I]t remains for everyone to take his own death *upon himself*. [. . .] Thus dying can never be taken, borrowed, transferred, delivered, promised, or transmitted. And just as it can't be given to me, so it can't be taken away from me" (44). Thus does an entire ethics of giving and taking become possible on the basis of death in Derrida.

33. Werner Hamacher, "Premises," in *Premises: Essays on Philosophy and Literature from Kant to Celan*, trans. Peter Fenves (Stanford, CA: Stanford University Press, 1996), 32 (emphasis in original).

34. Roland Barthes, "The Photographic Message," in *Image/Music/Text*, trans. Stephen Heath (New York: Hill and Wang, 1977), 16.

35. Paul Ricoeur, *Freud and Philosophy: An Essay on Interpretation*, trans. Dennis Savage (New Haven, CT: Yale University Press, 1970), 33.

36. Samuel Beckett, "Three Dialogues with Georges Duthuit," in *Proust and the Three Dialogues with Georges Duthuit* (London: Calder, 1987), 103.

37. The post-hermeneutical turn has appeared under the rubric of "reparative reading" (following Sedgwick), Heather Love's "close but not deep" sociological observation, "surface reading" (following a 2009 issue of *Representations* with an

influential introduction by Sharon Marcus and Stephen Best); is sometimes dubbed "the new modesty" in literary criticism or "the descriptive turn"; and has affinities with digital-humanistic strains of mapping, distant reading, antiformalist versions of affect theory, many modes of reception history and reader response criticism, and earlier polemics like Susan Sontag's "Against Interpretation." The members of this large tent, which admittedly contains local points of friction, share an impatience with depth, a presumption that texts disclose themselves on and at the surface with a neutral good faith (hence calls for critics to be "faithful" in return). However, in response to all these cries to dethrone Marxist, psychoanalytic, and deconstructive methodologies, many critics have pointed out that, as Elizabeth Weed words it, "these 'new' ways of reading rely on rather familiar indictments of the practice of critique," and in fact there is a robust history of "poststructuralist challenges to the very project of hermeneutical interpretation." Elizabeth Weed, "The Way We Read Now," *History of the Present* 2, no. 1 (2012): 95–106.

See Stephen Best and Sharon Marcus, "Surface Reading: An Introduction," in "The Way We Read Now," ed. Stephen Best and Sharon Marcus, with Emily Apter and Elaine Freedgood, special issue, *Representations* 108 (fall 2009): 1–21; Rita Felski, "After Suspicion," *Profession* (2009): 28–35; Heather Love, "Close but Not Deep: Literary Ethics and the Descriptive Turn," *New Literary History* 41, no. 2 (spring 2010): 371–91; and Sharon Marcus, Heather Love, and Stephen Best, eds., "Description across Disciplines," special issue, *Representations* 135, no. 1 (summer 2016), in particular Sharon Marcus, Heather Love, and Stephen Best, "Building a Better Description" (1–21), and Cannon Schmitt, "Interpret or Describe?" (102–18).

Best and Marcus's initial polemic has received a sizeable response. The sharpest articulations in opposition can be found in Ellen Rooney, "Live Free or Describe: The Reading Effect and the Persistence of Form," *differences* 21, no. 3 (2010): 112–39; and Garrett Stewart, *The Deed of Reading: Literature * Writing * Language * Philosophy* (Ithaca, NY: Cornell University Press, 2015). Most problematically from my perspective is Best and Marcus's alignment of formalism with their call for "just reading"—an account that relies on a pretheoretical and highly positivist notion of form, one that I would contend loses its capacity for speculation—and here I direct the interested reader to Rooney's fine critique of the difference between description and a robust reading for form.

Sedgwick's reparative reading is an oblique inspiration for this recent descriptive turn. It shares a rejection of a certain interpretive stance—infinite skepticism of surface expressions—which it aligns with paranoia. But in advocating for a reparative reading, Sedgwick sets in place a program that more closely resembles affect theory of the 1990s and 2000s in work like Steven Shaviro, *The Cinematic Body* (Minneapolis: University of Minnesota Press, 1993). See Eve Sedgwick, "Paranoid Reading and Reparative Reading, Or, You're So Paranoid, You Probably Think This Essay Is about You," introduction to *Novel Gazing: Queer Readings in Fiction*, ed. Eve Sedgwick (Durham, NC: Duke University Press, 1997), 1–37. For a critique of affect theory's resistance to closely reading texts, see "Ten Points to Begin," "A Tear That

Does Not Drop, but Folds," and "Film Theory's Absent Center" in Eugenie Brinkema, *The Forms of the Affects* (Durham, NC: Duke University Press, 2014). For a critique of surface reading and a polemic for the value of radical formalism in relation to pornography, see Eugenie Brinkema, "Form for the Blind (Porn and Description without Guarantee)," in "Porn on the Couch: Sex, Psychoanalysis, and Screen Cultures/ Memories," ed. Ricky Varghese, special issue, *Porn Studies* 6, no. 1 (2019): 10–22; and Eugenie Brinkema, "Irrumation, the Interrogative: Extreme Porn and the Crisis of Reading," in "Pleasure and Suspicion," ed. John Paul Stadler and Rachel Greenspan, special issue, *Polygraph* 26 (2017): 130–64.

38. Sedgwick, "Paranoid Reading and Reparative Reading," 17.

39. Kenneth Paradis, *Sex, Paranoia, and Modern Masculinity* (Albany: State University of New York Press, 2007), 24 (emphasis in original).

40. D. A. Miller, *The Novel and the Police* (Berkeley: University of California Press, 1988), 164.

41. Heidegger, *Being and Time*, sect. 251, 294.

42. Heidegger, *Being and Time*, sect. 262, 307.

INTERLUDE I. ABECEDARIUM

1. *ABCs of Death 2* (2014) follows the same twenty-six-letter chapter structure, whereas *ABCs of Death 2.5* (2016) is composed of films entirely for the letter *M*, chosen from the shorts that failed to be selected for the previous film, reasserting, however, the supremacy of alphabetic ordinality by being structured on the alphabetic measure of the final word for each title, running *M Is for Magnetic Tape* through *M Is for Mutant*.

2. Jacques Derrida, "Différance," in *Margins of Philosophy*, trans. Alan Bass (Chicago: University of Chicago Press, 1982), 3.

3. Brian Rotman, *Becoming Beside Ourselves: The Alphabet, Ghosts, and Distributed Human Being* (Durham, NC: Duke University Press, 2008), 93–94.

4. See chapter 9 in Eugenie Brinkema, *The Forms of the Affects* (Durham, NC: Duke University Press, 2014), for a reading of the abecedarium, Nietzschean recurrence, and joy in relation to Hollis Frampton's *Zorns Lemma*.

5. This destabilization of moral certitude has the formal consequence of shaking the stability of the abecedarium as a structure; for example, X takes no word in Belloc, only the admonition, "No reasonable little Child expects / A Grown-up Man to make a rhyme on X." (X is always something of a disaster for the abecedarium, requiring violence or a bit of whimsy.)

6. Inger Christensen, *alphabet* [1981], trans. Susanna Nied (New York: New Directions, 2001), 11.

7. Edward Gorey, *The Gashlycrumb Tinies, or, After the Outing* (New York: Simon and Schuster, 1963).

8. The children are not preyed on by death so much as they are vulnerable *to* the alphabet. As Eden Lee Lackner words it, "the *Gashlycrumb* children do not just die in

novel ways, but also do so in service to a poetic abecedarium, a traditional method for teaching the alphabet to young children. Gorey uses the format to subvert a safe childhood space, removing child-friendly verses and illustrations in favor of the specter of death, the most frightening monster of all. As both a concept and a narrative figure, death lurks around the edges, an end to each child's story."

Eden Lee Lackner, "A Monstrous Childhood: Edward Gorey's Influence on Tim Burton's *The Melancholy Death of Oyster Boy*," in *The Works of Tim Burton: Margins to Mainstream*, ed. Jeffrey Andrew Weinstock (New York: Palgrave, 2013), 153.

9. Michel Foucault, *The Order of Things: An Archaeology of the Human Sciences* (New York: Vintage, 1970), xvi.

10. Foucault, *Order of Things*, xvi.

11. Michel Foucault, *Les mots et les choses: une archéologie des sciences humaines* (Paris: Gallimard, 1966), 9.

12. Foucault, *Order of Things*, xvii–xviii.

13. Foucault, *Order of Things*, xvi.

14. Roland Barthes, *Roland Barthes by Roland Barthes*, trans. Richard Howard (New York: Hill and Wang, 1977), 147.

15. Barthes, *Roland Barthes by Roland Barthes*, 147.

16. Virginia Woolf, *To the Lighthouse*, ed. and intro. Margaret Drabble (Oxford: Oxford University Press, 1992), 47–48.

17. Barthes, *Roland Barthes by Roland Barthes*, 148.

18. Barthes, *Roland Barthes by Roland Barthes*, 148.

19. Roland Barthes, *The Responsibility of Forms*, trans. Richard Howard (Berkeley: University of California Press, 1985), 118 (emphasis in original).

20. Martin Heidegger, *Being and Time*, trans. John Macquarrie and Edward Robinson (New York: HarperCollins, 1962), sect. 240, 284; Jacques Derrida, *The Gift of Death*, trans. David Wills (Chicago: University of Chicago Press, 1995), 43.

21. Plato, *Phaedo*, in *The Collected Dialogues of Plato, Including the Letters*, ed. Edith Hamilton and Huntington Cairns (Princeton, NJ: Princeton University Press, 1989), 46 (63e–64a).

22. Plato, *Phaedo*, 46 (64a).

23. "Deleuze was apprised of this alphabetical schema and the specific themes beforehand, and while his responses seem quite spontaneous, comparison with his different texts reveals that throughout their exchanges, he frequently drew from a broad range of his own writings, either already published or in preparation. The sole condition Deleuze set for his participation in this project was that the film be made available posthumously. In 1994, however, Deleuze agreed to the transmission of *L'Abécédaire* on the European Arté channel (from late 1994 into 1995), since his physical condition had so deteriorated that he is reported to have said, 'C'est comme si j'étais déjà parti' ('it is as if I were already gone')." Charles J. Stivale, *Gilles Deleuze's ABCs: The Folds of Friendship* (Baltimore: Johns Hopkins University Press, 2008), ix.

The same phrase—"It is as if I were already gone"—appears in a statement Pierre-André Boutang gave to Olivier Le Naire in *L'Express* (and presumably is the source for Stivale's citation): "Normalement, les téléspectateurs n'auraient dû découvrir *L'Abécédaire* qu'après la mort de Gilles. L'an dernier, il a finalement accepté de lever cette condition en me disant: 'Vu mon état, c'est un peu comme si j'étais déjà parti.'" (Normally, the viewers would have discovered *The Abécédaire* only after Gilles's death. But last year, he finally agreed to waive this condition, saying, "Given my state, it's a bit like I'm already gone.") Pierre-André Boutang, "Socrate à la télé," *L'Express*, November 11, 1995, 58.

24. Samuel Beckett, "Malone Dies," in *The Selected Works of Samuel Beckett*, vol. II: *Molloy, Malone Dies, The Unnamable, How It Is* (New York: Grove Press, 2010), 276.

25. Samuel Beckett, "Dante and the Lobster," in *The Selected Works of Samuel Beckett*, vol. IV: *Poems, Short Fiction, Criticism* (New York: Grove Press, 2010), 88.

INTERLUDE II. RHYTHM & FEEL

1. Michel de Montaigne, "On Cruelty," in *The Complete Essays*, ed. and trans. M. A. Screech (New York: Penguin, 2003), 482, 483.

2. Roland Barthes, *Roland Barthes by Roland Barthes*, trans. Richard Howard (New York: Hill and Wang, 1977), 67.

3. Roland Barthes, "Reading Brillat-Savarin," in *The Rustle of Language*, trans. Richard Howard (Berkeley: University of California Press, 1986), 250. Originally published as the preface to Jean Anthelme Brillat-Savarin, *Physiologie du goût*, trans. C. Hermann (Paris: C. Hermann, 1975).

4. Jean-Luc Nancy, "Image and Violence," in *The Ground of the Image*, trans. Jeff Fort (New York: Fordham University Press, 2005), 15; originally published as "Image et violence," *Le Portique* 6 (2000). Jean-Luc Nancy, "The Forgetting of Philosophy," in *The Gravity of Thought*, trans. François Raffoul and Gregory Recco (Atlantic Highlands, NJ: Humanities Press, 1997), 59.

5. Nancy, "Image and Violence," 16.

6. Nancy, "Image and Violence," 16, 17.

7. Indeed, one distinction between the term *feeling* and related concepts like emotion, sentiment, sensation is precisely in its debt to the Saxon *felan* and not related Latin etymologies, such that, among other difficulties, "the untranslatability of 'feeling' in French reveals the peculiarities of a philosophy of affectivity or, at the least, a way of philosophizing, in English." For a robust articulation of the differences between feeling and emotion or feeling and sentiment, see the entry "Feeling / Passion / Emotion / Sentiment / Sensation / Affection / Sense" in Barbara Cassin, ed., *Dictionary of Untranslatables: A Philosophical Lexicon* (Princeton, NJ: Princeton University Press, 2014), 339–41.

8. de Montaigne, "On Cruelty," 484.

9. de Montaigne, "On Cruelty," 483.

10. At least two competing interlocutors (and thus analytic frameworks) are available for interpreting *À l'intérieur* on other grounds: one cinematic and inter-

textual, and one philosophical. On the one hand, the film pays repeated homage to Hitchcock's *Rear Window*: there is a foundational car accident; the physical restrictiveness of Jeffries's broken leg is permuted into the slow and difficult movements of pregnancy (a kind of auto-enfolding cast); the limited setting of Jeffries's apartment becomes the claustrophobia of a Parisian home; the protagonist is a photographer who, under threat of violence, uses her flash bulb to blind, document, but also paradoxically reveal herself to the intruder; and so forth. The philosophical interlocutor is any number of thought experiments testing the ethical permissibility of abortion, the most famous of which is Judith Jarvis Thomson's 1971 case of the violinist in "A Defense of Abortion": a second-person figure wakes to find themselves in a hospital providing life support to a famous musician ("You wake up in the morning and find yourself back to back in bed with an unconscious violinist," she writes, in a conceit interestingly reminiscent of the opening of *Saw*); you didn't give your consent to be in this situation but if you leave the musician will die. If you stay for nine months, he will be cured; the hypothetical "you" is unlikely to suffer harm, and no one else can take your place. Do you have an obligation to "stay connected"? We'll set aside the content of this competing rights experiment—Thomson's conclusion, incidentally, is that abortion deprives the fetus of the maternal body, to which it has no right or claim (in other words, go ahead and unplug the violinist)—and instead note that this intertextual ethic of umbilical bond is literalized, exteriorized, and formalized in *À l'intérieur* in multiple modalities.

11. Aristotle, "*De Poetica* (Poetics)," trans. Ingram Bywater, *The Basic Works of Aristotle*, ed. Richard McKeon (New York: Random House, 1941), 1467–68 (emphasis added).

12. Aristotle, "*De Poetica* (Poetics)," 1468.

13. Nancy, "Image and Violence," 16.

14. Étienne Balibar, "Uprisings in the *Banlieues*," *Constellations* 14, no. 1 (2007): 48.

15. Balibar, "Uprisings in the *Banlieues*," 51 (emphasis in original).

16. Michel Foucault, *Madness and Civilization*, trans. Richard Howard (New York: Vintage, 1965), 11.

17. Byung-Chul Han, *Topology of Violence*, trans. Amanda DeMarco (Cambridge, MA: MIT Press, 2018), 65 (emphasis in original).

LAPSUS

1. s.v. "Lapse," *OED Online: OED Historical Thesaurus*, based on *Oxford English Dictionary*, 2nd ed., 20 vols. (Oxford: Oxford University Press, 1989).

2. Jacques Derrida, "My Chances / *Mes chances*: Rendezvous with Some Epicurean Stereophonies" (1982), in *Psyche: Inventions of the Other, Volume 1*, ed. Peggy Kamuf and Elizabeth Rottenberg, trans. Irene Harvey and Avital Ronell (Stanford, CA: Stanford University Press, 2007), 344–76.

1. Jorge Luis Borges, "The Fearful Sphere of Pascal," in *Labyrinths*, ed. Donald A. Yates (New York: New Directions, 1964), 189–92.

2. G. W. F. Hegel, *Elements of the Philosophy of Right*, ed. Allen W. Wood, trans. H. B. Nisbet, Cambridge Texts in the History of Political Thought (Cambridge: Cambridge University Press, 1991), 26; Friedrich Nietzsche, *Thus Spoke Zarathustra*, in *The Portable Nietzsche*, trans. Walter Kaufmann (New York: Viking Press, 1954), 328.

3. Franz Kafka, "The Cares of a Family Man," in *The Complete Stories*, ed. Nahum N. Glatzer (New York: Schocken Books, 1971), 428, 429.

4. Ian Bogost, *Alien Phenomenology, or What It's Like to Be a Thing* (Minneapolis: University of Minnesota Press, 2012), 9.

5. Graham Harman, *The Quadruple Object* (Winchester, UK: Zero Books, 2011), 6.

6. Eileen Joy, qtd. in Jeffrey Jerome Cohen, *Stone: An Ecology of the Inhuman* (Minneapolis: University of Minnesota Press, 2015), 281n73. Originally published as a comment on Alex Reid, "The Object Industry," *Digital Digs: An Archeology of the Future* (blog), May 29, 2012.

7. Robert Smithson, "Entropy and the New Monuments," in *Robert Smithson: The Collected Writings*, ed. Jack Flam (Berkeley: University of California Press, 1966), 14.

8. Maurice Blanchot, *The Gaze of Orpheus*, trans. Lydia Davis (New York: Station Hill Press, 1981), 81.

9. Quentin Dupieux, qtd. in Todd Gilchrist, "*Rubber* Director Quentin Dupieux on Why He Made a Movie About a Killer Tire," *Wall Street Journal*, Speakeasy (blog), November 12, 2010, https://blogs.wsj.com/speakeasy/2010/11/12/rubber-director-quentin-dupieux-on-why-he-made-a-movie-about-a-killer-tire/.

10. Martin Heidegger, *The Metaphysical Foundations of Logic*, trans. Michael Heim (Bloomington: Indiana University Press, 1984), sect. 266–67, 206.

11. Roland Barthes, *Writing Degree Zero*, trans. Annette Lavers and Colin Smith (New York: Hill and Wang, 1967), 48.

12. Blanchot, *The Gaze of Orpheus*, 4.

13. Carl Andre, *Cuts: Texts 1959–2004*, ed. James Meyer (Cambridge, MA: MIT Press, 2005), 84.

14. Slavoj Žižek, "The Hitchcockian Blot," in *Looking Awry: An Introduction to Jacques Lacan through Popular Culture* (Cambridge, MA: MIT Press, 1992), 105.

15. Žižek, *Looking Awry*, 106.

16. Martin Heidegger, *What Is Called Thinking?*, trans. F. D. Wieck and J. G. Gray (New York: Harper and Row, 1968), 52–53.

17. Maurice Blanchot, *The Unavowable Community*, trans. Pierre Joris (Barrytown, NY: Station Hill, 1988), 15.

1. Because of the prominence of the figure of sacrifice, some of the most interesting readings of the film have been in relation to René Girard's theory of violence; see, e.g., Peter Paik, "Apocalypse of the Therapeutic: *The Cabin in the Woods* and the Death of Mimetic Desire," in *Mimesis, Movies, and Media: Violence, Desire, and the Sacred*, Volume 3, ed. Scott Cowdell, Chris Fleming, and Joel Hodge (London: Bloomsbury, 2015), 105–16.

2. One of the few readings of *Cabin in the Woods* to attend to this opening dialogue about the potential future child is Deanna Day, "Toward a Zombie Epistemology: What it Means to Live and Die in *Cabin in the Woods*," *Ada: A Journal of Gender, New Media, and Technology*, no. 3 (2013), doi:10.7264/N3MG7MDV. Day, however, problematically converts fertility into a sign of reproductive futurism via antisocial queer theory, and more problematically embraces (as does that discourse in various ways) the productive promise of failure, concluding of Marty and Dana's bringing about of the end of the human race, "Why attempt to preserve a mode of being that they know to be built with the blood of their friends? [. . .] Why continue to pretend that there is any desirable future in that cyborg vision?" In other words, the (critical) desire for a devastation of normative futurities is collapsed into approving polemics for a devastation of futurities in toto. Strategically refusing to accommodate discourses of futurity and a fantasy of the idea of the Child—a political technique that turns on resistance to a horizonal principle, as in Lee Edelman's *No Future*, one of Day's primary interlocutory texts—is a very different thing than this kind of broader call. Among the other things it does, then, the horror film gives explicit and graphic and protracted body to the charge of exploring that "what might happen" that Day and the critical line with which she engages promises. That "what might happen" includes extraordinary scenes of violence, and if critical positions are going to advocate for an affirmation of accelerated destruction, endingness, and a gleeful failure to preserve modes of being, then horror is the aesthetic site that insists that raw brutalizations are part of what those stances must own.

3. Søren Kierkegaard, *Fear and Trembling / Repetition*, ed. and trans. Howard V. Hong and Edna H. Hong (Princeton, NJ: Princeton University Press, 1983), 54–56, 62.

4. If resonant with postmodern horror in its relation to intertextual allusion and generic citation, *Cabin in the Woods* is more correctly a case of postmodern premodern horror; it does not move past the model of the genre as requiring a monster, and it locates that monstrosity in a straightforwardly metaphysical (and overtly Lovecraftian) world of ancient evil.

5. Steven Shaviro, *No Speed Limit: Three Essays on Accelerationism* (Minneapolis: University of Minnesota Press, 2015), 2.

6. Roger Zelazny, *Lord of Light* (New York: Eos/HarperCollins, 1967, 2004), 186.

7. Alex Williams and Nick Srnicek, "#Accelerate: Manifesto for an Accelerationist

Politics," in *#Accelerate: The Accelerationist Reader*, ed. Robin Mackay and Armen Avanessian (Falmouth, UK: Urbanomic Media in association with Merve, 2014), 362.

8. Nick Land, *The Thirst for Annihilation: Georges Bataille and Virulent Nihilism* (London: Routledge, 1992), 30.

9. Alain Badiou, "Beyond Formalization: An Interview with Alain Badiou, Conducted by Peter Hallward and Bruno Bosteels (Paris, July 2, 2002)," in *Badiou and Politics*, ed. Bruno Bosteels (Durham, NC: Duke University Press, 2011), 319.

10. Badiou, "Beyond Formalization," 319.

11. Badiou, "Beyond Formalization," 319.

12. Cf. A very different usage of terms in a reading of the film as political allegory via the concept of an "ideological matrix": Derrick King, "The (Bio)political Economy of Bodies, Culture as Commodification, and the Badiouian Event: Reading Political Allegories in *The Cabin in the Woods*," in "Joss in June: Selected Essays," ed. K. Dale Koontz and Ensley F. Guffey, special double issue, *Slayage* 11.2/12.1, nos. 38–39 (summer 2014), https://www.whedonstudies.tv/volume-12.html. Likewise, see also Bodo Winter, "Horror Movies and the Cognitive Ecology of Primary Metaphors," *Metaphor and Symbol* 29 (2014): 151–70, which articulates the graphic axis along which *Cabin in the Woods* progresses and offers schematics and diagrams of vertical structures in several horror films. However, while using something of the language of form, both authors make problematic versions of the claim for taking structure or structures as a local metaphor or long-form allegory.

13. David E. Nye, *American Technological Sublime* (Cambridge, MA: MIT Press 1994), 285.

14. Eugénie Shinkle, "Videogames and the Digital Sublime," in *Digital Cultures and the Politics of Emotion: Feelings, Affect and Technological Change*, ed. Athina Karatzogianni and Adi Kuntsman (Hampshire, UK: Palgrave Macmillan, 2012), 103.

15. Shinkle, "Videogames and the Digital Sublime," 103.

16. Shinkle, "Videogames and the Digital Sublime," 103.

17. Shinkle, "Videogames and the Digital Sublime," 104.

18. "grid, n.," OED Online, March 2019, http://www.oed.com.proxy.uba.uva.nl:2048 /view/Entry/81372.

19. "grid, n."

20. The former is true of any grid; as Krauss words it, "logically speaking, the grid extends, in all directions, to infinity." Rosalind E. Krauss, "Grids," in *The Originality of the Avant-Garde and Other Modernist Myths* (Cambridge MA: MIT Press, 1986), 18.

21. Rosalind E. Krauss, "The Originality of the Avant-garde," in *The Originality of the Avant-Garde and Other Modernist Myths* (Cambridge MA: MIT Press, 1986), 158.

22. Mark Colyvan, *An Introduction to the Philosophy of Mathematics* (Cambridge: Cambridge University Press, 2012), 91–92.

ii Alain Badiou, *Logics of Worlds: Being and Event 2*, trans. Alberto Toscano (London: Continuum, 2009), 4.

iii Heraclitus, Fragment 53, *Heraclitus: The Cosmic Fragments*, ed. G. S. Kirk (Cambridge: Cambridge University Press, 1954), 245.

v James Blish, SF *Gateway Omnibus: Black Easter, The Day After Judgement, The Seedling Stars* (London: Gollancz, 2013), 52.

vi Sappho 105a, qtd. in Anne Carson, *Eros the Bittersweet* (Princeton, NJ: Princeton University Press, 1986), 26.

x Maurice Blanchot, *The Instant of My Death*, with *Demeure*, by Jacques Derrida, trans. Elizabeth Rottenberg (Stanford, CA: Stanford University Press, 2000), 9.

xii Anna Bonifazi, "Inquiring into Nostos and Its Cognates," *The American Journal of Philology* 130, no. 4 (winter 2009): 481; James Phillips, "Distance, Absence, and Nostalgia," *Descriptions*, ed. Don Ihde and Hugh J. Silverman (Albany: State University of New York Press, 1985), 65.

xiv Jorge Luis Borges, "On Exactitude in Science," in *Collected Fictions*, trans. Andrew Hurley (London: Penguin, 1999), 325.

xvi Immanuel Kant, *Critique of the Power of Judgment*, 2d ed., ed. Paul Guyer, trans. Paul Guyer and Eric Matthews (Cambridge: Cambridge University Press, 2000). All quotations are from First Section, Second Book: *Analytic of the Sublime*: 132 ("absolute, non comparative"); 139 ("shapeless mountain"); 144 ("volcanoes"); 144 ("boundless ocean"); 151 ("stretches imagination to its limit"); 141 ("pleasure to find every standard"); 150 ("pleases immediately"); 151–52 ("feeling of the deprivation"); 156 ("imagination finds nothing").

xviii Bernhard Siegert, "(Not) in Place: The Grid, or, Cultural Techniques of Ruling Spaces," in *Cultural Techniques: Grids, Filters, Doors, and Other Articulations of the Real*, trans. Geoffrey Winthrop-Young (New York: Fordham University Press, 2015), 97; Le Corbusier, *The City of To-Morrow and Its Planning*, trans. Frederick Etchells (London: Architectural Press, 1971), xxii, 220; Krauss, "Grids," 10.

xix Grégoire Chamayou, *A Theory of the Drone*, trans. Janet Lloyd (New York: New Press, 2015), footnote 8 (247–54), 248, 249.

xxii Thomas C. Hales, "The Honeycomb Conjecture," *Discrete and Computational Geometry* 25, no. 1 (2001): 1, 2.

xxiii Charles Darwin, *The Origin of Species*, in *From So Simple a Beginning: The Four Great Books of Charles Darwin*, ed. Edward O. Wilson, [441–760] (New York: W. W. Norton, 2006), 599.

xxiv "table, n.," OED *Online*, http://www.oed.com.proxy.uba.uva.nl:2048/view/Entry/196785; "matrix, n.," OED *Online*, http://www.oed.com.proxy.uba.uva.nl:2048/view/Entry/115057; "base, n.1," OED *Online*, http://www.oed.com.proxy.uba.uva.nl:2048/view/Entry/15848; Claude Lévi-Strauss, *The Savage Mind* (Chicago: University of Chicago Press, 1966), 16–17; Jacques Derrida, "Structure, Sign, and Play in the Discourse of the Human Sciences," in *Writing and Difference*, trans. Alan Bass (Chicago: University of Chicago Press, 1978), 285; Michel Foucault, "Nietzsche, Genealogy, History," in *Foucault: Aesthetics, Method, and Epistemology*, ed. James D. Faubion, trans. Robert Hurley et al. (New York: New Press, 1998), 371–72.

1. The curious reader would be well rewarded to consider the history of surgical illustration more broadly and, more narrowly, the role of the anal fistula as a representational mode within that history. Michael McVaugh argues that the Middle Ages saw a shift in surgical conceptions of space, moving from the "two-dimensional" anatomy of the thirteenth and fourteenth centuries, in which the body was viewed as "a collection of systems that are not merely functionally discrete but spatially unintegrated," to a fifteenth- and sixteenth-century "three-dimensional" anatomy that took notice of spatial relationships independent of systematic interaction. McVaugh glimpses the beginning of the later anatomy in Arderne and gives pride of place to the fistula's channels as the conceptual opening into the spaces of the body that changed understandings of interiority, anatomy, and spatial integration. See Michael McVaugh, "Fistulas, the Knee, and the 'Three-dimensional' Body," in *Medicine and Space: Body, Surroundings and Borders in Antiquity and the Middle Ages*, ed. Patricia A. Baker, Han Nijdam, Karine van't Land (Leiden: Brill, 2011), 21–36. Cited here is the Middle English translation of John Arderne, *Treatises of Fistula in Ano, Haemorrhoids, and Clysters*, ed. D'Arcy Power (London: Oxford University Press for the Early English Text Society, [1910] 1968), 47–49. On Arderne's use of illustrations, see Peter Murray Jones, "'Sicut hic depingitur . . .': John of Arderne and English Medical Illustration in the 14th and 15th Centuries," in *Die Kunst und das Studium der Natur vom 14. zum 16. Jahrhundert*, ed. Wolfram Prinz and Andreas Beyer (Weinheim: Acta Humaniora/VCH, 1987), 103–26.

2. Watching *The Human Centipede*, it becomes almost impossible to shake the sense that it is restaging one of Freud's most famous footnotes from *Civilization and Its Discontents*, the oft-cited one about humans and dogs in reference to a structure of upwardness versus downwardness as it relates to smell and taste, shame and disgust. There, Freud wonders why "man should use the name of his most faithful friend in the animal world—the dog—as a term of abuse." The answer is that the dog is "an animal whose dominant sense is that of smell and [yet] one which has no horror of excrement." The note speculates that once man raised himself up from the ground, this "assumption of an upright gait" made the genitals, once concealed, now visible and in need of protection, "and so provoked feelings of shame in him," and that the centrality of the intermittent olfactory stimuli will be taken over by the permanent possibilities of visual excitation in sexual response. Sigmund Freud, *Civilization and Its Discontents* (standard edition), ed. and trans. James Strachey (New York: W. W. Norton, 1961), 54–55n1.

As though telling Freud's story in reverse, the declension back down from an upright gait to the ground (through the ruination of knee extension) re-conceals the genitals, and the intermittency of digestive processes take over where visual processes have been supplanted. *The Human Centipede* figures the physical organization of the dog form that Freud describes—dog lowness, dog movement, dog smells—with the residual disgust and shame of the upright human, a figure that retains the horror of excrement, which is to say a figure that does not want to get too close to its own digestive teleology. And, in fact, Heiter feeds this thing on the ground, tries to train the creature he has made, and complains at night that it whimpers so loudly he cannot get adequate sleep.

3. In the language of conventional horror tropology, Lindsay, though the last figure, is not the Final Girl of the slasher narrative, for she merely *persists* in the end, as opposed to functioning as the locus of audience sympathy battling violence in order to *survive*. For all that *The Human Centipede* is complexly in dialogue with the history of horror—from its relation to the mad scientist motif, the sequel's overt mother-son citations to *Psycho*, its indebtedness to the intertwined histories of Bataille-citing surrealist horror and the extremity of postmodern body horror—a generic approach misses the more radical scene of violence: that of the generality of the diagram.

4. "The Craft of Nombrynge," ed. E. R. Sleight, in *The European Mathematical Awakening: A Journey through the History of Mathematics, 1000–1800*, ed. Frank J. Swetz (Mineola, NY: Dover Publications, [1994] 2013), 27; reprinted from E. R. Sleight, "The Craft of Nombrynge," *The Mathematics Teacher* 32 (1939): 243–48.

5. Aristotle, *Metaphysica* (Metaphysics), trans. W. D. Ross, in *The Basic Works of Aristotle*, ed. Richard McKeon (New York: Random House, 1941), 787 (1029); Aristotle, *De Anima* (On the Soul), trans. J. A. Smith, in *The Basic Works of Aristotle*, ed. Richard McKeon (New York: Random House, 1941), 595 (431b, 432a).

6. Louis Althusser and Étienne Balibar, *Reading Capital* (New York: Verso, 2009), 17.

7. T. S. Eliot, *The Rock: A Pageant Play* (New York: Harcourt, Brace, 1934), 76.

8. There is initially another A, an anonymous man Heiter already possesses when the two girls unwisely seek refuge in the house of this bad host. The impersonality of position is given its first iteration as Heiter quietly whispers to him, "My friend, you don't match. I have to kill you." Intravenously injecting the agent of elimination, he softly says, "Don't take it personally."

9. John Bender and Michael Marrinan, *The Culture of Diagram* (Stanford, CA: Stanford University Press, 2010), 7.

10. See "Diagrams" (193–268) and "Networks" (269–83) in Jacques Bertin, *Semiology of Graphics: Diagrams, Networks, Maps*, trans. William Berg (Madison: University of Wisconsin Press, 1983).

11. s.v. "diagram, n.," OED *Online*, http://www.oed.com.proxy.uba.uva.nl:2048/view/Entry/51854.

12. Michel Foucault, *Discipline and Punish*, trans. Alan Sheridan (New York: Vintage, 1977), 205.

13. Deleuze wrote a great deal on the diagram, though in a sense apart from how

I am deploying the figure; in particular, for Deleuze, the diagram does not exhibit structure but involves a nonstructuring map of the relations of forces. He does write of the form's abstractions—and on this we partially concur, that the diagrammatic machine does not represent something real but "constructs a real that is yet to come, a new type of reality." We share the bondedness of the diagram to the word *abstract*, and I would likewise resist the notion that the diagram *represents* something prior, but my critique hinges on the figure of representation in that case. In short, Deleuze's diagrams are generative (a reason they have been taken up so enthusiastically in architectural theory) and constructive in a manner that I find problematic to think with here, given their insistence on the nonformed, on the informal, and on continuums of intensities and affects—the Deleuzian diagram does not have a conceptual space to address the rigorously formed, that which works through the violence of structure as such. This is, perhaps, a broader problem of the role of formalism in Deleuze. The quotation above is from Gilles Deleuze and Félix Guattari, *A Thousand Plateaus: Capitalism and Schizophrenia*, trans. Brian Massumi (London: Continuum, 1987), 157. See also Gilles Deleuze, *Foucault*, trans. Seán Hand (Minneapolis: University of Minnesota Press, 1988), which is in many ways a book about the diagram; and Jakub Zdebik, *Deleuze and the Diagram: Aesthetic Threads in Visual Organization* (London: Continuum, 2012).

14. Bernard Tschumi, *The Manhattan Transcripts* (London: St. Martin's Press, 1981), 32.

15. Roland Barthes, "The Plates of the *Encyclopedia*," in *A Barthes Reader*, ed. Susan Sontag (New York: Hill and Wang, [1964] 1982), 230.

16. *Oeuvres Complètes* XVII, from the chapter on fibers in Diderot's *Elements de physiologie*; quoted in Andrew H. Clark, *Diderot's Part: Aesthetics and Physiology* (New York: Routledge: 2016), 75.

17. Denis Diderot, "The Salon of 1765," in *Diderot on Art*, vol. 1: *The Salon of 1765 and Notes on Painting*, trans. John Goodman, intro. Thomas Crow (New Haven, CT: Yale University Press, 1995), 104.

18. "A line used in a work of art, a vibrating string, and a vibrating fiber all function in a similar manner in that they are essential in giving the object movement, sensibility, life, form, and communicability," goes Clark's summation of this thinking. Clark, *Diderot's Part*, 76.

19. Diderot, *Oeuvres complètes* XVII, 338, quoted in Clark, *Diderot's Part*, 77.

20. "De même que la ligne du serpent trouve sa parodie dans la ligne du ver, de même elle trouve sa caricature, dans la ligne torse," in Diderot, *Oeuvres complètes* XVII, 340; quoted in Clark, *Diderot's Part*, 76.

21. Roland Barthes, *Roland Barthes by Roland Barthes*, trans. Richard Howard (New York: Hill and Wang, 1977), 116; Roland Barthes, *The Pleasure of the Text*, trans. Richard Miller (New York: Hill and Wang, 1975), 31; Roland Barthes, *A Lover's Discourse: Fragments*, trans. Richard Howard (New York: Hill and Wang, 1978), 197.

22. Jean-Paul Sartre, *Nausea*, trans. Lloyd Alexander (New York: New Directions, 2007), 103.

23. William Hogarth, *The Analysis of Beauty*, ed. Ronald Paulson (New Haven, CT: Yale University Press, 1997), 22, 21.

24. Hogarth, *Analysis of Beauty*, 41.

25. Hogarth, *Analysis of Beauty*, 41, 42.

26. Hogarth, *Analysis of Beauty*, 42.

27. Marquis de Sade, *Juliette*, trans. Austryn Wainhouse (New York: Grove Press, 1968), 979. See also Roland Barthes, *Sade, Fourier, Loyola*, trans. Richard Miller (Berkeley: University of California Press, 1989), 136–37.

28. Michel Foucault, *The Order of Things: An Archaeology of the Human Sciences* (New York: Vintage, 1970), 6.

29. See Martha Hollander, *An Entrance for the Eyes: Space and Meaning in Seventeenth-Century Dutch Art* (Berkeley: University of California Press, 2002), 126.

30. s.v. "full, adj., n.2, and adv.," OED *Online*, http://www.oed.com.proxy.uba.uva .nl:2048/view/Entry/75327.

31. Emmanuel Levinas, *De l'évasion* [On Escape], intro. Jacques Rolland, trans. Bettina Bergo (Stanford, CA: Stanford University Press, 2003), 56.

32. Levinas, *De l'évasion*, 53 (emphasis in original).

33. Levinas, *De l'évasion*, 54.

34. Levinas, *De l'évasion*, 55 (emphasis in original).

35. Levinas, *De l'évasion*, 55.

36. Levinas, *De l'évasion*, 64.

37. Levinas, *De l'évasion*, 65.

38. Levinas, *De l'évasion*, 65.

39. Levinas, *De l'évasion*, 60.

40. Levinas, *De l'évasion*, 63.

41. Levinas, *De l'évasion*, 56.

42. Levinas, *De l'évasion*, 59.

43. As Levinas puts it, "Being is: there is nothing to add to this assertion as long as we envision in a being only its existence"—note, however, that he will criticize this view, the privileged stance of philosophy, locating in being, instead, a need that is not privation, a fullness of responsibility and not (merely) existence. Levinas, *De l'évasion*, 51.

44. Theodor Adorno, *Prisms*, trans. Samuel and Shierry Weber (Cambridge, MA: MIT Press, 1981), 248.

45. Alexander Düttmann, *Philosophy of Exaggeration*, trans. James Phillips (London: Continuum, 2007), 15 (emphasis in original).

46. Levinas, *De l'évasion*, 70.

47. See Derrida's critique of this form of dissymmetry in Levinas in Jacques Derrida, "Violence and Metaphysics," in *Writing and Difference*, trans. Alan Bass (London: Routledge, 1967).

48. Levinas writes: "Kierkegaardian violence begins when existence is forced to abandon the ethical stage in order to embark on the religious stage, the domain of belief. But belief no longer sought external justification. Even internally, it combined

communication and isolation, and hence violence and passion. That is the origin of the relegation of ethical phenomena to secondary status and the contempt of the ethical foundation of being which has led, through Nietzsche, to the amoralism of recent philosophies." Emmanuel Levinas, "Kierkegaard: Existence and Ethics," in *Proper Names*, trans. Michael B. Smith (Stanford, CA: Stanford University Press, [1963] 1996), 72.

49. Emmanuel Levinas, *Otherwise Than Being or Beyond Essence*, trans. Alphonso Lingis (The Hague: Martinus Nijhoff, 1981), 117; Emmanuel Levinas, *Totality and Infinity: An Essay on Exteriority*, trans. Alphonso Lingis (Pittsburgh: Duquesne Press, 1969), 299.

50. Levinas, *Otherwise Than Being*, 112.

51. Levinas, *Otherwise Than Being*, 112, 114.

52. Levinas, *Otherwise Than Being*, 6, 11.

53. Levinas, *Otherwise Than Being*, 114.

54. Levinas, *Otherwise Than Being*, 112.

55. Georg Wilhelm Friedrich Hegel, *The Science of Logic*, Cambridge Hegel Translations, ed. and trans. George di Giovanni (Cambridge: Cambridge University Press, 2010), 588.

56. Hegel, *Science of Logic*, 589 (emphasis in original).

57. Hegel, *Science of Logic*, 592 (emphasis in original).

58. Georg Wilhelm Friedrich Hegel, *Philosophy of Nature: Part Two of the Encyclopaedia of the Philosophical Sciences (1830)*, trans. A. V. Miller, with a foreword by J. N. Findlay (Oxford: Oxford University Press, 2004), 239. The translation is based on Nicolin and Pöggeler's 1959 edition and the *Zusätze* in Michelet's 1847 text.

59. s.v. "middle, adj. and n.," OED *Online*, http://www.oed.com.proxy.uba.uva .nl:2048/view/Entry/118140.

60. W. T. Stace was one of the earliest readers of Hegel to note the way in which triadic form as principle continually fails in relation to enacted philosophical method, writing, "A word of warning is, however, necessary. It must not be supposed that Hegel has actually succeeded in rigorously applying these principles throughout his system. The description of the dialectic method given above is an ideal description, a description of what the method aims at being or ought to be. In practice it is sometimes difficult to see how this description applies to some of Hegel's actual triads. For example, in the philosophy of spirit Hegel puts forward as one of his triads the notions of art, religion, and philosophy. Here art is supposed to be the thesis, religion the antithesis, philosophy the synthesis. It is very difficult to see in what sense religion is the opposite of art; and it is quite impossible to see that art and philosophy are related as genus and species, or that religion can be regarded as the differentia. Numerous similar examples might be given. There are even cases of 'triads' which contain four terms! These irregularities do not indicate, however, that our description of the dialectic method is wrong. What they do show is that Hegel has not himself been able to carry out his own dialectic method with absolute consistency in all cases. This is of course an imperfection in his system. Yet the fact that he has

made mistakes in the application of his principles does not necessarily invalidate the principles themselves."

What Stace has also described is the relation between the formalism of a diagram of the dialectical method—its idealism—and its lived, fleshed-out imperfections (where its sutures leak; where the surgical technique of joining fails). See W. T. Stace, *The Philosophy of Hegel: A Systematic Exposition* (New York: Dover Publications, 1955), 97.

More generously, J. N. Findlay was the great reader of the promiscuity of Hegel's triadicism and triplicities; in his *Hegel: A Re-Examination*, he writes that "the triads of Hegel's system vary vastly in their make-up. In some the second member of the triad is the direct and obvious contrary of the first, as where Being is opposed to Nothing, or Essence to Appearance. In others the opposition is of a much less extreme character [. . .]. In some triads the third member is an *obvious* choice as mediating between the other two [. . .]. In other cases, the third member of the triad is merely *one* of the things in which the first two members *could* be united [. . .]. In yet other cases the reconciling functions of the third member are not at all obvious [. . .]. There are many more triads in which the third member emerges out of the second member *alone,* than triads in which it emerges out of the two previous members conjointly." J. N. Findlay, *Hegel: A Re-Examination* (London: Routledge, [1958] 2013), 73 (emphasis in original).

61. Samuel Beckett, "How It Is," in *The Selected Works of Samuel Beckett*, vol. II: *Molloy, Malone Dies, The Unnamable, How It Is* (New York: Grove Press, 2010), 501.

62. Beckett, *How It Is*, 501.

63. Beckett, *How It Is*, 516.

64. Leo Bersani and Ulysse Dutoit, *Arts of Impoverishment: Beckett, Rothko, Resnais* (Cambridge, MA: Harvard University Press 1993), 59. For a useful and thorough review of the critical literature on *Comment c'est*, see Anthony Cordingley, *Samuel Beckett's* How It Is: *Philosophy in Translation* (Edinburgh: Edinburgh University Press, 2018).

65. Beckett, *How It Is*, 504.

66. Beckett, *How It Is*, 445.

67. Andrew Gibson, *Beckett and Badiou: The Pathos of Intermittency* (Oxford: Oxford University Press, 2006), 32.

68. Gibson, *Beckett and Badiou*, 32, 33.

69. Bersani and Dutoit, *Arts of Impoverishment*, 57.

70. Beckett, *How It Is*, 499.

71. Gibson, *Beckett and Badiou*, 273.

72. Gibson, *Beckett and Badiou*, 32.

73. I therefore disagree with the central thesis of the excellent *Horror in Architecture* by Joshua Comaroff and Ker-Shing Ong, in which they argue that "horror dramatizes the failure of abstraction"—our disagreement nearing a pole of agreement, for their study is nothing but an effort at a formal typology of horror via architectural figures of doubling, reiteration, incontinence, homunculism, solidity, distortion,

disproportion, &c. However, in place of the authors' interest in the failure of abstraction as "a moment in which the corporeal program of modernism is unequal to the complexity of contemporary buildings," horror reveals the violence of formalism in which abstraction not only does not fail but continually reasserts itself, even amid uneffaced metaphoricities: uneffacing as a practice of infinitizing the possibility of further formalizations. Joshua Comaroff and Ker-Shing Ong, *Horror in Architecture* (San Francisco: ORO Editions, 2013), 15, 134.

74. See the treatment of the literal / counterfigurative and its relation to science fiction and Romantic poetry in Seo-Young Chu, *Do Metaphors Dream of Literal Sheep?: A Science-Fictional Theory of Representation* (Cambridge, MA: Harvard University Press, 2010).

75. Jacques Derrida, "White Mythology," in *Margins of Philosophy*, trans. Alan Bass (Chicago: University of Chicago Press, 1982). Derrida's argument involves the circulation of the philosophical concept as doubly de-faced, in which "such efface-ment itself effaces itself" (211); a figure "becomes metaphor when put in circulation in philosophical discourse. At that point, the first meaning and the first displacement are simultaneously forgotten. The metaphor is no longer noticed, and it is taken for the proper meaning. [. . .] On this view, philosophy would be a self-eliminating process of generating metaphor" (211). The metaphysician, Derrida writes, is economical: choosing the most abraded, worn, polished words.

76. "The identification of the same in the I is not produced as a monotonous tautology: 'I am I.' The originality of identification, irreducible to the A is A formalism, would thus escape attention." Levinas, *Totality and Infinity*, 37.

77. Rorty registers this cranky complaint in several places, sometimes explicitly engaging with Levinas, sometimes attacking him through commentary on Derrida, deconstruction, or both. On "infinite responsibility," he writes, "the infinite and the unrepresentable are merely nuisances" to the public responsibilities of political organization. Richard Rorty, *Achieving Our Country* (Cambridge, MA: Harvard University Press, 1998), 97.

Attempting to appease the Hegelian charges against Derrida, Simon Critchley likewise warns in *The Ethics of Deconstruction*, "I have argued that there is a need for a political *supplement* to deconstruction, in the full sense of that word, as something which both makes up for a lack and adds to what is already complete. I believe that this supplement is necessary in order to prevent deconstruction from becoming a fail-safe strategy for reading—an empty formalism—which, as Rorty would have it, is a means to private autonomy that is publicly useless and politically pernicious." Simon Critchley, *The Ethics of Deconstruction: Derrida and Levinas* (West Lafayette, IN: Purdue University Press, 1999), 236–37.

78. Georg Wilhelm Friedrich Hegel, *Elements of the Philosophy of Right*, ed. Allen W. Wood, trans. H. B. Nisbet, Cambridge Texts in the History of Political Thought (Cambridge: Cambridge University Press, 1991), 162.

79. Beckett, *How It Is*, 412.

80. American Academy of Orthopaedic Surgeons, *Advanced Emergency Care and*

Transportation of the Sick and Injured, 2nd ed., ed. Rhonda J. Beck (Sudbury, MA: Jones and Bartlett Learning, 2012), 1268.

81. Adriana Cavarero, *Inclinations: A Critique of Rectitude*, trans. Amanda Minervini and Adam Sitze (Stanford, CA: Stanford University Press, 2016), 13 (emphasis mine).

POSTSCRIPT

1. Fredric Jameson, *The Political Unconscious* (Ithaca, NY: Cornell University Press, 1981), 42; Yves Bonnefoy, "Paul Valéry," in *L'Improbable et autres essais* (Paris: Mercure de France, [1963] 1980), 102; Bieberbach, quoted in Herbert Mehrtens, "Ludwig Bieberbach and 'Deutsche Mathematik,'" in *Studies in the History of Mathematics*, ed. Esther Phillips (Washington, DC: Mathematical Association of America, 1987), 202.

2. Robert Kaufman, "Everybody Hates Kant: Blakean Formalism and the Symmetries of Laura Moriarty," *Modern Language Quarterly* 61, no. 1 (2000): 131.

Useful accounts of both Lacan's and Badiou's periods of (rather strict, but differing) formalism(s) can be found across Peter Hallward and Knox Peden, eds., *Concept and Form*, vol. 2: *Interviews and Essays on the* Cahiers pour l'Analyse (London: Verso, 2012). Along with the first volume, which collates translated texts from the *Cahiers pour l'Analyse*, this second volume of essays and interviews with the journal's members and interlocutors explores the broader project of French structuralism and therefore constitutes an especially valuable exploration of the different formalisms (mathematical, philosophical) that animated twentieth-century philosophy and critical theory.

Starting from the negative, a useful encounter with form occurs via a theorization of *l'informe* in the three editorial introductions: "Formless 1. Groundless Interpretations: Thought and Formless" (17–26); "Formless 2. Within and Between: Literature and Formless" (105–12); and "Formless 3. The Interminable Detour of Form: Art and Formless" (185–92) in Patrick Crowley and Paul Hegarty, eds., *Formless: Ways In and Out of Form* (Oxford: Peter Lang, 2005).

In part because of the unwieldiness of the term, a selection of further reading on form might well point to the doors of a sizable library, but here are a few selected places to begin. For a thinking of form in Kant, see Rodolphe Gasché, *The Idea of Form: Rethinking Kant's Aesthetics* (Stanford, CA: Stanford University Press, 2003). Peter Steiner's *Russian Formalism: A Metapoetics* (Ithaca, NY: Cornell University Press, 1984) scrutinizes both the shared principles and the profound differences in the assemblage dubbed the Russian Formalists. A useful overview of the return to formalism and a compelling rereading of Adorno can be found across the entirety of Josh Robinson, *Adorno's Poetics of Form* (Albany: State University of New York Press, 2018). See Sam Rose, *Art and Form: From Roger Fry to Global Modernism* (University Park, PA: The Pennsylvania State University Press, 2019) for a treatment of the relation between formalism and (in) modernism. (Moving away from a "formalist modernism," Rose is partial to a "modest formalism," which is sometimes, tellingly, written as a modest *postformalism*.) In addition to the other scholarship grappling with the new formalism or various returns to the aesthetic cited elsewhere in these notes, the interested reader might consult the introduction to and essays in Verena Theile and Linda Tredennick, eds., *New Formalisms and Literary Theory* (Basingstoke, UK: Palgrave Macmillan, 2013). For a thinking of formal ontology and form's relation to a broad concept of speculative realism, see Tristan Garcia, *Form and Object: A Treatise on Things*, trans. Mark Allan Ohm and Jon Cogburn (Edinburgh: Edinburgh University Press, 2014).

3. Marjorie Levinson, "What Is New Formalism?" PMLA 122, no. 2 (2007): 559.

4. See Susan J. Wolfson, "Reading for Form," *Modern Language Quarterly* 61, no. 1 (March 2000): 1–16; and Susan J. Wolfson, *Formal Charges: The Shaping of Poetry in British Romanticism* (Stanford, CA: Stanford University Press, 1997). Tom Eyers, *Speculative Formalism: Literature, Theory, and the Critical Present* (Evanston, IL: Northwestern University Press, 2017).

5. Roland Barthes, *Mythologies*, trans. Annette Lavers (New York: Hill and Wang, 1972), 112.

6. Paul de Man, "Kant's Materialism," in *Aesthetic Ideology*, ed. Andrzej Warminski (Minneapolis: University of Minnesota Press, 1996), 128.

7. Oscar Wilde, "The Critic as Artist," in *The Artist as Critic: Critical Writings of Oscar Wilde*, ed. Richard Ellmann (Chicago: University of Chicago Press, 1982), 398; Viktor Shklovsky, *Theory of Prose*, trans. Benjamin Sher (Normal, IL: Dalkey Archive Press, 1998), 159.

8. See, for example, Fredric Jameson, "Video: Surrealism without the Unconscious," in *Postmodernism, or, The Cultural Logic of Late Capitalism* (Durham, NC: Duke University Press, 1991), 67–96, which stages a particularly vivid confrontation between a formal close reading and historicism in its grapple with the video piece *AlienNATION*. Jameson's essay turns on the question of how to read this work of experimental video, and what is most fascinating is that despite his efforts to move away from tracing formal movements, the seductive complexity of such a reading keeps insinuating itself: "But my attempt to tell or summarize this text makes it clear that even before we reach the interpretative question—'what does it mean?' or, to use its petit bourgeois version, 'what is it supposed to represent?'—we have to confront the preliminary matters of form and reading. It is not evident that a spectator will ever reach a moment of knowledge and saturated memory from which a formal reading of this text in time slowly disengages itself" (83). In the last few pages, Jameson suddenly returns to historicism and locates a "palpable referent," but a close reading of his appeal to figures of fragmentation and collation suggests that he never sheds the sense that occupies most of the essay: that in fact questions of form are not only the motor of reading but (possibly) the only way for reading as such to take place.

9. See György Lukács, *Soul and Form*, ed. John T. Sanders and Katie Terezakis, trans. Anna Bostock, intro. Judith Butler (New York: Columbia University Press, 2010). For Lukács, form is linked sometimes to historical conditions of emergence

and sometimes to a universal, timeless essence (in other words, his concept of "form" bears out the double sense of the term about which I have written in several places in this book): e.g., writing of the essay that it is "the mystical moment of union between the outer and the inner, between the soul and the form" (8).

10. Barthes, *Mythologies*, 111.

11. Claude Lévi-Strauss, "Structure and Form: Reflections on a Work by Vladimir Propp," trans. Monique Layton, in Vladimir Propp, *Theory and History of Folklore*, ed. Anatoly Liberman, trans. Ariadna Y. Martin and Richard P. Martin (Minneapolis: University of Minnesota Press, 1984), 167–88, 167.

12. Caroline Levine, *Forms: Whole, Rhythm, Hierarchy, Network* (Princeton, NJ: Princeton University Press, 2015), 3. Levine owns this move outright: "This book proposes a way to understand the relations among forms—forms aesthetic and social, spatial and temporal, ancient and modern, major and minor, like and unlike, punitive and narrative, material and metrical. Its method of tracking shapes and arrangements is not confined to the literary text or to the aesthetic, but it does involve a kind of close reading, a careful attention to the forms that organize texts, bodies, and institutions" (23); and "we cannot do without bounded wholes: their power to hold things together is what makes some of the most valuable kinds of political action possible at all" (27). If there were any doubt about her ultimate critical aim, it would be resolved in her contribution to the PMLA special section of responses to her book, which she titles "Three Unresolved Debates," the first of which she names *What Is Politics?* Caroline Levine, "Three Unresolved Debates," PMLA 132, no. 5 (October 2017): 1239.

Robinson, in *Adorno's Poetics of Form*, writes, "If the old formalism left itself open to the criticism that its dedication to form came at the expense of a concern with the social and the political, the new frequently describes itself as willing to subordinate its investigation of form to these social and political concerns. This new formalism, then, is a formalism understood as technique or investigative procedure, which explicitly rejects the self-imposed limits of the introspective old formalism" (3–4).

13. Catherine Gallagher notes a fundamental tension between a relegation of form to structure and a relegation of form to style, one that poses an irresolvable relation between abstraction and the concrete inherent in any thinking of form: "Form as structure comes into view only from a distance; form as style requires unusually close proximity. Structuralists tend to translate time into space; stylistics translates it into tense." Catherine Gallagher, "Formalism and Time," *Modern Language Quarterly* 61, no. 1 (March 2000): 231.

14. Constance Penley and Janet Bergstrom, "The Avant-Garde: History and Theories," in *Movies and Methods*, vol. 2, ed. Bill Nichols (Berkeley: University of California Press, 1985), 294.

15. Friedrich Schiller, Letter 22, in *On the Aesthetic Education of Man in a Series of Letters*, trans. Elizabeth M. Wilkinson and L. A. Willoughby (Oxford: Clarendon Press, 1983).

Although a thorough consideration of Laruelle on the decision would extend this endnote to the length of a chapter, it is minimally worth noting that Laruelle's account of the form of philosophical decision as the fundamental gesture of philosophy— that which is the cause of the appearance of philosophy itself—functions as the conceptual ground for regarding philosophy itself *as a form* that is solely analyzable within the syntax of formal operations (division, decision) that continually introduces formal variance (difference). The philosophical decision (of any philosophical system, Kant, Heidegger, Nietzsche, &c.) would be the decision to reflect on the world philosophically, a decision that therefore cannot be philosophically reflected (and can only thus be grasped by nonphilosophy). Laruelle's definition of Philosophical Decision—which runs "Principal and formalized invariant or structure of philosophy according to philosophy which does not indicate it without also simultaneously auto-affecting and affecting its own identity; instead, non-philosophy gives it a radical identity (of) structure or determines it in-the-last instance. Its synonyms: dyad and unity, ambiguity, unity-of-opposites, mixture, mélange—are likely even to have a double use, intra-philosophical and non-philosophical, which changes their sense"—thus has some great conceptual risks, including that an interest in *the singular form* of philosophical decision overrides the details of difference that render different philosophical decisions different, thus committing itself to a reductive and flattening project. It is in this way at odds with the project of radical formalism represented herein, which is marked, by contrast, by a resolutely proliferative drive. François Laruelle, "Philosophical Decision," in *Dictionary of Non-Philosophy*, trans. Taylor Adkins (Minneapolis: Univocal, 2013), 56.

See also François Laruelle, "Theory of Philosophical Decision," in *Philosophies of Difference: A Critical Introduction to Non-Philosophy*, trans. Rocco Gangle (London: Continuum, 2010), 196–223; Rocco Gangle and Julius Greve, eds., *Superpositions: Laruelle and the Humanities* (London: Rowman and Littlefield International, 2017); and Ray Brassier, "Axiomatic Heresy: The Non-Philosophy of François Laruelle," *Radical Philosophy* 121 (September/October 2003): 24–35.

16. Ellen Rooney, "Form and Contentment," *Modern Language Quarterly* 61, no. 1 (2000): 29.

17. Cleanth Brooks, *The Well Wrought Urn: Studies in the Structure of Poetry* (New York: Harcourt Brace, 1947), 194, 197.

18. Robert S. Lehman, "Formalism, Mere Form, and Judgment," *New Literary History* 48, no. 2 (2017): 246.

19. Aristotle, *Metaphysica* (Metaphysics), trans. W. D. Ross, in *The Basic Works of Aristotle*, ed. Richard McKeon (New York: Random House, 1941), 794.

20. See Wladyslaw Tatarkiewicz, "Form: History of One Term and Five Concepts," in *A History of Six Ideas: An Essay in Aesthetics*, trans. Christopher Kasparek (The Hague: Martinus Nijhoff, 1980), 220.

21. Tatarkiewicz, "Form," 220–21, 221.

22. Raymond Williams, "Formalist," in *Keywords: A Vocabulary of Culture and Society* (Oxford: Oxford University Press, 2015), 94.

23. Such wording is typical: "In sum, the deconstructive critique of metaphysics,

logocentrism, ontotheology, essentialism, and the like, corresponds in its structure and dynamics to Girard's critique of sacrificial practices. [. . .] It is as if Derrida describes as happening to the linguistic signifier something that Girard describes as happening at the foundation of cultural institutions. There is an opportunity here to relate what appears to many to be but a formalist critique, concerned only with texts, to real institutional practices, and accordingly, to substantive issues. There are possibilities for real knowledge in deconstruction, which has to be redeemed from some of its formalist or nihilist temptations." Andrew J. McKenna, *Violence and Difference: Girard, Derrida, and Deconstruction* (Urbana: University of Illinois Press, 1992), 12.

24. Angela Leighton, *On Form: Poetry, Aestheticism, and the Legacy of a Word* (Oxford: Oxford University Press, 2007), 3; Peter Osborne, "*October* and the Problem of Formalism," QP 28 (2013): 5 (emphasis in original).

25. Maurice Denis, "Definition of Neotraditionism," in *Theories of Modern Art*, ed. Herschel Chipp (Berkeley: University of California Press, 1968), 94.

26. Eugenie Brinkema, *The Forms of the Affects* (Durham, NC: Duke University Press, 2014), 36–37.

27. Craig Dworkin, *Reading the Illegible* (Evanston, IL: Northwestern University Press, 2003), 4, 5; Laura U. Marks, *Touch: Sensuous Theory and Multisensory Media* (Minneapolis: University of Minnesota Press, 2002), xxii.

28. Levine, *Forms*, 7. One sees similar moves elsewhere, as in Anna Kornbluh's "political formalism" in *The Order of Forms*, or her offer of a "social close reading" in *Realizing Capital: Financial and Psychic Economies in Victorian Form*. Anna Kornbluh, *The Order of Forms: Realism, Formalism, and Social Space* (Chicago: University of Chicago Press, 2019); Anna Kornbluh, *Realizing Capital: Financial and Psychic Economies in Victorian Form* (New York: Fordham University Press, 2014), 14.

For an extensive collection of responses, rethinkings, and critiques of Levine's *Forms* from a variety of perspectives, see the Theories and Methodologies dossier in *PMLA* 132, no. 5 (2017). In that issue, Marijeta Bozovic's "Whose Forms? Missing Russians in Caroline Levine's *Forms*" (1181–86) is particularly instructive in pointing out the limited scope, definition, and intellectual-historical take on "forms" in Levine's book, while also noting the way in which the formalist reading that comprises the final part is, in fact, not particularly concerned with the specificities of that object's textual form: "Levine's reading of *The Wire* in the last chapter is indicative: entertaining, clever, but also oddly light, and it reduces (or translates) *The Wire* to a Victorian novel" (1184).

29. Levine, *Forms*, 16.

30. Plato, *Republic*, in *The Collected Dialogues of Plato, Including the Letters*, ed. Edith Hamilton and Huntington Cairns (Princeton, NJ: Princeton University Press, 1989), 682.

31. Sibylle Baumbach, *Literature and Fascination* (Basingstoke, UK: Palgrave Macmillan, 2015), 67.

32. Denis Diderot, "Passions," *The Encyclopedia of Diderot & d'Alembert Collaborative Translation Project*, trans. Timothy L. Wilkerson (Ann Arbor: Michigan

Publishing, University of Michigan Library, 2004), http://hdl.handle.net/2027/spo
.did2222.0000.248 (accessed October 1, 2020). Originally published as "Passions,"
Encyclopédie ou Dictionnaire raisonné des sciences, des arts et des métiers (Paris,
1765), 12:142–46.

33. The first image in Mademoiselle's album is the famous photograph of the 1905
execution by *lingchi* of the Mongolian guard Fou Tchou-Li for the murder of his
master, Prince Ao-Han-Wan. One of the curious provocations of *Martyrs*, however,
is its insistence on reframing the history of martyrdom, falsely, as the sole province of
women. Accordingly, Mademoiselle's spoken narration runs: "Long Sheng Province,
1912. This woman didn't believe in God. She tried to steal a hen. It cost her dearly.
When this photo was taken, she was still alive. Look at her eyes." The film inverts every element in the record of torture: from male to female (suggesting that at least one
of the cuts of such a torture includes a cleaving from the category of sexual difference), and from political rebellion to domestic infraction (because of the great agony
of the process, and because of its contravention of filial obligation to the wholeness
of the body, the death of a thousand cuts was historically reserved for extraordinary
crimes, especially treason). It also misdates the photograph to 1912 when, in fact, Fou
Tchou-Li was one of the very last of the condemned to experience this punishment,
which was banned in the year of his execution in a sweeping revision of the imperial
Chinese penal code.

The photograph, however historically misdescribed, positively functions as a
point of connection to its appearance in works of philosophy, particularly among
thinkers grappling with precisely the question of a fascination with violence—most
notably Georges Bataille in his meditations on torture and drama, ecstasy and sacrifice. This photograph is discussed in his 1943 *Inner Experience*, and he also wrote
about and reproduced it in his final work, the 1961 *Tears of Eros*. In the earlier work,
not unlike Mademoiselle, Bataille also effects a historical swap: in place of lodging
Christ's sufferings at the center of a thinking of "non-discursive experience," he turns
to "the photographic image—or sometimes my memory of it—of a Chinese man
who must have been tortured during my lifetime. Of this torture, I had had in the
past a series of successive representations. In the end, the patient, his chest flayed,
twisted, arms and legs cut at the elbows and knees. Hair standing on his head, hid-
eous, haggard, striped with blood, beautiful as a wasp. I write 'beautiful' . . . something escapes me, flees from me, fear robs me of myself and, as if I had wanted to
stare at the sun, my eyes slip" (Bataille, *Inner Experience*, trans. Stuart Kendall [Alba-
ny: State University of New York Press, 2014], 121). Bataille likely saw this photograph
in 1934, probably in the third volume of the 1923 *Nouveau traité de psychologie* by
Georges Dumas. In *Tears of Eros*, Bataille notes, typographically registering his shock,
that Dumas uses the photograph as an illustrative example of—and we have never
moved past the burdens of this word, not even now, not even at so late a moment,
not even in the postscript—"*horripilation*: when one's hair stands on end . . . !"
(Bataille, *The Tears of Eros*, trans. Peter Connor [San Francisco: City Lights, 1989],
205). If invoked under the sign of horror, however, that affect is unstable, and in *Inner*

Experience, Bataille shifts, not unlike this book itself, from horror to the intensities of the amative: "The young and seductive Chinese man of whom I have spoken, left to the work of the executioner, I loved him with a love in which the sadistic instinct had no part: he communicated his pain to me or rather the excess of his pain, and it was precisely this that I was seeking, not to enjoy it, but to ruin in me that which is opposed to ruin" (121–22).

If *Martyrs*, then, conforms to Bataille's insistence in *Tears of Eros* that "The world evoked by this straightforward image of a tortured man is, to my knowledge, the most anguishing of worlds accessible to us through images captured on film" (205)—and if its logic of martyrdom hews to Bataille's reading of the photograph as what merges "the identity of these perfect contraries, divine ecstasy and its opposite, extreme horror"—it diverges from where his analysis lands: "And this is my inevitable conclusion to a history of eroticism" (207). The film also diverges from the nature of the photographic illustration: if for Bataille it is singular, it is also rendered neutral and ahistorical—the photographic subject is anonymous, his crime and time of death unremarked in the philosopher's photographic caption. *Martyrs*, by lodging the photograph in an album and narrative of an iterated "female [*sic*]" record of extraordinary suffering, makes it both less exemplary and more concrete (if also historically invented), but simultaneously cleaves it from eroticism to regard it as a pure capacity of bodily endurance: not inner experience or the departures of ec-stasis, but the outer morphological experience of formal transformation—the rapturous displacement or removal from a proper place (*existanai*: to displace, to put out of place, to put outside oneself) of the qualities of a form. What astonishes is this put-into-motion aesthetic capacity, the derangement of the martyr's corpus as it is rendered *nothing but* a form.

Much has been written on this photograph and Bataille's relation to it. See James Elkins, "The Very Theory of Transgression: Bataille, *Lingchi*, and Surrealism," *Australian and New Zealand Journal of Art* 5, no. 2 (2004): 5–19; Kent L. Brintnall, *Ecce Homo: The Male-Body-in-Pain as Redemptive Figure* (Chicago: University of Chicago Press, 2011), esp. 1–24; and Timothy Brook, Jérôme Bourgon, and Gregory Blue, *Death By a Thousand Cuts* (Cambridge, MA: Harvard University Press, 2008), esp. 222–42.

34. This figure and formulation, though attributed most often to Bacon, was part of a broader seventeenth-century discourse of torturing, hounding, vexing, interrogating nature; see Peter Pesic, "Nature on the Rack: Leibniz's Attitude towards Judicial Torture and the 'Torture' of Nature," *Studia Leibnitiana* 39, no. 2 (1997): 189–97; and Peter Pesic, "Wrestling with Proteus: Francis Bacon and the 'Torture' of Nature," *Isis* 90 (1999): 81–94.

35. Maurice Blanchot, "The Song of the Sirens," in *The Gaze of Orpheus*, trans. Lydia Davis (Barrytown, NY: Station Hill Press, 1981), 109.

36. Blanchot, "Song of the Sirens," 109.

37. Jacques Derrida, "La forme et la façon," preface to *Racisme et antisémitisme: Essai de philosophie sur l'envers des concepts*, by Alain David (Paris: Ellipses, 2001), 10 (emphasis in original).

38. Jacques Derrida, "Le Dernier Mot du racisme" [Racism's Last Word], trans. Peggy Kamuf, *Critical Inquiry* 12, no. 1 (1985): 290–99, 292.

39. Derrida, "Le Dernier Mot du racisme," 292.

40. Derrida, "La forme et la façon," 11.

41. Jacques Derrida, "Form and Meaning: A Note on the Phenomenology of Language," in *Margins of Philosophy*, trans. Alan Bass (Chicago: University of Chicago Press, 1982), 157.

42. Derrida, "Form and Meaning," 157–58 (emphasis in original).

43. Derrida, "Form and Meaning," 158 (emphasis in original).

44. Derrida, "Form and Meaning," 158 (emphasis in original).

45. Derrida, "La forme et la façon," 11.

46. Jean-Luc Nancy, "Image and Violence," in *The Ground of the Image*, trans. Jeff Fort (New York: Fordham University Press, 2005), 20.

47. Nancy, "Image and Violence," 24–25.

48. Nancy, "Image and Violence," 25.

49. Ovid, *The Metamorphoses*, trans. Allen Mandelbaum (New York: Knopf, 1993), 187 [Book VI, lines 387–91].

50. Sergei Eisenstein, *Disney*, ed. Oksana Bulgakowa and Dietmar Hochmuth, trans. Dustin Condren (Berlin: Potemkin Press, 2011), 15.

51. Eisenstein, *Disney*, 15.

52. Eisenstein, *Disney*, 15.

53. Roman Signer, interview with Konrad Tobler, "Der Schreck kommt erst im Nachhinein," *Tages-Anzeiger*, June 12, 2014.

54. Marquis de Sade, "The 120 Days of Sodom," in *The 120 Days of Sodom and Other Writings*, trans. Austryn Wainhouse and Richard Seaver (New York: Grove Press, 1966), 649.

55. de Sade, *120 Days of Sodom*, 674.

56. Herbert Breger, "The Art of Mathematical Rationality," in *Leibniz: What Kind of Rationalist?*, ed. Marcelo Dascal, Logic, Epistemology, and the Unity of Science 13 (Dordrecht: Springer 2008), 148.

57. Cf. the reading of Schelling's "account of endlessly generative deviations from the dynamism or flux of potencies" not as a negative process, but as what "describes the activity of the finite product or object with regard to its infinite production or manufacture, in ontological terms. Expressed positively, the genesis of forms in the world—*morphogenesis*—becomes coextensive with the excess of matter at the margins of either its concepts or its bodies, which are necessarily departing from their cause and in turn becoming the new ground for ever new organisms and phenomena"; in Julius Greve, *Shreds of Matter: Cormac McCarthy and the Concept of Nature* (Hanover, NH: Dartmouth College Press, 2018), 13.

58. Breger, "Art of Mathematical Rationality," 148.

59. Catherine Malabou, *Plasticity at the Dusk of Writing: Dialectic, Destruction, Deconstruction*, trans. Carolyn Shread (New York: Columbia University Press, 2010), 1.

60. Malabou, *Plasticity at the Dusk of Writing*, 2 (emphasis in original).

61. Gilles Deleuze, *Cinema 2: The Time-Image*, trans. Hugh Tomlinson and Robert Galeta (Minneapolis: University of Minnesota Press, 1989), 174.

62. Daney, quoted in Deleuze, *Cinema 2*, 176.

63. Deleuze, *Cinema 2*, 176.

64. Gilles Deleuze, *Cinema 1: The Movement-Image*, trans. Hugh Tomlinson and Barbara Habberjam (Minneapolis: University of Minnesota Press, 1986), 106 (emphasis in original).

65. Deleuze, *Cinema 1*, 106.

66. Deleuze, *Cinema 1*, 106.

67. Tim Palmer, *Brutal Intimacy: Analyzing Contemporary French Cinema* (Middletown, CT: Wesleyan University Press, 2011), 171, 133.

68. Jean-Luc Nancy, "The Forgetting of Philosophy," in *The Gravity of Thought*, trans. François Raffoul and Gregory Recco (Atlantic Highlands, NJ: Humanities Press, 1997), 59.

69. Emmanuel Levinas, "There Is: Existence without Existents," in *The Levinas Reader*, ed. Seán Hand (Oxford: Blackwell Publishers, 1989), 33.

LOVE AND MEASUREMENT

1. Michel Serres, *Rome: The First Book of Foundations*, trans. Randolph Burks (London: Bloomsbury, 2015), 166.

2. Serres, *Rome*, 166.

3. Serres, *Rome*, 166.

4. Vitruvius, *The Architecture of Marcus Vitruvius Pollio in Ten Books*, trans. Joseph Gwilt (London: Priestly and Weale, 1826), 11.

5. Dorrit Cohn, "Kleist's 'Marquise von O . . .': The Problem of Knowledge," *Monatshefte* 67, no. 2 (summer 1975): 129.

6. Wagner, *Tristan und Isolde*, Act II, scene 2. The opera premiered June 10, 1865, at the Royal Court and National Theatre in Munich.

7. Michael Pattison, review of *Amour Fou*, *Sight and Sound* 25, no. 3 (March 2015): 68.

8. Denis de Rougemont, *Love in the Western World*, trans. Montgomery Belgion (Princeton, NJ: Princeton University Press, 1940), 50, 54. Jacques Lacan, "The Function and Field of Speech and Language in Psychoanalysis," in *Écrits*, complete edition, trans. Bruce Fink (New York: W. W. Norton, 2006), 262.

9. Jean-Luc Nancy, "The Inoperative Community," in *The Inoperative Community*, ed. Peter Connor, trans. Peter Connor, Lisa Garbus, Michael Holland, and Simona Sawhney (Minneapolis: University of Minnesota Press, 1991), 39.

10. Aristotle, *De Poetica* (Poetics), trans. Ingram Bywater, in *The Basic Works of Aristotle*, ed. Richard McKeon (New York: Random House, 1941), 1459, sect. 1449a.

11. Michel Serres, *Le Système de Leibniz et ses modèles mathématiques* (Paris: PUF, 1968), 153; and quoted in Serres, *Rome*, 236.

12. Letter to Des Bosses, February 5, 1712, quoted in Serres, *Le Système de Leibniz*, 153. See G. W. Leibniz, *The Leibniz-Des Bosses Correspondence*, ed. and trans. Brandon C. Look and Donald Rutherford (New Haven, CT: Yale University Press, 2007).

Leibniz discusses scenography in numerous places, including in G. W. Leibniz, *Monadology and Other Philosophical Essays*, trans. Paul Schrecker (Indianapolis: Indiana University Press, 1965). For further readings of Leibniz on perception, ichnography, and scenography, see Gilles Deleuze, *The Fold: Leibniz and the Baroque*, trans. Tom Conley (Minneapolis: University of Minnesota Press, 1992); Jonathan Crary, "The Camera Obscura and Its Subject," in *Techniques of the Observer: On Vision and Modernity in the Nineteenth Century* (Cambridge, MA: MIT Press, 1990), 25–66; and the third section, entitled "The Supremacy of Space," in Edward S. Casey, *The Fate of Place: A Philosophical History* (Berkeley, CA: University of California Press, 1997).

13. Michel Serres, *Genesis*, trans. Geneviève James and James Nielson (Ann Arbor: University of Michigan Press, 1995), 19.

14. Louis Marin, *Sublime Poussin*, trans. Catherine Porter (Stanford, CA: Stanford University Press, 1999), 143 (emphasis in original).

15. The metric system itself was aimed at moving past the anthropometric modes of earlier measures: "Many Ancien Régime measures—especially those that related to the world of production—had at their origin an anthropometric meaning derived from human needs and human interests," from references to the size of the king's foot to "the quantity of labor a person could do in a given period of time. Thus, coal in one region of France was measured in a charge ('load') equal to the twelfth of a miner's daily output." Ken Alder, *The Measure of All Things* (New York: Free Press, 2002), 129.

The introduction of the metric system during the French Revolution thus aimed at abstracting measurement from both labor as lived practice(s) and from human proportions. The resistance—stubborn, often brutally furious—to the metric system then (as now) suggests the broader difficulty of nonanthropometric models of anything whatsoever.

16. Roland Barthes, *Critical Essays*, trans. Richard Howard (Evanston, IL: Northwestern University Press, 1972), xvii (emphasis in original).

17. Richard M. Proctor, *Principles of Pattern Design* (New York: Dover, 1990), 60.

18. Sue Thornham, *Spaces of Women's Cinema: Space, Place and Genre in Contemporary Women's Filmmaking* (London: BFI Publishing, 2019), 96.

19. Thornham, *Spaces of Women's Cinema*, 96.

20. Thornham, *Spaces of Women's Cinema*, 97. A more robust reading of the planimetric's formal features in relation to *Amour Fou* ("There is no place for diagonals. When there is a vanishing point, it is centred") can be found in Catherine Wheatley, "Small Is Dutiful," *Sight and Sound* 25, no. 3 (March 2015): 30–33.

21. Thornham, *Spaces of Women's Cinema*, 98. For a reading of wallpaper as both ornament and entrapment in a range of aesthetic objects, see Tomáš Jirsa, "Lost in Pattern: Rococo Ornament and Its Journey to Contemporary Art through Wallpaper," in *Where Is History Today? New Representations of the Past*, ed. Marcel Arbeit

and Ian Christie (Olomouc, Czech Republic: Palacký University Olomouc, 2015), 101–19.

22. Gilles Deleuze and Félix Guattari, *A Thousand Plateaus: Capitalism and Schizophrenia*, trans. Brian Massumi (Minneapolis: University of Minnesota Press, 1987), 109.

23. Henri Focillon, *The Life of Forms in Art* (New York: Zone Books, 1992), 66.

24. Derrida, *On Touching—Jean-Luc Nancy*, trans. Christine Irizarry (Stanford, CA: Stanford University Press, 2005), 292 (emphasis in original); Novalis, quoted in Derrida, *On Touching*, 292.

25. Deleuze and Guattari, *A Thousand Plateaus*, 269, 268.

26. Deleuze and Guattari, *A Thousand Plateaus*, 229 (emphasis in original).

27. "Sex, Death, and Geometry: A Conversation between Alain Guiraudie and João Pedro Rodrigues on *L'inconnu du lac*," *Cinema Scope* 55 (summer 2013): 33–37 (emphasis mine).

28. Richard Lippe, "Stranger By the Lake: What Is Love?," *CineAction* 92 (2014): 70–72.

29. Charles Harrison, "The Effects of Landscape," in *Landscape and Power*, ed. W. J. T. Mitchell (Chicago: University of Chicago Press, 2002), 224.

30. Harrison, "Effects of Landscape," 224.

31. Fabien Gris, "La solitude du silure et des petits poissons," *La Vie des idées*, July 24, 2013, http://www.laviedesidees.fr/La-solitude-du-silure-et-des.html.

32. Quoted in Bérénice Reynaud, "The Gleaners and Varda: The 2013 AFI FEST and American Film Market," *Senses of Cinema* 70 (March 2014), http://sensesof cinema.com/2014/festival-reports/the-gleaners-and-varda-the-2013-afi-fest -american-film-market/. Original interview published as "Alain Guiraudie im Gespräch mit Berenice Reynaud," *kolik.film* 20 (2013): 64–73.

33. Compare with the diagram of the film as a queer *Carte de tendre* in Nathan Friedman, "Diagram of the Amorous Search: Generating Desire with Guiraudie's *L'inconnu du lac*," *Scapegoat: Landscape, Architecture, Political Economy* 9 (winter/ spring 2015): 185. Deploying the Deleuzian notion of diagram to account for how the rigorously partitioned space opens up multiple possible configurations of desire, Friedman productively attends to the arrangement of bodies, elevations, and topol- ogies in the film via a set of elemental diagrams he has drawn. See also, relatedly, the assembled fragments and inset map of "Cruising Occitanie" by Cruising Pavilion (Pierre-Alexandre Mateos, Rasmus Myrup, Octave Perrault, and Charles Teyssou) in "Alain Guiraudie/Albert Serra," *Fireflies*, no. 6 (2018).

34. Jonathan Romney, "Dream Lovers," *Film Comment* 50, no. 1 (January–Febru- ary 2014): 64–67. Romney takes landscape not only as affective and scenographic, but also as integral to the project of thinking Guiraudie in relation to queer cinema. That Guiraudie's films queer rural landscapes in the same way that they make objects of desire from unconventional bodies is a common refrain in the critical literature on his work.

35. Ariane Nicolas, "'L'Inconnu du lac': Eros et Thanatos sont sur un bateau . . . ,"

Contre Champ (blog), Franceinfo, June 19, 2013, https://blog.francetvinfo.fr/actu-cine
/2013/06/19/linconnu-du-lac-eros-et-thanatos-sont-sur-un-bateau.html/. Nicolas
appropriates all subsequent spectatorial anxiety to the question of the specter of this
fish: "Avant même la scène du meurtre, Guiraudie introduit une tension dramatique
en la personne du silure, un poisson monstrueux long de 4 à 7 mètres (Henri ne sait
plus bien). Dès lors, la moindre scène de nage devient source d'angoisse." (Even before the murder, Guiraudie introduces a dramatic tension in the figure of the catfish,
a monstrous fish 4 to 7 meters long [Henri doesn't know]. From then on, the slightest
scene of swimming becomes a source of anxiety.)

36. Mark Wilshin, "My Summer of Love," *Dog and Wolf*, February 21, 2014, http://
www.dogandwolf.com/2014/02/stranger-by-the-lake-review/.

37. Pliny the Elder, *The Historie of the World: Commonly Called the Natural Historie of C. Plinius Secundus*, 2 vols., trans. Philemon Holland, folio (London: Adam Islip, 1601), book IX, chap. 15, 125; originally printed for the Wernerian Club (1847–48).

38. Pliny the Elder, *Historie of the World*, 125n3.

39. "You don't love me anymore?" "No; but I feel an infinite tenderness for you."
The specificity of this exchange in *Blue Is the Warmest Color* / *La Vie d'Adèle* extends
and slightly permutes this vulnerable wondering and negative answer: to Adèle's
pleading question, Emma, isolated in the frame against a featureless black background, merely shakes her head and remains silent; to Adèle's response, "Are you
sure?" Emma replies that she is, that she is with another lover now, that Adèle knows
that—and only then makes the promise of having an "infinite tenderness" for Adèle,
one Emma avows she will carry for the remainder of her life.

40. "779. Diese Farbe macht für das Auge eine sonderbare und fast unaussprech-
liche Wirkung. Sie ist als Farbe eine Energie; allein sie steht auf der negativen Seite
und ist in ihrer höchsten Reinheit gleichsam ein reizendes Nichts. Es ist etwas Wid-
ersprechendes von Reiz und Ruhe im Anblick. 780. Wie wir den hohen Himmel, die
fernen Berge blau sehen, so scheint eine blaue Fläche auch vor uns zurückzuweichen.
781. Wie wir einen angenehmen Gegenstand, der vor uns flieht, gern verfolgen, so
sehen wir das Blaue gern an, nicht weil es auf uns dringt, sondern weil es uns nach
sich zieht." Johann Wolfgang von Goethe, *Theory of Colours* (1810), trans. Charles
Lock Eastlake (Cambridge, MA: MIT Press, 1970), 310–11. Emphases are mine in the
English translation of the Goethe in the text.

41. Stendhal, *Love* (1822), trans. Gilbert and Suzanne Sale (London: Penguin,
1975), 45.

42. Jean-Luc Nancy, "Shattered Love" (L'amour en éclats), in *The Inoperative Community*, ed. Peter Connor, trans. Peter Connor, Lisa Garbus, Michael Holland, and
Simona Sawhney (Minneapolis: University of Minnesota Press, 1991), 100.

43. This is what is so problematically limiting in Linda Williams's "Cinema's Sex
Acts," in *Film Quarterly* 67, no. 4 (2014): 9–25. Her interest remains with evaluat-
ing *Blue Is the Warmest Color* in relation to prior debates about sexually explicit
codes—the old *Is it or isn't it?* that continually insinuates itself (various *its*: pornography, feminist, imperialist, queer). In doing so, however, the reading can unearth

nothing surprising about the film's form or its affective tensions, invested as it is in situating the film in relation to fixed categories of disciplinary evaluation.

44. Quoted in William Rubin, *"Primitivism" in 20th Century Art: Affinity of the Tribal and the Modern* (New York: Museum of Modern Art, 1984), 216–17, exhibition catalogue.

45. Eugenie Brinkema, *The Forms of the Affects* (Durham, NC: Duke University Press, 2014), 21.

46. Christopher Rivers, *Face Value: Physiognomical Thought and the Legible Body in Marivaux, Lavater et al.* (Madison: University of Wisconsin Press, 1994), 62.

47. Jane Kallir, *Egon Schiele: Love and Death* (Berlin: Hatje Cantz, 2005), 31, exhibition catalogue, Van Gogh Museum, Amsterdam.

48. "La Ville et l'Hôtel seront pour eux le théâtre où se joueront clandestinement leurs actions révolutionnaires. La Ville, l'Hôtel, la Forêt : trois zones occupées par des citoyens aux états civils variants—les couples, les célibataires en recherche de partenaire, les solitaires. Ces trois zones aux fonctions distinctes s'articulent dans un grand système hégémonique, un régime dystopique, ou, pour emprunter un concept foucaldien, trois hétérotopies qui intègrent ou rejettent les individus qui sectorisent et subliment les violences de la vie contemporaine." Guillaume Potvin, "*The Lobster*: La Ville, l'Hôtel, la Forêt," *Séquences: La revue de cinéma* 302 (May 2016): 22–23.

49. Yonca Talu, "Review: *The Lobster*," *Film Comment*, March–April 2016, 69.

50. Emmanuel Levinas, *Time and the Other and Additional Essays*, trans. Richard A. Cohen (Pittsburgh: Duquesne University Press, 1987), 36.

Although I disagree with its interpretation of the film's ending—which posits an unshown certainty by which "David chooses sameness and ultimately blindness"—there is a fine reading of similitude and alterity as formal problems related to narcissism and the animal in Sarah Cooper, "Narcissus and *The Lobster*," *Studies in European Cinema* 13, no. 2 (2016): 163–76.

51. Aristotle, *Ethica Nicomachea* (Nicomachean Ethics), trans. W. D. Ross, in *The Basic Works of Aristotle*, ed. Richard McKeon (New York: Random House, 1941), 935–1126, 1080.

52. Aristotle, *Ethica Nicomachea*, 1080.

53. Of Aquinas's theory of love, its use of the concepts of form and formal similitude, and its relation to Aristotle's theory of likeness, a great deal more could be said. In addition to Question 26, "Love"; Question 27, "The Causes of Love"; and Question 28, "The Effects of Love," in Thomas Aquinas, *Summa Theologiae*, vol. 19, *The Emotions*, 1a2ae.22–30, trans. Eric D'Arcy (Cambridge: Cambridge University Press, 2006 [1967]), the interested reader might begin with David Gallagher, "Thomas Aquinas on Self-Love as the Basis for Love of Others," *Acta Philosophica* 8 (1999): 23–44; Marko Fuchs, "*Philia* and *Caritas*: Some Aspects of Aquinas's Reception of Aristotle's Theory of Friendship," in *Aquinas and the Nicomachean Ethics*, ed. Tobias Hoffmann, Jörn Müller, and Matthias Perkams (Cambridge: Cambridge University Press, 2013), 203–19; and Daniel Schwartz, *Aquinas on Friendship* (Oxford: Clarendon Press, 2007).

54. Question 27, "The Causes of Love": "Primus ergo similitudinis modus causat amorem amicitiae, seu benevolentiae. Ex hoc enim quod aliqui duo sunt similes, quasi habentes unam formam, sunt quodammodo unum in forma illa, sicut duo homines sunt unum in specie humanitatis, et duo albi in albedine. Et ideo affectus unius tendit in alterum, sicut in unum sibi: et vult ei bonum sicut et sibi" (Aquinas, *Summa Theologiae*, 83).

There are nuances to this position and its variations across philosophical and theological accounts of love: in some accounts, similitude is sufficient as a formal condition for love, whereas at other times it is secondary to a primary self-love, such that the similitude valued in another would be already *of* qualities valued in the self. In Aquinas's example above, if A does not love one's own whiteness, by this model, a formal similitude of whiteness with B would not be the grounds for love between A and B.

55. Roland Barthes, *A Lover's Discourse: Fragments*, trans. Richard Howard (New York: Hill and Wang, 1978), 220.

56. Hélène Cixous, *The Book of Promethea*, trans. Betsy Wing (Lincoln: University of Nebraska Press, 1991), 65.

57. Barthes, *Lover's Discourse*, 222.

58. Gilles Deleuze, *Difference and Repetition*, trans. Paul Patton (New York: Columbia University Press, 1994), 2.

59. A compelling account of (and pressure put on) "the formalism of love"—in particular in its relation to repetition and return, pattern and structure—can be found in Lauren Berlant, "Love: A Queer Feeling," in *Homosexuality and Psychoanalysis*, ed. Tim Dean and Christopher Lane (Chicago: University of Chicago Press, 2001), 432–51. There, Berlant discusses both "the formalism of love as its central quality, quite apart from any representation of it, and apart from any institution associated with it," and "love as a conventional and historical mode of attachment to form, including in queer theory, where love is a site that has perhaps not yet been queered enough" (433).

60. Alain Badiou, with Nicolas Truong, *In Praise of Love*, trans. Peter Bush (London: Serpent's Tail, 2012), 25, 29, 22. This not-One is the ground of Badiou's philosophy of love: "Love contains an initial element that separates, dislocates and differentiates. You have *Two*. Love involves Two" (28). In some ways, then, Badiou's theory of love as a construction of a truth that involves seeing the world from the point of view of the Two is in collusion with the formal logic of the Hotel and its sketches of the value of life-as-Two, albeit with the provision that what the laws of the City see as a defense against an anxiogenic insufficiency of life as One, Badiou regards as a rupturing event that grounds a truth procedure.

61. Samuel Beckett, "Enough," in *The Selected Works of Samuel Beckett*, vol. IV: *Poems, Short Fiction, Criticism* (New York: Grove Press, 2010), 367, 369, 370.

62. Roland Barthes, *Journal de deuil* (Paris: Seuil-Imec, 2009), 247; Roland Barthes, *Mourning Diary*, trans. Richard Howard (New York: Hill and Wang, 2009), 235.

63. "To have a friend, to look at him, to follow him with your eyes, to admire him in friendship, is to know in a more intense way, already injured, always insistent, and

more and more unforgettable, that one of the two of you will inevitably see the other die." Jacques Derrida, "The Taste of Tears," in *The Work of Mourning*, ed. and trans. Pascale-Anne Brault and Michael Naas (Chicago: University of Chicago Press, 2001), 107.

64. That the lesser-known *Works of Love* must be read in relation to the pseudonymous texts is demonstrated across Amy Laura Hall, *Kierkegaard and the Treachery of Love* (Cambridge: Cambridge University Press, 2002).

65. Søren Kierkegaard, *Works of Love* (*Kjerlighedens Gjerninger*) (1847), trans. Howard Hong and Edna Hong, foreword by George Pattison (New York: HarperCollins, 2009), 318.

66. Kierkegaard, *Works of Love*, 319 (emphasis in original).

67. Kierkegaard, *Works of Love*, 319.

68. Kierkegaard, *Works of Love*, 319.

69. G. W. F. Hegel, "Love," in *Early Theological Writings*, trans. T. M. Knox, introduction by Richard Kroner (Philadelphia: University of Pennsylvania Press, 1975), 304.

70. Nancy, "Shattered Love," 98.

71. Kierkegaard, *Works of Love*, 321–22.

72. Kierkegaard, *Works of Love*, 322.

73. Barthes, *Journal de deuil*, 240; Barthes, *Mourning Diary*, 228.

74. Kierkegaard, *Works of Love*, 143.

75. Hegel, "Love," 304.

76. Hegel, "Love," 308.

77. Theodor W. Adorno, "On Kierkegaard's Doctrine of Love," *Studies in Philosophy and Social Science* 8 (1939–40): 417, 427.

78. Adorno, "On Kierkegaard's Doctrine of Love," 417 (emphasis mine).

79. Adorno, "On Kierkegaard's Doctrine of Love," 416, 417. Many thinkers have taken Adorno to task for a seemingly harsh reading of an acosmic and callous Kierkegaard, but its ungenerous approach productively highlights the terms of the necessary thought experiment: *What if* love were to be taken as this indifferent, callous, even cruelly violent notion? What becomes visible in an ethics governed by such a logic?

80. Adorno, "On Kierkegaard's Doctrine of Love," 427.

81. Adorno, "On Kierkegaard's Doctrine of Love," 416; Friedrich Wilhelm Nietzsche, *On the Genealogy of Morals*, trans. Walter Kaufmann and R. J. Hollingdale (New York: Vintage, 1967), 65.

82. Kierkegaard, *Works of Love*, 318.

83. Kierkegaard, *Works of Love*, 317.

84. Søren Kierkegaard, "At a Graveside," *Three Discourses on Imagined Occasions*, trans. Howard and Edna Hong (Princeton, NJ: Princeton University Press, 1993), 78–79.

85. Deborah Young, "*Amour*: Cannes Review," *Hollywood Reporter*, May 20, 2012, https://www.hollywoodreporter.com/review/amour-cannes-review-326962/. For her

part, Francine Prose writes that the film is "excruciating to watch," in a piece notably titled "A Masterpiece You Might Not Want to See." Prose opens her article with this particular gambit: "Michael Haneke's *Amour* is the ultimate horror film." Prose, "A Masterpiece You Might Not Want to See," *New York Review of Books*, January 7, 2013, https://www.nybooks.com/daily/2013/01/07/haneke-film-not-to-see/.

86. Walter Benjamin, "The Storyteller: Reflections on the Works of Nikolai Leskov," in *Illuminations: Essays and Reflections*, ed. Hannah Arendt, trans. Harry Zohn (New York: Schocken Books, 1968), 94.

87. Nor does the latter normally concern itself with the former; as Robin Evans writes in his classic 1978 essay, "Figures, Doors and Passages": "If anything is described by an architectural plan, it is the nature of human relationships, since the elements whose trace it records—walls, doors, windows and stairs—are employed first to divide and then selectively to re-unite inhabited space. But what is generally absent in even the most elaborately illustrated building is the way human figures will occupy it. This may be for good reasons, but when figures do appear in architectural drawings, they tend not to be substantial creatures but emblems, mere signs of life [. . .]." Robin Evans, "Figures, Doors and Passages," in *Translations from Drawing to Building and Other Essays* (Cambridge, MA: MIT Press, 1997), 56–57.

88. Garrett Stewart, "Haneke's Endgame," *Film Quarterly* 67, no. 1 (fall 2013): 18; Roy Grundmann, "Love, Death, Truth—*Amour*," *Senses of Cinema* 65 (December 2012), accessed May 11, 2020, http://sensesofcinema.com/2012/feature-articles/love-death-truth-amour/.

89. The best exception to the allegorizing critical line is thus found in the journal *Interiors*, which explores the intersection of cinema and architecture by diagramming floor plans of film scenes, indifferent to the semiotic densities of space. See Mehruss Jon Ahi and Armen Karaoghlanian, "Amour (2012)," *Interiors* (2013), accessed May 9, 2020, http://www.intjournal.com/0213/amour/.

90. Martin Heidegger, "Language," in *Poetry, Language, Thought*, trans. Albert Hofstadter (New York: Harper and Row, 1971), 201–2.

91. Heidegger, "Language," 201.

92. Barthes, *Lover's Discourse*, 148.

93. Nancy, "Shattered Love," 100.

94. Nancy, "Shattered Love," 82.

95. Plato, "Phaedrus," *The Collected Dialogues of Plato, Including the Letters*, ed. Edith Hamilton and Huntington Cairns (Princeton, NJ: Princeton University Press, 1989), 256e.

96. Anne Carson, *Eros the Bittersweet* (Princeton, NJ: Princeton University Press, 1986), 150.

97. Nancy, "Shattered Love," 87.

98. Barthes, *Lover's Discourse*, 65.

99. Michael Haneke, "Michael Haneke Talks about AMOUR," interview by Karin Schiefer, *AustrianFilms.com*, May 2012, accessed May 12, 2020, https://www.austrianfilms.com/news/en/michael_haneke_talks_about_amour/.

100. Nancy, "Shattered Love," 99.
101. Nancy, "Shattered Love," 99.
102. Nancy, "Shattered Love," 93.
103. Badiou, *In Praise of Love*, 22.
104. Nancy, "Shattered Love," 82.

Bibliography

Abish, Walter. *Alphabetical Africa*. New York: New Directions, 1974.

Adorno, Theodor W. "On Kierkegaard's Doctrine of Love." *Studies in Philosophy and Social Science* 8 (1939–40): 413–29.

Adorno, Theodor W. *Prisms*. Translated by Samuel and Shierry Weber. Cambridge, MA: MIT Press, 1981.

Ahi, Mehruss Jon, and Armen Karaoghlanian. "Amour (2012)." *Interiors* (2013). Accessed May 9, 2020. http://www.intjournal.com/0213/amour/.

Aikin, Anna Laetitia. "On the Pleasure Derived from Objects of Terror." In *Gothic Readings: The First Wave, 1764–1840*, edited by Rictor Norton, 281–83. London: Leicester University Press, 2000.

Alder, Ken. *The Measure of All Things*. New York: Free Press, 2002.

Alexander, Christopher. *Notes on the Synthesis of Form*. Cambridge, MA: Harvard University Press, 1964.

Althusser, Louis, and Étienne Balibar. *Reading Capital*. New York: Verso, 2009.

American Academy of Orthopaedic Surgeons. *Advanced Emergency Care and Transportation of the Sick and Injured*, 2nd ed. Edited by Rhonda J. Beck. Sudbury, MA: Jones and Bartlett Learning, 2012.

Ammons, A. R. *Corsons Inlet: A Book of Poems*. Ithaca, NY: Cornell University Press, 1965.

Andre, Carl. *Cuts: Texts 1959–2004*. Edited by James Meyer. Cambridge, MA: MIT Press, 2005.

Aquinas, Thomas. *Summa Theologiae*, vol. 19, *The Emotions*, 1a2ae. Translated by Eric D'Arcy. Cambridge: Cambridge University Press, [1967] 2006.

Arderne, John. *Treatises of Fistula in Ano, Haemorrhoids, and Clysters*. Edited by D'Arcy Power. London: Oxford University Press for the Early English Text Society, 1968. Originally published in Original Series, no. 139 (London: Richard Clay and Sons, 1910).

Aristotle. *Analytica Posteriora* (Posterior Analytics). Translated by G. R. G. Mure. In *The Basic Works of Aristotle*, edited by Richard McKeon, 108–86. New York: Random House, 1941.

Aristotle. *Analytica Priora* (Prior Analytics) (abridged). Translated by A. J. Jenkinson. In *The Basic Works of Aristotle*, edited by Richard McKeon, 62–107. New York: Random House, 1941.

Aristotle. *De Anima* (On the Soul). Translated by J. A. Smith. In *The Basic Works of Aristotle*, edited by Richard McKeon, 533–603. New York: Random House, 1941.

Aristotle. *The Basic Works of Aristotle.* Edited by Richard McKeon. New York: Random House, 1941.

Aristotle. *Ethica Nicomachea* (Nicomachean Ethics). Translated by W. D. Ross. In *The Basic Works of Aristotle*, edited by Richard McKeon, 927–1112. New York: Random House, 1941.

Aristotle. *Metaphysica* (Metaphysics). Translated by W. D. Ross. In *The Basic Works of Aristotle*, edited by Richard McKeon, 681–926. New York: Random House, 1941.

Aristotle. *De Poetica* (Poetics). Translated by Ingram Bywater. In *The Basic Works of Aristotle*, edited by Richard McKeon, 1453–87. New York: Random House, 1941.

Aristotle. *Prior Analytics.* In *The Complete Works of Aristotle*, vol. 1, revised Oxford translation, edited by Jonathan Barnes, 39–113. Princeton, NJ: Princeton University Press, 1984.

Augustine. *Confessions.* In *Augustine: Confessions, Latin Text with English Commentary*, edited by James J. O'Donnell. 3 vols. Oxford: Oxford University Press, 1992.

Bachelard, Gaston. *L'intuition de l'instant.* Paris: Le Livre de Poche, 1992.

Badiou, Alain. *Being and Event.* Translated by Oliver Feltham. London: Continuum, 2005.

Badiou, Alain. "Beyond Formalization: An Interview with Alain Badiou, Conducted by Peter Hallward and Bruno Bosteels (Paris, July 2, 2002)." In *Badiou and Politics*, edited by Bruno Bosteels, 318–50. Durham, NC: Duke University Press, 2011.

Badiou, Alain. *Logics of Worlds: Being and Event II.* Translated by Alberto Toscano. London: Continuum, 2009.

Badiou, Alain, with Nicolas Truong. *In Praise of Love.* Translated by Peter Bush. London: Serpent's Tail, 2012.

Badley, Linda. *Film, Horror, and the Body Fantastic.* Westport, CT: Greenwood Press, 1995.

Balibar, Étienne. "Uprisings in the *Banlieues*." *Constellations* 14, no. 1 (2007): 47–71.

Bantinaki, Katerina. "The Paradox of Horror: Fear as a Positive Emotion." *The Journal of Aesthetics and Art Criticism* 70, no. 4 (2012): 383–92.

Barthes, Roland. *Album: Unpublished Correspondence and Texts.* Translated by Jody Gladding. New York: Columbia University Press, 2018.

Barthes, Roland. *Critical Essays.* Translated by Richard Howard. Evanston, IL: Northwestern University Press, 1972.

Barthes, Roland. *Journal de deuil.* Paris: Seuil-Imec, 2009.

Barthes, Roland. *A Lover's Discourse: Fragments.* Translated by Richard Howard. New York: Hill and Wang, 1978.

Barthes, Roland. *Mourning Diary.* Translated by Richard Howard. New York: Hill and Wang, 2009.

Barthes, Roland. *Mythologies*. Translated by Annette Lavers. New York: Hill and Wang, 1972.

Barthes, Roland. "On Gide and His Journal." In *A Barthes Reader*, edited by Susan Sontag, 3–17. New York: Hill and Wang, 1982.

Barthes, Roland. "The Photographic Message." In *Image/Music/Text*, translated by Stephen Heath, 15–31. New York: Hill and Wang, 1977.

Barthes, Roland. "The Plates of the *Encyclopedia*." In *A Barthes Reader*, edited by Susan Sontag, 218–35. New York: Hill and Wang, [1964] 1982.

Barthes, Roland. *The Pleasure of the Text*. Translated by Richard Miller. New York: Hill and Wang, 1975.

Barthes, Roland. "Reading Brillat-Savarin." In *The Rustle of Language*, translated by Richard Howard, 250–70. Berkeley: University of California Press, 1986. Originally published as the preface to Jean Anthelme Brillat-Savarin, *Physiologie du goût*, trans. C. Hermann (Paris: C. Hermann, 1975).

Barthes, Roland. *The Responsibility of Forms*. Translated by Richard Howard. Berkeley: University of California Press, 1985.

Barthes, Roland. *Roland Barthes by Roland Barthes*. Translated by Richard Howard. New York: Hill and Wang, 1977.

Barthes, Roland. *Sade, Fourier, Loyola*. Translated by Richard Miller. Berkeley: University of California Press, 1989.

Barthes, Roland. *Writing Degree Zero*. Translated by Annette Lavers and Colin Smith. New York: Hill and Wang, 1967.

Bataille, Georges. *The Accursed Share: An Essay on General Economy*. 3 vols. Translated by Robert Hurley. New York: Zone Books, 1991.

Bataille, Georges. *Inner Experience*. Translated by Stuart Kendall. Albany: State University of New York Press, 2014.

Bataille, Georges. *The Tears of Eros*. Translated by Peter Connor. San Francisco: City Lights, 1989.

Baumbach, Sibylle. *Literature and Fascination*. Basingstoke, UK: Palgrave Macmillan, 2015.

Beckett, Samuel. "Dante and the Lobster." In *The Selected Works of Samuel Beckett*, vol. IV: *Poems, Short Fiction, Criticism*, 77–88. New York: Grove Press, 2010.

Beckett, Samuel. "Enough." In *The Selected Works of Samuel Beckett*, vol. IV, *Poems, Short Fiction, Criticism*, 365–70. New York: Grove Press, 2010.

Beckett, Samuel. "How It Is." In *The Selected Works of Samuel Beckett*, vol. II, *Molloy, Malone Dies, The Unnamable, How It Is*, 409–521. New York: Grove Press, 2010.

Beckett, Samuel. "Malone Dies." In *The Selected Works of Samuel Beckett*, vol. II, *Molloy, Malone Dies, The Unnamable, How It Is*, 171–281. New York: Grove Press, 2010.

Beckett, Samuel. "Proust." In *Proust and the Three Dialogues with Georges Duthuit*, 10–93. London: Calder, 1987.

Beckett, Samuel. "Three Dialogues with Georges Duthuit." In *Proust and the Three Dialogues with Georges Duthuit*, 94–126. London: Calder, 1987.

Beckett, Samuel. "The Unnamable." In *The Selected Works of Samuel Beckett*, vol. II, *Molloy, Malone Dies, The Unnamable, How It Is*, 283–407. New York: Grove Press, 2010.

Belloc, Hilaire. *A Moral Alphabet*. London: Edward Arnold, 1899.

Bender, John, and Michael Marrinan. *The Culture of Diagram*. Stanford, CA: Stanford University Press, 2010.

Benjamin, Walter. "The Storyteller: Reflections on the Works of Nikolai Leskov." In *Illuminations*, edited by Hannah Arendt, translated by Harry Zohn, 83–109. New York: Schocken Books, 1968.

Benson-Allott, Caetlin. "Old Tropes in New Dimensions: Stereoscopy and Franchise Spectatorship." In "Genealogical and Archaeological Approaches to 3-D." Special double issue, *Film Criticism* 37/38, no. 3/1 (spring/fall 2013): 12–29.

Berlant, Lauren. "Love: A Queer Feeling." In *Homosexuality and Psychoanalysis*, edited by Tim Dean and Christopher Lane, 432–51. Chicago: University of Chicago Press, 2001.

Bersani, Leo, and Ulysse Dutoit. *Arts of Impoverishment: Beckett, Rothko, Resnais*. Cambridge, MA: Harvard University Press, 1993.

Bertin, Jacques. *Semiology of Graphics: Diagrams, Networks, Maps*. Translated by William Berg. Madison: University of Wisconsin Press, 1983.

Best, Stephen, and Sharon Marcus. "Surface Reading: An Introduction." In "The Way We Read Now," edited by Stephen Best and Sharon Marcus, with Emily Apter and Elaine Freedgood. Special issue, *Representations* 108 (fall 2009): 1–21.

Blanchot, Maurice. *The Gaze of Orpheus*. Translated by Lydia Davis. Barrytown, NY: Station Hill Press, 1981.

Blanchot, Maurice. *The Infinite Conversation*. Translated by Susan Hanson. Minneapolis: University of Minnesota Press, 1993. *L'Entretien infini*. Paris: Gallimard, 1969.

Blanchot, Maurice. *The Instant of My Death*, with *Demeure: Fiction and Testimony*, by Jacques Derrida. Translated by Elizabeth Rottenberg. Stanford, CA: Stanford University Press, 2000.

Blanchot, Maurice. "The Song of the Sirens." In *The Gaze of Orpheus*, translated by Lydia Davis, 105–13. Barrytown, NY: Station Hill Press, 1981.

Blanchot, Maurice. *The Unavowable Community*. Translated by Pierre Joris. Barrytown, NY: Station Hill Press, 1988.

Blish, James. *SF Gateway Omnibus: Black Easter, the Day after Judgement, the Seedling Stars*. London: Gollancz, 2013.

Bogost, Ian. *Alien Phenomenology, or What It's Like to Be a Thing*. Minneapolis: University of Minnesota Press, 2012.

Bonifazi, Anna. "Inquiring into Nostos and Its Cognates." *American Journal of Philology* 130, no. 4 (winter 2009): 481–510.

Bonnefoy, Yves. "Paul Valéry." In *L'Improbable et autres essais*. Paris: Mercure de France, [1963] 1980.

Borges, Jorge Luis. "The Fearful Sphere of Pascal." In *Labyrinths*, edited by Donald A. Yates, 189–92. New York: New Directions, 1964.

Borges, Jorge Luis. "On Exactitude in Science." In *Collected Fictions*, translated by Andrew Hurley, 325. London: Penguin, 1999.

Boutang, Pierre-André. "Socrate à la télé." *L'Express*, November 11, 1995.

Bozovic, Marijeta. "Whose Forms? Missing Russians in Caroline Levine's *Forms*." *PMLA* 132, no. 5 (October 2017): 1181–86.

Brassier, Ray. "Axiomatic Heresy: The Non-Philosophy of François Laruelle." *Radical Philosophy* 121 (September/October 2003): 24–35.

Breger, Herbert. "The Art of Mathematical Rationality." In *Leibniz: What Kind of Rationalist?*, edited by Marcelo Dascal, 141–52. Logic, Epistemology, and the Unity of Science 13. Dordrecht: Springer, 2008.

Brinkema, Eugenie. "Form for the Blind (Porn and Description without Guarantee)." In "Porn on the Couch: Sex, Psychoanalysis, and Screen Cultures/Memories," edited by Ricky Varghese. Special issue, *Porn Studies* 6, no. 1 (2019): 10–22.

Brinkema, Eugenie. *The Forms of the Affects*. Durham, NC: Duke University Press, 2014.

Brinkema, Eugenie. "Irrumation, the Interrogative: Extreme Porn and the Crisis of Reading." In "Pleasure and Suspicion," edited by John Paul Stadler and Rachel Greenspan. Special issue, *Polygraph* 26 (2017): 130–64.

Brintnall, Kent L. *Ecce Homo: The Male-Body-in-Pain as Redemptive Figure*. Chicago: University of Chicago Press, 2011.

Brook, Timothy, Jérôme Bourgon, and Gregory Blue. *Death By a Thousand Cuts*. Cambridge, MA: Harvard University Press, 2008.

Brooks, Cleanth. *The Well Wrought Urn: Studies in the Structure of Poetry*. New York: Harcourt Brace, 1947.

Brophy, Philip. "Horrality: The Textuality of Contemporary Horror Films." *Screen* 27, no. 1 (January–February 1986): 2–13.

Burke, Edmund. *A Philosophical Enquiry into the Origin of Our Ideas of the Sublime and Beautiful*. Edited by T. O. McLoughlin and James T. Boulton. In *The Writings and Speeches of Edmund Burke, Volume 1: The Early Writings*, edited by Paul Langford, 185–320. Oxford: Clarendon Press, 1997.

Carnap, Rudolf. "Überwindung der Metaphysik durch logische Analyse der Sprache." *Erkenntnis* 2 (1931): 219–41. Translated by Arthur Pap as "The Elimination of Metaphysics Through Logical Analysis of Language." In *Logical Positivism*, edited by A. J. Ayer, 60–81. Glencoe, IL: Free Press, 1959.

Carroll, Lewis. "Sylvie and Bruno Concluded." London: Macmillan and Co., 1893.

Carroll, Noël. *The Philosophy of Horror, or, Paradoxes of the Heart*. New York: Routledge, 1990.

Carson, Anne. *Eros the Bittersweet*. Princeton, NJ: Princeton University Press, 1986.

Casey, Edward S. *The Fate of Place: A Philosophical History*. Berkeley: University of California Press, 1997.

Cassin, Barbara, ed. *Dictionary of Untranslatables: A Philosophical Lexicon.* Princeton, NJ: Princeton University Press, 2014.

Cavarero, Adriana. *Inclinations: A Critique of Rectitude.* Translated by Amanda Minervini and Adam Sitze. Stanford, CA: Stanford University Press, 2016.

Chamayou, Grégoire. *A Theory of the Drone.* Translated by Janet Lloyd. New York: New Press, 2015.

Christensen, Inger. *alphabet.* Translated by Susanna Nied. New York: New Directions, 2001.

Chu, Seo-Young. *Do Metaphors Dream of Literal Sheep?: A Science-Fictional Theory of Representation.* Cambridge, MA: Harvard University Press, 2010.

Cioran, E. M. *The Trouble with Being Born.* Translated by Richard Howard. New York: Arcade Publishing, 2012.

Cixous, Hélène. *The Book of Promethea.* Translated by Betsy Wing. Lincoln: University of Nebraska Press, 1991.

Clark, Andrew H. *Diderot's Part: Aesthetics and Physiology.* New York, Routledge: 2016.

Clover, Carol. *Men, Women, and Chain Saws: Gender in the Modern Horror Film.* Princeton, NJ: Princeton University Press, 1992.

Cohen, Jeffrey. *Stone: An Ecology of the Inhuman.* Minneapolis: University of Minnesota Press, 2015.

Cohn, Dorrit. "Kleist's 'Marquise von O . . . ': The Problem of Knowledge." *Monatshefte* 67, no. 2 (summer 1975): 129–44.

Collom, Jack, and Lyn Hejinian. *Situations, Sings.* Princeton, NJ: Zephyr Press, 2008.

Colyvan, Mark. *An Introduction to the Philosophy of Mathematics.* Cambridge: Cambridge University Press, 2012.

Comaroff, Joshua, and Ker-Shing Ong. *Horror in Architecture.* San Francisco: ORO Editions, 2013.

Cooper, Sarah. "Narcissus and *The Lobster.*" *Studies in European Cinema* 13, no. 2 (2016): 163–76.

Cordingley, Anthony. *Samuel Beckett's "How It Is": Philosophy in Translation.* Edinburgh: Edinburgh University Press, 2018.

"The Craft of Nombrynge." Edited by E. R. Sleight. In *The European Mathematical Awakening: A Journey through the History of Mathematics, 1000–1800,* edited by Frank J. Swetz, 26–31. Mineola, NY: Dover Publications, [1994] 2013. Reprinted from E. R. Sleight, ed. "The Craft of Nombrynge." *The Mathematics Teacher* 32 (1939): 243–48.

Crary, Jonathan. *Techniques of the Observer: On Vision and Modernity in the Nineteenth Century.* Cambridge, MA: MIT Press, 1990.

Critchley, Simon. *The Ethics of Deconstruction: Derrida and Levinas.* West Lafayette, IN: Purdue University Press, 1999.

Crowley, Patrick, and Paul Hegarty, eds. *Formless: Ways In and Out of Form.* Oxford: Peter Lang, 2005.

Cruising Pavilion (Pierre-Alexandre Mateos, Rasmus Myrup, Octave Perrault, and

Charles Teyssou). "Cruising Occitanie." In "Alain Guiraudie/Albert Serra." *Fire-flies*, no. 6 (2018): 57–64.

Darwin, Charles. *The Expression of Emotions in Man and Animals*. In *From So Simple a Beginning: The Four Great Books of Charles Darwin*, edited by Edward O. Wilson, 1255–477. New York: W. W. Norton, 2006.

Darwin, Charles. *The Origin of Species*. In *From So Simple a Beginning: The Four Great Books of Charles Darwin*, edited by Edward O. Wilson, 441–760. New York: W. W. Norton, 2006.

David, Alain. *Racisme et antisémitisme: Essai de philosophie sur l'envers des concepts*. Paris: Ellipses, 2001.

Day, Deanna. "Toward a Zombie Epistemology: What It Means to Live and Die in Cabin in the Woods." *Ada: A Journal of Gender, New Media, and Technology*, no. 3 (2013). doi:10.7264/N3MG7MDV.

Deleuze, Gilles. *Cinema 1: The Movement-Image*. Translated by Hugh Tomlinson and Barbara Habberjam. Minneapolis: University of Minnesota Press, 1986.

Deleuze, Gilles. *Cinema 2: The Time-Image*. Translated by Hugh Tomlinson and Robert Galeta. Minneapolis: University of Minnesota Press, 1989.

Deleuze, Gilles. *Difference and Repetition*. Translated by Paul Patton. New York: Columbia University Press, 1994.

Deleuze, Gilles. *The Fold: Leibniz and the Baroque*. Translated by Tom Conley. Minneapolis: University of Minnesota Press, 1992.

Deleuze, Gilles. *Foucault*. Translated by Seán Hand. Minneapolis: University of Minnesota Press, 1988.

Deleuze, Gilles, and Félix Guattari. *A Thousand Plateaus: Capitalism and Schizophrenia*. Translated by Brian Massumi. Minneapolis: University of Minnesota Press, 1987.

Deleuze, Gilles, with Claire Parnet. *L'abécédaire de Gilles Deleuze (1988–89); Deleuze From A to Z*. Directed by Pierre-André Boutang. Translated by Charles J. Stivale. Cambridge, MA: MIT Press/Semiotext(e), 2011.

de Man, Paul. "Kant's Materialism." In *Aesthetic Ideology*, edited by Andrzej Warminski, 119–28. Minneapolis: University of Minneapolis Press, 1996.

de Montaigne, Michel. "On Cruelty." In *The Complete Essays*, translated and edited by M. A. Screech. New York: Penguin, 2003.

Denis, Maurice. "Definition of Neotraditionism." In *Theories of Modern Art: A Source Book by Artists and Critics*, edited by Herschel B. Chipp, 94–100. Berkeley: University of California Press, 1968. Originally published in *Art et critique* (Paris, 1890).

de Rougemont, Denis. *Love in the Western World*. Translated by Montgomery Belgion. Princeton, NJ: Princeton University Press, 1940.

Derrida, Jacques. *Adieu to Emmanuel Levinas*, translated by Pascale-Anne Brault and Michael Naas. Stanford, CA: Stanford University Press, 1999.

Derrida, Jacques. "The Deaths of Roland Barthes." In *The Work of Mourning*, edited by Pascale-Anne Brault and Michael Naas, 31–68. Chicago: University of Chicago Press, 2001.

Derrida, Jacques. "Le Dernier Mot du racisme/Racism's Last Word." Translated by
　　Peggy Kamuf. *Critical Inquiry* 12, no. 1 (1985): 290–99.
Derrida, Jacques. "Différance." In *Margins of Philosophy*, translated by Alan Bass,
　　1–28. Chicago: University of Chicago Press, 1982.
Derrida, Jacques. "Form and Meaning: A Note on the Phenomenology of Language."
　　In *Margins of Philosophy*, translated by Alan Bass, 155–73. Chicago: University
　　of Chicago Press, 1982.
Derrida, Jacques. "La forme et la façon." Preface to *Racisme et antisémitisme: Essai de
　　philosophie sur l'envers des concepts*, by Alain David, 7–27. Paris: Ellipses, 2001.
Derrida, Jacques. *The Gift of Death*. Translated by David Wills. Chicago: University of
　　Chicago Press, 1995.
Derrida, Jacques. "The Law of Genre." *Critical Inquiry* 7, no. 1 (1980): 55–81.
Derrida, Jacques. "My Chances/*Mes chances*: Rendezvous with Some Epicurean Ste-
　　reophonies (1982)." In *Psyche: Inventions of the Other, Volume 1*, translated by
　　Irene Harvey and Avital Ronell, edited by Peggy Kamuf and Elizabeth Rotten-
　　berg, 344–76. Stanford, CA: Stanford University Press, 2007.
Derrida, Jacques. *On Touching—Jean-Luc Nancy*. Translated by Christine Irizarry.
　　Stanford, CA: Stanford University Press, 2005.
Derrida, Jacques. *The Problem of Genesis in Husserl's Philosophy*. Translated by Mar-
　　ian Hobson. Chicago: University of Chicago Press, 2003.
Derrida, Jacques. "Rams: Uninterrupted Dialogue—Between Two Infinities, the
　　Poem." In *Sovereignties in Question: The Poetics of Paul Celan*, edited by
　　Thomas Dutoit and Outi Pasanen, 135–63. New York: Fordham University
　　Press, 2005.
Derrida, Jacques. "Structure, Sign, and Play in the Discourse of the Human Sciences."
　　In *Writing and Difference*, translated by Alan Bass, 278–93. Chicago: University
　　of Chicago Press, 1978.
Derrida, Jacques. "The Taste of Tears." In *The Work of Mourning*, edited and trans-
　　lated by Pascale-Anne Brault and Michael Naas, 107–10. Chicago: University of
　　Chicago Press, 2001.
Derrida, Jacques. "Violence and Metaphysics." In *Writing and Difference*, translated
　　by Alan Bass, 79–153. London: Routledge, 1967.
Derrida, Jacques. "White Mythology: Metaphor in the Text of Philosophy." In *Mar-
　　gins of Philosophy*, translated by Alan Bass, 207–71. Chicago: University of Chi-
　　cago Press, 1982.
de Sade, Marquis. "The 120 Days of Sodom." In *The 120 Days of Sodom and Other
　　Writings*, translated by Austryn Wainhouse and Richard Seaver, 181–674. New
　　York: Grove Press, 1966.
de Sade, Marquis. *Juliette*. Translated by Austryn Wainhouse. New York: Grove Press,
　　1968.
Dickstein, Morris. "The Aesthetics of Fright." In *Planks of Reason: Essays on the Hor-
　　ror Film*, edited by Barry Keith Grant, 65–78. Metuchen, NJ: Scarecrow Press,
　　1996.

Diderot, Denis. "Passions." In *The Encyclopedia of Diderot and d'Alembert Collaborative Translation Project*, translated by Timothy L. Wilkerson. Ann Arbor: Michigan Publishing, University of Michigan Library, 2004. Originally published as "Passions," *Encyclopédie ou Dictionnaire raisonné des sciences, des arts et des métiers*, 12:142–46 (Paris, 1765).

Diderot, Denis. "The Salon of 1765." In *Diderot on Art*, vol. 1, *The Salon of 1765 and Notes on Painting*, translated by John Goodman, introduction by Thomas Crow, 1–188. New Haven, CT: Yale University Press, 1995.

Dixon, Wheeler Winston. *A History of Horror*. New Brunswick, NJ: Rutgers University Press, 2010.

Düttmann, Alexander. *Philosophy of Exaggeration*. Translated by James Phillips. London: Continuum, 2007.

Dworkin, Craig. *Reading the Illegible*. Evanston, IL: Northwestern University Press, 2003.

Eco, Umberto. *The Infinity of Lists*. Translated by Alastair McEwen. New York: Rizzoli, 2009.

Eco, Umberto. Interview with Susanne Beyer and Lothar Gorris. *Der Spiegel*, November 11, 2009.

Eisenstein, Sergei. *Disney*. Edited by Oksana Bulgakowa and Dietmar Hochmuth. Translated by Dustin Condren. Berlin: PotemkinPress, 2011.

Eliot, T. S. *The Rock: A Pageant Play*. New York: Harcourt, Brace, 1934.

Elkins, James. "The Very Theory of Transgression: Bataille, *Lingchi*, and Surrealism." *Australian and New Zealand Journal of Art* 5, no. 2 (2004): 5–19.

Evans, Robin. "Figures, Doors and Passages." In *Translations from Drawing to Building and Other Essays*, 54–91. Cambridge, MA: MIT Press, 1997.

Eyers, Tom. *Speculative Formalism: Literature, Theory, and the Critical Present*. Evanston, IL: Northwestern University Press, 2017.

Felski, Rita. "After Suspicion." *Profession* (2009): 28–35.

Findlay, J. N. *Hegel: A Re-Examination*. London: Routledge, [1958] 2013.

Focillon, Henri. *The Life of Forms in Art*. Translated by George Kubler. New York: Zone Books, 1992.

Foley, John Miles. "'Reading Homer' through Oral Traditions." In *Approaches to Homer's* Iliad *and* Odyssey, edited by Kostas Myrsiades, 15–42. New York: Peter Lang, 2010.

Foucault, Michel. *Discipline and Punish*. Translated by Alan Sheridan. New York: Vintage, 1977.

Foucault, Michel. *Madness and Civilization*. Translated by Richard Howard. New York: Vintage, 1965.

Foucault, Michel. *Les mots et les choses: une archéologie des sciences humaines*. Paris: Gallimard, 1966.

Foucault, Michel. "Nietzsche, Genealogy, History." In *Aesthetics, Method, and Epistemology*, edited by James D. Faubion, 369–92. New York: New Press, 1998.

Foucault, Michel. *The Order of Things: An Archaeology of the Human Sciences*. New York: Vintage, 1970.

Frege, Gottlob. *The Foundations of Arithmetic: A Logico-Mathematical Enquiry into the Concept of Number* (1884). Translated by J. L. Austin. Evanston, IL: Northwestern University Press, 1980.

Freud, Sigmund. *Civilization and Its Discontents* (standard edition). Edited and translated by James Strachey. New York: W. W. Norton, 1961.

Freud, Sigmund. "The 'Uncanny.'" In *Writings on Art and Literature*, Edited by Werner Hamacher and David E. Wellbery, translated by Alix Strachey, 193–233. Stanford, CA: Stanford University Press, 1997.

Friedman, Nathan. "Diagram of the Amorous Search: Generating Desire with Guiraudie's *L'inconnu du lac*." *Scapegoat: Landscape, Architecture, Political Economy* 9 (winter/spring 2015): 183–88.

Fuchs, Marko. "*Philia* and *Caritas*: Some Aspects of Aquinas's Reception of Aristotle's Theory of Friendship." In *Aquinas and the Nicomachean Ethics*, edited by Tobias Hoffmann, Jörn Müller, and Matthias Perkams, 203–19. Cambridge: Cambridge University Press, 2013.

Gallagher, Catherine. "Formalism and Time." *Modern Language Quarterly* 61, no. 1 (March 2000): 229–51.

Gallagher, David. "Thomas Aquinas on Self-Love as the Basis for Love of Others." *Acta Philosophica* 8 (1999): 23–44.

Gangle, Rocco, and Julius Greve, eds. *Superpositions: Laruelle and the Humanities.* London: Rowman and Littlefield International, 2017.

Garcia, Tristan. *Form and Object: A Treatise on Things.* Translated by Mark Allan Ohm and Jon Cogburn. Edinburgh: Edinburgh University Press, 2014.

Gasché, Rodolphe. *The Idea of Form: Rethinking Kant's Aesthetics.* Stanford, CA: Stanford University Press, 2003.

Gaut, Berys. "The Paradox of Horror." *British Journal of Aesthetics* 33, no. 4 (1993): 333–45.

Gibson, Andrew. *Beckett and Badiou: The Pathos of Intermittency.* Oxford: Oxford University Press, 2006.

Gide, André. *The Counterfeiters.* Translated by Dorothy Bussy. New York: Vintage Books, 1973.

Gilchrist, Todd. "'Rubber' Director Quentin Dupieux on Why He Made a Movie about a Killer Tire." *Wall Street Journal*, Speakeasy (blog), November 12, 2010, https://blogs.wsj.com/speakeasy/2010/11/12/rubber-director-quentin-dupieux -on-why-he-made-a-movie-about-a-killer-tire/.

Goethe, Johann Wolfgang von. *Theory of Colours.* Translated by Charles Lock Eastlake. Cambridge, MA: MIT Press, [1810] 1970.

Goethe, Johann Wolfgang von. *Faust: Part 2.* Translated by David Constantine. London: Penguin, 2009.

Gombrowicz, Witold. *Diary.* Translated by Lillian Vallee. New Haven, CT: Yale University Press, 2012.

Gombrowicz, Witold. *A Kind of Testament.* Edited by Dominique de Roux, translated by Alastair Hamilton, introduction by Maurice Nadeau. Champaign, IL: Dalkey Archive Press, 2007.

Gorey, Edward. *The Gashlycrumb Tinies, or, After the Outing*. New York: Simon and Schuster, 1963.

Greenberg, Clement. *The Collected Essays and Criticism, Volume 4: Modernism with a Vengeance, 1957–1969*. Edited by John O'Brian. Chicago: University of Chicago Press, 1993.

Greve, Julius. *Shreds of Matter: Cormac McCarthy and the Concept of Nature*. Hanover, NH: Dartmouth College Press, 2018.

Gris, Fabien. "La solitude du silure et des petits poissons." *La Vie des idées*, July 24, 2013. Accessed May 11, 2020. http://www.laviedesidees.fr/La-solitude-du-silure-et-des.html.

Grundmann, Roy. "Love, Death, Truth—*Amour*." *Senses of Cinema* 65 (December 2012). Accessed May 11, 2020. http://sensesofcinema.com/2012/feature-articles/love-death-truth-amour/.

Halberstam, Judith (Jack). *Skin Shows: Gothic Horror and the Technology of Monsters*. Durham, NC: Duke University Press, 1995.

Hales, Thomas C. "The Honeycomb Conjecture." *Discrete and Computational Geometry* 25, no. 1 (2001): 1–22.

Hall, Amy Laura. *Kierkegaard and the Treachery of Love*. Cambridge: Cambridge University Press, 2002.

Hallward, Peter, and Knox Peden, eds. *Concept and Form*, vol. 2, *Interviews and Essays on the* Cahiers pour l'Analyse. London: Verso, 2012.

Hamacher, Werner. "Premises." In *Premises: Essays on Philosophy and Literature from Kant to Celan*, translated by Peter Fenves, 1–43. Stanford, CA: Stanford University Press, 1996.

Han, Byung-Chul. *Topology of Violence*. Translated by Amanda DeMarco. Cambridge, MA: MIT Press, 2018.

Haneke, Michael. "Michael Haneke Talks about *Amour*." Interview by Karin Schiefer. *AustrianFilms.com*, May 2012. Accessed May 12, 2020. https://www.austrianfilms.com/news/en/michael_haneke_talks_about_amour/.

Hanich, Julian. *Cinematic Emotion in Horror Films and Thrillers: The Aesthetic Paradox of Pleasurable Fear*. New York: Routledge, 2010.

Hanslick, Eduard. *On the Musically Beautiful: A Contribution towards the Revision of the Aesthetics of Music*. Translated by Geoffrey Payzant. Indianapolis, IN: Hackett Publishing, 1986.

Harman, Graham. *The Quadruple Object*. Winchester, UK: Zero Books, 2011.

Harrison, Charles. "The Effects of Landscape." In *Landscape and Power*, edited by W. J. T. Mitchell, 203–40. Chicago: University of Chicago Press, 2002.

Hass, Robert. "Meditation at Lagunitas." In *Praise*. New York: HarperCollins, 1979.

Hegel, Georg Wilhelm Friedrich. *Elements of the Philosophy of Right*. Edited by Allen W. Wood, translated by H. B. Nisbet. Cambridge Texts in the History of Political Thought. Cambridge: Cambridge University Press, 1991.

Hegel, Georg Wilhelm Friedrich. "Love." In *Early Theological Writings*, translated by

T. M. Knox, introduction by Richard Kroner. Philadelphia: University of Pennsylvania Press, 1975.

Hegel, Georg Wilhelm Friedrich. *Philosophy of Nature: Part Two of the Encyclopaedia of the Philosophical Sciences (1830)*. Translated by A. V. Miller, with a foreword by J. N. Findlay. Oxford: Oxford University Press, 2004.

Hegel, Georg Wilhelm Friedrich. *The Science of Logic*. The Cambridge Hegel Translations. Edited and translated by George di Giovanni. Cambridge: Cambridge University Press, 2010.

Heidegger, Martin. *Being and Time*. Translated by John Macquarrie and Edward Robinson. New York: Harper and Row, 1962.

Heidegger, Martin. "Building Dwelling Thinking." In *Basic Writings*, edited by David Farrell Krell, 343–63. New York: Harper and Row, 1977.

Heidegger, Martin. "Language." In *Poetry, Language, Thought*, translated by Albert Hofstadter, 185–208. New York: Harper and Row, 1971.

Heidegger, Martin. *The Metaphysical Foundations of Logic*. Translated by Michael Heim. Bloomington: Indiana University Press, 1984.

Heidegger, Martin. ". . . Poetically Man Dwells . . ." In *Poetry, Language, Thought*, translated by Albert Hofstadter, 209–27. New York: Harper and Row, 1971.

Heidegger, Martin. *What Is Called Thinking?* Translated by F. D. Wieck and J. G. Gray. New York: Harper and Row, 1968.

Heidegger, Martin. "What Is Metaphysics?" In *Basic Writings*, edited by David Farrell Krell, 93–110. New York: Harper and Row, 1977.

Heraclitus. "Fragment 53." In *Heraclitus: The Cosmic Fragments*, edited by G. S. Kirk, 245–49. Cambridge: Cambridge University Press, 1954.

Hill, Adams Sherman. *The Principles of Rhetoric*. New York: Harper and Row, 1895.

Hills, Matt. *The Pleasures of Horror*. London: Continuum, 2005.

Hogarth, William. *The Analysis of Beauty*. Edited by Ronald Paulson. New Haven, CT: Yale University Press, 1997.

Hollander, Martha. *An Entrance for the Eyes: Space and Meaning in Seventeenth-Century Dutch Art*. Berkeley: University of California Press, 2002.

Hume, David. "Of Tragedy." In *Eight Great Tragedies*, edited by Sylvan Barnet, Morton Berman, and William Burto, 433–39. New York: Meridian, 1996.

Humphries, Reynold. *The American Horror Film: An Introduction*. Edinburgh: Edinburgh University Press, 2002.

Husserl, Edmund. *The Crisis of European Sciences and Transcendental Phenomenology*. Translated by D. Carr. Evanston, IL: Northwestern University Press, 1970.

Jameson, Fredric. *The Political Unconscious*. Ithaca, NY: Cornell University Press, 1981.

Jameson, Fredric. "Video: Surrealism without the Unconscious." In *Postmodernism, or, The Cultural Logic of Late Capitalism*, 67–96. Durham, NC: Duke University Press, 1991.

Jirsa, Tomáš. "Lost in Pattern: Rococo Ornament and Its Journey to Contemporary Art through Wallpaper." In *Where Is History Today? New Ways of Representing the Past*, edited by Marcel Arbeit and Ian Christie, 101–19. Olomouc, Czech Republic: Palacký University Press, 2015.

Jones, Peter Murray. "'Sicut hic depingitur . . .': John of Arderne and English Medical Illustration in the 14th and 15th Centuries." In *Die Kunst und das Studium der Natur vom 14. zum 16. Jahrhundert*, ed. Wolfram Prinz and Andreas Beyer, 103–26. Weinheim: Acta Humaniora/VCH, 1987.

Kafka, Franz. "The Cares of a Family Man." In *The Complete Stories*, edited by Nahum N. Glatzer, 427–29. New York: Schocken Books, 1971.

Kallir, Jane. *Egon Schiele: Love and Death*. Berlin: Hatje Cantz, 2005. Exhibition catalogue, Van Gogh Museum, Amsterdam.

Kant, Immanuel. *Critique of the Power of Judgment*, 2nd ed. Edited by Paul Guyer. Translated by Paul Guyer and Eric Matthews. Cambridge: Cambridge University Press, 2000.

Kaufman, Robert. "Everybody Hates Kant: Blakean Formalism and the Symmetries of Laura Moriarty." *Modern Language Quarterly* 61, no. 1 (2000): 131–55.

Kawin, Bruce. *Horror and the Horror Film*. London: Anthem Press, 2012.

Keenan, Dennis King. *The Question of Sacrifice*. Bloomington: Indiana University Press, 2005.

Kierkegaard, Søren. "At a Graveside." In *Three Discourses on Imagined Occasions*, translated by Howard V. Hong and Edna H. Hong, 69–102. Princeton, NJ: Princeton University Press, 1993.

Kierkegaard, Søren. *Concluding Unscientific Postscript to "Philosophical Fragments."* Edited and translated by Howard V. Hong and Edna H. Hong. Princeton, NJ: Princeton University Press, 1992.

Kierkegaard, Søren. *Fear and Trembling / Repetition*. Edited and translated by Howard V. Hong and Edna H. Hong. Princeton, NJ: Princeton University Press, 1983.

Kierkegaard, Søren. *Works of Love* (Kjerlighedens Gjerninger) (1847). Translated by Howard V. Hong and Edna H. Hong. Foreword by George Pattison. New York: HarperCollins, 2009.

King, Derrick. "The (Bio)political Economy of Bodies, Culture as Commodification, and the Badiouian Event: Reading Political Allegories in *The Cabin in the Woods*." In "Joss in June: Selected Essays," ed. K. Dale Koontz and Ensley F. Guffey. Special double issue, *Slayage* 11.2/12.1, nos. 38–39 (summer 2014). https://www.whedonstudies.tv/volume-12.html.

King, Stephen. *Danse Macabre*. New York: Gallery Books, 1981.

Kirby, Michael. *A Formalist Theatre*. Philadelphia: University of Pennsylvania Press, 1987.

Konstan, David. *The Emotions of the Ancient Greeks: Studies in Aristotle and Classical Literature*. Toronto: University of Toronto Press, 2006.

Kornbluh, Anna. *The Order of Forms: Realism, Formalism, and Social Space*. Chicago: University of Chicago Press, 2019.

Kornbluh, Anna. *Realizing Capital: Financial and Psychic Economies in Victorian Form*. New York: Fordham University Press, 2014.

Kracauer, Siegfried. "Hollywood's Terror Films: Do They Reflect an American State of Mind?" *New German Critique* 89 (spring–summer 2003): 105–111. Originally published in *Commentary* 2 (1946): 132–36.

Krauss, Rosalind E. "Grids." In *The Originality of the Avant-Garde and Other Modernist Myths*, 8–22. Cambridge, MA: MIT Press, 1986.

Krauss, Rosalind E. "The Originality of the Avant-Garde." In *The Originality of the Avant-Garde and Other Modernist Myths*, 151–70. Cambridge, MA: MIT Press, 1986.

Lacan, Jacques. "The Function and Field of Speech and Language in Psychoanalysis." In *Écrits*, complete edition, translated by Bruce Fink, 197–268. New York: W. W. Norton, 2006.

Lacan, Jacques. "*L'Étourdit*: A Bilingual Presentation of the Second Turn." Translated by Cormac Gallagher. *The Letter: Irish Journal for Lacanian Psychoanalysis* 43 (2010): 1–15. Originally published in *Scilicet*, no. 4 (1973): 5–52.

Lacan, Jacques. "Second Turn: The Discourse of the Analyst and Interpretation." In *L'étourdit* (1972), translated by Cormac Gallagher. Unedited seminar translations.

Lackner, Eden Lee. "A Monstrous Childhood: Edward Gorey's Influence on Tim Burton's *The Melancholy Death of Oyster Boy*." In *The Works of Tim Burton: Margins to Mainstream*, edited by Jeffrey Andrew Weinstock, 151–64. New York: Palgrave, 2013.

Land, Nick. *The Thirst for Annihilation: Georges Bataille and Virulent Nihilism*. London: Routledge, 1992.

Laruelle, François. *Dictionary of Non-Philosophy*. Translated by Taylor Adkins. Minneapolis: Univocal, 2013.

Laruelle, François. "Theory of Philosophical Decision." In *Philosophies of Difference: A Critical Introduction to Non-Philosophy*, translated by Rocco Gangle, 196–223. London: Continuum, 2010.

Lebensztejn, Jean-Claude, and John Johnston. "Star." *October* 1 (spring 1976): 86–103.

Le Corbusier. *The City of To-morrow and Its Planning*. Translated by Frederick Etchells. London: Architectural Press, [1929] 1971.

Lehman, Robert S. "Formalism, Mere Form, and Judgment." *New Literary History* 48, no. 2 (2017): 245–63.

Leibniz, Gottfried Wilhelm. *Consilium de Encyclopaedia nova conscribenda methodo inventoria (Project of a New Encyclopedia to be written following the method of invention)*. In *The Art of Controversies*, edited and translated by Marcelo Dascal, 130–41. Dordrecht: Springer, 2008.

Leibniz, Gottfried Wilhelm. *The Leibniz-Des Bosses Correspondence*. Edited and translated by Brandon C. Look and Donald Rutherford. New Haven, CT: Yale University Press, 2007.

Leibniz, Gottfried Wilhelm. *Monadology and Other Philosophical Essays*. Translated by Paul Schrecker. Indianapolis: Indiana University Press, 1965.

Leighton, Angela. *On Form: Poetry, Aestheticism, and the Legacy of a Word*. Oxford: Oxford University Press, 2007.

Lévi-Strauss, Claude. *The Savage Mind*. Chicago: University of Chicago Press, 1966.

Lévi-Strauss, Claude. "Structure and Form: Reflections on a Work by Vladimir Propp." Translated by Monique Layton. In *Theory and History of Folklore*, by Vladimir Propp, edited by Anatoly Liberman, translated by Ariadna Y. Martin and Richard P. Martin, 167–88. Minneapolis: University of Minnesota Press, 1984.

Levinas, Emmanuel. *De l'évasion* [On Escape]. Introduction by Jacques Rolland, translated by Bettina Bergo. Stanford, CA: Stanford University Press, 2003.

Levinas, Emmanuel. "Ethics as First Philosophy." In *Is It Righteous to Be? Interviews with Emmanuel Levinas*, edited by Jill Robbins, 103–238. Stanford, CA: Stanford University Press, 2001.

Levinas, Emmanuel. *Humanism of the Other*. Translated by Nidra Poller. Urbana: University of Illinois Press, 2006.

Levinas, Emmanuel. "Kierkegaard: Existence and Ethics." In *Proper Names*, translated by Michael B. Smith, 66–74. Stanford, CA: Stanford University Press, [1963] 1996.

Levinas, Emmanuel. "The Other in Proust." In *The Levinas Reader*, edited by Seán Hand, 160–65. Oxford: Blackwell Publishers, 1989.

Levinas, Emmanuel. *Otherwise Than Being or Beyond Essence*. Translated by Alphonso Lingis. The Hague: Martinus Nijhoff, 1981.

Levinas, Emmanuel. "There Is: Existence without Existents." In *The Levinas Reader*, edited by Seán Hand, 29–36. Oxford: Blackwell Publishers, 1989.

Levinas, Emmanuel. *Time and the Other and Additional Essays*. Translated by Richard A. Cohen. Pittsburgh: Duquesne University Press, 1987.

Levinas, Emmanuel. *Totality and Infinity: An Essay on Exteriority*. Translated by Alphonso Lingis. Pittsburgh: Duquesne Press, 1969.

Levine, Caroline. *Forms: Whole, Rhythm, Hierarchy, Network*. Princeton, NJ: Princeton University Press, 2015.

Levine, Caroline. "Three Unresolved Debates." *PMLA* 132, no. 5 (October 2017): 1239–43.

Levinson, Marjorie. "What Is New Formalism?" *PMLA* 122, no. 2 (2007): 558–69.

Liddell, H. G., and R. Scott, eds. *A Greek–English Lexicon*, 9th ed. Oxford: Clarendon, 1996.

Lippe, Richard. "Stranger by the Lake: What Is Love?" *CineAction* 92 (2014): 70–72.

Love, Heather. "Close but Not Deep: Literary Ethics and the Descriptive Turn." *New Literary History* 41, no. 2 (spring 2010): 371–91.

Lowenstein, Adam. *Shocking Representation: Historical Trauma, National Cinema, and the Modern Horror Film*. New York: Columbia University Press, 2005.

Lukács, György. *Soul and Form*. Edited by John T. Sanders and Katie Terezakis. Translated by Anna Bostock. Introduction by Judith Butler. New York: Columbia University Press, 2010.

Lüthi, Louis. *A Die with Twenty-Six Faces*. Amsterdam: Roma Publication, 2018.

Magistrale, Tony. *Abject Terrors: Surveying the Modern and Postmodern Horror Film*. New York: Peter Lang, 2005.

Malabou, Catherine. *Plasticity at the Dusk of Writing: Dialectic, Destruction, Deconstruction*. Translated by Carolyn Shread. New York: Columbia University Press, 2010.

Marcus, Sharon, Heather Love, and Stephen Best, eds. "Description across Disciplines." Special issue, *Representations* 135 (summer 2016).

Marin, Louis. *Sublime Poussin*. Translated by Catherine Porter. Stanford, CA: Stanford University Press, 1999.

Marks, Laura U. *Touch: Sensuous Theory and Multisensory Media*. Minneapolis: University of Minnesota Press, 2002.

McKenna, Andrew J. *Violence and Difference: Girard, Derrida, and Deconstruction*. Urbana: University of Illinois Press, 1992.

McVaugh, Michael. "Fistulas, the Knee, and the 'Three-dimensional' Body." In *Medicine and Space: Body, Surroundings and Borders in Antiquity and the Middle Ages*, edited by Patricia A. Baker, Han Nijdam, and Karine van't Land, 21–36. Leiden: Brill, 2011.

Mehrtens, Herbert. "Ludwig Bieberbach and 'Deutsche Mathematik.'" In *Studies in the History of Mathematics*, edited by Esther Phillips, 199–241. Washington, DC: Mathematical Association of America, 1987.

Melville, Herman. *Moby-Dick*. London: Penguin, [1851] 2012.

Miller, D. A. *The Novel and the Police*. Berkeley: University of California Press, 1988.

Munteanu, Dana LaCourse. *Tragic Pathos: Pity and Fear in Greek Philosophy and Tragedy*. Cambridge: Cambridge University Press, 2012.

Nagy, Gregory. "The Subjectivity of Fear as Reflected in Ancient Greek Wording." *Dialogues* 5 (2010): 29–45.

Nancy, Jean-Luc. "The Forgetting of Philosophy." In *The Gravity of Thought*, translated by François Raffoul and Gregory Recco, 7–71. Atlantic Highlands, NJ: Humanities Press, 1997.

Nancy, Jean-Luc. "Image and Violence." In *The Ground of the Image*, translated by Jeff Fort, 15–26. New York: Fordham University Press, 2005. Originally published as "Image et violence," *Le Portique* 6 (2000).

Nancy, Jean-Luc. "The Inoperative Community." In *The Inoperative Community*, edited by Peter Connor, translated by Peter Connor, Lisa Garbus, Michael Holland, and Simona Sawhney, 1–42. Minneapolis: University of Minnesota Press, 1991.

Nancy, Jean-Luc. "Shattered Love" (L'amour en éclats). In *The Inoperative Community*, edited by Peter Connor, translated by Peter Connor, Lisa Garbus, Michael Holland, and Simona Sawhney, 82–109. Minneapolis: University of Minnesota Press, 1991.

Ndalianis, Angela. *The Horror Sensorium: Media and the Senses*. Jefferson, NC: McFarland, 2012.

Neill, Alex. "On a Paradox of the Heart." *Philosophical Studies: An International Journal for Philosophy in the Analytic Tradition* 65, nos. 1/2 (1992): 53–65.

Neuhaus, Fabian. "urbanMachine." In *Studies in Temporal Urbanism: The urbanTick Experiment*, edited by Fabian Neuhaus, 7–22. London: Springer, 2011.

Newman, Kim. *Nightmare Movies: Horror on Screen since the 1960s*. London: Bloomsbury, 2011.

Nicolas, Ariane. "L'Inconnu du lac: Éros et Thanatos sont sur un bateau . . . ." *Contre Champ* (blog). Francetvinfo, June 19, 2013. https://blog.francetvinfo.fr/actu-cine/2013/06/19/linconnu-du-lac-eros-et-thanatos-sont-sur-un-bateau.html/.

Nietzsche, Friedrich Wilhelm. *The Gay Science*. Translated by Walter Kaufmann. New York: Vintage Books, 1974.

Nietzsche, Friedrich Wilhelm. *Nietzsche's Werke: Schriften und Entwürfe 1872 bis 1876*. Leipzig: Druck und Verlag von C. G. Naumann, 1896.

Nietzsche, Friedrich Wilhelm. *On the Genealogy of Morals*. Translated by Walter Kaufmann and R. J. Hollingdale. New York: Vintage, 1967.

Nietzsche, Friedrich Wilhelm. *Thus Spoke Zarathustra*. In *The Portable Nietzsche*, translated by Walter Kaufmann, 103–439. New York: Viking Press, 1954.

Noys, Benjamin. *Malign Velocities: Accelerationism and Capitalism*. Winchester, UK: Zero Books, 2014.

Noys, Benjamin. *Persistence of the Negative*. Edinburgh: Edinburgh University Press, 2010.

Nye, David E. *American Technological Sublime*. Cambridge, MA: MIT Press, 1994.

Odell, Colin, and Michelle Le Blanc. *Horror Films*. Harpenden, UK: Oldcastle Books, 2007.

Osborne, Peter. "*October* and the Problem of Formalism." QP 28 (2013): 1–24.

Ovid. *The Metamorphoses*. Translated by Allen Mandelbaum. New York: Knopf, 1993.

Paik, Peter. "Apocalypse of the Therapeutic: *The Cabin in the Woods* and the Death of Mimetic Desire." In *Mimesis, Movies, and Media: Violence, Desire, and the Sacred*, vol. 3, edited by Scott Cowdell, Chris Fleming, and Joel Hodge, 105–16. London: Bloomsbury, 2015.

Palmer, Tim. *Brutal Intimacy: Analyzing Contemporary French Cinema*. Middletown, CT: Wesleyan University Press, 2011.

Paradis, Kenneth. *Sex, Paranoia, and Modern Masculinity*. Albany: State University of New York Press, 2007.

Pattison, Michael. Review of *Amour Fou*. *Sight and Sound* 25, no. 3 (March 2015): 68.

Penley, Constance, and Janet Bergstrom. "The Avant-Garde: History and Theories." In *Movies and Methods*, vol. 2, edited by Bill Nichols, 287–300. Berkeley: University of California Press, 1985.

Perec, Georges. *Species of Spaces and Other Pieces*. New York: Penguin, 2008.

Pesic, Peter. "Nature on the Rack, Leibniz's Attitude towards Judicial Torture and the 'Torture' of Nature." *Studia Leibnitiana* 39, no. 2 (1997): 189–97.

Pesic, Peter. "Wrestling with Proteus: Francis Bacon and the 'Torture' of Nature." *Isis* 90 (1999): 81–94.

Phillips, James. "Distance, Absence, and Nostalgia." In *Descriptions*, edited by Don

Ihde and Hugh J. Silverman, 64–75. Albany: State University of New York Press, 1985.

Pinedo, Isabel Cristina. *Recreational Terror: Women and the Pleasures of Horror Film Viewing*. Albany: State University of New York Press, 1997.

Pirandello, Luigi. *Six Characters in Search of an Author*. Adaptation by Robert Brustein and the American Repertory Theatre Company. Chicago: Ivan R. Dee, 1998.

Plato. *Phaedo*. In *The Collected Dialogues of Plato, Including the Letters*, edited by Edith Hamilton and Huntington Cairns, 40–98. Princeton, NJ: Princeton University Press, 1989.

Plato. *Phaedrus*. In *The Collected Dialogues of Plato, Including the Letters*, edited by Edith Hamilton and Huntington Cairns, 475–525. Princeton, NJ: Princeton University Press, 1989.

Plato. *Republic*. In *The Collected Dialogues of Plato, Including the Letters*, edited by Edith Hamilton and Huntington Cairns, 575–844. Princeton, NJ: Princeton University Press, 1989.

Plato. *Symposium*. In *The Collected Dialogues of Plato, Including the Letters*, edited by Edith Hamilton and Huntington Cairns, 526–574. Princeton, NJ: Princeton University Press, 1989.

Pliny the Elder. *The Historie of the World: Commonly Called the Natural Historie of C. Plinius Secundus*, 2 vols., translated by Philemon Holland, folio. London: Adam Islip, 1601. Printed for the Wernerian Club (1847–48).

Potvin, Guillaume. "*The Lobster*: La Ville, l'Hôtel, la Forêt." *Séquences: La revue de cinéma* 302 (May 2016): 22–23.

Pound, Ezra. ABC *of Reading*. London: Routledge, 1934.

Powell, Anna. *Deleuze and Horror Film*. Edinburgh: University of Edinburgh Press, 2006.

Prince, Stephen. "Introduction: The Dark Genre and Its Paradoxes." In *The Horror Film*, edited by Stephen Prince, 1–12. New Brunswick, NJ: Rutgers University Press, 2004.

Proctor, Richard M. *Principles of Pattern Design*. New York: Dover, 1990.

Prose, Francine. "A Masterpiece You Might Not Want to See." *New York Review of Books*, January 7, 2013. https://www.nybooks.com/daily/2013/01/07/haneke-film-not-to-see/.

Reyes, Xavier Aldana. *Horror Film and Affect: Towards a Corporeal Model of Viewership*. New York: Routledge, 2016.

Reynaud, Bérénice. "The Gleaners and Varda: The 2013 AFI FEST and American Film Market." *Senses of Cinema* 70 (March 2014). http://sensesofcinema.com/2014/festival-reports/the-gleaners-and-varda-the-2013-afi-fest-american-film-market/. Original interview published as "Alain Guiraudie im Gespräch mit Berenice Reynaud." *kolik.film* 20 (2013): 64–73.

Ricoeur, Paul. *Freud and Philosophy: An Essay on Interpretation*. Translated by Dennis Savage. New Haven, CT: Yale University Press, 1970.

Rivers, Christopher. *Face Value: Physiognomical Thought and the Legible Body in Marivaux, Lavater et al.* Madison: University of Wisconsin Press, 1994.

Robinson, Josh. *Adorno's Poetics of Form.* Albany: State University of New York Press, 2018.

Romney, Jonathan. "Dream Lovers." *Film Comment* 50, no. 1 (January–February 2014): 64–67.

Rooney, Ellen. "Form and Contentment." *Modern Language Quarterly* 61, no. 1 (2000): 17–40.

Rooney, Ellen. "Live Free or Describe: The Reading Effect and the Persistence of Form." *differences* 21, no. 3 (2010): 112–39.

Rorty, Richard. *Achieving Our Country.* Cambridge, MA: Harvard University Press, 1998.

Rose, Sam. *Art and Form: From Roger Fry to Global Modernism.* University Park: Pennsylvania State University Press, 2019.

Rotman, Brian. *Becoming Beside Ourselves: The Alphabet, Ghosts, and Distributed Human Being.* Durham, NC: Duke University Press, 2008.

Rotman, Brian. *Signifying Nothing: The Semiotics of Zero.* Stanford, CA: Stanford University Press, 1987.

Rubin, William, ed. *"Primitivism" in 20th Century Art: Affinity of the Tribal and the Modern.* New York: Museum of Modern Art, 1984. Exhibition catalog.

Russell, Bertrand. *The Good Citizen's Alphabet.* London: Gaberbocchus, 1970.

Sartre, Jean-Paul. *Nausea.* Translated by Lloyd Alexander. New York: New Directions, 2007.

Schiller, Friedrich. Letter 22. In *On the Aesthetic Education of Man in a Series of Letters*, trans. Elizabeth M. Wilkinson and L. A. Willoughby. Oxford: Clarendon Press, 1983.

Schwartz, Daniel. *Aquinas on Friendship.* Oxford: Clarendon Press, 2007.

Sedgwick, Eve. "Paranoid Reading and Reparative Reading, Or, You're So Paranoid, You Probably Think This Essay Is about You." Introduction to *Novel Gazing: Queer Readings in Fiction*, edited by Eve Sedgwick, 1–37. Durham, NC: Duke University Press, 1997.

Serres, Michel. *Genesis.* Translated by Geneviève James and James Nielson. Ann Arbor: University of Michigan Press, 1995.

Serres, Michel. *The Parasite.* Translated by Lawrence R. Schehr. Minneapolis: University of Minnesota Press, 2007.

Serres, Michel. *Rome: The First Book of Foundations.* Translated by Randolph Burks. London: Bloomsbury, 2015.

Serres, Michel. *Le Système de Leibniz et ses modèles mathématiques.* Paris: PUF, 1968.

"Sex, Death, and Geometry: A Conversation between Alain Guiraudie and João Pedro Rodrigues on *L'inconnu du lac*." *Cinema Scope* 55 (summer 2013): 33–37.

Shaviro, Steven. *The Cinematic Body.* Minneapolis: University of Minnesota Press, 1993.

Shaviro, Steven. *No Speed Limit: Three Essays on Accelerationism.* Minneapolis: University of Minnesota Press, 2015.

Shelley, Mary. *Frankenstein: Or the Modern Prometheus*. Oxford World's Classics. Oxford: Oxford University Press, [1818] 2008.

Shinkle, Eugénie. "Videogames and the Digital Sublime." In *Digital Cultures and the Politics of Emotion: Feelings, Affect and Technological Change*, edited by Athina Karatzogianni and Adi Kuntsman, 94–108. Hampshire, UK: Palgrave Macmillan, 2012.

Shklovsky, Viktor. *Theory of Prose*. Translated by Benjamin Sher. Normal, IL: Dalkey Archive Press, 1998.

Siegert, Bernhard. "(Not) in Place: The Grid, or, Cultural Techniques of Ruling Spaces." In *Cultural Techniques: Grids, Filters, Doors, and Other Articulations of the Real*, translated by Geoffrey Winthrop-Young, 97–120. New York: Fordham University Press, 2015.

Signer, Roman. "Der Schreck kommt erst im Nachhinein." Interview by Konrad Tobler. *Tages-Anzeiger*, June 12, 2014.

Smithson, Robert. "Entropy and the New Monuments (1966)." In *Robert Smithson: The Collected Writings*, edited by Jack Flam, 10–23. Berkeley: University of California Press, 1966.

Smuts, Aaron. "Art and Negative Affect." *Philosophy Compass* 4, no. 1 (2009): 39–55.

Solomon, Stanley. *Beyond Formula: American Film Genres*. New York: Harcourt Brace Jovanovich, 1976.

Spadoni, Robert. *Uncanny Bodies: The Coming of Sound Film and the Origins of the Horror Genre*. Berkeley: University of California Press, 2007.

Stace, W. T. *The Philosophy of Hegel: A Systematic Exposition*. New York: Dover Publications, 1955.

Stein, Leo. *The A-B-C of Aesthetics*. New York: Boni and Liveright, 1927.

Steiner, Peter. *Russian Formalism: A Metapoetics*. Ithaca, NY: Cornell University Press, 1984.

Stendhal. *Love*. Translated by Gilbert and Suzanne Sale. London: Penguin, [1822] 1975.

Stevens, Wallace. "Connoisseur of Chaos." In *The Palm at the End of the Mind: Selected Poems and a Play*, edited by Holly Stevens, 166–68. New York: Vintage Books, 1990.

Stewart, Garrett. *The Deed of Reading: Literature * Writing * Language * Philosophy*. Ithaca, NY: Cornell University Press, 2015.

Stewart, Garrett. "Haneke's Endgame." *Film Quarterly* 67, no. 1 (fall 2013): 14–21.

Stivale, Charles J. *Gilles Deleuze's ABCs: The Folds of Friendship*. Baltimore: Johns Hopkins University Press, 2008.

Stoker, Bram. *Dracula*. Oxford: Oxford University Press, 2011.

Talu, Yonca. "Review: *The Lobster*." *Film Comment*, March–April 2016. https://www.filmcomment.com/article/review-the-lobster-yorgos-lanthimos/.

Tatarkiewicz, Wladyslaw. "Form: History of One Term and Five Concepts. In *A History of Six Ideas: An Essay in Aesthetics*, translated by Christopher Kasparek, 220–43. The Hague: Martinus Nijhoff, 1980.

Theile, Verena, and Linda Tredennick, eds. *New Formalisms and Literary Theory*. Basingstoke, UK: Palgrave Macmillan, 2013.

Thornham, Sue. *Spaces of Women's Cinema: Space, Place and Genre in Contemporary Women's Filmmaking*. London: BFI Publishing, 2019.

Thucydides. *The Peloponnesian War*. Translated by Martin Hammond. Oxford: Oxford University Press, 2009.

Tolstoy, Leo. "The Death of Ivan Ilyich (1886)." Translated by Hugh Aplin. Surrey: Alma Classics, 2013.

Tschumi, Bernard. *The Manhattan Transcripts*. London: St. Martin's Press, 1981.

Tudor, Andrew. *Theories of Film*. New York: Viking, 1973.

Tudor, Andrew. "Why Horror? The Peculiar Pleasures of a Popular Genre." *Cultural Studies* 11, no. 3 (1997): 443–63.

Tufte, Edward. *The Visual Display of Quantitative Information*. Cheshire, CT: Graphics Press, 2001.

Twitchell, James B. *Dreadful Pleasures: An Anatomy of Modern Horror*. Oxford: Oxford University Press, 1988.

Valéry, Paul. "Thoughts in the Rough." In *Collected Works of Paul Valéry*, vol. 14, *Analects*. Translated by Stuart Gilbert, introduction by W. H. Auden. Princeton, NJ: Princeton University Press, 1970.

Virgil. *Eclogues. Georgics. Aeneid: Books 1–6*. Translated by H. Rushton Fairclough, revised by G. P. Goold. Loeb Classical Library. Cambridge, MA: Harvard University Press, 1999.

Vitruvius. *The Architecture of Marcus Vitruvius Pollio in Ten Books*. Translated by Joseph Gwilt. London: Priestly and Weale, 1826.

Voltaire. "Remarques sur Sertorius." In *Oeuvres complètes de Voltaire*, vol. 9. Paris: Librairie de Firmin Didot Frères, 1855.

Weed, Elizabeth. "The Way We Read Now." *History of the Present* 2, no. 1 (2012): 95–106.

Wetmore, Kevin J. *Post-9/11 Horror in American Cinema*. London: Continuum, 2012.

Wheatley, Catherine. "Small Is Dutiful." *Sight and Sound* 25, no. 3 (March 2015): 30–33.

White, Carol J. *Time and Death: Heidegger's Analysis of Finitude*. Edited by Mark Railowski. New York: Routledge, 2016.

Wilde, Oscar. "The Critic as Artist." In *The Artist as Critic: Critical Writings of Oscar Wilde*, edited by Richard Ellmann, 341–407. Chicago: University of Chicago Press, 1982.

Williams, Alex, and Nick Srnicek. "#Accelerate: Manifesto for an Accelerationist Politics." In *#Accelerate: The Accelerationist Reader*, edited by Robin Mackay and Armen Avanessian, 347–62. Falmouth, UK: Urbanomic Media in association with Merve, 2014.

Williams, Linda. "Cinema's Sex Acts." *Film Quarterly* 67, no. 4 (2014): 9–25.

Williams, Linda. "Film Bodies: Gender, Genre, and Excess." *Film Quarterly* 44, no. 4 (summer 1991): 2–13.

Williams, Raymond. "Formalist." In *Keywords: A Vocabulary of Culture and Society*, 93–95. Oxford: University of Oxford Press, 2015.

Wilshin, Mark. "My Summer of Love." *Dog and Wolf*, February 21, 2014, http://www.dogandwolf.com/2014/02/stranger-by-the-lake-review/.

Winter, Bodo. "Horror Movies and the Cognitive Ecology of Primary Metaphors." *Metaphor and Symbol* 29 (2014): 151–70.

Wittgenstein, Ludwig. *Notebooks, 1914–1916*, 2nd ed. Edited by G. H. von Wright and G. E. M. Anscombe. Translated by G. E. M. Anscombe. Chicago: University of Chicago Press, 1961.

Wittgenstein, Ludwig. *Philosophical Investigations*. Translated by G. E. M. Anscombe. Oxford: Blackwell, 2001.

Wolfson, Susan J. *Formal Charges: The Shaping of Poetry in British Romanticism*. Stanford, CA: Stanford University Press, 1997.

Wolfson, Susan J. "Reading for Form." *Modern Language Quarterly* 61, no. 1 (March 2000): 1–16.

Wood, Robin. "The American Nightmare: Horror in the 70s." In *Hollywood from Vietnam to Reagan . . . and Beyond*, rev. ed., 63–84. New York: Columbia University Press, [1986] 2003.

Woolf, Virginia. *To the Lighthouse*. Edited and with an introduction by Margaret Drabble. Oxford: Oxford University Press, 1992.

Wright, Kristen. *Disgust and Desire: The Paradox of the Monster*. Leiden: Brill Rodopi, 2018.

Yeats, W. B. "Three Things." In *The Collected Poems of W. B. Yeats*. Hertfordshire, UK: Wordsworth Editions Limited, 2000.

Young, Deborah. "*Amour*: Cannes Review." *Hollywood Reporter*, May 20, 2012. https://www.hollywoodreporter.com/review/amour-cannes-review-326962/.

Zaborowski, Robert. *La crainte et le courage dans l'*Illiade *et l'*Odysée. Warsaw: Stakroos, 2002.

Zdebik, Jakub. *Deleuze and the Diagram: Aesthetic Threads in Visual Organization*. London: Continuum, 2012.

Zelazny, Roger. *Lord of Light*. New York: Eos/HarperCollins, [1967] 2004.

Žižek, Slavoj. *Looking Awry: An Introduction to Jacques Lacan through Popular Culture*. Cambridge, MA: MIT Press, 1992.

Index

A, 78–80; as A (Levinas), 196, 201, 403n76; "A" (Zukofsky), 86; *A* (Lenica), 80, 91–92; primacy of the letter, 82, 92–93, 211. *See also* abecedaria

À l'intérieur. See Inside (À l'intérieur) (Bustillo and Maury)

A, B, 93, 196–201, 262–63. *See also* A; A, B, C; attachment; one; two; relation

A, B, C, 201–215, 221–22, 229–44. *See also* A; A, B; *ABCs of Death, The*; abecedaria; attachment; *Human Centipede, The* (Six); middle term; relation

abandoning, 138–41; of a critique, 130; of form, 272; as giving, 140–41; of interpretation, 72; refused, 246–50; of the world, 251, 253

ABCs of Death, The, 82–83, 88–90, 92–95, 100, 389n1. *See also* abecedaria; alphabetical, the; death

abecedaria, 78–100; *A. B. C. (La Priere de Nostre Dame)* (Chaucer), 85; *The A-B-C of Aesthetics* (Stein), 85; *The ABCs of Death*, 82–83, 88–90, 92–95, 100, 389n1; *ABC of Reading* (Pound), 85; *Abeceda* (Nezval), 79, 87; *L'abécédaire de Gilles Deleuze*, 96–100, 390n23; "The Abecedarian's Dream" (Collom and Hejinian), 85–86; *alphabet* (Christensen), 86–87; *Alphabet* (Johns), 87; *The Alphabet of Death* (Holbein), 78, 88; *Alphabet Poem* (Lear), 85; *Alphabetical Africa* (Abish), 85; *A Die with Twenty-Six Faces* (Lüthi), 86; *The Gashlycrumb Tinies* (Gorey), 88, 389n8; *The Good Citizen's Alphabet* (Russell), 85; *A Moral Alphabet* (Belloc), 84–85, 389n5; *Nonsense Alphabet* (Lear), 85; *Semiotics of the Kitchen* (Rosler), 87; *Zorns Lemma* (Frampton), 84, 91. *See also* A; alphabetical, the; I; order; Q; X; Y

Abish, Walter: *Alphabetical Africa*, 85. *See also* abecedaria

abortion, 391n10. *See also* mother; pregnancy

abstraction, 240, 242–43, 245–46, 406n13; abstract formalism, 252; and the close-up (Deleuze), 56; and connections, 274; de-abstraction (of GPS), 173; and the diagram, 398n13; failure of, 402n73; formalization of, 164; and the graphic, 59–66; and mathematics, 312–13; and measurement, 413n15; pure, 277; and simplicity, 190; and the social, 347–48, 356; and subtraction, 209, 312; in *The Way Things Go*, 50–51. *See also* dragging; *Way Things Go, The* (Fischli and Weiss)

accelerationism, 161–62. *See also* speed

access, 186–88; and ichnography, 298

accidental: beyond the, 174; features of an object/person, 257, 336; layout of the ground, 174; poisoning, 197; urination, 354

Adorno, Theodor, 253; on Kafka and the shocking, 233; on Kierkegaard's model of love, 347–48, 356, 418n79

Aeschylus: *Seven against Thebes*, 8

affect: and angles, 297, 299; and art, 253; as degrees of pleasure and pain (Locke), 379n1; and history, 277–78; in literature, xv; waning of, 317; as the warmest color, 326; world without, 121. *See also* love

agency: of horror, 186; and violence, 180. *See also* horror; violence

Aikin, Anna Laetitia: on the pleasure derived from objects of terror, 15–16. *See also* paradox of horror

Akerman, Chantal, 300

Alexander, Christopher: on form diagram vs. requirement diagram, 63–64. *See also* diagram

Alphabet Reform Committee, 91. *See also* alphabetical, the

alphabetical, the, 78–100, 232–33, 235, 241, 280, 364, 389n1; desire to sabotage/reform, 91–92; and Rube Goldberg, 48–49. *See also* A; abecedaria; *Alphabet Reform Committee*; encyclopedia; I; order; Q; X; Y

Althusser, Louis, 251; "expressive causality," 10; "immediate reading," 24, 210

Ammonius: on deos vs. phobos, 7–8

Ammons, A. R.: "Corsons Inlet," 283

Amour (Haneke), 343, 350–69

Amour Fou (Hausner), 291–306, 312, 315, 413n20

Andre, Carl, 186; on holes, 136

animals: "A is for," 97, 99; bird (in apartment), 352, 363–64, 368–69; bird (electrocuted), 165, 173; bird (as graveyard distraction), 348–49; bird (neck-breaking), 39; bird (as symbol [and not]), 138, 363–64; boar (bristle), 3; chicken (attacked), 166; chicken (stolen), 409n33; dog (brother as), 331, 337; dog (dying, limb-cracked), 239; dog (fooled), 49; dog(-like), 109; dog (posing), 301; dog (stray), 89; dog (straying), 184–85; dog (as term of

abuse), 397n2; dog (triple), 207, 379n1; duty toward, 101; elephant (trunk of), 319; fabulous, 89; fiber as, 216; fish (cut-throat, murderous), 306–7, 311–12, 314, 414n35; fox (Nazi stripper), 90; generosity toward ("living with"), 130, 156; hedgehog (spines of), 3; horse (swerving), 184–85; horse (swimming), 311; imaginary, 89; lizard (eyelid of), 92; *The Lobster*, 330–41; pig (bristle), 3; pregnant, 187; purity of, 121; rabbit (in *Rubber*), 126–27; seeking a territory of death, 96; snake (as disgusting and without moral), 85; snakes (on a dog's necks), 379n1; that from a long way off look like flies, 89; very real, 89; wolf (mother as), 331–32; wolf (opposite of), 289; wolf (and penguin [as absurd couple]), 334; wolf (as returning), 319; worm, 216–17, 239–40

Anouilh, Jean: *Antigone*, 318–19. *See also Blue Is the Warmest Color/La Vie d'Adèle—Chapitres 1 & 2* (Kechiche)

anti-Semitism: and form, 266–68

Antonioni, Michelangelo, 54

apocalypse, 83, 93–94. *See also* ABCs of *Death, The*; *Cabin in the Woods, The* (Goddard/Whedon); totality

apology: for doubting the other, 292; for defecating into the other, 237; and violence, 83–84, 157

Aquinas, Thomas: on love as union, 335

arbitrariness: and the alphabet, 81, 91–93; of death, 46; of increment, 364; of love, 333; of origin, 241, 272; of signifying system, 337

archive: in *The Human Centipede III (Final Sequence)*, 226; pure (Deleuze), 97

Arderne, John of: on showing (and anal fistulae), 203. *See also* fistulae, anal; showing

Arendt, Hannah, 146; and the death of the monster, 382n24. *See also* violence

Argento, Dario: *Suspiria*, 22. *See also* Guadagnino, Luca

Aristotle, 252, 297; on aphaeresis, 209; on ekplektikon, 112–13; on extreme skepticism, 30; on form, 256–57; on friendship and similitude, 334–35; on horrible deeds and relation, 110; on love, 307, 312, 340; "*omne trium perfectum*," 109; on *reductio ad absurdum*, 45–46; on tragedy, 13

arousal: predicted, 13; self-reported, 12; as a tiresome field, 323

ars formularia, xvii–xviii, 274–75. *See also* Leibniz, Gottfried Wilhelm

attachment, 196–245, 391n10; affective, 166; to the dead, 207–8, 235–36; to form, 417n59; of prisoner to cop, 109–17. *See also* A; B; A, B, C; *Human Centipede, The* (Six); joining; relation

Audition, 210

Augustine, Saint: on trembling with love and horror (before God), 2

awkwardness: of body-moving, 246–50; and foot, 323; spatial, 114–18; of violence, 82, 103, 113–14

Bachelard, Gaston: on order and temporality, 64. *See also* order; temporality

Bacon, Francis: and the "torture" of nature, 264, 410n34. *See also* torture

Bad Taste, 210. *See also* taste

Badiou, Alain, 252; and "…except," 146; on humanity and infinity, 164; on love and truth, 340, 366, 417n60; on the passion for the real, 162–63. *See also* love

Badley, Linda: on horror and pornography, 380n11. *See also* horror; pornography

Balibar, Étienne: on the banlieues, 114–15. *See also* borders

Bantinaki, Katerina: "The Paradox of Horror: Fear as a Positive Emotion," 16. *See also* paradox of horror

bartering: of death (as impossible), 67; of form for neck, 6; of graphic violence for violence as graphic, 61. *See also* substitution

Barthes, Roland, 29, 215–17; on affectivity in literature, xv; on the alphabet, 81, 91–93; on bathmology, 103; on discourses full of gaps and lights, 136; on flies, 216–17; on form and structure, 253; on formalism and history, 253; on Gide's personality, 37; on "I love you," 359; on love's potential interchangeability, 335–36; on likeness and death, 344; on mourning and temporality, 346; on the naming of astonishing images, 215; on the photograph and its caption, 68–69; on the sequence of phenomena, 39; on shit vs. "shit," 219; on sketches, 216; on the task of art, 299; on two who love the same one, 361–62

Bataille, Georges, 162; and flies, 217; on love and community, 305; on horror, xxi; on the photograph of Fou Tchou-Li, 409n33

bathos, 103, 294

Baudelaire, Charles: and Poe (and modernism), 185

Baumbach, Sibylle: on fascination, 261

Baumgarten, Alexander: *aisthanomai*, 4

Bazin, André: on Chaplin's interaction with inanimate objects, 48

Beardsley, Monroe: on affective fallacy, 253

Beckett, Samuel: on an (idea-filled) abscess, 203; on death, 45, 99; and the diagram, 239; *Enough*, 342; on expression, 71; *Film*, 239; *Footfalls*, 239; *How It Is* (on enchainment and the other), 196, 238–43; and math, 240, 242; on people and things, 123; *Quad*, 239

bees: as geometers, 177. *See also* geometry; grid; hexagon: honeycomb conjecture

Behind the Mask: The Rise of Leslie Vernon (Glosserman), 161

being: and death, 74; as enchainment, 229–30, 234–36; as form, 268; and formula, 44; as the negation of negation, 140; as provisional, 58; and relating, 196–200. *See also* I; relation

belief: in deciphering, 71–72; and genre, 28; and violence, 400n48

Bell, Clive, 252

Belloc, Hilaire: *A Moral Alphabet* (Belloc), 84–85, 389n5. *See also* abecedaria

Benjamin, Walter, 146; on dying and the dead, 353. *See also* violence

Berger, John: *G.*, 86

Berlant, Lauren: on (the formalism of) love, 417n59. *See also* love

Bersani, Leo: on Beckett's *How It Is* (with Dutoit), 239–40; on cruising, 310. *See also* Beckett, Samuel

Bertin, Jacques: on diagrams, 212. *See also* diagram

Best, Stephen: on "just reading," 387n37. *See also* reading

Bettelheim, Bruno, 10

Bieberbach, Ludwig: on formalism, 251. *See also* formalism

Blanchot, Maurice: on abandonment as also gift, 140–41; on the corpse, 131; on friendship, 344; on the lightness following an evaded execution, 159; on the *Odyssey*, 265; on philosophical (vs. common) fear, 9; on shared solitude at death, 198; on the writer's double bind, 136

blankness, 29, 171, 190, 211, 277, 313, 324; and love, 305, 338, 359. *See also* emptiness; silence

Blish, James: *Black Easter*, 149

blood: black, 231; bleeding out, 102; as compositional element, 231; and cruelty, 269, 271; drinking of, 7; leaking out, 230, 401n60; as pigment, 188, 190

blue, 315–29; bluish gray, 292; Blue Period (of Picasso), 319; blueprint, 290; as contradiction, 315; and distance, 316; dress, 322, 329; glow of tanning beds, 53, 56; grass, 322; mailbox, 322; patient gowns, 246, 248; as rupture of the new, 321; as stimulating, 315, 317. *See also Blue Is the Warmest Color* (Maroh); *Blue Is the Warmest Color/La Vie d'Adèle—Chapitres 1 & 2* (Kechiche); color

Blue Is the Warmest Color (Maroh), 318–19, 321. See also *Blue Is the Warmest Color/La Vie d'Adèle—Chapitres 1 & 2* (Kechiche)

Blue Is the Warmest Color/La Vie d'Adèle—Chapitres 1 & 2 (Kechiche), 316–29, 415n39, 415n43; literary intertexts in, 318–19. *See also* blue; *Blue Is the Warmest Color* (Maroh); color; love; relation

Bogost, Ian: on the "self-expression of objects," 129. *See also* things

bones: broken, 20, 23, 334; "down to the bone," 336; singing, 33

Bonifazi, Anna: on *nostos* in Homer, 166. *See also* navigation; *Odyssey* (Homer)

Bonnefoy, Yves: on formalism, 251

borders: and banlieues, 114; of the cinematic frame, 169; closing off, 267; and line, 182; of text, 228, 274; violated in order to establish them, 117; without, 175. *See also* boundaries; map

Bordwell, David: on neo-formalism, 252, 258; on the planimetric shot, 301

Borges, Jorge Luis, 84, 89–90; on the point-for-point map of the Empire, 168; on the sphere, 125–26, 131–32

Bosquet, Alain: "La Trompe de l'éléphant," 319. See also *Blue Is the Warmest Color/La Vie d'Adèle—Chapitres 1 & 2* (Kechiche)

boundary: cartographic, 166; and form,

close-up: and abstraction (Deleuze), 56; extreme, 18, 60–61, 64, 137, 318; and intimacy, 318

Clover, Carol: as a fan (of horror films), 14; on "horror's system of sympathies," 13

Cohn, Dorrit: on "the most pregnant graphic sign in German literature," 291. See also *Amour Fou* (Hausner); *Marquise von O . . . , Die* (Kleist); punctuation

Collom, Jack (and Lyn Hejinian): "The Abecedarian's Dream," 85–86. See also abecedaria

color, 315–29; bodycolor, 324; *Color Grids* (LeWitt), 186; colorlessness, 60, 113, 308; "The Colour Out of Space" (Lovecraft), 133–34; corpus as, 324; eye (as of no import), 325, 336; impossible, 133–34; mere (Wilde), 253; as movement, 223; as shock, 329; skin as (and light), 323; and table, 181; and temperature, 55, 318; and temporality, 351; and torture, 270; and violence, 104. See also blue; brown; gold; green; orange; red; white; yellow

Colyvan, Mark: on bees and efficiency, 177. See also bees; grid; hexagon

Comaroff, Joshua: on horror and architecture, 402n73

comparisons, 355: as the best method, xv–xviii, 69, 274, 379n1; beyond all (the sublime), 169; and love, 359–63; of measured things (geometry), 312. See also difference; Leibniz, Gottfried Wilhelm; matching; sameness; similitude

complexity: of the anthropomorphic, 190; complexification of clarity, 64; of horror, 14, 58; indifference to, 175; of the "introverted" sublime, 170; unnecessary, 48–50, 53. See also Goldberg, Rube

connoisseurship: and horror films, 13, 39

consent: opposite of, 305; as presumed

(but misread [in *Amour Fou*]), 294–95, 298, 304. See also *Amour Fou* (Hausner); misreading

contagion: and art, 5; and taxonomy, 89

Corot, Jean-Baptiste-Camille: *Souvenir of the Environs of Lake Nemi*, 308–9. See also landscape

Courbet, Gustave: *L'Origine du monde*, 319. See also *Blue Is the Warmest Color/La Vie d'Adèle—Chapitres 1 & 2* (Kechiche)

crawling, 93, 231, 239–40, 242, 244, 246. See also dragging

creepiness, 2, 4

Critchley, Simon: on deconstruction and politics, 403n77

cruelty: alphabet as a, 92; and blood, 269, 271; essential form of, 107; of form, 363; of gravity, 119; mimed, 337; opposite of, 289; ordinary (of gender-based violence), 90; political, 163; pure ("anything beyond the straightforward death-penalty"), 101; schoolyard, 319; smell of, 348; of suggesting another try, 154. See also Montaigne, Michel de; torture

cruising, 306, 310, 314. See also *Stranger by the Lake (L'inconnu du lac)* (Guiraudie)

cut: behind the, 293; cesarean, 115, 117; death of a thousand cuts, 409n33; jump, 292; match, 137; as multiplication, 281. See also cesarean delivery; destruction

dance, 23. See also Mayerová, Milča

Daney, Serge: on scenographic flatness and holding one's gaze, 275. See also gaze; scenography; spectator

Darwin, Charles: on involuntary erections (of hairs, etc.), 3; on the power of the natural selection process, 177

database, 25, 28–29, 146, 181, 188. See also matrix

David, Alain: *Racisme et antisémitisme*, 266, 268–69. *See also* anti-Semitism; racism

Day, Deanna: on *Cabin in the Woods*, 394n2. See also *Cabin in the Woods, The* (Goddard/Whedon); infertility

de Man, Paul: on "speculative formalism," 253

de Rougemont, Denis: on passion, 295. *See also* passion

death: and the alphabet, 78, 87–100; and attachment, 207–8, 235–36; banality of, 294; and being (of a text), 65; as cause of death, 38, 41–42, 75, 386n13; as certain, but unexpected (but certain), 44; of children, 88, 389n8; and choice, 181, 182–84, 291–92; and community, 349; as death, 33; as deliverance from death, 101–2; and design, 68–77, 90, 242; by ennui, 88; failure due to, 166; fear of, 10, 141; fear of lack of, 10; and form, 58, 90–91; and friendship, 29, 66–67, 237, 344, 394n2, 417n63; at home, 351, 353, 359; and interpretation, 69–79; and the lake, 311; line of, 305; and life (as genre of), 58; and list, 34, 39–43, 59, 72, 88; and love, 342–69; as meaningless/valueless (Beckett), 45; as monster, 389n8; mourning, 342–69; non-substitutability of, 67–68; non-transferability of, 387nn31–32; as occasion (to reveal love to the living), 344, 358; and order, 36–100; for the other, 67, 94; of the other, 43, 198; penalty, 101; and philosophy, 41, 98; playing with (safely), 13; pluralization of, 29; and possibility, 31, 63, 73, 76, 292; and quotation, 29; as random but inevitable, 46; as refuge, 228; and silence, 198, 345–46; slowness of, 83, 99, 102–3; and temperature, 55–56; and temporality, 39–40, 42, 57, 62, 102, 350; as text, 68; and thresholds, 36–39, 43, 46, 48, 50, 54, 57, 60, 65, 69, 355; vs. torture, 101–2,

107; as unwanted, 34–35, 37, 40; and wetness, 36, 55; and witness, 159, 236, 344. *See also* mourning; murder/killing; suicide

decapitation: as a preferable option, 102; in *Rubber*, 127–28, 130

decision: and death, 350, 365; duration of, 338; horror as an act of, 279; love as an act of, 341, 367; philosophical act of, 255, 406n15; possibility of, 309; radical formalism as an act of, 281; reading as an act of, 281–82, 301. *See also* Laruelle, François

découpage, 51–53, 57. See also *Final Destination* (Wong); *Way Things Go, The* (Fischli and Weiss)

degradation: of the cultivation of form, 3; as an endless well of possibility, 225; moral, 261; of philosophy (by horror), 242. *See also* humiliation

Deleuze, Gilles, 216; *L'abécédaire de Gilles Deleuze*, 96–100, 390n23; and the "and . . . and . . . and . . ." (with Guattari), 301; on the close-up, 56; on concept-generation, 26; on the diagram, 398n13, 414n33; on the figural and the figurative, 93, 98; on Kleist's lines of flight (with Guattari), 304–5; on *The Passion of Joan of Arc*, 277; on spectacle and endurance, 275–76; suicide of, 99. See also *Salò, or the 120 Days of Sodom* (Pasolini)

Denis, Maurice: on severing aesthetics from subject, 258

depth: and *bathmos*: 103; breadthless (Euclid), 190; of breathing, 12; of focus, 300; and glass, 220; impatience with, 387n37; of insanity, 3; and intaglio, 189–90

Derrida, Jacques, 146, 275; on abandoning as giving, 140–41; on bricolage, 185; on close reading, 27; on death, 67, 94, 387n32; on form, 266–69, 281, 283; on friendship and death, 417n63;

Derrida, Jacques (*continued*)
  on friendship and mourning, 344; on
    genre, 28–29; on indirect reading, 255;
    on a lapsus, 120; on the letter *A*, 82; on
    Levinas's "host as hostage" relation,
    235; on mourning, 29; on oneself and
    the other, 196; on the parergon, 114; on
    philosophy and death, 41; on philos-
    ophy and metaphor, 243, 403n75; on
    racism, 266–69, 283; on sedimentation
    and returning to origins, 27, 29; on sui-
    cide (and the first kiss), 304
desire: and the diagram, 414n33; and
    disgust, 383n38; eluding, 360; and fear,
    314; and landscape, 309–10; and risk
    of censure, 332; to sabotage/reform,
    91–92; and suspicion, 310. See also
    Stranger by the Lake (*L'inconnu du lac*)
    (Guiraudie); wanting
destruction: and the anger of God, 147;
    and consumption, 193; as creation/
    generative, 127–28, 193–94, 272–73,
    279, 281; of design, 76–77; impulse to-
    ward, 3; of love, 305. *See also* cut;
    Human Centipede, The (Six)
diagram: and abstraction, 398n13; as
    (potentially) advisable (Wittgenstein),
    xv; as demonstration, 232; and desire,
    414n33; as diagramming, 221, 230; in
    Final Destination, 59–65; form dia-
    gram vs. requirement diagram (Alex-
    ander), 63–64; as generative, 398n13; in
    The Human Centipede, 203–6, 210–15,
    218–20, 225–26, 231–33, 244; and line,
    214; and melancholy, 66; and memory,
    66; and pedagogy, 225–26; and philos-
    ophy, 243; as sketch, 221; and violence,
    230–33, 245. See also *Final Destination*
    (Wong); *Human Centipede, The* (Six).
    See also cell; graphic, the; line; matrix;
    table
Dickstein, Morris: on horror films, 13
Diderot, Denis: on the line and the
    sketch, 215–16; on passion, 261. *See
    also* line; sketch

difference, 260, 295–96, 302–4, 312, 321,
    324, 344–50; and femininity, 334; little
    great (minimal), 340, 349–50, 353–57,
    364–65; narcissism of minor difference
    (Freud), 26; and pain (Heidegger),
    357–58; as shared quality, 89–90; and
    similitude, 330–41, 349–50; and spa-
    tiality, 356; as threat, 337–39. See also
    increment; *Lobster, The* (Lanthimos);
    matching; measurement; sameness;
    similitude; thresholds
digestion: and color, 223; inverted
    (vomit), 210; violence of, 193–94. See
    also *Human Centipede, The* (Six)
discovery: technique of, xvii–xviii. See
    also encyclopedia; Leibniz, Gottfried
    Wilhelm
disgust, 1–2, 26, 108, 210, 244; aesthetics'
    avoidance of feelings of, 14; and land-
    scape, 310; and navigation, 166; self-,
    261; taking pleasure in, 13, 382n30,
    383n38; and verticality, 397n2
Dixon, Wheeler Winston: on *Final Des-
    tination*, 48. See also *Final Destination*
    (Wong)
domesticity, 300–301. *See also* death: at
    home; pattern
doubt: in *Amour Fou*, 292; and being in
    two, 7; in *Martyrs*, 262–63, 283; and
    surprise, 283; and the unknown, xviii.
    See also *Martyrs* (Laugier)
Dracula (Stoker): and exchanged necks,
    3. *See also* neck
dragging: of bodies, 22–23, 239; and
    care/friendship, 246–50; through the
    flowers, 342; off vs. under (abstraction
    vs. subtraction), 209, 243. *See also* ab-
    straction; crawling
Dupieux, Quentin (a.k.a. Mr. Oizo). See
    Rubber (Dupieux)
Dutoit, Ulysse, and Leo Bersani: on Beck-
    ett's *How It Is*, 239–40. *See also* Beck-
    ett, Samuel
Düttmann, Alexander: on justified exag-
    geration, 233

Dworkin, Craig: on the "politics of the poem," 258

eating, 319; forced (gavage), 209–10, 243, 270; as violent consumption, 193. *See also* digestion
Eco, Umberto: on lists, 34
editing, 56, 69–70, 303; and ontology, 72; suspenseful, 19; and temporality, 61–62, 64. *See also* montage
Eisenstein, Sergei: on animation and "plasmaticity," 272; critical appraisal of, 254. *See also* montage: Soviet
ekplexis, 7, 110–11
Eliot, T. S.: on light, 210. *See also* light
emptiness, 41, 129–31, 338; of a circle, 126, 129; via consumption, 193; of the letter W (for Deleuze [initially]), 97; of Levinas's ethics (for Rorty), 243; and light, 170; of a tire, 134; void as more than, 73, 176–77. *See also* blankness; void
encyclopedia: and alphabetic order, 84, 365; "Chinese" (Borges), 89–90; Diderot's, 215; and infinity, 34; Leibniz's, xvii–xviii, 274–75. *See also* Leibniz, Gottfried Wilhelm
endurance: of endtime, 352; and martyrdom, 263–66; of the spectator, 264–66, 275–76, 409n33; of the threshold, 358; and waiting, 54. See also *Martyrs* (Laugier); spectator; temporality; violence; waiting
engraving, 189, 191. See also *Cabin in the Woods, The* (Goddard/Whedon); intaglio
Epstein, Jean, 254
erasure: of the dead, 66–67; of erasure, 403n75; and form, 254; and legibility, 66; of negative space, 328; repetition under, 26; and the rub, 126; and table, 182; of the very thing one does, 269
Erté: alphabet paintings of, 87, 93. *See also* abecedaria
Euclid, 298; "breadthless depth," 190; Euclidean transformations, 274

Evans, Robin: on architectural plans and human relationships, 419n87. *See also* relation
excrement: excreting the excrement of others, 210, 237, 241; explosive, 223; feces passing to the skin (via anal fistula), 202; and horror, 397n2; and shame, 397n2; shit vs. "shit" (Barthes) 219; as waste, 209–10. See also *Human Centipede, The* (Six)
Exorcist, The, 2
Experimental Jetset, 91. See also *Alphabet Reform Committee*
exteriority: and fear, 9; of form, 333; *Get Out* (Peele), 134; getting out, 228, 233; interior of the exterior, 117; as interiority, 104; vs. interiority, 357–58, 362; outside the outside, 113–14. See also *Inside (À l'intérieur)* (Bustillo and Maury); interiority; thresholds; topology
Exterminating Angel, The (Buñuel), 39
Eyers, Tom: on "speculative formalism," 253
eyes: color of (as of no import), 325; extreme close-up of, 18; eyelessness, 190; furious (red), 150, 269; open (in death), 113, 116; shielding of, 260, 279, 284; slippage of the, 409n33; wide, 260, 276–77; wild orby, 110. *See also* gaze; visibility; vision

failure: of abstraction, 402n73; in *Cabin in the Woods*, 148–87; to commit suicide, 357; due to death, 166; to enact sufficient violence, 147–53, 156, 161; of failure, 157; to fall to meaning, 367; gleeful, 394; in *The Human Centipede*, 222–23, 231; interface, 169–70; to make horror a verb, 2; and love, 365; mechanical, 293; as multiple, 167; of navigation, 165–70; and pleasure, 169. See also *Cabin in the Woods, The* (Goddard/Whedon)
falling, 119; bodies, 113, 213; off the grid (as impossible), 175, 180, 280; to meaning, 367; short, 131

fandom: and horror films, 13–14, 17–18, 222

fascination, 10; as double, 261, 271; about fascination, 16; violence of (with form), 260–84

Fassbinder, Rainer Werner: *Angst essen Seele auf*, 193

fear, 1–19; of death, 10, 141; and desire, 314; of fear, 9; fearful sphere (of Pascal), 125–26; of flowers, 300; and green, 7, 150; of letting society crumble, 162; and philosophers, 9; and pleasure, 13–19, 382n30, 383nn38–39, 384n42. *See also* horror; panic

feeling, 391n7; aesthetics of, 14; of exclusion, 118; vs. understanding, 324; of violence, 104–18. *See also* rhythm

femicide, 90. *See also* murder/killing

Fibonacci sequence: fibbed, 86–87. *See also* Christensen, Inger; order

Final Destination (Wong), 38–77, 280, 386n13, 386n17

Final Girls, The (Strauss-Schulson), 161

Findlay, J. N.: on Hegel's triadicism and triplicities, 401n60. *See also* Hegel, G. W. F.

finger: moving of (in silent skepticism), 30; pointing to with (designating), 50, 60–61, 73–74, 89, 183–84. *See also* showing

Fischli, Peter. See *Way Things Go, The* (Fischli and Weiss)

fistulae, anal, 202–3, 397

flesh: and letter, 219; and line, 215–19; overlapping of, 222, 238

flies: *Fly, The*, 208; killing of, 216–17

florid, 326. *See also* Klimt, Gustav; ornament

flowers: in *Amour*, 343, 351; and anthology, 83; arranging of, 291, 300–301; dragging through the, 342; and line, 218; and temporality, 351; and wallpaper, 299–301

form: and the body, 22–23, 278–81; cinematic, 179–80, 183; comparison of, 274; and death, 58, 90–91; at first sight, 324–25; formalism vs., 256; formalizing formalizing form, 184, 303; and freedom, 254; giving, 269, 282; and horror, 77; and limit, 266–68, 272; and meaning, 268; of the more, 344; and the new, 281; and philosophy, 257, 274–75, 406n15; problem of, 362, 366; and racism/anti-Semitism, 266–68; as reading form, 303; and reluctance, 58–60; and simplicity, 255; vs. structure, 253–56, 406n13; sufficiency of, 170; and violence, 24, 71, 104, 260–84, 402n73. *See also* formalism

formalism, 20–31, 132–34, 251–94; abstract, 252; activist, 252–54; bourgeois, 252; and constraint, 82, 96–100; Czech structuralism, 252; and death, 41; disaffordances of, 259; "empty," 243, 403n77; evaluative, 252; extreme, 252; game, 252; and history, 253; hyperformalism, 178–79; and love, 330–41, 350–69, 417n59; mathematical, 252; metaformalisms, 258; moderate, 252; neo-, 252, 258; new, 252, 254, 406n12; New, 252; normative, 252; not-, 253; philosophical, 252; and politics, 253–55, 258–59, 281, 406n12, 408n28; radical, 20–22, 30–31, 44, 109–10, 178–79, 230, 233, 253, 258–62, 281–83, 298, 310, 318, 333, 336, 348, 354, 366, 406n15; restricted, 252; Russian, 252, 254; speculative, 253; strategic, 254; vs. structuralism, 253–54; and temporality, 44, 255; of torture, 273; of violence, 104, 282; violence of, 402n73; and visibility, 44. *See also* form

Foucault, Michel: on Borges's "Chinese encyclopedia" and the alphabetical series, 89–90; on the form of the diagram, 212; on historical beginnings and disparity, 188; on the madman sent to sea, 117; on the mirror in *Las Meninas*, 220

Frampton, Hollis: *Zorns Lemma*, 84, 91

franchise, the: as formulaic, 42, 44; and sincerity, 42, 49, 72. *See also Final Destination* (Wong); *Human Centipede, The* (Six)

free will: as wounded/killed, 197. *See also* attachment; relation

Frege, Gottlob: as against formalism, 252; on zero, 19. *See also* zero

Freud, Sigmund, 10, 26, 146; on aesthetics' avoidance of feelings of repulsion/disgust, 14, 397n2; on melancholy, 346; on mortality, 33

Friedman, Nathan: on *L'inconnu du lac*, 414n33. See also *Stranger by the Lake* (*L'inconnu du lac*) (Guiraudie)

friendship: and death, 29, 66–67, 237, 344, 394n2, 417n63; and dragging, 246–50; and ethics, 160; and fear, 9; and fish tales, 311; *philia*, 307, 311–13; and reading, 71; and repetition, 160; and similitude, 334–35; and violence, 156, 158–60. *See also Cabin in the Woods, The* (Goddard/Whedon); Schiele, Egon

Fry, Roger, 252

Gaut, Berys: "The Paradox of Horror," 16. *See also* paradox of horror

gaze, 314; holding of one's, 275–76; at one who lingers, 308–9; technological, 11. *See also* eyes; vision

general: order of the, 213; violence (vs. particular), 83. *See also* genre

genre: dilemma of, 27–29; life as (of death), 58; vs. generic, 193, 232

geometry, xvii, 27, 274, 291–314, 362; of ethics, 249; and metaphor, 180, 313; and modern art, 174; as a problem of genre, 29; vs. scenography, 297–303, 306–14. See also *Cabin in the Woods,*

The (Goddard/Whedon); grid; hexagon; line; love; pattern

Get Out (Peele), 136

Gibson, Andrew: on Beckett's work and mathematics, 240. *See also* Beckett, Samuel

Gide, André: *The Counterfeiters* (*Les Faux-Monnayeurs*) ("drop by drop"), 36–39, 43, 46, 48, 50, 54, 57, 60, 65, 69. *See also* increment; thresholds

Gilman, Perkins: "The Yellow Wallpaper," 301. See also *Amour Fou* (Hausner); pattern; yellow

glass: and alphabet, 87; and depth, 220; grid/matrix, 28–29, 164, 175, 180, 184, 186, 220; and modernism, 210; "Simple Way to Find Your Glasses" (Goldberg), 48–50. See also *Cabin in the Woods, The* (Goddard/Whedon); matrix; mirror; transparency

glitches, 145, 167–70

Goddard, Drew. See *Cabin in the Woods, The* (Goddard/Whedon)

Goethe, Johann Wolfgang von, 296; on blue, 315–17, 328. *See also* blue; color

gold, 321, 324; counting of, 360; of flame, 56; of hair, 333; of light, 219, 221, 230, 292. *See also* color

Goldberg, Rube, 386n17; "Simple Way to Find Your Glasses," 48–50. *See also* chain reactions; *Final Destination* (Wong)

Gombrowicz, Witold: *Diary*, 199; on the primary task of creative literature, xv

Gorey, Edward: *The Gashlycrumb Tinies*, 88, 389n8. *See also* abecedaria

Gould, Glenn: and the action/feel of a piano, 105. *See also* feeling

Goya, Francisco: "The Sleep of Reason Produces Monsters," 10. *See also* monsters

graphic, the: in *Final Destination*, 59–66. *See also* diagram

Gray, Thomas: "Elegy Written in a Country Churchyard," 348

green: (and) fear, 7, 150; rot, 228; -white florescence, 111. *See also* color

Greenberg, Clement: on abstract expressionism, 254

grid, 19; in *Cabin in the Woods*, 28, 165–91, 280, 282, 303; and cinematic form, 179–80, 183; in *Final Destination*, 60–61; and infinity, 175–76, 180, 395n20; and line, 170, 172–74; and modernism, 174; as monstration, 180; and narrative, 176; as obligatory, 185; simplicity of the, 175–76; vs. table, 186. See also *Cabin in the Woods, The* (Goddard/Whedon); cell; diagram; matrix; table

Gris, Fabien: on landscape as stage in *L'inconnu du lac*, 309. See also *Stranger by the Lake* (*L'inconnu du lac*) (Guiraudie)

Grundmann, Roy: on *Amour*, 354. See also *Amour* (Haneke)

Guadagnino, Luca: *Suspiria*, 22–23

Guattari, Félix: and the "and . . . and . . . and . . ." (with Deleuze), 301; on Kleist's lines of flight (with Deleuze), 304–5. *See also* Deleuze, Gilles

Guiraudie, Alain: on *L'inconnu du lac* (as "scenographic"), 306–7, 310. See also *Stranger by the Lake* (*L'inconnu du lac*) (Guiraudie)

Hacker, Marilyn, 252

hair: blue, 320–21, 327, 336; and horror, 1–30, 120, 409n33. *See also* bristling; horror; neck

Halberstam, Jack: on monsters, 10

Hales, Thomas C.: on bees as geometers, 176. *See also* bees; grid; hexagon

Hamacher, Werner: on dying and understanding, 68

Hamilton, Ann: *abc*, 87. *See also* abecedaria; glass; wetness

Han, Byung-Chul: on the topology of violence, 117–18

Haneke, Michael: *71 Fragments of a Chronology of Chance*, 360; and emotional glaciation, 353, 355. See also *Amour* (Haneke)

Hanich, Julian: on horror, 384n42. *See also* horror

Hanslick, Eduard, 252, on the aesthetics of feeling, 14. *See also* feeling

happiness: death and, 98; death and a lack of, 85; and the sciences, xviii. *See also* death

Harman, Graham: on real objects, 129. *See also* things

Harrison, Charles: on anticipation in Corot's *Souvenir of the Environs of Lake Nemi*, 308–9. *See also* landscape

Harvey, Laurence, 224. See also *Human Centipede, The* (Six)

Hass, Robert: on thinking about loss, 288. *See also* loss

hatred: of formalism, 251–55, 284, 405n8; and love, 289–90, 297, 301, 304–5, 348, 361. *See also* formalism; love

Hausner, Jessica. See *Amour Fou* (Hausner)

Hegel, G. W. F., 275; on Kant's categorical imperative, 243; on love, 345, 347; and the syllogism, 236–37, 401n60

Heidegger, Martin, 275, 347; *Abbau*, 194; on death and dying, 33, 43–44, 62–63, 67, 74–77, 94, 387n31; and the interrogatory mark, 133; on losing (and Nietzsche's thinking), 139; on the nothing, 140; on pain and difference, 357–58; on the primordial truth of existence, 21; on sameness, 41–42

Hejinian, Lyn (and Jack Collom): "The Abecedarian's Dream," 85–86. *See also* abecedaria

Herbart, Johann Friedrich, 252

Heuvelt, Thomas Olde: *Hex*, 161

hexagon: and grid, 164–76, 179; honey-

increment, 25, 55–56, 119, 344–369, 379n1; bathmology, 103; little great (minimal) difference, 349–50, 353, 355–57, 365; and love, 361–62; and pregnancy, 153. *See also* care; difference; Gide, André; love; measurement; thresholds

indexes: as possible through alphabetic ordering, 84. *See also* abecedaria; alphabetical, the; order

indifference: to complexity (of the grid), 175; of the dead, 345; of the diagram, 236; of form, 363; to form, 322–23; as impossible, 296; of the lake, 313; of love, 346–49; of pain, 379n1; of pigeon, 364; of radical formalism, 259; and violence, 185–86, 306

infertility, 152–55, 157, 188, 394n2. See also *Cabin in the Woods, The* (Goddard/ Whedon); pregnancy

infinity, 280; and comparison, 362; and design, 68, 74–76, 90; desire to comprehend, 34, 62; and encyclopedia, 34; and God, 297; and humanity, 164; and horror, 280; infinite becoming, 339; infinite contingencies, 164–91; infinite deferral, 283; infinite degradation, 235; infinite destructibility, 281; infinite difference (love), 362; infinite exegesis, 69; infinite fascination (with form), 284; infinite finitude, 68, 75; infinite grid, 175–76, 180, 395n20; infinite incompleteness, 295; infinite letterform generation, 87; infinite library, 84; infinite literature, xv; infinite love, 341, 353; infinite potential, 299; infinite promise of reading, 325; infinite reconfigurability, 272; infinite responsibility, 234–35, 238, 403n77; infinite skepticism (of surface), 70; infinite tenderness, 315, 415n39; and lists, 34, 62, 186–87; and the middle position, 242; as (mere) nuisance (Rorty), 403n77; and the number line, 241; and the

other, 196; and violence, 178, 237–38, 241–42, 273, 281

insanity/madness: banished to the exterior of the interior, 117; of freedom, 305; and hair-bristling, 3. *See also* bristling; hair

Inside (À l'intérieur) (Bustillo and Maury), 106–18, 391n10

intaglio, 164, 189–91. See also *Cabin in the Woods, The* (Goddard/Whedon); engraving

interiority: calls from inside the house, 10; and the destruction of love, 305; vs. exteriority, 357–58, 362; interior of the exterior, 117; interior or the interior, 104. *See also* exteriority; *Inside (À l'intérieur)* (Bustillo and Maury); thresholds; topology

interpretation: all the way down, 284; continued (to prevent death), 69–79; and temporality, 210. *See also* reading

intimacy: and the close-up, 318; of pain, 357–58; refusal of, 300; and the spectator, 318

It Follows (Mitchell), 134, 161

Ito, Junji: *Uzumaki (The Spiral)*, 132

Jameson, Fredric, 253; on formalism, 251, 405n8; on political interpretation, xvi

John Dies at the End (Coscarelli), 161

Johns, Jasper: *Alphabet*, 87. *See also* abecedaria

joining: of bodies (in *Suspiria*), 22–23; of bodies (in *The Human Centipede*), 203–50; and parting, 315. *See also* A, B; A, B, C; attachment; *Human Centipede, The* (Six); relation

Jones, Ernest, 10

Joy, Eileen: on attention to things human and inhuman, 130. *See also* animals

jumping/leaping: a canyon on a motorcycle, 165, 170–74; of a dancer, 22; of hair, 11; jump cut, 292; temporal leap, 262,

Le Corbusier: on grids and intersecting lines, 174; on invariants, 254. *See also* grid; line

leakage, 190, 202, 230

Lear, Edward: *Alphabet Poem*, 85; *Nonsense Alphabet*, 85. *See also* abecedaria

Lebensztejn, Jean-Claude: on Derrida, 27. *See also* Derrida, Jacques; reading

legibility: and brightness, 210; and design, 64, 66; and erasure, 66; and form, 255; and simplicity, 310. *See also* light

Lehman, Robert: approach to art objects of, 256

Leibniz, Gottfried Wilhelm: *Consilium de Encyclopaedia nova conscribenda methodo inventoria*, xvii–xviii, 274–75; on making comparisons (as the best method), xv, 274, 379n1; and scenography, 297

Leighton, Angela: on form's significance, 257. *See also* form

Lemay, Erika: *Physical Poetry Alphabet*, 87. *See also* abecedaria

Lenica, Jan: *A*, 80, 91–92. *See also* abecedaria

Lévi-Strauss, Claude: on the bricoleur, 184–85; on structuralism vs. formalism, 253

Levinas, Emmanuel, 268; on being, 400n43; on death (and the other), 198; on escape, 227–31, 234–35; on femininity, 334; on Heidegger's philosophy, 43, 76, 387n31; on "I," 196, 201, 227, 403n76; *il y a*, 170; on Kierkegaardian violence, 400n48; on Kierkegaard's notion of noncontinuity, 234; *Otherwise Than Being*, 234–35; on sameness, 243; on shame, 229; *Totality and Infinity*, 234, 243; on true horror, 280

Levine, Caroline, 408n28; on strategic formalism, 254, 259

Levinson, Marjorie: on activist formalism vs. normative formalism, 252–53

LeWitt, Sol: *Color Grids*, 186

light: in *Amour Fou*, 296, 303; in *Blue Is the Warmest Color/La Vie d'Adèle*, 319, 327–29; and grid (in *Cabin in the Woods*), 170–73; in *The Human Centipede*, 210, 231; in *L'inconnu du lac*, 308–9; and love, 345, 350, 358, 365; and night photography, 55; rearranged/shifting, 329, 348; search for (in *Inside* [*À l'intérieur*]), 113; skin as (and color), 323; sunlight, 310; and torture (in *Martyrs*), 270–71. *See also* legibility

limit: fascination with, 265; and form, 266–68, 272; of imagination, 169–70; of the letter, 219; limitlessness of the not-All, 151; and love, 301, 360; and the ogee pattern, 299; of torture, 265, 276. *See also* pattern; surprise

line: and borders/boundaries, xxi, 182; of death, 305; and diagram, 214; and fiber, 2, 215–16, 399n18; filling in the, 188–89; and grid, 170, 172–74; and infinity, 178; and objects, 217–18; and roundness, 27; S-curve, 217–18, 299; in the sand, 183; sharing of interior, 323, 328; and sketch, 215–16; and violence, 178, 270–71; waterline, 307. See also *Cabin in the Woods, The* (Goddard/Whedon); grid

lists: and culture, 34; and death, 34, 39–43, 59, 72, 88; false, 37; and infinity, 34, 62, 186–87; of Leibniz, xvii–xviii; and loops, 57; and table, 182; and violence, 273–74. See also *Final Destination* (Wong)

Lobster, The (Lanthimos), 330–41

Locke, John: on affects as degrees of pleasure and pain, 379n1

loops, 89; and lists, 57; in *Micro Loup*, 132. *See also* circle; *Micro Loup* (McGuire); temporality; toroid; zero

loss: of blue, 320; of control (of reading), 325; of light, 308–9; of love, 315–29;

thinking about (Hass), 288. See also *Amour* (Haneke); death; lost; love; mourning

lost: getting, 166–67; love, 315–29; time, 119, 166. *See also* failure; loss; love; map

loup est revenu!, Le (Pennart), 319. *See also* animal: wolf; *Blue Is the Warmest Color/La Vie d'Adèle—Chapitres 1 & 2* (Kechiche)

love, 250, 291–369; antilove, 335–36; and blankness, 305, 338, 359; and breaking, 275; and death, 342–69; as double, 361, 366; and failure, 365; fetish, 348; and formalism, 253, 330–41, 350–69, 417n59; as geometral, 290, 297–98, 303, 305; and hatred, 289–90, 297, 301, 304–5, 348, 361; and horror, 2; *I-love-you*, 336–37, 359–60; and knowledge, 336; and light, 345, 350, 358, 365; and limit, 301, 360; lost, 315–29; as mathematical, 366; of mother, 359–62; as omnidirectional, 298, 303–4; opposite of, 289–90, 305; and the other, 334; and philosophy, 304; of self, 345; and similitude, 330–41, 347, 417n54; as something to live for, 158–59; and surprise, 317, 329; and truth, 340, 366; as uncontrollable, 305; as unknown, 314; and violence, 275, 306, 339, 354–55. *See also* affect; *Amour* (Haneke); *Amour Fou* (Hausner); *Blue Is the Warmest Color/La Vie d'Adèle— Chapitres 1 & 2* (Kechiche); hatred; *Human Centipede, The* (Six); *Lobster, The* (Lanthimos); *Marquise von O . . . , Die* (Kleist)

Love, Heather, 387n37. *See also* reading

Lovecraft, H. P.: "The Colour Out of Space," 133–34

Lukács, Georg: *Die Seele und die Formen* (*Soul and Form*), 253, 405n9

Lüthi, Louis: *A Die with Twenty-Six Faces*, 86. *See also* abecedaria

madness. *See* insanity/madness

Magistrale, Tony: on zombie and werewolf movies, 14

Malabou, Catherine: on plasticity, 255, 275

Malevich, Kazimir, 131, 174, 252

Mallarmé, Stéphane: and "…except," 146

map: failure of, 165; and grid, 174; of an ideal (diagram), 212; lake as, 310; mapping out, 60–65; point-for-point (Borges), 168; of process outcomes, 50; surgical, 213–14; surveyor's, 168. See also *Cabin in the Woods, The* (Goddard/Whedon); ichnography; navigation

Marcus, Sharon: on "just reading," 387n37. *See also* reading

Marivaux, Pierre de: *La Vie de Marianne*, 318–19, 325, 329. See also *Blue Is the Warmest Color/La Vie d'Adèle—Chapitres 1 & 2* (Kechiche)

Marks, Laura U.: on radical materialism, 258

Maroh, Julie: *Blue Is the Warmest Color*, 318–19, 321. See also *Blue Is the Warmest Color/La Vie d'Adèle—Chapitres 1 & 2* (Kechiche)

Marquise von O . . . , Die (Kleist), 291, 295. See also *Amour Fou* (Hausner)

Martyrs (Laugier), 262–84, 409n33

matching: with a romantic partner, 331–41; of tissues, 211, 235. *See also* difference; *Human Centipede, The* (Six); *Lobster, The* (Lanthimos); sameness; similitude

Matisse, Henri: on the terror of meeting a woman on the street, 322. *See also* blue; *Blue Is the Warmest Color / La Vie d'Adèle—Chapitres 1 & 2* (Kechiche)

matrix: 164, 175, 180–81, 184, 186–88. See also *Cabin in the Woods, The* (Goddard/Whedon); cells; database; mother; table

Maury, Julien. See *Inside (À l'intérieur)* (Bustillo and Maury)

Mayerová, Milča: *Abeceda*, 81, 89. *See also* abecedaria

McGuire, Richard. See *Micro Loup* (McGuire)

measurement, 306–14, 349–50, 359–62, 413n15. *See also* increment; *Stranger by the Lake (L'inconnu du lac)* (Guiraudie); thresholds

melancholy: of deceased silence, 346; and design, 66

memory: and the body, 18; of computer hardware, 170, 181; and the dead, 343–69; lapses of, 119; and love, 343–69; nostalgia, 166; saturated, 405n8; and the schematic, 66; of smells, 150. *See also* love; mourning; temporality

Mengele, Josef, 232. See also *Human Centipede, The* (Six)

metaphor, 10; and geometry, 313; and history, 127–28, 133; for nothing, 138; and philosophy, 243; vs. table, 180

metaphysics, xvii; and form, 268, 274–75; and horror, 242–46, 249; humiliation of, 21, 242–44, 249; in *Martyrs*, 263. *See also* Derrida, Jacques; philosophy

Micro Loup (McGuire), 132, 134–35. *See also* circle; *Rubber* (Dupieux); toroid/ tire; zero

middle term, 222–27, 234–42, 280; as ground, 236; as punishment, 237, 246; and the rhizome, 301. *See also* A, B, C; *Human Centipede, The* (Six)

Miller, D. A.: on paranoia and surprise, 72. *See also* paranoia; surprise

mimicry, 330; and the horror-film spectator, 12, 18, 382n25; in *The Human Centipede*, 225–26; in *Suspiria*, 22–23; tears tempting tears, 101. *See also* similitude

mirror, 220–21; back of the, 220, 233

miscarriage: and failure, 150; in *À*

l'intérieur, 106–7, 113; "M is for," 82, 88, 90. *See also* mother; pregnancy

misreading, 101–18, 294–95, 298, 304–5. *See also Amour Fou* (Hausner); *Inside (À l'intérieur)* (Bustillo and Maury); reading

Moby-Dick (Melville), 197. *See also* attachment; relation

modernism, 185, 272; vs. formalism, 254; and glass, 210; and grids, 174

monsters, 10–12, 74; as "?," 132; and chance (Barthes), 81; death as, 389n8; death of, 382n24; and grid, 164, 175, 180–81, 184, 186; as required, 384n42, 394n4. See also *Cabin in the Woods, The* (Goddard/Whedon); matrix; table

montage, 44, 61, 65, 111, 114, 254, 258, 264, 303, 310; Soviet, 53–54. *See also* editing

Montaigne, Michel de: *"De la cruauté"* (On Cruelty), 101–4, 107, 111–12, 116, 118

Morris, Sarah, 186

mother: /child relation, 249, 360, 398n3; love of, 359–62; matricide, 110–11; and matrix, 180, 187–88; vs. "mal," 365. See also *Inside (À l'intérieur)* (Bustillo and Maury); matrix; pregnancy

Mouffe, Chantal, 146. *See also* violence

mourning, 29, 156, 321, 342–69; and asymmetry, 346, 348. See also *Amour* (Haneke); death; friendship; loss; love

murder/killing: as easy, 146; as a favor (to a fly), 217; femicide, 90; matricide, 110–11; and measurement, 308; as not particularly easy, 144, 157. See also *Cabin in the Woods, The* (Goddard/ Whedon); death

Nancy, Jean-Luc: on blood, 269, 271; on the "common suicide" of lovers, 295; on love, 305, 318, 345, 359, 361, 365–67; on the realm of meaning, 279; on violence (and images), 103–4, 114, 269, 283 narrative: vs. form, 74, 183; and the grid, 176; and paranoia, 71–72; vs. spectacle, 59; and survival, 265

Natali, Vincenzo: *Cube*, 132

nationalism, 115, 117

navigation, 165–73. *See also* map

Ndalianis, Angela: on New Horror Cinema, 17–18

neck: breaking of (by an eagle), 39; dabbing of, 356; exchanged, 3; and horror, 1–30, 105, 108; puncturing of, 101–4, 110–11, 116. *See also* hair; horror

Neill, Alex, "On a Paradox of the Heart," 16. *See also* paradox of horror

Nelson, George: *A Problem of Design: How to Kill People*, 58

New Extremism, 262, 264, 279. See also *Martyrs* (Laugier); torture

Nezval, Vítězslav: *Abeceda*, 79, 87. *See also* abecedaria

Nietzsche, Friedrich Wilhelm, 146; and the circle, 126; on Kant, 348; on life and death, 58; as the philosopher of the shudder, 381n20; thinking of, 139

nightmare, 11, 185–86, 351; friendship as (for ethics), 160; logistical, 292

Noé, Gaspar: *Enter the Void*, 319. See also *Blue Is the Warmest Color/La Vie d'Adèle—Chapitres 1 & 2* (Kechiche); void

noise, 149, 151; dead friends as, 66; and mechanisms, 117; reduction of, 51; statistical (margin of error), 168; and the tire, 127; visual, 296, 299

nothing, 25, 131, 140, 321; almost, 139–40; expression of the expression of, 136; finding of (the), 138; good for (critique of violence as), 141; metaphors for, 136; a most lovely, 328; as positive/full, 136; vs. something, 170–73, 177, 179, 260, 280; tire's noisiness as divulging, 127. *See also* blankness; emptiness

Noys, Benjamin: *Persistence of the Negative and Malign Velocities*, 162

Nye, David: on the technological sublime, 169. *See also* sublimity

obligation: and grids, 185; over identity (Levinas), 196, 234; and order, 280. *See also* responsibility

obviousness, 39, 41, 47, 65, 75–76, 316, 326, 401n60. *See also* franchise, the

Odyssey (Homer), 7, 39, 166, 265

one, two, 211, 231, 246–50, 335; one out of two (hen ek duoin), 308, 312, 320, 328, 333, 335, 340, 366. *See also* A, B; relation; subtraction

Ong, Ker-Shing: on horror and architecture, 402n73

opposites, 289–90, 305, 409n33; and misreadings, 294. *See also* Serres, Michel

orange: singed skin as, 56. *See also* color

order: alphabetical, 81–100, 232–33, 235, 241, 280, 389n1; and death, 36–100; and disorder, 195; in *Final Destination*, 43, 51, 57–68; and Rube Goldberg, 48–49; and grid, 174; as impersonal, 398n8; ordinal drive, 59; and paranoia, 72; and temporality, 64. *See also* abecedaria; alphabetical, the; *Final Destination* (Wong); *Human Centipede, The* (Six)

ornament, 323, 326; and background, 302; vs. economy, 49. *See also* pattern

Osborne, Peter: on formalism as the "enduring problem," 257

Ovid: *Metamorphoses*, 51, 271, 274

Pabst, G. W.: *Pandora's Box*, 318. See also *Blue Is the Warmest Color/La Vie d'Adèle—Chapitres 1 & 2* (Kechiche)

Palmer, Tim: on *Martyrs*, 279. See also *Martyrs* (Laugier)

panic, 7–8; and misreading, 103; about panic, 10. *See also* fear

paradox of horror, 13–19, 382n30, 383nn38–39, 384n42. *See also* horror paranoia: paranoid reading (Sedgwick), 69–72

paraphrase: inability to, 21, 44, 71, 141, 356; as inadvisable, 244, 255–56, 324; reduction to, 23, 318. *See also* form; formalism; reading

Parnet, Claire, 96–98. *See also* Deleuze, Gilles: *L'abécédaire de Gilles Deleuze*

passion, 278, 305, 307, 348; absenting of, 316; and death, 295; and fascination, 261; and mechanics, xvii; *The Passion of Joan of Arc*, 277–78; for the real (Badiou), 162–63; as suffering, 295; vs. violence, 291

Passion of Joan of Arc, The (Dreyer), 277–78. *See also* passion

pattern: and grid, 181; and motion, 231; ogee, 299–300, 302–3; wallpaper, 296–303, 312. See also *Amour Fou* (Hausner); bees; geometry; grid; tessellation

pedagogy: and abecedaria, 84; and the diagram, 225–26; of violence, 12. *See also* primer

Perec, Georges: *La Disparition*, 84; on doors, 350; *W, or the Memory of Childhood*, 86

Phillips, James: on forms of longing, 166

philosophy: and abstractions, 243; as circle (Hegel), 126; crises of, 133; and death, 41, 98; ethics as first, 249; and fear, 9; and form, 257, 274–75, 406n15; and horror, 242–46, 249; and love, 304; and metaphor, 243; and violence, 234, 266–69. *See also* metaphysics

photographs: and caption, 68–69; in *Final Destination*, 54–56, 68–69; in *The Human Centipede*, 220; of martyrdom, 264, 266, 271, 409n33; and redness, 55–56. See also *Martyrs* (Laugier)

Pinedo, Isabel, 13

Pinsky, Robert: *ABC*, 85. *See also* abecedaria

plasmaticity: as fascinating, 272. *See*

also Eisenstein, Sergei; fascination; transformation

Plath, Sylvia: "Tulips," 150. *See also* flowers; red

Plato: on form, 256–57; on love, 307–8, 360; on the lure of the repugnant, 260–61; on tragedy, 13

Pliny the Elder: on the cut-throated silurus, 306, 311. *See also* animal: fish

Poe, Edgar Allan: and modernism, 185

poisoning: accidental, 197; of the chorus (in *Rubber*), 128–30, 136; slow, 83

politics: and deconstruction, 403n77; and formalism, 252–55, 258–59, 281, 406n12, 408n28; and horror, 159; as misreading, 304–5, 318. *See also* relation

Pollock, Jackson, 252

Ponge, Francis: *Le parti pris des choses*, 318–19. See also *Blue Is the Warmest Color/La Vie d'Adèle—Chapitres 1 & 2* (Kechiche)

Pope, Alexander: and bathos, 103

pornography: vs. horror, 380n11; speculative, 21; "torture porn," 262, 264–65. See also *Martyrs* (Laugier)

possibility: and death, 31, 63, 73, 76, 292; of decision, 309; and designation, 89; of form, 104; and fraudulence, 37; and the horrible, 2; and horror, 77; and inflexibility, 298; of love, 333; of return, 27; threshold of, 56; of violence, 237–38, 241–42. *See also* impossibility

posthumous release (as protection), 96–100, 390n23. *See also* Deleuze, Gilles: *L'abécédaire de Gilles Deleuze*

Pound, Ezra: *ABC of Reading*, 85. *See also* abecedaria

Powell, Anna: on corporeal responses to horror films, 5–6, 12; as a fan (of horror films), 14. *See also* horror; shuddering

pregnancy: as distended, 191; impregnation during unconsciousness, 291; and increment, 153; and matrix, 187; and temporality, 116. *See also* abortion; infertility; miscarriage; matrix; mother

preparation: for death, 95; vs. prepped, 186; and primers, 94; for surgery, 246

primer, 84, 94–95, 98, 211. *See also* pedagogy; preparation

Prince, Stephen: on the horror genre, 11

pro forma, 257, 267, 269. *See also* form

process: love as (agonizing), 339; reading as, 282–83

Prose, Francine: on *Amour* as "excruciating to watch," 418n85. See also *Amour* (Haneke)

Proust, Marcel: as in search of lost time, 166

punctuation: comma (as violence), 359, 362; dash (in *Die Marquise von O . . .*), 291

pure: abstraction, 277; animal as, 121; archive (Deleuze), 97; cruelty, 101; field of color, 276; form of visible difference (color), 321; formalism of violence, 104; geometry, 29; letter (Barthes), 93; power, 170; repetition of effect, 130–31

Pynchon, Thomas: *V.*, 86. *See also* abecedaria

Q: as omitted, 87; as unable to be gotten past, 92

question mark (?): as blunder, 133; a collection of, 185; as monster, 132

racism: and form, 266–68, 283; and language, 267. *See also* David, Alain

radical formalism. *See* formalism: radical

reading: close, 27, 62, 65, 68–77, 256–60, 325, 387n37, 406n12; and concept-generation, 27; distant, 387n37; and/for/with form, 21, 45, 65, 184, 254–60, 281–83, 341, 366; immediate (Althusser), 24, 210; indirect (Derrida), 255; just (Best and Marcus), 387n37; "new" ways of, 387n37; paranoid (Sedgwick), 69–72; as process, 282–83;

of reading, 69; reparative (Sedgwick), 387n37; surface, 387n37; and risk, 18–26, 29–30, 69–72, 92, 260–84; and surprise, 21, 27, 325; and temporality, 62, 322; without guarantee, 21, 140, 260, 282–83, 341. *See also* misreading

red, 150; in *The ABCs of Death*, 82–83; in *Cabin in the Woods*, 148, 150, 153; and cooperation, 231; and cruelty, 269, 271; in the distance (after Q), 92; eyes, 150, 269, 339; as failure, 148, 230–31; and floridity, 326; in *The Human Centipede*, 215, 221, 223, 230–31; in *Inside* (*À l'intérieur*), 106, 109, 111–12; Kiss/Intercourse (in *The Lobster*), 331; and photography, 55–56; vectors, 60–61. *See also* color

redistribution: and betting pools, 183; and violence, 108, 156–57

reductio ad absurdum, 45–47, 49, 75. See also *Final Destination* (Wong)

refusal: of abandonment, 246–50; as antidote, 282–83; of Antigone, 318–19; to describe symbolically/allegorically, 298; to exclude, 290; of the forced, 363; of intimacy, 300; of meaning, 365; to reduce reading to paraphrase, 255–56, 318, 324, 356; to remain faithful to accumulated saturations, 30; to sacrifice, 157–59, 160; to settle on interpretation, 299

relation, 50, 120, 196–369; and architectural plans, 419n87; bound but severable, 116–17; co-presence, 174–75; irrelationality, 314; non-relation as, 89; and the not-All, 151; and organization/co-operation (one, two), 211, 231, 246–50; and suicide, 295; and symmetry, 249, 361; and violence, 159, 240. *See also* care; chain reactions; friendship; Goldberg, Rube; I; one, two

repetition: of "180" (in the *Final Destination* franchise), 39; in *The ABCs of Death*, 93; and breaking, 275; in *Blue Is the Warmest Color/La Vie d'Adèle*, 319, 324; of (exhausted) concepts, 30;

repetition (*continued*)

and a desire for life, 40; of effect, 130–31; under erasure, 26; and friendship, 160; of grid, 172–79; of grid encounters (in *Cabin in the Woods*), 170; of "I love you," 359–60; of insistence, 358; as irritation-causing, 291, 304; in "Karma Police" (Radiohead), 121; and labor, 113; of loved-object-definition, 335; of "Letter is for Word," 93; of myths, 10; of a name (in *L'inconnu du lac*), 3075, 313–14; of negation (in *Rubber*), 136; and origin, 239; and pattern, 299–302; and sameness, 41; and speed/tempo, 112–15; of virus replication, 10; and visibility, 302–3; of (tired) words, 7. *See also* grid; pattern; tessellation

reserve: of knowledge, 98; without, 136, 149

responsibility: of being, 74, 234–36, 238, 400n43; guiltless, 234; infinite, 234–35, 238, 403n77; of love (in the midst of grief), 29; and margin of error, 168; and the other, 227, 234–36, 243, 246; public, 403n77; and the self, 229–30, 234, 387n32. *See also* obligation

return: of the dead, 17; of death, 29, 38; for a friend, 246–50; to home, 166; *Le loup est revenu!*, 319; to the originary foundation, 27; of the repressed, 6; to the site of trauma, 16; of the toroid, 50. *See also* circle

rhythm, 19; and explosions, 272–73; and kissing, 328; and pattern, 298; and posture (crawling), 239–40; and sex, 323; of torture, 270–71; of violence, 82–83, 101–18. *See also* feeling; *Inside (À l'intérieur)* (Bustillo and Maury)

Ricoeur, Paul: on interpreting, 70. *See also* interpretation; reading

risk: and anonymous connection, 310; of being overwhelmed by a formal detail, 321; of censure (as causing desire), 332; fish as symbol of, 311; in *The Human Centipede*, 246–50; of love, 290; and

the philosophical decision, 406n15; and reading, 18–26, 29–30, 69–72, 92, 260–84; and value, 260–61, 282, 284. *See also* care; *Human Centipede, The* (Six)

Rivette, Jacques: *L'Amour Fou*, 296, 305. See also *Amour Fou* (Hausner)

Rodchenko, Aleksandr: *Hanging Spatial Construction*, 186

Rodrigues, João Pedro: on *L'inconnu du lac*, 306, 310. *See also* geometry; scenography; *Stranger by the Lake* (*L'inconnu du lac*) (Guiraudie)

Rohmer, Éric: *The Marquise of O*, 296. See also *Amour Fou* (Hausner); *Marquise von O . . . , Die* (Kleist)

Romney, Jonathan: on landscape in Guiraudie films, 414n34. *See also* landscape; scenography; *Stranger by the Lake* (*L'inconnu du lac*) (Guiraudie)

Rooney, Ellen: on taking form seriously, 255

Rorty, Richard: on Levinas's ethics, 243, 403n77

Rosler, Martha: *Semiotics of the Kitchen*, 87. *See also* abecedaria

Rotman, Brian: on alphabetic ordering, 84; on the zero sign, 125. *See also* abecedaria; alphabetical, the; zero

Rubber (Dupieux), 50, 124, 126–32, 136–41, 280, 282. *See also* circle; toroid

Russell, Bertrand: *The Good Citizen's Alphabet*, 85. *See also* abecedaria

sacrifice: in *Cabin in the Woods*, 145, 147, 149, 156–57; false, 69–70; in *L'inconnu du lac*, 306; and pigeon, 363. *See also* substitution

Sade, Marquis de: cataloguing of violence (in *120 Days of Sodom*), 273–74; on limitations of the letter, 219

Salò, or the 120 Days of Sodom (Pasolini), 275–76. *See also* Deleuze, Gilles; Sade, Marquis de sameness, 41–42, 243, 274, 282, 302. *See also* difference; matching; similitude

Sartre, Jean-Paul: "L'existentialisme est un humanism," 318; *Les Mains sales*, 318; *Nausea*, 217. See also *Blue Is the Warmest Color/La Vie d'Adèle—Chapitres 1 & 2* (Kechiche); flies

Saw (Wan), 391n10

scenography, 275, 355; vs. geometry, 297–303, 306–14. *See also* geometry; ichnography; landscape

Schiele, Egon: "Friendship," 324, 328; vs. Klimt, 319, 325–26. See also *Blue Is the Warmest Color/La Vie d'Adèle—Chapitres 1 & 2* (Kechiche); Klimt, Gustav

Schiller, Friedrich: on form and freedom, 254

Schmitt, Carl, 146. *See also* violence

Scream franchise, 39, 161

Sedgwick, Eve: on paranoid reading, 69–72. *See also* paranoia; reading

Seneca: *Oedipus* (and horror), 8

Sensation Seeking Scale (Zuckerman), 12

Serres, Michel: on the compass, 303; on ichnography, 298; on love as geometral, 290, 297–98, 303; on opposites, 289–90, 294; on the question of being or relating, 200. *See also* being; I; ichnography; love; relation

Seventh Seal, The (Bergman), 39

sex: in *Blue Is the Warmest Color/La Vie d'Adèle*, 319–24; and form, 323; in horror, 17; in *L'inconnu du lac*, 311, 314; uninspired, 319. See also *Blue Is the Warmest Color/La Vie d'Adèle—Chapitres 1 & 2* (Kechiche); *Stranger by the Lake* (*L'inconnu du lac*) (Guiraudie)

shame: and care, 354; in Freud, 397n2; as a structural condition, 229–30; and structural division, 182

Shaviro, Steven: on accelerationism, 161. *See also* accelerationism

Shelley, Mary: *Frankenstein*, 2

Shinkle, Eugénie: on material breakdown in gaming, 169–70. *See also* failure

Shklovsky, Viktor: on art and emotion, 253

shock, 1; of blue, 319, 321; color as, 329; at hearing "I love you," 360; self-evidence as shocking (Adorno on Kafka), 233; "thermospasmic shock wave," 162

showing: *sicut hic depingitur*, 203, 210–32, 250. *See also* finger

shuddering, 1–8, 10–19, 26, 108, 380n11, 382n31; as the best part of humankind, 381n20; philosopher of the shudder (Nietzsche), 381n20; shudder-novel (*Schauerroman*), 2; of spectator, 5, 40, 108. *See also* bristling; horror

Siamese (conjoined) twins/triplets, 197, 207–8, 214, 224. *See also* attachment; *Human Centipede, The* (Six); relation

Siegert, Bernhard: on the grid and modernity, 174. *See also* grid

Signer, Roman: on rhythm in explosions, 272–73

silence, 26; and emotional expression, 330, 336–37, 339; and the dead, 198, 345–46; and mourning, 29; as response, 356, 358, 415n39; and skepticism, 30; in Trakl's "Die Sprache," 357; and voice, 313; written-over, 136. *See also* blankness

similitude: *ars formularia*, xvii–xviii, 274–75; between the dead and survivors, 65; and difference, 330–41, 349–50; and love, 330–41, 347, 417n54; and violence, 347, 362. See also *Lobster, The* (Lanthimos); matching; sameness

simplicity: in abstraction, 190; and form, 255; of grids, 175–76; of *The Human Centipede*, 233; and legibility, 310

Six, Tom, 207; as actor, 225–26. See also *Human Centipede, The* (Six)

Six Characters in Search of an Author (Pirandello), 185

sketch, 182; and line, 215–16; in *Blue Is the Warmest Color/La Vie d'Adèle*, 319, 321, 323; diagram as, 221. *See also* Diderot, Denis

slippage, 119; of the eyes, 409n33; homonymic, 127

smells: and children, 155; of cruelty, 348; foul, 202, 221, 243; and memory, 150; and shame, 397n2; and temporality, 351

Smithson, Robert: on minimalist artists, 131

Sole Survivor, 39

Solomon, Stanley: on horror, 383n32

soundtrack: in *Cabin in the Woods*, 171; in *The Lobster*, 332–33, 340; in *Rubber*, 127

Spadoni, Robert: on early Hollywood monster movies, 12

spatiality, 114–18, 350–69; and causality, 127; and increment, 354–55; and love, 358; and the spectator, 297; and surgical illustration, 397n1; and temporality, 356. See also *Amour* (Haneke); exterior; interior

spectacle, 260–66, 275–76; vs. narrative, 59. *See also* fascination; spectator

spectator: anguish of, 354; anticipation of, 309; anxiety of, 414n35; as detective, 39; endurance of, 264–66, 275–76, 409n33; enjoyment of terror/fright, 13–18, 208, 382n30; as "infected" by art (Tolstoy), 5; and intimacy, 318; investment by, 263; and mimicry, 12, 18, 382n25; orientation of (via form), 252; as riveted, 384n42; in *Rubber*, 128–31, 136, 138–139, 141; shuddering, 5, 40, 108; and spatiality, 297, 351–52, 363; speculation of, 203; and waiting, 54. *See also* fascination; paradox of horror; spectacle

speech: and love ("I love you"), 336–37, 359–60; as reflex for the dying, 365; replaced by gesture, 332, 336–37, 339; and

silence, 313; and violence, 40; without (infants), 116

speed: of breathing, 12; and change, 273; of death, 99, 102–3, 207; and feel, 105–6, 112; and GPS, 166; and repetition, 112–15; "S Is For," 89; slow motion, 332, 340; slowness (of crawling), 239–40; slowness (in *Inside* [À l'intérieur]), 112–17; and violence, 111, 118. *See also* accelerationism; temporality

Stace, W. T.: on the triadic form in Hegel, 401n60. *See also* Hegel, G. W. F.

Stanley, Richard: *Color Out of Space*, 134

stars: constellation, 146; missing, 146, 159, 165–66, 185, 189

Stein, Leo: *The A-B-C of Aesthetics*, 85. *See also* abecedaria

Stendhal: on love, 317. *See also* love

Stevens, Wallace: on order and disorder, 195

Stewart, Garrett: on *Amour*, 354. See also *Amour* (Haneke)

stiffness: of action, 105; of ceremony, 301; of characters in *Amour Fou*, 291; of exercise in *Amour*, 355; of hair, 1–3. *See* bristling

stitches: in (laughing), 191; of incisions, 93, 191, 209, 213, 273; and the other, 227; and sequence, 221. *See also* attachment; *Human Centipede, The* (Six); joining

Stranger by the Lake (*L'inconnu du lac*) (Guiraudie), 306–15, 414nn33–35. *See also* geometry; relation; scenography

stuckness: of constipation, 223, 237; of melancholy (in mourning), 346; of taste in one's mouth, 166

sublimity, 15, 168–70; failed attempts at, 103; introverted sublime, 170; and light, 308. *See also* Kant, Immanuel

substitution, 238, 241; in *Amour*, 360; and atonement, 149; in *Blue Is the Warmest Color/La Vie d'Adèle*, 319–21, 326; and endtime-endurance, 352; of gesture for speech (in *The Lobster*), 332; of intestines (in *120 Days of Sodom*), 273; in Levinas, 235; of lost fetus for regained one, 107–8; of lovers, 335–366; of worn words for new ones, 7. *See also* bartering; sacrifice

subtraction: and the diagram, 212; and knowledge, 209; two minus one, 308, 312, 320–21. *See also* one, two

suicide: in *The ABCs of Death*, 88; as authentic philosophical act (Novalis), 304; "common," 295; of Deleuze, 99; to escape a worse fate, 101–3; failed attempt at, 357; and the frustration of closure (in *Martyrs*), 263; as gesture of love (in *Amour Fou*), 291–95, 304. See also *Amour Fou* (Hausner)

surprise: and doubt, 283; and love, 317, 329; and paranoia, 72; and reading, 21, 27, 325. *See also* reading

Svenonius, Ian, 91. See also *Alphabet Reform Committee*

syllogism, 236–37. *See also* Hegel, G. W. F.

table, 180–83, 186–88. See also *Cabin in the Woods, The* (Goddard/Whedon); cells; grid; matrix

taste: *Bad Taste*, 210; getting a taste for, 169; *The Physiology of Taste* (Brillat-Savarin), 103; and shuddering, 6; as stuck in one's mouth, 166

Tatarkiewicz, Wladyslaw: on form, 257. *See also* form

taxation, 296, 300

taxonomy, 89–90

tears: of love, 319; as tempting tears, 101

Teige, Karel: *Abeceda*, 79, 87. *See also* abecedaria

temperature: and color, 55, 318; cooling off (love lost), 316; and death, 55–56. See also *Blue Is the Warmest Color* (Maroh); *Blue Is the Warmest Color/La Vie d'Adèle—Chapitres 1 & 2* (Kechiche)

tempo: and violence, 105–14. See also *Inside* (*À l'intérieur*) (Bustillo and Maury); rhythm; speed; temporality

temporality: in *The ABCs of Death*, 88; and blue (in *Blue Is the Warmest Color/La Vie d'Adèle*), 320–22; and closure, 222; and death, 39–40, 42, 57, 62, 85, 102, 350; and decision, 338–39; duration, 50–51, 54, 113, 270, 293, 322, 338; and editing, 61–62, 64, 113; end of (historical) time, 161; and endurance, 265, 270; and escape, 231; and the Fantastic (Todorov), 7; and flowers, 351; and formalism, 44, 255; the future (constructing), 162; and the grid, 174, 176; in *Inside* (*À l'intérieur*), 110–11; and interpretation, 210; just in time, 98, 102; and the list, 274; lost/missing time, 119, 166; and love, 317; and mourning, 345–46; and murder/suicide (in *Amour Fou*), 293; and narrative progress, 59; out of time (too late), 111–12, 315, 321; and order, 64; and pregnancy, 116; and reading, 62, 322; running out of time, 51, 83–84, 102, 308–9, 334; and the schematic, 61–65; simultaneity, 313, 344; and smells, 351; and spatiality, 356; and staging, 297; and tabling, 188; time stamps, 167; and violence, 118; wasted time, 101, 119, 154. *See also* lapse; speed; tempo; waiting

terror: and amazement, 16; as the "best part of humanity" (Nietzsche), 381n20; of meeting a woman on the street (Matisse), 322. *See also* fear; horror

tessellation, 176–79, 299–300, 303. *See also* bees; geometry; grid; hexagon; pattern

text: being of a, 65; death as, 68; world as, 72

things, 121–41. *See also* nothing; *Rubber* (Dupieux); *Way Things Go, The* (Fischli and Weiss)

Thompson, Kristin, 252

Thomson, Judith Jarvis: on abortion, 391n10. *See also* mother; pregnancy

Thornham, Sue: on *Amour Fou*, 300–301. See also *Amour Fou* (Hausner)

thresholds, 354; of action, 362; and death, 36–39, 43, 46, 48, 50, 54, 57, 60, 65, 69, 357; and light, 350, 358; of possibility, 56; and taxonomy, 89–90. See also *Amour* (Haneke); Gide, André; increment

Todorov, Tzvetan: on the Fantastic, 7

Tolstoy, Leo: on art as infectious, 5; "The Death of Ivan Ilyich," 198. *See also* contagion

topology: of the grid, 178; of the lapse, 119; and lines, 217–21; and psychoanalysis, 180; as structure (Lacan), 164; of violence, 117–18, 260, 352. See also *Cabin in the Woods, The* (Goddard/Whedon); exteriority; *Inside* (À l'intérieur) (Bustillo and Maury); interiority; *Rubber* (Dupieux); spatiality; toroid/torus

toroid/torus, 21, 131, 140; in *The Way Things Go*, 50, 54; in *Rubber*, 50, 124, 126–32, 136–41, 280, 282. *See also* circle; loops; *Rubber* (Dupieux); *Way Things Go, The* (Fischli and Weiss)

torture, 23; vs. death, 101–2, 107; ethics of, 279; as generative (from the perspective of form), 279; and the grid, 174; and knowledge, 264; and light, 270–71; limits of (tested by *Martyrs*), 265, 276; "torture porn," 262, 264–65. See also *Martyrs* (Laugier)

totality: dissection of, 60; *Totality and Infinity* (Levinas), 234, 243. *See also* apocalypse; *ABCs of Death, The*; *Cabin in the Woods, The* (Goddard/Whedon)

Trakl, Georg: "Die Sprache," 357–58

transformation: of form, 272–82, 298, 330–41. *See also* plasmaticity

transparency: and the grid, 174; of naked nerves (in *Martyrs*), 271; of slides (in *The Human Centipede*), 203–6, 210–15, 218–20, 244. *See also* glass; *Human Centipede, The* (Six); light; *Martyrs* (Laugier)

Tristan and Isolde (Wagner), 293–94. See also *Amour Fou* (Hausner)

truth: of existence (for Heidegger), 21; and love (for Badiou), 340, 366

Tschumi, Bernard: *The Manhattan Transcripts*, 212–13

Tucker & Dale vs. Evil (Craig), 161

Tudor, Andrew, 16; on "the empiricist dilemma" of genre, 28. *See also* paradox of horror

Tufte, Edward: on information-display design, 64

Twilight Zone, The: "Five Characters in Search of an Exit," 185

Twitchell, James: on being drawn to repellent art, 15; on etymologically derived affect over form, 23; on the experience of horror, 4–6. *See also* horrère; horror

twitching: of the body, 107, 113; of the tire in *Rubber*, 127

ugly, the: vs. the beautiful, 324; as excluded from the fine arts, 319; as included in the fine arts, 322, 326; lure of, 260–61. *See also* paradox of horror

universal: universality of existence (as true horror), 280; universalization, 151

unspeakable, 261; Y as (Parnet), 97

Valéry, Paul: on algebra and sensations, 121

Vauxcelles, Louis: on Matisse's *Nu bleu, Souvenir de Biskra*, 322. See also *Blue Is the Warmest Color/La Vie d'Adèle—Chapitres 1 & 2* (Kechiche); Matisse, Henri

Verlaine, Paul: *Amour*, 364. See also *Amour* (Haneke)

verticality, 190; interrupting horizontality, 173; and the matrix, 187; of the ogee pattern, 299; and shame, 397n2; of window, 246, 363. *See also* horizontality

victims: vs. martyrs, 263–64. See also *Martyrs* (Laugier)

violence: and agency, 182, 186; antiviolence (self-blinding as), 338; and apology, 83–84, 157; and belief, 400n48; and the body, 22–23; and choice, 183–84, 186–87; and comparison, 362; of consumption, 193–94; of correction, 338–41; defense of (justice/retaliation), 108; of the diagram, 230–33, 245; of digestion, 193–94, 209–10; of disemboweling, 218; of disinterestedness, 348; and ethics, 238; of fascination (with form), 260–84; and form, 24, 71, 104, 260–84, 402n73; and friendship, 156, 158–60; from "I love you," 360; of images (Nancy), 105–6, 114, 283; and infinity, 178, 237–38, 241–42, 273, 281; insufficient, 147–53, 156, 161; Kierkegaardian, 234, 400n48; law of, 182–83; limitless, 273; and line, 178, 270–71; and love, 275, 306, 339, 353–55; and objects, 126–32, 136–41; opposite of, 289; oral, 193; and order/position, 147, 221, 241; vs. passion, 291; pedagogy of, 12; and philosophy, 234, 266–69; and preparation, 186; and redistribution, 108, 156–57; rhythm of, 82–83, 101–18; and similitude, 347, 362; sonic, 171; and spectatorship, 128–31, 136; and speech, 40; of structure, 398n13; topology of, 117–18, 260, 352; transcendence of (as fantasy), 228; of transformation, 337; of violence, 183–84. *See also* death; torture

visibility: of death, 42, 353; of difference (color), 321; of form, 266–69, 275–76, 279, 282; and formalism, 44; and repetition, 302–3; of the tire's hole, 136. *See also* eyes; gaze; vision

vision: blocked, 11, 332, 338–39; not wanting to look, 18, 353, 409n33; short-sightedness, 331–32, 334, 336, 338–39; wanting to look, 18; as without finality, 283. *See also* eyes; gaze; visibility

Vitruvius: on ichnography, 290

Vogel, Henriette. See *Amour Fou* (Hausner); *Marquise von O . . . , Die* (Kleist)

void: *La Disparition* (*A Void*) (Perec), 84; *Enter the Void* (Noé), 319; as more than emptiness, 73. *See also* blankness; emptiness; silence

Voltaire: on horror and carnage, 2. *See also* horror

Vu, Huan: *Die Farbe*, 134

vulnerability, 333; of the dead, 346; of the human form, 273; and relationality, 249–50

waiting: in *Cabin in the Woods*, 154, 158, 182; and change, 50; for the decision of the other (in *The Lobster*), 332, 339; and endurance, 54; without guarantee, 321; and spectating, 54; for writing (*tabula*), 182. *See also* infertility; temporality

wanting: as wanting *nonetheless*, 307, 309. *See also* desire; *Stranger by the Lake* (*L'inconnu du lac*) (Guiraudie)

waste: consumption as, 193; the dead as graphic, 66; excrement as, 209–10, 210; and honey bees, 177; laying, 8, 111, 328; ridding, 43; rubbish as, 126; streaks of blood as, 109; of time, 101, 119, 154

Way Things Go, The (Fischli and Weiss), 50–54

Weed, Elizabeth: on "the 'new' ways of reading," 387n37. *See also* reading

Weil, Simone, 146. *See also* violence

Weiss, David. See *Way Things Go, The* (Fischli and Weiss)

West, Ti, 89. See also *ABCs of Death, The*

wetness: of the alphabet (in Hamilton's *abc*), 87; and death, 36, 55

Whale, James: *Frankenstein*, 132–33

white: classical sculpture, 324; knuckles
(OK Go), 166; lab coat, 210; light, 112–13,
232, 276; walls, xv, 324. *See also* color
White, Carol: on Heidegger and sameness, 41. *See also* sameness
whole: bounded (as necessary), 406n12;
and part, xvii, 207, 212, 237. *See also* A,
B, C; *Human Centipede, The* (Six)
Wilde, Oscar, 253
Williams, Linda: on *Blue Is the Warmest Color*, 415n43; body genres, 5–12;
as a fan (of horror films), 14. See also
*Blue Is the Warmest Color/La Vie
d'Adèle—Chapitres 1 & 2* (Kechiche)
Williams, Raymond: on form, 257; on the
term *form*, 59. *See also* form
Wimsatt, W. K.: on affective fallacy,
253
withnessless, 329, 344. *See also* loss;
love
witness: and death, 159, 236, 344; and
martyrdom, 265–66; and the spectacle,
276. *See also* spectacle; spectator
Wittgenstein, Ludwig: on diagrams (as
potentially advisable), xv; on drawing
boundary lines, xxi; Wittgenstein as
word, 97
Wölfflin, Heinrich: *Kunstgeschichtliche
Grundbegriffe*, 255
Wolfson, Susan: "activist formalism," 252
Wong, James. See *Final Destination*
(Wong)
Wood, Robin: on the horror genre, 10–11,
74
Woolf, Virginia: *To the Lighthouse* (and
the alphabet), 92

world: abandonment of the, 251, 253;
without affect, 121; *L'Origine du monde*
(Courbet), 319; as text, 72
Wright, Kristen: on the enjoyment of the
disgusting, 383n38. *See also* paradox
of horror

X: as a disaster for the abecedarium,
389n5; as for marking the spot, 60; as
unknown (Parnet), 97. *See also* abecedaria; Parnet, Claire

Y: as unspeakable (Parnet), 97. *See also*
Parnet, Claire
Yeats, W. B. "Three Things," 33
yellow: coat, 292–93; exudate, 202; in
Inside (*À l'intérieur*), 106, 111; "The
Yellow Wallpaper," 301. See also *Amour
Fou* (Hausner); color

Zangwill, Nick: on moderate formalism,
252
Zarlino, Gioseffo: on the "sounding
number," 254
Zelazny, Roger: *Lord of Light*, 161–62
zero, 125–26, 321, 342; definition of
(Frege), 19; fatalities, 147, 152; zero-
sum, 317. *See also* blankness; circle;
emptiness; loops; nothing
zigzag, 27, 29–30; "Z is for," 97. *See also*
Husserl, Edmund
Žižek, Slavoj: on *The Birds* without birds,
138. *See also* animals
Zorns Lemma (Frampton), 84, 91
Zukofsky, Louis: "A," 86. *See also* A;
abecedaria